Steel City Scholars

The Centenary History of the University of Sheffield

Steel City Scholars

The Centenary History of the University of Sheffield

Helen Mathers

Picture Editor
Anthea Stephenson

JAMES
X
JAMES

Designed by Robin Farrow
Typeset in 11/12.25pt Monotype Fournier
and 8/10pt Univers 57 condensed

Originated, printed and bound by
Butler & Tanner Ltd, Frome, Somerset

Published by
James & James (Publishers) Ltd
Gordon House Business Centre
6 Lissenden Gardens
London NW5 1LX

Half title: *Three generations of University architecture:
the original 1905 building, the Arts Tower, 1965, and the Howard Florey
building for Biomedical Science, 2004, which completed the fourth side
of the quad almost 100 years after the University's foundation.*

Title page: *Stained glass window by Wendy Taylor representing
the eight faculties of the University in 1994,* key below.

Pure Science	Engineering	Law
Social Sciences	University Crest	Medicine
Architecture	Arts	Education

Facing page: *Art Nouveau doors in Firth Hall.*
Page ix: *Facade of the Sir Frederick Mappin Building at St. George's.*

THE UNIVERSITY OF SHEFFIELD
CENTENARY HISTORY EDITORIAL BOARD

The Editorial Board wishes to express its thanks to Convocation
for a generous donation towards the cost of this project.

Preface

The difficulties of an official historian are formidable. He must not fail to include in his book details of all important appointments and all major bene-factions. He must record parallel and overlapping developments in a multitude of departments. And yet, somehow, he must contrive to order this mass of torpid material into a coherent and, if possible, an entertaining story.

From Darts *review of the first history of the University of Sheffield, 1955*

This Centenary History was co-ordinated by an Editorial Board which first met in the autumn of 2000. We were, from the start, in agreement that the History should be a single-volume, illustrated work in narrative form. It would tell the story of the University's first 100 years, together with that of its antecedents, the Medical School, the Technical School and Firth College. The History should be written to high standards of scholarship and serve as a work of reference, but should also be enjoyable and appeal to the general reader. Its approach would be comprehensive, ranging over the academic life of the University, the administrative challenges and achievements, and the experiences of staff and students.

It was hardly a surprise to be informed that our task was impossible. It has certainly proved very challenging. The educational historian Sheldon Rothblatt once described the modern university as 'like Proteus, many things at once'. Stephen de Bartolomé, a Sheffield Pro-Chancellor, asked 'What does Geography have in common with Psychiatry?' Yet the breadth of a University is its essence. We have made the attempt to evoke the essence of Sheffield in this volume; the reader must judge of its success.

Selection is inevitable and invidious. This is particularly true of the academic enterprise and of the activities of individual departments. While every faculty features in each chapter, some departments rise above the surface and become submerged again. Continuous, coherent history at this level must be the task of departmental historians; several examples (listed in the Bibliography) already exist and have been of considerable help in the preparation of this History. In the selection of outstanding academic achievement, the test of time and the appreciation of colleagues have often been the best guides. Some research attracts publicity and awards by its very nature, while other work of great scholarly value gains unfairly limited attention.

The period after 1970 covered by the final two chapters and the postscript includes the careers of many who are still in post and events which are still unfolding. The task of selection has proved even more difficult here. However, these chapters provide a context for contemporary events, an exercise which has not previously been attempted for the University's recent history.

'Much of the most valuable work of the University comes to life only in classes and tutorials', commented the University's *Gazette*. Yet there is no record of the countless hours of communication between lecturer and students; they are invisible to the historian. The student memories which we collected proved invaluable in this respect. Some members of staff and their classrooms came magnificently to life. The story of Professor Swift, who in the 1950s refused to let anyone into his lecture room after he had entered, even the student who had courteously stood aside to let him go in first, was told to us by several of those present, including the unfortunate student himself. He watched the lecture through a spy-hole devised for the purpose.

The previous history of the University, Arthur Chapman's *The Story of a Modern University*, was published for the Golden Jubilee in 1955. It covers the development of the University, from its earliest days, in great detail. Chapman, one of my distinguished predecessors as the University's Registrar, had access to all the surviving documentation, much of which he quoted verbatim. The book runs to 551 pages, and as a source for the current history it could not be bettered. Chapman also collected his documents in files which are in the University Archives. The approach of this Centenary History is very different from that of Chapman, but his work remains one of the most distinguished university histories of its day and irreplaceable for its careful study of the early development of the University of Sheffield.

We sought to extend the range of sources available for this History by inviting personal reminiscences from students and staff. David Bradshaw collected many early student memories via Convocation and an email questionnaire to post-1960 graduates elicited more than 900 responses. What is now a comprehensive collection of student memories has furnished innumerable anecdotes and impressions which enliven *Steel City Scholars*. We thank all the alumni who responded to our requests. Likewise, we thank the members of staff, both current and retired, who wrote accounts for us, took part in interviews and answered questions. In many cases, the information they have supplied was not available in any other way. Their names are listed either in the Notes or in the 'Sources and Acknowledgements' section on pp 396–9.

I have indeed been fortunate in the quality of the editorial team. I am grateful to Peter Mason, who has taken a number of stunning new photographs, and created a digital database of the illustrations – a project which will have value far beyond the History. Penny Draper compiled an Index on the splendid scale necessary for ease of reference in such a complex volume. The members of the Editorial Board have all provided services beyond proof-reading, including interviewing and collecting memories. David Bradshaw's work on the Convocation Centenary History Archive has been indispensable, and he has been a source of experience and guidance throughout. Roger Harper drew the maps which summarise the development of the University's estate at the end of each chapter, compiled an outline history of architectural developments, and assisted with the task of collecting illustrations and writing captions. Len Hill has not only written a comprehensive history of the biology departments but also assisted with research and compiled some of the appendices. Clyde Binfield edited the entire text, conducted many interviews, co-ordinated seminars, and initiated the brainstorming sessions which anchored the development of the project. He, John Roach and David Hey are distinguished historians whose great experience laid a firm foundation for the project and whose enthusiasm inspired confidence. Roger Allum gave advice on layout and compiled extra material, particularly for chapters 6 and 7, from his unrivalled experience of preparing the University's Annual Reports since 1980. John Hawthorne provided loyal administrative support to the project; both he and Michael Hannon, the Centenary Director and former Librarian, proved assiduous in checking details of the text.

Anthea Stephenson has been at work since the start of the project, sifting through the University's vast collection of photographs and illustrations, and using her knowledge of the Heritage collection to provide a visual record which precisely complements the text. Hamish MacGibbon and Robin Farrow of James & James have proved to be responsive partners in the publishing process. Above all my thanks are due to Helen Mathers, the author of this work. Helen's unstinting attention to detail, lucid style and excellent team-working have ensured that we have produced a History of our University of which we can all be proud. I hope that the reader has as much pleasure in reading it as we have had in its production.

David Fletcher
Chairman of the Editorial Board
January 2005

For the civic universities are . . . oases of withdrawal in a complex urban structure, centres of creative endeavour in the arts and sciences, repositories of informed knowledge and opinion, powerhouses of ideas, nurseries of new disciplines . . . And the future, . . . lies largely with them.

W. H. G. Armytage

Professor of Education at the University of Sheffield,
Civic Universities: Aspects of a British Tradition, 1955, p.311.

Contents

MAPS
by Roger Harper

ABBREVIATIONS USED IN THE TEXT

ADC   Academic Development Committee
AHRB   Arts and Humanities Research Board
ARCUS   Archaeological Research and Consulting Service
ASTMS   Association of Scientific, Technical and Managerial Staff
AUT   Association of University Teachers

BA   Bachelor of Arts
BEd   Bachelor of Education
BJur   Bachelor of Jurisprudence
BMet   Bachelor of Metallurgy
BMus   Bachelor of Music
BPS   British Pharmaceutical Society
BSc   Bachelor of Science

CERN   Conseil Européen pour la Recherche Nucléaire
CiCS   Corporate Information and Computing Services
CIDB   Commercial and Industrial Development Bureau
CVCP   Committee of Vice Chancellors and Principals

DMus   Doctor of Music

EEC   European Economic Community
ESRC   Economic and Social Research Council
EU   European Union

FBA   Fellow of the British Academy

FREng   Fellow of the Royal Academy of Engineering
FRS   Fellow of the Royal Society
FSSU   Federated Superannuation Scheme for Universities

GCSE   General Certificate of Secondary Education
GMC   General Medical Council

HEFCE   Higher Education Funding Council for England
HRI   Humanities Research Institute

IEE   Institution of Electrical Engineers
IMPETTUS Institute for Microstructural and Mechanical Process Engineering
IT   Information Technology

JIF   Joint Infrastructure Fund

LEA   Local Education Authority
LittD   Doctor of Letters
LLB   Bachelor of Laws
LLD   Doctor of Laws

MA   Master of Arts
MBChB   Bachelor of Medicine, Bachelor of Surgery
MEd   Master of Education
MEng   Master of Engineering
MMet   Master of Metallurgy
MMus   Master of Music
MRC   Medical Research Council
MSc   Master of Science

NASA	National Aeronautical and Space Administration	SERC	Science and Engineering Research Council
NERC	Natural Environment Research Council	SIRIUS	Structural Integrity Research Institute
NHS	National Health Service	SRC	Student Representative Council/Science Research Council
NPSA	Non-Professorial Staff Association		
NUS	National Union of Students		
		TQA	Teaching Quality Assessment
OTC	Officers' Training Corps		
		UCAS	Universities and Colleges Admissions Service
PGCE	Post Graduate Certificate in Education	UCCA	Universities Central Council for Admissions
PhD	Doctor of Philosophy	UFC	Universities' Funding Council
QAA	Quality Assurance Agency	UGC	University Grants Committee
RA	Royal Academician	UNECIA	Universities of England Consortium for International Activities
RAE	Research Assessment Exercise		
RCN	Royal College of Nursing	URC	Union Representative Council
RHA	Regional Health Authority		
RIBA	Royal Institute of British Architects		
		WEA	Workers' Educational Association
ScHARR	School of Health and Related Research	WUN	World Universities Network

---

CONVENTIONS

The titles 'Doctor' and 'Professor' have been used sparingly throughout. First name and surname have been preferred, especially in the later chapters, to avoid confusion and prevent repetition. As a general rule, heads of department and deans are professors, as are pro-vice-chancellors.

1

Prelude to a University:
1879–1905

THE CIVIC UNIVERSITIES

He gets degrees in making jam
At Liverpool and Birmingham.[1]

U NTHINKABLE AS IT MAY HAVE BEEN to many members of England's oldest universities, Oxford and Cambridge, there was a new spirit of higher education developing in the large provincial cities in the last decades of the nineteenth century. New universities were in the making. Often called 'redbrick', their better name is the 'civic' universities, since this exactly described their symbiotic relationship with the urban area which created them. Sheffield was one of a group of five, created from civic colleges, which received their charters in the first years of the twentieth century. They set out to educate the local workforce and were nurtured by the municipal pride of their city councils and by the ambitions of local manufacturers. If not actually in jam-making, degrees in engineering, mining, metallurgy, as well as in the pure sciences, were their defining aspect. Sheffield had one of the first degrees in metallurgy and a large school of engineering. Its inclusion in the first group of civic universities is a source of pride; Sheffield had sometimes lagged behind in matters of civic progress, but not in the case of higher education.[2]

The civic universities drew on the experience of teaching the physical sciences and engineering pioneered by University College, London, which had the first chairs of chemistry and of civil and mechanical engineering.[3] London and the civic universities were so different from the conventional English idea of a university,

Facing page: *Mark Firth, founder of Firth College. Bust by Edward Joy, 1879, now in the corridor adjacent to Firth Hall.*

1

nurtured at Oxford and Cambridge, that they created a completely new tradition of higher education. Sheldon Rothblatt, the distinguished historian of higher education, has spoken of a 'knowledge revolution' in the late nineteenth century, a movement from 'the museum concept of a university – a place to store and admire the wonderful achievements of the past' to 'a dynamic and open-ended concept of knowledge'.[4]

This 'dynamic' approach to knowledge had been a feature of British life throughout the industrial revolution, the essential power driving the transformation of the economy. But higher education had played little part in this process, since industry had relied for its training on apprenticeship, on the 'self-made' man and, to a lesser extent, on organisations like the Mechanics Institutes which provided library facilities and lectures for aspiring young men. Such an Institute was formed in Sheffield in 1832. In the 1860s and 1870s, however, the enterprise of British industry was challenged by innovations in Germany and America, whose universities turned out technologists and scientists of impressive skill. The challenge they posed, and the example they offered, was one of the forces creating the civic university.

The earliest northern civic college of higher education was Owens College, Manchester, set up in 1851. Its founder aimed at a model derived from Oxford and Cambridge, with emphasis on the classics, but there was little demand among Mancunians. The college struggled until it changed its syllabus to more practical subjects and secured the backing of a wealthy local industrialist.[5] Thereafter it went from strength to strength, establishing particular excellence in chemistry. Its success was such that it cannot really be compared with the other civic colleges. Owens College was formed earlier and had far more money and students.

Sheffield, Leeds, Newcastle and Bristol formed higher education colleges in the 1870s; Birmingham, Liverpool and Nottingham followed soon afterwards. Mason Science College, Birmingham, opened in 1880 but quickly secured generous funding and was the first to gain an independent charter, as the University of Birmingham, in 1900. Liverpool began life as University College in 1881 and also developed speedily, forming the federated Victoria University with Manchester and Leeds. These three became separate universities between the years 1902 and 1904.[6] Sheffield followed in 1905.

Industrial backing was essential to the early civic colleges, which relied for survival on a combination of municipal pride and overt commercial interest. The best-endowed were Manchester and Liverpool, with their enviable revenues from cotton manufacturers and merchants, and Birmingham, which had the great advantage of Joseph Chamberlain as chief fund-raiser. The two colleges in Yorkshire, Leeds and Sheffield, were much poorer, in a regular state of financial stress and more dependent on government and local authority grants. The applied sciences were expensive, requiring laboratories and workshops, the latest equipment and full-time staff to run them.

Although the applied sciences were at the core of their teaching, the civic colleges built up a balanced curriculum, with a range of arts and pure science courses. This was partly because of a parallel development, the University

2

Extension movement, which brought lecturers from Oxford and Cambridge to the north to deliver their brand of literature, history and popular science, often to huge and enthusiastic audiences. These lectures were usually run under the auspices of the local college, indeed in Sheffield's case they provided the impetus for the foundation of Firth College.[7] Those colleges which aspired to university status but began with the 'bread and butter' (technology and training) quickly realised that they might have to embrace what some of their founders thought of as 'useless knowledge' as well, if their ambitions were to be realised.[8] The Victoria University, for example, aspired to a balanced curriculum and could reject an applicant college which did not provide it. The Principal of Yorkshire College, Leeds, insisted, against the wishes of some of the governors, that arts subjects should be developed; he was rewarded when the College was admitted to the University in 1887.[9]

Courses in the arts and pure sciences attracted trainee teachers, who had become much more numerous since the 1870 Education Act, which created many more elementary schools and demanded a higher standard of teacher training. The traditional apprenticeship system of 'pupil-teaching' was supplemented by part-time study at the local college. Trainee teachers formed the largest number of day-time students in the early colleges and were welcomed with open arms, especially as they were publicly funded. W. H. G. Armytage, historian of the civic colleges, believed that the faculties of arts and pure science in the colleges and early universities owed their existence to them.[10]

Many women entered the civic colleges in the hope of becoming teachers, and the student generation which graduated in the early 1880s included the first women to achieve an English higher education qualification. One who lived in the Manchester area wrote, 'I experienced for the first time the gain that accrues from contact with lecturers of first-rate ability and vision. We P. T.s [pupil-teachers] had never previously had such a privilege, and the encouragement we received to read widely, to search and sift information for ourselves, was of the utmost value in our self-development.'[11] Sheffield's Firth College admitted women students on a par with men from its opening day in 1879. This was only a year after University College, London agreed to admit women to its degree programmes, the first to do so in England. Women had previously been educated separately and the movement for women's higher education had led to the development of separate colleges at Oxford, Cambridge and elsewhere. There was great opposition to the introduction of co-education at Owens College in Manchester, where there was a separate 'department of women' until the 1890s.[12] Women could be treated as second-class citizens in many ways, for example by the provision of separate entrances or different classes.[13] There is no evidence to suggest that any of this happened at Firth College. Women were, for example, freely admitted to the science laboratories and successfully completed scientific courses from the earliest days of the College.[14] The historian Julie Gibert believes that such civic colleges 'played an important though frequently unmentioned part in the advance of female education'.[15]

The medical schools were the other essential component of the civic college movement and were, indeed, the earliest examples of higher education in most cities. Sheffield's Medical School dates from 1828. In 1826 a report entitled *Thoughts on the advancement of academical education in England* commented:

> The opportunities of seeing the various forms of disease are so necessary to medical students that no universities . . . [can] pretend to give adequate instructions in the healing art.[16]

That is to say, the only English universities then in existence, Oxford and Cambridge, were unable to provide a full training for doctors because they could not offer sufficient clinical examples to study. The cities could furnish examples of 'the various forms of disease' in abundance and urban medical schools sprang up after this report. Most of these schools had a chequered existence until allying themselves with a local college, after which they and the college benefited from the sharing of facilities and teaching resources. The needs of medical students fitted closely with the ethos of the civic colleges, perhaps because, 'medicine counted as a practical science'.[17] The presence of the medical schools also encouraged each college to become a university, because once one civic (Birmingham) could award its own medical degrees, the others had to follow swiftly or risk their degrees being regarded as second rate.[18]

Before the colleges became universities they relied on the external London degree, created in 1858. Without this degree, higher education in the civic colleges might not have been possible and would certainly not have attracted able students and staff. This was the first time that degrees in subjects other than medicine became a possibility at provincial colleges. Owens College appointed the first civic college professor, in natural philosophy, in 1860. A new tradition of professors and departments, pioneered by London University, was challenging the colleges and fellows of Oxford and Cambridge.[19] These new professors were also keen to do research, perhaps 'to prove their value to the industrial patrons who provided their laboratories'. In this way, Sanderson argues, 'research came to be accepted as one of the dual functions of the university teacher'.[20] So 'the perpetual struggle between teaching and research' began.[21]

Members of the ancient universities could be snooty about the civic college movement, as J. H. Newman was when he spoke of 'utilitarians, political economists, useful knowledge people'.[22] But there were other distinguished academics who thought 'useful knowledge' the most important study of all, like Herbert Spencer, and T. H. Huxley of London University. This is one of the contributions that London and the civic universities made to extending the possibilities of higher education in England. Another was to democratise it by admitting a new type of student, of a lower social class. At Birmingham, for example, where detailed evidence is available for the early 1890s, 47 per cent of the students were from 'non-traditional' backgrounds, lower middle-class and artisan. All of these would have raised their social status by gaining a higher qualification.[23] They went on to jobs in teaching, medicine and qualified scientific work. The civics provided an opportunity for which many students had hardly dared to

dream, a college on their doorsteps which could enable them to succeed in desirable and fulfilling careers.

High Street, Sheffield, in the last decade of the nineteenth century.

> Decency, reverence for learning, keen appreciation of scientific power, warm liberality of thought and sentiment within appreciable limits, enthusiasm for economic, civic, national ideals, – such attributes were discoverable in each serried row . . . here was the sturdy outcome of the most modern educational endeavour, a noteworthy instance of what Englishmen can do for themselves, unaided by bureaucratic machinery.[24]

These were the ideals of George Gissing's fictitious 'Whitelaw' College. Although the reality was, inevitably, often different, they summarise the best of the early civic colleges and universities, of which Sheffield was a prominent example.

5

FIRTH COLLEGE

Mark Firth, one of Sheffield's most outstanding citizens, served as Master Cutler in three successive years (1867–69) and as Mayor of Sheffield in 1874. He donated a large public park and almshouses to the city, but his greatest gift was Firth College.

In 1871 Sheffield was a city of 240,000 people, which had doubled in size in the previous thirty years following the development of the so-called 'heavy trades', the manufacture of steel products in enormous quantities in the new forges and engineering plants of the Don Valley. The majority of the adult working population were engaged in metal working of some kind – 66 per cent compared with eleven per cent in professional and mercantile occupations.[25] This was a small middle class. A dense pall of smoke commonly lay over the whole city, with the exception of the western suburbs of Ecclesall, Broomhill and Ranmoor, which consequently became Sheffield's most desirable, and expensive, residential areas. The city centre barely extended beyond High Street and Fargate, which were surrounded by irregular, narrow streets, often lined with forges and workshops. There were few distinguished public buildings apart from the Cutlers' Hall opposite the Parish Church (now the Anglican Cathedral) and the Corn Exchange on Sheaf Street. Some improvements, including street-widening, began in 1875, but the present Town Hall was not opened until 1897.[26]

Mark Firth, who founded Firth College in 1879, had made his fortune as the head of Thomas Firth and Sons, one of the earliest and largest of the 'heavy' steel firms. His works in Attercliffe was 'one of the leading steel and gun forging firms in the world'.[27] His wealth took him from a house at the top of Wilkinson Street to a mansion, Oakbrook, on Fulwood Road, where he entertained royalty on two occasions. Like other leading manufacturers, he took his civic duties seriously, serving as Mayor of Sheffield and donating money to worthy causes. He belonged to the Methodist New Connexion and served as Treasurer to a ministerial training college built under the terms of his brother's will at Ranmoor. Many years later this building became a University hall of residence.[28] Mark Firth's own benefactions to the city included almshouses and a public park, both named after him. His finest gift was Firth College, which was inspired by a new vision of higher education.

The inspiration was the Extension movement, an army of Oxford and Cambridge lecturers who set out to convert the north to 'the advantages of University education'.[29] These dedicated pioneers travelled from town to town giving short courses of lectures, often in the evenings. The first Sheffield Extension classes, in 1868, were organised by the 'Ladies Educational Association' but they did not lead to regular visits.[30] The idea of having university lectures in Sheffield only took root after Mark Firth and the Revd. Samuel Earnshaw organised a public meeting and subscription which quickly raised over £1,000. Extension courses in political economy and English literature were held from January to April 1875. They took place in the Cutlers' Hall, with political economy in the evenings and English at twelve noon. The timing almost certainly reflects a desire to attract the ladies to English literature, while the more 'masculine' subject was held after working hours. Many women were encouraged to consider higher education by the Extension movement. One early woman student described University Extension as 'a gift from heaven'.[31]

The public response was gratifying. Almost 500 tickets were sold for each series of lectures. A regular programme of courses followed, although none achieved the enrolment of the first courses. Political economy, for example, went down to 130 and an attempt to introduce logic was a complete failure.[32] Clearly for some students the novelty had worn off and the reality of the university-style lecture was too daunting. The idea of price reductions for families was certainly optimistic. Regular patterns of attendance were, nevertheless, established. The lecturers made few concessions; their lectures were intellectually demanding and students were expected to produce coursework. R. G. Moulton, for example, a Sheffield Extension lecturer who spent twenty years in the north of England, produced extensive English course booklets for his students, with full reading lists and essay questions.[33] Samuel Earnshaw was moved to comment that 'the Cambridge lectures had, to his certain knowledge, produced a most marvellous effect in this town upon the upper middle class. The conversation now heard and the books now read were of a very superior kind.'[34]

However unlikely such a revolution might sound, it made a deep impression on Mark Firth. In 1877 he bought a city centre site, at the corner of what became Leopold Street and West Street, and engaged a prominent local architect, T. J. Flockton, to design a college building. Firth College was opened by Prince Leopold, hence the name of the street, in October 1879. The cost, some £20,000, was met by Firth and he also endowed the College with at least another £5,000.

The College was designed to facilitate University Extension lectures, and its large lecture hall commanded the whole height of the building; it could seat 400 on the ground floor, with another 170 in the gallery. It was a striking feature architecturally, top-lit by ornamental glass panes in the ceiling. Another lecture hall, for chemistry, seating 200, was sited in the basement and extended into the ground floor. This left little room for smaller classrooms; there were only two, in addition to a chemistry laboratory.

Even before the College was opened, however, its founder's vision had advanced. The first meeting of the Executive Committee, on 3 September 1879, agreed that the purpose of the College was 'the promotion of the moral, social and intellectual elevation of the masses, as well as of the middle and upper classes' by means of lectures and classes 'divested of the desultory character' of University Extension lectures.[35] 'Desultory' was an unfair description of the Extension classes, if applied to their academic rigour, but the courses were short-lived, seldom more than twelve lectures, and sporadic. The College founders aimed at permanency. Firth College courses would 'press onward and steadily aim at results which could not be accomplished in those lectures'. The College would have a principal 'who will introduce and steadily maintain method and system' and departments in various subjects, initially to include history, the sciences, economics and literature. The Executive hoped that the first principal would be a member of one of the three universities to which Firth College would be affiliated, Oxford, Cambridge and London. The College's primary objective was 'the cultivation of higher learning', but it was hoped that technical education could also be introduced. In addition, the College was to be open to men and women on equal terms.[36]

A close friend of Mark Firth, the Reverend Samuel Earnshaw was a gifted mathematician and Senior Wrangler at Cambridge who returned to Sheffield in 1847 to act as Assistant Minister of the Parish Church. He became a Trustee of Firth College and Vice President in 1879. His name is remembered in Earnshaw Hall of Residence.

Firth College, opened in 1879 on a site at the corner of West Street and Leopold Street. Originally two storeys high, a third storey had to be added in 1892. Designed by T. J. Flockton in the 'Renaissance manner', it has a close affinity with Clare College, Cambridge. 'The whole is treated with great freedom and without any subservient imitation of the prototype', commented Building News in 1879.

A. T. Bentley, the first Principal, was one of only three professors in place at the time of the College's opening in 1879. He left after only two years to become Registrar of the Victoria University.

This plan was nothing less than a university in embryo and, despite falterings on the way, the subsequent actions and decisions of the College authorities proved their commitment to this vision.[37]

A. T. Bentley MA, a lecturer at Owens College, Manchester, was appointed as the first Principal and Professor of Mathematics in October 1879. One of the other candidates (from a total of 38), Thomas Carnelly, so impressed Mark Firth that he offered to endow a chair of chemistry especially for him, with the cost of the laboratory being met by members of his family. A third College chair, in classics and ancient history, was awarded to Maurice Hutton BA, a fellow of Merton College, Oxford. The teaching staff was completed by three lecturers: Charles Harding Firth BA (Mark Firth's nephew) in modern history, Eugene Joel in modern languages and a theory of music teacher who rejoiced in the name of Thomas Tallis Trimnell. Ensor Drury was the first Registrar.

It will be noted that two of the lecturers had no university degree, but it must have been gratifying for the College to create 'professors' as part of its plan to award degrees. The College aimed to prepare students for the three stages of the London University external degree (Matriculation, Intermediate and Finals). Mark Firth also hoped that students might proceed from this to a further two years at Oxford and Cambridge to obtain an Honours degree.[38]

In practice, very few students attained even the London degree, since almost all were part-time. The majority of classes were held in the evening, with a respectable daytime programme in addition. In the first year there were 89 enrolments for daytime classes (including Extension courses) and 313 in the evening. Most of the students did not submit themselves for College examinations. It was, as W. M. Hicks later observed, 'a day of very small things'.[39]

There is little hard evidence about the social background of the students, but most would have been, as in other parts of the country, middle-class or skilled working-class, like Sheffield's self-employed 'little mesters'.[40] The College wanted to attract all social groups, but its fee levels, and possibly the nature of its courses, deterred some. At the opening ceremony Bentley, the new Principal, said that he wanted to charge fees which would be 'within the reach of all' as soon as funding was available.[41] Ordinary working men did not enter the College in any numbers until the opening of the Technical School in 1886, which offered not only lower fees but also courses of a practical nature. In the meantime, Firth College extended its range of sciences to include physics and biology as well as chemistry. Sheffield gradually gained, and retained, special notice for 'its education for the lower ranks of industry'.[42]

The College's early years were much more difficult than might have been expected. Morale was dealt a heavy blow in 1880, only a year after its foundation, when Mark Firth died at the age of 61. The College Council could no longer rely on him to cover costs and had to issue an appeal for subscriptions. In addition, the Council seems to have come into conflict with its Principal over 'the continuation of the University Extension methods', a conflict which might well have been resolved had Mark Firth still been in control.[43] Bentley wanted a greater commitment to systematic study and left, dissatisfied, to join the Victoria University after only two years.

The second Principal was a brilliant 25-year-old mathematician and physicist, John Viriamu Jones, who came to Sheffield from the University of Oxford. We know a good deal about his experiences from surviving Sheffield diaries and letters.[44] One of his first impressions was that 'systematic study' was attracting very few students. There were ten students in his first mathematics classes and five in physics, and in the advanced mathematics class on 9 November 1881 'no more than two, one male and one female, as in the Garden of Eden at the first. And they are both teachers, I being a teacher of teachers as an emperor is king of kings'. There was only one candidate for a scholarship examination, a sixteen-year-old who 'did not do well – but I think I shall give him an exhibition'. After a few months, Jones came to the conclusion that the College 'has to be restarted and raised, as it were, from the dead'. He spent considerable time, with little success, trying to tap the resources of philanthropic manufacturers like Thomas Jessop ('said to be a millionaire') and 'another rich man here, the great bookmaker, worth half a million I daresay. Perhaps

The first Registrar of Firth College, Ensor Drury, served the College, the Technical School and University College for a total of 23 years. However, in the early years of Firth College the Registrar's office was open for only two hours each day: much of the remainder of Drury's time was consumed by freemasonry and the 4th West Yorkshire Light Artillery Brigade.

Below left: The main entrance corridor of Firth College, containing (from the right) busts of Mark Firth, Samuel Earnshaw and A. T. Bentley.

Below right: In the College basement there was a raked science lecture theatre; here it is set up for a zoology lecture, with a diagram showing the structure of sponges on the blackboard.

Although John Viriamu Jones was Principal for only two years, 1881–3, he left behind an important legacy in the form of his enthusiasm for a university college to bring Firth College and the Technical and Medical Schools together. This bas relief is mounted in the corridor leading to the Edgar Allen building.

he might found a Professorship of Mathematics as dealing with Probability. They say great sinners found hospitals; why not a great betting man a Chair?'

On the other hand, the public lecture programme was a considerable success and science proved particularly popular. Jones lectured to an 'enormous audience' on electricity in March 1882 and Carnelly gave a lecture on colliery explosions, 'illustrated by some brilliant experiments' for which 'there was a very large audience, mainly men'.[45] These were typical of the programme offered and the response received. Jones, like the Extension lecturers, was messianic about the possibilities of adult education: 'I think next session I must go and give some lectures to the poor people at Brightside and Attercliffe and get them interested in many things beside the public house and betting'.

Distinguished research had begun under Professor Carnelly, who 'has already made the Chemical Laboratory of Firth College widely known by his investigation of the behaviour of solids raised above the melting-point under diminished pressure'.[46] Carnelly, however, left Sheffield to go to University College, Dundee, in March 1883 and later that year Jones himself was tempted by an offer he could not refuse, and returned to his native Wales as Principal of the new University College of Cardiff.

Firth College had lost two principals in four years. The third principal, however, not only retained the post for 22 years but proved to be the man that Firth College, and the University movement in Sheffield, really needed. William Mitchinson Hicks, who arrived in 1883, fought a resolute and successful campaign, often against the odds, to create the University of Sheffield. He became its first Vice-Chancellor. He was also Professor of Mathematics and Physics, 'whose delight was to amuse himself with stupendous equations in which one side covered several sheets of paper.'[47] He came to Sheffield from Cambridge, where he was a recipient of the 'high distinction' of the Hopkins Prize, and he continued his research on the so-called 'vortex atom' while Principal. Considering the parlous state of the College, which had only five members of staff when he arrived, the vision he maintained is remarkable. In 1888 he said,

> What is the ideal of a local college and technical school? . . . It is the place to which everyone, rich or poor, naturally goes for higher education in all its branches. It stimulates their intellectual interests. The town feels pride in the literary or scientific work done there, as a local product. Its school teachers have received their training there; its chemists, electricians, and trained foremen are drawn from its students; its leaders in industry and commerce are former members and present supporters; the medical profession has its home there; and in all directions it is inextricably bound up with the daily life of the place.[48]

Firth College's annual income never topped £2,500 in its first ten years, so the finances were precarious in the extreme. About a third of this income was derived from five-year pledges from individual donors, with the result that, in 1884, after the first five years, there was panic and heroic effort to acquire renewed subscriptions before the College Prospectus could be issued. In 1885, the salaries of two junior teaching assistants were paid by private subscription.

All the provincial university colleges encountered the same impasse, which was eventually overcome in 1889 by the provision of government grants. These grants, which saved the university colleges and enabled them to expand, were only secured after the most dogged of campaigns, led by W. M. Hicks and William Ramsay, the Principal of University College, Bristol. They received vigorous support from Oxford in the formidable shape of Balliol's Benjamin Jowett, who believed strongly 'that the university colleges were embryo universities' and that the cultural, as well as the technical, aspects of their work must be maintained.[49] The English colleges had good reason to feel neglected by the government, since grants were already awarded to Scottish, Welsh and Irish colleges, while the three colleges of the Victoria University (Manchester, Liverpool and Leeds), which had previously relied on local funding, had received government help within a fortnight of making their application in 1887. Ramsay and Hicks, however, had to fight for almost three years before the Chancellor of the Exchequer agreed to a total grant to the other colleges of £15,000 in March 1889.

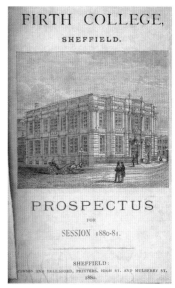

Title page of the Firth College Prospectus for 1880.

Firth College received £1,200, the same as Bristol and Durham, and less than any other college except Dundee. Although small, the grant was a considerable addition to the existing income and kept the College alive. Above all, it was income upon which the College could rely and which was likely to increase each year. The government also appointed a 'visitor' to report on the work of each college and recommend grant levels. This was the embryo of the University Grants Committee which, over many years, enabled universities to receive large sums from the Treasury (although never as much as they would have liked).

Life in Firth College

Before the grant, there were fewer than 200 students; thereafter numbers rose steadily to 360 by 1897, and there was a marked increase in the proportion of day-time students (see Appendix 4A). A student community began to evolve, with a few societies and men's and women's common rooms. As recalled by A. E. Dunstan, a student of the Intermediate BSc course from 1895–97, 'we were a community – we occupied the whole gallery at the Theatre Royal during the annual fortnight's visit of the D'Oyly Carte Company' and followed 'favourite professors when they delivered Extension lectures in various halls in the town'.[50] The students also produced a 'spasmodic journal', entirely hand-written, entitled *IT*, with articles contributed by any student whose arm could be twisted. Each edition was enlivened by the inspired cartoons executed by 'Scuta' (Leonard Shields). One article, 'Our College', was written in the form of a talk to 'Standard I' level elementary school pupils:

> A College, like Firth College, is a place where grown-up boys and girls go
> to learn . . . It is nicer to go to this sort of place than to a Board School,

because the head-master does not cane the boys and girls and not many of the teachers (called professors) keep the bad ones in after 1 o'clock . . . When you come to the place you see a big man with a kind face standing at the door, who looks very hard at you and . . . keeps a list of names and marks you late if you come in after nine . . . Boys who come late have to go and see the headmaster (called the Doctor) at 1 o'clock.[51]

The atmosphere of Firth College, for day-time students, seems to have been like that of an impoverished public school. A. E. Dunstan recalled that:

Work was hard and incessant – lectures mainly from 9 to 10, laboratories 10 till 1 and 2 till 5, followed by further lectures from 5 till 6 . . . The whole of Saturday morning was devoted to practical physics. Not much time for recreation! The evenings up to midnight were taken up with reading and the writing up of notes.[52]

The long teaching hours were necessary in part because many of the students came poorly prepared, from indifferent schools. There was no standard school examination system at that time.

Dunstan remembered Hicks as 'a man who evoked immense loyalty and affection from his colleagues and students' and Dr George Young as a 'brilliant chemist and a first class research worker' who was 'indefatigable.' Professor Leahy, who was in charge of mathematics from 1892, was 'an enthusiastic Irishman who always wrote diagonally down the blackboard'. He came to Sheffield from Pembroke College, Cambridge and was a man of wide-ranging interests. He published two books on old Irish literature, in addition to his mathematical work, and was on the Council of the Literary and Philosophical Society for many years.[53] Alfred Denny, the

Above: Jennings, by 'Scuta' in IT. Jennings, the College porter, had a cubby-hole in the entrance hall. Because the Department of Chemistry only had one member of staff, Professor Carnelly, Jennings also acted as laboratory assistant or chief technician.

Above right: Drawing by Schmidt from IT, 1894, showing students in the common room; the open door looks into the entrance hall.

Facing page, top left: Pleasant Monday Afternoon, chemistry practical class, by 'Scuta' in IT. 'Scuta' was a chemistry student, Leonard Shields, who later become responsible for the illustrations in The Magnet and The Gem.

Alfred Denny arrived as a lecturer in biology in 1884 and served for 41 years. He was promoted to Professor in 1888 even though he had no degree, but he was an excellent teacher and built up a significant zoological collection. This photograph of his laboratory shows some of that early collection in the background.

Professor of Biology, was described by a student as 'the best teacher in the College. He was a tiny man with a curious lisping voice. I was told he was the son of a museum curator in Leeds. At any rate he was part author of a classic, Miall and Denny on the Cockroach . . . He used to almost dictate slowly the important parts of the lecture but he filled it up with the most interesting quick speech "small print". He was a very good blackboard draughtsman and drew in our presence beautiful diagrams which most of us stayed behind to copy.'[54]

The staff was augmented in the later 1880s by a lecturer in Hebrew from St John's College, Cambridge and, following a public meeting which demanded that

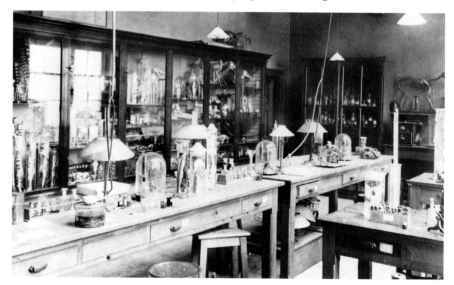

Arthur Leahy was appointed Professor of Mathematics in 1892, at the age of 35. A voluble and energetic Irishman he immersed himself in the activities of Firth College and its successors for the next thirty years. He acted as Public Orator and was responsible for drafting the ordinances and regulations of the new University.

H. W. Appleton by Sir William Rothenstein, 1919. Appleton, a lecturer in Classics, was appointed Professor of English Literature, Language and History in 1890. He was gradually relieved of some of these daunting responsibilities, but remained Professor of Ancient History until 1931.

the College appoint a 'competent man' as professor of literature, by the creation of a chair in English literature, language and history in 1890.[55] Twenty applications for this vast portfolio were received and H. W. Appleton, who was already lecturing at the College in classics, was appointed. This appointment of someone who was apparently from another discipline can be explained, since all the applications are preserved in the University archives. Appleton had completed a BA at Oxford in 1888, taking first class in classical moderations (part 1) and a double first in the finals schools of *literae humaniores* and modern history. This polymath was therefore qualified to teach all his various subjects at Firth College, but the fact that he achieved a chair only two years after graduation, with hardly any teaching or research experience, is indicative of the calibre of staff the College was able to attract in its early days. It is also a reminder that the title 'Professor' primarily denoted responsibility for organising the teaching of a particular subject. The modern understanding of the role and qualifications of a professor developed after Firth College became part of the University of Sheffield.[56]

G. C. Moore Smith took over English from Appleton in 1896, allowing him to concentrate on history. Moore Smith retained this chair until 1924 and is described by Chapman (the author of the University's Jubilee History) as 'one of the finest scholars Sheffield has ever known'. This may have been true in the early 1950s and he was Sheffield's first Fellow of the British Academy (FBA), but he never wrote 'a full-dress book, all his own, of his writing' since his volumes were editions of letters, poems and, in particular, Cambridge student plays.[57] He was a graduate of St John's College, Cambridge, who remained one of its most loyal alumni, returning there every vacation. He wrote many articles and reviews and was an acknowledged expert on seventeenth-century English literature. He contributed a great deal to the life of Firth College and devoted himself to its library, persuading

G. C. Moore Smith, *Professor of English Literature 1896–1924, by J. H. Dowd (1908). Dowd was a caricaturist and artist employed by a local newspaper; this drawing is in the University's collection.*

many of his Cambridge friends to donate books. It is clear, however, that a co-educational college was not his natural environment, since a former student of his recalled that 'if a woman turned up late, he listened with icy courtesy and impassive face to her stammering apologies. If a man was late he gave him a rare and friendly smile, realising, as one man to another, that a man sometimes had to be late'.[58] During lectures he declaimed his texts in a 'fine sonorous voice' so that, as another student recalled, 'we seemed to be enjoying an author with him, rather than being lectured to about an author'.[59]

One of the most striking features of Firth College was the lecture hall, which could seat around 600 people. It was described by a student in 1895 as 'quite a pleasing auditorium surrounded with bookshelves and provided with a spacious gallery. At the far end was a platform from which popular lectures were given in the winter months. Below the platform was a long green baize-covered table which served as a sort of common room plus study and was well-populated and covered with notebooks'.

16

Moore Smith wrote the words of the student song 'Floreamus', with music composed by Henry Coward, who was a part-time lecturer in music for thirty years from 1890. Coward was a supremely gifted choral conductor who brought his Sheffield Choir to a peak of perfection, winning international prizes and taking his 200 singers on a six-month world tour in 1911. The Sheffield Festival, a feast of choral music which he founded in 1895, attracted renowned guest conductors, among them Edward Elgar, who was so satisfied by the Festival performance of *The Dream of Gerontius* that he presented the Sheffield Free Library with the full score.[60]

Firth College set up one of the first Day Training Colleges for elementary school teachers in 1890.[61] These were recommended by the Cross Commission as an alternative to the residential colleges, which had been widely criticised. The curriculum was approved by the Education Department and regularly inspected. The Day Training College began with nine students and steadily expanded. It was run from 1894 by one indomitable woman, Mrs Lysbeth Henry, who was the first female member of staff and for several years performed all the work of the Training College alone, including supervision of students scattered throughout the city on teaching practice. Brought up in Scotland, she tried and failed to gain admission to medical school and took up teaching instead. She worked at the Central Schools in Sheffield and was promoted to Inspectress and, after her marriage, to lecturer at Stockwell and Southlands Training Colleges. After the death of her husband, she distributed her four children among boarding schools and relatives and returned to Sheffield as the 'Mistress of Method' at Firth College.[62]

Firth College's curriculum extended to mining, often as extra-mural lectures in mining areas like South Yorkshire. These took the now common form of 'a lecture of a popular nature, illustrated by experiments or lantern slides, followed by a class, the members of which worked on papers during the week which were sent by post to the lecturer and discussed at the class itself'.[63] A Professor of Mining was appointed in 1892 and a three-year part-time course in sciences relevant to mining developed. Thus began an association with miners' education which continued as long as the local industry itself lasted, into the 1980s. It was also a significant development of the Extension programme, which in the first ten years of Firth College had been chiefly confined to its own building. After a local newspaper campaign in 1887, the venues for Extension courses were expanded to include Broomhill, Sharrow, Attercliffe, Heeley and Brightside. In the working-class districts the lectures were free.

The popular lectures in the College's big hall were held on Saturday nights and became weekly affairs, attracting audiences of up to 400. There was no attempt to create a syllabus; they were simply 'star turns' by members of staff, with subjects ranging through ancient history, botany, zoology, metallurgy, music and painting. Some of the performers had a devoted following, like Anderson, Denny and Appleton. Henry Clifton Sorby, 'Sheffield's greatest scientist', was perhaps the most popular of all.[64] Professors were expected to contribute these lectures as part of the job; they continued to be a Saturday night feature until 1914.

Dr Henry Coward joined Firth College as a lecturer in music in 1890. One of the foremost chorus masters of his day, he composed many orchestral and choral works and conducted the Sheffield Festival Chorus at the opening of the University in 1905. Highly regarded by musicians such as Elgar and Parry, he was knighted in 1926.

The hall which was such a success on Saturday nights proved to be a liability to the College for the rest of the week. It would have been perfect for the mass higher education of today, but was far too big in the 1890s to be used for daytime teaching. The space it occupied left little room for the laboratories and classrooms which the College actually needed. Attempts to use the hall as a library-cum-physics laboratory were unsatisfactory, and practical work had to be done in spaces on the landings. Ernest Cotton, a physics student in the mid 1880s, recalled that:

> I myself worked in the basement, in the hall, in the staff cloakroom, on the staircase, in the lecture room and finally developing X-rays in the top floor laboratory. There was one moving coil galvanometer, so precious that it was kept under lock and key. A stop-watch was too costly to buy and the carrying out of Roentgen's experiment needed that Dr Hicks should construct his own Sprengel Pump.[65]

Another storey was added to the front of the building in 1892, a scheme dreamed up by Hicks and partially funded by Sir Henry Stephenson, who had already helped to found the Technical School.[66] Even that did not entirely solve the problem, but from 1895 the arts departments used the upper floors of shops on Church Street until the opening of a completely new building at Western Bank in 1905.

THE SHEFFIELD TECHNICAL SCHOOL

Just as Firth College can be seen as the microcosm of the University of Sheffield's Faculties of Arts and Pure Science, so the Technical School spawned the Faculty of Engineering. In addition, the School was the forerunner of Sheffield Polytechnic, later Sheffield Hallam University, which was founded after the Second World War. The Technical School, like Firth College, began by offering part-time studies and its ambitious evening class programme continued until the 1950s. These students were adults working in the steel industry. The number of day-time students was, for many years, much lower.

In several northern cities a technical school was the first institution of higher education, but in Sheffield an attempt to found the 'Sheffield School of Practical Science and Metallurgy' in 1862 foundered for lack of students after a year. It was supported by John Brown and Mark Firth, the two leading industrialists of the 'heavy' steel firms, but by few others. The need for technical and scientific instruction for Sheffield's cutlers and steelmakers may now appear glaringly obvious, but the tradition of learning on the job via apprenticeship seems to have become so well-established as to be unquestioned. Some firms may also have feared the loss of trade secrets.[67]

The establishment of Firth College provided a potential venue for technical education and the demand was demonstrated when the Central Higher School, from its new building adjacent to the College, ran successful evening classes in applied science and engineering in 1880.[68] Its accommodation was quite inadequate, but the challenge was taken up by the Principal at that time, John Viriamu Jones. His diary records that in November 1881 he met with his chemistry professor Dr Carnelly, C. H. Firth, now based in Oxford,[69] and Mr Willans, a local manufacturer who, unusually, had attended the Royal School of Mines:

> After some talking together we came to this conclusion – that nothing could be done at once better than to organise a course of lectures for next term in Metallurgy . . . This talk of ours was prompted by Alderman Mappin, Member of Parliament for Retford, a manufacturer of Sheffield, wealthy and conscious of the great need of this town for intellectual food. Accordingly, Charles Firth and I went to Thornbury, the home of Mr Alderman Mappin, and were fortunate enough to find him at home after the work of the day, which had consisted in opening a bazaar in Retford. We told him the conclusions we had come to, and estimated the cost of the proposed course of lectures at £100; this he then generously offered to provide.[70]

Sir Frederick Thorpe Mappin Bt. MP, gave £2,000 towards the foundation of the Technical School and was its first Chairman. He was 'its main driving force' and as a consequence often behaved as if the School belonged to him. He became a Vice-President of University College and in 1905, at the age of 84, a Pro-Chancellor of the University.

Frederick Thorpe Mappin had made his money twice over, first in his family's cutlery firm, Mappin Bros., and then in a large steel firm, Thomas Turton and Sons, of which he became chairman.[71] He retired from active business in order to concentrate on his public work as a Liberal MP. Like Mark Firth, he had been Master Cutler and Mayor and he too had a splendid home, Thornbury, on Fulwood Road. The Technical School became a pet project to which he gave much attention and considerable amounts of cash.

The 1886 Technical School building, designed by Flockton & Gibbs in a neo-Georgian style with Ionic brick pilasters, was built behind the former Grammar School. As shown here, it was increasingly hedged in by later buildings. It is the oldest purpose-built accommodation still occupied by the University.

The former Grammar School in Mappin Street, taken over by the new Technical School in 1884. It was demolished in 1912 and the main entrance to the Mappin Building now stands on this site. In the distance can be seen the first stage of the range of buildings which now runs along Mappin Street, erected in 1904.

Mappin has been credited as the founder of the Technical School,[72] but it would be fairer to acknowledge the efforts of a group of people, including the typefounder Henry Stephenson and the remarkable Sheffield scientist H. C. Sorby, as well as Viriamu Jones. The time was also propitious, since the government had just introduced grants for technical education, in response to increasing industrial competition from Germany and the USA. In 1883 Mappin and Jones secured from the City and Guilds of London Institute a grant of £300 for five years towards the appointment of a professor of metallurgy and mechanical engineering. William Greenwood and an assistant, William Ripper, began work in 1884.

Since the Firth College site could not accommodate the new school, in 1884 the College Council decided to buy and convert the vacant premises of the Grammar School in St George's Square. Mappin and Stephenson shouldered the lion's share of the fund-raising, going from works to works in a carriage and pair, even in deep snow.[73] Their efforts were poorly rewarded. The appeal raised little from Sheffield industry and the largest donors were themselves, the Duke of Norfolk and the Town Trust. Even the Cutlers' Company was unable to give more than £100.[74] Shortly afterwards the Drapers' Company of London offered £250 a year, inaugurating a commitment to support the school financially which lasted for many years.

A new building, on land behind the old Grammar School, was opened in February 1886, in a location which the *Sheffield Telegraph* thought would not 'impress its existence upon the popular mind', presumably because it was outside the town centre.[75] It was also hidden from the street by the old school. Large and well-equipped for such an infant enterprise, it had a metallurgical laboratory 'one of the most complete in Great Britain'.[76] The Firth College mistake had not been repeated, and the new premises were mostly made up of classrooms, workshops and laboratories, with two small lecture theatres seating 140 and 80 respectively. The total cost, for buying and adapting the old school, constructing the new building and purchasing equipment, was £11,025.

This sum was covered by the subscription fund, but only just, and the cost of running the school was a problem for several years. An extra appeal had to be made in 1889 to obtain testing equipment, but this time the response from local firms was more generous. Mappin and Stephenson were still the main subscribers, but the Technical School seemed already to be demonstrating its value to Sheffield industry. Shortly afterwards, grants under the new Technical Instruction Act (1889) made the future more secure.[77]

The school offered lectures, workshops and laboratory courses which could be taken separately, although students were encouraged to link them into a fuller programme. From October 1886 it was possible to obtain the qualification of Associate in Engineering or Metallurgy after three (occasionally two) years of study. Most students, however, took fewer courses and attended in the evening. Evening fees were kept low to attract artisans, a policy supported by town councillors (a few

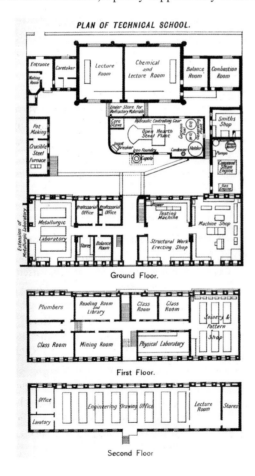

On this plan the former Grammar School on Mappin Street is at the top; below that is the open courtyard, and then the three floors of the 1886 Technical School.

Right: *John Oliver Arnold joined the Technical School as Professor of Metallurgy aged 31, after four years in the Navy and ten in the iron and steel industry. He dominated the department until 1919. In his rare leisure time he was a fearless yachtsman and Vice-President of the Sheffield Rifle Club.*

Professor Arnold built a high reputation as an experimental metallurgist, was twice awarded a Telford Premium and once a Telford Gold Medal. He received the Bessemer Gold Medal, above, in 1905, and was elected to the Royal Society in 1912.

of whom were themselves working men).[78] The Technical Instruction Act also made it possible for the Town Council to offer grants to the School, provided fees were reduced still further. Evening class enrolment made an immediate leap from 200 to 500 and continued to recruit well in subsequent years.[79]

The core of the Technical School's curriculum was practical metallurgy, and a Professor of Metallurgy, J. O. Arnold, was appointed in 1889. He was apparently told that, as his salary of £250 was 'a huge one for a young man' (he was 31), he must ensure that the new department was a success within a year.[80] Arnold proved to be outstanding in both teaching and research and he held the chair until 1919. He had close links with local industry and his metallurgy courses aimed to give the Sheffield working man instruction 'which would afford him a more comprehensive knowledge with respect to his everyday work . . . and throw further light on [practical] operations by application of the scientific knowledge of the day'.[81] Early photographs show workshops which replicated those of the local cutlery industry, with a crucible steel house and small-scale steel works containing a Siemens open hearth furnace and a one-ton Bessemer converter. Arnold was a demanding teacher and an early Sheffield example of the academic workaholic. When his students were working the Siemens furnace round the clock in shifts, Arnold had a bed put up in an adjoining office and was available to them at all hours. He 'never did things by half', according to his successor, J. H. Andrew.[82]

Arnold's department also taught geology, since 'those who identify crystalline materials and match the microtexture of aggregates should learn on rock structures'.[83] The leading influence here was H. C. Sorby who, although never a member of staff, was a prominent lay officer as President of Firth College 1882–97 and a member of the Council of both University College and the University. He was a supreme example of the Victorian gentleman scientist, enjoying a private income and establishing a laboratory in his home. His interests extended to chemistry and biology, as well as metallurgy and geology, and he devised a method of examining rocks microscopically which confirmed his reputation as 'the father of microscopic petrography'. He published more than 150 papers and was elected to the Royal Society at the age of 31. There was no chair of geology, however, until after Sorby's death in 1908, when the Sorby Chair was endowed under the terms of his will.[84]

William Ripper was promoted to the Chair of Mechanical Engineering after Greenwood left in 1889. His original career was as a Sheffield schoolmaster and his administrative skill is demonstrated not least by the fact that he was appointed head-

William Ripper was, together with Arnold, the dominant figure in applied science. From an apprenticeship in the Plymouth dockyards, he progressed through marine engineering to school teaching and became Professor of Mechanical Engineering in 1889. 'To him must go a large share of the credit for building up the technological side of the University'.

The Metallurgy workshops in Arnold's time, with Professor Andrew McWilliam on the right.

Clockwise from top left:

Henry Clifton Sorby, the 'gentleman scientist', who was deeply committed to both the Technical School and Firth College and a member of the Council of both University College and the University. He made serious contributions to several branches of science, became FRS in 1857 at the age of 31. President of the Royal Microscopical Society, he was founder-President of the Mineralogical Society and held a two-year Presidency of the Geological Society.

In 1878 Sorby bought a yacht 'The Glimpse' which he equipped as a floating laboratory. For the next twenty years he spent almost every summer on the coast and rivers of south east England carrying out a programme of marine biology. He was also an enthusiastic watercolour painter and made meticulous studies of seascapes and landscapes on these journeys.

Believed to have been Sorby's microscope. Also one of his boxes of rock samples, sliced so thin as to allow the rock structure to be examined by microscopic means. This revolutionary technique earned Sorby the title of 'Father of Microscopical Petrography'.

Sorby devised a unique method of preparing slides of whole animals, mounted so that their image could be projected to an audience. The slides are not only technically sophisticated but beautiful to look at and are well preserved in the University's substantial collection.

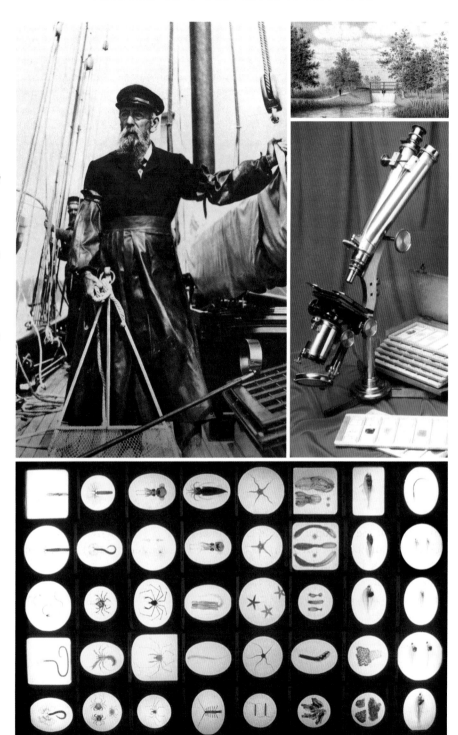

master of Walkley Board School at the age of 22.[85] He became Principal of the Technical School and University Vice-Chancellor during the First World War. His successful move from Board School to Technical School shows the calibre of the man and the links he developed with local manufacturers were just as close as those made by Arnold, who had come from industry. Like Arnold, with whom he sometimes clashed, he was an active researcher. Ripper invented a type of pressure indicator used on ocean-going vessels and worked on cutting tools and heat engines; he produced a classic textbook on the latter.

The Technical School added electrical engineering to the curriculum in 1889 and civil engineering in 1892. Facilities for these were so cramped, however, that in 1902 there were said to be 225 electrical engineering students accommodated in two small rooms, one of them a cellar.[86] The senior qualification offered by the School was the Associateship, which Arnold regarded more highly than the degree. It was a severe test including, for example, 'a practical and viva voce test on [the students] whole three years work in the Laboratory and at the Furnaces and Testing Machine'.[87] Only twenty Associateships had been awarded by 1897, some of those to evening students, whose achievement in passing while also working a full day was considerable.

Hall Overend, the 'father of the Medical School'. This bust, c.1820, by Edward Law, belonged to the Sheffield Literary and Philosophical Society from 1882 and was later donated to the Medical Library of the University.

THE MEDICAL SCHOOL

The Medical School is considerably the oldest establishment of higher or professional education in Sheffield, since it can be dated at least to 1828.[88] Although Scottish universities could award medical degrees in the eighteenth century, medical training in England was controlled by the Society of Apothecaries, which awarded its licence to practise, the LSA. The Apothecaries Act of 1815 made it possible for medical training to take place in English cities (with examination in London) and by 1830 medical schools had been founded in Manchester, Birmingham and Sheffield.[89] Six more followed by 1834.

Hall Overend, a Sheffield surgeon apothecary, began training medical students in Sheffield, perhaps as early as 1811. He was 'a superb teacher with initiative and drive' and played an important role in the intellectual life of Sheffield, presenting 'scientific and thought-provoking papers', often to the Literary and Philosophical Society, which he helped to found.[90] Although Overend successfully presented students for the LSA from 1815, he was never officially registered as a lecturer with the Society of Apothecaries and so cannot be described as running an official medical school. Even so, there is a strong case for regarding Overend as the father of medical education in Sheffield.

Overend's 'school' consisted of an anatomy museum, in which he conducted demonstrations of dissection. This was the one essential feature of a medical school at that time. The audience was not always confined to medical students; the *Birmingham Gazette* in 1762 advertised dissections at the house of Erasmus Darwin (grandfather of Charles) on the body of an executed criminal which were to continue 'every day as long as the body can be preserved'.[91] To obtain some of his

Sir Arnold Knight, the founder of the Medical Institution (later the School of Medicine). Knighted in 1841, he made an early study of grinders' asthma and founded the Public Dispensary.

Below from left to right: *Originally the Medical Institution and the Surgeons' Hall, this 1829 building in Surrey Street was designed by Samuel Worth (architect of the Cutlers' Hall) and James Harrison. Renamed the School of Medicine, its facilities became inadequate and in 1888 it moved into a new building in Leopold Street. The original building was later used as an army recruiting office and was demolished in 1965.*

School of Medicine boardroom and library.

Dissecting room in the School of Medicine, which was 'beyond words repelling'.

human specimens, Overend was almost certainly involved in grave-robbing, since bodies for dissection were so difficult to obtain before the Anatomy Act of 1832. Stories from several sources agree that he encouraged his students to look out for impending burials and sent them out at night with his horse and gig to recover the corpse.

In 1828 Overend's son, Wilson, who had undertaken some medical training in Edinburgh, successfully applied to become a lecturer with the Society of Apothecaries. He appears to have been more self-serving and less popular with the medical community than his father, who recognised that his small museum could not provide the facilities needed to improve standards of medical training. Hall Overend supported a campaign led by Dr Arnold Knight, who called a public meeting which agreed to found a single institution 'with proper rooms for the delivery of professional lectures, to be accompanied with scientific demonstrations and experiments on the principles and practice of Surgery and the *materia medica*'.[92] This idea was so popular that half the cost was subscribed on the spot. The proposed teachers' names were approved by the Society of Apothecaries in the same year, 1828. The Medical Institution opened in July 1829 in a new building on Surrey Street, which contained a museum/library, a lecture room with 100 seats and a dissecting room.

Wilson Overend refused to co-operate with the new Institution and he continued to run his own rival school, describing it as the 'Sheffield School of Anatomy and Medicine'. This was clearly not his father's wish, since he had seconded Dr Knight's resolution at the public meeting. Overend was in a very difficult position and appears to have retired from the scene; he died three years later in 1831.

The Wilson Overend school was destroyed by a riot in 1835 – and the adverse publicity which followed. According to the *Sheffield Iris*, which went to town on the story, the caretaker and his wife had been drinking with another man at the school's premises in Eyre Street, which housed the dissection room, until all were so drunk that the men put the wife out on the street where she shouted 'murder!'[93] A crowd broke into the building and found skeletons and partially-dissected bodies. This was a few years after Burke and Hare had been found guilty in 1829 of committing murder in order to supply Edinburgh surgeons with corpses for dissection. Public suspicion of anatomy museums had been aroused and the Sheffield crowd sacked

the building and burned its contents in the street. The riot was more 'first class entertainment' than serious protest, however, especially as the Medical Institution round the corner was almost untouched. The Riot Act was read, the dragoons arrived, the fire brigade cornered too fast, and the crowd was thoroughly drunk by the evening.

The initial courses of the Sheffield Medical Institution under Knight included midwifery, anatomy and the diseases of women and children. These were soon extended to cover physiology, chemistry, the 'practice of physic', surgery and medical jurisprudence: even at this date, knowledge of the law was necessary to doctors. Like all provincial medical schools, it was run by local doctors and surgeons who gave their teaching services free. From 1833, perhaps earlier, they were also designated as Proprietors, who agreed to give £20 a year. Lecturers had to be Proprietors, so they were, in effect, paying for the privilege of teaching. In return they became members of the governing Council and acquired dissection rights, but the rewards, set against the substantial outlay of time and money, were not enough for many. The Institution struggled to survive, in constant crisis caused by the regular resignations of the 'honorary' lecturers and the difficulty of recruiting new ones. The Institution was reorganised in 1850, but even the decision to appoint a paid member of staff, the Medical Tutor, did not improve matters. On at least two occasions, in 1865 and 1882, the Institution came near to closure. In 1865 the Institution advertised for lecturers in *materia medica*, physiology, anatomy and botany but received only one reply. For the teaching of botany, an essential aspect of pharmacology, it relied for thirty years on an amateur, a bank manager who lectured three times a week at 8.00 am in order to be at the bank by 9.00 am.

There are such considerable gaps in the records of the Medical Institution, which changed its name to the Sheffield School of Medicine in 1868, that it is impossible to give a detailed account of its early history. We know more about its leading figures, in particular Mariano Martin de Bartolomé, who was the President of the School for 22 years.[94] He was a Spaniard with an Edinburgh medical degree, who came to Sheffield in 1838 and practised from 3 Eyre Street in the city centre. He also had patients and a few student apprentices at the General Infirmary. He is said to have ridden there on a fine black horse and to have jumped the gate when he found it closed. Bartolomé estimated that he gave more than 3,000 lectures at the School of Medicine. He was sufficiently respected by his colleagues to be presented with his portrait in 1888.

During the second half of the nineteenth century, a good deal of work went on nationally to improve and systematise the medical curriculum. For example, the General Medical Council was created in 1858, 'a watershed marking the beginning of the end for apprenticeship medical training and the rise of scientific college education'.[95] The abolition of apprenticeship (in 1874) was hard for some consultants to accept. In Sheffield it led to the formation of a Clinical Committee, which agreed that hospital training fees could be collected by the Committee and divided annually among the clinical teachers. Dr Keeling's house, with its 'excellent refreshments', where meetings were held for 27 years, was central to the success of the

Mariano Martin de Bartolomé's biography reads like a romantic novel. He was the son of the Governor of the Province of Segovia, who had to flee Spain in 1832 for political reasons. The family went to the Channel Islands, where Mariano met his Sheffield-born wife. She paid for his medical training in Edinburgh and he became Physician to the Sheffield Royal Infirmary and President of the Sheffield Medical School for 22 years.

Bartolomé's microscope, made by the firm of Powell and Lealand, one of the top optical instrument makers in the country and medal winners at great international exhibitions. It was presented to the University in 1998 by his grandson Stephen on the occasion of the opening of the School of Nursing and Midwifery in the newly named Bartolomé House.

Arthur Jackson made a major contribution to the development of the Medical School. He followed his father, Henry Jackson, in being appointed Surgeon to the Infirmary. He once said 'the Sheffield School of Medicine is my child. I have no other'. Arthur Hall believed that the survival of the Medical School in the 1880s was due to him.

negotiations: 'hostilities simply melted away amidst such surroundings'.[96] Some doctors refused to accept the training fee, thus creating a fund which endowed scholarships and medical school developments.

The range of subjects in the medical curriculum was gradually extended, but there was debate about the preliminary sciences (physics, chemistry and biology) which was resolved by 1877 in favour of an examination to be passed before the start of the medical curriculum.[97] By 1885 this curriculum lasted four years, with an initial examination in anatomy, chemistry and physiology, and a final examination in medicine, surgery and midwifery. Its greater scope and length, together with the abolition of apprenticeship, gave an enhanced role to the medical schools, which some, including Sheffield, found difficulty in fulfilling.

The Sheffield School of Medicine was in a poor state in 1881, when records resume after a fifteen-year gap.[98] In addition to the problem of retaining and recruiting lecturers, there were few students and the building had been neglected. Arthur Hall, who was a student in 1883-4, recalled that,

> There was no laboratory of any kind. Except for the library, every place was in a state of decay. The anatomical theatre had not been used for years . . . The dissecting room was beyond words repelling . . . its contents were two trestle tables for the 'subjects', one or two stone tanks containing a few remains of dissected parts . . . and a dirty stone sink with cold water only, for all cleansing purposes. However, it did not matter much, because during the first three months of this winter session, in which we juniors were to study Anatomy, no 'subject' for dissection could be got for us![99]

The students were a motley crew who sat and smoked in a 'filthy den' the 'moral atmosphere of [which] was coarse and vulgar beyond imagination'. This description

The Medical School cricket team in the 1880s, with Mariano Martin de Bartolomé in the centre in a top hat and Arthur Jackson in the back row, third from the right.

28

accords with the account of the medical historian Newman, who suggests that inde-
cency and vulgarity were rife in medical schools until the late nineteenth century.[100]
It was one of the reasons for the resistance to accepting female students, who would
spoil the fun. Some of these students were the aptly-named 'chronics' who made no
academic progress but were allowed to continue at the School indefinitely on
payment of £30 a year. Arthur Hall left in disgust after one year, but returned later
and made an exceptional contribution to the School, as we shall see.

Bartolomé and the Council were trying to get a new building at this time. They
recognised the overwhelming need for change, especially as some of the students (in
their first two years) were now full-time. The new Secretary, Arthur Jackson, was
also galvanising efforts to improve the school. The way forward appeared almost
accidentally in 1882, when the Chemistry lecturer resigned and the Medical School
Council realised that, rather than run their own classes from inadequate premises,
the students could be directed to the chemistry classes at the new Firth College.
Thus began an association from which the Medical School was, initially, the main
beneficiary. The advantages to Firth College of widening its provision were,
however, clear to the farsighted. Viriamu Jones looked forward to a day when the
College would have three faculties, Arts, Pure and Applied Science, and Medicine,
and this vision became a guiding principle to W. M. Hicks.[101] A joint prospectus was
issued from 1884 onwards.

Encouraged by this promising relationship, the Council of the Medical School
decided in 1883 to build as close as possible to Firth College. A public subscription
for the new building attracted the support of leading figures, but the fund grew
slowly, for reasons which are hard to explain. At this time, much larger medical
institutions, such as the voluntary hospitals, were quickly securing substantial funds.
Sheffield had all the potential advantages of the urban medical school, as the Archbishop of York pointed out at a public meeting in 1886:

*The Medical School in its new
premises on Leopold Street. The
foundation stone was laid by M. M. de
Bartolomé on 17 June 1887. The
architect was J. D. Webster, who had
already designed the Children's
Hospital, the Jessop Hospital and
additions to the Royal Infirmary.*

> Sheffield is an excellent field for the acquisition of surgical and medical
> knowledge, inasmuch as it has a population of 300,000, which is rapidly
> increasing, possesses in its different hospitals about 400 beds supported by
> voluntary subscription, and from the nature of its industries and the
> powerful machinery therein employed daily witnesses accidents of the most
> varied and complicated nature.[102]

After four years, building began on a site close to the corner of Leopold Street,
directly opposite Firth College. Opened in September 1888, the School's premises
were twice as big as the previous building, with 'large and lofty' rooms, including a
library, classrooms, museum, dissecting room and a large tiered lecture theatre. Hall
described it as 'still but a glorified School of Anatomy' because it had no laboratories and the anatomy lecture theatre was far too big. However, all the preliminary
sciences were taught by Firth College and one or two of the Medical School's classrooms were adapted for extra laboratories. In this way the two institutions became
inextricably intertwined.

Arthur Hall was a gifted teacher, researcher and practitioner. His connection with the Medical School began in 1890 and he went on to become Professor of Physiology, Professor of Pathology and Professor of Medicine. He did outstanding research on encephalitis lethargica. He is shown here in his room at Leopold Street, c.1904, with plans for the new Western Bank building pinned above the fireplace.

Arthur Hall believed that the link with Firth College was 'the first glimmer of light at the dawn of a new day in the life of the School'. Medical student numbers increased encouragingly and the teaching improved markedly in the next few years. Tutors in medicine, surgery and midwifery were appointed to give a series of demonstrations to students taking final examinations and a full-time Tutor, subsequently Lecturer and Professor in Anatomy, Christopher Addison, began work in 1894. Addison was the school's first full-time lecturer, an able man who later left medicine for a distinguished career in politics. One of his students, A. E. Barnes, remembered that he was 'the students' friend', but tackled the 'chronics' by persuading the most hopeless to leave and giving such fine coaching that the others passed the examination.[103]

Arthur Hall was crucial to the Medical School's development. After his disastrous year as a Sheffield student, he qualified at St Bartholomew's in London and then returned, becoming Honorary Physician to the Royal Hospital and Assistant Demonstrator to the School of Medicine at the age of 24.[104] He also joined the Council of the School, with which he was associated for the next 46 years. 'He planned and very largely directed' its transformation into the Faculty of Medicine and his vision of its future needs led him to play a unique role. He was never a full-time member of staff but decided to build up various subjects as a lecturer until they became capable of supporting a full-time post. Thus, he taught physiology and equipped a modern laboratory, handing over to a full-time lecturer (later professor), C. Myers-Ward, in 1898. Hall then set to work on pathology, a subject in which he was an amateur; Barnes remembered his demonstration as 'the worst laboratory class I ever attended'.[105] The department was handed over to a full-time expert in 1906 and subsequently became a centre of excellence.

The number of students continued to rise and their behaviour improved, because of the leading example of Addison and perhaps also because they were given more respect. Hall recalls that wire netting which had covered the notice-board was removed and that the students were given free access to the library from 1891. When Arthur Jackson died in 1895, his widow endowed the Chair of Anatomy, a gift which ensured the future of that subject within the Medical School. Together with the new Favell Physiology Laboratory, this gave the Medical School confidence in its future as part of University College, Sheffield.

Christopher Addison (later Lord Addison) began his career in Sheffield as a Junior House Surgeon and was appointed full-time Medical Tutor in 1894 with the aim of improving clinical teaching in the Medical School. In 1897 he became first Arthur Jackson Professor of Anatomy in the chair endowed by Arthur Jackson's widow. In 1901 he left for Charing Cross Hospital Medical School and subsequently for a career in politics.

The London University beadle is scandalised by a request from a college student, Oliver Twist, that he be granted an honours degree (from the 1894 edition of IT).

THE FOUNDING OF
UNIVERSITY COLLEGE, SHEFFIELD

As soon as his campaign to secure government grants had concluded successfully, Hicks took up the idea of a single college which would have full power to award its own degrees. The fact that London University laid down the syllabus for the degree courses taught by Firth College was a source of professional dissatisfaction to the College lecturers. In addition, the College had little control over students registered externally with London University. Distance learning is not a modern phenomenon; it was quite possible for Sheffield students to take London courses in this way and some did so, depriving Firth College of the teaching income.

There was an alternative, since Owens College, Manchester, had united with University College, Liverpool and later with the Yorkshire College in Leeds to form the Victoria University. The Victoria University awarded its own degrees, including some in subjects not available in London, like engineering. Because it was a proper university, it had greater public prestige and entitlement to extra government grants. Sheffield was an adjacent northern city, so the Victoria University seemed to Hicks to be the natural home of Firth College and its associate Schools.

OLIVER TWIST REDIVIVUS
CHARLIE ASKING FOR MORE
"1st CLASS HONOURS, PHYSICS, PLEASE"

Sir Henry Stephenson, by Sir Arthur Stockdale Cope RA. Following the death of Mark Firth, the fledgling College survived only because of the energy of Sir Henry and his fellow trustees. He was first Vice-President of Firth College from 1881 and served it and its successors until his death in 1904. The University commemorates his name in a hall of residence, a fellowship and a lecture series.

'Nearly! A few more strokes'll do it', says Vulcan, depicted by 'Scuta' in IT as a Sheffield metalworker trying to bring about the unification of the Technical School, Firth College and the Medical School into University College. His sledgehammer is labelled 'Subscriptions'.

The campaign proved disastrous, however. A foretaste came when Henry Stephenson published statistics in the *Sheffield Independent* in 1893, comparing the student numbers, income and endowments of Sheffield, Liverpool, Birmingham and Leeds. They showed that the income of Firth College was minuscule

COLLEGE	DAY STUDENTS	EVENING STUDENTS	TOTAL ANNUAL INCOME	ENDOWMENT
Liverpool	240	Not registered	£14,015	£189,000
Birmingham	515	426	£10,275	£125,000
Leeds (incl. Tech. Sch.)	316	457	£22,965	£94,000
Sheffield (Firth Coll.)	103	136	£3,871	£18,133

Source: *Sheffield Independent*, 22 June 1893.

compared to the other colleges and its student numbers much smaller. Stephenson hoped, naively, to prove that Sheffield was making good use of its money. The figures for endowment income were so poor, however, that the newspaper published a crushing editorial suggesting that the attempt to join the Victoria University should drop.[106]

Hicks continued to argue that Sheffield, like the other colleges, would attract more income and students once it was a true university college. He directed his efforts towards increasing the endowment funds and formally uniting the three Sheffield schools, a slow business which was given sudden impetus by the projected visit of Queen Victoria to Sheffield in 1897. Although in her Diamond Jubilee year, this was her first visit to Sheffield. The Duke of Norfolk, who was Lord Mayor, agreed to be the first President of the University College and to support the launch of a Jubilee Endowment fund. According to Arthur Hall, who launched the fund in a letter to the *Sheffield Independent*, it would be 'a permanent memorial to the greatness and glory of our Gracious Majesty Queen Victoria's reign, of which so marked a feature has been the spread of education with all its moral and intellectual attributes'.[107] As was usual, this fund did not quite reach its target of £50,000; a cartoon in the student magazine *IT* showed a cutler laboriously forging the University College blade, with a hammer inscribed 'subscriptions' and the caption 'A few more strokes'll do it'.[108]

The establishment of the new college, which Arthur Hall hoped would be called Queen's College, involved protracted legal negotiations over the property of the three institutions. The Charter was granted on 11 May 1897, just in time for the Queen's visit on 21 May.

UNIVERSITY COLLEGE, SHEFFIELD, 1897-1905

The new College was not called Queen's College, or even Hallamshire College, for reasons which are unclear. All three of its constituent parts were represented at the highest level, with Stephenson, Mappin, Sorby and Dyson, the Professor of Medicine, as vice-presidents. Hicks was the first Principal and Stephenson the Chairman of the thirty-member Council.

In addition to the Council, the College had a new governing body, the Court. This was a large and unwieldy gathering of regional representatives: local mayors, chairmen of county councils, local members of Parliament, the head teachers of grammar schools 'of good standing', at least twenty city councillors and representatives of a great many local organisations, in addition to large donors to the College. The Court was not, of course, a decision-making body but a means by which members of the local community could influence its development. The Senate, consisting of the professors and other heads of departments with the Principal as chairman, was created to oversee the educational work of the College. The three organs of university governance instituted at this time were carried forward into the University in 1905 and survive, in modified form, to this day.

More should be said about Sir Henry Stephenson, who was the chairman of Council until his death in 1904, as well as the College's chief benefactor.[109] He was the head of Stephenson, Blake and Co, typefounders, a member of the Town Council and Mayor in 1887. His abiding interest in education led him to become a founding member of the Executive Council of Firth College and one of the instigators of the Technical School. He seldom missed even the dullest meeting, according to Chapman, and his 'massive common sense' and 'unusual clarity of thought' combined with his urbanity and personal generosity to surmount many a tangled problem. On his death he was described as the 'second founder' of University College.

The Technical School became the Department of Technology in the new College, but there was concern from the start about the elementary level of some of the courses provided, especially to evening class students. Were they appropriate to a university college? A compromise was reached by creating a Technical Department for the relatively advanced day-time students, leaving the Technical School for the others. Both were run by Professor Ripper but the Senate had no control over the work of the Technical School. Instead, the Technical Instruction Committee of the City Council kept a check on its work and ensured that it continued to qualify for their grants. This arrangement was clearly a compromise, disliked by Chapman, who writes of an *imperium in imperio* (empire within an empire).[110] The hostage to fortune was the power it gave to the city's Director of Education to interfere in the affairs of the University; one used without mercy in the 1920s and 1930s, as we shall see.

One goal remained: entry to the Victoria University. The University College was in a much stronger financial position now and the creation of a united College was a strong argument in its favour. Hicks and the College Council had good reason to believe that their facilities and range of courses were at least as good as those of Leeds at the time it was admitted to the Victoria University.

Hicks had exchanged regular letters since 1895 with the Vice-Chancellor of the Victoria University. He had pressed for a statement about the qualifying factors Sheffield would need and, although he was never given a promise, received the impression that the creation of a single university college would be the decisive factor. However, when the College Council formally applied for admission to the

'Scuta' laments the rejection of the College by Victoria University:

Graduate – Victoria University
Small Boy – Firth College

Small Boy: *Please may I call you mother now?*

Graduate: *How much have you got in your money box little boy?*

Small Boy: *£15,000, ma'am.*

Graduate: *No, run away my little man and come back when you have twice as much.*

33

University, in September 1897, it received a distinctly cold response. Questions were raised about the semi-independence of the Technical School and about financial and academic fitness. Representatives of the Victoria University Board of Studies made a formal inspection and many statistics were demanded and produced but, in June 1898, Sheffield's application was rejected.

This rejection was delivered in the most callous and humiliating way possible.[111] The University College Council discovered the decision by reading the morning newspapers. These contained a full transcript of the Victoria University's report, agreed unanimously the previous day, detailing all the faults found with Sheffield's application. The College itself received no communication until the following day, when a one-sentence letter of rejection was sent to the Registrar.[112] The College had to obtain a copy of the report from one of the newspapers.

The rigorous and judgmental nature of this report, even about matters for which evidence must have been slight, had just as much wounding power as the external appraisals of today. It is unnecessary to list all the faults found, or even the responses made by the Council in a detailed rebuttal.[113] The most serious were that some of the courses in arts, pure science and medicine were not 'sufficiently full' to meet the requirements of the University's degree examinations and that, apart from the Technical Department, the College buildings were inadequate. 'A large sum of money must be spent upon the purchase of an adequate site and the erecting [sic] of buildings'. Finally, the proportion of 'advanced' students was too low; only five honours students and one medical student were said to have graduated in the last few years.

It is difficult, years later, to judge the justice of this report. Sheffield University College's provision was extremely limited and the number of students achieving a degree very small. But it was by no means alone in this. All university colleges were struggling with the same problems and attempting to achieve a critical mass of courses, students, facilities and staff. The College can only be judged fairly by contemporary standards, and by those criteria Hicks and the University College Council had good reason to feel unjustly treated.

The College was able to rebut some of the facts in the report, but the strongest arguments came from a comparison of Sheffield's provision with that of the other colleges of the Victoria University, especially Leeds. Sheffield's arts and science staffing, for example, 'is stronger than at Leeds, even as shown in the Calendar for the current session'.[114] Sheffield's limited number and range of advanced students was no less than in Leeds, where the number of graduates in the previous four years totalled eleven, in engineering, chemistry and physics. The staff of the chemistry department were incensed at the suggestion that they had no facilities for carrying out research and pointed to five original research publications in the previous eighteen months, compared with five from Leeds and only two from Liverpool.

On the subject of its buildings, the College Council showed its practical, Sheffield face. The city had never gone in for extravagant buildings and the Council prided itself on its decision to make do with the accommodation it had and to wait for smarter accommodation until it could afford it. 'The finances are in a thoroughly stable and sound position, and no part of the income is expended on the service of debt'.[115]

It seems likely that University College, Sheffield, would have been welcomed if it had been judged by the criteria applied to the Yorkshire College, Leeds, when it was accepted for entry in 1887. Something had changed in the subsequent ten years. Historians have concluded that by 1897 the Victoria University had reached the limits of its development and was finding it increasingly difficult to manage the affairs of three separate colleges.[116] Liverpool was already considering withdrawal and gave its reasons for leaving in 1901 as, 'the machine is already overstrained; the organisation is already cumbrous and unwieldy. If other colleges were admitted – if their admission were forced upon the University by a successful appeal to the Privy Council – the organisation would break down.'[117] Leeds, more reluctantly, sought independent status in 1904, leaving Manchester alone as the Victoria University.

The leaders of the University College were furious at their treatment, not only the rejection itself but also the damaging press publicity. Hicks could only write to the *Sheffield Telegraph* asking its readers to 'suspend judgement' until 'our counter statement is before them'.[118] They considered an appeal to the Privy Council, but decided instead to attempt further 'friendly consultation' with the Victoria University. The reply from the Vice-Chancellor, Dr Nathan Bodington of the Leeds College, was anything but friendly. The University refused to state the conditions which would lead to Sheffield's acceptance and so Hicks and his colleagues abandoned all hope of a change of heart.

This episode blighted the closing years of the nineteenth century, especially for Hicks. But in the end the break-up of the Victoria University served Sheffield well. The way was clear for individual civic universities; Sheffield became one of them only seven years later.

University College football team, 1897.

Life in University College, Sheffield

When the College opened in 1897 there was 'an outburst of energy and enthusiasm' among staff and students.[119] A new journal, *Floreamus*, edited by Moore Smith, began. Since it was a staff-led venture, it was more serious than *IT* but introduced the College song with a special 'Scuta' cartoon. This song, which had six verses, was thereafter sung at student social gatherings, from the Musical Society to sports prize-givings.

A Students' Union had been in some form of existence at Firth College since 1895 and socials in the early days of the University College were designed to bring the three groups of students together, with mixed results. *Tableaux vivants* at the

Cover of 'A College Song', with music by Henry Coward and words by G. C. Moore Smith.

A College Song.

1 O the life of a Student's the life made for me,
   By the Cam or the Isis, the Seine or the Spree !
   But the best of all Students, or more is the pity,
   Are the Students who gather in Sheffield's black city !

   CHORUS.
   O Studiose,
   Magna cum voce
   Dic, ' Floreamus ! '

2 Do we envy the drudges who toil but for gold,
   With their minds ever shrinking, their hearts growing cold ?
   The Student who lives with the great ones of yore
   Has more in his garret than they in their store!
                          Chorus.—O Studiose, etc.

3 For life's little hardships, 'tis little we care :
   We've a world of our own and they can't enter there.
   We have Newton to lead us, and Shelley to sing,
   So, if the flies sting us, Amen, let them sting !
                          Chorus.—O Studiose, etc.

4 There's a joy that descends on the Student alone
   When he conquers a poser and feels himself grown,
   When he sees a bit deeper in nature or man,
   And thinks a bit harder than simple folks can.
                          Chorus.—O Studiose, etc.

5 And when work is put by, and he lifts up his eyes,
   How dear to the Student green fields and blue skies !
   The dark purple moor where he lies with his friend !
   The leaping and laughter ! the talk without end !
                          Chorus.—O Studiose, etc.

6 Then here's to our College, its friends and its founders !
   And here's to sound learning, and all its expounders !
   And here's to all Students, wherever they be,
   And, last but not least, here's to you and to me !
                          Chorus.—O Studiose, etc.

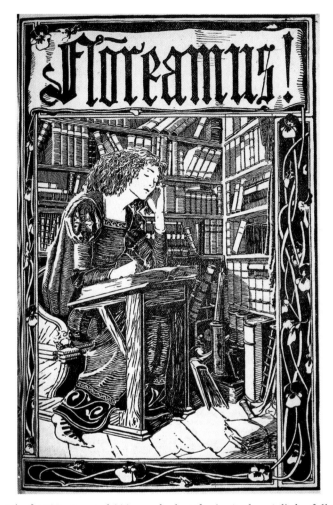

1897 'Scuta' cover of Floreamus *showing a female student in Pre-Raphaelite style.* Floreamus, *a chronicle of University College first appeared in 1897 and was edited by G. C. Moore Smith. Later it became a student magazine, which survived until 1928.*

Easter social of 1898 attracted 300 people, but the 'united social' the following year was attended by more women than men.[120] Perhaps the women preferred this kind of social, which seems to have been modelled on a parlour evening, with a piano solo, recitations, songs and a game entitled 'Clumps'. Medical students preferred 'smoking concerts' and a few of the male students, at least, wanted some single-sex debates and concerts.[121] The Medical School was alone in excluding women at this time and the success of co-education is the strong impression given by both *IT* and *Floreamus*. A full-page 'Scuta' drawing of a female student was used on the first cover of *Floreamus* in 1897.

Women students acquired a new common room in 1897 and the first women's hall, St Peter's on Ashdell Road, opened in 1901. Dorothy Russell Potter, who lived there in its earliest years, remembered a 'home from home' for about twenty women run by Mrs Fenn, a motherly woman who 'took a delight in giving frequent evening and garden parties to which our friends were invited and which we all thoroughly

William Tusting Cocking was Secretary to the Medical School from 1889. 'From the very infancy of its rebirth Cocking became the one person really responsible for [the School's] successful organisation and management' (Hall). Cocking died aged 50 from tuberculosis, almost certainly contracted from a patient.

Mrs Lysbeth Henry, the first woman member of staff, was responsible for training students intending to become elementary school teachers and bore the imposing title 'Mistress of Method'. Her original intention to study medicine was thwarted by the lack of places for women, but her daughter, Lydia Henry, was the first female graduate in Medicine in 1916.

enjoyed.'[122] The house was spartan, with 'a scarcity of bathrooms and hot water' but had 'sunny rooms, shady trees and sloping lawns' and was a happy, friendly and supportive place in which to live.

The majority of students, by a factor of three to one, were still those taking technical courses in the evening. The number of day students, however, was steadily rising. Most of these students were training as teachers and, in general, the development of University College emphasised the vocational. This was partly because of the influence of businessmen on the College Council.[123] It was the Council, for example, rather than the Senate, that decided, like other civic colleges at the time, to run language classes designed especially for aspiring teachers or 'commercial students'.[124] Two new professors of French and German began work in 1901; Professor A. T. Baker was to serve the French department for 35 years, a 'many-sided teacher and scholar'.[125] There seems to have been no expectation that language courses would be taken for their own sake, but on this occasion the commercial languages course was a failure and Extension courses in French and German a great success.

The Law School started in 1899, funded in the early years by the Sheffield Law Society. The initial lecturers were two distinguished Sheffield lawyers, Robert Leader and Edward Bramley. After a shaky start, they established an annual student cohort of twelve to fifteen.[126] The Medical School continued to improve under the energetic leadership of Tusting Cocking as Dean and of Arthur Hall. The teaching of bacteriology received an enormous boost after the arrival of John Robertson as Medical Officer of Health for Sheffield. In 1897 he set up a bacteriological laboratory for the use of the School and the city in West Street, and acted as unpaid lecturer there, as well as being Professor of Public Health. When he left the city in 1903 a full-time lecturer, Charles Porter, was employed at his laboratory.

Following the creation of a Dental Department at the Royal Hospital, a small Dental School with three part-time 'honorary' lecturers began work in 1898. The day training college for primary teachers, set up in 1890, had forty to fifty students by 1897, and had become a vital component of the College, providing between one-third and one-half of all the students on arts and science courses.[127] Most were following a two-year teaching certificate; few aimed at a degree. The programme was inadequately funded. The sole education lecturer, Mrs Henry, must have been, as Chapman says, a 'remarkable woman'. Energetic efforts to improve elementary education were made at the turn of the century by government and local School Boards. The level of provision at the day training college was criticised in 1899 and the College Council agreed to provide a teaching assistant – on the inevitable condition that savings were made elsewhere.[128]

The demand for training places was becoming so acute that it was impossible for University College to accommodate it, especially given the numbers of non-matriculated students. In 1905 the City Council, with powers granted by the 1902 Education Act, took control of the training college. New premises were provided in the recently vacated Royal Grammar School on Collegiate Crescent, a new Principal (V. W. Pearson) was appointed and Mrs Henry became Lady Superintendent.

There were 132 students in its first year of operation. This was the start of the City of Sheffield Teacher Training College. It continued for some time to have a relationship with the University of Sheffield, but later became part of the Sheffield Polytechnic and exists today within Sheffield Hallam University.

The loss of such a significant number of students seems, in retrospect, unfortunate and avoidable. The University persisted with another group of sub-degree level students in the Technical School. Hicks and Ripper insisted on keeping these students, especially since the attitude of local manufacturers had changed. From scoffing at the idea that the College could be of service to them, they had now become 'its stoutest supporters'.[129] The Technical School expanded into an additional new building on Charlotte Street, later Mappin Street, in 1904. This was the first part of the range of buildings which now face St George's Church.

Accommodation problems at the main College site were not so easily solved. The library, for example, housed in shelves around the big hall of the Firth College building, could only be used when nothing else was going on in there. The bookcases were locked, the only librarian was Professor Moore Smith, and the grant for purchase of books and journals, already low, was reduced to £40 in 1903. The Senate objected strongly but the College Council refused to move. Its attitude can only be described as philistine. 'Some of the more powerful lay members did not understand what a library was', comments Chapman.

In 1904 W. P. Wynne accepted the chair of chemistry in blissful ignorance of the state of his new department. In a speech made 21 years later, he recalled that if he had seen it, he would have gone straight back to London, since:

> There was no staff and all lecture apparatus and laboratory records had been removed by my predecessor, being his private property. Picture my first lecture in that dismal, underground lecture room . . . [with] a horsehair chair, rather the worse for wear, set out behind the lecture table.[130]

This was the chair used by Professor Carleton Williams who, suffering from gout, gave his lectures sitting down. Chemistry was at a particularly low ebb in 1904, since both Williams and George Young, the organic chemistry lecturer, had resigned. Wynne began 'a struggle' which led to a great improvement in the facilities of the Chemistry department. As one of the students' best friends among the staff, he was also horrified by the lack of permanent facilities for athletics and began a campaign which eventually ended the years of moving between rented fields in inconvenient locations, as we shall see.

Physics, by contrast, was flourishing under the direction of Hicks. Electronics was becoming a major subject and Hicks had published a useful handbook on dynamics. One of his students recalled that,

> His lectures were perfect logical demonstrations well illustrated with bench experiments. He collected the notebooks every month and read them and corrected errors. This was a hard intellectual course, the hardest in the

The Same Old Turn *from* IT *referring to the impoverished state of the Athletic Union. The refrain is 'Times was when cash & I were well acquainted'.*

William Palmer Wynne FRS was Professor of Chemistry 1904–31. He revived the department and was also a major figure in University affairs, as Dean for 20 years and a member of the University Council and Finance Committee. A powerful advocate of better sporting facilities, he regarded the award of honorary athletics colours to him by the student body as one of his greatest honours.

A Shady Nook, *a student impression of the Chemistry laboratory in 1896, taken from* IT.

college . . . Hicks did not use the symbols of the calculus but whenever he came to subjects requiring the calculus demonstrated the problem from first principles.[131]

William Michael Gibbons was appointed Registrar in 1902 at the age of 29. He served in that post for 42 years and instituted a highly disciplined and meticulous regime that was spoken of with awe by administrative staff many years after his retirement.

By 1904/05, there were more than 500 day-time students in the College. The great majority were local, drawn from homes within a thirty-mile radius, and taking part-time courses. Very few were registered for the University of London degree, and only four gained a BA or BSc in that year.[132] Twenty-eight passed courses in the Medical School. The largest group of students attended in the evening after a day's work – 1,162 in the Technical department. This student profile did not change until the First World War and it is only since the Second World War that it has become what it is today, with the majority of undergraduates in the 18 to 22 age range, drawn from the whole of the British Isles, as well as overseas.

Once French, German and economics were added to the curriculum, the pressure on space in Leopold Street forced the College Council to seek new premises. An early idea was to house the entire College at St George's Square, as a letter from the architects Gibbs & Flockton in 1900 shows.[133] The 'Arts and Science department' would have been accommodated in new buildings fronting St George's Square and the Medical School in buildings on the 'south west corner' of the Square and Portobello. A Central Block would have contained the 'Great Hall, Library, Museum, Council Room etc'. This plan collapsed because of the difficulty in obtaining all the land. The result, to the regret of many, was that the College was developed on two separate sites. The new Western Bank building opened in 1905, the year that the University College was granted a Charter as an independent university.

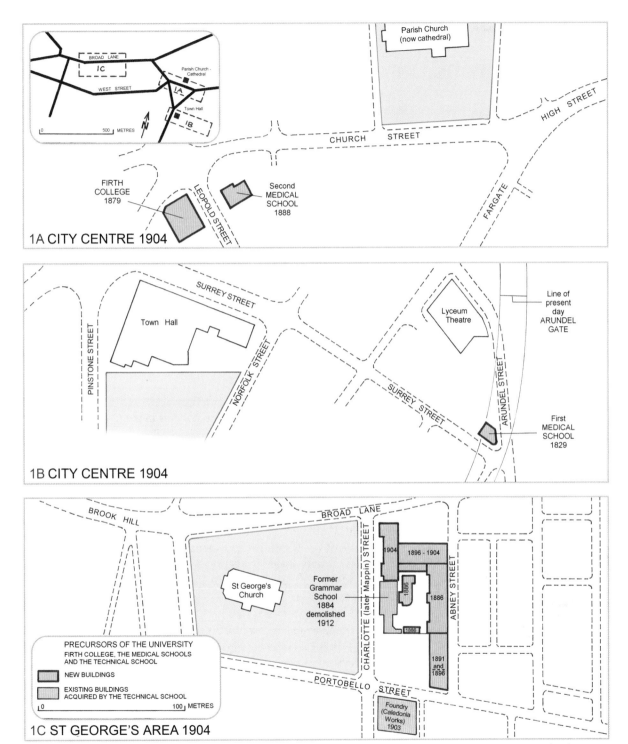

1A CITY CENTRE 1904

BROAD LANE

1C

WEST STREET

Parish Church - Cathedral

1A

Town Hall

1B

0   500   METRES

Parish Church (now cathedral)

CHURCH STREET

HIGH STREET

FARGATE

FIRTH COLLEGE 1879

LEOPOLD STREET

Second MEDICAL SCHOOL 1888

1B CITY CENTRE 1904

SURREY STREET

PINSTONE STREET

Town Hall

NORFOLK STREET

Lyceum Theatre

Line of present day ARUNDEL GATE

SURREY STREET

ARUNDEL STREET

First MEDICAL SCHOOL 1829

1C ST GEORGE'S AREA 1904

BROOK HILL

BROAD LANE

St George's Church

Former Grammar School 1884 demolished 1912

CHARLOTTE (later Mappin) STREET

1904

1896 - 1904

1886

1886

1886

ABNEY STREET

1886

1891 and 1896

PORTOBELLO STREET

Foundry (Caledonia Works) 1903

PRECURSORS OF THE UNIVERSITY
FIRTH COLLEGE, THE MEDICAL SCHOOLS AND THE TECHNICAL SCHOOL

NEW BUILDINGS

EXISTING BUILDINGS ACQUIRED BY THE TECHNICAL SCHOOL

0   100 METRES

Maps © Crown Copyright Ordnance Survey

41

varie

In

of

2

The University's Early Years and the Impact of War: 1905–18

Introduction

I
N THE FIRST DECADE OF THE TWENTIETH CENTURY the civic university colleges came of age, gaining university status. 'Vocationalism and efficiency' were the watchwords of the pre-war years, a national mood which helped to create and foster civic higher education, especially on its technical side.[1] Imperial College, London, was founded and Birmingham University's Great Hall at Edgbaston was adorned with friezes which depicted 'boilers, pistons, lathes, presses, drilling, forging . . . and colliers with a coal tub – the Midlands at work'.[2] The trend was sufficiently pronounced to cause anxiety in the courts and quadrangles of Oxford and Cambridge. In 1903, Cambridge was still insisting that its naval engineering students should study Greek and lost a large endowment as a result. Changes were made in response to the needs of modern industry and commerce. Oxford introduced an engineering degree in 1908, the last English university to do so. By 1914 both universities were attracting large donations from industry.

This was one of the few times when the civic universities were blazing a trail, for the Oxbridge ideal was deep-rooted and returned to haunt the academic upstarts after the First World War.[3] Even before the war the civics endured a certain amount of carping from the establishment. A government report of 1902 suggested that the standard of student in the university colleges was so low that 'the teachers have no alternative but to reduce to a pulp the mental nutriment with which they feed the pupils' and that no graduate of first-class ability from Oxford or Cambridge could be safely advised to take a post in one for fear of 'muffling his intellect'.[4] As late as 1919, Professor Ripper in Sheffield chided the governors of a local grammar school

Western House was 'a beautiful square stone mansion built of fine grained sandstone varied in colour by many markings. Some of the stone from this house was used by Mr Gibbs in lining the entrance and staircase of the University'. (Hunter Archaeological Society report)

for advertising their wish to appoint only a graduate of 'the older universities' as headmaster.[5] In practice, however, the civics were nurtured by graduates of Oxford and Cambridge, on both the academic and the administrative sides. They inevitably transplanted the educational ideals of the *alma mater* to the virgin territories. The quadrangles of Sheffield and Manchester, the provision of a liberal education in the arts and even the social sciences are examples of this. But the imitation did not extend very far, because the circumstances of the civics were so different. None, for example, copied the Oxford and Cambridge collegiate model, combining teaching and residence, because none, in the early days, had sufficient numbers of resident students. In designing Edgbaston, Joseph Chamberlain looked to the universities of Germany and the United States for inspiration.[6]

In the early days of the new university charters, the atmosphere was optimistic; there was slow but steady growth combined with energy and drive. Government inspectors in 1907 were much more complimentary than those of 1902:

> There is a university spirit incapable of definition which pervades the several University Colleges in a greater or less degree, influencing the intellectual growth of their students and producing, as we think, results of the highest importance.[7]

THE NEW BUILDING AT WESTERN BANK

Building decisions made during their early years dictated the long-term future of the fledgling universities. Birmingham, for example, chose in 1900 to develop a greenfield site of 25 acres at Edgbaston, which became the first true university campus in Britain.[8] Although its medical school remained in the city centre, Birmingham had substantial room to grow, in contrast to almost every other civic university. Sheffield moved from its city centre premises in 1905, but the new site was not extensive and was bounded on two sides by a public park, which necessitated City Council permission when the University wanted to build its first

The University buildings, as constructed in 1905 with the anticipated University library, built in 1909. Earlier designs envisaged a tower and the fourth side of the quadrangle to the right; that tower was built several decades later while the fourth side of the quadrangle did not appear until 2003.

44

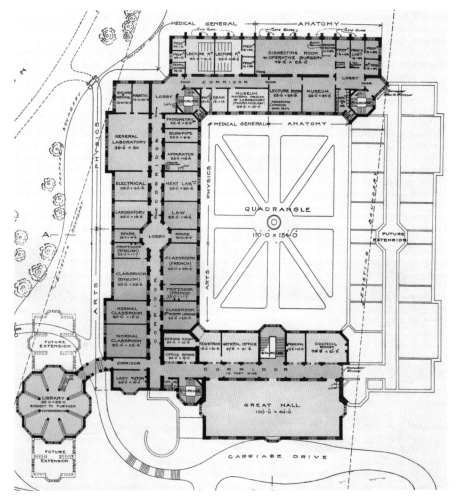

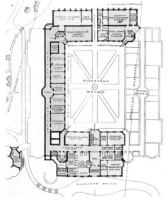

Plans for the ground and first floor levels of the new buildings, with Weston Park to the left and an outline of the planned fourth wing to the right. Even at this stage the library, later funded by Edgar Allen, is indicated in the form and situation it was to take in 1909. Future extensions to the library are envisaged in the drawing.

extension, a library, in 1909. Manchester and Liverpool both had substantial sites close to the city centre, but encountered the problem of space for expansion after 1918. The site occupied by Leeds, at Beech Grove Hall, was of campus size but, until 1927, it had almost no money to build on the scale needed.[9]

The Council of University College, Sheffield had been seeking a larger site since 1897. Among those considered was Wesley College on Clarkehouse Road, which was vacant, but proved unsuitable.[10] The possibility of a new building at the top of the Botanical Gardens, fronting on to Clarkehouse Road, foundered on the refusal of the staff of the Medical School to move further from the two hospitals, the Royal Infirmary on Infirmary Road and the Royal Hospital on West Street.[11]

The medical lecturers were prepared to accept a site at Leavy Greave, St George's, or Western Bank. At both St George's and Leavy Greave it proved impossible to buy some of the necessary land. Western House, which was bordered on two sides by Weston Park, was for sale and in 1903 the College agreed to buy and

Edward Mitchell Gibbs, who designed
Western Bank, trained at Sheffield
School of Art and the Royal Academy
in London. He worked in the practice
of the prominent architect Alfred
Waterhouse before returning to
Sheffield and in 1878 joining Thomas
Flockton's practice as a partner.

demolish it.[12] The site was small and half a mile from the Technical School, hardly
perfect, but the Council obtained the financial support of large donors like Sir
Henry Stephenson, Sir Frederick Mappin and Dr H. C. Sorby for the purchase.
Sorby gave an additional £3,500 for adjacent land to be used for later development.

The design of the new College building, by E. M. Gibbs, was based on the traditional collegiate quadrangle, but Sheffield's had one side missing, because only
three were needed – one for arts and pure science, one for the Medical School and
one for ceremonial purposes and administration. The original plan allowed for a
fourth side to be erected later but this decision was reversed in 1913. The foundation
stone was laid on 30 June 1903 by the Lord Mayor of London, Sir Marcus Samuel,
who had a splendid procession of military escorts and three state carriages. Large
crowds gathered and a garden party for some 2,000 guests was held in Weston Park.

By the time the building was ready for occupation, University College had
become the University of Sheffield. Western Bank was the perfect setting for the
infant university, except in one respect. The choice of site maintained the physical
distance between the Applied Science departments and the rest; inevitably detrimental to the intellectual and social life of both. It also determined the future
building plan, ensuring that the University, as it developed, would encroach on residential areas nearby. There was no space for expansion. On the other hand, it is hard
to see how the Council could have chosen better, given the scarcity of vacant land
in all the areas within reasonable reach of the hospitals.

A smartly dressed Edwardian crowd at
the laying of the foundation stone,
being addressed from the dais by the
Lord Mayor of London, Sir Marcus
Samuel. Seated immediately to the
right of the stone is the Duke of
Norfolk, behind it is the architect Gibbs
and Professor Hicks and, to the Duke's
right, Sir Henry Stephenson.

THE "HAT" IN THE WORKSHOP.

THE PROPOSED UNIVERSITY BUILDING.

You should support the University because:

1. The UNIVERSITY will be for the people.
2. The UNIVERSITY will bring the highest education within the reach of the child of the working man.
3. The UNIVERSITY will help the local industries.
4. The UNIVERSITY will be the centre where the treatment of accidents and diseases will be studied.
5. SHEFFIELD is the only large City in England without a University. Sheffield cannot afford to remain in this position.
6. The UNIVERSITY will not only benefit this district, it will assist the nation in its trade competition with other nations.

Ask at your works or shop for a copy of the Pamphlet on the University Movement.

OBTAINING THE CHARTER

When the federal Victoria University began to break up, early in 1902, the university college of Leeds proposed a 'Yorkshire University' based in Leeds. The University College Council in Sheffield were quick to point out that Leeds could not claim to represent Yorkshire.[13] At this stage, Sheffield would have been happy to become a joint partner in a 'Yorkshire University' and sent a petition to the Privy Council to this effect in June 1902. The Leeds college, wary of creating another federal university, refused to consider this proposal. Civic pride now dictated that Sheffield apply immediately for a separate Charter, lest Leeds become, by default, the only 'Yorkshire University'. In the most friendly spirit, 'come what may, we must be on an equality with Leeds', said Sir Henry Stephenson.[14]

The College Court met on 18 May 1903 to debate the issue. Hicks argued that the power of awarding independent degrees would attract good staff. At present, he said, 'the professor had nothing to show that the result was his work, and all artists liked to paint their names on their pictures'.[15] Alderman Franklin, making the case for applied science degrees, stated that 'there is no better investment for a business man than the encouragement of science'. Professor Anderson of the arts faculty held that a university was 'the fountain from which teachers are poured forth into the schools'. At both this meeting and a public meeting held that evening, the resolution to apply for a Charter was passed unanimously.[16]

This was the moment when Sheffield grasped a big opportunity and made it happen against the odds. In March 1903, Frederick Mappin thought it would be

Left: The appeal for funding for the University extended across all classes and received warm support from the working people of the city, who the Sheffield Independent felt made 'a very creditable display of the proper sense of citizenship'. (Cartoon 4 June 1904)

Above: Handbills of this kind put the University case across and seem to have had the desired result. In September 1902 the Vice-Chancellor of Leeds wrote to Hicks: 'I found a collection being taken in a pupil teacher centre in North Derbyshire for the new University. It shows that the people believe in it whatever the local authorities may do.'

The Charter was met at Victoria Station by the Pro-Chancellor George Franklin and conducted with police outriders and a procession of carriages to Firth College, where the birth of the new University was announced.

THE PROCESSION WITH THE ROYAL CHARTER FOR THE NEW UNIVERSITY LEAVING VICTORIA STATION JUNE 3RD 1905.

impossible to persuade the City Council to provide the funds that would be needed.[17] A few weeks later, realising the commercial and prestige value of a civic university, the Council supported the movement with a promise to increase its financial aid to the proposed university by a penny rate. This was an increase of more than 300 per cent, a strong vote of confidence. Such large funds were essential, since the Senate estimated that a capital sum of £10,000 would be needed for equipment, with another £10,000 annually for recurrent expenditure. The University College had recently raised £51,000 by public appeal for the Western Bank building, but a packed public meeting decided to extend the appeal to a new target of £170,000.

The original donors increased their offers, and resolutions in favour of the Charter were passed by a myriad of local organisations. The amount of local support received during the campaign was striking, reminding us that the University was truly a creation of the city and could not have existed without its backing. The fundraising included house-to-house visiting in the more prosperous streets and weekly collections in many places of work, to which thousands of workmen contributed. The Moody-Manners Opera Company held a 'University Opera Week' at the Theatre Royal in November 1904 with an ambitious programme. Eight operas, or operas in excerpt, were performed, four of them by Wagner. The students attended *en masse* on the Friday night and presented flowers to the 'diva', and all profits from the week were donated to the university fund.[18]

On 3 March 1904 the Privy Council sent two letters containing most welcome news. The first copied a letter to the Principal of Leeds, refusing its claim to become the 'Yorkshire University' and the second promised a Charter to Sheffield 'subject to a substantial realisation of the hopes mentioned', that is the appeal fund.[19] A year later, donations to the fund had risen to £130,000 and the Charter was granted. It was sealed on 31 May 1905.[20] The University of Sheffield had come into being.

An enthusiastic crowd of staff, students and civic leaders met George Franklin, the new Pro-Chancellor, when he arrived at Sheffield Victoria station with the Charter. A procession of decorated carriages, headed by the Band of the Hallamshire Rifles, led the Charter through the city to a ceremonial reception at Firth College. The women students had 'vehicles decked with gold-petalled flowers and streamers, yellow and black' (the University colours) and joined with the men in making a tremendous noise on 'pipes of Pan-demonium'.[21]

On 12 July, the University was honoured by a state visit from King Edward VII, who opened the Western Bank building. This was a civic occasion of the greatest importance, with street decorations, triumphal arches and a procession of open carriages watched by crowds which included 40,000 school-children. The opening ceremony of the new University was held in the new quadrangle, framed on its open side by a specially erected and extravagantly domed pavilion. Over 3,000 guests were entertained by the Sheffield Festival Chorus and heard speeches from the new Vice-Chancellor, Hicks, the new Chancellor, the Duke of Norfolk, and from the King himself. It appears that his prepared text was lost and, spontaneously, he confined himself to one sentence: 'I have great pleasure in declaring these beautiful buildings open and in expressing my fervent hope and desire for the long continued prosperity of the University of Sheffield.' This was, as Chapman comments, more effective than a longer speech.[22]

Hicks became the first Vice-Chancellor in recognition of his dedicated, sustained contribution to the creation of the University, over more than twenty years as Principal of the College. He had been Professor of Physics throughout that time and did not wish to combine the two roles within the new University. He decided to retire to his chair after he had presided over the inaugural ceremonies. His successor, Sir Charles Eliot, had already been selected and took over from Hicks on 15 July.

Sir Charles Eliot, Vice-Chancellor 1905-12, was a brilliant polymath, with scholarly interests in both zoology and Far Eastern languages and philosophy. From Sheffield, he moved to the University of Hong Kong as Vice-Chancellor.

THE INFANT UNIVERSITY

Arts and science were housed in the west wing of Western Bank and medicine in the north wing, both of which faced the park; the contrast with the shock Professor Wynne received on his arrival at Firth College in 1904 could not have been greater. Possession of this distinguished new building must have been a golden moment for the staff, although apparently some complained that they were rattling around. A basement refectory (opened in 1906) and common rooms in the administrative wing

The University's ceremonial mace presented in 1909 by George Franklin. Made in silver-gilt, it was designed by W. W. Scott with the York rose along the shaft and the arms of the city and University on the bowl. It was used for the first time at the conferment of an honorary degree on the Prince of Wales when he opened the Edgar Allen Library.

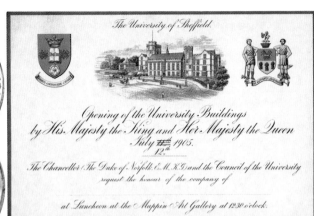

Description of the University Buildings.

The new buildings of the University are of red brick and stone. The are constructed in the Tudor style of architecture, and form three sides of a quadrangle, the arrangement being similar to that followed by most of the Colleges at Oxford and Cambridge. A tower has been erected at one side of the quadrangle, octagonal turrets at two of the other corners ; the site of the third turret together with the fourth side of the quadrangle being left vacant in order to provide for future extensions. The building on the south side, which faces Western Bank, contains the large Hall of the University ; this hall is to be known by the name of the Firth Hall, after the founder of Firth College. The Firth Hall is designed to accommodate an audience of about 800 persons, it is 100 feet long, and 40 feet in width ; it is lighted by 18 windows, and has an open-work oak roof, which in its arches and mouldings is of the Tudor period of architecture. In the same building are the Administrative Offices, the Council Room, the Common Rooms and Refectories ; the Council Room, and the Professors' Common Room are, like the Firth Hall, panelled in oak ; plaster ceilings dating from the sixteenth century, the gift of the Duke of Norfolk, are in the Vice-Chancellor's Room and the Professors' Common Room ; the Council Room has also a plaster ceiling of modern date. The buildings on the west and north sides provide for the needs of the different departments, that on the west sides for the departments in the Faculties of Arts and Pure Science, that on the north for the departments in the Medical Faculty. In the centre of the quadrangle is a granite fountain, the gift of H. K. Stephenson, Esq., the Treasurer of the University. Provision has not yet been made for a Library ; but it is intended that this shall be erected in the grounds that adjoin Weston Park : ...

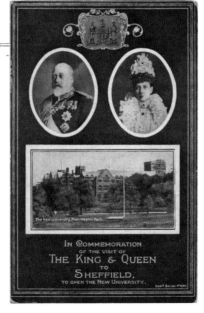

Facing page, clockwise from top left: Henry Fitzalan Howard, 15th Duke of Norfolk, was an ideal choice as the first Chancellor. Generous to social and welfare causes in the city, he had a particular commitment to education and his financial support was crucial to the creation of the Technical School. In addition to significant donations to the University fund he gave two handsome 16th century ceilings to Western Bank.

Every school-child in Sheffield received one of these medals commemorating the visit of the King and Queen to open the University.

Invitation card for the opening of the University, showing the more ambitious scheme for the buildings rather than the one actually in place in 1905. The original date had to be changed at a late stage.

The royal procession arriving at Western Bank.

The King and Queen left the exotic domed dais among a sea of hats while the Festival Chorus sang Sullivan's 'O Gladsome Light'. The Royal party proceeded to Weston Park where the King presented colours to the King's Own Yorkshire Light Infantry.

Badges worn by stewards and others officiating at the Royal Visit.

Left, clockwise from top: *From the programme produced for the opening of the new University building by King Edward VII and Queen Alexandra, 12 July 1905.*

The great event was marked by a proliferation of postcards of all kinds.

A souvenir serviette printed with the programme for the visit.

Firth Hall, the main assembly hall of the University, was distinguished by a fine series of timber roof trusses in American oak. This shows the original open tracery (now hidden by a suspended ceiling) and the early gasoliers. The marble bust of Mark Firth stands in its new location.

on the south side of the building provided a central meeting point; social activities for both staff and students were held in the new Firth Hall. This was the only part named after Mark Firth; the building itself was known simply as 'Western Bank' until the mid-1980s when it was given the name 'Firth Court'.

Firth Hall was part of a suite of rooms on the first floor presided over by the administrators, headed by the Registrar, W. M. Gibbons, and the new Vice-Chancellor, Sir Charles Eliot. He was the choice of the University Council, without reference to the Senate, and a rather surprising one, since his background was not in education, but the diplomatic service.[23] He had recently left his post after a serious dispute with Lord Lansdowne over events in East Africa.[24] Eliot was, however, formidably intellectual, conversant with at least twenty languages and an accomplished amateur biologist. He never had a popular touch within Sheffield itself, but his appointment can be regarded as far-sighted. Eliot had the ear of civil servants and politicians and could speak for Sheffield on the national, and even the international, stage. He inaugurated a tradition, for the following two vice-chancellors, Fisher and Hadow, had similar strengths and backgrounds. Eliot's intellectual interests, like theirs, were almost a hobby, 'the surplus products of a career devoted to public affairs . . . the irrepressible exuberance of a man of genius', in the words of the public orator.[25]

The new Council of the University was enlarged to 37 members to include the dean of each faculty and a representative of the Senate. The influential deans at this time were Appleton (Arts), Leahy (Pure Science), Cocking (Medicine) and Ripper (Applied Science). Large donors were no longer entitled to a seat on the Council, a right which had been criticised for allowing undue influence. The academics, especially the deans, now had a greater say in the running of the University. In the first year they outnumbered the civic representatives by fifteen to nine. Sheffield City Council was now, and for some years to come, making the largest university grant of any provincial local authority.[26] The Technical School continued to be managed by its Committee, now called the Applied Science Committee and under the nominal control of the University Council, but in fact a body with independent power. The Applied Science faculty still had a separate budget and its own Secretary.

Staff numbers increased to forty, but their work was very different from that of a modern university lecturer. Even within Western Bank, the majority of the students were still studying below degree level and were part-time. The different groups of students demanded a wide range of courses, but usually formed into small classes, which created a heavy load of preparation and teaching for the lecturers. The numbers of full-time students increased steadily, as Appendix 4A shows. The importance of part-time students to Sheffield was so great that the university ordinances originally made provision for part-time degrees in metallurgy and engineering. These were not unique, since Liverpool had an evening BA, but they were controversial. The ideal of the full-time degree student was not easily relinquished and has, indeed, endured to the present day. Sheffield's degrees, in its first seven years, had to be ratified by the other three northern universities, a system which Professor Wynne described as 'serving seven years for Rachel'.[27] The 'Joint Matriculation Board' established for this purpose went on to become an examining board run by all four universities. The Board rejected the part-time engineering degree, but a metallurgy degree, including one year of full-time study for employees in the Sheffield cutlery and steel trades, survived. Teachers had made a request for a part-time arts degree, and Eliot tried to provide staffing for it, but it proved unsustainable.

The full-time degrees in place by 1905/06 included the full spectrum of Bachelor's, Master's and Doctoral degrees in Arts, Science, Medicine, Engineering

Senior members of the University almost hidden by palms at a degree ceremony on the stage of the Albert Hall in 1911. This hall stood opposite the later City Hall.

53

F. G. Belton, first President of the Student Representative Council.

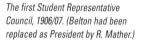

The first Student Representative Council, 1906/07. (Belton had been replaced as President by R. Mather.)

and Metallurgy. The first congregation to award Sheffield degrees took place on 2 July 1908 in Firth Hall. The faculties were consulted about the colours of academic hoods; Engineering chose purple, Metallurgy, predictably, steel grey, and Pure Science apricot. Lots had to be drawn at the Senate when Arts and Medicine both opted for red. Medicine won and Arts chose 'crushed strawberry'.[28]

The University took the opportunity, perhaps too readily, to reward its longest standing supporters with honorary degrees. The Chancellor, the Duke of Norfolk, became the first Sheffield graduate by receiving his degree before the ceremony. He, along with George Franklin (Chairman of Council) and Charles Harding Firth (benefactor of the library and former History lecturer), were honoured with doctorates. W. M. Hicks, W. Ripper, and J. O. Arnold received 'substantive' doctorates and many other members of staff 'ex-officio' Master's degrees.[29] Last, but surely not least, came twelve students who had passed the first Sheffield final examinations and fifty former Sheffield students who had graduated as external students of other universities, especially London, and now received Sheffield degrees 'ad eundem' (as equivalent to their original degree). The decision to confer these degrees was a happy one which, as Chapman comments, 'united the students of the old College with the new University'.[30]

Later that same month, the British Medical Association met in Sheffield and a second congregation was held to honour fifteen distinguished medical practitioners, headed by Simeon Snell, the University's Professor of Ophthalmology. After these degree congregations, the numbers of degree students leapt from 150 to over 200 and the following year (1909) to 280. Perhaps local people needed to see the ceremonies and the caps and gowns before realising that a degree was a prize worth aiming for.

Student activities

In 1906 the first Student Representative Council (SRC), uniting all sections of the new University, was founded. A third-year chemistry student, F. G. Belton, strongly encouraged by Professor Wynne, took the lead in organising the first elections, held in February 1906. Both the Sheffield newspapers reported on the 'excitement and enthusiasm' of the voting:

> Study at the university has this week proved a hollow mockery, for how could the youths and maidens study when they were passing through the throes of a general election? With the whole university divided into about thirty hostile factions, all excitedly urging the claims of their respective candidates; with mass meetings (at one of which the ladies became wildly excited) enlivening the dinner hour; and with the walls of corridors and rooms liberally dashed with electoral literature, the election dominated the thoughts . . . Never at any Parliamentary election has feeling run so high. Never have candidates and their partisans heaped upon each other such abuse and vituperation.[31]

The *Sheffield Daily Telegraph* commented on the fact that 'female suffrage [was] permitted' and that there were women candidates.[32] The first Executive Committee included three women. The result of the voting was announced to a rowdy gathering in the University entrance hall, with 'Floreamus' sung as the customary conclusion to events.

The male and female students had separate common rooms on the ground floor of Western Bank, but social life was relaxed with frequent student parties for which the women did the catering.[33] The Council would not allow Firth Hall to be used for student dances, however, despite the strict and formal dancing conventions of the day. At Liverpool University the men wrote names on the ladies' programmes and ladies were not supposed to dance more than twice with the same man.[34] Perhaps the Council were influenced by newspaper gossip like the cartoon in the *Morning Leader*, 1905, which was headed 'Don't Crush' and showed a queue of women purchasing train tickets to Bangor in response to announcements that 'at least six professors' at the University College had 'married lady students'.[35] Cooler heads prevailed after six years, when a chemistry lecturer, C. R. Young, took personal responsibility for the arrangements. The Chemistry staff were the students' particular friends at this time and for many years thereafter. Professor Wynne joined the Council in 1911 and persuaded the members to delegate the licensing of dances to a Discipline Committee, on which he took a leading role. Thereafter the dances, in which he was one of the most enthusiastic participants, flourished.

Wynne was also determined that the students should have a permanent playing field. As Treasurer of the SRC he put money aside for this purpose and also persuaded the Council to contribute. It proved impossible to find a suitable site near the University and the SRC had to settle on a field at Cow Mouth Farm in Norton, over six miles away and fifteen minutes from the nearest tram terminus. It did, however, have space for men's hockey, football, rugby, cricket and two tennis courts.[36] Wynne organised a student subscription to pay for levelling the field and the first ball was kicked by the Pro-Chancellor, George Franklin, at an opening ceremony in October 1910. His speech, as reported by the *Sheffield Daily Telegraph*, was extraordinary, considering the occasion:

> Mr. George Franklin . . . strongly condemned the excessive addiction of English people to sports. He was one of those, he said, who held that we in this country spent too much time upon our sport and games, and too little time upon the solid work that lay before us. He wanted to say quite frankly that the amount of time wasted in cricket and football might be very well applied to more useful purposes. In saying that he did not want to under-value for one moment the splendid opportunities now opened up to them by the playing field . . .[37]

Mr and Mrs George Franklin, left and centre, at the opening of the Athletics Grounds in 1910.

Franklin's attitude contrasted strongly with Wynne's and dramatically with that of Albert Hobson, the University's Treasurer from 1910, who, although severely disabled, was a strong supporter of university athletics.

The field had at first no changing facilities and in 1913 two adjacent houses were rented, one of which served as the groundsman's house. A regular income for the ground was secured by C. H. Wilson, President of the SRC in 1912, who arranged for an 'athletics and social subscription' to be levied as part of the university fees paid by students.

Student life receives little coverage at this time in *Floreamus*, which under Moore Smith's editorship was a stodgy publication. There was no student newspaper to replace *IT* after an attempt to found *The Blade* collapsed after one issue. *The Blade* did contain one good joke:

> Professor of Logic: 'I put my hat down in the room. I cannot see it anywhere; there has been nobody in besides myself; ergo, I am sitting on it.'[38]

The Chemistry Department

A very urbane-looking President C. H. Wilson in evening dress. He graduated MBChB in 1914. During his presidency he persuaded the University that part of the student registration fee should be paid over to the SRC for the support of athletic and sports facilities, which transformed their financial position.

Of the departments in Western Bank at this time, we know most about Chemistry, because descriptions were written by several members of staff.[39] Wynne was already 'an eminent chemist' when he came to Sheffield in 1904, a Fellow of the Royal Society. He was highly respected by his colleagues, who elected him Dean of the Faculty of Pure Science for twenty years running. Wynne was an excellent lecturer, always using a single sheet of notes and lavishly illustrating with 'experiments that never failed'. Despite his eminence, he chose to teach the junior students, leaving the advanced teaching and research supervision to his lecturers. He was, in the words of Chapman, who joined his department in 1920, 'the affectionate father of a large and lively family'.

W. E. S. Turner was appointed to a lectureship by Wynne and Hicks in 1904. His interview with Hicks was 'of the most friendly and informal character'; Hicks assured him that his job was secure and apologised that he could not immediately refund his travelling expenses, since the Registrar was away. 'After diving into both trouser pockets he succeeded in finding only one and a half pence'.[40] Both Wynne and Turner arrived in Sheffield in time to influence and improve the final plans for the construction of the chemistry laboratories at Western Bank. Two main laboratories, a large lecture theatre and a classroom, together with smaller laboratories and fume cupboards, were situated on the top floor of the west wing, next to Biology. Professor Wynne enforced a high standard of maintenance, described as 'apple-pie order', in the laboratories and was a hard taskmaster, sometimes standing by the door with his watch to check that staff arrived on time. The regular teaching day lasted from 9.00 am to 5.30 pm, with Monday and Thursday evening classes, taught by the lecturers. It was such a hard-working department that at least one resignation is said to have resulted from the adverse comparison with the Physics department, two floors below, which opened from 10.00 am until 4.30 pm. The standard of teaching demanded by Wynne was rigorous; one lecturer 'had the soul-destroying task, week after week, of going through students' notebooks, annotating them and preparing a progress report for the Professor'.[41]

The Chemistry laboratories were featured in the Gentleman's Journal, *26 July 1913. They were located on the top floor of Western Bank.*

Wynne and Turner took the University's commitment to local industry seriously and Turner devised a course of physical chemistry for metallurgists which was the first of its kind. Practical analysis classes and courses in electro-chemistry followed. Departmental research suffered because of the teaching load in the early years, but from 1908 enthusiastic research students from the new honours school began to transform the laboratories. Seven years later members of the department had published more than twenty papers.

There were several women among the early chemistry students and a few went on to undertake research. Emily Turner completed her degree in chemistry, mathematics and education in 1909 and an MSc in chemistry in 1910.[42] During the war, she became a temporary lecturer, along with two other former students, Dorothy Bennett and Annie Mathews. Turner described herself as one of Wynne's 'chemical children', acting as his unpaid secretary out of hours.[43] She and Bennett took charge of the main first-year laboratory and formed the back-bone of the department's first year teaching for many years. Bennett remained until 1934 and Turner until 1953.

Some aspects of student life never change.

On one occasion staff and students came together to perform a most suitable play, Ben Jonson's *The Alchemist*, for a Town and Gown 'conversazione' (open day). A Chemical Society started in 1905, but not with quite the bang intended, as Turner recalled:

> I gave the first lecture entitled 'Combustion: Slow and Rapid'. I had as my able assistant Mr. Jarrad and we had aimed at bringing down the house with a final experiment in which the explosion of a mixture of hydrogen and oxygen was started off by a trace of colloidal platinum. We . . . had rehearsed the experiment with perfect success earlier in the day and felt entirely confident . . . that there would be a deafening explosion; so we ducked immediately below the bench level. We had also stuffed our ears

Annual Examinations.

———

" GREAT SCOT ! WHAT A PAPER ! "

Conversazione of the Chemical and Biological Societies.

PEARLS AND PARASITES.

FOR more than a fort-night before the Chemical and Bio-logical Societies' Conver-sazione there was a feeling of suppressed excitement amongst the students, and everywhere preparations for the coming event might be seen. One morning, two or three days before the Con-versazione, the Advanced Chemical Labora-tory was suddenly transformed into a kitchen, various stu-

FAIR EXHIBITORS

From Floreamus, 1905.

Right: The Chemical Society, 1905/06, with Professor W. P. Wynne centre front and W. E. S. Turner and A. N. Meldrum, the only other two members of staff, at either side of him. On the far right is Dorothy Bennett who returned to the department as a lecturer in 1916. She and Emily Turner were known as the 'Tartrate Twins'.

with cotton wool. No explosion occurred and there was tremendous applause as Jarrad and I sheepishly raised our heads again above bench level with coils of cotton wool streaming from our ears.[44]

Chemistry demonstrators past and present will sympathise.

Education students

In its first year, the University established a Department of Education under John Alfred Green. He came from Bangor University College, where he was head of the day training department, but was a former Sheffield pupil-teacher and student of Firth College.[45] In an amusing article written for *Floreamus* soon after his appointment, he regretted his department's generic and somewhat misleading title, since every professor was engaged in education and 'it is a little extraordinary to hear discussions on whether or not a degree course shall include Education!'[46] Education was approved as a full degree subject in 1906 and the one-year post-graduate diploma in secondary education began in 1907.

To begin with, this new department concentrated on secondary school education. The day training college for elementary schoolteachers had become independent in 1905, following severe criticism by the Board of Education.[47] This was not a happy state of affairs for the University, because the loss of students also meant the loss of considerable government grants.[48] Eliot, the new Vice-Chancellor, was also concerned that the Sadler Report on Education in Sheffield had stressed the need for 'a close and organic connection' between the University and the training college.[49]

This connection had been retained for the matriculated 'three-year' teaching students, since it was impossible for the training college to teach to degree level. However, the University was unable to claim Board of Education grants for these students unless the college was linked to the University. An elaborate scheme, devised in 1906, re-established this link, but it lasted no longer than 1908.[50] The two-year diploma students responded unsatisfactorily to courses taught by University lecturers in general science, history and English literature. An inspectors' report of 1907 criticised the 'methods of instruction' of these courses, which were said to 'presuppose a higher degree of education than [the students] at present possess.'[51]

The ill-starred attempts to teach diploma students stopped at this point. The University decided instead to set up a separate training college, within the Department of Education, for degree-level elementary teaching students. This was eligible for the Board of Education grant and an intake of 100 students was approved. Demonstration schools for teaching practice were made available and a female lecturer in education was appointed, along with teachers of needlework, drawing, reading, voice production, school hygiene and music. From 1908, the new Sheffield Teacher Training College dealt only with two-year students.

The compromise seems a happy one, but it is worth noting that no other civic university tolerated the diversion of the diploma students into a different college. In Manchester, for example, elementary training courses of real quality and innovation were developed for all levels of student.[52] The exact nature of the problem in Sheffield is unclear, but it was certainly caused in part by the University lecturers' unwillingness, or inability, to teach at a sub-degree level. The University training college was a success and by 1910 had achieved its maximum intake. The degree course was extended, by national agreement, to four years in 1911. Students who pledged to work in local authority schools were given a grant for the full four years, an offer which proved so attractive that universities were flooded with trainee teachers.

Emily Turner was one of the first two MSc graduates of the University in 1910. (The other was Dorothy Bennett.) She was a lecturer in the Chemistry department, 1916–53.

THE FACULTY OF APPLIED SCIENCE (THE TECHNICAL SCHOOL)

J. A. Green, Professor of Education 1906–22, by Sir William Rothenstein (1918).

Although it changed its name to the Faculty of Applied Science, the Technical School was relatively unaffected by the creation of the University. It maintained its own traditions, including different term dates, and a well-respected qualification, the Associateship, which, in the eyes of the faculty, was superior to the degree that was also offered from 1905. The departments were already drawing students from far afield. The first international student was Z. T. K. Woo in 1904. A fellow student recalled 'my surprise when . . . I saw a hansom cab pull up [in St George's Square] and two Chinese step out, wearing frock-coats, top-hats and carrying umbrellas and grey gloves, apparently making their formal call on Professor Ripper'.[53] Woo was awarded one of the first three B Met degrees in 1907 and also received the M Met at the first degree congregation in 1908. However, the vast majority of students, about 85 per cent, were local and continued to attend in the evening; many of them became leading metallurgists and engineers.

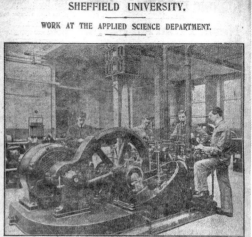

SHEFFIELD UNIVERSITY.

WORK AT THE APPLIED SCIENCE DEPARTMENT.

TESTING A COMPOUND AIR COMPRESSOR DRIVEN BY AN ELECTRIC MOTOR.

Above: *Metallurgy workshop in 1908.*

Right: *Students at work in Engineering in 1908.*

Apart from his professorial duties L. T. O'Shea was instrumental in establishing the Officers' Training Corps in the University and was its Commanding Officer from 1911 until departmental pressures forced him to stand down in 1917. The OTC still awards the O'Shea Cup for rifle shooting.

The daily life of the faculty was recorded by a reporter from the *Sunday Chronicle* in 1908. He toured the workshops, describing the practical training of the students whose faces were 'besmeared lavishly with a mixture of soot, steel filings and lubricating oil'. In the 'large, well-lighted but evil-smelling' metallurgy workshop 'a half-dozen young men [were] busily engaged boiling various coloured liquids over gas burners . . . The whole place seemed to exude steel . . . I breathed steel filings, I handled steel samples and I literally fell over a steel rail on the staging'.[54]

There were three laboratories in the Electrical Engineering department by 1905 and the Department of Mining was also growing, spawning a Sub-Department of Fuel Technology in 1907. L. T. O'Shea became its Professor and a new Professor of Mining, F. A. Armstrong, arrived in 1913 with a distinguished research record. He took a 'deep personal interest' in the miners, who came from all over the West Riding to attend his classes. Most of the teaching work of the department was extramural, but a lot of effort in the pre-war years went into creating opportunities for some students to take full-time degree courses and become colliery managers.[55] Armstrong had great difficulty securing better facilities on the St George's site and the campaign for a new building carried on after the war. It finally succeeded in 1925, too late for Armstrong who died at the height of his powers in 1921.[56]

The Metallurgy department still used the original Technical School building, the old Grammar School, which adjoined the new (1904) building in a temporary but incongruous juxtaposition. According to the memories of its clerk, E. J. Thackeray, Metallurgy had 'two very old and dilapidated chemical laboratories, one or two lecture rooms, microscopical and geology laboratories, a two hole crucible steel house . . . and, across the road . . . a model steel works.'[57] In 1908 the department took on the study, research and teaching of non-ferrous metallurgy, after a request from local manufacturers of silver, electro-plate and Britannia metal goods. The accommodation had to be expanded and Sir Joseph Jonas, the new Chairman of the Technical Committee, began a successful fundraising campaign in 1910. The old

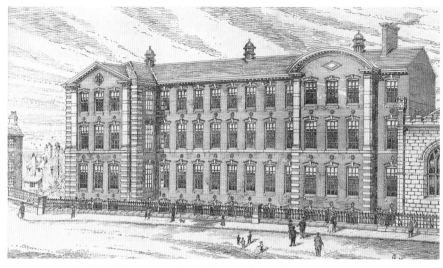

The first phase of a new building for the applied sciences on Charlotte (later Mappin) Street, erected in 1904. This architect's drawing shows the new wing adjacent to the old Grammar School.

Grammar School building was demolished and the foundations of a central block and wing to match the 1904 extension were laid. This distinguished building, which is still the central feature of the St. George's campus, was opened in 1913.

Arnold, the Professor of Metallurgy, carried out valuable research in these years, including contributions towards the development of new forms of steel, like vanadium (used for motor car parts), phospho-magnetic steel and electrical steels. His research became so important to industry that, by 1909, he had to accede to local firms' demands not to publish it, for fear of alerting foreign competitors, especially in America and Germany.[58] Some ill-guarded remarks about high-speed steels at a meeting of the Royal Institution led to a resolution from eleven local firms to the Applied Science Committee demanding that University staff should be compelled to make their lectures 'subservient to the trade interests'.[59] The Committee could not, of course, agree to this, but Arnold, after contemplating resignation, agreed to apologise to them.[60]

Among the ruins of demolished houses, an assembly of local dignitaries watched the foundation stone of the 1913 extensions to the Applied Science buildings being laid by Judge Benson, Master of the Drapers' Company, which had made a substantial donation of £15,000 towards their cost.

Clockwise from top left:

The completed Applied Science building. A contemporary newspaper report described it as 'a fine range of buildings . . . just sufficiently decorative to give them distinction without robbing them of their essential business character'. All the various Applied Science buildings were variations on an English Renaissance theme: if, as originally intended, the entire University had been built on this site the familiar 'Tudor' face of the University might never have existed.

The newly completed Applied Science buildings, looking in the direction of West Street.

Main gates of the Applied Science building. The cartouche, bearing the University coat of arms, and the flanking laurel wreaths were carved by Frank Tory .

Coats of arms of the University, the Drapers' Company and the City of Sheffield, from windows in Mappin Hall.

Mappin Hall with its handsome panelling, fine plaster ceiling and bust of Frederick Thorpe Mappin, who died in 1910.

At the same time, in February 1909, these firms also alleged that Arnold had conducted research several years earlier for one firm, Jonas and Colver, and had failed to communicate the results to their local competitors. The recognised procedure, to avoid this kind of accusation, was for the results of research carried out by the department to be communicated to all the local firms. In the case of the Jonas and Colver research, Arnold argued that he had conducted it during the long vacation, in a hired laboratory, using the firm's equipment and so the normal rules did not apply.[61] This was a thin defence, particularly since Jonas, the head of the firm, was also a prominent member of the Applied Science Committee, but it seems to have been accepted by his colleagues.

The ethical conflicts caused by the civic universities' close connection to competitive industrial innovation have been analysed by Michael Sanderson, who shows that similar issues arose at most of them.[62] They were almost inevitable and Sanderson acquits the universities of venality by commenting, 'so much did the universities owe to the business communities of their respective cities that these occasional naiveties of over-pushing businessmen or lapses by academics scarcely seem to provide evidence of the debauching of the universities by their involvement with industry'.

Arnold threatened resignation again in 1916, this time because he resented the power Ripper had over him as Dean of the faculty. There may well have been a personal clash between himself and Ripper, but Arnold's demand for a separate Faculty of Metallurgy was granted in 1917, just as Ripper became acting Vice-Chancellor.[63] Within the new Faculty of Engineering, there were two chairs; Ripper took Mechanical Engineering and J. Husband Civil Engineering.

THE FACULTY OF MEDICINE

The Medical School entered on a new and fruitful period of development after its establishment in the north wing of Western Bank.[64] The most prominent staff during this time were progressive and well attuned to the opportunities and challenges of higher education. J. S. MacDonald, for example, the Professor of Physiology from 1902 to 1914, came to Sheffield from Liverpool, where he had taken part in the establishment of that university and so became 'a source of infinite strength' during Sheffield's own transition period.[65] Arthur Hall continued to be the guiding light as he led the implementation of a science-based curriculum. It was he who recognised that the laboratory, rather than the anatomy theatre, should be the centre of pre-clinical medical training.[66]

Hall's vision not only firmly closed the door on the nineteenth century medical curriculum but was also particularly suited to a civic university. The medical faculty became closely involved in the practical healthcare issues of the city, for example through the bacteriological laboratory set up by John Robertson, who was both Sheffield's Medical Officer of Health and the University's Lecturer in Public Health. He persuaded the city to become the first to introduce compulsory notification of tuberculosis and carried out the requisite bacteriological examinations in

The Anatomy dissecting room was deliberately built with unusually large windows between substantial brick buttresses to give the best quality of daylight for dissection work. The same principle was applied in the Physiology department so that it had ideal conditions for microscopy.

J. B. Leathes, Professor of Physiology 1914–33, by Sir William Rothenstein (1918). An early champion of clinical biochemistry, he was one of the most distinguished members of the early medical faculty. A gifted teacher and strong supporter of the University, he also served the profession on a national level as Chairman of the Education Committee of the GMC. On his retirement, Floreamus declared 'a great man is passing from our midst'.

the medical school laboratories. Hall believed that Robertson 'demonstrated for the first time to the citizens of Sheffield that the presence of an efficient School of Medicine in their midst had a real and tangible value in connection with the health work of the city'.[67] This work continued and developed after Robertson left Sheffield in 1903, as the University laboratory performed routine bacteriological tests for the local hospitals.[68]

The income generated by this work, together with the Hunter bequest of 1909, allowed the medical school to develop the Department of Pathology. Of the three successive full-time professors of pathology in the years 1906–15, Louis Cobbett was a tuberculosis expert and H. R. Dean was an immunologist with an interest in vaccine therapy. It is a striking indication of the strides made by the medical school that in 1903 a Jessop Hospital doctor was reluctantly compelled to teach a course in vaccination; by 1912, the department was conducting vaccine research.[69] In 1915, the Pathology chair passed to J. S. C. Douglas, another immunologist who supervised large numbers of routine tests, for example those generated by the Venereal Diseases Act of 1916. In so doing, like his predecessors, he eschewed purely academic research in favour of a 'service-oriented' approach which chimed with the work of other parts of the University, especially the Applied Science faculty. This was criticised by some of the medical profession for its lack of 'purity' but University lecturers gained vital research material from their 'service' work and were genuinely committed to 'developing lines of research and teaching that would be of direct use to other institutions in the city'.[70]

The result was that members of the Sheffield medical faculty had a high profile locally and were entrusted with work of crucial public interest. In 1919, for example, when the government introduced compensation for refractory workers suffering from the lung disease silicosis, the faculty was asked to adjudicate on borderline cases.[71]

Like Pathology, the Physiology department also owed its early development, and its philosophy, to Arthur Hall.[72] Hall and J. S. MacDonald, the Professor from 1902, promoted chemical physiology, a new field which appeared to promise immediate medical benefits. By 1911 they had also reformed the teaching of pharmacology, a neglected subject which had previously been taught as 'materia medica' and botany.[73] The faculty's strong chemical profile was consolidated by the appointment of J. B. Leathes to succeed Macdonald in 1914. He was well known for his work on metabolic biochemistry, a Fellow of the Royal Society and a major catch, 'the greatest acquisition which the faculty has had since the University was founded', according to Hall.[74] Leathes was keen to work in a civic university, accepted the limited salary and was so content that he remained at Sheffield for the rest of his teaching life. He established close links with the local hospitals, by offering diagnostic and investigative services, and was appointed Honorary Physiologist to both the Royal Infirmary and the Royal Hospital in 1919, a post which Hall believed to be nationally unique at the time.[75] Hall overcame some initial opposition from hospital consultants, the result of professional jealousy, by demonstrating the enormous research advantages which the collaboration offered.

In 1909 the hospital consultants' control of clinical training was challenged when the government's Board of Education introduced grants which had the aim of putting the universities in ultimate control, by demanding that all clinical teachers be members of university staff. The consultants' resistance was resolved by a compromise, in which the Clinical Committee was reconstituted as a committee of the University. In practice the control of bedside hospital teaching remained with the hospital doctors.[76]

In 1905 the medical faculty resolved, for the first time, to admit female students.[77] Women had made slow progress in entering medicine, despite the pioneering efforts of Elizabeth Garrett Anderson, whose name had been added to the British medical register in 1865.[78] The struggle to admit women to co-educational institutions was protracted; even University College, London, did not admit female medical students until 1917. In Sheffield there is little evidence of strong opposition; the resolution to admit women was passed unanimously in 1905 and a generous annual scholarship of £100 was offered 'by a friend of the University' to a female student of the medical school.[79] There was no rush, however, as the scholarship was not awarded until 1908, when Elizabeth Ethel Jenkins and Lydia Henry, the daughter of Lysbeth Henry, began their studies. Elizabeth Jenkins did not complete the course, but Lydia Henry graduated seven years later, in 1916, having missed a year because she contracted a streptococcal infection in the dissecting room.[80] She and Florence Millard were the first female graduates in medicine at the University of Sheffield. Dr Millard continued to practise until the age of seventy; Lydia Henry went on to a distinguished wartime career at Royaumont Hospital in France.[81]

The faculty also had a female member of staff from 1909, Elizabeth Eaves, who was appointed by Leathes to teach physiology. She went on to study part-time for a medical degree, but never practised as a doctor, remaining a mainstay of the department for 38 years, until her death in 1947.[82] Lucy Naish, one of the first women doctors in Sheffield, became the second 'Lady Tutor in Anatomy' in 1916 and went on to teach osteology for twenty years. The wife of a later Professor of Medicine, A. E. Naish, and mother of eight children, she evokes the vivid memory of a battered brown suitcase containing a large selection of bones for teaching purposes, which she habitually carried around with her.[83]

DEVELOPMENTS AT WESTERN BANK, 1909–14

The Library

The Edgar Allen Library was added to Western Bank in 1909, a striking feature with its octagonal shape and pointed roof. Edgar Allen's donation was announced at the opening ceremony in 1905, but there were delays caused by the design and by the need to use part of Weston Park as the site. Although the University offered other land in compensation, there were objections from local people, for example that 'the proposed Octagon library building will not only spoil the outlines of our chaste university buildings, but also ruin the park and its entrance at that point'.[84] The

Above: *William Edgar Allen's fortune was made in steel, principally through trade with the continent, made easier by his exceptional grasp of languages. In addition to the University Library he funded a lectureship in geography; in the city his charitable giving included churches, hospitals and a physiotherapy treatment centre. This small bronze plaque was struck to mark the opening of the Library, which appears on the obverse.*

Above right: *There was some public concern about the size and scale of the proposed library building and in 1906 a full sized timber framework was erected on the site to show the actual scale of the building. (Sheffield Independent, 13 November 1906)*

Right: *This was one of the earliest specially designed University libraries in the country. Gibbs, who had studied University buildings in North America and Britain, designed an octagonal library rather like a cathedral chapter house in the same Tudor style as the main building.*

Commemorative silver bowl made in the same year as the opening.

controversy, smoothed over, foreshadowed later battles between town and gown about encroachment on land.

The University, and before that the College, had lacked a proper library. Its small book stock (only 10,000 volumes in 1905) had been shelved at the sides of the biggest lecture theatres. In 1909 it acquired not only a separate library, but 'one of the earliest specially designed university libraries in the country'.[85] It was a beautiful building and proved to be a tranquil and inspiring place in which to work, with space for 104 readers. Gibbs and Flockton, the architects, planned that it would shelve 114,000 volumes, with the stack in use, but in fact it never held more than 80,000 and was full by 1929.[86]

When Professor Moore Smith resigned as Honorary Librarian in 1907, the job was advertised as a full-time post. It was offered to Thomas Loveday, a professor of philosophy in Cape Town who was keen to return to Britain. His application, preserved in the archives, shows that his experience of librarianship was limited to 'an interest in Bibliography', experience of a 'valuable family library' and familiarity with the Dewey cataloguing system 'since it is in use at the large Public Library in Cape Town'.[87] Loveday was, however, a fine scholar with a beautiful

The Library was opened on 26 April 1909 by the Prince of Wales, seen in this drawing by J. H. Dowd receiving an honorary degree from the Duke of Norfolk. Also in the drawing, from the left, are Sir Charles Eliot, W. Edgar Allen, the Princess of Wales and George Franklin.

The Library had a central control desk, from which the reading bays radiated. Over each bay was the sculpted head of a prominent personality associated with the establishment of the University. Electric lighting was used throughout; the option of gas was not even considered, as it had been for Firth Hall.

Below: Programme for the opening of the new Library.

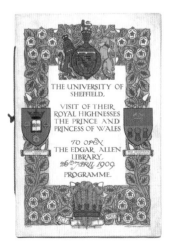

printed testimonial from the Vice-Chancellor of Oxford. He relinquished the job four years later to become Lecturer in Philosophy.[88] Loveday was the last non-specialist scholar to run the Library; he was succeeded by Arthur P. Hunt, who had extensive experience of academic library work, including the Bodleian and Balliol College, Oxford. Hunt managed the Edgar Allen Library with dedication for thirty years, until his retirement in 1941.

A new faculty and new departments

The Law department, which had been run since 1899 by Robert Leader and Edward Bramley, was reorganised in 1906, when the two 'honorary' lecturers took a back seat and a full-time senior lecturer, W. F. Trotter, was appointed. Bramley then worked steadily towards creating a Law faculty which would provide training and qualifications equivalent to those offered by Oxford, Cambridge and London.[89] In the first stage, Sheffield became a partner in the Yorkshire Board of Legal Studies, the channel for grants from the Law Society, previously monopolised by Leeds. Then a Faculty of Law, awarding the LL B degree, was created in 1908 and Trotter became the first Professor. Finally, an Act of Parliament was promoted in order to allow Sheffield graduates to reduce their period of articled service from five years to three. This already happened elsewhere and so the act became a means by which Sheffield asserted its equality with older universities: after listing them, it stated 'graduates of the University of Sheffield . . . shall be entitled to all such privileges, as fully as any of the last-mentioned universities'.[90]

These changes required considerable and sustained effort by the department and the Registrar; a final one proved the most demanding of all. In July 1913, Gibbons and the Registrar of Leeds were frantically trying to get permission to offer a one year, sub-degree, course in law which had been pioneered by the Law Society. After delaying his holiday, Gibbons discovered that they would need the personal assent of the Master of the Rolls, the Lord Chancellor and the Lord Chief Justice.[91] His gesture was futile; it took another year before all the negotiations were completed and agreement reached. A bulky file of the correspondence contains telegrams in which legal language is rendered almost impenetrable by the lack of sentences:

> Draft proposed order adopted as amended by sub-committee Bramleys letter read Society insist Clause 8 in principle including some form control curriculum and examination unofficially informed probably certificate University ordinarily accepted as evidence under last part Clause 8 [92]

This was sent by the University's solicitors, Munby and Sparkes, who after more than a year's work charged Leeds and Sheffield just over £27 each.

In addition to the Faculty of Law, 1908 saw the foundation of two new departments, Geography and Architecture.[93] The Geography department began after a speech given to the annual Court dinner by the President of the Royal Geographical Society, which inspired Edgar Allen to offer £150 annually towards a lectureship. By

Edward Bramley at the beginning of a long connection with the University which began in the Department of Law and included service as Treasurer and then as Pro-Chancellor throughout the 1940s.

This house, formerly at the corner of Hounsfield Road and Western Bank, contained the departments of Law and Economics.

autumn 1908, a degree within the Faculty of Pure Science had been recognised (the Arts faculty degree came later) and a lecturer, R. N. Rudmose Brown, was appointed. He had already made his mark as an explorer and been awarded a Scottish Geographical Society medal for his work in the Antarctic. This inspired appointment was probably the result of contacts which the Vice-Chancellor had built up as a former colonial administrator and keen traveller. The new department flourished under Rudmose Brown, who became Professor in 1931 and remained at the University until 1945.

The Architecture department had been much longer in the making, for the Sheffield Society of Architects had been keen to promote 'architectural education in its highest grades' even in University College days.[94] In 1907 they agreed to underwrite the costs of appointing a lecturer and W. S. Purchon began work in 1908, teaching a three-year certificate course and later a five-year advanced diploma for 'pupils' in architectural offices. The demand was greatest from these part-time students, and before 1914 student numbers were respectable for an untried course.[95] During the First World War, however, the students disappeared and the lecturer was forced to take work at the steel firm, Firth's. This, compounded by a post-war dearth of students, disrupted the department's progress so much that its survival was in question for most of the 1920s. Its shaky start contrasts with that of Liverpool, which had an outstanding Architecture department from the end of the nineteenth century.

The social sciences developed towards their modern form between 1880 and 1914, although separate university departments often did not emerge until after the Second World War.[96] For example, Sheffield did not have a Psychology department until 1960, but the subject was taught within the Education and Philosophy departments. Professor Green of Education collaborated with Thomas Loveday in writing an influential introductory psychology textbook for teachers.[97] Economics became a separate discipline much earlier because of the pioneering example of the Cambridge economics and political science tripos, set up in 1902.[98] Sheffield created a Department of Economics in 1910, with Douglas Knoop as the first lecturer. This was the initiative of the Vice-Chancellor; Eliot's enthusiasm was greater than that

Left: *Robert Neal Rudmose Brown, first lecturer in Geography, was the botanist aboard the 'Scotia' on the 1902 Scottish National Antarctic Expedition; he is shown, left, with colleagues in the shipboard laboratory. In the great age of Antarctic exploration this gave him considerable cachet when he arrived in Sheffield. In 1909 and on several later occasions he joined expeditions to Spitsbergen in the Arctic where he conducted significant research.*

Right: *The Scottish Antarctic Expedition vessel 'Scotia'.*

In 1913 Douglas Knoop was awarded an Alfred Kahn Travelling Fellowship enabling him to study the economies of other countries for a year. On the sum of £660 he toured many parts of Europe, North Africa, Indonesia, China, Japan and the United States. These images are from his impressive collection of slides and photographs.

W. G. Fearnsides, Sorby Professor of Geology 1913–45, became widely known to industrialists and coal owners in the region and nationally. In due course he was elected to the Royal Society and to the presidential chair of the Geological Society.

of any of the professors of arts or sciences, who could envisage no 'direct benefit' to their work.[99] Knoop became the first Professor of Economics in 1920 and a staff member of exemplary loyalty; he remained until his retirement in 1948. He took a keen interest in Freemasonry, publishing three histories with his colleague G.P. Jones and reprinting many masonic pamphlets.[100]

A separate Department of Geology was created in 1913, with rooms in the new extension at St George's Square and a chair endowed by the will of H. C. Sorby. W. G. Fearnsides became the first Sorby Professor, another felicitous and long-term appointment, since he led the department until 1945 and became a major figure in the world of geology and a prime ambassador for the University. The greater part of the legacy, £15,000, was allocated by Sorby to a fellowship which would enable 'men of proved ability [in any scientific field] to devote themselves to research' without other distractions.[101] Clearly Sorby understood the pressures of academic life! He had nurtured this idea since 1871 and had been encouraged in his plans by Hicks, who wished to cultivate 'the spirit of research' and 'raise the academic tone of the place'.[102] The holders of the Sorby Fellowship proved the wisdom of its conception; many of them completed notable research projects and went on to senior posts at Sheffield and elsewhere. For example, the first Fellow, J. F. Thorpe FRS, 1909–13, previously a senior lecturer at Manchester University, published 'a notable series of papers' in organic chemistry before being appointed to a chair at Imperial College.[103] Sorby's legacy, which was administered by the Royal Society, was largely sufficient to maintain the Fellowship until 1975. Thereafter it had a more spasmodic existence, although it was revived in 1984 to celebrate its 75th anniversary, with financial support from both the University and the Worshipful Company of Goldsmiths.[104]

There is interesting evidence about the workload of academic staff in draft returns on teaching hours requested in 1911 by the Board of Education. These drafts were not, in fact, returned to the Board because the Vice-Chancellor, Eliot, resented the 'rude questions' as 'ungentlemanly'.[105] For the same reason, he refused to require staff at Western Bank to clock in at nine each morning. One can imagine how he would have responded to the far more intrusive questions asked by the higher education funding councils of later generations. The drafts show that the staff taught for most of the week, even when they had considerable administrative responsibilities. Professor Wynne, for example, who was also Dean of Pure Science, devoted twenty hours to routine teaching. The research output of the University was impressive given the teaching load, an average of 87 publications in each year between 1910 and 1914.

The inevitable result of the increasing number of departments, staff and students was that the accommodation in Western Bank, which had seemed so generous in 1905, required an extension by 1912. With the help of Sir William Clegg, a City Council grant of £10,000 was obtained, despite some opposition from both the public and councillors who felt the University had already been very generously treated.[106] This sum helped to pay for a new block at the north-east corner, into which the biological departments moved in 1914, creating more space for Chemistry in the west wing.

Naturally there were some less successful enterprises. These included the evening arts degree and proposals for a theology department, which foundered because of the lack of supporting courses, even though Charles Eliot offered to teach Hebrew and Aramaic himself. Commercial languages, unpopular at Firth College, did not revive at the University despite considerable effort. The Council (composed of laymen), rather than the Senate (academics), played the largest part in establishing the modern languages departments, which would account for the commercial bias. Despite this, the Professor of French, A. T. Baker, was not only a gifted teacher but also an 'incessant researcher' who built up a department with traditional academic strengths. He held special classes for teachers of French and served on the Joint Matriculation Board for 26 years. A member of staff from 1901 until 1936, Chapman regarded him as 'one of the finest souls we have ever had here'.[107]

Continuing the tradition established by Firth College, the University offered a wide range of part-time courses. Saturday night lectures by members of staff in Firth Hall were very popular, with an average attendance of 427 in 1905/06.

In 1913 the architects came forward with suggestions for a second quadrangle to the east; various design alternatives were considered, one of which is shown here. In the event only the short terminating block with a handsome oriel window was built at that time.

71

Professor Denny had the largest audiences, averaging 608, for a course of lectures on 'Evolution and Adaptation in the Animal World', held at Owler Lane Council School.[108] When the Workers Educational Association (WEA) was established in 1907, the University collaborated on an extensive adult education programme. The WEA, closely associated with the labour movement, promoted higher education for working men and women, who attended in the evenings or mornings, depending on shifts.[109] Its lecturers were University professors with a strong commitment to its ideals. Appleton, Green and Knoop, and several vice-chancellors, starting with Sir Charles Eliot, gave strong support. A Joint Committee was established in 1910 to run 'tutorial classes', which offered an experience akin to university-level study for the WEA's most ambitious and able students.[110] Gibbons became the joint secretary to this Committee and Douglas Knoop was a conscientious member, attending over seventy per cent of meetings for many years. He and Thomas Loveday taught the first two tutorial classes, in industrial history and philosophy, which, along with economics, were three of the most popular subjects. The classes were demanding for both tutor and student, consisting of a one-hour lecture followed by an hour of intensive discussion. The written work requirement, twelve essays per session, was stringent, but one literature tutor claimed to have received an average of 11.5 essays per student.[111] Until at least the Second World War, the Sheffield Joint Committee ran one of the biggest university tutorial class programmes in the country.

A new Vice-Chancellor, 1913

In 1912 Sir Charles Eliot resigned in order to return to his enduring love, the Far East, as Vice-Chancellor of Hong Kong University. He later became Ambassador to Japan and died there in 1931. As Sheffield's Vice-Chancellor he was little interested in the details of everyday administration, which fell to Gibbons (who married Eliot's sister). Knoop reported that Eliot was 'more often to be found in his marine zoology laboratory (. . . near the Library) than in the Vice-Chancellor's room', although no trouble was too much for causes like the WEA which ignited his enthusiasm.[112] He was not fond of making speeches but was considered to be a congenial host at Endcliffe Holt.

The following year, H. A. L. Fisher replaced him as Vice-Chancellor. Fisher was a Fellow of New College, Oxford, and a popular and authoritative exponent of European history. Like Eliot, however, he had a need for active service as well as the lettered life. 'When the first excitements of the intellectual life have worn themselves out', he wrote, 'the ordinary Englishman . . . struggles to find an escape from the library into the open air of the common life. Administration, politics, travel, philanthropy lure him away from his books'.[113] Fisher's father had been Private Secretary to the Prince of Wales; his background gave him no experience of a northern city, but he was enthusiastic about the applied sciences and as supportive as Eliot of the WEA and adult education. For example, in the early months of the First World War, he gave a series of public lectures which inspired a national 'War Lectures' programme. This did a great deal to educate ordinary people about the causes of the war.[114]

Fisher, coming straight from Oxford, was keen to introduce student halls. During his speech at the degree ceremony of 1914, he expressed his hope that Sheffield would soon have

> a flourishing residential life, because I believe it to be a profound fallacy to suppose that the residential system, because it flourishes in Oxford and Cambridge, where the students are mainly rich, is not adapted to a university where the students are mainly less well-off. On the contrary I believe the truth to be exactly the opposite. I believe that the poorer the student is, the more contracted his home, the more desirable is it for him to receive the social education and advantages and the opportunities of uninterrupted intellectual labour at night which are afforded by the college or the hostel system.[115]

H. A .L. Fisher was Vice-Chancellor for less than four years, 1913–17, and his national duties took him away from Sheffield for much of that time. He was unexpectedly appointed President of the Board of Education in 1916. Later he returned to Oxford University to write his great History of Europe.

This was visionary at a time when there were no student halls, apart from the tiny, private, St. Peter's hostel for women. The vast majority of students lived at home, with a few in lodgings. The idea of student halls was foreign to Sheffield; two 'ratepayers', writing to the *Sheffield Daily Telegraph* in 1914, suggested that the Duke of Devonshire might provide accommodation at Chatsworth House and that the students 'could weekend' at Hardwick Hall. 'Welbeck is well worth considering, as there is a splendid riding track . . .'[116]

The sarcastic implication that students would be housed in the lap of luxury was wide of the mark. Needless to say, Fisher had no such ambitions. He spoke only of a 'modest university quarter' and directed his first efforts towards a hall for women which would be owned and run by the University. This was partly in order to offer a safe and supervised environment for young, middle-class, single women who, before the 1914–18 war, were still considered to need chaperones. Fisher said he wished to attract 'young women of the professional class, the daughters of doctors, solicitors, clergymen and the like' and Gibbons noted that 'many parents hesitate to send their daughters to a University where they have to live in lodgings'.[117]

Several sites for a new building were considered. They included one at Fulwood, which Fisher rejected because it was too far for women to attend evening meetings, and Endcliffe Grange. The Grange had grounds extensive enough for a hall for fifty, but the war prevented completion of negotiations to purchase it. After the war, the Grange proved too expensive and it was to be almost fifty years before it was finally used for Earnshaw Hall. The first women's hall was based in Oakholme Lodge from 1918, a much smaller building than had been hoped for.

Stephenson Hall Church Hostel, situated at 276–278 Western Bank on the site of the present Alfred Denny building, was opened by the Archbishop of York on 12 October 1912.

The first men's hostel was founded in 1912 by Lady Stephenson in her husband's memory, as the 'Stephenson Hall Church Hostel'. It was aimed at men who intended to take holy orders in the Church of England and was housed at 276–278 Western Bank, moving in 1914 to 'Westbourne' on Severn Road. Like the St Peter's hostel, the University's only claim on Stephenson Hall was its annual grant. Despite Fisher's ambitions, it was not until after the war that the University gained ownership of any halls of residence.

Above: *Student behaviour at degree congregations drawn by J. H. Dowd and published in a local paper in July 1912. It makes modern students look positively decorous.*

Right: *Shrove Tuesday Carnival procession assembled on the staircase leading up to Firth Hall.*

Student fun

Innocently entitled 'Gay Doings', the local press reported the 'students' night' at the Alexandra Theatre pantomime in 1913. This was evidently an annual event:

> About a hundred [male students], dressed in all manner of costumes, as pierrots, clowns, women, and babes – with 'Lloyd George' seated in a coffin – left the University about half-past five. Their procession was headed by a traction engine which drew a waggon-load of students and the rest of the merry company rode on the tops of half a dozen four-wheelers. They went through the principal streets of the city and arrived at the theatre in ample time for preliminary skirt dances in front of the curtain and for the ripening of the hilarious spirit. Both boxes were filled with students, and the rest crowded together in the front rows of the stalls. The choruses went with riotous swing; every time the music was suited to the rhythm, the whole body of men stood and swayed together from side to side. When there was no music there was shouting.[118]

For many years, the students also attended the degree ceremony *en masse* and, apart from the fancy dress, enjoyed themselves in just the same way. In 1917, for example:

> Those male students who were in attendance . . . entertained [the visitors], prior to the commencement of the business, with the singing of popular ditties . . . interspersed with the customary cat-calls, sounding of motor-

horns, whistles and other mechanical instruments of torture, under the auspices of the 'Medical Choir' !!! It was a weird and wonderful combination, and as the procession of candidates, members of the governing bodies, Deans and Professors, filed up the hall to their places, they were greeted with 'The animals went in one by one' . . . The presentation of the various candidates was accompanied by cheers, jeers, groans and laughter, and other signs of 'approval' . . . The popularity of some of the girl students was most apparent, a fact which did not seem to cause the slightest embarrassment to the fair recipients. 'The end of a perfect day' was the appropriate finale to the 'choir's' efforts at the end of the proceedings.[119]

The civic universities and the onset of war, 1913–14

FULL-TIME STUDENTS IN SELECTED INSTITUTIONS OF HIGHER EDUCATION IN ENGLAND, 1913–14

UNIVERSITY/COLLEGE	ARTS	PURE SCIENCE	MEDICINE	ENGINEERING	TECHNOLOGY	OTHERS	TOTAL
Birmingham	396	114	172	111	74	-	867
Bristol	272	103	112	?	-	-	487
Cambridge	?	?	382	?	?	?	3,679
Durham	?	?	?	?	?	?	370
Leeds	184	124	157	59	89	-	613
Liverpool	270	168	301	97	25	-	861
Manchester	385	314	215	70	-	21	1,005
Oxford	?	?	?	21	?	?	4,025
Sheffield	132	53	46	68	50	-	349
University College, London	374	195	128	125	19	-	841
King's College, London	103	64	190	94	13	-	464
University College, Nottingham	143	71	7	31	10	1	263

(- no students; ? no figure by faculty available, only total student numbers) Source: Sanderson, *The Universities in the Nineteenth Century*, pp 242–4.

In 1913/14, Sheffield was still the smallest civic university, smaller even than Bristol (which became a university in 1909) if judged by the number of full-time students. The table above indicates the tiny size of the medical school and the relatively low numbers taking arts and pure science courses. This was partly because Sheffield had allowed the day training college to become independent in 1905, thus losing students training to teach in elementary schools, while most of the other civics had retained them. In addition, Sheffield had larger than average numbers of part-time students. There were approximately 1,450 evening students in 1913/14 and a high number of part-time day students – about 260, an addition of 74 per cent of the full-time total. The comparable percentage at Liverpool, for example, was 25.[120] Both Sheffield and Liverpool took pride in the large number of local students and their

75

success in attracting those who could not afford any other form of higher education. This could not have been achieved without evening classes, but in the long term the introduction of day-time classes was preferable for the sake of both students and staff.

The years before the war saw heightened social tension, industrial unrest and recession. Trades unionism affected the universities, especially the junior staff, whose status, pay and working conditions were often pitifully poor. Their numbers were becoming greater as universities expanded. A meeting of the junior staff in Liverpool in 1909 has been seen as the embryo of the Association of University Teachers (AUT), founded just after the war, in 1919.[121]

When the First World War broke out in August 1914, undergraduates and staff alike volunteered *en masse* for the front line. Many of the brightest intellects, the most promising hopes for the future, were swept indiscriminately into the trenches and perished at the Somme and subsequent military disasters. This was a catastrophe for the universities, as well as the country, but the patriotic fervour of the moment overwhelmed vice-chancellors as well as students. In a symposium entitled *British Universities and the War*, published in 1917, H. A. L. Fisher described the common experience:

> No measure of compulsion was needed to bring the Universities into the great National Crusade against the German crime . . . it was not an easy decision to make – this resolve to abandon all the pleasant prospects of an easy and honourable career for the chance of wounds or death, but the young men of our Universities made the choice for the most part instantaneously, and the rest of the country followed.[122]

Sir Alfred Dale, the Vice-Chancellor of Liverpool, refused to write of 'our losses, grievous as they are' because 'pride triumphs over pain'. Professor J. A. Green at Sheffield spoke of the mass enlistment as 'a wonderful time to live through'. The lack of discrimination with which the eager recruits were accepted was later regretted by some of those responsible. Until 1917 the universities had difficulty even in retaining those staff and students with technical and scientific skills essential for the war effort. This can only be described as a national disgrace, the product of the same narrow outlook which had created only 3,000 university places in science and technology, while Germany had 25,000.[123] The German government had a national blueprint for the development of technical education; Britain relied almost entirely on local effort. Few government ministers had the vision of Haldane, the Secretary of State for War, who helped to found Imperial College in 1907 and enthusiastically promoted technical higher education.[124]

In the event, chemists, engineers, physicists and metallurgists working in university laboratories and workshops triumphed over these obstacles to make a crucial contribution to victory. In 1914 there were 'very serious gaps in [Britain's] military technical capacity' because the country depended on Germany for many types of glass, synthetic dyes, medicinal drugs and even the components of explosives like TNT and gases like chlorine.[125] The ingredients of other vital chemicals, like saltpetre used to make nitric acid, were imported from other countries and thus vulnerable to German submarine attack. At the start of the war the government seemed to assume that private firms would meet all its needs. The potential of the universities' knowledge and facilities was not fully harnessed until 1916, when Lloyd George became Prime Minister and created the Ministry of Munitions to co-ordinate the national effort.

The list of inventions and technical breakthroughs is a long one. There were developments by staff at every university, often working in collaboration. Michael Sanderson concludes that these were 'a tribute to the inherent soundness of our higher scientific education'.[126] The war greatly enhanced the prestige of the universities, particularly of their scientific and technical education.

THE UNIVERSITY IN WARTIME, 1914–18

The changes in the University during the First World War were so far-reaching that it is surprising that any normal academic work continued at all. There was the immediate loss of substantial numbers of students and staff to the front line and to other war work. Intimations of this began two days before war was declared, on Sunday 2 August 1914, when Fisher was asked by the War Office to supply names of staff and students willing to accept commissions into the army. He sent out 300 circulars that day and by Thursday had received 100 positive replies, including forty from staff.[127] A total of 153 students enlisted at the start of the war, almost half joining the Sheffield City Battalion. As the war progressed, and particularly after conscription was introduced in 1916, male students who were fit for service left when they reached their eighteenth birthday. Only selected medical students were exempt, in order to complete their training. The Officers' Training Corps enlisted more than 100 'new and enthusiastic' recruits among the younger students preparing for their own place in the 'great world drama'.[128] Women students joined the Red Cross and some helped with agriculture, harvesting wheat and corn during the summer vacation. Of those who went to fight, 157 graduates and students were listed as killed, dead of wounds, or missing. 21 members of academic staff and ten laboratory assistants joined the armed forces, together with 38 honorary medical staff who went to the military hospitals. Four academics and four laboratory assistants did not return.

Enlistment at the Corn Exchange, Sheffield, 12 September 1914. 53 members of the Officers' Training Corps were among the first to enlist. The notice on the pillar to the right reads 'To Berlin via Corn Exchange Sheffield'.

Above: *The Marquess of Crewe, who succeeded the Duke of Norfolk as Chancellor, inspecting the OTC on 29 June 1918.*

Right: *Soldiers marching through the city centre.*

Professor Ripper as acting Vice-Chancellor, a position he held from 1917–19. In addition he remained professor, dean of Engineering, vice-chairman of the Committee on Munitions of War and director of the faculty's munitions work. For his war work he was awarded the high distinction of Companion of Honour. This portrait is by Rothenstein.

The duties of staff absent on war service were shared out, sometimes between departments. Thus the Department of German was handed over to J. D. Jones, the lecturer in English, and the Greek lecturer's job was divided between the Vice-Chancellor and three other lecturers. Some departments employed women lecturers and research assistants for the first time. A female team in Chemistry supervised the production of large quantities of an anaesthetic drug, ß-eucaine. Four women were recruited to conduct research in glass technology.[129] Some of these posts were lost after the war but several became permanent, supported by enthusiastic heads of department. Women proved their capabilities to such an extent that it was difficult to ignore their contribution once the war was over.

Professors' wives ran the 'Sheffield University hospital supply depot' in Western Bank. There a large number of women worked voluntarily, turning out 'necessaries and comforts for the troops'.[130] A Surgical Appliance branch was formed at St George's Square, with about fifty volunteer wood and metal workers. Fisher also appealed for teachers to help Belgian refugees learn English. Some were housed in the original Stephenson building on Western Bank which, funded by members of staff, became known as the University Belgian Hostel.

The Scientific Advisory Committee, set up by W. E. S. Turner of the Chemistry Department, offered local manufacturers the benefit of University expertise to solve technical problems.[131] The University was drawn, inevitably, into the production of armaments in Sheffield. The city's steel and engineering industry was, in Arnold's phrase, 'the greatest British Naval and Military Armoury' and crucial to the war effort.[132] The Sheffield Committee of Munitions of War met daily from May 1915 to co-ordinate the efforts of steel firms. They used a handsome room in the Applied Science building, which later became the John Carr Library. Many firms were working flat out to produce munitions, but more were needed and the Committee, led by Ripper, Herbert Hughes and A. J. Hobson, and assisted by Gibbons, organised a census of the local works, classifying them and allocating suitable war work to them. For example, firms specialising in art silver work had to adapt to the production of steel helmets. Altogether the Committee co-ordinated the production of over eleven million articles, including 27,000 gauges, 973,000 shrapnel-proof helmets, half a million shells and over one million exploder containers.[133] The Engineering department was responsible for the production of gauges for the Admiralty, which 'demanded extreme perfection of workmanship', and carried out research for the Ministry of Munitions.[134] It also trained over 1,000 non-recruitable men in shell-turning. The Metallurgy department developed the production of cupro-nickel, used in the manufacture of bullets, and trained over 500 workers. The Electrical Engineering department was 'engaged almost continuously' in the work of aeronautical inspection and helped to train anti-aircraft gunners through a simulation erected in Firth Hall. The contribution of the Applied Science faculty to the war effort was regarded as so significant that it received a royal visit in September 1915.

The University was disrupted and demoralised in the middle of the war by the sudden loss of senior and longstanding leaders. George Franklin, the Chairman of Council since 1904, Herbert Hughes, an indefatigable member of Council, and the Chancellor, the Duke of Norfolk, died within a few months of each other, between September 1916 and February 1917. W. M. Hicks, known affectionately as 'Daddy

Clockwise from top left: The University trained non-recruitable men to machine shells in its own workshops; over 1,000 men went through the course and passed into the local munitions factories.

Some of the fifty voluntary workers in the 'Sheffield University Hospital Supply Depot' in 1916, making such items as bandages and dressings.

In September 1915 the University received a visit from King George V, who inspected the laboratories and workshops in Applied Science and attended a meeting of the Sheffield Committee on the Munitions of War. He is seen here descending the steps to Mappin Street.

Women being trained on lathes for munitions work, 1915–16.

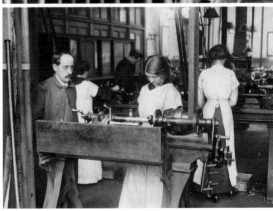

Portrait of Sir Joseph Jonas (1916) which now hangs in Mappin Hall. He did a great deal to develop the applied sciences and also promoted the establishment of chairs of French and German for their business value. Jonas was much liked in the city and the University and his steelworkers showed their belief in him by continuing to refer to him as 'Sir Joseph' despite his being formally stripped of his title in 1918.

Hicks' by the students of his later years, retired at the same time.[135] Moreover in December 1916 the Vice-Chancellor, Fisher, was summoned to join Lloyd George's new government as President of the Board of Education. This was a complete surprise to Fisher but he made a success of the job, despite his lack of parliamentary experience. Perhaps this was because he was, as Lloyd George said, an educationalist and not a politician.[136]

The gap which had now appeared at the head of the University was filled temporarily by Professor Ripper, since it was hoped that Fisher would return after the war.[137] It seems that Ripper was the unanimous and immediate choice as acting Vice-Chancellor; his 'tolerant and kindly spirit' was generally appreciated.[138] However, the pressures now placed on him were exceptionally heavy, since he did not relinquish any of his huge burden of war work. Ripper remained Vice-Chancellor until 1919, but the situation eased when H. K. Stephenson was allowed to return from the front in September 1917; he became senior Pro-Chancellor and Chairman of Council.

Before he left, Fisher was instrumental in setting up the Department of Russian, just before the 1917 Revolution. Fisher's European historical interests convinced him that a Russian alliance would be 'of prime necessity' to the future political security of Britain.[139] Many Sheffield steel firms also had commercial links with Russia and the entire cost of the department was borne by Vickers & Son. Although trade with Russia became increasingly difficult after the war, the department survived, under a lecturer, G. A. Birkett. A Department of Spanish, promoted for commercial reasons by Herbert Hughes, was established in 1918.

One of the many distressing aspects of the war was the effect on University members with German connections. Julius Freund, Professor of German since 1908, was interned as an alien and had his chair removed by the University Council in December 1916, despite his vehement protests from prison.[140] The chair of German lapsed and was not reinstated until 1953; until then the department was run by lecturers. Sir Joseph Jonas, who was one of the mainstays of the Applied Science faculty and the chairman of its committee, was born and educated in Germany and had been the German Consul to Sheffield for many years. His fortune came from

Professor Wynne with the all-female Chemistry team who produced the anaesthetic ß-eucaine, which had formerly been manufactured exclusively in Germany.

supplying steel for rifles and he had close business connections with the German Mauser Rifle Company, to whom he supplied information about British government rifle contracts in 1913. In 1918 he was tried for treason and although he was acquitted of the charge of intentionally threatening British security, he was found guilty of misdemeanour. Jonas was stripped of his knighthood and forced to resign from his public offices, a punishment which in Sheffield was generally thought to be excessive. However, his actions were clearly most unwise at a time of such tension in Anglo-German relations.[141]

The Glass Department

Most of the University's war work ended with peace in 1918, but one enterprise proved so timely and essential that it became a permanent and unique feature of the University. When W. E. S. Turner was Secretary of the Scientific Advisory Committee he noted that a disproportionate number of enquiries were coming from the glass industry. The industry was in crisis because specialised glass had been imported from Germany and Austria. Hundreds of industries used laboratory glass and both naval and military commanders needed binocular glass.[142] Suddenly called upon to produce home-made versions, glass manufacturers could not ignore the absence of scientific expertise within an industry which had relied for centuries on the rule of thumb. Nearly all the manufacturers were ignorant of the exact composition of the materials they used and of the nature of their chemical reactions when heated. Turner was astonished, on analysing a sample of 'pure' arsenic sent in by a manufacturer, to discover that it was forty per cent sand.[143] Measurement of temperature was unknown in an industry which regarded its processes 'in terms of secret recipes handed down from father to son'.[144] Turner acted with rapidity and thoroughness, visiting 23 firms in South Yorkshire and producing a report in May 1915 which advised the University to make immediate provision, both for courses of instruction and research into glass manufacture. He pointed out that no other university or college was addressing the needs of the glass industry and that there were many glass firms in the vicinity of Sheffield.

Fisher and Wynne responded with equal alacrity, and by the autumn of 1915 the Department of Glass Manufacture (later Glass Technology) began work with a full-time lecturer/demonstrator and two part-time assistants. Turner was appointed lecturer-in-charge, although he still had considerable responsibilities in the Chemistry department. The aim of his report had been to make the case for a glass department, not to write his own job description, but his obvious enthusiasm and suitability for the job spoke for him.[145] The following year he founded the Society of Glass Technology, quickly making himself a national figure and Sheffield the natural centre of glass research and development. Turner became engrossed by his new subject, as he explained in 1937:

> As the work of development proceeded I became, not unnaturally, involved
> in an increasing number of problems and interests. The great joy of

The Marquess of Crewe was installed as Chancellor in 1917; he held the post for 27 years, until 1944.

81

Above: *William Rothenstein was already a notable artist nationally, particularly as a portraitist, in 1917 when his old friend H. A. L. Fisher invited him to come to the University, as Professor of Civic Art. In 1920 he was made Director of the Royal College of Art and the growing pressure of this job forced him by 1926 to give up the Sheffield chair. Sadly it was never refilled and the University's academic involvement with art and design ceased at that point.*

Right: The Violinist *by Rothenstein was presented to the University by his daughter, Mrs A. B. Ward, who had married Alan Ward, owner of a well-known bookshop in Sheffield. It now hangs in the Department of Music.*

In addition to his many other commitments Rothenstein was an official War Artist. This drawing entitled On the Peronne Front *was reproduced in* Floreamus, June 1918.

teaching students who, as adult men, clamoured for information . . . the initiation of researches, and last, but very important, the foundation of the Society of Glass Technology and all that it involved brought me to the state, ere long, of realising how fascinating is the subject of glass; and soon all thought of relinquishing it at the end of the war passed away. I had, indeed, for better or worse, become part of the glass industry.[146]

Turner's achievement, with the support of the University, was nothing less than the creation of a new discipline.[147] It was a perfect example of applied science and of the function of a civic university. The department was initially housed in two rooms borrowed from Chemistry and moved in 1917 to new premises at St George's Square, partially financed by the glass industry. These could never be made big enough because of tenants' rights on the surrounding property. By 1920, there were fifteen staff members and the department was forced to move to Attercliffe, three miles from the main University site, to take over a vacant glassworks which could provide facilities for research.[148] The staff had no choice but to accept the disadvantages of their isolation and the travelling which became a part of their day, since teaching still took place in the St George's Square building. Fortunately the glassworks was near Attercliffe station. This arrangement was, naturally, seen as a temporary one but the department stayed in Attercliffe for eighteen years. Turner became Professor of Glass Technology in 1920; he led the department with unquenchable enthusiasm until 1945.

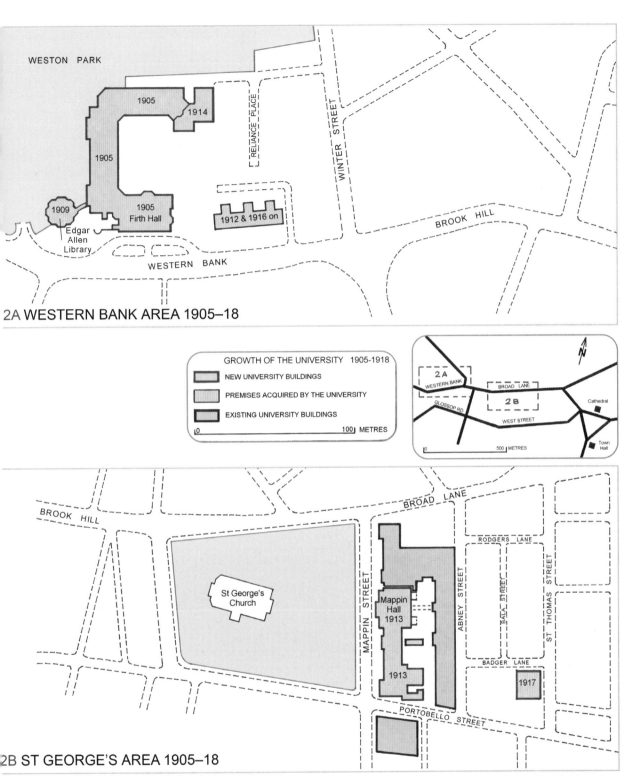

2A WESTERN BANK AREA 1905–18

Within map 2A:

WESTON PARK

1905

1914

1905

1905

1905 Firth Hall

1909 Edgar Allen Library

RELIANCE PLACE

WINTER STREET

1912 & 1916 on

BROOK HILL

WESTERN BANK

GROWTH OF THE UNIVERSITY 1905–1918

NEW UNIVERSITY BUILDINGS

PREMISES ACQUIRED BY THE UNIVERSITY

EXISTING UNIVERSITY BUILDINGS

0 100 METRES

Inset location map:

2A WESTERN BANK

GLOSSOP RD

BROAD LANE

2B

WEST STREET

Cathedral

Town Hall

0 500 METRES

N

2B ST GEORGE'S AREA 1905–18

Within map 2B:

BROOK HILL

BROAD LANE

RODGERS LANE

St George's Church

MAPPIN STREET

Mappin Hall 1913

1913

ABNEY STREET

BALM STREET

ST THOMAS STREET

BADGER LANE

1917

PORTOBELLO STREET

Maps © Crown Copyright Ordnance Survey

3

The Frustrating Inter-war Years: 1919–39

Introduction

I N 1921 MICHAEL SADLER, THE VICE-CHANCELLOR OF LEEDS, reportedly said that he would not 'lay heavy odds' on the survival of the universities of Leeds or Sheffield.[1] They were crippled by the conjunction of a sudden influx of post-war students with a financial slump which killed off all attempts at fundraising. Liverpool suffered in the same way, although Birmingham, not for the first time, was much better off. Sheffield's administrators spent the 1920s struggling to balance the books and failing to find the capital even for modest expansion schemes. For Sheffield, A. H. Halsey's description of the inter-war years as 'bleak' is correct.[2]

The dependence of the arts and pure science faculties on students who intended to become teachers meant that they were badly affected by the reduction in the number of teacher training grants in the 1930s. Enrolments of full-time technology students did not rise significantly except in the immediate post-war years.[3] The only boom in student numbers at Sheffield was in the medical faculty, which at this period was subsidising the rest of the University. The number of women students fell in the 1930s because of the reduction in teacher training grants, at a time when there were few other professional opportunities for women.[4]

University teaching standards, in general, were not high. An enquiry by the National Union of Students (NUS) at Manchester, Birmingham and Nottingham in 1938 found that the teaching was conducted almost entirely by lectures, with tutorials confined to honours students in the later years.[5] Few students could afford to buy textbooks and libraries had not invested in multiple copies.[6] Lecturers faced

Facing page: View of Sheffield from Crookes (1923), by the Sheffield-born artist Stanley Royle, shows the University buildings in the centre ground of the picture. The brick buildings to their right housed the mail order business of J. G. Graves, a benefactor to the University. This view is familiar to the generations of Sheffield students who have lived in flats and lodgings in Crookes.

impossible odds; one was quoted as saying that his ideals for the lecture 'had assumed the facilities of older and richer universities; without them . . . I had to turn myself into a textbook'.[7]

In the 1920s, the Honours course often lasted four years but, as school certificate standards rose, it was agreed that students who had passed the Higher School Certificate could waive some or all of the Intermediate courses and so complete Honours in three years. The Honours degree soared in popularity after 1921, when the Burnham salary scale for teachers began to reward honours graduates. In the 1930s, the 'Ordinary' or 'Pass' degree, made up of several subjects and inferior to the Honours degree, was abolished in most universities. At Sheffield it was replaced in 1933 by the 'General' degree, taken in three subjects. The trend towards specialisation was not universally welcomed; the National Union of Students in 1938 recommended a General Honours degree and the abolition of restrictions preventing inter-faculty combined degrees.[8]

Postgraduates became more numerous with the introduction of the PhD after the war.[9] The PhD had first been offered in Germany and the United States in the mid-nineteenth century. British universities introduced it in order to attract research students away from the graduate schools of those countries. The five northern universities, including Sheffield, agreed to the joint introduction of a PhD in 1917. The new degree proved to be more successful at attracting home students than those from abroad. Until 1926 Sheffield averaged only three PhDs a year, initially in the arts but then most often in applied sciences. Library resourcing proved to be the biggest hurdle. 'In 1925–6 all the grant-aided Universities and Colleges of Great Britain put together did not spend as much on books as the four American universities of Illinois, Michigan, Minnesota and North Carolina.' [10]

The Committee of Vice Chancellors and Principals (CVCP), which had existed in nascent form since 1912, spoke up for the struggling universities and was rewarded by a government grant of £1 million per year from 1919.[11] To administer this hugely increased budget, the Chancellor of the Exchequer, Austen Chamberlain, created the University Grants Committee (UGC).[12] Sir William McCormick became its chairman and established an organisation which not only gave the universities essential, if basic, funds, but did so in a way which was perceived to be fair. The relationship was, according to one vice-chancellor, 'the right footing of partnership and mutual consultation'.[13] Another praised the UGC's 'tact and sympathy' and the fact that it 'preferred "influence" to any semblance of "control", and . . . abstained from any cast-iron system of uniformity of treatment'.[14] Quinquennial visits by the UGC to each university were established at this time.

To complete this organisational revolution, the Association of University Teachers (AUT) was also formed in 1919.[15] The AUT brought academic staff (including professors, a source of contention to begin with) together and campaigned on a range of issues. Sheffield was involved from an early stage; F. Raleigh Batt, a Law lecturer, drew up the rules and one of the earliest meetings was held at Sheffield in April 1919. The focus of the early campaigns was the introduction of salary scales and increments. Professors' salaries were the subject of private negotiation and varied widely.[16] In some cases they were supplemented with a proportion of departmental fee income. In Sheffield, Leathes had the highest basic salary (£1,200 in 1920–24) but the addition of fee income raised Wynne's earnings to £1,875. Only three other professors earned more than £1,000 before 1936; the system of allocating fee income was gradually phased out. Lecturers' salaries were unacceptably low nationwide and the UGC reported in 1922 that a large number were compelled to seek outside work. Staff payment systems continued to be haphazard until salary scales were introduced for professors in the late 1930s and for lecturers not until 1946.

Women academics were paid less than men and found it almost impossible to rise above the rank of lecturer. Birmingham was unusual in appointing its first female professor, in Italian, in 1921; there was only one other female professor at a civic university at the time and even in 1951 there were only three.[17] A study of university women at this time concludes that 'any notions of steady assimilation or easy integration tend to disappear in the face of the detailed historical evidence.'[18]

The post-war students

'A prolonged epidemic of dancing' is Chapman's description of the post-war years. He meant this literally, but it could be a metaphor as well. The students were happy and determined to make up for lost time, not least in matters of love. The university authorities found 'students dancing in the Firth Hall during the daytime and even in the corridors' and were outraged by requests for alcohol and tobacco to be allowed on the premises.[19] Firth Hall was locked and in 1922 the academic staff protested to the Vice-Chancellor about the 'detrimental effect' on academic work of midday dances during the week, with the result that he wrote to the Student President to suggest that they be discontinued.[20]

Many of these students were ex-servicemen, several years older and correspondingly more mature than undergraduates coming straight from school. They had deferred their university education and were now determined to make the most of it, both socially and academically. They were also numerous – 846 undergraduates in 1919/20, compared with 388 the previous year, and almost 1,000 in 1920/21. Postgraduate numbers also escalated. The University struggled to cope. Staff numbers were insufficient and the teaching accommodation was inadequate. Sciences were particularly popular and two large asbestos huts were erected in the quadrangle to relieve the Chemistry and Physics departments. Even so, when A. W. Chapman arrived as lecturer in Chemistry in 1920, the students' apparatus was stacked in the corridors and he had to conduct 'advanced classes for forty in a laboratory which thirty students made uncomfortably full'.[21] The Applied Science departments had to deal with daunting numbers of part-time students, in addition to the increased full-time load.

Even so, this was a good time for the lecturers because, 'after the academic stagnation of wartime, it was mentally and spiritually refreshing'.[22] They taught some bright and enthusiastic students, including future leaders of their profession, like

Olive Dickinson was President of the Students' Union in 1922, the first woman to be elected during normal times, although two women held the office during the First World War. Floreamus commented that this was not a move towards petticoat government: 'It is a compliment to Miss Dickinson's own marked ability and not to the women students of the University'.

The 'temporary' asbestos huts for Chemistry and Physics survived until 1962. The photograph is also a graphic reminder of the characteristic smoke-laden atmosphere of industrial Sheffield in the period before the Clean Air Act.

Right: Elementary laboratory in the Physics hut.

Donald Bailey who later designed the Bailey bridge.[23] This helped to compensate for the large numbers, the cramped conditions and salaries which had not been increased for many years. The flood of students also abated quickly, so that by 1926 total numbers had dropped to under 900; they remained at that level until 1945.

THE HADOW YEARS 1919–30

During the 1920s the vice-chancellor was William Henry Hadow, another distinguished public servant with wide intellectual and social interests. Having obtained first-class degrees at Worcester College, Oxford, in both classical moderations and *literae humaniores*, he went on to study music, an unfashionable subject for Oxford scholars, and gain a BMus in 1890. He became a composer and music critic, whose achievements are commemorated today in Hadow House, the home of the Music department. He was an arresting lecturer, always without notes, but his immediate grasp of the essential facts could make him appear peremptory in conversation. Douglas Knoop reported that no member of staff developed an intimate acquaintance with him; both he and Chapman recall that Hadow would 'march backwards and forwards the whole time, talking at the top of his voice' when meeting visitors.[24] He showed, however, an unfailingly shrewd understanding of the students and both his private and his university correspondence reveal great personal warmth.

Hadow had been Principal of Armstrong College, Newcastle for ten years before coming to Sheffield.[25] He was thus the first vice-chancellor to arrive with previous experience of higher education in a northern city. He believed in the tradition of the civic university, writing to Sir Robert Hadfield in 1919:

> I have always maintained that, while one of the functions of a University is the pursuit of scientific research as far as it will go, another function is the satisfaction, so far as possible, of local needs . . .[26]

Sir Henry Hadow, *by Sir William Rothenstein, at the time of his appointment as Vice-Chancellor in 1919. He combined his duties at the University during a time of financial stringency with a Chairmanship at the Board of Education. 'Only an exceptional man', such as Hadow, 'could have stood the strain'.*

Armstrong College was one of the worst-endowed civic institutions, so Hadow was well prepared for the financial restrictions and frustrations of life in Sheffield. Nothing, however, could have prepared him or any other vice-chancellor for the demands of the post-war years. In the optimism of 1920, Hadow launched a public appeal for £500,000, to build new student facilities and classrooms. This was proceeding well until the slump of the following year, which hit the city hard. Firms which had pledged regular contributions were unable to make them, with the result that the University's building schemes had to be postponed year after year. Worse still, there was insufficient income for maintenance and an economy committee was set up, which in 1921 was forced to make cuts to the already inadequate academic resources. Laboratory allocations were reduced, the Library was starved of funds and some junior staff members were dismissed. By 1926, the University was also faced with a major reduction in its grant from the City Council.

The University had influential friends on the City Council, especially the Pro-Chancellor, W. E. Clegg, who had married the widow of Joseph Jonas and was the leader of the majority Conservative/Liberal alliance party. In the early 1920s Sheffield Council's higher education grant (the product of a penny rate) was the

The Prince of Wales on a visit to the University in 1923, accompanied by the Lord Mayor Sir Henry Kenyon Stephenson (Pro-Chancellor) and Sir Henry Hadow, far right.

Sir William Clegg supported the University in his role as leader of the Sheffield Liberal party. He was also chairman of the Applied Science Committee and was made a Pro-Chancellor following the death of Sir Albert Hobson in 1923. This cartoon from the Sheffield Mail marks that event.

A pugnacious-looking Percival Sharp.

most generous in the country, continuing at the same level even after the institution of the UGC grant.[27] While the Council was being munificent to the University, however, it was failing to meet increasingly militant working-class demands for housing, social services and aid to the unemployed. The Labour Party made significant gains at every local election until it achieved a majority in November 1926. Clegg and seven of his friends were ousted from the aldermanic bench.

Despite its close links with local industry and honourable record in adult education, the University was not a popular cause with the Labour party. Hadow commented privately that the Labour Council did not understand the University because 'to most of them education is bounded by the Secondary school'.[28] Certainly its priorities lay elsewhere, and the university grant appeared an easy target. In particular, the City Council was expected to fund sub-degree-level students, like the part-time engineering, mining and metallurgy students in the applied science departments. This grant now became the subject of a tortured struggle between Gibbons, the Registrar, and Percival Sharp, the new Director of Education, who relentlessly pursued him for every possible saving. As their correspondence shows, Sharp went to the limits of his responsibilities and beyond; one letter to Gibbons in 1925 begins with an apology, 'that my anxieties and worries arising out of university finance should have impelled me to the use of angry language when talking with you over the telephone'.[29] Sharp's estimates of the University's costs were based, quite unreasonably, on comparison with the cost of the Central Commercial College, where the students were younger, needed fewer facilities and followed a less advanced curriculum than those at the University.

This attitude was particularly unfair because there was no technical college in Sheffield at the time and so the University was, in effect, performing that service for the local authority at St George's Square. Any other form of technical college would have been far more expensive and the City Council did not, in the event, make such funding available until 1948, when the Technical College (later the Polytechnic) was founded. The combined arguments of university administrators and academics failed to win the day in 1927, however, and the grant was reduced by more than half. To add insult to injury, the City Council decided to appoint Sharp as a representative on the Applied Science Committee, in order to 'give valuable service to the administration of the University'.[30]

It is not hard to imagine how Gibbons felt about this treatment, although in public his 'discretion was impenetrable'.[31] As an administrator he was a good deal more polite than Sharp and just as meticulous. During these years he 'relentlessly drove himself and his tiny staff in the collection of the masses of data required . . . and in the preparation of the successive statements of the University's case to the City authorities and to all the other bodies to whom the University appealed'.[32] His task was probably not aided by Hadow, who had many commitments and tended to avoid confrontation. At the height of the tension in 1927, Hadow told his colleagues: 'If I demur to some of [Sharp's] statements it is not in order to challenge the spirit in which they are made, but to indicate that in my opinion there is another side to the case'.[33]

The University suffered as a result, in its reputation as well as its finances. It was criticised in the press for spinelessness, the *Sheffield Daily Telegraph* pointing out that some of the money lost was the right of the University under Board of Education rules.[34] Cecil Desch, Professor of Metallurgy, told Gibbons that 'the University has humiliated itself by its abject surrender, without any advantage gained. We lose so large a sum of money that the work will be crippled, and get nothing whatever in exchange, whilst we submit to the most humiliating bureaucratic control'.[35]

Predictably, Sharp proved to be a disruptive presence on the Applied Science Committee. The following year he pursued Dr Wall, the head of Electrical Engineering, accusing him, in a flurry of letters and documents, of concentrating on

An early aerial view of the University in 1920/21. The main tram route followed Hounsfield Road from the bottom right hand corner of the picture, then divided to go up Western Bank and along Winter Street. On the right, the pale coloured building at the tramline junction is the Scala Cinema, then under construction.

91

research for his own 'personal benefit' at the expense of teaching. Hadow's carefully detailed responses did not satisfy his inquisitor, who continued to bombard him with intrusive questions and accusations.[36]

By 1927/28, Hadow and Gibbons were forced to adopt even more stringent economies and a detailed scrutiny of the teaching hours of every member of staff. The arguments of the University's friends, however, caused a change of heart at the end of that difficult year. The City Council awarded an extra grant, together with an offer to extinguish the University's debts in due course. An increase in the Treasury quinquennial grant in 1930 enabled the current books to be balanced, so that when Hadow retired he was able to pass on to his successor, Sir Arthur Pickard-Cambridge, the 'long overdue' chance to raise staff salaries.[37]

THE STUDENTS OF THE TWENTIES

Hadow's tolerance gradually prevailed against the restrictions imposed on the students by Gibbons. The Vice-Chancellor refused to take the word of some professors who told him that the Student Representative Council was 'in open mutiny' and he approved the students' demand for a beer and tobacco licence.[38] The behaviour of these students would certainly have been seen as daring by their parents' generation. The girls were no longer chaperoned and enjoyed easy social relationships with men. Some of them smoked, like Amy Johnson, who arrived to study for an arts degree in 1922. Amy's letters during her first year in Sheffield are full of the excitement of freedom: 'I'm having the time of my life'.[39] She refused to accept the restrictions of life in Hall and chose to live in lodgings, starting off in Sharrow and moving many times. She revelled in the dances in

> a beautiful hall in the Univ., the floor's lovely and we had a proper orchestra, sitting-out rooms etc. Being a fresher I was told I needn't expect any dances as the senior men didn't bother themselves with newcomers. But I got my program [sic] full at the very beginning . . . It was quite a triumph for a fresher!

She had 'the most topping time' playing hockey for the first eleven. Amy's letters to her older boyfriend reveal that he became her lover during her university years. This was probably exceptional among her generation of female students, but none could understand the attitude of a Discipline Committee which refused to allow dances after midnight.

This rule lasted until 1925 and the secretary of the Entertainments Committee had to send 'respectful' requests for dances in Firth Hall until 1935.[40] The students had no premises outside the main University building in which to organise their own social facilities, an issue which had been a running sore for years. During the war the SRC protested forcefully about the fact that Gibbons had given the 'Belgian House' (for refugees) to the Workers Educational Association, even though the students had asked to use it as a Union building.[41]

Amy Johnson, one of Britain's most famous inter-war aviators, graduated from the University in 1925 with a BA degree in Latin, French and Economics. Her reputation was established by her solo flight to Australia in the Gypsy Moth 'Jason' in 1930. She died in 1941 after crashing into the Thames estuary while carrying out war work for the Air Transport Authority.

After the war, the SRC was led by men who had known the social facilities of the armed services. Their demands for a student club brought a gratifying response from the University Council in 1919, with an offer to appeal for funds for a 'substantial building' which would also serve as a memorial to students killed in the war.[42] This initiative, which would have done so much to satisfy the students, did not survive the financial crisis of 1921–28. Instead, two less than satisfactory buildings were adapted as student clubs. No.4, Leavygreave (on a site now occupied by the Hicks building) was equipped for the men with its own refectory, lounge and smoke room, and a 'Committee room common to both sexes'.[43] The women were given No.1, Northumberland Road. These clubs were the only students' union buildings until 1935.

The early twenties saw the birth of the student union movement, with the founding of the National Union of Students (NUS) in 1922. The University of Sheffield Union was formed in October 1921 and the SRC was renamed the Union Representative Council (URC) two years later. In the early days fewer than ten per cent of the students were members of the Union.[44] The formation of Union social committees probably did a great deal to change attitudes – Entertainments, Debates and Publications committees were all in place by 1923, together with the Rag Committee.

Earl Beatty, Commander of the Grand Fleet during the war and subsequently First Sea Lord, was treated to 'chairing' on his visit to receive the honorary degree of LLD on 23 July 1920. The students staged a rag in his honour in the form of a mock degree congregation before the real ceremony.

The Rag

The 'Charity' or 'Hospital' Rag started with the medical students' high-spirited attempts to raise money for local hospitals on 'Hospital Saturday' in 1920:

> The collectors 'searched the pockets' of the football and theatre crowds, not once, but many times; and every tavern was a happy hunting-ground . . . to the 'Medicals'.[45]

The Prime Minister David Lloyd George was awarded the honorary degree of LLD on 17 October 1919. He was 'chaired' round the quadrangle by medical students and, left, received an enthusiastic welcome outside the main entrance on Western Bank.

Facing page, clockwise from the left:

The first Rag in 1920 concentrated on raising money for the hospitals, a theme that continued for many years as Rags became bigger and more elaborate.

An ambulance bought with proceeds from the November 1923 Rag is presented to the hospitals outside the main entrance to Western Bank.

Scenes from Rag processions and boat races on the Don during the 1920s and 1930s.

The name 'Rag' was an established school and student term for having fun by dressing up or playing practical jokes. Sheffield students played the 'Prohibition Rag' on a visiting lecturer from the United States in 1920, who instead of making his planned speech on Prohibition, found himself bundled into a vehicle and conveyed to the 'Three Merry Lads' at Lodge Moor.[46] In February 1922 the Rag started with a procession:

> Preceded by mounted police and headed by a gruesome banner bearing the picture of a skeleton, which heralded the fact that Medicals were in the vicinity, it wended its way by a tortuous route around the town. Stretching for quite a quarter of a mile, it consisted of a conglomeration of strange-looking individuals . . . Many side-shows, such as concert-parties, &c, succeeded in bringing about a complete state of 'Bedlam' at the Town Hall, until the time for the grand procession to Bramall Lane Football ground.[47]

A second Rag in 1922, during which Amy Johnson and her friends dressed up as Red Indians, brought in students from the other faculties and together they raised £2,500 for the hospitals. Over the next few years, traditions which were to last for decades began. The Rag magazine, originally called *The Star*, first appeared in 1926 and changed its name to *T'Wikker* (after the local street and Arches) in 1930. 85,000 copies were printed in 1928. 'Immunity labels', denoting that a shop or motorist had paid up and should not be harassed for money, were first sold in 1927. Douglas Haigh, a student in the early thirties, recalls ' a boat race in tin bath tubs down the river Don' and that 'a six-foot medical student called R. B. Davies used to prance up and down the rocks on the roundabout . . . and other roads, dressed as a short-skirted fairy with a star-ended wand . . . He later became a much-respected general practitioner in Sheffield!'[48]

The Pavilion, the Gymnasium and the Appointments Board

Sir Albert Hobson, the Master Cutler in 1903, was a supporter of the University from its foundation and acted as Treasurer 1910-16 and Pro-Chancellor from 1916 until his death in 1923. His portrait hangs in Firth Hall opposite a case containing the war medals awarded to his two sons, who were killed in action.

Athletics, for some reason renamed 'Harriers', was popular after the war but the Athletics Committee was frustrated by the lack of a proper pavilion at Norton, which meant that it could not arrange inter-university matches at the ground. Before his death in 1923, Sir Albert Hobson decided to fund a new pavilion in memory of his two sons who had been killed in action during the war. It was eventually completed in 1928, with extra funding from the University Council, and the first inter-university sports match was held there a few days later. Professor Wynne and W. E. Clegg, the Pro-Chancellor, did a great deal to promote the pavilion and Wynne ensured that it had a maple dance-floor. Tea on Saturdays followed by a dance became a regular part of the University's social activities. The pavilion was so close to Wynne's heart that when he retired, he insisted that the money raised for his present should provide a grand pavilion clock.

Hadow was proud of both the pavilion and the university gymnasium, which also

SHEFFIELD + UNIVERSITY
MEDICAL FACULTY'S EFFORT
FOR THE
HOSPITALS
THEY HELP YOU
CAN'T SHELP-EM

GIRL PAT

THE RAG OFFENSIVE OF 1935 MAKES ITS FIRST CONTACT WITH THE ENEMY

The Hobson Memorial Pavilion at the time of its opening in 1928. The clock presented by Professor Wynne following his retirement was mounted over the central window in 1931.

opened in 1928. There was much concern in the 1920s about the 'physique of the nation' and the lack of attention to physical training in schools and universities.[49] Despite the University's perilous financial situation, Hadow secured a grant from the UGC for about half the cost of the gymnasium and it was built on a site just below the main Western Bank buildings.[50]

The students signed up enthusiastically for Physical Education (P. E.) classes, but after only a few weeks attendances had plummeted to such an extent that the classes were abandoned.[51] For more than a year the gymnasium was only used for badminton, while the authorities wondered what to do. The students themselves provided the answer, by inviting 'Sergeant' Harry Cofield to run a different type of class. Instead of P. E., which was redolent of school and of army training, Cofield structured the classes around games training. Gymnastic exercises, boxing, fencing and football training were introduced successfully and Cofield became the backbone of the gymnasium; he remained at the University until 1967.

Jobs for graduates were not a foregone conclusion in the 1920s, especially for arts and pure science students who did not want to teach. Mark Rampion, one of the heroes of Aldous Huxley's novel *Point Counter Point*, was a 'scholarship boy' at the University of Sheffield in the 1920s who was 'horrified' and 'depressed' by the prospect of teaching. His escape was to marry a rich woman who could support his career as a writer and painter.[52] Another graduate who was determined not to teach, Amy Johnson, struggled to find her feet and took secretarial, shop assistant and advertising jobs before embarking on flying.

In 1924/25, Senate proposed the building of a gymnasium with the following words: 'It would be a great thing if Sheffield could in this matter be a pioneer in English university education – the University should add to its equipment a gymnasium with an adequate staff of teachers who might do for the bodily development of our students what the classroom and laboratory do for their minds'.
Designed in a Tudor style to match the existing buildings, the gymnasium was constructed in the front gardens of four houses on Western Bank. The windows were situated nine feet from the ground in order to ensure privacy.

Aware of the need for greater enterprise, the University set up an Appointments Board in 1928. J. R. Clarke, the Physics lecturer, was the Secretary and students were represented on the committee. Clarke worked enthusiastically to build up careers information and to liaise with possible employers. This was the start of the University Careers Service, which gained its first full-time staff member in 1947.[53]

Student halls of the twenties

Hadow was as keen on student halls as his predecessor, Fisher, had been and just as liable to overblown rhetoric on the subject. 'Much of the best part of education consists in the corporate life of the students, and though this can be materially assisted by the organisation of clubs and societies, it reaches its highest point in the daily intercourse which a hostel is specially well qualified to give', he wrote in 1919.[54] Like Fisher, however, Hadow was to be frustrated in his larger ambitions for the halls. He came closest to success with the women's halls. By 1920 demand for places in Oakholme Lodge heavily exceeded its capacity and the University was offered the chance to purchase Tapton Cliffe, a large house on Fulwood Road, for £3,000. This was a substantial gift from the owner, Frank Atkin, since the house's true value was over £8,000.[55] It became the second women's hall, for 22 students, and opened in January 1921.

Two years later there were still 48 women living in lodgings and a third hall opened in 1924 when the University acquired Endcliffe House on Endcliffe Vale Road, the former home of Sir Joseph Jonas. This building, which ultimately became Halifax Hall, originally took twenty students. Kay Rogers and Margaret Wolsten-holme, who shared a room there, remember that it had 'an ornate Victorian fireplace' with a fire which was a 'brute to light' and a ration of one scuttle-full of coal per day.[56] The warden, Miss Grace Hadley, greeted Kay with a Pekinese in her arms. She led prayers before the evening meal. Katharine Jex-Blake, the former mistress of Girton College, Cambridge, visited just after Endcliffe opened and commented that no other town took better care of its women students than Sheffield.[57]

Hadow sometimes moderated the discipline applied to women in hall. In 1926 Miss Hadley suspended a resident for several weeks because she had come in late on three occasions. Hadow thought the punishment excessive, but wrote tactfully, 'I have, as you may imagine, had a great deal of experience of students who come in

'Sarge' Cofield who ran the gymnasium with military efficiency. He was an expert fencer.

Left: *Tapton Cliffe, the second women's hall.*

Right: *The Library at Tapton Cliffe.*

Above and right: *Endcliffe House was a substantial family residence built around 1840 and significantly extended in 1891. These photographs taken in 1935 show the exterior and the common room, making it clear that the atmosphere of the women's hall (later named Halifax Hall) was still that of the pre-war years.*

late; Oxford was full of them . . . but I am not sure whether so long a period of suspension is not a little more than meets the case.'[58]

Hadow and the University Council would have liked to create halls with at least forty members, 'large enough to allow some such corporate life as a College at Oxford or Cambridge can bestow'.[59] This proved to be impossible, for either men or women, before the 1930s. In 1919, however, there was strong hope of establishing a large men's hall in the Ranmoor College building on Fulwood Road, between Gladstone Road and Graham Road, which had originally been a college established by the Firth family for training Methodist New Connexion ministers. The University had already opened negotiations to buy the College when it learned that the Education Committee also wished to use it as a hostel. This was the first occasion on which Hadow and Percival Sharp confronted each other directly. When their dispute was referred to H. A. L. Fisher at the Board of Education, he, conscious of his previous connection with the University, asked for independent advice, which unfortunately supported the City Council.[60] The University finally acquired this building for a hall in 1947, abandoning it in 1968 for a second, newly-built, Ranmoor House on a different site.

The sole men's hall, Stephenson, which was intended primarily for Anglican ordinands, was re-established in a third home, Tapton Elms on Taptonville Road. It could house only twenty men and the greater ambitions for the men's halls were not realised until the 1930s, when the financial crisis was over and a new vice-chancellor had arrived.

Hadow retired in 1930, just as he embarked on his first marriage, at the age of seventy. He achieved as much as any vice-chancellor could have done in the unpropitious 1920s and left a more than promising legacy for his successor. In the extravagant language of honorary degree orations, 'by the exercise of wisdom, patience and application, he has at length rolled his almost Sisyphean burden to the summit, and glimpsed at least the outline of a kindlier and less laborious universe which those who follow will enjoy'.[61] Throughout his time at Sheffield, Hadow was chairman of the Consultative Committee of the Board of Education (1920–34),

Facing page: *Women students at Tapton Cliffe in 1926.*

98

during 'its greatest creative period', when it produced 'three reports which changed the face of education in England and Wales'.[62] These were *The Education of the Adolescent* (1926), *The Primary School* (1931) and *Infant and Nursery Schools* (1933). Hadow's legacy to education at all levels was immense.

ARTHUR PICKARD-CAMBRIDGE
AND THE BUILDING PROGRAMME 1930–38

Sir Arthur Wallace Pickard-Cambridge, Vice-Chancellor from 1930 to 1938, by George Harcourt RA. Chapman commented that he and Lady Pickard-Cambridge knew all the members of the academic staff, their wives and families; they also 'made the acquaintance of large numbers of undergraduates and were personally and informally known to nearly all of them'.

Dr Arthur Chapman, at this time a lecturer in the Department of Chemistry. He became the first warden of Crewe Hall and is pictured in his study there. In 1944 he was appointed Registrar of the University.

Arthur Pickard-Cambridge was a classical scholar who had spent nearly all his working life at Oxford. He was much less well prepared for the demands of Sheffield than Hadow had been and admitted that 'he was something of a fish out of water in the industrial community of Sheffield.'[63] He had, moreover, little interest in the concerns of business and spoke his mind with a brusqueness which sometimes caused offence. Pickard-Cambridge never became a public figure in the mould of either Hadow or Fisher, but this had the advantage of concentrating his energies. Chapman observed that, 'unlike Hadow, [he] spent most of his working days in the University building and made it clear that he really was accessible to all members'. He and his wife took pains to get to know every member of staff and their genuine interest in the students was characteristically but affectionately reciprocated in the Vice-Chancellor's nickname, 'Pickled-Cabbage'.

Steeped in the culture of Oxford, Pickard-Cambridge was even more obsessed than Fisher and Hadow had been with the need for student halls. His first memorandum to the Council on the needs of the University in 1931 gave top priority to the building of a new men's hall. He reported that Leeds and Manchester both had much better hostel accommodation and that Sheffield was losing applications as a result.[64]

Thus a note of materialistic competition was added to the idealistic rhetoric that was such a feature of discourse about halls at this time. A. W. Chapman wrote:

> In the life of the Hall the small intolerances that divide specialist scholars are rubbed away; the literary man realizes by experience that the technologist is not the barbarian he might be thought; the medical student finds that the classics make a contribution to general culture that he can ill afford to despise, and men can test their opinions in frank and easy discussion with those of different outlook.[65]

Chapman became the first warden of Crewe Hall, which the Council decided to build in June 1932 in the grounds of Oakholme Lodge, from which the women had recently departed. The Lodge itself became the warden's house and the stables were converted into a library. Crewe was the university's first purpose-built hall and could accommodate 100 male students. Its design was inspired by Oxford colleges, with quadrangles and rooms mostly grouped round staircases, which were seen as better for 'housing vigorous young men'.[66] It was also planned to have a single entrance to enforce 'gating' times but this idea was abandoned, for reasons of cost,

in favour of trusting the students 'to keep reasonable hours and behave maturely', an experiment which Chapman deemed a success. The hall was opened in September 1936 and named Crewe after the University's Chancellor, the Marquess of Crewe.

The community life at Crewe evolved over the first two years. There were dances, 'the most successful in the whole university',[67] in the dining hall, which was designed to be cleared of furniture in thirty minutes, and a debating club. Courts for tennis, squash and fives, sports of which Pickard-Cambridge clearly approved, were built in the grounds. Upon its opening Pickard-Cambridge wrote, 'I look upon the Hall as one of the best things that has been done in my time here' which 'is going to do more for the University than any changes that have taken place in it for years.'[68] His belief that the hall would be 'a real centre of corporate life' for the University as a whole was not entirely borne out by events, but his vision of a University residential quarter in the Endcliffe area proved far-sighted. By the end of the 1960s, there were four other large halls in the immediate vicinity of Crewe.

In relation to the women's halls, Pickard-Cambridge's task was very different because the proportion of women students began to decline in 1927, shortly after the creation of Endcliffe House. There were vacancies in the women's halls in 1929, mostly caused by the falling number of students sponsored by the Board of Education.[69] The majority of women students aimed at a teaching career, so this affected all universities, but the decline in Sheffield was far greater than the national average. The University Council took the opportunity to create a single, more manageable, hall by enlarging Endcliffe House to take about sixty women. The new hall, renamed 'University Hall for Women', was ready in 1934 and Oakholme and Tapton Cliffe were closed.[70]

The University Hall had single rooms, each with a gas fire, desk, bookcase and washing basin. The gas fires, in particular, made it 'Utopia' to inmates who had

The design for Crewe Hall was the result of an architectural competition, won by John C. Procter of Leeds. It was the first major University building not designed by E. M. Gibbs, who had in effect retired in 1928. The design departed from the Tudor style favoured by Gibbs on the main campus. The photographs show the exterior and the dining room.

A study bedroom in the University Hall for Women (later renamed Halifax Hall), complete with The Laughing Cavalier, *taken in 1935.*

struggled with the old coal fires.[71] The women were looked after with great care by a staff led by Miss Violet Murray, the warden until 1936, and then by Miss D. M. Bennett. A Board of Management included Mrs Pickard-Cambridge and other University wives. Vera Rose, a resident from 1934, says that, 'in my opinion we were completely spoilt and the wardens did everything in their power to make it a happy home.'[72] Two guests were officially invited to the Hall dances on behalf of each student and the warden greeted each of them as they arrived. The rules for entertaining callers were more lenient than in the pre-war years, but still strict:

> We were free to have visitors in our rooms, when we provided the food. If we wished to entertain a boy friend we had to invite a chaperone and men must have gone by 7.30 p.m. so that students could be on the corridor in 'dishabille'. If a boy came in the evening, he rang the doorbell and a maid ushered him into the library whilst she went to fetch the student. [73]

Curfew was 11 pm and it was obviously unusual for the residents to be out later than that, since Vera Rose recalls that once when she was given a late key 'Miss Bennett asked me to knock on her door to let her know that I had returned safely'.

The women's common room, situated to the right-hand side of the main entrance to Western Bank. This photograph dates from 1935 but the room appears to have changed little since it was built.

This kind of concern is unthinkable to later generations of students, used to halls of 400 or more. University Hall was undersubscribed until 1939, when women medical students were evacuated from London at the start of the Second World War and Stephenson Hall had to be commandeered as well to take some of the extra women. [74]

WESTERN BANK IN THE 1930s

A story written for *Arrows* in 1932 depicts a 'dream' in which the building is transformed – 'the windows were clean and the cigarette packet I threw away a month ago had disappeared'; 'the library . . . was actually warm!' and in the refectory 'the tea was hot and served in china cups'.[75] Some aspects of life at Western Bank were squalid. The men's common room in 1936 is remembered as 'knee deep in fag-ends' and occupied almost exclusively by medical students.[76] The women's common room in Western Bank, by contrast, sought to preserve the decencies of life. The Women's Tutor had an office inside the entrance and laid the law down, insisting 'that we behaved correctly and, in particular, that we were suitably dressed' (including stockings at all times).[77] The role of the Women's Tutor was limited to such trivialities that one Tutor, Lucy Storr-Best, resigned as a result.[78]

On their first day, freshers unlucky enough to be caught were 'dunked' in the fountains of the quadrangle and degree ceremonies were interrupted by the antics of the students, who, as in previous eras, attended in force. Sometimes the interruptions were a cry of 'Mornin' Sir' to the Chancellor each time he conferred a degree, but others were more imaginative. Francis Knight remembers that some students secreted themselves in the hall with 'a unique collection of musical instruments' and sang 'The animals came in two by two' as the procession filed in.[79] Margaret

The University porter, Dyson, carries the mace at a ceremony in Weston Park in 1924 to mark the 21st anniversary of the laying of the foundation stone.

Below left: A student view of the role of the porter from Arrows 14, 1933.

Dyson's successor, Sedgewick, joined the University in 1926 and like Dyson became an integral part of the institution. Arrows reported that a fresher could get information on almost any topic from the porter: 'he need only tap on the door of the lodge and, between telephone calls, sit at the feet of the sage'.

THE PORTER IN THE PORTER'S LODGE.

We depend upon our Porter for everything we do,
When you are in trouble he's the man to see your through,
Your father and your mother and your sister too,
Is the Porter in the Porter's Lodge.

You dash off to a lecture every time you hear a bell,
You try to learn so much that your brain begins to swell,
And now you want a man to tell the Prof. to go to—lunch
Ask the Porter in the Porter's Lodge.

You want to send a message to the girl you're out to woo,
She's in the Women's Common Room—to enter is taboo,
Who's the only man you trust to take your billet-doux?
The Porter in the Porter's Lodge.

You slipped into the fountain as you were passing by,
You've got all wet and slimy and you feel you're going to die,
You want another pair of pants while yours hang out to dry,
Get the Porter's from the Porter's Lodge.

And when at last we're dead and gone—it must be soon or late,
And when we go to Heaven—if that should be our fate,
Who'll be standing with St. Peter just inside the golden gate?
The Porter from the Porter's Lodge.

Chorus: Porter, Porter, Porter,
Gee, whatever should we do without
The Porter at the Porter's Lodge.

UNIVERSITY·OF·SHEFFIELD
SHOWING EXTENSIONS
LANCHESTER & LODGE · ARCHITECTS

1936 perspective of the winning scheme for the proposed University extensions by T.A. Lodge, which were never built. The intention was to move to a markedly different style from that of Gibbs's original buildings. The scheme reflects the more monumental stripped-down classicism characteristic of the period: however, the block linking the original buildings to the new ones attempts to speak both architectural languages.

Wolstenholme saw white mice running among the audience and even 'a goat let loose to walk up the hall with "Diploma of Education" pinned to its horns. We usually blamed the Medics or the Rugger Club for these pranks'.[80]

On these occasions the Western Bank porter, known to everyone as Dyson, doubled as mace-bearer, dressed in robes and a velvet hat. Described as 'the man who really counted in the university', he lived on the premises.[81] In addition to his other roles, he was the students' friend: 'a chat with him in the porter's box, or in his "cubby-hole" on the bottom corridor was a great refresher in dark times'.

By 1930 the teaching accommodation was becoming overcrowded again, particularly for the medical school. Pickard-Cambridge planned an ambitious extension, which would go as far as Winter Street and provide a much larger 'Great Hall'. He thought Firth Hall was too small and, in any case, by 1932/33 one end was screened off with a curtain to provide extra teaching space.[82] Five architects submitted plans to a competition to design the extension, which had several phases. If built, the winning design by T. A. Lodge would have completed the second quadrangle with a large assembly hall and a new entrance, dominated by a tall tower, on Winter Street. In the event, finance only became available for the first phase, accommodation for Botany, Zoology and Geography, to which these departments moved in 1941.

The Library

The Edgar Allen Library was the heart of the University for many students and members of staff. From the desk in the centre, the librarian could deal with enquiries and issue books, while also keeping a watchful eye on readers, including those in the galleries above. A firm 'no talking' would break off forbidden conversations. The central desk led via a spiral staircase to the stack below, which was designed to have two storeys, although only the basement floor was built and in use before 1920. The shelves should have been steel, but false economy led to the instal-lation of 'old bookcases and lengths of planking' which were narrow and impossible to adjust to take folios and quartos.[83] When this stack was full, the intermediate floor was constructed in 1925, but with the same wooden shelving, a 'constant source of trouble and exasperation' for the unfortunate librarians. When completely full, the stack held only 60,000 volumes and not the 87,000 originally planned for.

It was inevitable that the Edgar Allen Library would at some time prove too small for the growing university; as it was, this stage was reached by 1929, only twenty years after its opening. When a large donation of books from Sir Charles Firth's library was anticipated, the Library Committee's urgent plea to the Senate led to the decision to turn the nearby general lecture room into a History Library.[84] The History Library (now the Tapestry Room) provided another pleasant reading area and space for 20,000 volumes, but at the cost of losing an important lecture theatre.

With library accessions running at more than 6,000 volumes a year, the respite was temporary. Pickard-Cambridge was keen to use Firth Hall for a library once the 'Great Hall' was built. This dream never came to fruition, but the Library Committee came up with the imaginative solution in 1936 of excavating beneath the Western Bank building in the area adjacent to the library stack, in order to enlarge it.[85] This new stack, fitted correctly with steel shelving and so referred to as the 'steel basement', was opened before the end of the year. Together with changes made to the History Library, the capacity of the library was increased by 40,000 volumes at minimal cost.

The Library introduced a turnstile in 1934, after repeated complaints about loss of books.[86] Turnstiles were novel at the time, but had been successfully imple-mented at Reading, Leeds and University College, London. The Library Committee, evidently anticipating student objections at the checkout, suggested that the turnstile assistant could be 'ex-army or ex-police officer'.

In memory of the 200 students and staff who died in the First World War, the University commissioned a memorial from H. St J. Harrison, a part-time lecturer in Architecture. Sited in the Edgar Allen Library, it was unveiled by the Chancellor, the Marquess of Crewe, as part of the University's coming-of-age celebrations in 1926. It now stands in Firth Hall corridor.

ARTS, EDUCATION AND ARCHITECTURE DEPARTMENTS 1919–39

Sir Henry Hadow's contacts in the musical world were unrivalled and if the finances had been available, Sheffield might have had Adrian Boult, 'one of the two or three best conductors in England', as a professor of music in the early 1920s.[87] Lacking the funds for this, Hadow had to content himself with making a joint lecturer appointment with the Education Committee. G. E. Linfoot, the holder of this post, had a strenuous job description: to work in schools as well as the University and to perform 'public musical work in the City'.[88] Linfoot revived the university orchestra, gave music lectures to the Education students and later added a 'History of Music' course to the BA degree programme.

The chance to create a chair in music came in 1926, when Mr and Mrs Rossiter Hoyle, friends of Hadow's who were keen supporters of Sheffield music, bequeathed £16,000 for the purpose. Again Hadow was ambitious, trying to secure Ralph Vaughan Williams and then settling on Dr Percy Buck as a visiting professor

Sir Charles Harding Firth began his career as Lecturer in History in the early days of Firth College and ended it as Regius Professor of Modern History at Oxford. He was a nephew of Mark Firth and donated a large part of his substantial book collection to Sheffield.

F. H. Shera was Professor of Music from 1928 to 1948. He carried a heavy teaching load, gave a series of public lectures each session, directed the University Orchestra and Choral Society and served as Public Orator. He was equally memorable for his personality 'with its eloquent chuckles and sudden sparkles of wit; above all, that warm companionableness which he has always shown alike to colleague and student'.

of 'high eminence' to set the chair 'on a proper footing'.[89] In 1928, F. H. Shera, who was a native of Sheffield and 'a man of enormous energy and a genius at inculcating musical appreciation', became the first full-time J. Rossiter Hoyle Professor of Music.[90] This was an immense source of satisfaction to Hadow, who had thought the prospect of establishing a chair in music 'not worth considering' in 1920. Shera retained the chair until 1948 and inaugurated the degree of Bachelor of Music in 1932.

The Department of Architecture's prospects also took a giant stride forward in 1928. Three lecturers-in-charge had come and gone in the years 1920–27 and student recruitment was so uncertain that the University *Calendar* described course arrangements as 'purely provisional and liable to be amended or cancelled without further notice'.[91] Not surprisingly, this did not please the architects' professional body, the RIBA, which agreed to help fund a full-time lectureship in architecture, offered to Stephen Welsh in May 1928. He remained at the University until 1957, becoming Professor in 1948. Student numbers were low throughout the thirties, with many still part-time, but the trend towards full-time attendance increased and the degree received external recognition for its 'marked improvement' in 1934.[92] The department was then housed at the top of the main turret of Western Bank in two studios, the upper one of which had a large glazed roof light. Alec Daykin, who was a student in the late 1930s, remembers that, 'since all the usual offices and amenities were on the ground floor, there were frequent and justified complaints from members of the Chemistry department, whose lives were endangered by

The Architecture studio at the top of the turret in Western Bank.

Architecture students in a hurry swinging by the handrails at the corner landings as they hurtled down.'[93]

In 1920 Appleton (who, it will be remembered, taught History and English simultaneously in Firth College days) became Professor of Ancient History, a post he held for the final eleven years of his 42-year service. J. B. Black was appointed to the first chair of Modern History.[94] His successor in 1931 was G. R. Potter, who left an indelible impression on successive generations of students. During the lectures of his early years they 'gazed with awe as the Professor, wrapping both arms in his gown, would lean back against the front of his desk and speak for the entire hour'. Their assumption that simply drinking at this fount of wisdom (no essays were set) would be sufficient to pass the examination was rudely shattered at the final lecture, when they were told to study Lodge's *Modern History*, which proved to be 'a thick dusty tome with pages little thicker than rice paper' and tiny print.[95] For first-year students it was a cathartic experience. Potter was a well-known figure in the University until long after his retirement in 1965. His most highly-regarded publications were completed in those post-retirement years, including the one for which he is best known, on the Swiss reformer, Zwingli.

Stephen Welsh, Professor of Architecture 1948–57 and head of department from 1928, established a large and highly successful Department of Architecture. A student population of forty before the Second World War had increased to 200 by 1952. Brash and outspoken in personality, he demanded, and received, a high standard of work from both students and colleagues.

From 1934, the number of students in Arts and, particularly, Pure Science began to fall, as Appendix 4C shows. The main reason was the decreasing number of teacher-training students, who were the backbone of those faculties. After twenty years of intensive training and recruitment, supply had matched demand by the mid-thirties and the numbers of grants awarded in return for a commitment to work as teachers were reduced. Donald Tomlin remembers the solemnity of the 'Commitment' ceremony in 1937, 'in front of the Vice-Chancellor himself in full regalia':

> The commitment document was formally read out to the assembled students (about sixty in my year) and . . . we filed up onto the stage to the vice-chancellor's table, where everybody had to read the document to the VC. (How bored he must have been by the end).[96]

In fact, Pickard-Cambridge was not bored. He relished this ceremony, since he took a deep interest in teacher training. He inspected schools and insisted on being involved in the selection of Education students, breathing mercilessly down the neck of the new Professor, G. H. Turnbull, in the process.[97] He also gave tea parties for the 'committed' students which Vera Rose found 'quite an ordeal':

> The girl students were expected to wear hats. Usually you were sitting next to someone you didn't know. After a suitable interval a bell was rung and you were expected to move and talk to somebody else . . . I smoked a cigarette (always provided in those days) to hide my embarrassment.

Prospects for the education, arts and pure science faculties were transformed by the Second World War. Chemistry, in particular, became the largest single department.

Physics lecturer J. R. (Joe) Clarke with a class in 1929. The high percentage of overseas students is striking, but there is only one woman. During the later 1920s and 1930s there were noticeably fewer female Science students.

THE PURE SCIENCE DEPARTMENTS 1919–39

In the early 1920s, A. W. Chapman remembered, he had to dash repeatedly up and down 87 stairs between students being taught in the Chemistry hut and in the laboratories.[98] In the 1930s, the department averaged six honours graduates a year and was delighted if the research school reached a total of four. Despite this, research breakthroughs still occurred, like the discovery of optical activity of diphenyl compounds by Kenner and Christie. Professor Wynne retired in 1931 at the age of seventy and was then invited to move to Cambridge, where he conducted research until well over eighty. He also served on the UGC from 1934 to 1943, using his wide experience to allocate grants to the universities. He died in 1950.

The Professor of Physics after Hicks's retirement was S. R. Milner, described by a colleague as 'the most lovable of men'.[99] He formulated the first 'self-consistent classical theory of magnetism'. The most memorable staff member was J. R. ('Joe') Clarke, a lecturer from 1920 to 1954. A Sheffield graduate, he enlisted early in the War and sustained two head wounds in 1915 which almost proved fatal. A large portion of his skull was replaced by a metal plate in a pioneering series of operations carried out in Sheffield by A. M. Connell, the Professor of Surgery.[100]

Clarke was a great favourite of the students. One of his honours students recalls that he covered the roll-over blackboards with his calculations so fast and furiously that they could hardly keep up.[101] Sometimes Clarke himself lost track and finished with the wrong answer, which he cheerfully admitted and suggested that the students work out where he had 'gone wrong' from their own notes. Unusually for

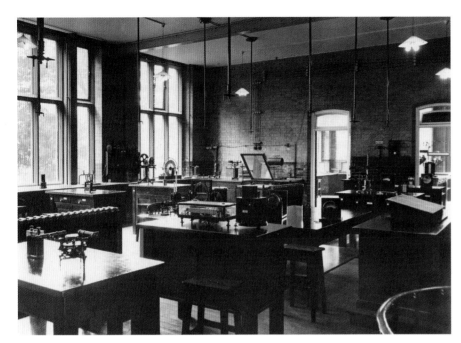

An advanced Physics laboratory in Western Bank, overlooking Weston Park, in 1935. Various items of equipment shown here, such as the Wimshurst machine on the windowsill, remain in the University's collection of old scientific instruments.

his time, he requested student feedback on his teaching. When one of them questioned his approach to laboratory teaching, Clarke said that his intention was:

> to get people used to handling equipment and to observe properly . . . The end result was either right or wrong. If it was right, you had handled and observed correctly, if wrong you hadn't. When I asked you to repeat something it was generally because you had missed a vital clue or made a clumsy observation. If you now look twice at everything you do, read, observe, I've done my job.

This practical pedagogy suited the student, Donald Tomlin, and, no doubt, many others. There was little assessment of written work, apart from laboratory notebooks. Students were expected to work through the 'examples' in textbooks, but were only tested on their learning during the examination. The emphasis was on facts and technical skill rather than critical scientific analysis.

In the Mathematics department, Dr C. A. Stewart used to update his lecture notes by cutting out sections and patching in new ones. They were known to the students as 'Stewart's doilies' and formed the basis of a published textbook in later life. The Professor of Mathematics from 1923, P. J. Daniell, was famous in his own field and, indeed, is still remembered.[102] He has a 'permanent and honoured place in the history of mathematics' for the 'Daniell-Kolmogorov theorem' and the 'Daniell Integral'. Under this unusual approach, integration is made the primary concept, rather than differentiation or measure. This is the opposite of the procedure taught, for example, in calculus, but Daniell's approach made many converts.

Sheffield University Biological Society in 1924/25, remarkable for its all-female personnel, with the exception of the chairman of the society B. H. Bentley who at this time was head of the Department of Botany and from 1931 to 1938 also its professor.

Alfred Denny retired as Professor of Zoology after 41 years of service in 1925. He was succeeded by H. G. Cannon and then by L. E. S. Eastham in 1932. Eastham became the University's first pro-vice-chancellor in 1946. There was no chair of Botany when Denny retired, but this was created, along with a chair of Geography, in 1931. B. H. Bentley and R. N. Rudmose Brown, the longstanding lecturers in those subjects, became professors.

THE FACULTY OF MEDICINE 1919–39[103]

A Joint Hospitals Council was created in Sheffield in 1919, including several representatives from the medical school and with the Vice-Chancellor as chairman. This produced a much more positive and co-operative relationship between the hospitals and the University, the first fruits of which were the appointment of Professor Leathes as Honorary Physiologist in both the Royal Hospital and the Royal Infirmary.[104] The best aspect of the new Joint Council from the University's point of view was that the control of clinical teaching passed wholesale to the medical school. Appointments to clinical teaching posts were, at last, made by the faculty.

In 1919, the Royal Infirmary agreed that the proposed new Professor of Pharmacology should have his own beds there and treat selected patients for the purposes of research.[105] This opportunity was grasped with both hands by Edward Mellanby, who took the chair in 1920. He also had a background as a physiologist and his research focussed on the physical effects of dietary deficiency. He was working on rickets – physical deformities in children which are now almost unknown in this country but, at the time, as Hadow commented, wrecked 'the happiness, the career and even life of so many of our children'.[106] Hadow helped to find the site for a field laboratory, corrugated iron huts at Lodge Moor, where Mellanby could keep the dogs he used for his research. Within a short time, he had discovered that feeding a small amount of milk, together with unlimited bread or oatmeal porridge (the standard diet of many Sheffield children) would infallibly produce rickets in puppies. He also found the cure – small doses of cod liver oil. This was a major breakthrough, as his colleague A. E. Barnes explained, when looking back on Mellanby's career:

> When the writer was a boy, leg deformities were extremely common in Sheffield. Indeed among the writer's own relatives (lower middle class) there was one with a rickety chest, one with skull deformities and another old lady with defective vision originating from 'zonular' cataracts produced by rickety convulsions . . . When we think of the operations for bent legs, the difficult childbirth from pelvic deformities, the chest deformities, and the 'fits' seen by every student, we can realise what the world owes to Edward Mellanby.[107]

Mellanby went on to contribute to experiments which demonstrated the ways in which 'vitamins' (a word invented at this time) in food were essential to healthy growth. In all his researches, which continued until the end of his life, he was assisted by his wife, May, who had an independent reputation as a dental histologist and later an honorary lectureship in physiology. She demonstrated that dental disease in children could be linked to lack of vitamins and the mother's pre-natal diet.[108] Mellanby's reputation as a scientific clinician, together with that of Leathes, led the Medical Research Council to choose Sheffield in 1923 as the only provincial centre to produce and test insulin. At the time insulin was a new therapy; Mellanby's most famous patient, Stuart Goodwin, had suffered from *diabetes mellitus* for three years and was on the Allen Starvation regime. He told Mellanby that he had two choices: to die of starvation or in a diabetic coma. Insulin made in the Physiology department restored him to health; his thankyou card to Mellanby is 'likely to be the earliest surviving record of insulin therapy given to a patient within this country'.[109]

Appreciation of Sir Edward Mellanby's work in Sheffield was such that local general practitioners made an unprecedented gift of £1,000 to him for the equipping of a field laboratory at Lodge Moor. Much of his experimental work was carried out in these picturesquely-sited asbestos huts.

Edward Mellanby was Professor of Pharmacology from 1920 to 1934. He then became Secretary of the Medical Research Council until 1949. The picture shows a visit by the Master Cutler to the University in March 1930 with Gibbons (Registrar) on the left, May Mellanby, Edward Mellanby, the Master Cutler and a member of the departmental staff.

Goodwin's gratitude to the University was to extend far beyond his card, as this History will record later.

Clinicians in the city could not fail to be impressed by the practical value of university research. In 1920 the local general practitioners donated £1,000 to Mellanby's field laboratory. Arthur Hall was justifiably proud of this success. In 1925 both the Royal Hospital and the Royal Infirmary agreed to the appointment of a pathologist to work in the same way as Leathes and Mellanby.

The emphasis that Hall and Leathes placed on the integration of science and clinical care within medical practice led to their decision to change the pre-clinical course in order to make it less theoretical. Hall had always disliked this aspect of the early medical course. During his own time as a student at Cambridge, physiology was taught, he said,

> as if the students were to be physiologists, rather than merely medical men. From an educational point of view [the lectures] were simply a waste of time, for we could not understand half the terms used. That anatomy or physiology had any remote connection with them never occurred to us.[110]

In 1919, the pre-clinical (2nd MB) study of anatomy and physiology was reduced to three terms, followed by continued study of these subjects in the clinical context until the fifth year. Robert Platt, who was then a student, did not think this integration particularly successful because 'students, however irrationally, like to feel that they have finished with something before embarking on something else'. He was amused 45 years later, however, to find the idea being proposed as something new in medical education.[111]

After 1919, clinical training itself became much more systematic and progressed from the 'apprenticeship' model. Where previously students had attached themselves to one consultant who acted as their tutor and took them round the wards to observe the daily caseload, now medicine and surgery were taught in small groups by systematic lectures, with cases chosen to illustrate the needs of the curriculum. This was clearly preferable, although it reduced the contact with any particular consultant. That relationship was still of great importance. Frank Ellis, a student in the 1920s, had to resit surgery and worked through the summer vacation with Professor Connell at the Royal Infirmary. His reward was to assist at many of his operations and even, under supervision, to remove appendices and a gall bladder.[112] Other memories of this period include the external examiner who was researching the little-understood spleen. He asked his frightened candidate to describe the functions of the spleen, to receive the stammering reply, 'I'm afraid sir, I've forgotten'. 'Good Lord', responded the examiner, 'now nobody knows'.[113]

Portrait of Sir Arthur Hall by Ernest Moore, painted in 1936. The artist made two copies of this picture, one to hang in Firth Hall among the portraits of the people who made crucial contributions to the University's early development, and one to hang in the Faculty of Medicine.

In 1928 the Medical School celebrated its Centenary, with a special degree ceremony, a 'conversazione' (open day) and a formal dinner.[114] Self-congratulation is a feature of these occasions, but it does appear from all the evidence that the school had achieved genuine eminence by this time: 'one of the bright spots in recent years in British medicine'.[115] Hall's own efforts were the most important reason for this and he retired in 1931 with the tributes which he deserved.[116] In the decade which followed, the medical school doubled its student numbers. Hall was succeeded as Professor of Medicine by A. E. Naish, the 'most inspiring and impressive teacher' in the school at that time.[117]

One of Hall's many successful strategies was the decision to focus the research of the school on medical chemistry. This had led to the appointment in several disciplines of professors with a common interest in chemical approaches – Leathes in Physiology, Mellanby in Pharmacology and Douglas in Pathology. On Douglas's death in 1931, the chair of pathology was awarded to the Australian Howard Florey, a radical choice because his research was physiological and dealt with 'the causes of pathological changes, not merely the effects'.[118] At that time, there was a division within pathology between the traditional 'morbid anatomists' and the new experimental pathologists. The judgement of Hall, Leathes and Mellanby in appointing Florey was triumphantly vindicated, since he proved to be the leading research pathologist of his day.[119] He revolutionised the activities of the department and, after only three years, went on to become Professor of Pathology at Oxford – a post he secured because of Mellanby's strong advocacy at the Appointment Committee.[120] (By 1934 Mellanby was Secretary of the Medical Research Council). In Oxford, Florey and his team purified penicillin and demonstrated its therapeutic potential in 1940. He was awarded the Nobel Prize for medicine in 1945 together with Ernst Chain and Alexander Fleming. Fleming had discovered penicillin in 1928 but could not purify it; he was thus unable to exploit its antibiotic potential.[121]

Howard Florey with his children during his period at Sheffield in the 1930s.

The Sheffield connection with penicillin therapy in fact pre-dates Florey's arrival. Cecil George Paine, a member of the Pathology department, made a crude filtrate from a penicillin-producing mould supplied by Fleming. He successfully used it to treat eye infections in two babies in 1930, but did not recognise the significance of his discovery.[122] Paine did, however, inform Fleming of his success and

C. G. Paine made the first documented use of penicillin as a therapy at Sheffield in 1930. His contribution was overlooked until the 1980s when two members of staff, Milton Wainwright and Harold Swan, reconstructed the story and found the proof in Paine's dusty case notes in the Royal Infirmary.

C. G. Paine and penicillin therapy

CASE REPORTS AND POINTS ARISING

A search was accordingly made (HTS) in the surviving Royal Infirmary ward journals of the late Mr A.B. Nutt, with whom Paine claimed to have achieved clinical successes. Mr Nutt's journals for 1930 still exist but not those for the subsequent year. Two relevant case histories were found. They are illustrated as figs. 2 and 3, and are likely to be two of the five ophthalmic cases recollected by Paine and referred to by Florey in *Antibiotics* in 1949.[5]

Figure 2. Case notes of 1930 recording penicillin therapy. Source: Sheffield Royal Infirmary case records, South Yorkshire County Records Office, Sheffield.

The first case (fig.2) concerns a three-week-old male baby, Peter, who was admitted to Mr Nutt's female ward on 28 August 1930. This baby is recorded as suffering from bilateral ophthalmia neonatorum of gonococcal origin with a copious discharge from the eyes "since some time after birth". The following is a transcription of the notes under the admission date of 28 August 1930.

45

C. G. Paine and penicillin therapy

Figure 3. Case notes of 1930 recording penicillin therapy. Source: as for fig. 2.

neonatorum", the eyes being "full of pus" and the culture growing "diphtheroids". The total entry is as follows under the admission date of 4 December 1930.

On admission
Both eyes swollen and full of pus
Culture diptheroids
Penicillin hourly
22.12.30 Both eyes clear
Home
Lot AB Zinc
TID
8

Here, the information is clearly stated that penicillin was given hourly and that treatment was effective enough to allow the baby to be sent home eighteen days later with clear eyes. It is, of course, unsatisfactory to have been left with diphtheroids as

47

told Florey about it when he was working at Western Bank. Even Florey showed no interest at the time and did not begin his own work on penicillin until 1938.

Mellanby and Leathes left the University in the early 1930s, succeeded by Edward Wayne in Pharmacology and G. A. Clark in Physiology. Their legacy of successful research was maintained; H. N. Green, Professor of Pathology from 1935, pioneered the immunological theory of cancer[123] and Hans Krebs came to the University as Lecturer in Pharmacology in 1935. Krebs was to be awarded the Nobel Prize in 1953 for the discovery of the citric acid cycle, a breakthrough which occurred in Sheffield. He and Florey would have made ideal research colleagues, but Krebs arrived in Sheffield a few months after Florey had left.[124] Krebs was a German Jewish refugee who had already discovered the ornithine (urea) cycle at Freiburg before being forced to flee the country in 1933. He had found a temporary home in Cambridge when Wayne invited him to Sheffield, where he stayed for nineteen years. Wayne gave him 'invaluable advice' and 'generous freedom' to continue his research.[125] Pickard-Cambridge made a series of successful funding applications to the Rockefeller Foundation, which maintained its support for Krebs for eleven years.[126] Krebs was happy in Sheffield and married a local schoolteacher. During his first eighteen months at the University, aided by his postgraduate student William Arthur Johnson, he discovered the 'citric acid cycle', the chemical reactions during respiration which convert glucose and oxygen into carbon dioxide, water and energy.[127] The cycle is a basic function of every kind of animal and plant but, failing to recognise its importance, *Nature* declined his paper for lack of space and it was published instead in *Enzymologia*.

114

The Scala cinema on Brook Hill, purchased by the University in 1952 to provide Krebs with the extra laboratory space he needed. It was located next to the new Chemistry building and was demolished in 1969.

Hans Krebs in his laboratory with a group of postgraduate students.

Although his work was closely related to pharmacology, Krebs was in essence a research biochemist. In recognition of this, the new Department of Biochemistry was created for him in 1938 and he became Professor in 1945.

Struggling enterprises: Pharmacy and the Dental School

Pharmacy, which has become a major programme in several universities, failed to take root in Sheffield despite the efforts of both Hadow and the British Pharmaceutical Society (BPS) to establish a course in the 1920s.[128] Professor Wynne offered the help of the Chemistry department but the secretary of the BPS demanded a separate department and three lecturers. This was out of the question. 'Nothing in this University . . . has started in [this] highly developed state', said Wynne.[129] At a climactic meeting in August 1928, the Society rejected the only house the university was able to offer and demanded expensive equipment. In the University's parlous financial state at the time, the breakdown of talks was inevitable.

The Dental School in 1920 was still in an unsatisfactory state, entirely dependent on 'honorary staff' and with 'lamentably insufficient' premises at the Royal Hospital.[130] It had been kept going for twenty years by the enthusiasm of two men – Frank Harrison, following its establishment in 1898, and G. H. Froggatt. The students were still studying for London University qualifications until 1922, when Sheffield degrees were introduced. New dental mechanic workshops were provided in Western Bank in 1925 and the premises at the Royal Hospital were expanded and re-equipped in 1928.

The new Dental Mechanics Laboratory at Western Bank in the 1920s. It may not look very exciting now but a contemporary pamphlet described it as 'among the best in the country ... highly commended by examiners and others interested'.

To improve, the Dental School needed its own salaried staff and Pickard-Cambridge worked hard to provide a full-time professor, G. L. Roberts, who arrived in 1935. A full-time lecturer followed in 1937. Margaret Barnes, an under-graduate at this time, recalls that they had to buy their own equipment for the Dental Mechanics course – 'plaster knives, fret-saws, scrapers and files'. The school had a 'Long Room' with twelve dental chairs, a gas room and an X-ray room, but needed hospital premises suitable for instruction – which those at the Royal Hospital were not. In 1935 Sir Charles Clifford, a long-standing member of the University Council, proprietor of the *Sheffield Telegraph* and a wealthy man, offered to purchase Broom Bank, a house on Glossop Road, for a new dental hospital.[131] The following year he died, leaving more than £77,000 for the 'general purposes' of the University – one of the largest benefactions it had yet received.[132] Everything was set fair until it was discovered that Broom Bank was on the site reserved for a large new general hospital to replace the Royal Hospital and the Infirmary. The plans had to be abandoned, and war prevented the building of the Charles Clifford Dental Hospital (on a different site) until 1950.

THE APPLIED SCIENCES 1919–39

During the time that he held the posts of Vice-Chancellor, Professor of Mechanical Engineering, and director of the University's war effort, W. Ripper found time and energy in 1918 to create the 'trades technical societies'. From his close contacts with manufacturers and workmen, he was aware of the need for what would now be called 'staff development'. Sheffield industry was still predominantly carried out in small workshops, the workforce was scattered and there was little chance to exchange ideas on innovation and good practice. Under Ripper, the faculty took its responsibilities to this workforce, none of them 'students' in the formal sense, seriously. The trades technical societies held evening lectures, conducted variously by university staff and local craftsmen, to introduce technical innovations and their scientific background. The University also provided laboratory facilities for metal-testing and furnace treatment. By 1948 there were 23 societies serving the various metal trades and it was estimated that 15,000 workers had attended meetings since their formation.[133] One of the Engineering lecturers, W. H. Bolton, took charge of the administration after Ripper's retirement; he had an office in St George's Square with two staff.

The Ripper Medal awarded by the Sheffield Trades Technical Society.

Professor Arnold had overworked to the point of nervous breakdown by 1919 and was compelled to retire.[134] He had built up the best Metallurgy department in the country, but latterly it had failed to move with the times and there was keen demand for new blood from some of the younger members of the faculty, like Husband and Fearnsides. Unfortunately, the rest of the staff took it for granted that Arnold would be succeeded by Andrew McWilliam, his deputy for many years. Fearnsides and Husband set out to overturn this foregone conclusion.[135] At the faculty meeting which would have crowned McWilliam without a contest, they produced the name of an alternative candidate, C. H. Desch, Professor of Metallurgy at the Royal Technical College in Glasgow. The meeting 'was adjourned in haste' and the post was advertised. McWilliam offered the skill of the 'practical'

The opening evening of the advisory council of the Sheffield trades technical societies in Mappin Hall on 5 October 1929. Sir Henry Hadow is in the chair, with Ripper and Desch to his left hand. The bust of Sir Frederick Mappin overlooks the proceedings.

Cecil Henry Desch FRS, Professor of Metallurgy 1920 to 1931. He was President of the Cutlery Research Association and Vice-President of the Iron and Steel Institute and was also, unusually, interested in sociological issues. He served on the Council of the Institute of Sociology and chaired a committee which carried out a social survey of Sheffield.

J. H. Andrew, Professor of Metallurgy 1932 to 1950. He modernised the curriculum and was so successful in making the case for better facilities that, at the time he left, he could claim that the department was one of the best equipped in the world.

man, while Desch was the scientist and theorist who could develop the department's research. Both were needed and Hadow tried hard to raise enough money to create two chairs, but failed. Desch, liberally supplied with inside information by Fearnsides, was appointed. McWilliam died less than three years later.

Desch had such a 'pure' approach to research that he may not have been the ideal replacement for Arnold, but he did what he could to renovate the department – a difficult job in the cash-strapped 1920s. He was also an outstanding lecturer and so encyclopaedic in his knowledge that it was said that he never forgot anything he read. He had written a famous book on 'metallography' and 'solved the problem of the breaking of springs in aircraft engines'.[136] Desch attracted good students, including the first metallurgy PhD, J. W. Jenkin. By his own account, Jenkin was in despair with only three weeks to go before the last date for submission.[137] 'Press on, my lad', was Desch's advice. 'It is surprising how in such a short time as three weeks some idea may occur to you that will illuminate the whole project'. This optimism proved justified and the thesis was typed at break-neck speed by Desch's clerk, Edgar Thackeray, directly from Jenkins's dictation.

Desch could also be 'somewhat reserved'. 'When visitors were invited to his home it was not unknown for him to disappear into his study for the evening, leaving his wife to be the perfect hostess', recalled one of his successors, A. G. Quarrell.[138] Desch had courted his wife, who had herself studied chemistry, with a home-made album of drawings showing the internal structure of metals, some of them surprisingly beautiful.[139] Two female students gained Associateships in Metallurgy during his time and both went on to work in the Brown-Firth laboratory.[140]

Desch's successor, J. H. Andrew, who arrived in 1932, made the more far-reaching changes. After his first term, he produced a hard-hitting report to the Vice-Chancellor, describing the curriculum as 'totally inadequate' and the equipment as 'antiquated'.[141] He also criticised recent research as being of 'a physical and highly theoretical nature', not suited to the 'direct practical' needs of Sheffield industry. His proposals for team-working were typical of a man who, in direct contrast to Desch, was gregarious and approachable, not least at home where he and his wife regularly entertained students and staff 'in a very generous manner'.[142]

Such was Andrew's conviction and energy that the University Council granted him immediate and substantial funds. In addition, he raised external funding to reconstruct the foundry and install modern plant and persuaded Sir Robert Hadfield to endow a new laboratory, opened in September 1938. The research programme developed to such an extent that by 1940 almost every student graduating with honours stayed on as a postgraduate.[143]

In 1920, the faculty created a new department, Fuel Technology, after the death of L. T. O'Shea, the Professor of Applied Chemistry. Fuel Technology dealt with the preparation and use of all types of fuel, although under its new head, R. V. Wheeler, it had close links to the Mining department. Wheeler was an expert on mine explosions, and at his laboratory in Buxton could give 'terrifyingly realistic' demonstrations to visiting miners about the inflammability of coal dust, emphasising the need for vigilance underground.[144] Much of his research was devoted to

THAT WIRELESS WIZARD,
MR. F. LLOYD, TOLD US WE
MIGHT SOON BE ABLE TO
SEE BY WIRELESS.

Left: *The Little Gem concert party, which played at the opening night of the Wireless Relay Station.*

Above: *In November 1923 the first wireless relay station in Yorkshire was opened in the Applied Science building. Frederic Lloyd, President of the Sheffield and District Wireless Society, had pressed Sheffield's case very strongly with the BBC and his success was considered quite a coup. Lord Reith, Managing Director of the BBC, spoke at the opening and the University conferred the honorary degree of MEng on Lloyd in 1929. (Sheffield Mail, 18 February 1927)*

improving safety in mines; in this field he had already become a leader. He held the post of Director of the Safety in Mines Research Laboratory while at Sheffield. He had previously conducted coal research for the Home Office and in that role met Marie Stopes, at that time a coal research scientist. 'I received a slight thrill reading that you have dissolved coal', wrote Wheeler to her; she reciprocated by inviting him to comment on her manuscript of *Married Love*.[145] Dr Stopes delivered five lectures on coal in the department during its early years.

Wheeler's research was of international importance. He was also a writer of 'great clarity and edited in detail every paper with which he was associated'. There were more than 200 of these during his time in Sheffield, which ended with his premature death in 1939, aged 56 – caused, Chapman suggests, at least partly by 'persistent overwork'.

Like several of his predecessors, Wheeler found himself caught between university and industry. In 1932, he publicly supported the Salerni Carbonisation process and came into conflict with local firms which championed the competing Low Temperature process.[146] Sir Henry Stephenson, the Pro-Chancellor, himself an industrialist, rebuked Wheeler for taking sides and was supported by the Vice-Chancellor. Wheeler's own thoughts have not survived, but the frustration of his position as an expert obliged to appear 'objective' can be imagined. The requirement to remain aloof from individual firms was often incompatible with the needs of research. Fearnsides built up a practice as a consultant to deep pit mining and refractory firms because 'only as their employee could I have been entrusted with unpublished secret information, about failures as well as successes'.[147]

Ripper, one of the two original staff of the Technical School, finally retired in 1923 after 39 years. The University Council was reluctant to let him go, even then, and he was appointed 'Adviser in Technology'. Husband was still Professor of Civil Engineering, a longstanding member of staff who was remembered by one student

119

R. V. Wheeler, Professor of Fuel Technology from 1920 to 1939. A subsequent member of staff in the department described him as 'the miners' greatest friend since Sir Humphrey Davy', in his role as Director of Research Stations for the Safety in Mines Research Board from 1922 to 1939.

for his 'lecture on the Tay Bridge disaster, explaining how important it was to allow for the effect of side wind when designing such structures'.[148] F.C. Lea, whose 'staunch Methodist belief and practice ruled his management of the department' took Ripper's post in Mechanical Engineering in 1923.[149] This left Electrical, the third branch of Engineering, without a chair and there is evidence that T. F. Wall, the lecturer in charge, resented this to the point of resignation in 1931.[150] He was persuaded to stay, but a chair of Electrical Engineering was not created until 1955, long after his departure. Both Lea and Husband retired in 1936 and the faculty was then reorganised, with H. W. Swift as Professor and senior lecturers in charge of each of the three branches of Engineering.

Government grants sustained the Glass Technology department's research in its early days. These were administered under a 'Delegacy' chaired by Frank Wood. When this source of funding ceased, in 1925, Wood invited subscription from the industry; almost every glass manufacturer in the country, as well as a number abroad, contributed. The department's exile on Darnall Road, however, continued, in most inadequate accommodation and on a site next to the canal, where the sewers were liable to overflow onto the road in heavy rain.[151] In 1935, the 'Elmfield' house and estate, in an open and attractive location on Northumberland Road, came on the market. It was purchased for £2,200 and an appeal, led by Turner, raised £40,000 to adapt and greatly extend the property. It was opened in June 1939, the first fitting location for the work of Turner's eminent department. The Professor's wife died later that year and Turner commissioned a beautiful mosaic in her memory on one wall of the department's new glass museum. Later he donated £1,000 for exhibits of 'artistic and decorative character' showing the 'beauty of glass' in the museum.[152]

The vast majority of Applied Science students still attended part-time in the evening. Stanley Ellam, for example, left school at fourteen, got a job in an engineering workshop and attended four years of evening classes at a local college before being admitted to the University on a County Council Exhibition. For three

Students working with Dr T. F. Wall, lecturer in charge of Electrical Engineering.

or four nights a week, he 'had to go home, wash and change, have tea and catch a train or bus by 6.15 pm to arrive at St. George's by 7.00 pm'.[153] After five years' study, he gained his Associateship and the Mappin Medal.

> I certainly would have liked to have had the privilege of a full-time course, but for me and for many others it was out of the question. We had a job to hold down, a job acquired by luck and hard work and no employer gave time off for such things. We missed not only the wider education of University life, but even the social life of our compatriots as all our free time was spent in study. However, I would not have had it otherwise and l look upon my time at St George's Square with satisfaction.

The number of evening students was higher than it had ever been, 2,000 annually, in the years before the Second World War. This made huge demands on the staff, but the City Council was, at long last, planning to build a Technical College which would take some of the more elementary work away from the University. The Associateship which Ellam acquired was seen by many as equivalent to a degree, but in 1938 the faculty decided to enhance its higher-level qualifications by offering a degree in Engineering by part-time evening study. It appears that this idea did not survive the opposition of the Vice-Chancellor, who persisted in the belief that a degree could only be awarded after full-time study because 'a degree meant far more than passing examinations. It denoted that the holder had become a member of a society which was engaged in intellectual work.'[154] The contrary, unsuccessful view, put by some members of the faculty, was that gaining a degree by evening study

Left: The main staircase in Elmfield.

Above: *The original Elmfield dated from 1888 and was modified and extended to form a new building for Glass Technology, with financial support from the glass industry. The foundation stone, in the form of a four hundredweight glass block, was laid by Sir Geoffrey Pilkington on 9 November 1937. The architect of the new building was H. B. Leighton.*

Metallography class, 1935.

121

122

Clockwise from facing page, top left:
The Wood memorial window commemorated Frank Wood, who had been President of the Society of Glass Technology and Chairman of the Glass Research Delegacy from 1923 to his death in 1934. The window was removed and re-mounted in the new Applied Science Library on Mappin Street when the glass technologists moved from Elmfield to the Hadfield building in 1993.

Portrait of Professor Turner commissioned in 1938 to mark his election as a Fellow of the Royal Society. Painted by the prominent portraitist Edward Halliday, it was exhibited at the Royal Academy in 1939. The artist was at pains to include objects and books that reflected Turner's eminent research and publications.

Mosaic Map 'Glassmaking through the Centuries' which was commissioned by W. E. S. Turner and his children in 1939 in memory of his first wife Mary Isobel Turner. It was made at the Whitefriars glass foundry under the direction of their chief designer James Hogan, who had also been responsible for the Wood window. The mosaic was also transferred from Elmfield in 1993.

In endowing the Museum Turner wished to demonstrate the aesthetic properties of glass and its long craft tradition. On his travels to glass manufactories around Europe and America Turner was often presented with specimens of their work, many of them experimental and in some cases unique. He built up a fascinating collection of twentieth century glass which remains one of the strengths of the Museum. The photographs show a few items from the collections.

A selection of English and continental drinking glasses.

Monart bowl made by John Moncrieff of Perth, Scotland, 1924–39.

Cameo vase made by Richardson and Sons, Stourbridge, around 1870.

123

J. G. Graves made his fortune by establishing an early mail order business and was a lavish benefactor to both city and University. In 1934 he offered to fund the building of a new Students' Union 'as a personal gift to the students of the University, present and future, in the hope that it may add to their pleasure and comfort in their student years, and help towards pleasant memories of Sheffield and its people in the years to come'.

A. A. Yousef, President of the Union Representative Council 1935/36.

'would connote certain qualities of character of special value in the engineering industries'.[155] After the war, the process of running down technological evening study began.

THE STUDENTS' UNION BUILDING

The building of Crewe Hall was the great achievement of Pickard-Cambridge's early years. It enhanced the lives of the few who lived there but, as Wynne pointed out in 1931, a Students' Union building would benefit all:

> I for one think that the Union, if and when it comes into being, will – just because its educative influence will be open to every student – exercise a more profound effect on their lives and minds than the provision of a large hostel which can benefit only a small proportion of our students, the majority of whom live at home in Sheffield or its near neighbourhood.[156]

The men's and women's clubs established in 1920 were stop-gaps and had become embarrassments by 1928, when a Senate report listed the failings of the Men's Club, a decrepit building with few amenities other than billiards, and recommended the erection of a new building with facilities for both men and women.[157] Pickard-Cambridge concurred, saying that the value of a proper Students' Union 'in the social and (in a broad sense) the educational life of the students can hardly be over-estimated' and that the 'miserable building' currently in use was 'utterly unworthy of any great University'.[158] Plans were drawn up by Stephen Welsh, the head of the Architecture department, for a new building on a site in front of the men's club. In 1934, J. G. Graves, a member of the University Council and a wealthy and increasingly philanthropic businessman with mail order premises on Western Bank, offered to fund the new building.

The new Union was designed to have three sections, 'one for men, one for women and one for activities which will be common to both', and opened in 1936.[159] It contained a large assembly hall, called Graves Hall, with a stage suitable for dramatic performances; there were also common rooms, meeting rooms and a refectory. There was, however, no bar. Donald Tomlin, one of the first generation of students to use the Union, recalled that the only alcohol allowed was 'Cidrax or cider', courtesy of the porter:

> The porter served up glasses in his tiny office at the side of the dining room entrance. A glass cost 3d (about 1p) but if you could show you were in a party of more than four, a flagon bottle of Bulmer's cider cost 10d (about 4p). The cider was very weak . . .

There was no competition here for the 'West End' or the Leavygreave pub where, in the late 1930s, 'the widow in charge provided bread, cheese, pickled onions and a pint of beer served in a blue earthenware jug – all for one shilling'.[160]

The Graves Union building was constructed in brick in a neo-Georgian style which complemented the Georgian terrace houses next to it. A contemporary newspaper report noted the 'particularly striking . . . modern-art electric light fittings . . . wireless has been installed to serve a number of loudspeakers, the apparatus being designed to reproduce gramophone records and to relay speeches'.

The majority of students were, as ever, more interested in social facilities than activism. Even in the later 1930s and in contrast, say, to Cambridge or the London School of Economics, politics was apparently the concern of a tiny minority.[161] There was support for the socialist side in the Spanish Civil War among Union officers in 1938, yet the following year only twenty students attended a meeting to debate the British government's decision to introduce conscription.[162] The 'Cosmopolitan Society', however, an attempt to bring overseas and home students together in the face of growing international tension, had a healthy membership. In 1928 the Indian students had formed their own, short-lived, separate Union, but by 1936 an Egyptian, A. A. Yousef, was elected President of the URC.[163] Pickard-Cambridge saw this as an 'election freak' but it was, in fact, the result of a campaign to force the University to recognise the problems of overseas students.[164] There were, apparently, incidents of racism towards students in lodgings, and some were too poor to afford medical care.[165] Yousef returned to Cairo before the end of his presidential year, but his campaign helped to alert the authorities to the issue of student health, with far-reaching results.

The Union campaigned for free medical examination of students, including a chest X-ray to detect early signs of tuberculosis, which had recently killed two students. In 1937, the University introduced the 'medical' and by 1942 it was compulsory for all first years. This was the start of the Student Health Service, one of the first set up by any British university and truly pioneering in offering a free service eleven years before the start of the National Health Service.[166]

This was one of the major achievements of Pickard-Cambridge's last two years at the University. In 1937 and 1938 he also worked to improve the students' sports facilities, securing £6,000 from the UGC to build a swimming pool, and improving the Norton athletics ground. Another twenty acres were purchased to construct a running track, and new rugby and soccer pitches.[167] The swimming pool, planned for the Crewe Hall garden, was never built.[168]

Retrospect

Once the post-war bulge had passed, the number of full-time students remained remarkably static, at between 830 and 887 each year from 1926–40. Two active and concerned vice-chancellors were unable to achieve any expansion, an experience which was common to all the civics, especially the least well-endowed, Sheffield and Leeds. The formation of the UGC was good news, but the new focus on higher education as a national system was beginning to cut into the local roots of the civic universities. Yet they still relied on local authorities for two-thirds of their income – the UGC supplied barely a third.[169] The inter-war years were a period of faltering confidence, when universities like Sheffield struggled to build on their strengths and were distracted by the example of their entirely different cousins, Oxford and Cambridge.[170] By 1940, 'it was commonly accepted that the universities, in particular the civics, had sunk to unacceptably low depths during the previous two decades.'[171]

There are two highlights of the inter-war years. One is the accumulation of excellence in the medical school, where Leathes, Mellanby, Florey and Krebs graced the laboratories of Western Bank. The second is the student bonhomie, the inception of long-lasting traditions like the Rag and the consistent efforts of the staff to provide improved facilities for them. Crewe Hall and the Graves Students' Union building are Pickard-Cambridge's memorials.

The University was so small that the office staff of Western Bank could greet each student by name.[172] Looking back in old age, one Student President of the 1930s reckoned that he knew 85 per cent of his fellows. The tiny size of the University was, to him, its strength; 'I certainly loved it, and still do'.[173]

Sid Teale and the Varsity Follies played for many student dances in the 1930s.

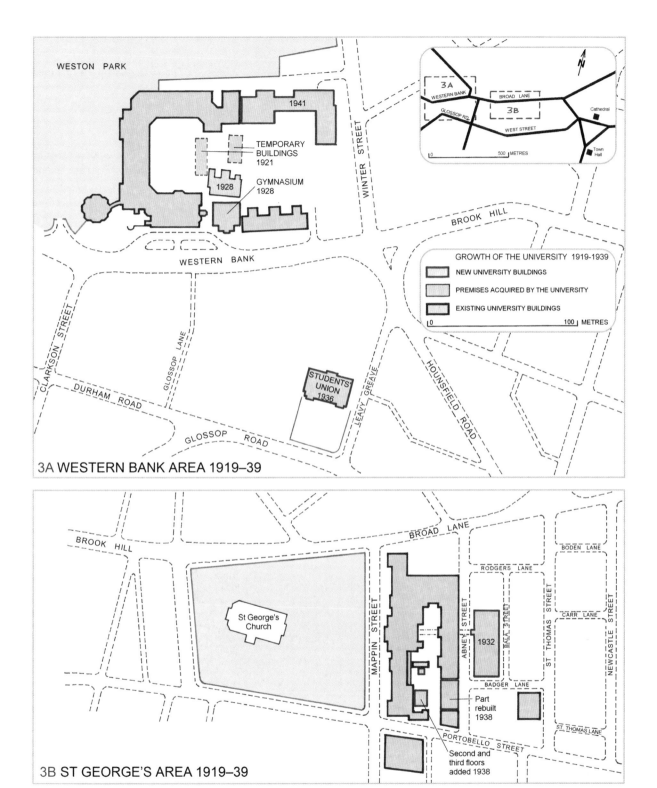

3A WESTERN BANK AREA 1919–39

3B ST GEORGE'S AREA 1919–39

Maps © Crown Copyright Ordnance Survey

127

4

Wartime and the Seeds of Expansion: 1939–59

THE NEW VICE-CHANCELLOR

I N 1938 PICKARD-CAMBRIDGE WAS SUCCEEDED by Irvine Masson, a dour Scot who had been Professor of Chemistry at Durham and was elected FRS in 1939. It was fitting that a chemist should, for the first time, hold the highest office in a university where chemistry was such an important subject, but Masson was ill-suited to some aspects of the role of vice-chancellor. He had few social graces, and a 'besetting reserve' easily mistaken for aloofness.[1] 'Masson was a monk, a hermit almost, he didn't associate with anybody at all', according to Gerard Young, a local industrialist and future Pro-Chancellor.[2] The new Vice-Chancellor found public speaking nerve-wracking and was reluctant to take part in Sheffield public life. During the war, his refusal to attend meetings of the Education Committee caused comment in the local newspapers.[3]

Masson's skills were administrative, and his ability to master and clarify complex financial and statistical data made him the ideal partner for the industrious Gibbons in eking out the University's resources as war approached. His review of the University's building programme brought Pickard-Cambridge's unfinished projects, including the swimming pool and the Western Bank extensions, to a sudden halt. The extension to house Zoology, Botany and Geography was the lone survivor; Medicine had more room to breathe in the north wing after this was opened in 1941.

There was no fun under Masson. He decreed silence at degree ceremonies and made strenuous attempts to enforce it. Searches were instituted to prevent students from bringing in musical instruments, with limited success. On one occasion a

Facing page: Table suite of a rosebowl and two candleholders commissioned by Convocation and Sheffield University Association to mark the University's golden jubilee in 1955. It was made by Mappin & Webb to the design of W. C. Smyth whose original drawings are held in the University's Hawley Collection.

129

Irvine Masson presided over a major expansion of the University after the war. For this and for his war-work, as Director of a research station of the Ministry of Supply (based in the Department of Chemistry) and Chairman of the Amatol Committee on the supply of explosives, he was knighted in 1950.

Facing page: The quadrangle during the war with the fire ladder, hydrant covers, and tops of the air-raid shelters clearly visible. The fountain, presented by H. K. Stephenson at the time of the opening, and the layout of the paths are as designed in 1905.

Major F. Orme, the Commander of the Senior Training Corps, was a former student who gained the BMet with honours and the Mappin Medal in 1914. He joined the staff of Metallurgy in that year and retired as a senior lecturer in 1959. He is seen here in his role as captain of the Rifle Team.

student 'cut up an old trombone, secreted it about the person of himself and friends, and then joined it up again with rubber tubing and tape once inside the hall'[4]. Graduation moved to the City Hall in 1947 and it was only after this that the required 'solemn' atmosphere was achieved, perhaps because groups of students were not allowed to gather in any particular part of the Hall.[5]

Members of staff were also discouraged from enjoying themselves. University folklore recalled, for decades thereafter, a reception where Masson, a teetotaller, served neither alcohol nor any other refreshment.[6] On the other hand, it was Masson's idea to open a Staff Club in a house on Brook Hill (now known as 'Club 197'). This was the first time that a vice-chancellor had attempted to facilitate social contact between staff working at St George's and at Western Bank.

THE EFFECT OF THE WAR ON THE UNIVERSITY

Masson arrived at the time of the Munich crisis. The following year was one of tension, as precautionary air-raid shelters were dug at the halls of residence and in the Western Bank quadrangle. 'The detour necessary to avoid falling down into the bowels of the earth' provided medical students with another excuse for being late for 9 o'clock lectures.[7] The government, mindful of the waste of talent in the first two years of the 1914–18 war, organised a Central Technical and Scientific Register, for which all universities had to list the expertise they could offer. Some staff were categorised as 'reserved' (from military service) as a result.

There was no mass conscription of students when war broke out in September 1939. Instead, all male students aged eighteen or over, the call-up age, had to appear before the University Joint Recruiting Board. In general, those studying medicine, science and technology were allowed to finish their degrees, while those taking other subjects could be asked to defer completion of their course and join the forces immediately. Not surprisingly, this boosted applications for the 'reserved' subjects, which were also sponsored by state bursaries from 1941. This factor, together with the increase in women students, who were not called up until 1942, meant that student numbers remained relatively stable throughout the war.

The students, however, were regarded as military trainees and expected to join the Senior Training Corps, commanded by Major Orme, and to take part in regular manoeuvres.[8] These became more taxing as the war went on; by 1943 the aim was to 'turn out a fully trained, tough private soldier'.[9] Reluctant students were 'shaken up and made to realise that there is a war on'. Their training included 'sampling the joys of tear gas in a mobile gas van' and tackling an assault course containing 'thickets with hidden trip wires; winding, pitch-black tunnels' and a gully which they had to cross on a rope while 'smoke blinded them and water from the stream shot up into their faces as charges [of explosive] went off'.[10]

Arts and Law students had to devote 200 hours and 21 days a year to this; students of reserved subjects did 108 hours and 14 days – still a considerable commitment. Attendance was monitored by the University, which was expected to report cases of back-sliding, as well as failure to progress academically, to the Ministry of Labour.

Angel Street from Snig Hill, *by Hillby Henry Rushbury (1940) shows streets close to King Street where Robert Brian decided his exam had probably been cancelled.*

In the years 1942 to 1944, an average of 47 male students were reported annually – some medical students for failing only one examination.[11] A report to the Ministry resulted in immediate conscription; a striking example of the way in which the University's administration was enlisted into the war effort. However, there is no indication that the Senate committee which undertook this job did so reluctantly; medical students, indeed, complained in 1940 that their attendance rules were more strictly enforced than at other universities.[12]

Blackout had to be installed at the start of the war; at Western Bank it was permanent, creating 'Styxian gloom' and excessive use of gas-lighting.[13] (Parts of Western Bank were still gaslit.) University buildings were sandbagged by a team led by the Physics lecturer J. R. Clarke. One student who volunteered to help found that he was then judged competent to lead gangs of building labourers doing the same job around the city.[14] All male students were ordered to fire-watch in pairs through the night from the top of the Western Bank Tower. On one occasion a team rushed to extinguish a fire on the roof of a house in Glossop Road, only to discover that their presence was not welcome since the house was a brothel.[15]

The University escaped lightly from the Sheffield Blitz on 12 December 1940, although many nearby buildings were hit, including the Jessop Hospital, the Mappin Art Gallery and St Mark's Church. In the circumstances, the decision to close the Western Bank building, which might have been used as a refuge, was rather feeble.[16] Robert Brian, trying to reach the University the following morning to take his chemistry practical examination, got as far as King Street, which 'had vanished, tram upon tram lay shattered and all power lines were down'. After clambering over 'mountains of debris' he concluded that the exam must have been cancelled.[17]

At Crewe Hall, the night was spent in the air-raid shelter, where a system of air conditioning had been rigged up, operated by a bicycle. This treadmill was pedalled by a continuous stream of volunteers.[18] All the gas mains in the area were severed. 'Hoppy', the formidable matron of Crewe, improvised barbecues in the kitchen yard and managed to serve a full Christmas dinner four days later. She continued to cook on open fires and primus stoves throughout the following term.[19] The King

Left: *A typical float from the 1941 Rag, referring to the war.*

Right: *Student sporting events continued as long as possible in war-time; this picture from the* Sheffield Telegraph *shows the line-up for the ladies' javelin final in May 1940.*

and Queen visited the devastated city, and reached the University at such short notice that students had to be summoned from the Refectory to greet them.[20]

The halls were full throughout the war, not only because travelling was more difficult but also because students were moved to Sheffield from other parts of the country. The first were a group of women medical students evacuated from University College, London, with their teachers, for the year 1939/40. Some were housed in Stephenson Hall, which was specially equipped with wardrobes and an iron; some were in the women's hall and others in Crewe, which thus became 'the first case of a mixed students' hostel in England' due to the continued presence of men.[21] The women were sorry to leave and thanked everyone for 'the universal friendliness and help with which we were received'. The second group was some 600 state bursars, funded by the government to study science and technology and drafted to Sheffield from all over the country. Many were from southern schools which had never sent a boy to a northern university before and were doubtful about the education which they would receive. As Chapman observed, these students, when favourably impressed, became ambassadors for Sheffield in their home towns and contributed to the increase in applications from further afield after the war.[22]

The proportion of women students rose from twenty per cent at the start of the war to almost 33 per cent by 1944. In that year it was impossible to house all the new students, even with extra accommodation lent by the City Council. For girls whose parents disliked the idea of lodgings, Mrs Masson organised a 'hostess' scheme whereby selected Sheffield families provided them with 'conditions approximating to home life'.[23] Students in residence during the war helped with domestic work, as it was impossible to recruit sufficient staff.

Normal student activities went on for as long as possible. Dances were held and the Rag continued until it was banned, to the great annoyance of the students, in 1942. During the 1940 Rag, a student splendidly attired as a Maharajah (he was in fact an Indian prince) was given a red carpet welcome at Victoria Station (having boarded the train at Darnall). He was then weighed in pennies on a fairground machine erected at Barker's Pool, in imitation of the weighing of the Nizars of

Hyderabad in precious stones.[24] A second Rag stunt, the conversion of a suite of public lavatories into 'Tutankhamun's Tomb', had to be abandoned when the Sheffield Watch Committee refused to allow a charge of 3d for a guided tour. 'Hitler's coffin' was a feature of the 1941 Rag, with the public eagerly queuing to knock nails in at one penny a time.[25]

In addition to its magazine, *Arrows*, the Union published a fortnightly news-sheet during the war, which had become known as *Darts* ('little arrows') by the autumn term of 1943.[26] The name was temporary, but it stuck. Until 1946 *Darts* was produced on a duplicator, probably the fearsome one operated by Dorothy, the Union clerk, who first cleared the office, put on an apron and manoeuvred the machine into position before turning the handle. 'This ceremony', *Arrows* reported, 'causes a dislocation in Union life comparable to washdays in domestic households'.[27]

In 1942, government pressure to speed up the production of graduates led to the introduction of a four-term year at every university. By then the war had reached a desperate stage and students were spending their free time on voluntary war work or military training. The lazy, contemplative summer holiday was a thing of the past. Even so, the 'vacation term' is a particularly striking example of the way in which this world war, much more than the first one, impinged on life *within* the University. Initially introduced for those taking 'reserved' subjects in 1942, it was extended to all students the following year. The University Council particularly resisted shortening the medical degree, since that would inevitably reduce clinical experience on the wards, but was forced to comply in 1943.[28]

The demands of the 'vacation term' removed nearly all of the time which lecturers normally relied upon for research and 'doing those things by which they legitimately augment their stipends', as the Finance Committee put it.[29] Despite this, the Committee refused to increase staff pay, because the government was making no special grant towards the accelerated teaching year.

Some members of staff volunteered for service at the start of the war and some younger ones were called up. Others vanished mysteriously and unexpectedly. J. R. Clarke, for instance, was called away in the middle of a teaching term to advise on the magnetic properties of ships. John Colman of Zoology disappeared and later summoned one of his students to a job at Bletchley Park as an Enigma code-breaker.[30] Sixteen staff were released full-time during the war to work on government projects, but the majority remained in post because a great deal of war work was going on within the University. Masson directed a Ministry of Supply team based in the Chemistry department, which studied the physical properties of amatol explosives, with the aim of improving the blasting power of large bombs and mines.[31] A second chemical research team worked on precautions against chemical warfare, and a third enhanced the quality of the charcoal used in fuse powders for shells.

The Physics department made a considerable contribution to the development of radar, which proved to be crucial to the war effort. Indeed, the Second World War has been called 'the physicists' war' because of the major innovations in radio

Sir Donald Bailey, who had graduated from the Department of Civil and Structural Engineering in 1923, standing on a Bailey bridge at Caen in 1944.

communication and nuclear power. Professor Willie Sucksmith, who came from Bristol to take over the department in 1940, played an important role in designing the magnets for the valves essential to radar.[32] Sucksmith was a 'brilliant experimentalist', who had been elected FRS for his research on magnetism. He created a stimulating atmosphere where young scientists could forge ahead with research. Some graduates, like Donald Tomlin and Henry Turner, went directly from Sheffield to work in radar research establishments. A new subject, radio physics, was added to the degree programme for the duration of the war, almost doubling the teaching load of the department.

Just as they had been during the First World War, the St George's buildings were a hive of activity. Staff and students of Metallurgy worked up to three shifts a day in the summer of 1940, producing forgings for tank parts and sheet metal for helmets. After the Blitz damaged local factories, the workshops were turned over to the production of hundreds of thousands of small tools.[33] The Engineering faculty produced aircraft and gun components and trained hundreds of munitions workers, many of them women. From 1942 to 1944, women students assembled thousands of anti-tank mine fuses in a converted laboratory in the Western Bank building. Margaret Rogers remembers the sessions as a 'pleasant interlude' during which they sang popular dance tunes as they worked.[34] The Department of Glass Technology, in addition to advising industry and government on specialised glasses, set up a lamp-working school and trained men as glass blowers.

After the introduction of the four-term year, it proved impossible for the Engineering faculty to staff both their production and teaching duties. Additional workers, including a production manager, were employed after Professor Swift vented his frustration to the Council in November 1942.[35]

Professor Sucksmith working in the laboratory. A plain-speaking Yorkshireman, he was particularly supportive to research students.

Medical research with conscientious objectors

The war created innumerable challenges in medical and biological research. The Pathology department formed a research unit to investigate the treatment and causes of shock after major injury, with such success that members of the unit advised casualty clearing stations in Germany during the final stages of the war.[36] Highly publicised research using conscientious objectors was conducted by the Sorby Research Fellow, Kenneth Mellanby (a nephew of Edward Mellanby, the former Professor of Pharmacology) and, later, by Hans Krebs.[37] The conscientious objectors were no ordinary research subjects because, as Krebs recalled, they 'were willing to take risks, making it clear that they had not evaded war service because of its unpleasantness and danger'.[38]

Kenneth Mellanby conducted pioneering wartime research on parasitic infections, for which he was awarded the OBE.

Mellanby's first investigation was the cause of scabies, a parasitic infection rife in barracks and camps and believed to be transmitted by shared bedding and clothing. The scabies mite was inserted under the skin of Mellanby's volunteers and the reaction observed. One of them, Wilfred Harrison, recalls that he suffered from an itch on the wrist, where the mite was, but even after its removal, 'the itch increased and made sleep restless . . . it was discovered that I had not been infested with the intended male, but with a female mite, and it had laid eggs which were now maturing into an infestation, not just on the wrist but extensively. I was stripped naked and painted all over with benzyl benzoate that smarted fiercely in every open scratch, wound or pore'.[39] Mellanby shared the discomfort, since, according to one of his students, he walked around with mites in a matchbox strapped to his leg.[40] His conclusions were that an infected person could pass on the disease only through close physical contact, but not via blankets.[41] The health authorities were able to halt the sterilisation of bedding, saving both time and money.

The objectors were an ideal research group, 'intelligent and co-operative people living under closely controlled conditions'.[42] They were put on experimental diets, designed to discover how the nation could cope with food restrictions, with the result that 'national wheatmeal' became a staple part of the diet. Mellanby and twelve volunteers also lived on 'lifeboat rations', without water, to establish the best minimal diet for shipwrecked sailors.

Dr Mellanby's assistant at the Sorby Institute from 1940 was Walter Bartley who, hoping to escape the bombing in Brighton, arrived in Sheffield on 12 December just as the Blitz started. The next morning he met a dishevelled young woman, Mella Roth, the daughter of the Institute's cook, whose home had been destroyed during the night. Bartley, together with the entire Roth family, moved into the Institute and Mella later became his wife. After the war, Krebs encouraged Bartley to take a degree in physiology, in which he gained first class honours, followed by post-graduate research and a post with Krebs's MRC Unit in Oxford. He returned to Sheffield as Professor of Biochemistry in 1963 and later became Dean and pro-vice-chancellor. Such a progression, from technician to pro-vice-chancellor, may be unique. Kenneth Mellanby was appointed OBE for his wartime research and joined the army as an adviser on parasitology in 1943. Krebs continued the Institute's dietary research and demonstrated the minimum amount of vitamin C needed to prevent scurvy.

Walter Bartley joined Mellanby's Unit in 1940 and became Professor of Biochemistry in 1963. After his retirement in 1981, he returned 'quietly' to the department to work as a research technician.

The retirement of Gibbons

W. M. Gibbons, the Registrar since University College days, retired in 1944 after 42 years in the post. Such longevity in a senior position is extraordinary; Gibbons was 71 on his retirement, having been persuaded to stay on at the start of the war. In 1942 he received an Honorary Doctorate of Laws and he devoted the substantial subscription raised at the time of his retirement to the 'Gibbons Prize' for a graduate in the Faculty of Arts.

Gibbons was the ideal Registrar for the early days of a poor university. He kept an iron grip on the purse strings and managed his office in an economical, not to say cheeseparing, way. Eric Bagnall, a member of his staff, used to remark that Gibbons 'turned every penny over twice'. He was a demanding boss, employing the minimum number of subordinates and working them extremely hard. 'Office hours were elastic, often extending far into the evening; legend has it that the wife of one member of staff used to haunt the office in the evening . . . in order to catch an occasional glimpse of her husband'.[43] Chapman, his assistant, described Gibbons in 1968 as 'an exacting and often difficult master'.[44] He could, however, be delightfully tactful towards the academic staff, writing to a professor who had submitted a long-winded report in 1935:

William Gibbons became the Registrar to University College, Sheffield in 1902, aged 29. He remained Registrar until 1944, a record of 42 years service in the post which seems unlikely to be equalled. This drawing was made by Sir William Rothenstein in 1918.

John Bycroft, from a portrait etching by Andrew Freeth at the time of his retirement in 1952. He served the University for 45 years, acting as private secretary to Eliot and Fisher and shouldering an extra burden of work on the Munitions Committee (1914–18) and the FSSU. He was given the title of 'University Accountant' in 1939 and became the first Bursar in 1944.

Busy people are sometimes a little annoyed – no doubt unreasonably – with a longish document. We wonder whether you can curtail the draft without impairing the case, which is a good one.[45]

From 1913 Gibbons was the mainstay of the national staff pension scheme, the Federated Superannuation System for Universities (FSSU), acting as its secretary. His efforts ensured the success of FSSU, which grew from 22 institutions in 1915 to 184 by 1944.[46] The extra daily workload which he shouldered was considerable and his effort in continuing past retirement age was Herculean. The University owes him an enormous debt, amplified by the fact that he aged 'too rapidly' after his retirement; he died in 1952.[47]

He had to be replaced by two men: A. W. Chapman, who took over as Registrar, and John Bycroft, who became the first Bursar. Bycroft had worked for Gibbons since 1907 and acted as Bursar for the last eight of his 45 years of service. The Vice-Chancellor praised him as the type of finance officer, rare even then, whose concern was to find the money for valuable academic enterprise, rather than to judge its worth by its potential income.[48] A former secretary, Margaret Bennett, has observed that, despite her 'laborious work' with a 'stone age' letter book, 'it was an honour and privilege to work for such a man'.[49]

Mrs Bennett evokes the 'almost intimate' feeling which still characterised the University in the 1940s, when every administrator knew the students personally. 'Students crossing the quadrangle had no idea that eyes were noting who was with whom and we had a fair idea who was "going all the way" – mostly medics and mostly the exception!'

Aerial view from the mid-1950s showing the third and fourth huts being constructed below the quadrangle (behind the gymnasium and the houses where arts subjects were taught), the Graves mail order warehouse (bottom left), and the Students' Union building on Glossop Road.

The 1944 Beaumont design for the development of the campus proposed tall high-density blocks which would have overwhelmed the smaller scale of the original buildings. This preliminary sketch suggests a grandiosity which would have substantially changed the image of the University.

OVERCROWDING, TEMPORARY BUILDINGS AND THE POST-WAR STUDENTS

VE Day was announced to students and staff over the loudspeakers on Monday 7 May 1945. A crowded impromptu dance in Firth Hall was followed by a torchlight procession round the city centre singing, 'Come and Join Us'. At Barkers Pool the procession merged with the huge crowd of local people singing 'There'll always be an England'.[50]

Young people called up for war service had received a compelling education in life, but their higher education had been delayed by as much as six years. Male arts students had suffered the most serious delay, since their subjects were not 'reserved'. When they returned to the University, some ex-servicemen had wives and children and all were desperate to start their careers.[51] They worked hard and were grateful for what they had. 'Such people would have had no patience with the student unrest of the late sixties', comments a fellow student, David Payne, who had arrived straight from school and believes that their example inspired younger students, like himself, to work harder.[52] The two very different groups of students appear to have learned from each other and certainly relished this time of peace and normality. The University's large collection of student memories from these years recalls the austerity of food rationing, the lack of money and the overcrowding of university buildings, but, above all, the happy atmosphere and the close camaraderie between students and staff.

These post-war students were the first to come in significant numbers from homes distant to Sheffield.[53] There were enough overseas students to warrant the appointment of a tutor to foreign students in the Arts faculty and the creation of a Diploma in English Studies for foreign graduates in 1946.

The University provided a refuge to a succession of Dutch students invited to stay in Sheffield for three months as part of their recovery from the occupation. Its

Left: *Chemistry seen from Broad Lane across the site of the future Brook Hill roundabout. The Portland stone-faced building is already complete and extensions to it are under way.*

Right: *View from the weathercock on the Western Bank building in 1949, with the backdrop of the Jessop Hospital, St George's Church, and the Applied Science buildings.*

A Crewe student in his room in 1945. Note the utility furniture and slide rule.

terrible reality was recalled in 'Reawakening', a story published in *Arrows* in 1946, which describes the student's previous daily existence – a walk of many miles to find husks of maize, the only food, the secret sale of forbidden newspapers and the desperate attempts to help Jews in occupied Holland.[54] This story was one of several war reminiscences published in the University magazines. A tutor in surgery's account of his experiences as a Japanese prisoner-of-war objectively analyses the threat he faced under four headings: possibility of execution, infectious disease, dietary deficiency disease and hazardous surgery[55].

Because of the slow demobilisation, many ex-servicemen did not arrive at the University until 1946. From then until 1950 there were about 500 a year, some forty per cent of the total. Student numbers increased from 918 in 1945, to 1,355 in 1946, 1,704 in 1947, 1,910 in 1948 and 1,987 in 1949. Thereafter the numbers were held for some time at about 2,000 students. Pure science subjects were in the greatest demand, with seven applications for every place in 1949, between four and five for arts, medicine and engineering, three for metallurgy and only one for law.

With no new buildings, the University was forced to erect even more huts for physics, chemistry and engineering. Every spare house in the area was pressed into service in the drive to double the accommodation of the arts departments within two years, 1945 to 1947. The University was operating on an 'emergency footing' and 'under desperate difficulties', without modern buildings or equipment.[56] It was also short of staff, since there had been, in Chapman's phrase, a 'general post' of academics in 1945, caused by the glut of retirements of staff who had agreed to stay on during the war.[57] Many posts were on offer, with the result that some younger academics moved elsewhere. The difficulty of finding replacements in an under-supplied market, combined with inflated student numbers, led inevitably to heavier timetables and larger classes. Sheffield's student load in 1947/48 was more than double what it had been in 1938/39; much higher than the national average growth of 54 per cent.[58] In these circumstances, even an increase in staff numbers of fifty per cent by 1948 was not sufficient.

Finding suitable housing for this glut of students became a serious problem. The number of places in hall was entirely inadequate, even when new annexes to the women's hall were found and Ranmoor College at last became a men's hall in 1947 (this was the first incarnation of Ranmoor House, superseded in 1968).[59] A second purpose-built men's hall, the final site for Stephenson, did not open until 1952. Women who were without a hall place continued to rely on the 'hostess system'. For the men, it was lodgings. The majority of these were adequate, and many landladies became second mothers to students who lodged with them for the full three years. Douglas Rimmer and his room-mate, to take just one example, were 'fed like turkey-cocks' and taken out to the local pub.[60] Sheila Banks, however, isolated in a house at Beauchief in her first year and then moved to 'awful' cold digs in Nether Edge, was so unhappy that she considered abandoning her course.[61]

The redoubtable Tessie Ball was appointed as warden of lodgings in 1947 after student complaints that twenty per cent of the accommodation was unacceptable (with some lodgings being described as racist).[62] By her own account, she began work without a telephone, staff or a car and visited all 230 registered lodgings in her first three months. She sometimes had to work until the early hours in order to find new lodgings for the extra students.[63] Miss Ball made exacting demands on landladies before allowing them to display a certificate signed by the Vice-Chancellor. She could also be unsympathetic towards students who complained about 'digs' which she had personally approved. Her belief was that lodgings offered 'a more normal way of living' than flats or even Hall.

Some lodgings were a long way from the University and students returned to them for their evening meal. Thereafter, and at weekends, they were stuck with the facilities provided by their hosts. Few seem to have returned to the University in the evening, where in any case, there were no social facilities available for them in the

Tessie Ball, Warden of Lodgings from 1947. She initially visited landladies scattered across the city without a car, until Chapman agreed to provide her with a taxi. This turned out to be an ancient Rolls-Royce. Seventeen years later she wrote, 'There are still landladies who remember me arriving in this vehicle'.

A mock nineteenth-century cricket match was part of the entertainment at the Crewe Hall garden party in June 1949.

Union until 1949, when a coffee bar opened. Many gathered in local pubs. Entertainment of the opposite sex in lodgings was hazardous, since the rules continued to be strict. Tessie Ball apparently thought that the halls had become too lax, because Crewe Hall had agreed to admit girls at 1.30 pm on a Sunday. She noted that curtains were swiftly drawn across windows, a sure sign of something 'untoward'.[64]

The lucky few who secured a place in Crewe, Ranmoor or the Women's Hall report a time of idyllic happiness. For Ron Savigear, Ranmoor was 'one of the great experiences of my life' when he was 'part of something special'.[65] Ranmoor was a home from home for fifty men, where the benign traditions established by Chapman at Crewe were adopted by his deputy, Bill Maddocks, a lecturer in metallurgy, when he became the new hall's first warden. These were civilised places where order was only disrupted by practical jokes, like the deliberate flooding of a staircase.[66]

Right: *Torchlight procession to Barkers Pool, Rag 1948.*

Below: *Rag procession in 1953 with a tram waiting next to the Scala Cinema at the intersection with Western Bank.*

Far right: *A Rotherham tram decorated with the Rag Fairy, 1947.*

Left: *Hans Kornberg, the editor, and Bernard Hart, Chairman of Rag, getting ready to sell Twikker in 1948. Kornberg, on the right, was heavily involved in Students' Union activities, and went on to gain a PhD in 1953, and to be elected FRS. He became Professor of Biochemistry and Master of Christ's College, Cambridge, and was knighted.*

Above: *The cover of the scandalous 1949* Twikker. *The Yorkshire Star felt it constituted 'a grave breach of good taste and that neither the University nor the cause being helped could tolerate its continued sale'.*

Ex-servicemen were among the inhabitants. Some of the more prosperous and dashing wore 'cavalry twill' and 'well cut tweed jackets', although Alec Barron, a President of Crewe, recalls that he and his friends wore their 'demob suits' — 'creations of failed tailors in moments of alcoholic rapture' and that his was a purple three-piece.[67] One member of Crewe donned tails from Moss Bros to gate-crash the Cutlers' Feast, the pinnacle of Sheffield's social calendar. He arrived in a taxi and easily passed himself off as a guest.[68] It was impossible to impose the restrictions of pre-war social life on such students. Women were allowed to visit much more freely and a bar was installed in Crewe Junior Common Room (JCR).

By 1949 the students had voted to have a bar in the Union, even though the only available space was the stage used for student productions. The Union was desperately overcrowded, as was the Western Bank Refectory, the only other place to eat at lunchtime. Every student of those days recalls the long queues for lunch, which was a set meal served by waitresses in uniform. Coffee was taken in the JCR 'into which students packed like passengers on a Japanese commuter train'.[69] Those worst affected by these arrangements were medical students on clinical attachment to the Royal Infirmary, which refused to provide catering for them. They had to walk up the hill from Infirmary Road, queue, eat and walk back down in time for the afternoon session. Self-service was not introduced until 1958.

Men outnumbered women by four to one throughout the post-war decade and the numbers of women did not rise appreciably until the 1960s. The atmosphere was still distinctly male, with lecturers quite commonly beginning 'Gentlemen . . .' The sexism of student magazines like *Darts* and *North-Wing* was sometimes blatant. The Rag magazine *Twikker*, like all Rag magazines, grew racier and more *risqué* after the war. There was an attempt at a clean *Twikker* in 1948, but the following year *Twikker* was deemed to have gone too far and was banned. Chapman and Masson ordered its recall and the destruction of all copies, apparently because the Lord Mayor, who traditionally bought the first copy, was upset by it. Members of the Education Committee described it as 'a disgrace to education' during a debate on the City

The newspaper caption reads 'After long arduous hours of morning study, students . . . take advantage of the warm sunny weather to relax in the terraced grounds of the Students' Union during their lunch hour'.

Council's grant to the University.[70] The banned magazine, meanwhile, changed hands for £1 a copy, since most of the edition had already been sold.[71] From the perspective of a later generation, it is hard to understand what the fuss was about. When *Twikker* returned, after an enforced gap of three years, it quickly reverted to its old ways.

The Rag did not take place for four years during the war and was inspired by an energetic need to make up for lost time when it resumed in 1946. The Union President fulfilled his promise to eat his hat (made of liquorice) if the target sum was reached and the famous conductor John Barbirolli connived at his own 'kidnapping' in the middle of a City Hall concert. The Professor of Music, F. H. Shera, persuaded the audience to pay a 'ransom' to enable the concert to continue.[72]

Despite the success of the Rag with the Sheffield public, which was both generous to the cause and tolerant of the students' high spirits, Masson continued to be suspicious of it and of outbreaks of student spontaneity in general. C. R. Tottle recalls that Masson used to inspect the Rag floats before departure from Western Bank, but only on the side facing the steps, with the result that the other side displayed all the *risqué* slogans. Jean Beeley was entranced by her first experience of Rag day, summing up its appeal to students – 'we let ourselves go as never before'.[73]

THE POST-WAR DEVELOPMENT PLAN

When the war ended in 1945, the University faced the same challenges as in 1918, but this time it was not left to struggle alone. Indeed, the government was determined that the universities would not only survive, but expand. As early as 1943, plans for social improvement, epitomised by the Beveridge report, were being drawn up and universities were to be in the vanguard of reforms in education.

Encouraged by the UGC, Masson drafted a list of buildings which the University would need. They included a new medical school, new library, an arts block, a staff house and more student halls.[74] A Sites Committee began to consider how to acquire the necessary land, a Development Committee was formed and an architect, J. S. Beaumont, was invited to draw up sketch plans (see p 139). The aim was to expand to 1,500 students (twice the pre-war figure) but to 'make good the existing departments before embarking on new ventures'.[75]

This relatively modest plan was overturned in 1946, after the Barlow Report on Scientific Manpower recommended doubling the numbers of qualified scientists. Sheffield was offered the chance to plan for expansion to 2,800 undergraduates by 1956.[76] This was a radical step. The decision dictated the University's development over the next ten years, and beyond, ensuring that the emphasis would be on the expansion of science. It reflected the record numbers applying for places in pure science after the war and the fact that they were 'gateways' to other subjects, like medicine. Chemistry was described as 'a notorious university bottleneck' for this reason.[77] In these circumstances, and with a registrar and a vice-chancellor who were both chemists, it is not surprising that provision for chemistry assumed the highest priority. Beaumont was invited to revise his 1944 plans to accommodate the extra science students and produced a scheme which gave top priority to new chemistry and physics buildings, together with a new medical school and engineering extensions.

This plan sited the Medical School at the junction of Broomspring Lane and Glossop Road, opposite the site intended for the 'new Infirmary'. The new science buildings would form a 'second quadrangle' next to Winter Street, approached by an archway from the main building. Arts would be housed in an extension to Western Bank, the entrance of which would be moved to the corner with Winter Street, 'emphasised by an imposing doorway, a large vestibule, a wide staircase and a lofty tower'.[78]

The proposed sites for these buildings were not readily available. The Winter Street/Bolsover Street area was a busy community with shops and a cinema. Smart Victorian houses stood on the proposed medical school site. In order to acquire these, the University promoted a Parliamentary bill, which awarded powers of compulsory purchase in June 1948. Only one of the owners, a man with four houses on Western Bank, petitioned Parliament against the compulsory purchase. The University's response was to describe his houses as 'very mean' and 'rather dreary' in contrast to the 'dignity' of the proposed redevelopment.[79]

Some compulsory purchase orders were never used, and all of the owners were allowed at least seven years to vacate. Chemistry was awarded the only ready-made site, the result of bomb damage on Brook Hill. This first post-war building began construction in 1949, but proceeded slowly because of the discovery of an underground stream. Now known as the Dainton building, it was ready for use in 1952,

Left: *The Earl of Harewood, guarded by the well-remembered City Hall lions, addressing the congregation after his installation as Chancellor.*

Right: *John Masefield meeting the new Chancellor, the Earl of Harewood, at the installation ceremony and degree congregation held in 1946. Masefield, then Poet Laureate, gave an inspiring address describing his vision of a university.*

by which time extensions were already needed. A new engineering and mining building was started in 1950.

Although the UGC's provision was generous, in 1947 the University Council decided to supplement it by launching a Development Fund to raise money from local benefactors and businesses. It was a propitious moment. Despite, or perhaps because of, the privations of the war, idealism about higher education was strong. The first glamorous post-war civic occasion was the installation of the new Chancellor, Lord Harewood, the husband of the Princess Royal. The City Hall was full and, after the years of austerity, the audience was enraptured by the 'blaze of colour and pageantry' in the procession.[80] The Poet Laureate, John Masefield, who received an honorary doctorate, made a speech which included this inspirational passage:

> There are few earthly things more splendid than a university. In these days of broken frontiers and collapsing values . . . wherever a university . . . exists, the free minds of men, urged on to full and fair enquiry, may still bring wisdom into human affairs.[81]

The Earl of Halifax, seen here in a photograph by Cecil Beaton, was Chancellor from 1947 to 1959. A Viceroy of India and Ambassador to the USA, he was Foreign Secretary 1938–40, when the Second World War began. On his death in 1959 the University Hall for Women was named Halifax Hall after him.

The Development Campaign proved to be the most successful since 1905, passing £300,000 within a year and eventually reaching over £400,000. Two open days brought over 10,000 Sheffield people swarming through Western Bank, St George's and the halls. Lord Harewood's death within two years and the appointment of Lord Halifax, a former Foreign Secretary, as his successor led to a second installation ceremony, of even greater pomp, in July 1948. The *Sheffield Telegraph* was moved to report that Halifax's speech was 'pregnant with the religious fervour that backgrounds his life'.[82] The wit of the Public Orator, Denis Browne, was given the accolade of 'true brilliance' by the future Prime Minister Anthony Eden, an honorary graduate.

The 'success beyond expectations' of the Development Fund has to be compared with almost £1 million given by the UGC during the same period. Only eight per

cent of the University's recurrent income came from the local authorities by 1949.[83] The University had local support, but its policies and finances were increasingly directed by the strategies of the national higher education system.

ARTS, ARCHITECTURE AND THE SOCIAL SCIENCES IN THE 1940s AND 1950s

The post-war emphasis on science could have sidelined developments within the arts, and there were many who feared that it would, especially in a university with Sheffield's scientific and technical traditions.[84] However, the arts were also in great demand after the war and social sciences were set for expansion. Masson and the University Council had recognised this when they included a new chair of Philosophy and a new School of Social Studies in the development plan of 1944.

Ellinor Black, the first Director of the School of Social Studies. She made important contributions to the work of the Joint University Council for Social Studies and the International Association for Schools of Social Work.

The discipline of social studies was already taught at other universities, notably the London School of Economics, its primary focus being the training of social workers. Academic sociological study was in its infancy and scarcely recognised as a separate discipline, hence Douglas Knoop's claim that his department, Economics, already covered it.[85] The Senate would have preferred to offer a full degree programme, but the complications of organising this led to the decision to begin, in 1949, with a two-year certificate course in social administration and a postgraduate diploma.[86] The lack of a degree gave Social Studies a somewhat nebulous status and the School's first director, Ellinor Black, did not become a professor. Most of its students were women, for whom 'social welfare' work had become an attractive career option. It seems to have been more like the day teacher training college of the 1890s than any contemporary department in the University. This phase of the school's existence lasted until 1959, when the Department of Sociological Studies was created under a new Professor, Keith Kelsall. Ellinor Black died on the eve of her retirement in 1956.

Psychology was a subject which had featured in university medical and educational curricula for many years. It too had a strong claim to become a separate

147

F. F. Bruce, the first Professor of Biblical History and Literature. His appointment in 1947 coincided with the discovery of the Dead Sea Scrolls, a favourite lecture topic. He left Sheffield in 1959 for a particularly prestigious chair in Manchester.

department and a chair was duly advertised in 1947. The supply of suitable candidates was so meagre, however, that the post could not be filled and the discipline operated under the auspices of the Philosophy department until 1960. Yet the younger generation of psychologists was bursting with enthusiasm. One of them, Harry Kay, who became the first professor in 1960, wrote:

> After 1946 the numbers of university psychology students and researchers shot up, and a mixed lot we were, many of us having spent up to six years in one wartime job or other. Former army officers and veterans from the Pioneer Corps, naval officers and merchant navy seamen rubbed shoulders with ex-Spitfire pilots, conscientious objectors and members of the Land Army.[87]

The war had kindled the interest of many of them, since the army conducted extensive psychological tests with its recruits.

The Department of 'Biblical History and Literature' came into being in 1947 after an 'unholy' row, described in a gloriously indiscreet account by G. R. Potter, Professor of History.[88] Masson and Clapton, the Professor of French, were vehemently opposed to the pet project of Leslie Hunter, the determined and shrewd Bishop of Sheffield, who wanted a Department of Theology which could train Anglican ordinands. At the same time, the Professor of Education, G. H. Turnbull, wanted to provide for the training of teachers of religious instruction in schools. Given the University's non-sectarian, indeed secular, traditions, a Theology department was too contentious, but the Senate decided that a department with the focus of Biblical history and literature would be acceptable. It is likely that Masson was reconciled to this by his own serious interest in the textual study of ancient manuscripts.[89]

Architecture students in their new home, the old Sunday School buildings in Shearwood Road

The interviews for a lecturer-in-charge caused a further dispute. The Bishop, perhaps predictably, preferred a clergyman, while the majority of the panel opted for F. F. Bruce who, as a member of the Plymouth Brethren, was both a Nonconformist and a layman. Bruce proved to be an ideal head of the new department. With an 'unparalleled range of knowledge in biblical themes . . . and effortless familiarity with everything done in his field', he rose above sectarianism.[90] He found his new job 'enjoyable beyond words' and became his department's first professor in 1955.[91]

Architecture, a struggling department with a maximum of forty students before the war, took off when the war ended. Stephen Welsh, who was promoted to the first chair of architecture in 1948, was so dominant that he inspired fear in his students and even his staff, but he was an energetic leader. Many ex-servicemen were attracted to architecture; Alec Daykin (then a junior lecturer) recalls that they were 'keen and mature . . . and not prepared to suffer fools gladly'.[92] The department grew to 150 students by 1947 and 200 by 1952, by which time it was the largest department in the Faculty of Arts. In 1946 it moved from its lofty premises in Western Bank to recently vacated Sunday School buildings in Shearwood Road, adjoining the Baptist Church. A nursing home (the original site of Claremont) commanded the top of the *cul-de-sac*, which was new territory for the University at that time. The Sunday School had large, high-windowed rooms, perfect for studio work, and there was a basement to house the library.

Most of the arts departments were accommodated in houses on Western Bank and Leavygreave. Lectures were held in Western Bank and there was a strict 75 per cent attendance rule, which applied to the whole university. When Kenneth Haley, the new History lecturer, passed round an attendance list in 1948, he was surprised to find that his class included George III, Charles James Fox and the younger Pitt.[93] G. P. Jones, who taught economic history, pulled a wheeled blackboard over the door to prevent the entry of late-comers, until the inevitable day when he himself was late and could not get in.[94]

Francis Berry is remembered by generations of students for his dramatic performances. He was promoted to a personal chair in 1967 but moved to Royal Holloway College in 1970 when he married aged 54.

John Tyler is remembered by post-war history students as a 'superb teacher' with a powerful intellect. Born locally, the product of generations of 'little mesters', he was the 'best-read man in the University'.[95] William Carr was appointed after the war, in 1949, and gave almost forty years service to the University. As a German speaker, his war service had included interpreting at interviews with suspected Nazis. He was also a front-line soldier during the Normandy campaign and had a strong bond with the ex-servicemen. He became one of 'the foremost historians of modern Germany', publishing several standard works and a 'masterly' biographical study of Hitler.[96]

The Professor of French until 1949 was G. T. Clapton, 'one of the charismatic figures of university teaching' and remembered by former students for his trenchant views and encyclopaedic knowledge.[97] Clapton's successor, Harold Lawton, who was to become one of the first pro-vice-chancellors, had survived a 'hellhole' prison camp in the First World War and used his command of French during the Second to prepare RAF personnel and British secret agents for landings in German-occupied France. He was awarded the *Légion d'Honneur* when he reached his hundredth birthday in 1999.[98]

William Empson in 1955, shortly after his arrival in Sheffield, when he was engaged in the preparation of the masque for the Queen's jubilee visit.

The Poets of the English Literature department

> ... Witty and lucky and plucky this man.
> He came as a legend, he left as a myth.[99]

This is William Empson, as described by Francis Berry. Both were poets in the English Literature department; Empson was internationally famous and Berry was well-reviewed for work such as 'Murdock' and 'The Galloping Centaur'. Berry gave 'hypnotic' performances of his works, in public and during lectures, sweeping dramatically across the room, pausing for moments of rapt contemplation and gazing into space 'with visionary eyes'.[100] He loved to take part in drama and once rushed to catch the last train to Grindleford (where he lived in a cottage named after a character in Beowulf) wearing his 'Oresteia' costume of tunic and short Greek kilt.

Facing page: The first year Chemistry laboratory before its transfer to the new building.

In William Empson's case the drama lies in his life. He came to Sheffield as Professor of English Literature in 1953 with his fame assured by *Seven Types of Ambiguity* (1930), a classic work of criticism, and volumes of poetry which were acclaimed by the literary world, including fellow poets like T. S. Eliot.[101] It was said by some in Sheffield that Empson himself was the eighth type of ambiguity. His poetry could be complex, since it deployed a scholarship which ranged through mathematics, psychology, anthropology and oriental languages. Unlike Berry he was a reluctant performer, but he made mesmerising recordings of his poetry for the BBC in 1952.

For all his abstracted air, Empson was a man of the world. In 1929 he had the catastrophic experience of being sent down from Cambridge, forfeiting a fellowship, because contraceptives were found by staff clearing his college room.[102] A few months later he wrote some 'mock-heroic' verses entitled 'Warning to undergraduates'. He spent most of the 1930s teaching at universities in the Far East. In 1937 he arrived at the University of Peking just as the Japanese invaded China. The universities were forced to make the 'long march' out of the occupied territories and Empson 'refugeed' with them, lecturing in remote places and quoting memorised poetry because there were no books. By the time he left China in 1939, his affinity with the country was such that he became a Chinese editor for the BBC. He returned to Peking University in 1947 and witnessed the civil war and the Communist siege of Peking, which forced him to cross the lines in order to lecture on *Macbeth*. He fully supported the Chinese revolution and stayed on, under the increasingly repressive Maoist regime, until 1952. Famously dishevelled in appearance, and living in well-attested squalor in a Broomhall basement flat, he relied on his devoted secretary, Mrs Baehl, to organise his departmental life. It was said that she used to check his wastepaper basket, lest he had discarded important documents.

As a teacher, Empson could be intimidating; he wrote 'exhaustive marginalia' on essays and his lectures were not pitched to the understanding of the average first-year student. However, they were 'unforgettable: . . . it was impossible to make notes as he ranged over all sorts of subjects, just musing aloud while we students scrambled to make the connections'.[103] Yet he enjoyed the company of his students and became devoted to the department, whose status soared. He stayed until his retirement in 1971.

THE PURE SCIENCES IN THE LATER 1940s AND 1950s

The Department of Geography

David Linton oversaw a period of growth in the Department of Geography in the post-war years, when student numbers trebled. He was an eloquent lecturer and wrote a number of classic scholarly papers. The editor of Geography *for many years, he became President of the Geographical Association and President of the Institute of British Geographers.*

Geography gained its second distinguished professor when David Linton succeeded Rudmose Brown in 1945. During the war Linton's skills in aerial photography brought him leadership of the Intelligence department charged with identifying war targets, like the 'Scharnhorst' discovered lurking amongst the Norwegian fjords.[104] Linton was assisted by Alice Garnett, who had been a lecturer in the department since 1924 and had published 'one of the most scholarly and important monographs'

The huts below the quadrangle, where the overspill from Chemistry and Physics was housed. When students were sitting exams in them on hot days it was common practice for the porters to spray the roofs with cold water to keep the temperature down. Behind are the cottages housing arts subjects with the gymnasium to their left. Firth Hall is top right and beyond is the Graves mail order warehouse.

Professor R. D. Haworth (right), Firth Professor of Chemistry 1939–63. Elected FRS in 1944 for his original observations on humic acid, he recruited a group of eminent scientists to the department. The department's heady expansion was said to have been facilitated by Haworth's friendship with the Bursar, R. M. Urquhart, forged during many hours watching cricket and football at Bramall Lane.

of the Institute of British Geographers in 1937.[105] The department developed special research interests in geomorphology, climatology and social geography. Alice Garnett ran a meteorological station on Kinder Scout which was visited every Sunday to change the charts.

The attractive new premises on B floor of the 1941 extension were 'the envy of many other university departments of geography' and included an extensive map collection.[106] However, the accommodation was designed for student numbers about one quarter of those which the department had attracted by 1950; within six years an annexe had been created from two adjacent houses on Winter Street. Alice Garnett brought the headquarters of the Geographical Association to Sheffield and persuaded the City Council to house its library. In the 1950s it was based at the Duke Street branch library, an easy journey by tram for geography students, who could escape the crush in the Edgar Allen library.[107] David Linton left a very flourishing department in 1958 to take up a chair in Birmingham.

Alice Garnett waited until 1962 to receive her own chair – only the second in the University's history awarded to a woman.[108] She retired in 1968 after 44 years service, which included nine years as the University's senior tutor to women students.

Physics and Chemistry

Facilities in both Chemistry and Physics were abysmal after the war. Geoffrey Ardron, who started a physics PhD in 1946, recalls that he built the high voltage

By 1954 Chemistry was already the largest department in the University and immediately filled the new building designed by J. S. Beaumont. The building contained three lecture theatres, many laboratories and a library named in honour of Professor W. P. Wynne.

induction furnace he needed with navy surplus components and anything he could scrounge. He worked in a basement laboratory in Western Bank and demonstrated to the physics students in the main laboratory, which was still a hut in the quadrangle.[109] Professor Sucksmith seems to have rather enjoyed 'making do'.

The Chemistry department was still partially housed in huts in the quadrangle dating back to 1920, now supplemented by new ones. Its main laboratory within Western Bank was separated from the huts by 84 steps, a number not easily forgotten by those who climbed up and down them several times a day. The desperately-needed new building was in use from 1953 and officially opened in 1954, a wonder to the local press, who were amazed that the blinds and blackboards could go up and down at the touch of a switch.[110] Although the 'Palace of Chemistry' could accommodate 240 students and sixty research staff, it was already too small. The University had decided to expand the department by another fifty per cent and construction of a new wing began almost immediately.

An 'outstanding chemist', Robert Haworth, was Professor of Chemistry from 1939 and guided the department through these years of heady development.[111] He facilitated such inspired appointments at senior level as T. S. Stevens, a future FRS, in 1947 and George Porter, the new Professor of Physical Chemistry, in 1955.[112] Porter, who had been brought up at Thorne near Doncaster, had established his research reputation at Cambridge University. His flash photolysis experiments with R. G. W. Norrish had demonstrated for the first time the way in which molecules split and reassemble during chemical reactions. He improved these techniques in

George Porter was awarded the Nobel Prize for Chemistry in 1967, knighted in 1972 and became a Life Peer in 1990. He left Sheffield in 1966 to become Director of the Royal Institution where his talent for the popularisation of science was used to full effect. Much of his later research was directed towards producing pollution-free fuels.

Pegasus, the University's first computer.

Sheffield, gathering a group of physical chemists whose research reduced the time required for reactions to be measured. Porter, together with Norrish and Manfred Eigen of Germany, was awarded the Nobel Prize for Chemistry in 1967.

Mathematics and the dawn of computing

In 1948 the new Professor of Mathematics, A. G. Walker, created statistics and mathematics laboratories which would 'bring Sheffield into line with other progressive universities'.[113] The first Lecturer in Statistics was appointed. The 'calculating machines' in the statistics laboratory, 'both hand and electrically operated', were reported in breathless terms by the *Gazette* in 1948; this was the first mention of machines whose descendents would later dominate university life.[114] In 1949 there was great public interest in a lecture and exhibition, particularly of tables compiled by Charles Babbage, the Victorian inventor of calculating machines.[115]

In 1955 Deryck Allen became the University's first Professor of Applied Mathematics. His strong interest in computing and 'enviable gift of being able to see far ahead' inspired the decision to team up with the United Steel Companies (USC) to buy the University's first computer, the Pegasus, in 1956.[116] Because there was no room for it at Western Bank, 'Pegasus' was installed at Redlands, a USC building on Tapton House Road, in 1958. The functions of 'Pegasus' were confined to arithmetical calculations and its programs [sic] had to be fed into the machine on punched paper tape, with the results typed onto a teleprinter. A small bank of program tapes, the forerunners of software, was available, but for any non-standard computation a new tape had to be programmed from scratch and errors ironed out. The possibility of errors was a major frustration, since detecting them could 'take as long as writing the program in the first place'.[117] Nothing daunted, the first programming training courses for staff were held in 1958, and basic computing principles were included in the undergraduate mathematics and engineering curriculum. Computing's potential to aid research in all disciplines requiring statistical analysis of data was recognised, but the need for trained staff to write the programs limited its use in the early days. Medical statistics were, however, given special attention from the start. When the Department of Statistics was created in 1955, with the financial support of the USC, its advisory service was in heavy demand from the hospitals and medical departments.[118]

MEDICINE AND THE BIOLOGICAL SCIENCES IN THE LATER 1940s AND 1950s

There was 'a revolution in the medical school' in the post-war years.[119] This revolution was almost entirely administrative, caused by the Goodenough Report of 1944 and the foundation of the National Health Service in 1948. The NHS brought voluntary and public hospitals into one nationalised system and governing bodies were created for the hospital groups, in which the University was more strongly represented than in previous days. The Goodenough Report had the more powerfully direct effect on the universities, however, since it investigated the organisation of medical schools.[120] Having analysed the system by which clinical practice was taught by the 'honoraries' (medical practitioners who derived their income from private practice and were not paid by the hospitals or the universities) it recommended, not surprisingly, that this system had no future. Medical schools needed full-time professors, who would have clinical duties but whose first responsibility would be to their universities. Sheffield had already pioneered a chair of this type, Pharmacology under Mellanby and then Wayne.

The substantial funding necessary for these new chairs was provided by the Ministry of Health. The University Council decided in 1945 to start with a chair of medicine, hoping that by acting quickly it would beat other schools to the best candidates. They were rewarded with a shortlist of great distinction from which Charles Stuart-Harris was appointed.[121] His research on infectious diseases like influenza and bronchitis was definitive and an MRC unit in virus research, under the direction of himself and C. P. Beattie, was established in 1954. Stuart-Harris was a demanding and single-minded leader, nicknamed the 'smiling tiger'. His office was in a dark corner of the Royal Hospital and so functional that a visiting American professor mistook it for the technician's room. Yet Stuart-Harris dominated the medical school until his retirement in 1972. He became a national figure, serving on committees of the UGC, the MRC and the World Health Organisation, and was knighted in 1970. A favourite story recalls an occasion when Stuart-Harris and his colleague Jerry Daly were flying to a conference in Aberdeen. The aeroplane failed twice to take off and appeared to be less than sound mechanically. Daly turned to the professor and said, 'I think we're in trouble here', to which the response was, 'Indeed we are, Daly, it looks as if we shall miss the first paper!'

Student numbers in the post-war medical school doubled in twelve years; from 175 in 1940 to 370 in 1952. It was decided that a full-time administrative dean was needed and J. G. McCrie was recruited from Leeds Medical School in 1947. He 'made a quite outstanding contribution to the development of the Faculty of Medicine'.[122]

The full-time chair in child health was awarded to Ronald Illingworth in 1946. When he arrived at the Children's Hospital it was largely run by visiting general practitioners; by the time he left in 1975 it was one of the best-equipped in the country and its paediatric practice commanded international respect.[123] His own reputation was founded on compassion for children forced to stay in hospital. Traditionally, child patients were routinely isolated from their parents on admission to hospital and permitted few visits. Illingworth pioneered a humane visiting regime, in the face of intense local and national opposition.[124] He allowed parents to stay with their children and built the facilities to make this possible. Illingworth's classic texts on child development, which remained in print for many years, include *The Normal Child* (1953), *Common Symptoms of Disease in Children* (1967) and *Development of Infants and Young Children* (1963). Some of his books were aimed at parents rather than professionals, since he believed that the education of parents was the best guarantee of the health of children.

Charles Stuart-Harris, Sir George Franklin Professor of Medicine from 1946 to 1972. He served as a member of the Medical Research Council and on the World Health Organisation committee on poliomyelitis, and was knighted in 1970.

Ronald Illingworth, the pioneer of academic paediatrics in Sheffield, was a prolific writer, publishing 650 articles and 14 books, some with his wife and collaborator, Cynthia. Most of the books were instant bestsellers and translated into many languages.

The full-time chairs in two other disciplines came somewhat later; obstetrics and gynaecology was awarded to Charles Scott Russell in 1950 and surgery to Richard Pomfret Jepson in 1954. Russell did not give his inaugural lecture in Masson's time because Lady Masson thought his subject unsuitable for a public lecture.[125] He was among the first to demonstrate that maternal smoking in pregnancy can damage the development of the baby.

The medical school had taken a leading public health role in its early days by staffing the routine bacteriological testing laboratories and by engaging the Medical Officer of Health as Professor of Public Health. In 1946 the Department of Bacteriology transferred the testing laboratories, established in 1898, to the city authorities. This had been planned by J. W. Edington, the first Professor of Bacteriology, who was killed with his wife in a head-on car crash in 1939. Under one of Edington's successors, Colin Beattie, the department expanded into the new field of microbiology, appointing a lecturer, S. R. Elsden, to study 'the bacteria that do good'.[126] This research was so successful that a separate Department of Microbiology, only the second in the country, was created under Elsden in 1952.

Biomedical research

The Department of Physiology, which was 'dreadfully run down' after the war, took a major step forward when David Smyth, an Ulsterman, was appointed Professor in 1946. Smyth had already spent the academic year 1939/40 in Sheffield when he was evacuated with the students of University College, London. He had done some research in Krebs's laboratory, an experience which 'meant a very great deal' to him.[127] Under Smyth and Krebs the departments of Biochemistry and Physiology worked together closely and Smyth developed his long-term interest in intestinal absorption, inspired by the research of two lecturers, Quentin Gibson and Gerald Wiseman. Smyth persuaded the international physiological world that a long-held orthodoxy about 'peptic transport' was wrong and that the textbooks should be rewritten. Intestinal absorption dominated the department; Smyth appointed further staff who could contribute to the research and by 1960 there were only two colleagues who were not involved in it.[128]

In the newly created Department of Biochemistry, under Krebs, the atmosphere was relaxed and the minutes of its meetings, 1947–58, are often amusing.[129] 'There was a tentative suggestion that sunny days should be declared holidays'; Mr Bartley suggested 'that flowers would be preferable to empty whisky bottles in the front garden of No 7, Winter Street. Nothing was said about full whisky bottles'. A mirror had at last found its way into the women's cloakroom – 'a sign of real progress in the University'.

In 1945 the Medical Research Council (MRC) decided to create research units on a long-term basis, to avoid the vagaries of funding applications. Krebs, who by then had published 98 papers, was selected to lead a unit based in Sheffield. He recounts with disbelief in his autobiography that, even though the MRC[130] offered to pay half his salary, Masson hesitated to accept because he was worried about the 'dual allegiance' Krebs would have to the University and the MRC. Eventually Krebs's argument that both institutions existed to foster research prevailed. The Unit was given rooms in the Winter Street extension of Western Bank. For several weeks no-one noticed that, through a printing error, their Unit appeared on its new letterhead as 'Unfit for Research in Cell Metabolism'.

Krebs regarded his new research team as 'a close-knit social unit, indeed a family'.[131] The nucleus of this team was 'highly skilled, intensely dedicated and deeply loyal' and somewhat to his surprise, for he was a demanding taskmaster, several members stayed with him for many years.[132] They worked in a large laboratory where ideas and techniques could easily be exchanged and a strong, often robustly critical, camaraderie developed. Krebs had no belief in small laboratories, which he thought less stimulating, less safe and far less educational.

The team was highly successful and the Unit became internationally famous at a time when biochemistry was developing at a ferocious pace and proving its relevance to every biological subject. Krebs received many tempting offers to leave Sheffield, including one from Harvard in 1951, which offered 'a stimulating environment and splendid opportunities' as well as far more space.[133] Krebs was frustrated by his 'grossly inadequate' Sheffield premises and he drafted a memorandum, almost an ultimatum, to the University demanding more room. The result was the conversion of two rooms in the Scala cinema, at the corner of Winter Street and Brook Hill, both with a floor area of 1,000 square feet. The Scala became known as the 'Krebs Empire'. The new premises made it possible to introduce an honours school of biochemistry. Shortly afterwards, in 1953, Krebs was awarded the Nobel Prize for Medicine.

One of Krebs's reasons for rejecting the Harvard offer was the impossibility of taking his research team with him to America. Unfortunately for Sheffield, the loyalty of his staff held firm when Oxford came courting in 1954 with the offer of the Whitley Chair of Biochemistry. The Unit moved, lock, stock and barrel, to Oxford, with all but one of the research staff.

This haemorrhage was inevitably a devastating blow to those left behind, struggling to teach the new honours degree. The financial loss was also considerable, although Krebs left a highly equipped workshop. Who was to follow him as professor? Biochemistry had its own contenders but the radical decision was made to appoint Quentin Gibson from Physiology to the vacant chair. This altered the thrust of the department's research towards physical biochemistry and, in particular, towards Gibson's interest in the chemistry of haemoglobin. Gibson's star rose quickly and he, too, departed; this time for the United States in 1963.

During the 1950s departments like Physiology and Biochemistry began to appoint significant numbers of staff whose background was scientific rather than medical. Although Physiology continued to shoulder a heavy burden of pre-clinical medical teaching, courses for non-medical students were growing in popularity.

The vibrancy of biomedical research at this time led to a department in the new subject of genetics. One of only seven in the country, it was established in 1954

David Smyth, Professor of Physiology 1946–73 and elected FRS in 1967. He served as a pro-vice-chancellor 1962–66, and was in later years actively concerned about the ethics of animal experimentation. After his retirement he wrote Alternatives to animal experiments *(1978).*

under a lecturer, J. M. Thoday, whose standing in the field was so high that he was appointed to the chair at Cambridge in 1959. Alan Roper became Sheffield's first Professor of Genetics in the same year. Roper had obtained his PhD in the Unit for Cell Metabolism and was thus another example of the 'Krebs connection'. Five Sheffield professors worked with Krebs – Alan Roper, David Smyth, Walter Bartley and, later, Rodney Quayle and Frank Woods. Another five from his Sheffield Unit became professors elsewhere, among them Hans Kornberg, who discovered the 'glyoxylate cycle' while working in Krebs's Oxford Unit, and was awarded a knighthood and the chair of Biochemistry at Cambridge.[134]

The new Dental School, 1953

G. L. (Laurie) Roberts became Professor of Dental Surgery in 1935 at the age of 31 and was the chief instigator of the Charles Clifford Dental Hospital, opened in 1943. He is seen here (left) with John Osborne in 1939, when they were the only paid members of his department's staff.

Broom Bank on Glossop Road had been purchased for a dental hospital in 1936, but its development was dogged by the fact that the house was on the proposed site of a new general hospital. These plans pre-dated the war, even though the Hallamshire Hospital was not completed until 1978. In 1947 Broom Bank was demolished, a decision criticised by the local press as the loss of a short-term chance to adapt it for the purposes of the hospital.[135]

The plans of Professor Roberts of the Dental School, however, were ambitious. He initially hoped that the Broom Bank site would be used for a complex containing both the dental hospital and the radium centre, but this proved impracticable. Instead, a new site for the dental school was found on Wellesley Road. When it opened in 1953 it was 'one of the finest dental schools in the country' with laboratories, teaching rooms, a library and common rooms as well as one floor devoted to general treatment and a second, with forty dental chairs, for 'conservative restoration of teeth and peridontal work'.[136] The NHS provided most of the funding, but some of Sir Charles Clifford's legacy was used to buy equipment and the hospital was named after him.

Dental mechanics' workbench in the original premises in the north wing of Western Bank.

THE INSTITUTE OF EDUCATION

Teacher training came under the spotlight of the McNair Report (1944), which was prompted by concern about the poor standard of training in some of the smaller training colleges. The proposed solution was to link each college with a university Education department for the purposes of support and validation – a huge challenge for the universities, particularly as the early schemes would have turned Education departments into the 'ultimate government' of teacher training.[137] Foreseeing problems similar to those encountered in the early days of the Day Training Colleges, the CVCP rejected these schemes and proposed 'Institutes of Education' instead. Colleges were to keep their separate identity, but work in partnership with universities and make co-operative arrangements for examinations.

The Sheffield Institute, founded in 1948, proved to be a demanding but rewarding commitment for the Education department. Attempts by Professor Turnbull to combine the management of both proved impractical and an Institute

The Charles Clifford Dental Hospital was made possible by a bequest of over £77,000 from Sir Charles Clifford. He gave constant support to the University as a member of Council, through the Sheffield Telegraph newspaper, of which he became managing director, and as a donor to its appeals.

director, N. R. Tempest, was appointed in 1949. By 1952, seven local colleges had enrolled as members, boards of studies for each subject in the training course had been established, and examinations for the two- and three-year courses agreed. Headquarters were established at 304 Western Bank, where the Institute provided social and library facilities, attractive not just to students but also to serving teachers, who began to enrol as individuals. The Institute developed an Advanced Certificate in Education for these teachers.[138] Tempest left in 1954 to return to Liverpool and H. C. Dent became the new director. Dent was a prolific and respected educational historian, whose publications included histories of teacher training and of university education. For many years the editor of the *Times Educational Supplement*, he was already in his sixties when he came to Sheffield.[139]

The problem of combining staff and students of both degree and sub-degree level institutions continued. It would only be solved when teaching became a graduate profession, but that development lay in the future.

THE DEPARTMENT OF EXTRA-MURAL STUDIES

The connection between the University and the Workers Educational Association (WEA) remained as strong as ever; indeed Sheffield had the highest number of tutorial classes in the country in 1945.[140] The Vice-Chancellor and the Registrar

Maurice Bruce, the first director of Extra-mural Studies.

took personal pride in the University's contribution to adult education, which was still co-ordinated from Western Bank.[141] Extra-mural departments already existed in some universities and, by 1946, there was an urgent need for one in Sheffield. The only premises available for the new department were in the basement of St John's Methodist Church on Crookes Valley Road. Books collected for the use of classes, which had been stored in a Western Bank cellar, were moved to form the nucleus of an excellent teaching library. A director, Maurice Bruce, was appointed in 1947.[142]

Bruce revived the tradition of the public lecture, inviting well-known speakers and attracting large appreciative audiences. He was 'at his very best' when addressing them, since 'he always valued the big occasion'.[143] Such an occasion, gleefully noted in the University's *Annual Report*, was the lecture series in 1948 commemorating the centenary of '1848: the year of revolutions', when the lecture theatre was full to overflowing and many people were turned away.[144] Other successful lecture series featured 'New Light on the Ancient World' and recent scientific developments. Many of the University's own lecturers participated, although Bruce annoyed some by suggesting that the biggest 'crowd-pullers' came from outside Sheffield.[145]

The core of the department's programme was its weekly adult classes, which required less commitment than the three-year tutorial classes. In addition to the 'liberal' programme, the education of manual workers was a steel cord running through the department, sustaining and developing the traditions of the WEA.[146] The Miners' Day Release scheme became Extra-mural's most important commitment. It started in 1952 when Bert Wynn, the secretary of the Derbyshire Area of the National Union of Mineworkers (NUM), agreed to fund the wages of members taking a day's release from the pit.[147] The NUM traditionally fostered the education of the miners, whose school education was often minimal but who had a keen interest in political, social and industrial issues. In its final form, the day release programme lasted three years, initially with a strong emphasis on industrial relations and economics, later with the addition of cultural studies. It was devised by Ken Alexander of the Economics department and led for many years by Royden Harrison and Michael Barratt-Brown. At its peak, eight out of fourteen departmental staff taught on the programme full-time.

The impact of the Day Release scheme on the lives of its students was immense, summed up by Jim Macfarlane who recalled that when his first tutor said, "'It'll widen your horizons', I thought, that's the first time I knew that I had horizons'. " Jim Macfarlane went on to take a degree, like many others, and then to become a tutor on the course. The majority of students stayed in the pit, but a considerable number went on to leadership of trades unions and local councils. At least ten, among them Dennis Skinner and Eric Varley, became Members of Parliament as did two tutors, John Mendelson and J. T. Park. Kenneth Alexander became a professor at Stirling and then Chancellor of the University of Aberdeen, Royden Harrison went to the chair of social history at Warwick, and Michael Barratt-Brown became the first Principal of the Northern College at Wentworth Castle, the 'Ruskin of the North'.

Extensions to the Engineering buildings down Broad Lane, designed by J. S. Beaumont, architect of the Chemistry building. These buildings reflect the influence of the European modern movement in their emphasis on horizontality with the banding of the windows in the upper storeys and their clean functional lines.

THE APPLIED SCIENCES IN THE LATER 1940s AND 1950s

While the University was building up its extra-mural programme, the tradition of evening classes within the Applied Science faculty was drawing to a close. After the war the long-planned College of Technology, funded by the City Council, took over the sub-degree work of the departments of Metallurgy and Engineering. The transfer of engineering evening classes began in 1949; metallurgy followed in 1951.

This change appears to have been a great relief to the staff, although the full-time lecturers had not been required to teach evening classes since 1942. The central

Laboratory in the new Engineering building.

161

administration, too, felt that the programme had gone on 'too long', but it may be doubted whether its potential students felt the same way.[149] The College of Technology could not compete, especially in its early days, with the expertise and facilities of the University, and the Associateship for industrial employees was a respected local qualification. A campaign to retain the Metallurgy Associateship resulted in an unhappy compromise: selected students from the College could obtain it by attending the University for one year full-time. This lasted until 1965, when the College (Sheffield Polytechnic from 1969) established its own degree in metallurgy.[150] W. H. G. Armytage of the Education department was among many who believed that the transfer of the Associateship in Metallurgy was 'one of the major disasters in this university's history'.[151] A link with the University's adult education roots was severed. This binary divide within the city was not inevitable; some, like Manchester, managed to avoid it.[152]

A more symbolic change in 1948, but a cause of grief to traditionalists, was the disbandment of the Applied Science Committee. Its functions had mostly been subsumed into the central administration but, spiritually if not practically, it had retained some of the fierce independence of the old Technical School. (One man who personified this was Edgar Thackeray, a clerk in the faculty since 1904, who retired after fifty years service in 1954.)

Arthur Quarrell (left) at an Open Day in 1955 explaining exhibits to W. G. Ibberson, the Master Cutler, who was a former student and leading member of Convocation.

The Trades Technical Societies, founded by Ripper in 1918 and still meeting in the University, enjoyed a heyday after the war. These were among the ways by which the University kept in touch with the concerns of local industry, although Arthur Quarrell was keen to promote links at managerial level. Quarrell had worked with the steel industry, especially on alloy steels, and been a member of important industry committees before becoming Professor of Physical Metallurgy in 1950. The friendships he had forged in the industry meant that, 'if I wanted anything I asked for it and I got it'.[153] Quarrell was not impressed by the facilities when he arrived, which compared unfavourably with industry, and he also wanted to improve research. He persuaded local companies to fund several senior research fellowships in ferrous metallurgy.

There was increasing emphasis on postgraduate study and research. Actively encouraged by the UGC, three new postgraduate schools were founded in the early 1950s. Physical Metallurgy was the first and by 1956 'a large proportion' of metallurgy students were postgraduate.[154] The undergraduate degree was more general under Quarrell. A Postgraduate School of Mining supplemented the longstanding undergraduate programme from 1952. Despite the aim of 'improving the supply of better trained minds for UK industry', the majority of students in this school came from overseas.[155] The School of Applied Mechanics was inaugurated by a new professor, W. A. Tuplin, in 1951. He developed a scheme of short courses for industry on gear design, friction and 'servomechanisms' which were very successful. 'A roll-call of the sponsoring firms reads as a Who's Who of British industry'.[156] Tuplin was a mainstay of the Institution of Locomotive Engineers and kept a steam locomotive cab as a hut in his garden, inspiration for his many important articles on the subject of gears.

Just as in science, so there were unprecedented numbers of engineering students in the late 1940s and 1950s, and an urgent need for new accommodation. In 1950, the UGC gave the largest grant the University had yet received for extensions. Professor Swift planned a building which would house three times the pre-war number of students and a much increased population of staff, together with their equipment.[157] The site was next to the Applied Science Building, running down Broad Lane. The slope of the site made it possible to provide basement rooms with considerable headroom for the heavy machinery. When opened in 1955, it housed the whole Department of Civil Engineering and part of Mechanical Engineering. An annual intake of ninety undergraduates was provided for, together with twenty postgraduates. Even in 1956, however, the intake was actually 115 and planning for more extensions began. A Mining block opened in 1957 and another for Fuel Technology and Chemical Engineering in Newcastle Street in 1960. These developments were facilitated by the closure of several roads beyond Mappin Street.

Professor Swift retired once the new building was opened, his job complete. He had run the Engineering faculty since 1936. His meticulous timekeeping was legendary, and his 'First World War pocket watch' was 'the undisputed standard time throughout the faculty'.[158] He was replaced by separate professors for each of the three engineering disciplines. Electrical Engineering, now the biggest department in the Mappin building, did particularly well thereafter. Professor Alex Cullen was well-known in the field of electromagetism and microwaves and set the department on such an advantageous course that it had a second chair by 1967. In 1959 Cullen was awarded £30,500 to construct a ZETA machine for thermonuclear energy research, the first in a university.[159]

Students found some of the engineering courses heavy going, due to the number of lectures and their expectations of rote-learning.[160] The timing of their break, 12. 30 to 1. 30 pm, continued to mean that they missed lunchtime activities in the Union. The first female engineering student, Jean Harrop, who endured 'a lot of leg-pulling', started her course in 1948. The *Sheffield Telegraph* claimed amazement at discovering that she was not 'Amazonian' but slim and only 5 feet 2 inches tall.[161]

W. E. S. Turner retired as the first Professor of Glass Technology in 1945 and was succeeded by Harry Moore. Turner's legacy was so substantial that, to his regret, the department's work could no longer be contained within Elmfield. The increasing amount of industrial consultation and advice was swamping the work of the academic department. A three-way split was arranged. In 1955 the 'British Glass Industry Research Association' (BGIRA) was formed for the industrial section; it moved into new laboratories nearby, on Northumberland Road, in 1959. Lord Halifax, who opened the building, described the work as 'the best kind of co-oper-ation between university, research and industry'.[162] The Society of Glass Technology, formed by Turner in 1916, had its own staff of five by 1953 and moved to Thornton, the home of Dr Gibbons, the late Registrar, on Hallamgate Road.

When Fearnsides retired as Professor of Geology in 1945, the subject was taught as an applied science, a crucial aspect of studies in civil engineering, metallurgy and mining.[163] Most of its students took geology as part of a general degree and few

Violet Dimbleby, who graduated from the University in mathematics, physics and chemistry in 1912, returned as a research assistant to Turner in 1918 in the field of chemical analysis and chemical testing of glass, often working on problems referred by the glass industry. She retired in 1955.

Above: *Teams from the Geology Department completed the first geological maps of Kilimanjaro on two expeditions in 1953 and 1957. This photograph taken from the report shows the kind of terrain that had to be surveyed. The report noted early signs of 'global warming'; the ice at the summit was disappearing because of the rise in external temperature.*

Right: *1957 was the International Geophysical Year and the second Kilimanjaro expedition formed part of Britain's contribution. This picture shows those members of the team who were staff of the Geology department: from the left, Peter Wilkinson, W. H. Wilcockson, Derek Humphries and Charles Downie.*

were allowed to attempt honours (there was only one candidate in 1945). The limited facilities were confined to what one postgraduate described as 'a sort of large glorified hut on the roof of the Mappin Street building' with classrooms on the floor below.[164] Fearnsides himself donated equipment worth £2,840 in his final years, continuing to believe that what Sheffield lacked in resources it made up for by the opportunities for fieldwork in coalmines and on the Derbyshire limestone and millstone grit.[165] Fred Shotton succeeded to the Sorby chair, followed by Leslie Moore in 1949. Moore was 'a larger than life character with a deep West Country accent, who was a brilliant motivator'.[166] Both professors increased the number of honours candidates; one woman student, however, was refused entry in 1949 even though she had come top in the first year examinations. She had to take a geography degree before returning to geology and went on to become the first research student

W. H. Wilcockson conducting a petrology class, in which several of the students seem to have mastered the art of smoking a pipe at the same time as looking down a microscope.

164

in palynology.[167] A former student, Dave Sampson, became director of Geological Services in Tanzania, and invited the department to make the first geological map of Kilimanjaro. The field trips in 1953 and 1957, led by W. H. Wilcockson and involving six members of staff, were gruelling due to the loneliness and barrenness of the terrain and the need to examine every detail. Peter Wilkinson, for example, spent thirteen weeks camping above 10,000 feet without descending. Many of the climbs were pioneering; the result was a map of the whole region. In the 1970s Wilkinson was invited by the Tanzanian government to survey the 'next sheet', Arusha, which he completed in four trips with the aid of colleagues.[168]

Refractories, 'man-made aggregates of minerals', had become a separate discipline by the 1950s and moved out of Geology to form a new department under James White. He became the first Professor of Refractories in the country, sponsored by Dyson Industries, in 1956. White and Bill Ford carried out 'some of the seminal refractories research in the UK', especially on direct-bonded bricks, which became a Sheffield speciality.[169]

THE END OF THE MASSON ERA, 1952

Masson's period of office lasted from 1938 to 1952, a challenging time in the University's history. Government-dictated expansion in the post-war years could hardly be managed except by the use of temporary buildings and the overworking of staff. In addition, the role of the civic universities was changing as they became national, rather than local, institutions with students drawn from much further afield. Some vice-chancellors, like Moberly at Manchester, resisted this; others, like Mountford at Liverpool, embraced and made the best of it.[170] 'Bruce Truscot', the Liverpool professor whose *Red Brick University* (1943) created much debate within the civics, prescribed 'residence and cosmopolitanism' as the only way for these universities to progress.[171]

It is hard to know how much Masson controlled events, and how much they controlled him. Most of the expansion of the post-war years seems to have been forced on him. By the time he retired, the University was twice as big as when he arrived, but its buildings were badly overcrowded and the only new accommodation was in converted churches and houses. Much of the delay in starting new buildings was due to post-war constraints, but other universities completed buildings in the later 1940s.[172] Masson was a serious man more suited to 'making do'. He also exercised his office in an over-punctilious way. Fuel economy was a national concern and a favourite story within the University was that Masson was returning home late from a function in town and saw a light burning in the Department of Biochemistry. The next morning he phoned Professor Krebs to complain about the waste of electricity. Krebs replied that if Masson ever passed his laboratory and found the lights turned off, he wished to be informed immediately, since he expected his research team to be there day and night.[173]

Masson improved the University's administration by abolishing the outmoded Applied Science Committee and extending the influence of the Senate on Council.

At the outbreak of the war Lady Masson, seen here with Lord Halifax, founded the University Tea Club, still active as the University of Sheffield Women's Club. Flora Masson was a prolific watercolourist and a member of the Sheffield Society of Artists.

165

Sligachan River with Sgurr nan Gillean, left *and* Peacock feathers, right, *both by Flora Masson, from a collection of her paintings donated to the University by Sir Irvine Masson after her death.*

He also created two institutions which did a great deal to improve collegiality across the University. The first was his support for the production of the *University of Sheffield Gazette*, a digest of events, personalities and departmental activities, which was distributed among the staff and ran from 1948 until 1980.[174] It was published up to three times a year and contained lengthy articles, some commissioned from members of staff. Secondly, the opening in 1952 of the Staff Club at 197 Brook Hill did, as Masson hoped, bring colleagues from St George's and Western Bank together. Bernard Argent, a Metallurgy lecturer, remembers that in the 1950s 'people from all departments, including the engineers, found time to take lunch there'.[175] Coffee cost 3d per cup.

THE RELUCTANT VICE-CHANCELLOR

Masson was succeeded by J. M. Whittaker, who in 1952 became the second mathematician (after Hicks) to run the University. Whittaker may fairly be dubbed the reluctant Vice-Chancellor, since, in retirement, he told an interviewer that, 'basically I'm not and never have been much interested in university administration'.[176] In 1951 he had been Professor of Pure Mathematics at Liverpool University for nineteen years, but was still only 46. It seemed that there was no other direction in which his career could advance. He was head-hunted for two posts in London, which he refused, but when the Sheffield post became vacant he decided to apply because 'I thought that, really, I must break down sooner or later' and he was 'extremely attracted' by the Sheffield countryside.

Whittaker never gave up his interest in mathematics and several colleagues have testified to coming upon him in his office, working out a calculation at an empty desk. He was also an enthusiast for historic coins, furniture and fine art. As Vice-Chancellor, he proved to be a fluent public speaker who was happy to attend dinners

166

and committee meetings and rebuild bridges with civic leaders – something the Appointing Committee was actively seeking after Masson.[177] Whittaker succeeded so well that he was given the Freedom of the City, a rare honour. He was not interested in national university politics and never became involved in it. Instead, he immersed himself in the life of Western Bank, and he and his wife, Iona, 'a born hostess', became popular members of the Sheffield social scene.[178] Although not an instinctive autocrat, he found it more convenient to keep firm control of all the university committees. He remarked that he always took the chair, 'not from an excessive sense of duty, but simply in order to save myself trouble, because my experience was that if I was in the chair it would almost certainly go the way I wanted. If I wasn't there then it might not. It would be far more trouble for me to put right than to take the chair. '

The Jubilee celebrations 1954/55

The Jubilee celebrations gave Whittaker an opportunity which he grasped with both hands. The commemoration of fifty years since the signing of the University Charter took place in the academic year 1954/55. The Queen, then young and newly-crowned, was invited to visit the University and Whittaker decided to put on a unique performance. The following account is Whittaker's own, from the interview he gave in retirement:

> It occurred to me that when Queen Elizabeth I visited the universities of Oxford and Cambridge, it was the custom for the students to present a masque and this custom was continued in Stuart times but was gradually petering out and came to a complete stop under the Commonwealth. Now I thought that we might revive this because as it happened we had exceptional resources who I was perfectly certain could produce a good show. We had in the first place William Empson, an eminent poet who could write it. Then we had a brilliant student producer, Peter Cheeseman. At that time he intended to be a teacher but it was obvious that he'd got the theatre in his blood . . . Well then we had a girl contralto singer of real operatic quality. She was a big blonde girl who would be perfectly cast as a goddess [Pamela Brown] . . . Then we had a member of staff, Gilbert Kennedy. . . who had a great deal of experience composing and conducting theatrical music . . . Then we had architects [Alec Daykin and colleagues] who had experience of designing sets for theatres.
>
> So we put it up to the Queen that we would like to present a masque. This was in something like May or June 1954 and the actual Jubilee was to be in June '55 when we expected Her Majesty to come. So we received a message that this would be very welcome. Her Majesty would be delighted to come in June '55 and see the masque. Well, then we had an absolute bombshell. Her Majesty would be delighted to come and see the masque but unfortunately she couldn't do so in June '55, she could only come at the end of

The new Vice-Chancellor, Dr J. M. Whittaker.

167

Left: *The glass pavilion from which the royal party watched the masque.*

Right: *The Queen leaving the masque with Lord Halifax.*

October 1954. Now this was, as you can imagine, an appalling spanner in the works. In the first place it lessened the time that we had to a few months. Moreover this included the long vacation, when Empson was going to lecture in America and of course the students would normally be down. But what was far worse was that the masque would have to be presented in the open air, having regard to the number of people that would be expected to come, the prominent industrialists who subscribed to us and that sort of thing, besides the academics. And, of course, it's one thing to present a show in the open air in June and quite different to present it at the end of October. However there was nothing for it. The Queen was coming and she said she'd like to see a masque, so a masque she was going to see.

Fortunately, the members of staff whom Whittaker had selected managed to work to this new deadline and the masque was ready in time. Empson's concept drew on the Elizabethan tradition in which the Queen was flattered as a god. In *The Birth of Steel* she becomes the goddess Minerva, who descends from the sky to show the medieval alchemist, Smith, how to fashion a silver sword and so creates modern steel technology.[179] Empson squared the political circle (he was, after all, a Maoist) by arguing that it was 'somehow politically right. I mean, it combines queen-worship with pro-worker sentiment and fair claims for the university backroom boys'.[180]

Rehearsals for a cast of hundreds, which included a 66-strong orchestra, a brass band and a large choir, were held every night. Pilkington's offered to build an elevated glass pavilion in the quadrangle, so that the Queen could view the masque under cover. However, it was not possible to heat the pavilion and the weather turned nasty:

> The day before she was coming we had a dress rehearsal and it was a really filthy night, the sort of night that you get in late autumn when the rain is coming down in sheets . . . How Kennedy kept his orchestra going under these conditions, I simply cannot conceive. However he did and we could just hold our hands in prayer and hope that it would be better. The next night, it was really, honestly, like a miracle. It was the warmest night that you ever get in Sheffield in the height of summer and this, as I say, was at the very end of October. There was no rain and the heating problem wasn't at all severe and Her Majesty saw it. Afterwards we went to tea and she was quite delighted.

The whole event lasted less than an hour. The following evening, partly to mollify those guests who could not be accommodated the day before, the masque was repeated in a concert which concluded with the 'goddess' singing 'Rule Britannia', written by Thomas Arne for a masque for the Prince of Wales in 1740.

The stress of preparing for this event left vivid memories for Peter Linacre and Eric Bagnall of the administrative staff. They were in charge of the Loyal Address to be presented to the Queen, which had been carefully prepared and placed on an office table. A week before the event, they could not find it and concluded that it had somehow dropped into a wastepaper basket. 'So', Linacre remembered, 'we went down the back lane and emptied about nineteen sacks of rubbish and eventually found the brown paper packet'. Bagnall took the Address home to iron it before it was fit to present to the Queen.[181]

The most positive effect of the Jubilee, in Linacre's view, was that the University was tidied up. Huts which had been in the quadrangle since 1920 were demolished, pavements were relaid and electric lighting replaced the gas mantles in Firth Hall and the corridors. The gas mantles in Firth Hall, 'three great things hanging from the roof', had been 'a pestilential nuisance for many years', especially for students sitting examinations there.[182]

Dr Arthur Chapman, the author of the Jubilee history.

In April 1955, A. W. Chapman's history of the University was published, to general admiration if not universal acclaim.[183] *The Story of a Modern University* is strongest in its account of the University's earliest days, which for detailed and accurate research is matched by the histories of few other universities. Its focus on the central administration, with copious quotes from letters and minutes, at times creates a turgid narrative. As a work of reference, however, it is exemplary, with an impeccable, comprehensive index compiled by Chapman's secretary Margaret Hemmings. As the first warden of Crewe Hall, Chapman's account of its early days sparkles with enthusiasm and, when read today, rekindles the charm of an era which is completely lost.

Chapman's emphasis on the pure and applied sciences was criticised by Eric Laughton, the Professor of Latin, who complained that it compounded the low

Dr Edward Bramley watching the outcome of the toss, and bowling the first ball at the staff-student cricket match which inaugurated the Bramley Playing Fields. He was 87 at this time and went on to celebrate his 101st birthday. 'Sarge' Cofield is the umpire.

public awareness of the University's achievements in the arts.[184] It is, however, undeniable that by 1955 Sheffield's greatest advances had all been made in the scientific and medical faculties. Chapman's history fairly reflects that fact.

The Bramley Fields, 1955

Edward Bramley was a prominent local solicitor who had helped to found the Law department and had even been a student of Firth College. As Pro-Chancellor, he made it his business to look out for land suitable for development near to the University. In 1940 he discovered that four small dams were to be declared redundant by the City Council. With the picturesque names of Misfortune, Ralphs, New and Godfrey, they ran stepwise above the Old Great Dam (now Crookes Valley Boating Lake) and straddled Northumberland Road.[185] After protracted negotiations, which lasted until 1951, Bramley secured the University's right to purchase the dams and fill them in.

In one astute move, Bramley created sixteen acres of land for sports facilities within five minutes walk of Western Bank. This open space, protected from urban sprawl, greatly expanded the vista of greenery on the westward side of the campus and created an arresting view down the valley towards the town centre. In a grandiose, but not entirely inappropriate, comparison, Whittaker suggested that the immediate environment of the University, where its buildings and playing fields were close to civic open space and local shops, churches and houses, was more like Oxford and Cambridge than other civic universities.[186]

The opening of the first Bramley Field (on New Dam) was a fitting celebration of Charter Day, 31 May 1955. A staff-student cricket match was played on the field, at which Dr Bramley, then aged 87, bowled the first ball.

ARCHITECTURAL VISIONS 1952–59

When Whittaker took office, the University had a substantial debt for the first time in many years, and Masson had told his final meeting of the University Court that there was little prospect of achieving many of the planned capital projects in the next quinquennium, 1952–57.[187] Among these were a new library and a new

Students' Union building, both desperately needed. Masson's prediction proved to be correct, but those years were, nevertheless, notable for the enormous strides taken towards fulfilling a vision which others, especially the Pro-Chancellors Edward Bramley and Gerard Young, refused to abandon. Bramley articulated this vision at the 1951 Court meeting:

> A striking university centre, not far from the middle of the city, extending from Northumberland Road to Bolsover Street on the north side of Western Bank . . . On the southern side of Western Bank our buildings will stretch roughly from below J. G. Graves's premises down to Favell Road, and also along Winter Street and Bolsover Street to Weston Street. There will also be the playing fields close by . . . [and] a Hostel centre in most pleasant surroundings extending along nearly the whole of Oakholme Road and a great deal of the north side of Endcliffe Vale Road.[188]

By the end of the 1950s, all that Bramley envisaged for the Western Bank area was built or under construction. In addition, Winter Street had been closed altogether and the J. G. Graves premises had been sold to the University. The 'hostel centre', with two completely new halls, was in hand, and came to fruition in the 1960s.

The City Council started this ball rolling in 1952, by offering a plot of vacant land at the Winter Street entrance to Weston Park, which was ideal for the new library. The library had previously been planned for the other side of Western Bank, next to the Graves Union building, but this land was still covered by housing, which, although compulsorily purchased, could not come into immediate use. The City Council also promised to close Winter Street, once the houses were demolished, so that it could be incorporated into the University site. Gerard Young proposed an architectural competition to design the future layout of the whole area, of a size which Whittaker compared to that of 'the medieval city of Cambridge'.[190] (Oxbridge comparisons seem inescapable at this time – the final plan was likened to a 'modernised Oxford'.)[191]

Every dean was told to provide detailed specifications for the accommodation of his faculty and the competing architects were asked to envisage 3,000 students, a 'daring' target at the time.[192] The competition aroused great interest within the profession. Sheffield's plans offered an exciting opportunity for the post-war generation of young architects – the timing was right and the subject, a new image for a young university, was right too. Ninety-nine submissions were received, all of which were put on public display. The entrants included architects who were to become prominent within their profession – James Stirling, Colin St John Wilson, Alison and Peter Smithson. The winner, announced at the Court meeting in December 1953, was the London firm of Gollins, Melvin, Ward and Partners, a group of young architects of 'high promise'.[193] The firm had already designed the new College of Technology in Pond Street.

The architects summarised the chief features of their winning plan as 'the tall, free-standing Arts Department Block . . . with the low square Library its foil; and

Dr Gerard Young, member of Council from 1947, Treasurer, and Chairman of the Buildings Committee throughout the period of the University's greatest expansion.

171

The model of Gollins, Melvin and Ward's design which won the major architectural competition in 1953 for the expansion of the University.

Architects' drawing of the final version of the development plan in 1957. The various changes between the model stage and the plan as executed included the reorientation of the Arts Tower by ninety degrees.

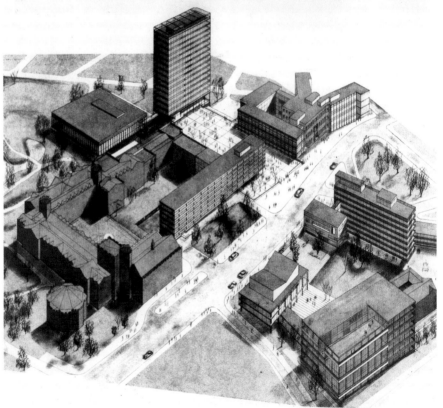

the combined Administration and Physics building [as] the link between the existing University and the Chemistry block'.[194] A new Medical School was to take pride of place on the other side of Western Bank, with an extension to the Students' Union running down Hounsfield Road.

One of the unsuccessful competitors wrote, magnanimously, to the *Sheffield Telegraph* to praise the design as 'the most lucid statement of advanced contemporary architectural thought so far set down in this country'.[195] This reflects the general response, although *The Builder* criticised the fact that the buildings, whatever their function, all looked like each other.[196] To the University Council it was 'a master plan which has thrilling possibilities', although there were worries about the height of the Arts Tower (then planned to be thirteen storeys).[197] To anyone who knows the post-1960 campus, the surprise must be that this was, indeed, the 'master plan', since so few buildings materialised in the way envisaged. The Arts Tower's position was moved by ninety degrees to bring it into closer proximity to the Library. The 'Administration and Physics' building ultimately became the Biology building of the late 1960s, considerably reduced in width. The original plan was to put this building on stilts, creating an 'open ground floor' as a gateway to Tower Court, which thus would have been like an enclosed quadrangle. When the plans were reconsidered in 1957, the University's planning officer, Roy Johnson, grasped the chance to create an open court with the resited Arts Tower as its focus.[198] The Biology building in its final form, however, is compromised by the fact that the original concept was changed so much.

On the other side of Western Bank, nothing resembling the original plan was ever built. This was mainly because of pressure from the UGC to plan for much greater expansion, especially in science and technology. By 1957, the University Council, which had only recently thought that 3,000 was a daring target, had agreed to aim for 4,600 students by 1966. New science buildings were needed and the plans were revised extensively. In addition there were problems with the projected site for the Medical School because it was so close to existing houses on Glossop Lane (now the path between University House and the Octagon), which had 'rights of light'.

The medical school never had a new building at Western Bank. In the 1946 Beaumont plan it had been placed opposite the projected 'new Infirmary' on Glossop Road and was moved back to Western Bank in the Gollins plan because of the uncertainty of the hospital's development.[199] The majority of its departments stayed in the Western Bank building until the early 1970s, expanding into space vacated when other new buildings opened. Medicine also benefited from the long-planned completion of a new teaching block for Surgery and Therapeutics at the Royal Infirmary in 1955, described as 'the first-born of the union between the teaching hospitals and the University'.[200]

The projected 'Physics and Administration' building was on the site of fine Georgian houses which were still serviceable to the Arts faculty and so it was decided to build a tall Mathematics and Physics block at the top of Hounsfield Road. University House, planned for that site but not as tall as the Physics building, was moved to the problematic Glossop Lane site. Extensions to house the extra

THE LAST OF THE UNIVERSITY TRAMS

On 5 May 1957 the last No.194 tram to Crookes ran past the University. The students sent a 'mourning party' to the terminus in its honour. Having gathered round the tram front with accordion and guitars, they sang the National Anthem and a song entitled 'Death to the Internal Combustion Engine'. This picture appeared on the front page of Darts.

chemistry students were planned in two new wings of the Chemistry building, running as far as Bolsover Street.

The new roadscape

By 1956, demolition had begun in Winter Street and also in Bolsover Street, which had to be widened to become the new main road from Walkley. Buses on Bolsover Street replaced the Walkley tram which had previously rattled past the east side of the Western Bank building. A steel chimney for the University's new boiler house, 111 feet tall, was erected on the proposed site of the Arts Tower in 1958, with Whittaker apologising that it would 'assault the skyscape' for at least five years before incorporation into the Tower.[201]

Just as the University was beginning major construction work next to the Students' Union building, the Sheffield Corporation decided that the volume of traffic and number of accidents dictated that Western Bank should be widened to a dual carriageway. Lecturers, students and administrators alike were horrified at the prospect of a larger, faster road carving through the new campus, especially as an alternative scheme existed in which the extra traffic was routed through a tunnel under Brook Hill.[202] Arthur Chapman and Roy Johnson put a brave face on their inability to reverse this decision, telling the *Sheffield Telegraph* in 1959 that the new central reservation was a boon, making it easier for students to cross the road.[203] In fact, the University lost considerably, not least the grass verges and trees which had lined Western Bank on either side. It took a change of heart by the Corporation and a piece of brilliant thinking to reunite the campus ten years later.

The Main Library

Below: *The caretaker's house at the bottom of Back Lane, shortly to disappear to make way for the new Library.*

Right: *T. S. Eliot at the opening ceremony for the Library.*

Sheffield, Liverpool and Manchester had pioneered purpose-built libraries before the First World War, but Sheffield's beautiful Edgar Allen building was hopelessly inadequate by 1930. By 1944, Liverpool and Manchester had already rebuilt, but Sheffield's *ad hoc* solution, the 'steel basement', was full and working conditions in the library were taxing the patience of its staff and readers on a daily basis.[204] Books

were constantly moved, the numerical sequence of shelving had broken down, and seating space was so cramped that it was filled as soon as the Library opened, and disappointed students were forced to go to the Central Library in town to find a place to work.

The English lecture theatre was converted into an overflow library soon after the war, but the only permanent solution was a new building. The new librarian, Sidney Peyton, produced specifications, which included a large reading room with immediately accessible shelves for the most heavily-used books, a capacious stack, a catalogue hall, a periodicals room and plenty of separate workrooms and offices for the staff.[205]

The first plans, for a site on the south side of Western Bank, had to be abandoned but they were in all crucial respects similar to those used for the new site on Winter

The new Library:

Clockwise from top left, the reading room looking towards Weston Park, the principal staircase from ground level, the catalogue hall and the exterior.

175

Sidney Peyton, University Librarian from 1941 to 1956. Peyton received the honorary degree of LittD in acknowledgement of his role in bringing the new Library to fruition.

Street.[206] Both sites were hilly and used the slope to build a four-tier stack beneath the main reading room. The great advantage of Winter Street was the outlook over Weston Park, utilised to its full advantage by the Gollins design of 1953, which placed the Reading Room on a level with the park, approached by two flights of stairs from the main entrance, twenty feet below. This internal route is one of the Library's finest features – 'an extended, generous, enticing and apparently gradual rise from cloakroom level'.[207] A mezzanine floor was included, with turnstiles, the 'pamphlet store' and offices for the Librarian and secretaries. On the main floor, the catalogue hall led to a periodicals room (on the right) and to the reading room, lined by bookshelves on the entrance side and with plate glass windows overlooking the park. This huge room, 152 feet by 53 feet and two storeys high, embodied Peyton's dream, that 'readers may work undisturbed, for there is no through passage-way nor are any administrative functions performed within it'.[208] The generous, even over-generous, allocation of space was typical of Peyton's concern for students who had nowhere else to work. As his successor, J. E. Tolson, explained, 'only a small proportion live in halls of residence and enjoy the amenity of a private room as well as the hall library . . . it is not always our books that students want, but often simply a quiet place where they can work or read on their own'.[209] It may be noted that Philip Larkin, a contemporary university librarian, found that the provision of an unsupervised hut with 200 seats relieved his Hull library considerably.

The Library was designed for the long term and to hold one million books – 200,000 on opening and an assumed increase of 10,000 books a year for eighty years. Peyton's foresight was crucial to ensuring that the Library remains serviceable in the 21st century, despite the huge expansion of the University. One mistake was the decision to make the stacks windowless, poky and inaccessible. Peyton did not intend readers to use them, since all books were to be brought up by the librarians. Even the highest stack (number four) would have been inaccessible from the reading room had not Dr Whittaker, at a late stage, insisted that a staircase should be built between the two.[210] This stack proved after some years to be essential for the periodicals collection; stack three also came to be used by readers, but both proved to be pretty cramped workspaces.

For several years, the library staff waited whilst a cavernous hole was dug in Weston Park – the foundations for the stacks. When the Library was complete, at Easter 1959, it was too late to move the books before examinations started. The result was that the Library contained only twelve rare books at the opening ceremony on 12 May. Empson's friend T. S. Eliot opened the Library, describing it as 'the most modern in the country'.[211] The assembled librarians of every other university (except Cambridge, noted *The Guardian*) appear to have agreed.[212] The empty reading room proved a magnificent location for a higher degree ceremony attended by 800 people. Honorary degrees were awarded to T. S. Eliot and Hans Krebs, and Sidney Peyton, who had by then retired as Librarian, deservedly received a LittD.

A hectic shuttle of vans moved the books, in numerical sequence, in July 1959. Special permission was given for the vans to drive through the park and the staff worked in two teams, one at the old and one at the new library, every day for three

J. E. Tolson, the Librarian from 1956 to 1974. He supervised the move to the new Library and later helped to found the Postgraduate School of Librarianship.

weeks. Jim Tolson, the new Librarian, was from time to time heard singing among the bookshelves. One of his staff recalled that, 'on the proud day when the Library finally opened for business, we revelled in all the extra space and the ease of movement around the building with lifts and trolleys'.[213] There were no lifts in the Edgar Allen Building.

Western Bank after the Library move

With the library removed, the administrative staff, crammed into a few offices on the Firth Hall corridor, had room to breathe. Edgar Allen's octagonal building was the subject of an inspired conversion. The upper gallery bays of the old Library were enclosed in glass to create a suite of offices for the Vice-Chancellor and his staff. The librarians' desk on the lower floor was moved and the spiral staircase covered over to create the Registrar's department.

The old History Library became a new Council Chamber, always referred to as the Tapestry Room, and the true legacy of Jack Whittaker. As a connoisseur of fine art, he decided to decorate the walls with tapestries to rival those at Hardwick Hall. He found a 1720 Beauvais tapestry in a shop in London and chose a second which complemented the first so well that a visiting architect was convinced that both had been made for the room.[214] To enhance the effect, he also bought a fine pair of mirrors, made for a great northern house. The Beauvais tapestry, sited to overlook the Council members, became the focus of many a meditation during meetings, with the aggressive-looking man in red appearing to be admirably cast as the UGC on the warpath. The second tapestry was stolen in the 1980s and has never been retrieved.

THE 'SCHOLARSHIP' STUDENTS

By the end of the 1950s, the post-war influx of mature students had passed, although National Service remained a requirement until 1960. Some universities, like Oxford and Cambridge, encouraged applicants to complete their military obligation first; at others, including Sheffield, it appears that the majority deferred their National Service until after graduation. Thus the majority of students were aged 18–21, the profile which has endured ever since. Most students lived away from home and most were in receipt of a local authority grant. (In 1951, 85 per cent already had a grant; the 'pledge' to teach was abandoned in that year.) This created a new breed – the scholarship boy or girl who did not plan to teach. Alf Walker recalls:

> Me Mam and me knew nothing about universities, but a man at County Hall in Lincoln offered to pay so I thought I might as well go . . . I decided on Sheffield because it was first to accept me. I studied economics because I didn't need School Certificate Latin.[215]

Some grants were insufficient for hall fees, but Alf could afford to live in Crewe Hall. 'There was a library with wood panelled walls, a real coal fire and deep arm

chairs in green leather; I'd never sat in a deep leather arm chair before . . . There
were tennis, squash and fives courts, table tennis, a darkroom and congenial
company. Crewe Hall was perfect'. Angela Dixon was just as enthralled by the
University Hall (which changed its name to Halifax in 1959 in honour of the Chancellor who died that year). Even in the late 1950s they wore black undergraduate
gowns for every meal and often paraded in them during their 'constitutional, post-
prandial' walk to the Botanical Gardens.[216] There was a conservatism about many
things, including dress and food. Brian Lowthian remembers that in the new
Stephenson Hall, opened in 1952, there was 'uproar' when curry was served at the
evening meal. 'No-one would eat it. Most had no idea what it was. Some said it was
a way of foisting bad meat on us'.[217] Alf Walker and all his friends wore 'the sports
jackets and grey flannels we arrived in, our only clothing indulgence a striped
student scarf'. Brian Lowthian bought no new clothes during his six years in
Sheffield.

For entertainment, there were the Hallé concerts at the City Hall, popular with
many students, together with the cinema and pubs like the 'Fox and Duck' in
Broomhill. 'For special celebrations', Alf Walker and his friends took the box next
to the stage at the Attercliffe Palace, where they used 'pea-shooters to make the bare
ladies of the cast move, as they stood in poses the Lord Chancellor decreed should
be unmoving'.[218]

Men still greatly out-numbered women, but there were far more overseas
students than before the war. In 1956 Narayan Swamy, the secretary of the Indian

Narayan Swamy (centre), a research student in civil engineering, had a successful career at Sheffield, retiring as a professor in 1994. One of his duties as President of the Union in 1957 was to act as ex officio macebearer at a special honorary degree ceremony in hospital for G. H. B. Ward, the noted campaigner for public access for walkers.

Society, was elected Union President – not only the first Indian student to be President, but also the first from Engineering for a long time. The University reception for overseas students arriving at Midland Station started in 1957.

By the late 1950s, the Students' Union was so crowded that Graves Hall was simultaneously used for eating and for meetings. Debates were well attended and there was, for example, a student march to oppose apartheid in 1959. The pressure on the Union was slightly eased in 1955/56 by the purchase of 13 Leavygreave for the use of committees, and by the promise of UGC funding for a new Union building. While haggling went on over the plans for this extension, students heard that the University planned to run the kitchen there. Complaining that this would make their food more expensive, the students boycotted the Western Bank Refectory in January 1958 and were photographed by the press brewing tea on the steps of the building.[219] Female students served extra snacks in the Union and some science students made fish and chips in the lab. The story made all the newspapers, including the *Manchester Guardian* and *The Times*.

This was the first substantial student protest against the University authorities, but not, of course, the last. The tide was turning.

The new Stephenson Hall was opened in May 1952 by the Chancellor, Lord Halifax, who commented that 'corporate life . . . must be the essentially true part of education'. The pictures show the new extensions and dining hall.

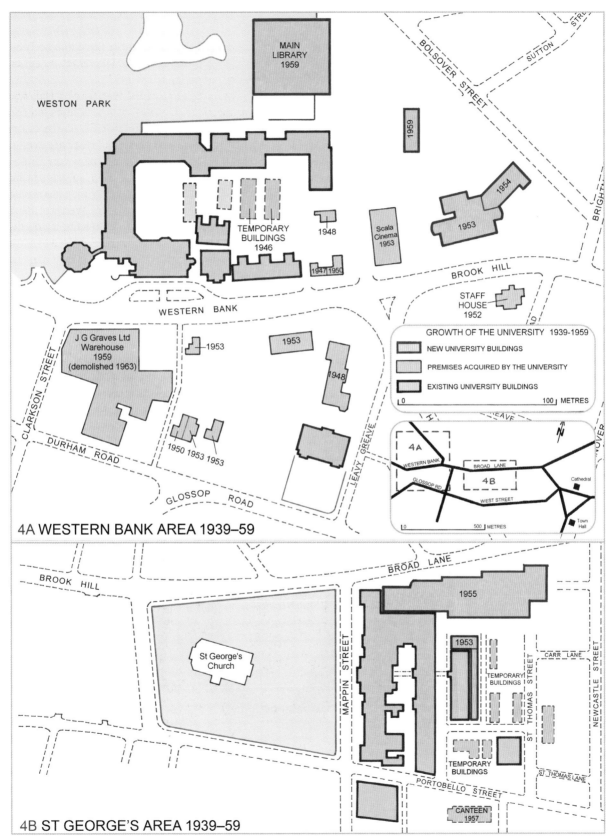

MAIN LIBRARY 1959

WESTON PARK

1959

1954

1953

TEMPORARY BUILDINGS 1946

1948

Scala Cinema 1953

1947/1950

BOLSOVER STREET

SUTTON

BRIGHT

BROOK HILL

STAFF HOUSE 1952

WESTERN BANK

J G Graves Ltd Warehouse 1959 (demolished 1963)

1953

1953

1948

CLARKSON STREET

DURHAM ROAD

1950 1953 1953

GLOSSOP ROAD

LEAVY GREAVE

GROWTH OF THE UNIVERSITY 1939–1959

☐ NEW UNIVERSITY BUILDINGS

☐ PREMISES ACQUIRED BY THE UNIVERSITY

☐ EXISTING UNIVERSITY BUILDINGS

0   100 METRES

4A

WESTERN BANK

GLOSSOP RD

BROAD LANE

4B

WEST STREET

Cathedral

Town Hall

N

0   500 METRES

4A WESTERN BANK AREA 1939–59

BROAD LANE

BROOK HILL

1955

St George's Church

MAPPIN STREET

1953

ST THOMAS STREET

CARR LANE

TEMPORARY BUILDINGS

NEWCASTLE STREET

TEMPORARY BUILDINGS

ST THOMAS LANE

PORTOBELLO STREET

CANTEEN 1957

4B ST GEORGE'S AREA 1939–59

Maps © Crown Copyright Ordnance Survey

5

Tower Blocks and Transformation: The Sixties

THE 'ROBBINS' ERA

A NEW AND MOST DISTINGUISHED Chancellor was inaugurated in May 1960. R. A. Butler was the statesman whose Education Act (1944) 'recast the national education service' for the post-war period and built on the educational initiatives of two Sheffield vice-chancellors, Fisher and Hadow.[1] Butler had only one disadvantage to overcome – he was not a Yorkshireman like his predecessor, Lord Halifax.[2] His speeches at graduations often focussed on his famous Act, which could be tedious for staff, but one Registrar had its true significance brought home to him by the student who said, 'But that thrilled me enormously. You see, I was a product of his Act'.[3] It was the improvement in secondary education after 1944 which delivered the sixth formers clamouring for university places in the 1960s.

The Conservative government of which Butler was Home Secretary in 1960 was committed to funding the expansion of higher education on a grand scale. By 1962, local authority grants, which included the payment of tuition fees, were guaranteed for all university students. Butler himself had made 'unprecedented' funds available to the UGC for the first wave of post-war buildings when he was Chancellor of the Exchequer (1951–55).[4] The Robbins Report of 1963 is usually regarded as the engine of expansion, but eight new 'plate glass' universities were already building on their green-field sites by 1963.[5] Some technical colleges had been upgraded and every civic university had been expanding for at least seven years. The Robbins Report, however, was 'the first attempt to co-ordinate the development of a system of higher education in modern Britain' and enshrined the principle that a place in

Facing page: Four Rings by Austin Wright, made in 1960 and acquired for the University in 1982 from an exhibition of Wright's work organised by the University Fine Art Society.

183

Portrait of Lord Butler by Martin Rose, 1977.

higher education should be available for every 18-year-old who could benefit from it.[6] It set an even more ambitious expansion target, to which the existing universities responded by offering to provide 20,000 more places than Robbins proposed.[7] Some bids were therefore doomed to disappointment. Sheffield wanted to expand to 5,540 places by 1967 but was told that only 5,200 would be required. This was just 331 more than the pre-Robbins target.[8] The civic universities overall, however, accommodated 25,000 extra students between 1962/63 and 1967/68. Many of their courses were in the arts and social sciences; the demand for science was over-estimated by politicians, especially the Labour governments of 1964–70 which created eight technological universities and thirty polytechnics, instituting the 'binary divide' which lasted until 1992.[9]

The over-provision in science and technology meant that even in 1966 Sheffield had some vacant places; nationally there were 1,600 vacancies.[10] The University gave Lord Robbins an honorary doctorate in 1967, but in many ways his Report made things more difficult. The Bursar, R. M. Urquhart, recalled that in 1959 he said 'that we could merrily proceed on our expansion on the assumption that two out of the extra three students would be in science or technology; then came Robbins, and the UGC said, "I'm sorry boys, it's a free for all"'. Plans already half-way to fulfilment made it inevitable that there would be too much provision for Metallurgy and Chemistry, and probably Fuel Technology and Physics as well.

The lack of applicants was a crushing disappointment to those who had championed the expansion of science and technology. Frederick Dainton, then Vice-Chancellor of Nottingham and later successor to Butler as Sheffield's Chancellor, was asked to lead a national enquiry into the reasons and concluded that there was a 'swing away from science' among sixth-formers who perceived it as too intellectually demanding.[11] In Sheffield, perhaps unfairly, some of the negative impact was blamed on the fact that the University had no 'national profile' at this time.[12] Whittaker was not interested in 'mixing myself up in the sort of thing that goes on in London' and refused to become involved in the CVCP. He had been appointed to improve the local profile of the University, which he did very well. However, an interest in national politics and national decision-making was becoming crucial for a vice-chancellor – and had always been advantageous.

Sheffield's expansion started before the Robbins Report; indeed the increase in undergraduate numbers was 39 per cent during 1960–65 and rather less, 34 per cent, during 1965–70. By 1969 the popularity of arts and social sciences led to the adjustment of its student targets upwards by 5 per cent (from 38 to 43 per cent) and correspondingly downwards for science (from 62 to 57 per cent).[13] Student numbers not only increased dramatically, by 87 per cent during the sixties, but were more evenly distributed between the faculties.

Staff numbers, inevitably, did not rise at a corresponding rate and there were many instances of overcrowded classes, especially in the early sixties. Later on, UGC funding was generous; for example 125 new academic posts were funded in the years 1965–67. By the end of the decade the staff-student ratio was restored.[14] Many of the new appointments were young lecturers, who brought freshness and a radical outlook to the campus. The number of women staff also rose appreciably in all faculties except Engineering (see Appendix 4), although the ratio of female to male staff was still no more than one in ten before the 1970s. Halsey and Trow, in their famous study of sixties academics, found the same to be true nationwide and concluded that women 'were a small minority . . . who tend to concentrate in the lower ranks'.[15]

THE SIXTIES BUILDING BOOM

By 1960 the south side of Western Bank was 'one vast building site'.[16] The Hicks building for Mathematics and Physics was under construction on Hounsfield Road at the same time as the foundations to University House and the Union extensions were being laid. All over the site, houses had been demolished until only the Graves Students' Union building remained in splendid isolation, deprived of some of its windows while the link building was constructed. The Union remained open, but for almost two years it could only be reached via a 'Bailey bridge' which entered the building at ground floor level. Built in two days by twenty members of the OTC, it was dubbed 'the bridge of sighs' by *The Star* because the girls had trouble going

The 'vast building site' photographed in April 1960 showing the new Students' Union site in the centre foreground with the Hicks Building going up to its right. The new University Library is clearly visible and the Haworth wing of Chemistry is under construction next to the Scala Cinema.

185

Sheffield Newspapers picture of a Bailey bridge being built by the OTC to give access to the Union building during construction work. To the left, the Hicks Building is making good progress.

over it in stiletto heels. The unsympathetic response from the OTC was that 'the bridge was designed for tanks, not women'.[17]

The University's building boom coincided with high local demand for building labour and materials, as housing estates mushroomed all over Sheffield, and the site for the Hicks building proved to have unforeseen technical problems. The Mathematics, Physics and Statistics departments finally moved in during the summer of 1962. The hopes of staff who had been working in condemned houses and inadequate accommodation in Western Bank were fulfilled. For the first time, Mathematics staff had private rooms with blackboards and there was a student lounge 'to enable students of all departments to meet and discuss problems over refreshments'.[18] The first on-campus university computer was installed on the top floor; one early user found that the best way to untangle the rolls of paper tape was to suspend them from the window. The computer was in great demand; an engineering student doing a final-year project remembers the special privilege of being let into the computer room after hours by the operator – and buying him a beer afterwards.

By 1961 mealtime queues in the Students' Union stretched outside the building, but relief on a splendid scale came the following year. The new University House had two refectories and two coffee bars (which were, despite the student protests, run by the University). A link block containing 'the longest Union bar in the country' joined University House to the original Graves building.[19] The students now had a Union building of generous size; one which has adjusted and expanded to meet the demands of subsequent years. The Union was the centre of most students' social lives; the Saturday night 'hops' in the Lower Refectory were almost

186

compulsory. In the early sixties the group might be The Stan Hardcastle Quartet and the dance still ended with the singing of student songs. Glenn Miller and Joe Loss were popular, especially with 'public school types'.[20] The end of this era, and with it the lingering impact of the post-war generation, came quickly. The 1963 Treasurer of the Entertainments Committee recalls that Sheffield was one of the first Unions to book nationally-famous pop groups. 'We were regarded as the leader – the new Union building had just opened and we could draw in good crowds'.[21] The Lower Refectory throbbed to the amplified beat of top-rated bands like The Drifters, Manfred Mann, Cream and the Kinks. Joe Cocker, who was brought up on Tasker Road in Crookes, and The Who played at the Union Ball in 1968.

University House contained a spacious new Senior Common Room on floor five, in which Dr Whittaker took great pride. It became a popular meeting place, and not just at lunchtime. Staff dances were held and there was plenty of conviviality even on Saturday mornings.

The red-letter year in the development of the campus was 1962. In addition to University House and the Hicks building, the Bursar's department (on the site of the old gymnasium) was completed in January and major extensions to Halifax Hall in July. Other buildings were nearing completion, but even at this rate construction was not keeping pace with demand.[22] The 3,000 student mark was reached by 1960, with 4,600 envisaged for 1966 and 5,200 before 1970. Extensions were being planned

Hicks Building shortly after completion in 1962, when Hounsfield Road still joined Western Bank, and Ward's Bookshop and its neighbours occupied the corner site. The right of way along Leavygreave was maintained by separating the lecture block from staff rooms and laboratories and connecting them by a bridge. Western Bank looks deserted by comparison with 2005.

Above: *The upper refectory, University House.*

Right: *The exterior of University House from Glossop Road. Designed by Gollins, Melvin and Ward it is an elegant composition of ground floor columns, a blue engineering brick panel at the first level and stylish glazed and balconied upper storeys. The effect is one of lightness and balance.*

Sir Stuart Goodwin, the founder of the University's Athletics Centre.

before the original buildings were completed. The Hicks building, for example, had two floors added to the plan after building had started, and the construction of extra workshops on Hounsfield Road began as soon as the main block was finished.

The constant revision of plans and the need to control escalating costs put enormous pressure on the staff and lay officers in charge of planning and development. Gerard Young, the chairman of the Buildings Committee until January 1967, Roderick Urquhart, the Bursar from 1952 to 1966, Roy Johnson, the Planning Officer, and Arthur Connell, the University Treasurer, proved more than equal to the challenge. With the help of Stephen Welsh, Professor of Architecture, Urquhart devised guidance notes for architects, surveyors and engineers, 'which spelt out exactly what we wanted them to do, and how they were supposed to do it, and produced schemes for regular reports on costs'.[23] These reports gave the Buildings Committee control and 'in the end the excess costs on buildings became the exception rather than the rule'. Gerard Young, who gave unstinting time to the University, was 'a wonderful stimulator', preparing a set of New Year resolutions for the Committee every year. Even so, they found that it was impossible to go from drawing-board to new building in less than four, often five, years. The job of supervising building progress became so large that the office of Director of Works was created, to which Noel Costain was appointed in 1964.

The Goodwin Athletics Centre

Sometimes all that was needed was the generosity of a grateful man. Sir Stuart Goodwin, the head of Neepsend Tool and Steel Corporation, had been seriously ill in his youth and restored to health by the Department of Pharmacology in Edward Mellanby's time (see Chapter 3, p111).[24] Almost forty years later, he approached Gerard Young with the unexpected offer of £30,000 towards the cost of building a sports hall on the Bramley Fields. He had learned from 'Sarge' Cofield that the University would have to demolish the outdated gymnasium on Western Bank to make way for the Bursar's department.[25] The result was 'the best gymnasium in the country', opened in October 1960.[26] Cofield was the king of vastly improved facilities: the hall, 120 feet long, could be adapted for physical training, indoor athletics, tennis, basketball, badminton, hockey, football, golf and cricket nets and enabled him to coach fencing to international standard. Its versatility even extended to a pit for high jump and pole vault. A new roadway alongside Elmfield led to the gymnasium and to an adjacent block of changing rooms containing forty showers.

Once involved in the sports project, Sir Stuart was hooked. He discovered that the University had no swimming pool (since that project had been abandoned in 1939) and he determined to remedy this as well. Gerard Young was presented with two cheques for £30,000 – equal amounts from Sir Stuart and his wife to cover the cost of £60,000. He sprang a third surprise when, at the opening ceremony for the gymnasium, he announced a final phase to provide squash and fives courts, and indoor cricket wickets.

The swimming pool, together with a second gymnasium, opened in 1963. Within five years, Sir Stuart and Lady Goodwin's gifts, totalling £173,000, created athletics facilities which were the envy of other universities and a major attraction to prospective students. In gratitude, the students made Sir Stuart the Honorary President of the Union. 'We were on cloud nine', said one basketball enthusiast who had used the old gymnasium in his first year.

Cofield persuaded members of staff to take an interest in the sports teams. Urquhart became President of the hockey team and Chapman of swimming while Tim Eley, the Assistant Bursar, took on rugby, Leslie Moore, Professor of Geology, the football team and Harry Kay, Professor of Psychology, presided over women's hockey. All were invited to the annual Athletics Dinner, which was 'done up to the standard of the Dorchester hotel banquet' with excellent speakers and 'all the spit and polish that Cofield could muster'.[27] When Cofield retired, after 37 years, in 1967, Sir Stuart named the pool 'Sarge Cofield Swimming Pool'.

A chillingly familiar sight – examinations in the gym.

Left: The Olympic-size swimming pool funded by Sir Stuart and Lady Goodwin and named in honour of 'Sarge' Cofield.

Below: The new Goodwin Athletics Centre and the playing pitches. Elmfield is to the left.

The Arts Tower rising over the University and the city. According to Professor Armytage, every time the planning group for the building met, the height went up by two storeys. It finally reached nineteen storeys and was the tallest university teaching building in the country.

The Arts Tower

The building for Arts envisaged by Gollins, Melvin and Ward in 1953 went through several radical changes during the planning stages. It was moved to become the focal point of 'Tower Court' and its specifications extended to some Architecture and Social Science departments. Members of the design group, which had academic representation from the three faculties, amused themselves drawing plans in a choice of shapes.[28] Whittaker's took the form of a 'DSO' Medal with lecture theatres in a wedge, the same shape as his office in the old library, which, he believed, maximised the available window space.[29] After all this invention, the group finally decided simply to build a 'cube of steel, glass and concrete'.[30] Six more storeys were added to the original thirteen, including two for which Young and Connell found funding when the UGC refused to pay. If they had not done so, 'we would have been in a hell of a mess', according to the Professor of Ancient History, Robert Hopper.[31]

Public interest was intense even before the first hole was dug. Tower blocks were new and exciting and the building boom was changing the cityscape. The Arts Tower's commanding position on high ground ensured that it would be seen from any viewpoint. Some of its occupants would themselves be at the forefront of the renaissance. The Architecture departments were allocated the upper floors because, Urquhart told *The Star*, it would give them 'a very good view over Sheffield to see all the town planning which is going on'.[32]

With foundations on solid rock thirty feet below Tower Court, the Arts Tower took almost four years to build. It was 'topped-out' in October 1964 in a ceremony which tested the nerve of everyone except the Vice-Chancellor. The only means of joining the builders for the traditional glass of beer on the roof was the open hoist on the outside of the building. Roy Johnson recalled that it was a 'pretty rickety thing' which 'just shot up' without any speed control. Many entered it with trepidation, but Whittaker hardly turned a hair.

Eighteen departments and 160 staff were housed in the Arts Tower. Lecture theatres for 1,000 students were on the lower ground floor, which extended underneath Tower Court. It was an arrangement much admired by the architectural correspondent of the *Financial Times*, who commented that it ensured the maximum amount of courtyard at ground level and enhanced the dramatic effect of the Tower's position as the focal point of the Western Bank campus.[33] The entrance hall had the same generous ceiling height as the Main Library, to which it was linked by a bridge from the mezzanine floor.

For Robert Hopper, the move into the Tower, during the 1965 summer vacation, came as a 'blessed relief'.[34] Departments which had been scattered between houses were together for the first time, with at least one floor allocated to each. Many of the staff had private offices, also for the first time, although only those of professors were fully carpeted.

The building was opened by the Queen Mother in June 1966 at a ceremony which everyone enjoyed because she was not only charming but also well prepared. Peter

Left: *Dr Whittaker carrying out the 'topping out' ceremony.*

Right: *The Chancellor, Lord Butler, greeting the Queen Mother on the occasion of the opening of the Arts Tower in June 1966.*

Beneath the Arts Tower, the lower foyer provides access to thirteen lecture theatres. In later years a student café was also created at this level.

Linacre, who had organised several royal visits, admired the fact that she 'did everything she was supposed to do' despite arriving late.[35] The Professor of Spanish, Frank Pierce, said that his admiration for the Queen Mother on this occasion 'almost made me into a monarchist'.[36] The Main Library reading room was once again used for a degree ceremony, at which the Queen Mother was made a Doctor of Music. This unexpected choice was disarmingly accepted with the words:

> I shall always particularly value this doctorate of music because the Vice-Chancellor was so persuasive in presenting me for the degree that he almost succeeded in convincing me that I fully deserved it.[37]

Every kind of tower, from the Tower of Babel to the Leaning Tower and, inevitably, the ivory tower received a reference in her speech until she plumped for 'the tower of light and learning' as the metaphor for Sheffield's new building.[38]

Among the users of the tower of light and learning, the major talking point was the vagaries of the Paternoster lift. It had been recognised early in the planning stages that vertical transport would be a problem, especially on the hour, when large numbers of students and staff would be moving between teaching rooms. There was room for only four lift shafts, no matter how many floors there were. It was decided to use two for high-speed lifts, primarily to the upper floors, and the other two for the Paternoster, a revolutionary solution since few had been built and none of the size needed in Sheffield. The Paternoster's mechanism was best described by the *Yorkshire Post* as 'like the big wheel in fairgrounds'.[39] It moved slowly without stopping, taking two people in each of 38 cars, and allowed easy movement between floors. The idea that it would 'continuously circulate', a favourite phrase in University publicity, became a bad joke when it was realised how easily the Paternoster could be brought to a stop. The trip wire on each compartment, essential for safety reasons, could be triggered by any troublemaker and every stop caused a substantial delay while longsuffering porters investigated the cause. The unhappy inhabitants of the cars at such times could be stuck in a position where it was impossible to climb out. George Porter recalled an occasion when he and his wife attended a tea party given by the Vice-Chancellor on the thirteenth floor:

> We travelled smoothly in the new wondrous Paternoster lift until, as our heads appeared above the thirteenth floor, we were able to see our host receiving the guests. As he turned to greet us the lift stopped, leaving us about neck level to the floor. The Vice-Chancellor immediately joined us, though necessarily at a higher level, and during the twenty minutes which passed before the lift could be started again, graciously served us with tea on the floor. This is typical of Sheffield hospitality.[40]

Responding to a question about memorable parts of the University, nearly all former students mentioned the Paternoster. Second and third year students liked to scare 'freshers' by emerging from the top of the shaft doing a handstand to 'prove' that the cars turned right over. For some the memories are very good: 'if you could persuade one of your female friends to accompany you, there was time for a good kiss as you went round [in the basement]'; 'by judicious use of the trip wire you could get stuck in one of the cars with a particularly attractive girl, which gave time for a chat-up'.

Stories of the Tower's 'sway' persist; it is slight but measurable and certainly perceptible on windy days to the architects, who have inhabited the top floors for the whole of its existence. The Tower also creates a wind tunnel underneath the bridge to the Library and visitors were frequently drenched by the fountains which originally adorned moats at the main entrance. One librarian had an alarming experience during a particularly cold winter when a long icicle from the side of the Tower shattered his window in the Library and landed on his desk.[41]

The end of the building boom

The initial finance for the building boom was provided by the UGC in 1957/58, and supplemented by a University appeal in 1960 which raised £500,000. The UGC continued to provide regular funds until 1964, when it suddenly announced that Sheffield would have no building allocation whatsoever for 1966. This was a shock and several projects were put on hold, although planning for the Biology building was sufficiently advanced to allow construction to begin in 1965. Built in stages, it took six years to complete.

A casualty of the UGC cut-backs was the treasured theatre project. A distinctive oval design, 'like a great ostrich egg', had been developed by Gollins, Melvin and Ward for a 614-seat arena on Western Bank to serve as a concert and assembly hall, theatre and cinema.[42] The idea of a larger, multi-purpose replacement for Firth Hall

The planned University theatre was, unfortunately, a victim of UGC cutbacks. The 'great ostrich egg' would have been an eye-catching feature of the campus. This model is partly cut away to show the internal layout as well as the exterior.

had been nurtured since the days of Pickard-Cambridge and included in the Beaumont development plan of 1946. In 1958 a site was earmarked next to University House and a covered way planned to link the theatre to the House's catering facilities.[43] The UGC agreed to allocate £175,000 and completion of the theatre by 1965 was confidently predicted.[44] Early in 1963, however, the UGC revoked the funding, apparently because the hectic pace of university expansion left nothing for luxuries like a theatre. The local press, which had taken a great interest in the plans, complained that 'a university is more than a collection of lecture halls, libraries and laboratories' and that recreation was as important as academic work.[45] It also hoped, of course, that the theatre would be a general amenity for Sheffield – as it would have been. The Drama Studio, which opened in 1970 (pp. 244–5), was the compromise outcome of a dream which had once been much greater.

The proposed site of the theatre was later landscaped and became a popular spot to congregate outdoors in hot weather. A more spacious site for an assembly hall, which was finally used twenty years later, became available when the University was offered the empty premises of J. G. Graves Ltd, directly opposite the Western Bank building. Urquhart and Whittaker decided that it could be adapted for the use of Biology and secured UGC funding to buy it, before discovering that the cost of the conversion would be 'ridiculous'.[46] The only other option was demolition. In truth, the building was an eyesore, festooned with drainpipes; 'just about the ugliest building in Sheffield'.[47] The University was happy to get rid of it, but it was certainly unfortunate that, for the next twenty years, this key site had no other use than as 'the country's most expensive car park'.[48] It was finally used for the Octagon Centre in 1982/83.

HOUSING THE SIXTIES STUDENTS

The new halls at Endcliffe

During the sixties the number of places in student halls rose from under 600 to well over 2,000. This was entirely due to the energetic Buildings Committee and to the support of Jack Whittaker – all the halls were planned in his time, although the final two were not completed until after his retirement. He and Young recognised that Crewe and Stephenson were 'much too small' and that halls taking several hundred students each were needed.[49] They rejected the alternative solution, apparently adopted by some other urban universities, of leaving students to find their own housing.[50]

Looking up Clarkson Street with the J. G. Graves building to the right.

In 1955, two Architecture lecturers, Victor Jackson and Alec Daykin, were commissioned to produce a masterplan for an extensive residential campus at Endcliffe, utilising the properties of Endcliffe Grange and Endcliffe Vale House next to Halifax Hall.[51] They hoped to build new halls there and to close the bottom of Oakholme Road, so that Stephenson and Crewe Halls would become part of the 'parkland' site. There would have been a chapel, with a fine central mall and a perimeter road servicing the halls at the rear.

This vision ran into opposition from local residents (exercised behind the scenes by people with influence).[52] The University was allowed to demolish two large houses (the last decade, Urquhart commented, that it could have done so) but had great trouble with its plans for the 'third men's hall'. Some denizens of Endcliffe Crescent, an exclusive and tranquil Victorian enclave to the rear of the site, objected to the destruction of trees and other amenities to build a hall just beyond their garden walls.[53] Attempting to limit the impact on the ground, the Buildings Committee decided to build a tower block.[54]

The result was that Sorby Hall pleased neither the Buildings Committee nor the neighbours. Its height, ten floors, was intrusive; far more than a low level development would have been. Initially favourable reaction from Endcliffe Crescent turned to objection just as contracts were exchanged. Young afterwards regretted the attempt at compromise, and regarded Sorby as 'a nasty building'. The Committee did not make the same mistake for the adjacent 'fourth men's hall', which became Earnshaw. A new architect, Tom Mellor of Lytham St Anne's, was employed to develop a low-level scheme. It proved so successful that he was also invited to work on the 'second women's hall', which became Tapton.

Sorby Hall was ready for the start of the 1963/64 session, but, as Arthur Connell recalls, there was a last minute crisis caused by the discovery that the specially-designed beds would not fit in the lifts. The problem was solved by 'Sarge' Cofield, who 'marshalled the rugby club . . . and said, "This is your training for the beginning of the season, boys – get those beds up those stairs!"'[55] Sorby is remembered with affection by many students as 'a delightful place to live and study'. Societies and balls sprang into being and there was generous staffing, led by Arthur Quarrell as Warden with Deryck Allen as his Deputy.

Sorby Hall was ten storeys high and accommodated 378 male students. Its name honoured H. C. Sorby in the Jubilee year of the founding of the Department of Geology. This contemporary picture shows Sorby Hall when first built, down to the original blinds and curtains, red and blue on alternate floors. The architects were Hadfield, Cawkwell and Davidson, also responsible for the Halifax Hall extension.

Above: *Halifax Hall with the 1963 extension to the right.*

Right: *The architect of Earnshaw, Tom Mellor, successfully used the saw-tooth arrangement of the façade to maximise the view and the building's orientation. It contrasts with the slab block of neighbouring Sorby by using medium rise in brick around landscaped courtyards.*

The extension to Halifax Hall, started in 1961 and completed in 1963, was designed during the ill-fated flirtation with towers at Endcliffe. This was kept to seven storeys, however, and the Hall's impressive garden was preserved almost intact (a new road was built round its perimeter). The large dining hall, with plate glass windows, was designed to take maximum advantage of the garden view. The *Sheffield Telegraph* commented that 'bluestocking hairdos' would be a thing of the past thanks to 'a hair-dressing room with salon-type driers where they can style their own fashionable sets'.[56]

The design of Earnshaw Hall, opened in 1965, was imaginative and felicitous, blending in with the environment. It consisted of small four-storey residential units, each with between fifty and eighty study-bedrooms, and a separate single-storey block with the central facilities of dining and common rooms. The 'tooth-edge façade' on the bedroom blocks created rooms with a pentagonal shape. The name commemorated Samuel Earnshaw, 'the distinguished mathematician who succeeded Mark Firth as President of Firth College'.[57] According to Leslie Moore, the first warden, it was the most lavish hall the University had built, with the best staff-student ratio.[58] A former student recalls that they were 'waited on hand and foot' and had their rooms cleaned and beds made every day.

Hall rules continued to be strict throughout the sixties. Professor Moore seemed to one student 'like a disapproving headmaster who didn't entirely regard us as sensible adults'. The most unpopular rules, naturally, concerned visits by the opposite sex. At Halifax, known as the 'Virgins' retreat' to some, men were not officially allowed private visits until 1967. However, according to former residents, boyfriends were often smuggled in and out after hours and Dr Mowat's assumption that 'her girls were good girls' was 'far from the truth'. A favourite, quite possibly apocryphal, story among Sorby students was that Professor Quarrell was walking his basset hound in the grounds of the hall when he saw a naked woman standing at a bedroom window. He raced back to apprehend the culprit, but she was never discovered. The moral of this story was 'shut the curtains'. There were expulsions from hall, including one Sorby president, for entertaining out of hours.

Despite the jokes, many students found the restrictions patronising. A student who helped to stop 'initiation' ceremonies at Stephenson in 1963 said that 'the rules on entertaining women seemed to be designed to encourage regression toward childhood rather than adult behaviour'. Rules were one of the main reasons why some students chose not to live in hall.

When asked about sex in the sixties, fear of pregnancy was often mentioned as a deterrent by students from the pre-Pill years: 'buying condoms was still a hugely embarrassing experience'. Even students from the mid-sixties often responded that 'sex had not been invented'. However, attitudes were changing. One woman reports her 'thrill' at discovering that the Student Health Service gave the Pill to unmarried women (from 1967). Sorby students campaigned for a condom vending machine, which was approved by the Warden in 1970.[59] By then, the University authorities were no longer acting *in loco parentis* for those under 21, since the age of majority was lowered to 18 in 1969.

Students go self-catering

The majority of students were still living in 'digs' all over Sheffield in the early sixties. Journeys to the University could be long and there are vivid memories of bus rides through industrial areas where 'the lurid glow from the furnaces looked like the gates of hell through the thick smog on winter nights'. 'I can remember during the half-hour walk from my digs in the morning going past very dirty and noisy cutlery factories and tasting the sulphur in my mouth'. These are the last such student memories, since the Clean Air Acts dispelled most of the smog by 1963.[60] Many lodgings were a true 'home from home' and students often stayed in them for the full three years. To take one example, a house in Pitsmoor was 'absolutely marvellous . . . [not] as well equipped or comfortable as the digs others had in more middle class areas . . . but [the landlady] was an ace cook and stood no nonsense in the nicest possible way'. A few were highly unsuitable. There was an acute student accommodation crisis in the early sixties, partially solved by the new halls, but also by twisting the arms of the householders of Sheffield. Staff were asked to take students into their homes at the start of each year until 1966. Five members of the academic staff were designated 'censors' in 1961 to assist the Warden of Lodgings in her attempts to regulate behaviour in lodgings.

The Staff-Student Committee was in the forefront of changing all this. It challenged the assumption that students would not live anywhere which did not serve them with breakfast and a hot evening meal, and urged the authorities to consider the entirely novel possibility of self-catering student flats.[61] A working party of staff, staff wives and students investigated the arrangements at other universities and concluded that conversion of suitable properties for small groups of about six was the ideal. The first student flats, available only to postgraduates, were in eight converted terraced houses in Victoria Street, near the Jessop Hospital. Opened in 1966, each flat offered five single bedrooms, a bathroom and a kitchen with a separate 'food locker' for each student.[62] In 1968 Florey Lodge, an annexe of Halifax Hall, also became self-catering.

Revolutionary changes were made to the accommodation rules during the sixties. In 1961 it was a big concession to allow students over 21 to find their own accommodation.[63] The Union adopted a policy of 'free choice of accommodation for all' in 1966 and this was conceded for all students over 18 in 1969. The accommodation did not even have to be university-approved, although this was still available.[64] Tessie Ball's era had passed and she retired as the Warden of Lodgings, to be replaced in 1969 by Jack Dorgan, with the new title of Accommodation Officer.

By 1967 1,700 students were living in self-catering flats, with demand exceeding supply. They had freedom, although privately-owned flats could be dreadful. 'They were tips; student houses nowadays are palaces in comparison', was one comment. Another student shared a flat in Shirecliffe Hall, a 'stately home' which was in fact due for demolition and rat-infested. Despite this, he was happy there. Lodgings had become 'universally unpopular', according to a student survey,[65] and by 1967, for the first time in many years, there was no shortage of them.

The first mixed halls – Ranmoor and Tapton

The next hall, opened in 1968, was the biggest in the University and amongst the largest in the country with 617 study-bedrooms. It was called Ranmoor House; the old Ranmoor House had closed when Sorby opened. The new Ranmoor was also on Fulwood Road, on a site of ten acres bought from the Freemasons, who retained their headquarters to the rear.[66] It was designed as a men's hall and was originally going to be run as two smaller units. Like Earnshaw, it had a number of four-storey blocks, linked by covered ways and paths to a central catering and recreation block. The design was considerably more utilitarian than Earnshaw, however, especially in the bedroom size and the internal concrete and brickwork finishes which, it was said, were 'aimed at producing a robust, masculine character'.[67] A clinic with twenty beds was part of the plan and all other University sick bays closed when Ranmoor Clinic opened.

Despite the economies, students from the first intake to Ranmoor recall that 'it was like going to a five star hotel', apart from the 'sea of mud' in grounds which had not yet been landscaped. It became the first mixed hall, with men in the west wing and women in the east wing, because of the delay in opening the 'second women's hall', Tapton, due to cut-backs in UGC funding. The need for women's accommodation was acute and so it was decided to divide Ranmoor between male and female students for its first year, 1968/69. The formidable Edith Mary Johnston, of the History department, was appointed women's warden and Deryck Allen was men's warden. The mixing proved successful and was extended to Tapton, even though this meant abandoning the idea of the second women's hall.[68] The proportion of hall places was said to reflect the proportion of sexes in the University.

Tapton Hall was built on the former Hallamgate Works on Crookes Road, at some distance from the other halls. It was the last residential hall to be built by the University and the smallest of the new ones, accommodating 266 students. Perhaps for that reason, its profile was initially lower than that of Ranmoor, which gained something of a radical reputation, especially once its blocks went mixed (individual floors continued to be segregated for some time). Ranmoor was large enough to have a vibrant social life – Hall Balls were ambitious and the Folk Club was 'probably the best in Sheffield'.[69]

Ranmoor House was built on a nine acre site and was restricted by the vendor of the land to four storeys and a distance of 75 feet from Fulwood Road. Designed by Hadfield, Cawkwell and Davidson it was the first University building which employed prefabricated building techniques, using large precast concrete panels.

Tapton Hall, where the architect Tom Mellor again favoured the saw-tooth façade he had used at Earnshaw.

Chapman and the foundation of UCCA

Arthur Chapman retired as Registrar in 1963. He had served Sheffield 'with a rare devotion for more than forty years' and was appointed first OBE and then CBE.[70] His triple roles as Senior Lecturer in Chemistry, first Warden of Crewe, and Registrar were unequalled. More than 1,000 members of the university community subscribed to his retirement gifts. He received an honorary degree in 1964, for once the actor and not the stage-manager.[71] Chapman was a meticulous and enthusiastic ceremony-organiser, insisting on full rehearsals.

'A great Registrar and a great personality', Chapman also left an important legacy to the whole of higher education, through his contribution to the creation of UCCA (later UCAS), the central application system. Chapman was a member of a committee set up by the CVCP in 1957 to introduce order into the chaos of individual university admission systems. Each university had its own application form, there was no limit on the number of applications a candidate could make, and universities were often not informed when an offer had been firmly accepted elsewhere. With the expansion of higher education, this system would become untenable. The committee proposed the solution of a centralised system, and Chapman chaired a working group which devised its essential elements. His succinct report, produced in only six months, outlined:

> a central office through which every candidate would apply to enter one of the institutions of his choice. The office would distribute his applications to the institutions, record their results, inform the candidate and, wherever necessary, carry out a clearing-up operation after the main selections are over. The principal tool of the central office would be a data-processing system using an electronic computer which can make practicable an otherwise impossibly large and complicated task.[72]

Keith Kelsall, Professor of Sociological Studies, was a member of the working group; he had previously conducted an enquiry which showed the extent of the admissions problem.[73] Staff at Western Bank assisted Chapman, particularly Peter Linacre who, a colleague said, was 'built into the bricks' of UCCA.[74] They monitored the 'running in' year, 1962/63, during which 'nobody knew what they were doing', and eased many teething problems.[75] Sheffield's contribution to UCCA was thus of central importance to its early success. Chapman continued to work on UCCA even after his retirement.[76] Peter Linacre took pride in the fact that Sheffield often received the largest number of UCCA applications. Every golden disc ('Top of the Unipops') commemorating this achievement was hung prominently above his desk.

The Academic Development Committee

There have been many hundreds of committees in the life of the University, but probably only one which deserves its own section in this History. The Academic

Development Committee (ADC) was not only unique and genuinely innovative when it was formed in 1964, but has remained central to the deliberations of the University ever since. The Committee is composed of academics elected by Senate and has responsibility for academic planning. The vice-chancellor is a member *ex officio* but not the chairman. This was a revolution since, as the historian V. H. H. Green points out, the charters of civic universities tended to concentrate power in the hands of the established order and 'prevented younger men and women from having any significant say in the government of the university or in moulding academic policy'.[77]

The story of the ADC goes back to 1956 when some of the 'young Turks' among the professoriate were becoming disenchanted with their lack of influence on university decision-making.[78] Senate had a large membership that was dominated, in their opinion, by the 'old guard', whose outlook was that of the parochial pre-war University. In addition, they felt that the academic view was inadequately represented on Council and central committees. Frank Pierce, Robert Hopper and Harry Armytage became the ringleaders of a plot to get two academics elected to Council via a nomination of the Court. The Court was a large formal annual assembly and it had seldom known such excitement or, indeed, an election of any kind. Robert Hopper and the much-loved Physics lecturer, Joe Clarke, were returned at the top of the poll.

This episode was embarrassing for Whittaker and his officers, but they responded to the palace revolution by increasing the academic representation on committees. Gerard Young, in particular, accepted the value of more academic input. Senate, however, continued, in the view of some younger professors, to 'waste its time by emotional discussions . . . [which] never really changed any decisions that had been made by other bodies'.[79] A ginger group from all faculties held evening meetings at members' homes to co-ordinate policy offensives.[80] Their primary aim was a forum for long-term strategic planning free from the petty details of day-to-day housekeeping. Their recommendation for a small sub-committee of Senate, to be called the Academic Development Committee, was adopted in 1964. Nine members were chosen by Senate in an election which had no reserved places for deans or pro-vice-chancellors. The result was not, in fact, a clean sweep for the ginger group and the first ADC was a fair representation of all the Senate. It included, for example, veteran professors Eric Laughton and David Smyth. Harry Kay, the new Professor of Psychology, was the first chairman, a young, forward-thinking strategist who, in Laughton's opinion, was 'ideal' and 'absolutely impartial'.[81] He may be regarded as the founder of the ADC. Kay's respect for its achievements can be judged by the fact that he immediately created a replica at the University of Exeter when he became Vice-Chancellor there in 1973.[82]

One of the ADC's first acts was to examine Sheffield's degree structure in the light of the Robbins Report's encouragement for broader first degrees, and the fact that the new universities were providing a wider range of honours courses. At Sheffield and some other civics, forty per cent of students still emerged with an ordinary degree.[83] Honours students were selected on the basis of the Intermediate examination; they took four subjects in the first year (three in Pure Science), and then went on to a single honours programme.

The Intermediate examination had been designed for students who arrived with School Certificate qualifications and had become outdated, since 'A' Level courses were introduced in the early 1950s and students were thus better prepared for university-level study. The examination was abolished in 1965/66, except in the Law faculty, where the 'Intermediate' had recognised professional standing. In other faculties it was replaced by the 'first university examination'. All students now read for an honours degree, with the option of a 'Pass' for those who performed poorly in the final examinations.

At the same time, new honours degrees were created in subjects which had not previously had one, like Music, Russian, Prehistory & Archaeology, and Statistics. The ADC was keen to promote more general and interdisciplinary studies and the Faculty of Pure Science retained a general honours degree until 1988. An attempt to create an interdisciplinary 'Bachelor of Philosophy' degree failed, but the spirit of generalism survived through the creation of dual honours degrees. Bernard Crick, the new Professor of Politics, was one of those who strongly advocated duals, although he had to admit by 1970 that provision outstripped demand. He developed one of the most successful dual degrees, History and Politics, but there were always more candidates for single honours Politics.[84] Single honours degrees remained popular throughout the University and the majority of students graduated with them after the revolution of 1965/66.

THE BURGEONING SOCIAL SCIENCES

The sixties were the decade of expansion in the arts and, particularly, social sciences. Many of the new post-Robbins universities focussed on these subjects and applications soared, both to them and to Sheffield. A Faculty of Economics and Social Studies was created in 1959 and expanded at an incredible pace, 740 per cent by 1969. Three new departments, each with a chair, were created: Business Studies in 1962, Economic History in 1963, and Political Theory and Institutions in 1965.

From 1967 the faculty was known simply as 'Social Sciences', but Economics nurtured each of the three new departments and was still the dominant subject, at least for first-year students.[85] The first Dean was the Economics Professor, Jack Gilbert, whose routines were legendary. At the start of a lecture he 'walked in, deposited an upturned bowler on the table, mounted the platform and peeled off his gloves, deposited them in his hat, reached for a pole to open the window, then commenced'.[86] A colleague described him as 'a constant in an era of bewildering and rapid change'.[87]

Economic History had a proud tradition in Sheffield, going back to the first Economics Professor Douglas Knoop and his successor G. P. Jones (1948–57). Sidney Pollard came to Sheffield to work under Jones as the first Knoop Research Fellow in 1950 and was subsequently elected to the first chair. Pollard's career was, in the words of his colleague Colin Holmes, 'a resounding triumph over adversity'.[88] His parents were driven from their home in Vienna to the Leopoldstadt ghetto in 1938 when Pollard, then called Siegfried Polliak, was thirteen. They secured a place for him on the *Kindertransporte* to Britain, but did not themselves survive the Holocaust. Pollard never lost the feeling of 'not wholly belonging anywhere', but his outstanding academic abilities in mathematics and economics led to his acceptance by the London School of Economics and graduation with first class honours in 1949. His first work was *A History of Labour in Sheffield* (1959), which made a seminal contribution to the new genre of labour history. His versatility was demonstrated in works of business history, like *The Genesis of Modern Management* (1965), which he deemed his most satisfying, and surveys like *The Wasting of the British Economy* (1982). Pollard soon had the largest postgraduate school of economic historians in the country; the department was so popular that seven lecturers had been appointed by 1965.[89]

Sidney Pollard was Professor of Economic History from 1963 to 1980, having joined the Department of Economics in 1950. He spent several years at the University of Bielefeld in Germany in the 1980s, before returning to Sheffield.

Bernard Crick, the first Professor of Politics, came from the London School of Economics in 1965 where he had already published a classic text, *In Defence of Politics*.[90] In his own entertaining account, he arrived two hours late for his interview and so 'felt I couldn't very well refuse' when offered the chair.[91] He was only 35 at the time. Crick was an unconventional and combative character who liked nothing better than a heated debate with Union officers or baiting the 'old guard' at Faculty board meetings. He was famously discovered sleeping in his room in the Arts Tower; his family home was in London.[92] He was the ideal person to build up a new department since he maintained a high profile, writing regularly for *The Observer*, and was 'an academic entrepreneur', inviting leading thinkers from London to visit the department.[93] Crick's lectures 'dazzled' many students and influenced their thinking for years to come.[94] Royden Harrison, the author of *Before the Socialists*, transferred from the Extramural department to join Crick; within a few years he was appointed Professor of History at Warwick.

Bernard Crick encouraged mature students into the department and enjoyed teaching them so much that he left Sheffield for Birkbeck College, London, in 1971.

Bernard Crick is to the left, pictured with Michael Foot MP and Anthony Arblaster. He considered Sheffield to be 'a solid and commonsensical place, with no false airs but great competence'. It is entirely typical of Crick that his Who's Who entry used to list his club as the fictitious Attercliffe Working Men's (Non-Political) Club. His many publications include a biography of George Orwell (1980).

David Blunkett in his student days with the redoubtable Ruby, not always the most reliable of guide-dogs and fond of chasing the ducks in Weston Park.

George Clayton was Newton-Chambers Professor of Applied Economics 1967–83, Dean of Social Sciences 1968–71, Pro-Vice-Chancellor 1978–82, and Warden of Sorby Hall 1971–80. 'An urbane and democratic pillar of the University', in the words of his Times obituary.

At Sheffield, his most celebrated mature student was David Blunkett, the future leader of Sheffield City Council and member of Labour governments as Education Secretary and Home Secretary. Bernard Crick arranged for him and his guide-dog Ruby to have the use of a room on the Politics floor of the Arts Tower. Blunkett recalls that, because the Paternoster was impossible for them and the lift usually full, they often started the day by climbing all ten flights of stairs.[95] Fellow students helped him by reading books onto tape and he used a Braille typewriter to transcribe recorded lectures. He became a City Councillor while still a student. His graduation in July 1972 was accompanied by tremendous applause, spiked with gasps when it appeared that Ruby was going to pull him over the edge of the City Hall stage. Ruby loved flowers and the stage was lined with them.

The Politics department had another blind student, Brian Campbell, at the same time as Blunkett. The University's first blind student was Edward Kaulsuss, also mature, who graduated in 1945 to 'one of the greatest rounds of applause ever given by the students'.[96]

Sociological Studies took off in the early sixties, with buoyant student demand for its new honours degree. The department was regarded as one of the best in the country, a tribute to the work of its first professor Keith Kelsall, who introduced the honours school.[97] The workload for lecturers was demanding: Trevor Noble recalls that, 'I was in no way exceptionally burdened, but in my first year in the department I was required to present a 48-lecture main undergraduate course, a 22-lecture applied sociology option, plus seminars for both, [and] tutor four first-year tutorial groups'.[98] Kelsall was also Dean and followed his 'Kelsall Report' for the CVCP with a 'gigantic survey' of 6,000 women teachers.[99] He was one of the founding members of the British Sociological Association. The social policy and social administration side of the department's work was the responsibility of Eric Sainsbury and Kathleen Ovens, who supervised the postgraduate programme for trainee social workers which replaced the old Certificate in Social Studies in 1962.

A new Department of Business Studies had been created under Douglas Hague in 1957, at a time when business studies was emerging as a subject for academic research and teaching at postgraduate level.[100] In the early sixties the government was keen to create two business schools of Harvard standards of excellence. Manchester and London were selected for this role, a decision which angered some in the University, like Gerard Young.[101] There was however, an ongoing debate in the faculty about the proper response of a university to this practical subject. This emerged after Hague had left (for Manchester) and a new professor, A. J. Merrett, proposed that the chair's designation should be changed from 'Applied Economics' to 'Finance' and the department merged with Accountancy. The proposal was rejected; a decision which significantly changed the direction of the department. After Merrett's departure for London, his successor George Clayton adopted a more conventional approach.[102] During his sixteen years in the chair, Clayton advised institutions all over the world on financial policy-making and wrote influential, and highly readable, publications on the United Kingdom's financial system, the banking and insurance sectors, and exchange rate policies. He was a lecturer of 'relaxed charm' and a colleague who was 'always a team player', undertaking the deanship a year after his arrival and acting as the first chairman of a multi-professorial unit, the Division of Economic Studies, which linked the economics departments in 1970. George Clayton also served as a pro-vice-chancellor in the difficult years 1978–82 and as a 'resolute and fair-minded, good humoured, and sociable' Warden of Sorby Hall.[103] He was a deservedly popular man.

Roy Marshall, Professor of Law 1956–69. His distinguished career led to a CBE in 1968 and a knighthood in 1974.

THE LAW FACULTY TAKES OFF

Law celebrated fifty years as a faculty in 1959, but the cygnet had taken all of those years to become a swan. In 1956/57, there were still only thirteen full-time students in the faculty. Like other subjects, its students had disappeared during the war but, unlike other subjects, they did not reappear in large numbers thereafter. The problems were largely external but frustrating to Denis Browne, the Professor and Dean since 1936, who moved to the Queen Victoria Chair of Law at Liverpool in 1955. Browne, who was intensely sociable and friendly, was held to be one of the University's wittiest Public Orators, renowned for 'scintillating, polished and graceful speeches of almost matchless quality'.[104]

He was succeeded by Roy Marshall, aged 36, a practised administrator, who came from University College, London, where he had already been appointed Sub-Dean of the Law Faculty at the age of 29.[105] Born in Barbados, he was a Barbados Scholar at the University of Cambridge from 1938. At Sheffield he set to work on the Law department, recognising that the course would not catch on unless it was made attractive to undergraduates who might wish to study the subject for its educational value, without committing themselves to following the legal profession.[106] He widened the syllabuses, employed more staff and increased the number of tutorials, believing that 'the give and take of discussion is the basis of sound Law teaching'.[107] Recruitment improved by leaps and bounds, reaching an intake of fifty to the LLB degree by 1965. Marshall attracted some able students from his own country, like Baden Prince, a most successful Student President in 1963 and later a conciliation officer for the Race Relations Board.[108]

In 1958 the department moved from Leavygreave to more spacious, but scarcely adequate, premises in Shearwood Mount, a former nursing and maternity home next door to the Department of Architecture. David McClean, who arrived as a lecturer in 1961, said the facilities were a 'culture shock' for people who had come from Oxford, or even from bigger civics like Manchester.[109] The basement flooded and the lecturers had tiny rooms which looked like 'a rather crowded bus' when students were squeezed in for tutorials. Roy Marshall, however, was particularly happy with the great improvements to the Library.[110]

The former nursing home at the top of Shearwood Road which was the home of the Law Department from 1958, and later taken over by English Literature.

Marshall's dynamic energies soon extended beyond his Sheffield commitments. He served on many race relations committees and from 1963 to 1965 was seconded to the University of Ife, Nigeria, as founding Dean of Law. In 1969 he left Sheffield to become Vice-Chancellor of the University of the West Indies. Later he became Secretary-General of the CVCP and Vice-Chancellor of Hull. He maintained his

Frank Pierce was Professor of Spanish 1953–80, Dean of Arts 1964–67, and a founder member of the Academic Development Committee. He published several major books on medieval Spanish literature. His energy and zest for life caused George Clayton to comment, 'He was the sort of person who could enter a revolving door behind you and come out in front of you'.

Geoffrey Bownas, the first Professor of Japanese Studies 1966–80, developed his skill in oriental languages during war service with the Intelligence Corps. This photograph shows him, centre, at the opening of the Centre for Japanese Studies.

links with Sheffield throughout, as a visiting professor. To mark the hundredth birthday of Edward Bramley, the founder of the Law department, Marshall's chair was named the 'Edward Bramley Chair of Law' in December 1967.[111] Some of the lecturers whom Marshall recruited – John Wood, Graham Battersby and David McClean – stayed with the department for many years and proved crucial to its continuing success and growth.

ARTS, ARCHITECTURE AND EDUCATION BEFORE AND AFTER THE ARTS TOWER

The University's first female professor succeeded F. F. Bruce in the chair of Biblical History and Literature in October 1959. Aileen Guilding had been a lecturer in the department since 1948 and published a major study of St John's Gospel in 1960.[112] Deteriorating health forced her to resign the chair in 1965. It was two years before the appointment of her successor, James Atkinson, widely known for his work on Martin Luther and the Protestant Reformation.[113] He quoted Luther on every possible occasion, and was an inspirational speaker and memorable Public Orator. As a Canon of the Church of England, Atkinson was the first ordained professor; and the first to take the new title of 'Biblical Studies'. It was his abiding belief that the church needed continuous reformation through 'returning again and again to the biblical texts'.[114]

It was no coincidence that Frank Pierce was Dean of the faculty during a buoyant period for modern languages. Pierce was Hughes Professor of Spanish, a gregarious Irishman, who was 'an enthusiastic proponent of Hispanism' in the widest sense.[115] The department flourished under his leadership with 'a distinctive dedication, enthusiasm and mateyness . . . that has hardly been matched anywhere'.[116] The department's *velada teatral*, a social evening of music and drama to which local teachers and pupils were invited, was very popular and the annual dinner was, apparently, unforgettable.[117] It took place in a Derbyshire hostelry where Pierce could indulge his passion for conversation liberally laced with real ale.

Professor Pierce's enthusiasm for all things Hispanic (in Latin America as well as the Iberian peninsula) was matched by Professor Mainland's enthusiasm for all things Germanic. He taught Dutch and even Danish, and the departments became, respectively, Hispanic and Germanic Studies. Bill Mainland himself was 'an expert and profound scholar' of Schiller; like Pierce he was 'a superbly entertaining companion'.[118] The Department of Russian, which had lapsed after the war, was revived in 1966 and went from strength to strength. Italian was less successful and its staff were incorporated within Hispanic Studies in 1970.[119]

The Centre for Japanese Studies was created not simply to teach a new language, but to focus on the geography, politics and culture of Japan and East Asia. Its origins lay in the Geography department, whose Professor, Charles Fisher, had been captured by the Japanese during the war. Not many captives would thereafter have wished to study their culture, as Fisher did. He became a 'powerful propagandist' for Asian Studies and was the 'key person' in the foundation of the

Sheffield department.[120] Fisher suggested to Whittaker that Sheffield should make a bid to the UGC for Japanese Studies following the 1961 Hayter report, when funds were available to create centres for non-European 'area studies'.[121] The growing importance of Japanese manufacturing industry made a connection with Sheffield particularly promising.

Unfortunately Fisher left the University in 1964, one year after the Centre for Japanese Studies was established. Its situation was somewhat uncertain until the first Professor, Geoffrey Bownas, was appointed in 1966. A talented linguist, Bownas had been trained in Japanese during the war and had set up an honours degree in Japanese at Oxford. The Centre decided to offer dual degrees; Japanese with, for example, Geography, History or Economics. It also ran programmes for business executives and members of the Foreign Office; the students included three future ambassadors to Japan. As a result of this link to the heart of government, the University was chosen to administer the Japan Foundation Endowment, offered by the Japanese government in 1973 to further the study of the country's language and culture in British universities.

Language laboratories were a novel feature of the Arts Tower; within ten years of their opening an archive of one thousand tapes covering thirty languages had been amassed. An English Language/Linguistics joint degree was established in 1972, followed by Linguistics with French, Greek, Italian, Russian and Spanish three years later.

The Centre created a generation of scholars of Japanese on a scale which had not existed before. By the time Bownas retired in 1980, it was the largest department of its kind in the country.

There were thus some impressive success stories in the Arts faculty of the sixties, but there was also an internal battle between 'old guard' professors and new recruits. 'We collapsed into agreement', said Empson after one long faculty meeting.[122] Some very small departments were preserved, like English Language, Latin and Greek, but other opportunities were lost.[123] Harry Kay, for example, believed that a leading department of Archaeology could have been created when Colin Renfrew, an expert on ancient Greek archaeology, was an Ancient History lecturer.[124] Renfrew conducted summer digs in Milos (near Crete) and in the Orkney Isles; one member of staff remembers having to drive directly from one to the other with the equipment.[125] It proved impossible to provide a chair for Renfrew and he departed for Southampton in 1972 to become Professor of Archaeology. His international career took him to Cambridge in 1981 as a professor and later director of the Institute for Archaeological Research.[126] Sheffield was given a second chance, when Keith Branigan was appointed Professor of Archaeology in 1976 and went on to create an outstandingly successful department.

The Survey of Language and Folklore

English folklore studies have been the focus of high-powered and well-funded research centres in Europe and North America, but in England itself have often been shrugged off as 'rustic', 'recondite' and 'either unacademic or irrelevant'.[127] John Widdowson, a lecturer in English Language, did not underestimate the scale of the task when his passion for the study of folklore, particularly in its linguistic forms, led him to set up the Survey of Language and Folklore in 1964. It started with an Extramural course on 'The Growth of English', which spawned an ongoing

Above: *The cover of the first edition of Lore and Language.*

Right: *John Widdowson, founder of the National Centre for English Cultural Tradition and Language. Its archive is rich in printed and recorded research material and its Traditional Heritage Museum reflects Sheffield life over the last 150 years. Seen here at an Open Day at the Museum, he is serving behind the counter of a reconstructed local shop.*

programme of courses and a large group of local enthusiasts. A Survey team was established in 1968 to collect examples of local speech, childlore, customs, folk narratives and traditional music, drama, arts and crafts. Widdowson started a journal, *Lore and Language*, in 1969. Under his direction, the Survey had permanent life and its work led to a host of publications. The Centre for English Cultural Tradition and Language was inaugurated to organise the teaching, co-ordinate the research and house an unparalleled library, archive and collection of tape recordings. The Survey's collection of traditional artefacts was ultimately housed in its own Traditional Heritage Museum on Ecclesall Road, which opened in 1989.

Despite the success of his work, Widdowson felt that folklore continued to be a poor relation in academic life, though he was grateful for the support of professors like Richard Wilson and, later, Norman Blake. Wilson, the first Professor of English Language, presided over the development of this small department for almost three decades, 1946–73. He produced two classic works on Middle English language and literature and was 'an amiable and gentle teacher'.[128] One student recalls teaching methods which were unusual at the time: 'he told us to concentrate on listening, not to take notes, and then gave us verbatim handouts of the lecture at its conclusion'.

The new Faculty of Architecture

Architecture was growing so fast that it had generated three new departments by 1967 and was dominating the Arts faculty. Alec Daykin remembers that he and a colleague, Marshal Jenkins, came up with the idea of a separate faculty, which was inaugurated when the staff moved to the Arts Tower in 1965.[129] Despite the allocation of several top floors, there was not enough room for everyone. Daykin made constant trips between Shearwood Road, the Arts Tower and even St George's, where he taught architectural aesthetics to engineers.

The new Department of Building Science was developed by Professor John Page, appointed in 1960 to strengthen the technological teaching. It was the first such department in the country and, appropriately from its base in the Arts Tower, performed 'much of the ground breaking work on urban wind flows'.[130] In the new Department of Town and Regional Planning, the first Professor was J. R. 'Jimmy' James in 1967.[131] James came to Sheffield from the Ministry of Housing, where he had been Chief Planner, 'the most prestigious planning post in the land', and had already been appointed OBE and CB. He proved to be an inspirational leader. At once 'a very practical visionary' and a skilful negotiator, he had a gift for motivating students and developed an attractive and successful Postgraduate Diploma in Town and Regional Planning, the core of the department's work. There was also a BA degree for which there were 600 applications for eleven places in 1968. In 1970 James launched the Centre for Environmental Research, the first of its kind in Britain, which brought representatives of local industry, government and higher education together to improve the research on environmental problems in relation to planning.[132]

The third new department, Landscape Architecture, was the first in Britain to be devoted entirely to Landscape, previously taught as part of architecture or town planning degrees. Funding was provided by the Granada Foundation and its excellent standards were set by the first Professor, Arnold Weddle (1967–82). Weddle required his staff to be fully involved in practical landscape projects and 'stretched the students to the limit so as to make them better able to cope with real life'.[133] He wrote the standard textbook *Techniques in Landscape Architecture* in 1967, and pioneered an approach which gave priority to scientific understanding of the environment, long before 'biodiversity' or 'sustainability' were fashionable concerns.

Landscape Architecture is the closest Sheffield has come to recreating the Chair of Civic Art, held by Rothenstein in the years 1917–1926. Whittaker was keen to establish a department of fine art in the Arts Tower, but this scheme unfortunately did not come to fruition.[134]

Below from left to right:

The heads of department of Britain's first Faculty of Architectural Studies:

J. R. 'Jimmy' James, Professor of Town and Regional Planning 1967–78. He came to Sheffield from the Ministry of Housing, where he worked for Richard Crossman and was described in his famous Diaries as 'one of the most attractive of my civil servants.'

Arnold Weddle, Professor of Landscape Architecture 1967–82.

John Needham, Professor of Architecture 1957–72.

John Page, Professor of Building Science 1960–84.

W. H. G. (Harry) Armytage was a lecturer in the Education department from 1946 and Professor 1954–81. He was a Pro-Vice-Chancellor (1964–68) and first Dean of the Faculty of Education from 1972. Typical of his enthusiasms was a vigorous campaign in the 1960s for a University of Scunthorpe on the grounds that 'what's good for Scunthorpe is good for Britain'.

Education in the days of Armytage

The colossus of Education at this time was Harry Armytage. He had been the professor since 1954, but it was in the sixties that his influence within the University as a whole began to be felt. He was a man of commanding presence and overflowing goodwill. To encounter him on the campus was to receive a lesson, or a story, or advice which could change your life. As Pam Poppleton recalled, 'By the time he had finished, it sank in that you had agreed to give a lecture, organise a course, write a book or take the next flight to Michigan'.[135] He was very much a 'person man', in Norman Blake's phrase. To students he was supportive, while setting high standards. His teaching skills were inspirational and showed the value of the unexpected. One teacher never forgot a demonstration lesson when the pupils were mesmerised by a bowler hat which Armytage appeared to have hung by magic on the blackboard. In fact he had affixed a small nail just before the lesson.[136]

Armytage was also a prolific historian; in Gary McCulloch's view he was 'the last great liberal historian of education', with an astonishing breadth, the product of irrepressible interest as well as a taste for the recondite.[137] This led, for example, to a book on civic universities which traced their origins to the sixth century AD, and to works of ambitious scope, including *Four Hundred Years of English Education* and *Heavens Below*, a study of Utopian experiments. His internationalism inspired works on the American, French, German and Russian influences on English education. His great enthusiasm for the history of his adopted city led to a biography of A. J. Mundella, the local Victorian Liberal MP, and to studies of the development of science and technology in *A Social History of Engineering* and *The Rise of the Technocrats*. He was one of the few people who could converse knowledgeably with anyone he met on the campus about their field of study – and he did.

One of Armytage's colleagues, John Roach, has remarked that there are two kinds of leader. There is the leader who 'leads by, in a sense, pushing down the people below him and shining all the more brightly because they are diminished' and there is the leader who brings on his subordinates.[138] Armytage was the second kind. 'He gave his colleagues great freedom, he interfered very little, and, when he did, it was much more to encourage than to criticise'. This regime created a flourishing department.

Following the educational historian Harold Dent, the distinguished heads of the Institute of Education were Boris Ford (1960–65), the editor of the seven volumes of *The Pelican Guide to English Literature*, and John Roach, like Dent an educational historian.[139] In the 1960s the institute and the department continued to be separate institutions. The department's training work until 1965 focused on the successful one-year postgraduate certificate in secondary education. The Robbins Committee, however, added a new commitment when it suggested the establishment of a four-year Bachelor of Education (BEd) degree. The aim was to give the most ambitious college students the chance of a degree; but this required sensitive co-operation between the universities and the colleges. John Roach was in the eye of this storm through his work with the colleges and had to change the initial decision to teach the fourth year entirely within the University.[140] Not for the first time, the University found itself in difficulties when it tried to offer an undergraduate course in teaching.

The Extramural department continued to be successful. In 1968 it finally moved from its inadequate rooms in the basement of St John's Methodist Church. Evening classes could not be held there 'because of the strenuous activities of the Church's Youth Club overhead' and the accommodation was shared in a 'strange, though very friendly, partnership with Forensic Pathology'.[141] The new premises were, most appropriately, in Broomspring House on Wilkinson Street, once the home of Mark Firth.[142] A library block was built in the garden and the director, Maurice Bruce, became a professor.

'Teaching machines' and the department of Psychology

The Department of Psychology was in the forefront of the development of 'programmed learning' in the 1960s. Harry Kay was so far ahead of the game that he developed the first programs for use on his own design of 'teaching machines'. Computers had the potential to make the job much simpler and Sheffield acquired the first in any British Psychology department in 1966. The Elliott 903 took many months to customise and 'required cumbersome preparations' before use, from 'checking and winding up substantial lengths of paper tape' to 'correctly setting approximately thirty switches'.[143] Staff and graduate students had to acquire programming skills in order to use it, but by 1969 had advanced so far that they were already considering the prospects of 'on-line' computing, and hosted an international conference in Sheffield to plan the way ahead. The programs had particularly

Below left: The Department of Psychology's first computer – the Elliot 903.

Below: Harry Kay (left) was Professor of Psychology 1960–73 and a Pro-Vice-Chancellor 1967–71. He is seen here with one of the early teaching machines in the cellar of his department. Kay was described by a colleague as 'a man of the future with great vision which he was not afraid to use, and the skills to implement it'. He left Sheffield in 1973 to become Vice-Chancellor of the University of Exeter.

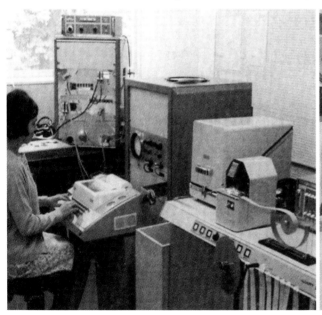

Janos Reeves, second left, the first
full-time producer in the University's
CCTV service, was a refugee from the
repressive Communist regime in
Hungary.

Janos Reeves, second left, the first full-time producer in the University's CCTV service, was a refugee from the repressive Communist regime in Hungary.

strong potential for use in technical training and in 1967 Kay received funding from the Ministry of Labour to set up the Programmed Instruction Centre for Industry.

Harry Kay's influence on the ADC was one reason why the University became interested in teaching methods, something which had previously been taken for granted. 'Lessons in confidence for the professors' were held, during which lecturers were advised at all costs to 'avoid a dull monotonous drone'.[144] The first videotape recorder was bought in 1966 and closed circuit television facilities were installed in new lecture theatres, for example in the new Metallurgy building. By 1969 the University had acquired a mobile TV Unit with a full-time producer, Janos Reeves. It quickly proved its worth by producing teaching tapes, including classroom observations for the Department of Education and equipment demonstrations for such diverse departments as Electronics and Anaesthetics.[145]

Psychology finally became a separate department in 1960. Its first premises were a house on Mushroom Lane which was soon full to bursting, with Harry Kay's rat colony in the attic (inevitably known as the 'rattic') and some research laboratories consigned to cramped and damp cellars. One member of staff looking for a quiet space in which to study the imprinting of chickens had to destroy a 'giant bright orange fungus, about six feet long and four feet wide' before he could start work.[146] The department was young and full of enthusiasm. Students gathered with staff for morning coffee and afternoon tea, where ideas and developments were openly and avidly discussed. Peter Warr carried out a 'communication tracer study' and concluded that the flow of information within the department passed chiefly through the coffee area.

These heady days, when the department 'felt like a close-knit family' and the social programme was as hectic as the work schedule, inevitably diminished in intensity as the department got bigger, but the humane and democratic culture established by Harry Kay survived. The department was also very successful. In addition to the Programmed Instruction Centre, a Social and Applied Psychology Unit was established in 1968 with funding from the MRC. Directed by Peter Warr, it was the first in the country to analyse decision-making and human interaction in the workplace. A second computer was installed for this work and in time the Unit gained 'world pre-eminence' as the Institute of Work Psychology.[147]

The Postgraduate School of Librarianship and Information Science

In 1963 the Library Association decided to fund a second national postgraduate school (the first was in London).[148] Sheffield was chosen, in part because of the excellence both of the new university library and of its public library system. The school was based in a fine Victorian house, 16 Claremont Crescent. From the start, under the stimulating leadership of Wilfred Saunders, the school set high standards, aiming to 'break the mould' of previous training courses. Graduates of science and technology, for example, who had previously avoided librarianship, were attracted by courses in scientific information and made up forty per cent of the first student cohort. The school was the first to offer these courses, to add 'Information Science' to its title (in 1967) and to offer MAs in both Librarianship and Information Science (from 1968). In 1973 a MA in Social Sciences Information was added.

'Wilf' Saunders, Director of the Postgraduate School of Librarianship from 1963 and Professor of Librarianship and Information Science 1968–82. Skilled at securing funds, he came to Sheffield as Deputy Librarian in 1956 and proved an outstanding choice to head the new School.

Entry standards were high, for the department's graduates were to be the future innovators, not only in libraries but in information studies generally. The department quickly gained national and international influence and was in the forefront of computerisation in university libraries.[149] The journal *Social Science Information Studies*, edited from within the school, became *The International Journal of Information Management*. In the 1970s, the school was also for some time a leader in the new field of user studies, with a separate research centre run by Peter Mann.

The potential of the centre to aid university research was demonstrated by David Smyth of Physiology. In 1965, he was trying to cope with the abundance of literature published in his field, intestinal absorption, by producing a monthly list of article titles and decided that 'Wilf' Saunders might help him do it better. They applied for a grant from the Office for Scientific and Technical Information (OSTI), and this led to the foundation of the Biomedical Information Service. By 1980 it was producing 113 monthly lists for researchers in the University and beyond.[150]

THE PURE SCIENCES

The Chemistry department

Numbers in the Pure Science faculty doubled, from 641 to 1220, during the decade and the Chemistry department grew from one building to four, as three major wings were opened by 1968, filling the site between Brook Hill and Bolsover Street.

T. S. (Tommy) Stevens was awarded the University's first ever personal chair in 1963 after his election to the Royal Society. A gifted storyteller, he was a linchpin of the Department of Chemistry for twenty years, 1946–66.

Robert Haworth retired in 1963 but thereafter continued his research with an intensity 'otherwise associated with elemental fluorine'.[151] George Porter left Sheffield in 1966, shortly before he was awarded the Nobel Prize. He became the Director of the Royal Institution, a tribute at once to his scientific eminence and his outstanding abilities as a public face of science.[152] He was a regular 'TV professor' and an ideal choice to supervise the Royal Institution's Christmas lectures, which were started by Michael Faraday in 1825. Porter gave them himself in 1969 and 1976 and was followed by two other Sheffield scientists, Charles Stirling in 1992 and Tony Ryan in 2002.[153] Two of the department's readers, T. S. Stevens and A. S. C. Lawrence, gained the first personal chairs awarded in the University; indeed Senate's decision to create personal chairs in 1963 was due to Stevens's election as FRS. Senate decreed that, 'Appointment to a personal chair should represent the University's recognition of the exceptional esteem in which it holds the recipient. Mere ordinary chair-worthiness is not in itself sufficient'.[154]

By 1967, when Stevens and Lawrence had also retired, the Chemistry department was in an unsettled state. It was large and there were four new professors, David Ollis, Ronald Mason, Jan Hoytinck and Roy McWeeny. The multi-professorial department was new to the University, and its administration did not adapt easily to it. It insisted on one voice, that of the head of department, and one signature for the acquisition of resources. If there were tensions between professors, they were greatly magnified when one of them was placed in overall command, even though this role was rotated.

The personality of David Ollis, Professor of Organic Chemistry 1963–1990, proved to be a particularly volatile ingredient to this new brew. He was highly ambitious and utterly focused on research and teaching; his door displayed a notice saying that he was not available for meetings between 8.00 am and 8.00 pm. One administrator was told that his only available time for a meeting was 11.00 pm.[155] Such a man was not prepared to compromise with colleagues and became at times unbearably dominant.[156] As an organic chemist, Ollis was first class, 'one of the leaders of chemistry in the UK', who was elected FRS in 1972.[157] He 'elevated the whole standard of organic chemistry in Sheffield' when he arrived from Bristol University in 1963 with his own group of research students. As his reputation grew, he lured researchers from all over the world, usually running a group of about 24. He liked to say that 'you need only one outstanding research student to establish your reputation'. He had many, including Richard Roberts, who was awarded a Nobel Prize in 1993. To students like Roberts, who could live up to his exacting standards, Ollis was 'a tremendous inspiration'.[158]

David Ollis, Professor of Organic Chemistry 1963–90.

Many remember the Chem Soc Review, in which staff let their hair down in sketches which everyone enjoyed – 'The Waiter, the Porter and the Upstairs Maid' with Professors Porter, Ollis and Mason in particular. Ronald Mason, a popular Welshman, left the department in 1970 for the University of Sussex: he was elected FRS in 1975 and knighted in 1980. Mason came as an inorganic chemist and then developed an interest in biological chemistry. This was a significant new area (Richard Roberts actually won his Nobel prize for research in molecular biology)

and in Sheffield it developed outside the Chemistry department. However, the Theoretical Chemistry section was successfully launched by Roy McWeeny.[159]

The Physics department

One year before Sputnik 1 and the dawn of the space age, Tom Kaiser arrived in the Physics department, having already published the definitive paper on meteor ionisation.[160] He persuaded the University to acquire a hilltop at Edgemount Farm, High Bradfield, and covered it with radar aerials in order to study the upper atmosphere.[161] There, his colleague David Hughes remembers, 'many happy nights were spent bouncing radar pulses off meteors and the aurora borealis.' Instruments developed by the Space Physics group were carried on Skylark rockets launched at Woomera, Australia, in 1962, 1965 and 1966.[162] Kaiser also designed survey instruments for the first all-British satellite, Ariel 3, launched in 1967, which were the first to overcome radio interference problems. Work on Ariel 4, in 1971, led Kaiser to visit the British Antarctic Survey headquarters and establish VLF receivers which have provided a valuable long-term database for understanding the ionosphere.

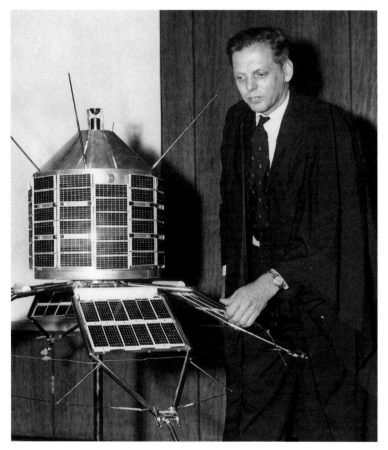

Tom Kaiser, Professor of Space Physics 1966–87, was a brilliant innovator in the field of space science and was awarded the Gold Medal of the Royal Astronomical Society for his lifetime's work in this field in 1994. Strongly left-wing, prior to arriving in Sheffield he had been forced to leave Australia and later Jodrell Bank because of his political activities. This 1966 photograph shows him with the model of Ariel 3.

Bill Galbraith, Professor of Nuclear Physics 1966–88, estimated that he drove 60,000 miles in ten years commuting from Sheffield to research facilities at Daresbury, Cheshire. Later he used the high energy accelerator at CERN in Geneva where he was a full-time senior research fellow in 1979. Galbraith served as Pro-Vice-Chancellor 1982–86.

Joe Gani, Professor of Probability and Statistics 1965–74, founded four journals and the Applied Probability Trust; the Trust publishes the journals and continues to be based in Sheffield. A truly international scholar, with over 250 papers to his name, Gani also worked for long periods at universities in Australia and America.

Willie Sucksmith retired once Physics had safely transferred to the Hicks building. Departmental folklore insists that he designed the high window sills to prevent lecturers staring out of the window. His interest in solid state physics was maintained and developed by colleagues like John Crangle, who was fascinated by magnetism, a theme of ongoing departmental research. Crangle worked with explosive materials, like liquid hydrogen which was housed in a special room in the Hicks building.

Other colleagues had to travel to their research facilities. George Bacon, the head of department from 1963, was 'the father of neutron scattering in the UK' and continued to perform his research at the Atomic Energy Research Establishment at Harwell, where he had previously worked.[163] He had built a neutron diffractometer there. Bill Galbraith, who held the chair of nuclear physics, worked with high energy electron beams generated at the new SRC Laboratory at Daresbury in Cheshire. He and colleagues from Glasgow produced 'internationally recognised work which now forms part of the particles data tables, the Bible of high energy physics'.[164]

The Manchester-Sheffield School of Probability and Statistics

The passionate mathematician Dr Whittaker had supported the creation of a Department of Statistics in 1955 but it was struggling, with 'one lecturer, one research assistant and six vacant posts', when Joe Gani became the first Professor in 1965.[165] Gani was born in Egypt to a Greek Jewish family, emigrated to Australia, and had worked there and in the United States before coming to Sheffield. He built up the department to twenty academics through sheer personality and skill. Although he remained in Sheffield for only nine years this period was, he said, 'one of the most constructive and happy of my life'.[166] Whittaker had kept all his promises, even though he was 'the only person who ever interviewed me and made promises . . . by jotting them down on what seemed to be the back of an envelope'.[167] For instance, a research assistant, Mavis Hitchcock, was provided for the *Journal of Applied Probability*, which Gani had founded in 1964.

Gani defined applied probability as 'the art of building probabilistic models of all kinds of real-life situations (like dams, queues, epidemics)'.[168] One example is the model he later developed for the spread of HIV among intravenous drug users. Applied probability was a new field in the sixties and statisticians were in short supply. In 1967, when Manchester University lost its professor, there was no obvious successor and, having failed to persuade Gani to move from Sheffield, they accepted his proposal of a joint School. It proved surprisingly successful and has survived to the present time. Sheffield's department has also become one of the largest in the country. Joe Gani, undoubtedly one of the international leaders of applied probability, left Sheffield in 1974 to return to Australia, but retained his connection through the Applied Probability Trust, which he founded.

Left to right:

Ian Chester Jones, Professor of Zoology 1958–81 and Dean of the Faculty of Pure Science 1965–68. One of the founders of the field of comparative endocrinology, he built up a department with an international reputation for the study of vertebrate and insect hormones.

Roy Clapham, Professor of Botany 1944–69 and acting Vice-Chancellor 1965–66. Elected a Fellow of the Royal Society in 1959, he published The Flora of the British Isles *in 1951 and had a world-wide reputation as a taxonomist and ecologist.*

Robert Barer held the Arthur Jackson Chair of Human Biology and Anatomy from 1963 to 1982. He was a pioneer of cell biology and the instigator of major changes in the research and teaching of the Anatomy department. At the end of the war he was the first allied officer to enter the typhus-infested Sandbostel concentration camp – a formative experience.

BIOLOGY AND THE BIOMEDICAL SCIENCES

Keeping animals in a department meant that life was never boring. A Zoology technician, Roger Webb, was idly poking 'Big Sammy', a large lungfish, with a thermometer when Sammy bit the end off and swallowed the mercury. Webb waited for him to keel over, but he lived for many more years and the Professor never found out.[169] 'Big Sammy' was the prize exhibit in Ian Chester Jones's collection, used for his research on the endocrine systems of different animals. Chester Jones, Professor of Zoology from 1958 to 1981, was 'one of the father figures' of comparative endocrinology. He attracted so many enthusiasts among his staff that the Zoology department became one of the world's leading research centres in this field.[170] Chester Jones was extrovert, loud-voiced and informal, in contrast to Roy Clapham, the Professor of Botany, who was 'aloof, reserved and almost patrician'; both were kings of their castles.[171]

Under Francis Davies, a classical anatomist who had extensively revised and updated *Gray's Anatomy*, the Department of Anatomy was devoted to the teaching of pre-clinical medical and dental students. When Davies retired in 1963, the new Professor, Robert Barer, completely changed the department's priorities. His interests were in the structure and function of the cell, and he reduced the time that pre-clinical students spent on the traditional dissection of the cadaver by half.[172] A successful special honours degree linking anatomy and cell biology, 'one of a handful in the country', was introduced.[173]

Barer secured funding from the Nuffield Foundation and the Sheffield Town Trust for an extensive research programme in cell biology. In laboratories in a new building, 3 Clarkehouse Road, he housed two electron microscopes and a young team of enthusiastic and energetic researchers who produced a steady stream of papers. It was 'a melting pot of unconventional talent' with a powerfully creative camaraderie. This laboratory 'was one of three or four worldwide' making revolutionary developments in anatomy.[174]

Barer's department was divided between the new high-tech laboratory and the old dissecting suite in Western Bank, where technicians like 'David and Gilbert' still

Robert Kilpatrick, Lecturer in Pharmacology from 1955, Professor of Experimental Pharmacology 1965–66 and of Clinical Pharmacology 1966–75, Dean of the Faculty of Medicine 1970–73 and Chairman of Academic Development Committee. He moved to Leicester to establish its new Medical School in 1975, and served as President of the General Medical Council 1989–95. He was knighted in 1986 and made a Life Peer as Lord Kilpatrick of Kincraig in 1996.

presided over macabre preparations in surroundings which had changed little since 1905.[175] ('Straight out of *Doctor in the House*', commented one medical student.) Anatomy symbolises in the starkest form the changes which were coming over the biomedical sciences. Although they continued with pre-clinical teaching, Anatomy, Physiology and Biochemistry focused more intensively on their own special honours degree programmes and their own students. The only exceptions were Bacteriology, Pathology and Pharmacology. Attempts to establish a single honours pharmacology degree were unsuccessful at this time, although clinical pharmacology flourished under Robert Kilpatrick, who later became President of the General Medical Council. Bacteriology found its niche as a 'medical microbiology' research department under Colin Beattie.[176] His studies of the flu virus with Charles Stuart-Harris created a spin-off Department of Virology and his research on toxoplasmosis had achieved an international reputation by the time he retired in 1967.

The Genetics department was led by Alan Roper, a gentle, diplomatic Sheffield graduate who had studied for a PhD in Krebs's department and moved into the new field of genetics at Glasgow University.[177] He recalls that the department was developed against a background of resistance from some of the establishment; Clapham in Botany, for example, regarded Genetics as a 'service' department and 'not a discipline'. It took Roper seven years to establish a degree in Genetics and Microbiology, the first scientific dual honours degree. This started in 1966 and quickly became popular. Single subject degrees started in 1973.

The department was housed in a small building in the grounds of the Institute of Education on Glossop Road, and it was here that clinical genetics began in 1960. The normal human chromosome complement (46) had been established in 1956 and with this an understanding of chromosomal abnormalities like Downs' Syndrome. A clinic for the parents of Downs' Syndrome children, directed by Eric Blank, was so successful that, in 1964, the University and the health authority jointly funded a move to much larger premises. These were at Langhill on Manchester Road, formerly the home of Sir Stuart Goodwin. The Centre for Human Genetics was 'the only one of its kind in Britain', and became the Sub-Department of Clinical Genetics, in the Faculty of Medicine, in 1970.[178]

Genetics, biochemistry, cell biology and microbiology were the new subjects included in the Integrated Biology first year course, which began in 1966. The idea was to extend the introductory course beyond the original subjects of botany, physiology and zoology. This meant that the new subjects benefited at the expense of the original ones. Alan Roper, for one, loved teaching this course, which resulted in many more students being attracted to his degree. The Integrated Biology course lasted until 1981. Some of its components were unexpected, particularly chemistry, taught by the Chemistry department. It was an unpleasant surprise to quite a few first-year students to discover that the first three weeks of a biology degree included the study of quantum mechanics.

The biology departments grew to such an extent that even the rooms in Western Bank vacated by other departments, like Mathematics and Physics, could not contain them. A new Biology building, at the entrance to Tower Court, was

Alan Roper, Professor of Genetics 1959–89. Apart from his academic contribution in establishing the subject of genetics he was widely respected for his personal and diplomatic skills and served as chairman of the Academic Development Committee and from 1971 to 1975 as a Pro-Vice-Chancellor. His own research on fungal production of antibiotics was taken up by cancer researchers to 'revolutionary effect'.

The Biology building, later named after the first professor, Alfred Denny. The concrete framed structure was faced with the same red brick as the 1905 buildings; the animal and plant growth rooms, which did not require windows, account for the solid band of brickwork at the top. The block behind, facing the Arts Tower, was built in the Edwardian gothic style to match the previous extensions.

completed in stages between 1965 and 1971. The first phase provided two lecture theatres and a large teaching laboratory, and the departments of Zoology, Physiology and Pharmacology were rehoused in subsequent stages. Many new specialist facilities, including animal houses, aquaria and a radio-isotope suite were provided, together with a new anatomy dissecting room. At Western Bank Biochemistry, Botany, Microbiology and Human Biology & Anatomy expanded into the vacated space.

Krebs's old department, Biochemistry, was struggling once again in 1963, since many of the senior staff, including Professor Gibson, had joined the brain drain to the United States.[179] Walter Bartley, who had gone to Oxford with Krebs, returned as the replacement for Gibson. He was 'an excellent and supportive delegator' who enabled his staff to follow their own research interests and so achieve distinction.[180] He recreated the department by selecting colleagues who could reflect the new range of biochemical research. They included Rod Quayle, from Krebs's Oxford Unit, who was in Biochemistry for only two years before becoming Professor of Microbiology. The permeability of some of the boundaries in biology was noticeable, but amalgamation of departments was still a long way off.

THE MEDICAL SCHOOL

There is a real sense in which Medicine, unlike other faculties, was treading water during the sixties. Intake rose from sixty to eighty in 1962, but a further increase to 120 had to be postponed. Every attempt to expand was thwarted by the continuing serious delays in building the Hallamshire Hospital. The UGC approved designs in 1961 for a Medical School on Beech Hill Road to house some of the clinical departments and the faculty office.[181] Unfortunately this was closely integrated with the plans for the hospital next door and the building contract for that was not signed until December 1969. No part of the new Medical School was ready for occupation until 1973.

The sixties medical school was thus still based in Western Bank; it comes alive in the memories of former students.[182] The small numbers meant that 'we had access to a wealth of patients throughout the city hospitals'. 'Clinical training was second to none'; and many lecturers were unforgettable. Sir Frank Holdsworth of Orthopaedics 'sometimes made us tremble in our shoes with his lacerating sarcasm (roll over Lancelot Spratt!) but he exercised razor-sharp logic and helped us to arrive at answers which we never forgot'. For many years voted the best lecturer in the medical school, he developed the first accident and orthopaedic service in Sheffield.[183]

The students spent hours each day travelling between the various hospitals; some even walked to the Northern General (three miles away) to save the fare. The students' residences provided relaxation; 'Charcot's Joint' at the Infirmary was the only place to watch 'Top of the Pops'. It was, however, 'unbelievably awful' – 'the floors, doors and stairs creaked, the furniture was battered, and there was a permanent sulphurous atmosphere from the ancient boiler'. 'It should have been

Alec Jenner, the second Professor of Psychiatry (1967–92) is seen here (second left) with Harry Kay from the Department of Psychology at the opening of the Medical Research Council Unit at Middlewood Hospital in 1969.

condemned' in the 1950s, but in fact survived until the 1970s. 'Bedside Manor' for the Royal Hospital had good, homely food; the residence for the Jessop Hospital for Women was known as 'Chorionic Villa' – like 'Charcot's Joint' a name which, they imagined, 'only medics will understand'!

Clinical teaching and research

It is impossible here to do justice to the extensive clinical teaching and research of the Sheffield hospitals. The focus will therefore be mainly on the work of the full-time professors. The first of these in the Department of Psychiatry was Erwin Stengel, appointed in 1959 (he had been in the department since 1956).[184] Stengel was another of Sheffield's refugees from the Nazis; he fled from Vienna in 1938 and was forced to requalify 'in a foreign country and in a language not his own'. He owed much of his success in Sheffield to 'his intellectual stature, the breadth of his knowledge and his clinical skill as a psychiatrist'. One psychology student recalls that 'his method of teaching was to interview patients in a huge tiered lecture hall, and I was always amazed by their willingness to undergo Stengel's interrogation and reveal the most embarrassing details about their personal problems'.[185] Stengel was in the forefront of moves to integrate psychiatry with general medicine because of 'the ubiquity of psychological problems in all fields of medical work'. Although he himself was a most happy person, his particular expertise was suicide. He was a co-president of the Samaritans, 'a wonderful man', who on his retirement did much voluntary work, most notably in Wakefield Prison.[186]

After Stengel retired in 1967 Alec Jenner, who had previously worked at Sheffield, returned from Birmingham University to succeed him. Jenner was already the director of a successful MRC Unit studying the psychiatric impact of certain metabolic disorders. This Unit, with all its staff, transferred to Middlewood Hospital and continued its fundamental research, which included the identification of two new disorders and a study of the periodic nature of some psychotic illnesses.[187] One of the Unit's members was Dorothy Rowe, who went on to write best-selling popular guides to psychology.[188]

The full-time chair of public health was established in 1949 and held by John Knowelden from 1960 to 1984.[189] He established a Medical Care Research Unit which has continued to flourish. Knowelden was one of the first to use randomised control trials to establish the effectiveness of an innovation, in this case early discharge after hernia repair.

The Children's Hospital's national reputation in the 1960s was based on the work of four outstanding consultants: Ronald Illingworth, John Lorber, Robert Zachary and John Emery.[190] In 1968 the Congenital Anomalies Research Unit with forty staff, funded by the Wolfson Foundation, was established as a national centre for pioneering treatment developed by Lorber and Zachary.[191] Babies born with the genetic anomalies of hydrocephalus (an enlarged head) and spina bifida (deformed spine) had previously been regarded as untreatable. Zachary, the surgeon in the team, operated on them immediately after birth and Lorber developed a meticulous

Erwin Stengel, the first full-time Professor of Psychiatry (1959-67). He bequeathed this bronze to the University in 1980.

As a young Viennese doctor working at a psychiatric clinic, Stengel met Freud's maid and, introduced by her, was able to consult Freud about the treatment of one of his patients. The maid gave him a pot belonging to Freud which Stengel greatly valued and brought to England when he fled the Nazis in 1938.

John Lorber, left, and Robert Zachary, right, of the Congenital Anomalies Research Unit.

regime of post-operative care, which could last several years. Both Zachary and Lorber had unusual backgrounds which, in Emery's view, contributed to their devotion to this task: Lorber was a Hungarian refugee from the Nazis and Zachary suffered from scoliosis, another spinal deformity.[192] Their commitment brought babies to Sheffield from all over the country and their centre became internationally renowned. Tragically, it became clear that the quality of life for some of these children would be irreversibly poor and that they could never live independently. At this point, Lorber took the difficult decision to advocate selection for surgery, so that a baby whose prognosis was very poor would not be treated. Zachary, on the other hand, wanted to treat every baby. This created 'one of the most active and in some ways acrimonious disputes relating to child care' of the century, with members of the profession ranged on both sides.[193] The issue was not, and perhaps could not be, resolved. By the 1980s, however, the development of prenatal diagnosis meant that far fewer babies were being born with these conditions.

Medical Physics: radiology and the beginning of 'clinical engineering'

Medical Physics was established as a sub-department in 1960 to develop work in radiological physics which had begun in Sheffield in 1915, after radium was first used as a treatment for cancer.[194] The Sheffield Radium Centre was established in 1931, thanks largely to the efforts of two Sheffield graduates, T. E. Allibone, who designed the new X-ray machine, and Frank Ellis, the first director.[195] In 1945 the Centre moved to Broom Cross, a large Victorian house on Tree Root Walk, where the physicists initially worked in the attic, before a new building was erected in the grounds to house a two million volt clinical therapy machine, powered by a Van de Graaff generator. This huge machine, which was christened 'Bertha', 'put Sheffield in the forefront of megavoltage therapy in England' but was 'a real tyrant of a baby to look after'.[196] She needed a 'twice daily feed of solid CO_2' and changing her belts was a laborious and long-winded process. In 1970, the radiotherapists moved into the new Weston Park cancer hospital on Whitham Road, the dream of 'a full treatment and laboratory service in a well equipped specialist hospital', which had come to fruition after thirty years of planning.[197]

The potential for 'medical electronics' and 'bioengineering' to transform many other areas of medicine was becoming obvious, and collaborative projects began. For example, a 'radio-pill' to transmit information from inside the body was developed with the Department of Surgery.[198] A team at the Jessop Hospital invented a pioneering method of monitoring the baby's heart rate during labour.[199] Medical physicists became accepted and essential members of many hospital care teams.

The first director of the sub-department was Harold Miller, who came to the Radium Centre as its sole physicist in 1942. He built up a training and support service in radiotherapy which extended across the whole Trent region.[200] His 'quiet determination' was crucial to the success of the Weston Park hospital project and he was promoted to Associate Professor in 1972, shortly before his retirement in 1975.

THE APPLIED SCIENCES

The Professor of Fuel Technology from 1953 to 1964 was a colourful character called Meredith Thring. He was jealous of the new Engineering building (opened in

Felix the fire-fighter being demonstrated to a group of guests including the Duke of Edinburgh, far right, at the opening of the Fuel Technology building in November 1961. Meredith Thring is standing between the Duke and the Lord Mayor.

The Metallurgy building, later known as the Hadfield building, marked the easternmost extent of the University in 1964/65. The concrete-faced wall was left in an unfinished state for many years in the expectation that a second phase of the building would be erected, but this never happened. Lecture theatres are on upper floors because of the need to house workshops at ground level.

The abstract sculpture in the Metallurgy department foyer was designed by C. E. Sansbury and made in the department's workshops under his supervision.

1955) and twisted arms within the University's administration until he got a new building himself.[201] The Fuel Technology building was opened by the Duke of Edinburgh in 1961, an occasion which proved memorable. Thring invented robots and had announced his plan for 'Freda the mechanical housemaid' whose aim was to 'help housewives in the home by doing jobs like laying the table'.[202] Alas, little more was ever heard of Freda. However, 'Felix the fire-fighter' was a prototype demonstrated with success, although he exceeded his remit. When let loose in the yard, Felix moved immediately towards the strongest source of heat, which was the sun. Unfortunately the Duke of Edinburgh was standing in his path and had to be rescued just in time to avoid a drenching by Felix's extinguishers.[203] For some reason this part of the story failed to appear in the newspaper accounts.

Thring's enthusiasms for nuclear and rocket propulsion and flame research built up a department of impressive standing. He and his successor, J. M. Beer, often conducted their research at a safely isolated location – partially submerged concrete bunkers at Buxton in Derbyshire, originally built to store munitions and leased by Thring from the Ministry of Defence. Jim Swithenbank also conducted rocketry research there which proved of great value to NASA in the USA.[204] This included pioneering work on the design of aircraft to go into orbit.

Metallurgy got a new building in 1966, a tower which was described by an Oxford professor as 'by far and away the best in the country'.[205] Like all the St George's buildings, it received generous funding from Sheffield industry and Arthur Quarrell's contacts were crucial in securing this. He was ably supported by Robert Honeycombe, an Australian who became Professor of Physical Metallurgy at the age of 34 in 1955. Honeycombe's research on alloys led to his appointment to a chair at Cambridge in 1966.

The Department of Glass Technology joined the Faculty of Metallurgy in 1962 and, under Ronald Douglas, explored new uses of glass with huge potential. These included the generation of laser beams and the theoretical possibility that fibre-optic glass cables might be able to 'convey hundreds of thousands of telephone calls simultaneously on the same fibre'.[206] Douglas's knowledge of glass was immense, his enthusiasm for research infectious and his expectations of staff very high.[207] He and Quarrell were the last of the baronial heads of department, whose word was law. A 'carpeting' in Douglas's office could be a harrowing experience. He and a colleague, Amal Paul, could not agree about the interpretation of some experimental data. After a long meeting between the two, Douglas exploded, 'That Dr. Paul! It took me ten years to convince him and now that I have changed my mind, he won't change his!'[208]

It was increasingly difficult to describe the faculty as 'Metallurgy' when the departments of Glass Technology, Refractories and Ceramics played such an important part in its work. Quarrell fought hard to keep a name with such strong significance for Sheffield, but it was changed to 'Materials Technology' in 1969, shortly before he ceased to be head of department.[209]

The faculty hosted that most arcane of departments, Theory of Materials, from 1966 to 1983. The applied mathematics of the structure and performance of mate-

Bruce Bilby, FRS, Professor of Theory of Materials 1962–84.

Left: The first fifty years of Glass Technology were marked by the presentation to the department of two commemorative glass panels by the Worshipful Company of Glass Sellers in 1966.

rials was taught by Bruce Bilby, a former Sorby Fellow and Professor from 1962, who, despite his wish to communicate, found it difficult 'to come down to the level of ignorance that most students started from'.[210] His appearance, 'like Father Christmas', was as striking as that of Jock Eshelby, who joined him in 1966, a small Scotsman who habitually 'wore a hat that looked like a rugby sock'.[211] The department was undoubtedly top heavy in its tiny teaching load and staff of one programmer, one lecturer and two professors. These two professors, however, were both Fellows of the Royal Society. A student, Alex King, recalls the demanding nature of Eshelby's lectures:

Jock Eshelby, FRS, Reader, and Professor of Theory of Materials 1971–82. As a child he decided to test the thermal shock resistance of glass by putting a hot tea pot on his mother's best glass-topped coffee table. When it cracked he recalled, 'I subsequently received a discouragement from performing experiments that has lasted me the rest of my life'.

> He would walk into the lecture hall, apparently already halfway through his lecture . . . clear a patch of the board and start deriving a theorem. Running out of space, he would clear another patch, not necessarily connected with the first, and fill that up. Eventually, small pieces of the theorem would be scattered more-or-less at random across the chalkboard, stochastically mixed with the detritus of the previous lecture, and with random parts missing – erased to make space for more . . .[212]

Sometimes, even Eshelby had lost the thread by the end of his lecture.

The teaching of mining in universities was in precipitate decline by the early sixties, and in 1962 the National Coal Board withdrew support from four of the nine departments it sponsored. Sheffield was confident that its position remained strong, since it had produced almost half Britain's mining undergraduates and more than half its

All the holders of the Sorby Chair of Geology assembled for a commemorative dinner in Sorby's honour in September 1963. From the left, Leslie Moore, 1949–77, William Fearnsides, 1913–45, and Frederick Shotton, 1945–9. Behind is the portrait of Sorby painted by Mary Lemmon Waller to mark the award of his honorary doctorate by the University.

One example of the work of the Control Engineering department, created in 1968. This tunnelling machine illustrates the 'fundamental fascination of mining control problems'.

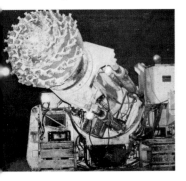

postgraduates in the previous four years.[213] However, by 1965 when Professor Frank Atkinson retired, the days of even Sheffield's undergraduate degree were numbered and the chair was withdrawn. The Dean, Alex Cullen, said that this decision gave him more heartache than anything else he had done.[214] There were high hopes for the postgraduate school, but this lasted only three more years and closed in 1968. Some of the staff moved to the Department of Geology, due to its expertise in rock mechanics, and others to Civil Engineering. The independent Safety-in-Mines Research establishment remained in Broad Lane, across from the Engineering departments. It later became the Health and Safety Executive Research Laboratories.

The centenary of Henry Clifton Sorby was celebrated in 1963 with 'a distinguished gathering of the upper geological crust'.[215] All three holders of the Sorby Chair of Geology were present. The perilous state of mining studies impacted on Geology, but fortunately large numbers of students were taking geology as a pure science subject by the sixties. Professor Moore reported that 'the departure of three coaches from St George's Square with the first year class safely aboard is a gratifying sight'.[216] The department had established new specialist research laboratories at the time of the Centenary, but its plans for a new building were later stopped for 'academic reasons'.[217]

When Professor Tuplin of Applied Mechanics retired in 1968, it was decided to close his department in favour of a new Department of Control Engineering. Feedback mechanisms like servos, valves and, increasingly, computer control, were a fertile research field and the university moved into it very early. The new Professor was Harry Nicholson, who moved from Electronic Engineering and was an encouraging boss who was 'very attuned to opportunities'.[218] A Master's course was developed and, later, the first undergraduate degree in the country.

The Department of Civil Engineering, under Norman Boulton and his successor Bill Eastwood, grew from forty undergraduates and three postgraduates in 1954 to more than 200 undergraduates and eighteen postgraduates by 1966.[219] Nearly all the technology departments expanded during the sixties. It was, after all, the era of Harold Wilson's 'white heat of the technological revolution'. Even so, as a proportion of the University's intake, the number of applied science students fell from 22 per cent in 1961 to 19 per cent in 1967.

Engineering students of the sixties remember Professors Eastwood, Benson and Cullen as particularly good teachers and cannot forget Eng Soc dinners which were so riotous that a different venue had to be found each year, since they would never be allowed back. Ma Butler's on Broad Lane was the place for hot food, or possibly Margie's café opposite the Hicks building, which served all-day breakfasts and tea in pint-sized mugs. Both were more popular than the University's St George's Coffee Bar, with its watery soup.[220] Many of the staff found time to go to the Senior Common Room for 'dinner' at long tables with staff from all over the University. They recall the pleasure of talking to colleagues from other departments, conversations which could generate powerful ideas and formulate research projects. Those who chose to stroll down West Street for their lunch had to run the gauntlet of wolf-whistles from the 'buffer girls' (cutlery workers). 'Very embar-rassing', remembers Peter Robson.[221]

Mappin Hall was converted into an Applied Science Library in 1967, a move which was resisted for some time because it had, quite by chance, an excellent acoustic for chamber concerts.[222] A compromise was reached by which the loss of Mappin Hall was balanced by improvements to the acoustic of Firth Hall. A false ceiling was built over the original hammer beams, into which sound disappeared. Gerard Young was happy to have 'transformed Firth Hall from a gloomy, noisy and worn-out Edwardian barn', but the conversion was costly and not to everyone's taste. Mappin Hall reverted to its original design after the purpose-built Applied Science Library opened in 1992.

WHITTAKER MAKES WAY FOR ROBSON, 1965/66

By his own account, Whittaker took more interest in the recruitment of professors than almost anything else. He believed that 'the appointment of professors was the most important thing that a university did. If you got hold of a good professor then . . . he would collect good people and so the whole thing would be in a very flour-ishing condition.'[223] His favoured method was 'asking around', especially to 'people at Oxford and Cambridge who would be in a position to know the field'. This could be (and was) criticised, but there is no disputing the results. Whittaker's recruits included three future vice-chancellors, two future heads of Cambridge colleges and the Nobel prize-winner, George Porter.

Whittaker decided to retire early at the age of 60 in 1965, not a surprising decision in view of his statement that 'my natural interests are all of a scholarly nature and I find it increasingly difficult to give my whole attention to adminis-trative problems'.[224] During the next few years he taught mathematics at Birm-ingham, Cairo and Teheran Universities, but he kept a permanent home in Endcliffe, where he died in 1984. He and his popular wife, Iona, held a magnificent retirement party in University House to which, at their own expense, more than 1,100 guests were invited.

Whittaker was a shy man who never quite attained ease as a vice-chancellor, but among his many strengths was his encouragement of a team of able people, both lay officers and administrators, to whom he delegated some important work. Sheffield was fortunate to have officers of the calibre of Young and Connell and adminis-trators like Urquhart (who departed only a year after Whittaker, to become Registrar at Southampton). Professor Clapham made an impressive acting vice-chancellor during an interregnum which included the departure of another registrar. George Clark, Chapman's successor, stayed less than two years, for family reasons. His temporary replacement was Frank Hooley, well known locally in a political context as 'Hooley for Heeley'; he was elected as a Labour MP in 1966.

The search committee for a new vice-chancellor, under the chairmanship of Gerard Young, set out to scour the world for the best person, determined to take the time necessary to do the job properly. As Arthur Connell recalled, the committee

Left to right:

Jack and Iona Whittaker in the garden of the Vice-Chancellor's Lodge at the time of his retirement. He confided to the Sheffield Telegraph that he was anxious to 'settle down again to the study of complex variables'.

Hugh 'Norrie' Robson was a Scot whose career had taken him to Australia as Professor of Medicine at the University of Adelaide. In the next thirteen years he established the new department and became a specialist in blood diseases; he admitted later that treating terminal leukaemia, especially in children, was something he no longer felt able to do and the call to Sheffield was the new challenge he needed.

made lists of the qualities to be desired in a vice-chancellor, until every member had 'a settled, if somewhat irrational, conviction that one day we would meet a man and straightway say, "This is a vice-chancellor"'.[225] The committee, which had five academic representatives, drew up lists of names, sent scores of letters to colleagues at home and abroad, and conducted several interviews. The search lasted nine months before its members heard about Hugh Norwood Robson, Dean of the Faculty of Medicine at the University of Adelaide. Robson came over to Sheffield and was interviewed privately at the Hallam Tower Hotel on Fulwood Road. Connell recalled that he and Young first took him up to the Penthouse to see the view of the university's residential quarter and the Derbyshire moors beyond. Robson commented, 'You know, there's a precedent for taking those about to be tempted on to high places'.[226] During the afternoon which followed, every member of the Committee became convinced that they had met their man.

Professor Robson, who was always known as 'Norrie', returned to Sheffield on the Oriana in January 1966. 'A bevy of beautiful young women' accompanied him, since he and his wife had two teenage daughters and an Australian nurse for their son Michael, who was only sixteen months old.[227] The sudden move to a British winter and an unknown city was challenging and Robson arrived in the middle of an academic year, but he impressed everyone by his efficiency in his new role. Robson quickly mastered complex briefs and was also very good-humoured. He liked to tell how, during his first week in Sheffield, he had to entertain the Soviet Cultural Attaché, who was due to present books to the Library. After lunch, he conducted the visitor across the campus at a brisk pace, only to stop short and mutter to a colleague, 'Where is the damned library, anyway?'[228]

Robson instituted informal weekly discussions with his pro-vice-chancellors, over coffee and sandwiches. Eric Laughton recalls that 'no subject, however trivial, was barred'. The lack of an agenda gave everyone a wider-ranging perspective on the University and the Vice-Chancellor had the chance to talk things over with trusted colleagues. But he was most certainly in charge. Beyond the affability, and central to Robson's personality, lay determination, ideals and the highest standards. He had true *gravitas* and came to be considered by many colleagues, at Sheffield and beyond, as 'an ideal vice-chancellor'.[229] Yet he was never pompous. A typical story is that he once drove down to St George's in his own car, and the car park attendant, not recognising him, said, 'I'm sorry, Sir, only people from St George's are allowed in here'. Robson replied, 'Oh are they? I'm so sorry', and parked somewhere else.

A new Registrar joined the staff five months before Robson. Alexander Monteith Currie, previously Academic Secretary to the University of Liverpool, was also a Scot and he and Robson forged the closest of working partnerships. Currie was a man of 'colossal energy', with an ebullient personality and an excellent sense of humour.[230] The Registry was extremely busy, but Currie brought relaxation to its rather austere atmosphere. He recalled that,

Sheffield United had a brilliant but quixotic forward, inconveniently – indeed inconsiderately – called Tony Currie. The back page Monday

Below: *Alex Currie, OBE, Registrar and Secretary 1965–78.*

Left: *The other face of Alex Currie, appearing, centre, in the Staff Dramatic Society's production of* The Tempest *with Alan England and Stan Collier.*

229

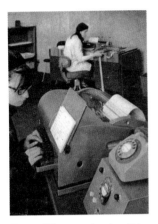

The new Telex system introduced into the Library in 1967. Before email or fax this was the best means of fast print communication. Used principally for book orders and inter-library loans, messages were typed and produced on teleprinters at both ends.

morning headlines succinctly summed up his performance on the previous Saturday at Bramall Lane and were eagerly collected by Peter [Linacre] and his staff. I remember one particularly bleak Monday when he smirkingly brought me up the rubric, 'Another lack-lustre Currie performance'.[231]

There is a real sense that a new team came in to bat in the mid-sixties. That team had an outlook which was more national and less parochial, with the ability to take Sheffield into the first division of universities. Despite all the recent building, Currie's first impression was that, in comparison to Liverpool, Sheffield was:

> a slightly homespun place. A place that had built itself up, certainly, but still was very close to origins that showed it had had to watch the pennies. All those temporary huts [demolished soon after Currie arrived, to make way for the Biology block] . . . were still there from the First World War. . . . [In Western Bank] I remember an over-powering smell of carbolic soap! It was a lovely building but it was sparse and there didn't seem to be many luxurious trimmings about it.[232]

Both men did as much as they could, given the increasing government restraints. Compared with the cuts to come, they were in clover but under Labour the UGC came under the control of the Department of Education & Science and thus became its agent rather than 'the neutral mediator between universities and government' which it had been created to be.[233] Limitations on growth were imposed from 1967 and universities like Sheffield were forced to improve their proportions of arts-based students at the expense of places in science.[234] The development plan previously agreed, with a timetable of ten years, was brought to a sudden halt, damaging staff morale and delaying buildings in the later part of the schedule. Unfortunately, this affected departments which were expanding fast, like Psychology, although the Geography building was allowed to proceed.

Relations between Officers and Students

In December 1966 the Labour government announced the imposition of a considerable increase on the fees of overseas students, to start in 1967. This was firmly and unanimously opposed by the CVCP, but universities could only avoid imposing the increase by bearing the cost themselves. This option was considered in Sheffield, but reluctantly dismissed. The issue, which became a running sore because of further large increases in the 1970s, badly damaged relations with overseas students. It 'upset Norrie greatly', according to his wife.[235] He saw the fee rise as 'a blatant form of discrimination'.[236]

The Students' Union, in which overseas students had been active for many years, took the view that the University had reserves it could draw upon if it wished. Four universities did, in fact, choose this course of action. Anti-racism was a consistent theme of student protest from now on. The University offered help in cases of

Lord Butler at a meeting with students in the lower refectory in University House in April 1969.

hardship and supported an Overseas Students Bureau in the Union to give 'advice and practical help'.[237]

1968 is well known as the year in which the force of student rebellion began to knock the breath out of university administrations in Britain. The Vietnam War had provoked student opposition on a vast scale in America and this crossed the Atlantic for an anti-war demonstration in London in October 1968 when students occupied the London School of Economics.[238] There was strong reaction to the LSE's decision to dismiss two lecturers who had supported the occupation.[239] The Chancellor, Lord Butler, who was a member of the LSE Board, was heckled at a higher degrees congregation in April 1969, and at one point Sheffield students voted to offer the LSE lecturers employment out of Union funds. This was swiftly voted down by a larger meeting and even a planned boycott of lectures did not take place. A considerable number of academic staff supported their LSE colleagues. All this coincided with a government report on lecturers' salaries which was received with 'astonishment and derision' in the universities and with a national strike by ASTMS, during which many university technicians downed tools.[240]

Every vice-chancellor who avoided the excesses of the LSE or Essex at this time breathed a sigh of relief. There were occupations at ten other universities at least, including Leeds, Birmingham and Manchester.[241] To a certain extent Sheffield was lucky, but attitude and skill helped, and his colleagues were quick to praise Robson's handling of student issues. Robson was neither reactionary nor out-of-touch with students. His own teenage daughter, Eleanor, married the President of the Students' Union, Julian Allitt, in 1969. Even before he arrived in Sheffield, Robson was

Engagement photograph of Eleanor Robson, daughter of the Vice-Chancellor, and Julian Allitt, Student President, from the front page of Darts 22 May 1969.

231

Helen Davidson, the first female Union President since 1930, after her election in 1969.

quoted as saying that, 'a little beer and a little horseplay by students are not a bad thing' and 'it will be a sad day for this country when our youth loses its high spirits, and worse still if we ever lose our sense of humour'.[242] He was to demonstrate this on many occasions, for example when students managed to penetrate the Concorde hangar in Bristol during the 1968 Rag week and he received the inevitable official complaint. When asked, 'What are you going to do about your students?' he is said to have responded, 'What are you going to do about your security?'

Robson's response to student aggravation was to refuse to be provoked even by personal attack and to be 'ready for a constructive discussion'.[243] On occasion this meant that he remained in a meeting lasting several hours, often with the ringleaders of a campaign. Harry Armytage, who was chairman of the Staff-Student Committee, used to say 'stick with them' and this is what both he and Robson did.[244] The Staff-Student Committee also proved to be a forum which, in Alex Currie's words, 'helped to leak a lot of that trouble away'. By the mid-sixties, the membership of this committee comprised eight students and nine staff.

All universities became more democratic in response to an NUS campaign demanding student representation on university committees. Sheffield had little difficulty with student involvement in welfare committees, like health and accommodation, but problems arose over committees responsible for academic decisions, especially Senate. It was early in 1970 before a special meeting of Senate finally agreed to admit three students, who would be eligible for election to Senate committees and faculty boards.[245] By 1972 student representatives had full membership of Council. As a by-product, democracy was extended to the Non-Professorial Staff Association (NPSA), whose committee representation was much improved.[246] Senate agreed to encourage all departments to hold regular staff meetings and to give all academic staff access to the papers and minutes of Senate and faculty boards.[247]

The sixties were vintage years for Rag stunts. In 1967 three students painted 'HMS TWIKKER' in whitewash on the bows of the QEII when she was moored in the Queen's Dock on Clydeside.

Far right: Students painted a zebra crossing the full width of a new stretch of the M1 near Chesterfield during the 1967 Rag; the police were not amused.

Rag Day and its procession, late 1960s; students stayed up all night preparing the floats.

STUDENT CULTURE IN THE SIXTIES

'Intro Week', originally called 'Freshmen's week', started in 1960 and included a vice-chancellor's reception, held over three nights so that Whittaker could greet each student personally.[248] 1960 was also the year in which the SRC launched an organised attempt to show prospective students around the campus. This grew into Student Reception, a working committee of the Union with its own offices and a large number of volunteer recruits. It became the biggest service of its kind in the country, with a Sabbatical Officer from 1968. The efficiency and warmth of its welcome encouraged many interviewees to choose Sheffield over other universities.

Early sixties alumni recall a packed meeting in Graves Hall at the time of the Cuban missile crisis (1962) 'when the future of the world hung in the balance'. It was too serious for a Rag stunt. Students who plastered newspaper stands in the city centre with the headline 'War declared' were suspended.[249] Geography students who had built an 'intercontinental ballistic missile on a huge artic. lowloader' as a float were told by the Rag Committee that it was too frightening to use. They 'worked all night to cut windows into it and turned it into Dan Dare's spaceship' instead. Despite such moments, the students of the sixties and seventies were a favoured generation. They had new facilities, grants and leisure; hardly any of them needed to take a job during term-time. Social life centred on the Union or hall bars or on pubs like 'The Raven' on Division Street or 'The Red Deer' on Pitt Street. Union societies flourished. Morris Dancing, Jazz Club, Folk Group, Theatre Group, Gilbert and Sullivan, Bridge Club, climbing and a wide variety of sports clubs are all fondly remembered. Chaplaincies in the main Christian denominations attracted young adherents and offered not only a home from home but also an expansion of conventional horizons. A former student who overcame claustrophobia by going caving with the Speleological Society asked, 'Does the university still see itself as developing the whole person? Sheffield did that for me'.

Conservative styles of dress were still normal in the early sixties – grey flannel trousers, sports jacket, shirt and tie for the men; skirts for the women. University

Jim Holmes and Dennis O'Neill (right) performing in the piano marathon outside the cathedral in the 1969 Festival. O'Neill went on to become an international opera star.

Baden Prince, a law student from Antigua, became President of the Union in 1962. He is seen here with Rosemary Maxwell, his Vice-President. In 1966 he was appointed as the first Race Conciliation Officer for Greater London.

scarves were essential, the most popular being the Union scarf in longitudinal stripes of blue, yellow, black and white, or the University scarf in black and gold. Only the scarves survived the fashion revolution of the sixties. Miniskirts arrived in Sheffield (although a long time after they appeared in Carnaby Street) followed by women's trousers (it is said that two women were ejected from a physics lecture for wearing trousers in 1965). Men abandoned their jackets and flannels for jeans and teeshirts; 'some people were the real hippy types with afghan coats and flowery shirts'. Hair styles changed dramatically; long hair and beards were normal by the end of the decade. Cigarette smoking was common, but the youth drug culture so widely reported was encountered by relatively few in Sheffield.[250]

Sexism had yet to be invented; every edition of *Darts* featured the 'dolly pic', usually a glamorous student. The new absence of deference towards staff spilled over in some articles. When Professor Eastwood complained that students did not attend his lectures after the all-night 'Spider Walk', the Union Secretary responded: 'I find it regrettable that Prof Eastwood should presume to tell people that his lecture is particularly worthwhile. He is in no position to judge its value'.[251] This Secretary held one of the two new Sabbatical posts, which were added to the Presidency in 1963. Funded jointly by the Union and the University, the Sabbaticals were paid a Bursary of £750. That did not stop them biting the hand that fed them – and the biting was to become even more vicious in the 1970s.

234

The Arts Festival

In the sixties and early seventies, the Students' Union was central to an initiative which is now almost forgotten. To celebrate the vast new spaces of University House and the Library, the Union decided to stage an Arts Festival after the final examinations in 1963. Baden Prince, then Student President, came up with the idea and inspired a large number of volunteers to help. Five hundred students took part and the programme included concerts, ranging from classical to jazz to cabaret, and dramatic productions. An international theme introduced classical Indian music, Kathak dancing and Calypso bands. Sculptures by Epstein and Henry Moore were displayed on the campus.[252]

In subsequent years, the Festival continued its tradition of eclecticism and controversy.[253] The showing of two 'blue' films was criticised in the local press in 1967 and the extremes of 'avant garde' theatre provoked some adult gasps. The most successful events were the film festival, the late-night Festival Club and the folk concerts, which opened the Festival in later years with packed-out gatherings in Paradise Square. Although its organisation was often a scramble, the Festival's events proliferated to the point where a 'Festival Diary' was essential. Student productions grew more ambitious and included operas like *Carmen* and *Dido and Aeneas* and plays like Eliot's *Murder in the Cathedral*.

The intention was to be a civic, rather than just a university, event and so the name 'Sheffield Festival' was adopted in 1965. The City Council made a small grant

Reclining Figure, by Henry Moore, loaned for the first Arts Festival in 1963 by the Tate Gallery and displayed outside Western Bank.

Below left: Jacob and the Angel, by Epstein, loaned for the same Festival, was displayed in the glass-fronted entrance to the Library. It proved controversial and its loan was terminated when a Muslim steelworker threw stones through the window at it because it offended his religion.

Below right: Stainless steel sculpture, by A. P. Armitage, erected opposite the Students' Union in 1965 to mark the RIBA Conference at the University.

each year; Bill Galbraith of Physics was the chairman.[254] In the mid-seventies the Festival was wound up when the Council withdrew its support. By then the City was funding other arts activities, not least the new Crucible Theatre. Gerard Young chaired the development committee, knowing, he said, 'nothing about theatres, but by then quite a bit about building'.[255]

The Western Bank Concourse

Once the Hicks Building and University House were open, the dual carriageway running through the Western Bank campus was not only divisive, but also a serious hazard.[256] By 1966 there were 10,000 crossings a day, but the only pedestrian crossing was much higher up the road. In the Union feelings were running high, with calls for direct action in the form of a 'human barricade' after an accident in which a student broke a collar-bone.

Roy Johnson, the Planning Officer, had produced 'dozens and dozens of schemes' when one day:

> I just happened to be looking at a plan and it occurred to me that the level outside the Arts Tower . . . was virtually the same as the level of the bridge leading into University House. The solution was staring me in the face. I could connect those two on the same level, . . . chop out a piece of Western Bank and replace it with a bridge.[257]

It was fortuitous that Johnson had this idea before the foundations of the Biology building had been dug. He and Young decided to site the ground floor at this level and construct steps up to Western Bank. They had the foresight to refuse to build 'one of these corporation underground pedestrian ways', tunnels, which were the favoured sixties solution and have since become very unpopular.[258] The City Council was persuaded to help with finance and eventually gave £50,000 of the £160,000 cost.

The design of the flyover, and the concourse created thereby, was an engineering triumph which won a Civic Trust award as 'an excellent example of generous and constructive thinking, turning what was a serious nuisance and hazard into a distinct asset'.[259] Ove Arup and Partners designed a bridge with two halves, one for each carriageway, separated by a light-well. Central supports proved to be the best way of avoiding the effect of a tunnel, since they emphasised 'the space underneath the bridge rather than the bridge itself'.[260] Construction was undertaken one carriageway at a time and the new concourse opened in September 1969.

This project involved the demolition of all the remaining houses in the area and completed a major restructuring of the landscape, to create the physical contours of the campus today. This restructuring, together with the new buildings and the huge increase in student and staff numbers, makes the sixties a uniquely important decade in the University's history. Harry Kay, the chairman of ADC, summed up the achievement:

The campus in 1968, just before the Concourse was created. The Biology building is under construction.

237

Right: *The bridge designed by Ove Arup and Partners created a major visual as well as physical link between the buildings of the central campus which were separated by Western Bank. The scheme was only possible because of the support and co-operation of the City Council.*

Below: *The bridge supports, adapted for student use.*

Sheffield, to me, seemed to grow enormously in stature during [the sixties]. It made the best of a very, very difficult site . . . linking its Union half to its Western Bank half . . . It was the sort of place where the Professor of Chemistry, distinguished FRS that he was, would know just how well or how badly Sheffield Wednesday had played on Saturday. It was the sort of place where its links with its community, down in the steelworks and so on, were strong . . . Sheffield was moving forward in such a way that I felt there was more internal vigour in the place than in many of the universities which I had the privilege of visiting as external examiner and as member of the UGC sub-committees. In short, one was very proud to be a member of a university of this kind.[261]

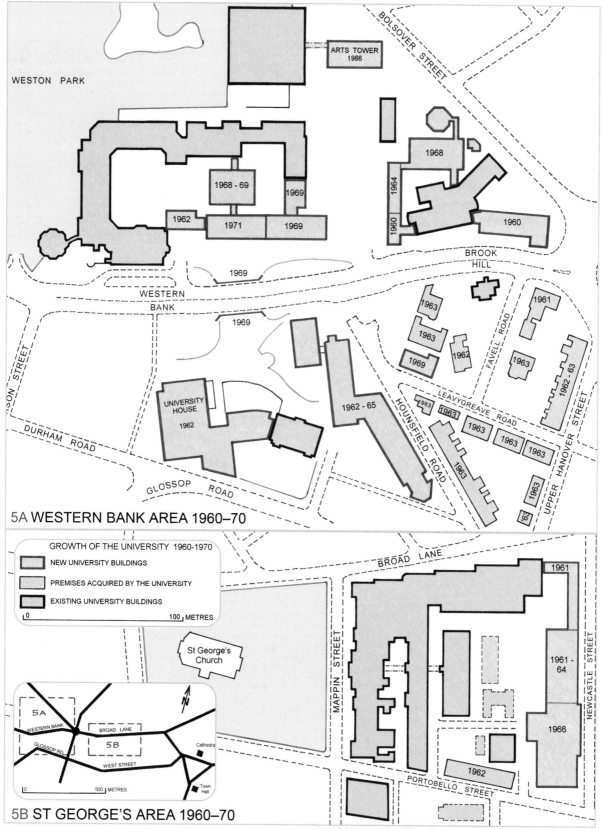

5A WESTERN BANK AREA 1960–70

WESTON PARK

ARTS TOWER
1966

BOLSOVER STREET

BROOK HILL

1968-69
1969
1962
1971
1969

1968
1964
1960
1960
1960

1969
WESTERN BANK
1969

1969

UNIVERSITY HOUSE
1962

1962-65

HOUNSFIELD ROAD

DURHAM ROAD

GLOSSOP ROAD

1963
1963
1969
1962
1963
1963
1961
1963
1962-63
LEAVYGREAVE ROAD
FAVELL ROAD
UPPER HANOVER STREET
1963
1963
1963
1963
1963
1963
1963
1963
'63

GROWTH OF THE UNIVERSITY 1960-1970

- NEW UNIVERSITY BUILDINGS
- PREMISES ACQUIRED BY THE UNIVERSITY
- EXISTING UNIVERSITY BUILDINGS

0 ____ 100 METRES

St George's Church

BROAD LANE

MAPPIN STREET

NEWCASTLE STREET

1961

1961-64

1966

1962

PORTOBELLO STREET

5A
WESTERN BANK
GLOSSOP RD.
BROAD LANE
5B
WEST STREET
Cathedral
Town Hall

0 ____ 500 METRES

5B ST GEORGE'S AREA 1960–70

Maps © Crown Copyright Ordnance Survey

6

Constant Change is Here to Stay:* the Seventies and Eighties

The 'confidential files' episode

'NORRIE' ROBSON BECAME CHAIRMAN OF THE COMMITTEE of Vice Chancellors and Principals (CVCP) in 1972, the first (but not the last) time that a Sheffield Vice-Chancellor assumed this important role.[1] He was also a key member of the Association of Commonwealth Universities and regularly commuted to London, fully justifying the faith of the appointing committee that Robson would put Sheffield on the national map.[2] This he insisted on doing even at some cost to his health, which was not robust. He was once taken ill in London with appendicitis and insisted on returning to Sheffield in great pain to be operated on by Ron Clark of the Department of Surgery.[3] He had to contend with Margaret Thatcher as Education Secretary during the Conservative government of 1970–74. According to Robson, she once summoned the vice-chancellors together and barked, 'Stand forward those of you who have medical schools'. They were 'visibly shaking' as she demanded to know why their universities were not taking more women into medicine.[4]

Her next demand was 'get your students in order', with which vice-chancellors would have loved to comply, if only they could. 1970/71 was dominated by the rather extraordinary episode of the 'confidential files'. National paranoia about student and staff files began when a member of Warwick's Council gained access to that university's files to check on the left-wing activities of two members of staff.[5] Offices on many campuses were occupied while students searched for compromising files. In Sheffield, 2,500 students packed a Union general meeting in March 1970 at which Robson patiently explained that he could not open files because they

Facing page: The Quadrangle *by Paul Waplington, 1983.*

* *Notice on the office wall of the Registrar & Secretary, 1978–82.*

241

contained confidential references, but they did not record political views and were never shown to the police.[6] In an atmosphere of hostility and distrust, he took the great risk of making a joke. With Currie standing beside him, Robson disclosed that there were indeed secret files in Sheffield: some were held in caves in Derbyshire and the really important ones had been microfilmed and kept in 'a hollow tooth of the Registrar'.[7] There was silence before someone giggled and then the audience burst out laughing. A Senate proposal to appoint an external assessor who would examine files on the students' behalf was accepted by another packed meeting three days later. At the July degree congregations the relieved Chancellor, Lord Butler, praised the behaviour of Sheffield students, saying, 'I hardly know of any student population which has behaved in such a responsible and effective way'.[8]

Fears that university authorities would use information about the political activity of staff to block selection or promotion led to the formation of the Council for Academic Freedom and Democracy in 1970. One of its leading lights was Anthony Arblaster who, after a brief but colourful career at Manchester University, lost his temporary lectureship; whereupon Bernard Crick offered him a refuge in Sheffield's Politics department.[9] Arblaster's book *Academic Freedom* (1974) became the Bible of the movement. Although he and left-wing colleagues held political views which they believed were not supported by the majority of staff, the slogan of 'academic freedom' had the capacity to unite across the political spectrum.[10] Even a Conservative like Colin Renfrew, of Archaeology, wrote to *The Times* about staff selection issues.[11]

Lecturers were among the objectors to the award of an honorary degree to Lee Kuan Yew, the Prime Minister of Singapore, in 1971, due to his country's dismal human rights record.[12] The ceremony in Firth Hall took place against a background of chanting, but Robson refused to have the demonstrators ejected from their own university building.[13] The award was described by the moderate Union President, Abdul Gani, as 'a political gesture' and it even provoked objections in the House of Commons.[14] During the years 1971–74 such conflict was, however, uncharacteristic. Shortly afterwards, this period came to be seen as the calm before the storm.

Norrie Robson addressing a packed Union General Meeting on 5 March 1970.

The Geography building, designed by Whitfield and Partners. The City Council agreed to allow the building to be landscaped as part of the park, with no boundary fences. This feature was among those praised by the Civic Trust, which awarded the building a commendation in 1972/73.

BUILDINGS OF THE ROBSON ERA

The Geography Building

The Geography building, discussed and delayed since the early 1960s, opened in 1970 on a beautiful site next to Weston Park. A fine town house, Westonville, was demolished, as well as shops and a row of terraced houses, but the new building was a worthy successor. It was truly innovative, designed to take advantage of its position, with 'a cluster of hexagonal units of different heights' at the end of a main six-storey wing containing a library, a map room and teaching laboratories.[15] This wing featured a central glass-enclosed lift surrounded by the main staircase, while a large brass compass was inlaid into the floor of the main foyer. The hexagons housed drawing offices, research rooms and staff offices.

The design of the Geography building won a Civic Trust commendation in 1972/73. It was a desirable home for a department which had grown fast during the sixties and was by 1970 producing over 100 graduates annually, and awarding degrees within three faculties. It was also running a noted MSc in applied geomorphology which attracted many overseas postgraduates. Alice Garnett, who had done so much to aid this expansion and the idea of a purpose-built home, retired in 1968.[16] Ron Waters was head of department when the new building opened.

Alice Garnett, who joined the staff of the Geography department as a lecturer in 1924 and retired as a professor in 1968. Her total service to the University was 53 years, since she continued to study air pollution at her research unit for nine years after her retirement. She was awarded an honorary degree in 1980.

243

Above: *This Baptist Church, built in 1871, was imaginatively converted into the Drama Studio in 1970. It created a flexible space that has since been in constant use by groups from both the University and the community.*

Right: *The interior of the Drama Studio.*

The Drama Studio

After the demise of the Theatre plan in the 1960s, *ad hoc* arrangements continued until it occurred to Alec Daykin of the Architecture department that the old Baptist Church on Shearwood Road, which was used as a furniture store, could be converted into a theatre.[17] Daykin made a model which envisaged a great deal of flexibility. Much of the audience seating could be moved and the acting area adapted to provide different kinds of staging, including thrust, proscenium and Elizabethan. The project committee were captivated by the model and had great fun trying out the various layouts. Frank Pierce promoted the idea within the Senate and the Drama Studio was born.

An orchestra pit and stage traps were provided, together with effective lighting. The result was a flexible theatre which has proved to be suitable for everything from Shakespeare to contemporary plays and from musicals to ballet. 'The Drama Studio was a luxury which would have been the envy of many provincial theatre companies – superbly kitted out and very versatile', recalled a student member of the Theatre Group at this time. 'A fantastic resource', said another, who went on to work in the theatre. Stephen Daldry, who became a leading national theatre and film director, was a member of Theatre Group and is remembered by some for the moment when

244

Above: *Stephen Daldry, who read English at the University (1979–82), went on to become a highly successful theatre and film director.*

Far left: *The British premiere of the opera* Masaniello Furioso *by Reinhard Keiser was staged at the Studio in November 1973 in the presence of the German Ambassador Karl-Gunther von Hase.*

Left: *Bill Royston and Helen McCallum in J. M. Barrie's* Seven Women, *a 1987 Staff Dramatic Society production which took first prize in the Sheffield and District Amateur Theatre Association Awards – one of many successes for the Society. Royston was also awarded the prize for outstanding performance.*

he wore both a tutu and a military jacket in *The Ruling Class*. In addition to the Students' Union and Staff Dramatic Society, the English and modern languages departments used the Studio for their own productions. The Music department seized on the opportunity in ambitious style, by staging a baroque chamber opera. This became an annual event under Professor Basil Deane and his successors, while the enthusiasm of local community music and drama groups for the Studio ensured that it was booked throughout the year.

Alex Currie was an enthusiastic actor and while he was Registrar, the Staff Dramatic Society was virtually run from the Registry. It was almost a condition of appointment that his staff helped out, front or back stage, and there are happy memories of the productions. For example, pantomimes for University children were held for several years. Some of the actors came to remember their roles – and their costumes – with 'a mixture of affection and embarrassment', but John Ebling of Zoology was shameless enough to send a Christmas card sporting a photograph of himself wearing Tudor doublet and hose.[18]

The Drama Studio was managed for its first 25 years by Bill Royston, who not only presided over many successful productions but was himself a consummate actor, taking roles like King Lear and Richard III. Rehearsal rooms were later created in the old Sunday School behind the Studio, previously used by the Architecture faculty.

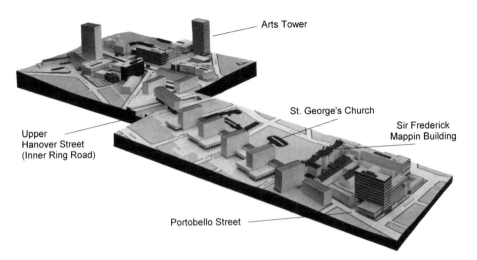

Model of the Portobello Strip development plan by Arup Associates. A glazed bridge over Upper Hanover Street was proposed to overcome the problem of a busy dual carriageway which effectively divided the campus. It would have been open to members of the public as well as the University.

Arts Tower

St. George's Church

Sir Frederick Mappin Building

Upper Hanover Street (Inner Ring Road)

Portobello Street

The Portobello strip and Crookesmoor

The University produced an extraordinarily ambitious Development Plan in 1966, looking ahead to the possibility of 10,000 students by the 1980s.[19] The plan suggested 'zoning' a development area stretching from Crookesmoor Road and Harcourt Road on the north-western edge to Newcastle Street and West Street at the eastern end. If this scheme had gone ahead, the University would have stretched from Parker's Road in Broomhill to beyond St George's Square. The perceived advantage was a 'wider', as well as more united, campus.[20] One of the most important features was the 'Portobello strip', running from Upper Hanover Street beside the Jessop Hospital and St George's Church as far as Mappin Street, so linking the St George's area to the buildings around Western Bank. Every vice-chancellor has regretted the divided campus and Robson presided over an ambitious attempt to unite it.[21]

In 1970 a competition was held for the 'strip' and won by Arup Associates, the designers of the Western Bank concourse.[22] Their cuboid buildings, all for Technology, reflected contemporary architectural enthusiasm for grid-based system planning. The most, indeed the only, exciting feature was a large bridge in the form of a 'generous glazed concourse' straddling Upper Hanover Street and linking the two parts of Leavygreave. This bridge, however, was never built and no section of the 'strip' was developed until the 1990s. The plan did, however, influence the design of the first new building on Leavygreave Road, to house the new ICL 1906S main-frame and other major computers. The Computing Centre, completed in 1976, had a reception and offices at first-floor level with the main-frames and the plant room needed to drive them below.

The Psychology building was opened a year earlier, in 1975, on a site at the top of Western Bank, between Northumberland Road and Mushroom Lane. In size and location, this building reflected the stature which the department had achieved under Harry Kay. It was intended to be the first of several dedicated buildings for social science and arts departments in the vicinity, since the 1966 plan envisaged zoning the campus according to faculty.

The decision to place the faculties of Social Sciences and Law in the Northumberland Road/Crookesmoor area continued to guide planning even after 1973, when the development zone there was reduced somewhat.[23] The retained area was bounded by Moor Oaks Road and contained Elmore and Marlborough Roads and parts of Crookesmoor Road. Unlike Portobello, Crookesmoor and Broomhill contained desirable homes with articulate owners. They did not appreciate the 'blight' of university zoning which, in effect, prevented them selling their homes on the open market. Those who were not reprieved in 1973 organised themselves to resist university encroachments and started an impressive campaign, with strong local press coverage and eloquent arguments against the University's plans.[24] The Crookesmoor/Mooroaks Residents' Association, led by Terry Cooper and the 'redoubtable' Angela Coe, mother of the Olympic champion Sebastian Coe (later Lord Coe), demanded meetings with Costain and Currie.[25] They joined forces with the Broomhill Action and Neighbourhood Group (BANG), which was trying to prevent the further intrusion of the Hallamshire Hospital into the suburb regarded by John Betjeman as the finest in England. The era of the unquestioned physical expansion of the University was over.

The protests eventually forced the University to curtail most of its plans for the area and should probably have prompted a rethink in 1974. However, at that time there was one large site at the bottom of Conduit Road (originally Crookesmoor House), which proved irresistibly attractive because the University already owned it. It was, in truth, a long walk from the main campus, but the Glass Technology buildings, the Goodwin Athletics Centre and the Psychology building formed an almost continuous link to it. A new Law and Economics building had been

The Psychology building, opened in 1975 by the Prince of Wales, was designed by Renton Howard Wood Levin Partnership, architects of the successful Crucible Theatre. The main entrance to Psychology faces the busy Western Bank while the quieter side, containing the larger windows, overlooks the Bramley playing fields.

Above: *The Crookesmoor library.*

Right: *The Crookesmoor building, designed by Whitfield and Partners, combines hexagonal units with a long low-level library, all facing inwards to a small quadrangle. The site was enhanced by the retention of established trees. The building originally housed Law, Economics and Economic History; by the mid-1990s Law was in sole possession.*

scheduled for this site since 1966. Local opponents suggested that it would be an 'office block' in a residential area.[26]

The design of the Crookesmoor building was in fact attractive and of an appropriate scale for the surrounding houses. It was also sensitively landscaped on completion in 1977. Roy Johnson claimed that it was inspired by a monastery,[27] but a closer model was the admired Geography building with its hexagons, designed by the same architect, William Whitfield. Crookesmoor has seven separate units, the largest crowned by a turret, with interconnecting covered walkways. A large library had space for 65,000 books and there were several lecture theatres, as well as common rooms and offices for the staff of Law, Economics and Economic History.

One 1970s student thought the view from the Crookesmoor building so spectacular that it would be 'a good place to be buried'! Another, however, found the library cold in winter, because the radiators were placed near the ceiling 'taking advantage of the fact that heat falls'. For the University, its location made parking difficult, and it was immediately apparent that there could be no expansion of the facilities without knocking down neighbouring houses. Compulsory purchase orders were served on some of these in 1978, but the opposition campaign shifted into a higher gear and the City Council reduced its support, despite arguments made by the University about its major contribution to the local economy.[28] Even the Students' Union President, and David Gosling, Dean of the Faculty of Architecture, spoke against the expansion when a public enquiry was finally held in

August 1979.[29] The compulsory purchase orders were revoked and there has since been no further development of new sites at Crookesmoor.

This disappointment should not overshadow the achievement of the 1960s and 1970s development plans. The University created a campus which stretched from the borders of Broomhill to the edge of the central business district, with a great deal of variety in between. This campus is comfortably integrated into the city; a quality which has become part of the educational experience.

THE DEPARTURE OF ROBSON

Soon after Robson became chairman of the CVCP, the government published a white paper *Education: A Framework for Expansion* (December 1972), which envisaged 22 per cent of school leavers in higher education by 1981. It was the last time that the Robbins ideology formed the basis of public policy.[30] University budgets for the quinquennium 1972–77 were accepted without too much demur and expansion plans were drawn up, in Sheffield's case for 10,000 students by the early eighties. This climate of optimism was destroyed within a year by the energy crisis, the miners' strike and the three-day week. In January 1974 the UGC withheld compensation for inflation and reduced grants for furniture and equipment. Robson's last months as the chairman of CVCP were spent trying to recover some of the lost ground. Sheffield was forced to draw on its reserves, but proved conspicuously lucky in being given the go-ahead for both the Crookesmoor and Computing buildings. The money allocated to Sheffield by the UGC was ten per cent of its entire budget for non-medical building purposes.[31]

In 1973 Hugh Robson was invited to become Principal of his *alma mater*, Edinburgh University – an offer he could not refuse. He left Sheffield in the summer of 1974, with a knighthood for his services to education (received at the same time as Roy Marshall, who was by then secretary-general of the CVCP). At the time, Robson described the role of vice-chancellor as that of the 'conductor of an orchestra whose score has not been written'.[32] He also likened himself to the general practitioner who listened to the concerns of his community, even if he could not solve every problem.[33] These were modest aspirations from a man who knew that most of the events in the university world were outside his control. Yet he achieved as much as could realistically be hoped for, mostly by 'going to London', at a time when the government's attitude to higher education was either unreliable or actively unhelpful. (Downright hostility came later.)

Edinburgh was delighted to reclaim Robson, but his first year was marred by student disruption on a scale far greater than Sheffield had seen. His diplomacy improved the situation, but he was to have only three years as Principal there. In December 1977, he had a stroke in his office and died a few days later at the age of 60. In his memorial oration Edinburgh's Rector, Magnus Magnusson, referred to the 'healing qualities' and 'selfless dedication' of 'this very special man' and hoped that they would remain as inspirations to the universities he had guided, Edinburgh and Sheffield.[34]

Geoffrey Sims, Vice-Chancellor 1974–90, came to Sheffield from the University of Southampton with a distinguished record in electronics as well as considerable experience of university management.

THE NEW VICE-CHANCELLOR, GEOFFREY SIMS

Professor Geoffrey Sims came from the University of Southampton, where he had become head of the Electronics department in 1963, a time of 'explosion' in the possibilities of the subject, with an 'exciting' atmosphere generated by relatively young professors.[35] The department quadrupled in size under his leadership. After four years as a dean and experience as a deputy vice-chancellor, he pondered his future and decided to accept a post as vice-chancellor, should he be offered one.

There was a short-list of three to replace Robson in 1974. Sims was competing with a distinguished Oxford historian, who was considered by some to be too old for the post, and an internal candidate, John Wood from Law.[36] For the first time, the appointment committee included not only a representative of NPSA (the Non-Professorial Staff Association) but also the Union President John O'Leary. O'Leary's involvement was unique to Sheffield, according to Currie, who believed that it demonstrated the maturity of its staff/student relations. This was, indeed, a feature of O'Leary's year of office, but the next two Presidents had appalling relations with Western Bank.

Darts depicts Geoffrey Sims signing the Union petition against education cuts, and the education minister Fred Mulley (a Sheffield MP) surrounded by a crowd of students protesting against the introduction of differential fees for overseas students.

Geoffrey Sims believed strongly in university autonomy and freedom. 'Its maintenance is crucially important', he said at the time of his appointment, 'interfere and civilisation will suffer'.[37] The new man at the helm was instinctively dedicated to the interests of his staff and was a natural community builder, both internally and externally. Early on, he went out of his way to salve wounds created by the University's expansion plans. A University Council investigation reported in 1975 that future development should not have an 'unacceptable effect' on the local community.[38] Sims cultivated strong relationships with city leaders, and the Extra mural department found him an enthusiastic champion of its efforts to bring university education to the wider community.[39]

The qualities of the 'people person', Sims's self-description, were strongly in evidence. He was unassuming and approachable, described by many colleagues as a very nice man. He disliked rocking the boat, preferring to make it his business to keep it afloat, intact. This proved to be a very considerable, in some cases impossible, task during the years of his vice-chancellorship, which lasted until 1990. Sims's tenure coincided with times of great uncertainty as universities learned, painfully, to deal with governments which had suddenly decided to play with them, as a cat plays with a mouse.

Ever since 1919, the universities had been able to rely on the support of the UGC and its system of quinquennial planning. Although funding was often tight, the system provided a secure base which nurtured the universities until the 1970s. Then this base was destroyed. First there was the refusal to compensate for inflation in 1974, which led in Sheffield to the freezing of vacant academic posts and the cutting of expenditure. Then, in 1976, the Labour government introduced a system of 'annual cash limits' which spelled, in effect, the end of quinquennial planning. This caused severe administrative strain because the limits were announced late in the preceding year and, again, did not sufficiently allow for inflation. Cuts continued each year, with the result that the University, despite making savings, had used up its cash reserves by 1979.[40]

Lord Dainton, the University's future Chancellor, was chairman of the UGC at this time and recalls that the period became one of 'improvised salvage' because of the double-digit inflation and national balance of payments problems.[41] At the same time, university staff were fighting for increases in salaries which had failed to keep pace with inflation. The only control Sheffield had left was over student intake, but that was a cause of concern by 1974, chiefly because of a decline in pure science applications.[42] Sheffield could have capitalised on the increasing popularity of vocational subjects, but a virtual standstill on student numbers was imposed in 1976. It was a very difficult time to be Director of Finance. When John Barker retired from this post in 1980, his successor, Terry Thomas, ruefully counted the new clichés for financial stringency – 'steady state', 'cash limit', 'level funding', 'zero growth' – which had become part of the vocabulary of the University.[43] He attributed the 'almost break-even situation' in 1980 largely to Barker's management and sound judgement. Two Barkers were crucial, in fact, because the Treasurer during the seventies was Chris Barker, a loyal member of Council since 1964 and its Chairman from 1980 to 1987.

THE STUDENT SITUATION

To compound these management problems, Sims (like Robson on his arrival in Edinburgh) found himself confronted by unprecedented student disruption in his early years. The value of the student grant was being eroded by the effects of inflation and government policy and in 1973 Sheffield's Union held the country's largest rent strike in protest.[44] The grant was raised by £20. The following year was marked by severe strain in the relationship between the Union and Western Bank.

Top: Hamish Ritchie and Below: David Bland, who helped to end the student occupation in 1977. They contributed in many other ways to the academic management of the University: Ritchie was head of the Department of Germanic Studies and a pro-vice-chancellor (1975–79), Bland was a self-confessed 'maverick' who nevertheless became the first non-professorial pro-vice-chancellor (1984–88).

The concourse bridge as a platform for student views. The banner reads 'All quiet on the Western Bank. Currie get your peace pipe out.'

'Sticking with them', the favoured policy, proved impossible when Pat Hughes was President (1974/75), because compromise was not part of his language. In an annual report, which he insisted on presenting to the Court unedited, Hughes described the University's attitude to the Union as 'nominal', 'hostile' and 'cynical' and spoke of the betrayal of students.[45]

The issue of overseas student fees erupted again in 1975 when government policy forced an increase of £70.[46] Both the CVCP and UGC continued their opposition to fee differentials, but in the very testing financial climate of the mid-seventies, only Bradford University refused to implement them. Most universities, consequently, felt the full force of student anger. In Sheffield it was expressed through a series of occupations, the first that the University had experienced. In November 1975, after overseas students accosted the visiting government education minister, Fred Mulley, and were told by him to 'go home', there were 'token' occupations of the Tapestry Room, to prevent Council from meeting, and the telephone exchange.[47] A year later, the Labour government announced that the fees for 1977 would be at least double those of 1975. After Council reluctantly agreed to implement these, in February 1977, the protests erupted into an eight-day occupation of Western Bank.[48] Even 'moderates' like the new President, Bob Hamilton, had become convinced that direct action was necessary.[49] One former student recalled that he was persuaded to join by a Singaporean student in his hall and 'had never laid out my sleeping bag in such a posh location before'!

The vast majority of the academic staff, although sympathetic to the cause, were angered by the action and cancelled some classes, with Sims's support.[50] There was unprecedented tension when, on the seventh day, a Union General Meeting voted by 1,425 to 1,088 to continue the occupation. That evening, the pro-vice-chancellor

Hamish Ritchie recalled, he was at home watching *Starsky and Hutch* when he had a phone call from a member of the ADC, David Bland, who said that the students were ready to talk. The Vice-Chancellor was unavailable, so the two of them went into Western Bank and spent several hours listening. Ritchie addressed the mass meeting, telling the students that their point had been made, and they agreed to leave the building. The occupation was over by the time staff arrived next morning. Ritchie, who had previously weathered occupations at the University of Hull, chaired a staff/student working party which in 'endless meetings' devised a system of reduced fees for students who had already started their courses.[51] His report was accepted by both Senate and the Students' Union, but the issue did not, and could not, go away while the government continued to target overseas students.

Even before the February occupation, Geoffrey Sims had described the proposed fee rise as 'vicious and ill-conceived'.[52] He also suggested that government policy of increasing fees to cover 25 per cent of total university income would put academic standards at risk throughout the system. By 1977, both he and Alex Currie had decided to campaign publicly for the abolition of all student fees, on the grounds that the administrative costs were disproportionate and that entry to university 'should be conditional only on a student's ability'.[53] Few other university managers were prepared to go as far as this.

'We were all political in those days', recalled one 1970s student, but the majority limited their activity to attending the emergency general meetings which packed out the Lower Refectory, especially when lectures were cancelled. Student action impinged only indirectly on the lives of most academics but it had a major impact on the administrative staff who worked in Western Bank. They were upset by the occupations and could never be sure when another one was going to take place. Large groups of angry students could be very intimidating and there was genuine fear, even though no violent incidents took place. The danger that Senate and Council members might be trapped in the Tapestry Room for hours led to the opening up of a trap door to the basement. A staircase already existed from the days when this room was the History Library with a stack beneath.

During the eight-day occupation, the Vice-Chancellor was exiled to the medical school and Alex Currie was forced to take up temporary residence in the Hicks building with his staff, from which he angrily looked across at the invaded offices of the Registry. It was impossible for men of his generation to avoid contrasting their own youthful experiences of discipline and hardship during the war, and the sheer relief of being at university, with the negative and rebellious attitudes of the current students. They also felt 'a sense of despair', because of the complete lack of room for financial manoeuvre.[54] Currie's name was scrawled in graffiti on the campus. 'This put a public edge on [my job] which I found disturbing', he recalls. Of course, he was not alone. When registrars met at this time, it was almost as if they had escaped from a battlefield and were capping each other's stories – 'they were frying bacon at my desk', for example.

Alex Currie left Sheffield in 1978 to return to his native Scotland, as Robson had done. He took up the post of Secretary to the University of Edinburgh, but Robson,

Francis Orton, the University's first Academic Secretary (1966–78) and Registrar & Secretary from 1978 until 1982. He brought experience and skill in financial planning to these roles, responding to the spending limits of the 1970s with a statistical model for resource allocation – the Orton Line.

with whom he had formed such a good working partnership, had died by the time he arrived. Despite the trouble caused by some of its students, Currie remembered his years in Sheffield as among the happiest of his career.

He was succeeded by the Academic Secretary, Francis Orton, who was faced with a further occupation in November 1979. By then, the new Conservative government had decided to make overseas students pay the full cost of their degree courses. The education minister Rhodes Boyson was reported as saying that he could see no reason 'why the British taxpayer should act as the milch cow of the world'.[55] Orton took the tough line of seeking a court order to evict the students – which was only given after the University had produced documentary proof that it owned the building.[56] A new hardship fund was set up, but the number of registrations by overseas students plummeted immediately – by 35 per cent in October 1980.[57]

A further diversion during this period was the McColgan affair in the summer of 1978, when Sheffield featured regularly in the national newspapers.[58] Mike McColgan of the German department had a dubious publication record and had been held at the 'bar', that is, denied further progress on the salary scale, for several years. McColgan claimed that the University was trying to dismiss him and argued that, although other lecturers were in the same position, he had been singled out because of his left-wing political activities, which included supporting the student occupations. He was a keen, if unorthodox, teacher and a campaign to prevent his sacking, orchestrated by the AUT and the Campaign for Academic Freedom, received the backing of most of his students, who organised a petition. The University set up a hearing under the chairmanship of John Wood of the Law department, which decided to allow McColgan another two years to produce acceptable publications.

The McColgan affair was seen as a victory for the Campaign for Academic Freedom and the AUT. Hamish Ritchie, the head of his department, is philosophical about the outcome. 'Mike was a nice guy [who] just believed that revolution was more important than normal academic work . . . When I arranged for him to go away on study leave, I enjoyed reading his reports in *The Guardian* from the trouble spots of the world (never from Germany where he was supposed to be)'.[59] Having been reprieved, McColgan left academic life to retrain as a lawyer.

Student life in the seventies

'Accommodation crisis looms' was a stock headline brought out by the local newspapers every year in early September. Dorothy Freeman, the Accommodation Officer, kept a store of extra mattresses to put in the halls. She also stepped up the recruitment of landladies, since lodgings were essential, despite being the second choice of most students. Among her many stories was that of the student who asked his landlady where he could get hash, to which she replied, 'I'll make you some' and cooked him a mutton stew.[60] The Student Accommodation Committee worked hard to increase the number of self-catering places. UGC finance was seldom available, but Sheffield adopted new schemes, for example joint loan finance.[61]

Several complexes of student flats were built as a result, including Taptonville I (1973), Taptonville II (1976) and Riverdale (1976). They were designed by Roy Johnson and built at minimal cost to a basic design and limited room size (8.77 square metres). The original plans had double rooms, which were changed to single rooms after student protest. The budget was tight: the size and specifications of the rooms had to be reduced until agreement could be reached with the Students' Union on the rent. When he saw them, Pat Hughes commented that Irish pig sties offered greater space. Later he called the Riverdale flats 'doss houses . . . with their cell-sized units and brickwork internal finish'.[62] Financial constraints appear to have resulted in buildings with which no-one was entirely happy. The so-called 'doss houses' were in an extremely attractive location, right next to Endcliffe Park. The residents of this beautiful road had gathered a petition with 1,700 names opposing the development.[63]

It was said at this time that Broomhill was becoming a 'student ghetto'.[64] Wherever possible, the University was converting properties it already owned, although new and stricter fire regulations sometimes made this difficult. Student squatting in properties which the University could not convert became a problem.[65] The Wolfson Flats (52 students) were built on Westbourne Road in 1978/79, and a handsome pair of early nineteenth-century houses on Endcliffe Crescent were demolished to build the Woodvale Flats with 142 places. With these developments, the University believed by 1980 that it had solved its accommodation crisis.[66] Later construction in Broomhill and Endcliffe was, with the exception of the 1992 Crescent Flats, restricted to the grounds of the halls.

A controversial decision, especially to those who had lived there, brought the demise of Crewe Hall in its original form. Crewe was too small to be economically viable in the university of the 1970s, and demand for flats was so strong that it was converted for self-catering in 1973. W. R. Maddocks, the warden, wrote an obituary for Crewe as 'a place of beauty and pleasant living'.[67] The formal dinners and the male camaraderie passed into history but Crewe, with its extensive and beautiful grounds, remained an attractive place for students to live.

The mixing of sexes within university flats was allowed from 1975 and Sorby was adapted to become a mixed hall in 1978.[68] Most seventies students report that hall rules were liberal – 'the only rule at Ranmoor seemed to be "no going on the roof "'. At Tapton, 'the staff seemed highly amused' when 'an early morning fire alarm resulted in large numbers of bleary eyed men appearing from the female half (their beds were wider for some reason).' Such stories were duplicated for every other hall. Such tolerance could be difficult for students brought up with different values – a Greek student recalled Ranmoor as 'the lonely hall . . . I felt like a stranger in a new city'.

This was an unusual comment: most seventies graduates recall Sheffield with great affection. The proximity of the Peak District is mentioned by many, together with the close links with the city, which combined 'the pleasures of being students' with those of 'being part of a very friendly community'. Many made life-long friends and partnerships. Most students could survive on their grant (especially if

Dorothy Freeman cherished her regular landladies and organised outings to thank them for their services at a time when increasing student numbers raised the threat of an accommodation crisis at the beginning of every session. This group is on the way to Lathkill Dale and a pea and pie supper.

Thank-you landladies

Rag events from 1973 and 1974.

topped up by their parents) and it was most unusual to take a job during term-time – 'we didn't appreciate how lucky we were'. Long coats (especially Afghan) were fashionable, as were kaftans, beads, tie-dye shirts, combat jackets, even crimplene flares ('yes, I had some in pale blue, I admit it'). Some of the men were butterflies: 'I did think I looked good in my velvet jacket, stack-heeled shoes and lilac loon pants [with] 28-inch bottoms which completely covered my shoes'. Any male student wearing a shirt and tie was thought odd and hair was even longer than in the 1960s, complemented by 'siders'. Punk arrived in Sheffield quite late – certainly after 1977.

Cannabis, and sometimes LSD, were more easily obtainable, but still passed the great majority of students by. Drinking was a daily event for many and pubs like the 'Old Grindstone' and 'Nottingham House' (the 'Notty') are frequently mentioned. In the Union, the 'Ents' Committee continued to stage incredible concerts for £1 a ticket – Led Zeppelin warming up before Wembley, The Who, David Bowie at the Union Ball, Procol Harum, Slade and Roxy Music at Ranmoor. Paul McCartney turned up 'on spec' with his new band Wings. The concert was sold out by word of mouth in less than two hours. Even this event was eclipsed for some by Sha Na Na, straight from Woodstock.

The chairman of Rag Committee in 1973/74 dreamed up a sales incentive

Members of Student Reception at a residential conference in 1978.

256

scheme for *Twikker* – a free pint for every 25 magazines sold. Scottish and Newcastle were happy to supply the beer in return for publicity. There were no pin-ups in the magazine after 1975, following protests from the Women's Liberation group, although the jokes and advertisements continued in the established tradition. Rag stickers were used to enthusiastic excess by one group on West Street. A well-dressed lady pulled up outside a bank in a Rolls-Royce and unwisely went inside, leaving ' a plague of locusts' to descend on it and cover the whole car with stickers. The lady 'went bananas' and could not even remove enough to drive away. Later she sent the garage bill to the Rag Committee. A stunt remembered by several observers is the Paternoster toilet cubicle, created by a student who got himself locked in the Arts Tower overnight and spent the next day going round and round on his throne, reading a newspaper. On another occasion a streaker 'flashed past' on a complete circuit of the Paternoster, before doing 'a wild run round the main concourse'.

On a more uplifting note, Student Community Action organised children's adventure playgrounds and other caring projects in deprived parts of the city. Student Reception went from strength to strength and was described by *The Star* as 'the most successful in Britain'.[69] In 1979 *Darts* was voted Student Newspaper of the Year by the *Daily Express* and was highly commended by *The Guardian*. A Lesbian and Gay Society was started in 1973, six years after homosexuality was legalised. A 'Boycott South Africa' campaign directed against firms investing in apartheid led to large numbers of students boycotting Barclays Bank and South African products. The December 1979 meeting of the University Court decided, in a tied vote, to sell all its shares in such companies.[70] Nelson Mandela was appointed first honorary President of the Union in 1984.

Student Community Action volunteers organise games for local children at the University playing fields.

New Union and University services for students

The Union building was becoming overcrowded by the mid-seventies. Union President Andy Tucker told the Court that the queues for lunch lasted fifteen minutes and that the meal often had to be eaten in the corridor.[71] He and fellow officers mounted a protest in the form of an invasion of the less crowded Senior Common Room, arguing that there was no justification, except 'social prestige', for it to be reserved for staff. The confrontation led the University to set up a working party on social space, which recommended the construction of an extra floor on University House. This was completed by the end of 1978, along with extensions to the Union Bar and a new Porters' Lodge. There was even hope that funds for a large new building on the Clarkson Street car park would become available.[72]

In the 1970s student welfare services of all kinds multiplied. The University already had an excellent Student Health Service, whose founding director Peter Gifford retired in 1977. He was succeeded by R. M. 'Bob' Kinsey, famous for his bow tie and, apocryphally, for putting every female who walked across his threshold on the Pill. A Social Welfare Committee, for both staff and students, was established in 1976/77, together with the sabbatical Union post of Academic and Welfare Secretary. (Entertainments and Athletics also gained sabbatical posts at

Dr Bob Kinsey, Director of the Student Health Service from 1977 to 1988.

The University Nursery.

this time). There were campaigns for a University counselling service and a nursery. The counselling campaign was protracted, because of serious misgivings from some academic staff who feared that the service would transgress the 'personal tutor' role of lecturers.[73] There was already a 'Tutor for Students', Mary Sharrock, whose role had originally been dubbed the 'Tutor for Fresher Women'.[74] The girls recalled the way she mothered them: 'an excellent source of comfort and support in difficult times'. She responded to distress calls at all hours from both students and parents, and on one occasion found a girl 'squatting with the disapproved boyfriend and his dog in a clapped-out car in a [remote] car park'. Sheer numbers, however, made a specialist counselling service essential. The Vice-Chancellor agreed, but it was not until 1984 that the University set up a service in a house on Brook Hill and appointed Jenny Bell as Counsellor. She was succeeded in 1987 by Colin Lago, formerly head of the Counselling Service at Leicester Polytechnic where there were three full-time and two part-time counsellors for the same number of students as in Sheffield. Not until the 1990s was money found to staff the service adequately.

The campaign for a university nursery, led by student parents like Mary Holding, was enterprising, imaginative and strident. Babies began to appear in lectures and were even, on one famous occasion, dumped on Currie's desk. In 1976 the University agreed to establish and finance a nursery, for both students and staff, in a house on Brunswick Street. Its management caused severe problems during the first decade.[75] The difficulty of financing the nursery from either Union or University funds meant that, when the UGC refused to provide grants for nursery provision in 1980, there was a real threat that the nursery would close down. The Union mounted another campaign; John Westergaard, among others, allowed TV crews to film a lecture attended by young children who had all been issued with noisy toys . . .[76]

Mary Sharrock, Tutor for Students and Warden of Halifax Hall, 1977–87, was very supportive to students in her charge. This photograph shows her, centre back, with a group of overseas students. She was also a popular tutor of English Literature classes for the Extramural Department.

Lord Dainton, universally referred to as 'Fred', was Chancellor of the University from 1978 until his death in 1997. Having been knighted in 1971, he was made a life peer in 1986. This picture shows him with his wife Barbara, herself a significant scientist, on the occasion of the conferment of an honorary degree upon her by the University.

The nursery was reprieved and managed jointly by the Union and the University until 1984. It was then that Union managers took a decision which made the nursery commercially viable.[77] It was expanded to provide the first private nursery in the city offering a full-day service to working parents. Fees were means-tested, so that students and single parents were subsidised by those on comfortable incomes, making it 'the cheapest nursery in the country' for needy parents. With 64 places, managed by the Union, it continued to be successful thereafter.

The new Chancellor

When Lord Butler was officiating at degree ceremonies, Alex Currie would sit behind the Chancellor's chair handing him cue cards. Currie collected them afterwards to use as notes to the milkman who, he recalled, was startled to be told, 'I admit you to the University of Sheffield'. Butler retired as Chancellor early in 1978. The chosen successor, Frederick Dainton, could hardly have been more appropriate. He was a Sheffield lad, brought up in Ranby Road, Greystones, as the ninth child of a master stonemason. The tools his father used throughout his working life were given to Fred Dainton by a former employee in 1990, and displayed in the Chancellor's Room.[78]

Dainton was a spectacularly successful product of the state education system. He progressed from the Sheffield Central Secondary School to Oxford University, to which he travelled each term on a 3-speed 'sit up and beg' Raleigh bicycle. He gained a first class degree in Chemistry, went to Cambridge to do research, became Professor of Chemistry in Leeds and was Vice-Chancellor of the University of Nottingham when he was invited to return to Oxford as Dr Lee's Professor of Chemistry. At the same time he contributed to national developments as chairman of such bodies as the government's Council for Scientific Policy, the University Grants Committee and, in 'retirement', the British Library Board, responsible for the construction of the new £500 million building at St Pancras.

'Sir Fred' was delighted to serve the University of his native city, and his pleasure in the role was transmitted to everyone around him. He gave a different speech at every degree congregation and spoke to graduands individually, remarking that 'it has always seemed to me that there was no point in having a degree ceremony unless it was made memorable for each individual, his or her family and friends'.[79]

Dainton's contacts, which were legion, international, and advertised to everyone, because he was an inveterate name-dropper, were of tremendous value to the University. He raised its national profile at a time when this was vitally important. Geoffrey Sims recalled that it was he who first broached the subject of the Chancellorship with Dainton, on the main staircase of the Athenaeum. It was an inspired suggestion even though, at 65, 'Sir Fred' (who became Lord Dainton in 1986) was considered by some to be too old.[80]

THE TRAUMATIC 1980s

The University celebrated the Centenary of Firth College in 1979 and launched a Centenary appeal. Under Fred Dainton, the UGC had agreed to raise the number of students at Sheffield to 8,000 by 1981/82, but the election of the Conservative government in May 1979 was the signal for an unprecedented assault on university funding. The 1980s were the most painful decade in the history of higher education in this country, from which universities emerged, by force, with a transformed ethos which embraced far greater public accountability, commercial responsiveness and a much higher proportion of non-UGC income. Pure research and student/staff teaching ratios were the most significant losers, not to mention the many academics in post whose careers were blighted or destroyed, or the younger generation whose careers never started.

In December 1979 universities were told that their grants for the next three years would be held at the level of 1979/80 and that student numbers should also be kept at this level. Income from overseas students was to be increased by recruitment at previous levels despite the recent fee rise – an impossibility.[81]

The government was committed to drastic reductions in public expenditure, but in its early years policy-makers were also convinced that the higher education

Left: *From* Darts *9 February 1980.*
Right: *Student demonstration against the cuts in student grants, 1981.*

market was set to contract because of the falling birth-rate.[82] By the time it was clear that this demographic time-bomb would not detonate, due to increasing demand and achievement among 18–21-year-olds, a great deal of damage had been done to universities. At a time of high unemployment, many would-be students had failed to obtain the education they needed. The cuts of the 1980s took place against a background of year-by-year increases in applications to Sheffield. All the civic universities were popular, and Sheffield was top of the UCCA league in 1988 and 1989. It was a continuing frustration that many good applicants had to be turned away.

The 1979 announcement was followed by threats of further cuts in 1981. Sheffield took pre-emptive action in March 1981 by imposing a freeze on the refilling of posts, and advertising premature retirement schemes for the first time.[83] Even so, no-one was prepared for the drastic measures announced to the university world on 1 July 1981. 'Nothing was ever the same again', recalled Reg Goodchild, then an Assistant Registrar.[84] The worst affected universities, Aston, Bradford and Salford, were ordered to adjust to a loss of income, over three years, of 31, 33 and 44 per cent respectively.[85] Salford's Registrar, known to many in Sheffield, was 'ashen' with despair. The staff at Western Bank were almost relieved to emerge with a cut of 'only' fourteen per cent and a UGC commitment to maintain student numbers at 6,860.

'Saying that Sheffield hasn't come off too badly [is] almost like consoling someone in the dock and saying you haven't got life, but you're sentenced to ten years', said Gwyn Rowley, Secretary of the AUT.[86] Lecturers were 'bitterly angry' at the cuts. There was particular shock for the Arts faculty, which was ordered to cut its student numbers by 270 (having been told as recently as 1978 that arts and social science numbers should rise).[87] Conversely, science and medicine received some support, since the UGC wanted their numbers to increase.

Universities were left to find their own way of making these cuts. Some wealthy universities had enviable reserves of property and investments to fall back on.

Graeme Davies (head of table, left) chairing a meeting of the ADC; this one met to consider the final draft of ADC5 in November 1985.

Sheffield had very little and so was forced into contraction, while making every effort to maximise income. All universities made use of the initially generous UGC-supported early retirement schemes but, as Geoffrey Sims recognised, these carried the great danger of 'random staff wastage' and a disproportionate loss of staff in some departments.[88] This was not avoided at Sheffield or anywhere else. Senate agreed to a 'moratorium on posts', in which a vacancy would be filled 'only in exceptional circumstances and if it is related to academic need'.[89] In practice the exceptions were few and the invitations were sent to everyone of appropriate age. Patrick Collinson recalled that in 1984 he had no sooner arrived as Professor of Modern History than he was invited to leave again. A phone call put this straight, but throughout the University there were 128 academic and 66 non-academic premature retirements by 1984.[90]

The ADC grasped the rudder to steer the University through these choppy waters; it shouldered the brunt of the planning and produced a series of excellent reports (ADC1 – ADC6), which ensured that painful changes at least had a coherent rationale.[91] If the University had not had the ADC at this time (and many universities had nothing comparable), it would have had to invent it. The members took on an enormous burden of extra work; in the first year of the crisis they met formally on 31 occasions, in addition to fact-finding discussions in every department.[92] Ron Waters was the chairman from 1979 to 1982, followed by Graeme Davies from 1982 to 1985 and thereafter Ron Johnston. The significance of the role was such that Davies and Johnston each went straight from the chairmanship of ADC to the vice-chancellorship of another university.

The ADC tried to protect the highest achieving parts of the University. Its first plans in 1982 were based on a scattergraph, known to administrative staff as the 'Orton Line', which represented the favourability of staffing levels in each department according to a number of criteria, especially teaching loads. Thus a real attempt at fairness and objectivity lay behind the order to some departments to cut staff, while others were permitted to maintain them.[93]

One glimmer of hope, at exactly the right moment, was an unexpected legacy from Hossein Farmy, a 1938 graduate who built up a fortune in the United States and left £535,000 to the University in May 1982 – its largest bequest at the time.

Peter Banks, Professor of Biochemistry and a future pro-vice-chancellor, spoke for many when he wrote to *The Times* on 12 December 1981:

> The universities exist to preserve our past culture and to lay the foundations of our future wealth and civilisation by teaching and research . . . The future of the nation depends upon its universities [to] remain vigorous centres of innovation and train a greater proportion of our young people than at present.

Campaigns against the cuts were supported by staff and students alike: in May 1982 the whole university community took part in one of the largest demonstrations in the country. Staff and students came into conflict, however, over the state of the library, which had suffered from budget cuts for several years. There was an overnight 'work-in' there in February 1982, organised by Union President K. K. Tan. Tan opposed occupying administrative offices, saying that students were living in 'cloud cuckoo land' if they thought the cuts and redundancies could be reversed, but a week after the library 'work-in' he was over-ruled and there was another occupation at Western Bank.[94] After six days 'one of the biggest ever' Union General Meetings, which crowded out the concourse, ordered the militants to give up. Drastic action, including the threat of heavy fines on the Union, swiftly ended a further occupation in 1984 and after that 'work-ins' in the Library became the protest of choice.[95] Western Bank now had the measure of student militants. The

Geographers at the heart of Western Bank:

Left: Ron Johnston, the influential chairman of ADC and pro-vice-chancellor who went on to become Vice-Chancellor of Essex in 1992. Appointed to a chair at the age of 32, he gained an international reputation for his work on the British electoral system, and was identified as one of the three most cited geographers. He received the Vautron Laud Prize, said to be the equivalent of a Nobel Prize in Geography. He was also a keen bell-ringer and wrote two standard works on the subject, one of which, inevitably, was An Atlas of Bells.

Centre: Pro-vice-chancellor Ron Waters, 1974–78. His research in the field of periglacial geomorphology helped to modify traditional, more simplistic, views of the ways in which British landscapes were fashioned by ice flows.

Right: Stan Gregory, pro-vice-chancellor 1980–84. He was also a physical geographer and well known for his forthright views: when he became pro-vice-chancellor he told Sims, 'I shall say what I think'.

continuing government attack on the level of student grants also led to regular marches throughout the 1980s, usually with the support of the University Council.

The universities hoped that the painful adjustments of 1981–83 would satisfy the government. There was some respite; Sheffield even received funding for building projects in 1983/84, among them the new MRC Applied Psychology Unit. 230 'new blood' posts for academics under 35 were announced and Sheffield got four of these. More money was found for the Library in 1984 and 1985.[96] But the government had acquired an appetite for squeezing universities. They were asked to take in extra students from 1984, with no extra money. Rod Quayle, the Vice-Chancellor of Bath and a former Sheffield professor, described this as 'lunatic planning'.[97]

By 1985 it was clear that financial support for universities would continue to decline. The UGC announced a new model for grant allocation, with teaching to be funded per student, according to national criteria rather than those of individual institutions. Research was to be selectively funded. Thus the first Research Assessment Exercise (RAE) was launched in May 1985, with returns required by November. Every university had to report not just on research achievement, but also on teaching and research objectives, forecasts of student numbers, and anticipated finances for the years 1986–1990. It was a 'gargantuan review exercise' which stretched staff to the limit.[98] It also introduced a new form of external assessment and selective funding which was to affect the goals of every department, the work of every academic and the status of every university.

To add to the pressure, the government's green paper, *The Development of Higher Education into the 1990s*, broached the possibility of closure of institutions and urged universities and industry to work together to ensure that courses reflected the demands of the economy. This paper was widely seen as 'narrow and utilitarian'

2,000 students and staff marching up Cambridge Street on 20 May 1982 to attend a rally protesting against Government cuts. This was estimated to be the largest demonstration by a single university.

The occupation of Firth Court, February 1983. The message on the blackboard reads 'All offices and services are closed today'. The placard at the front reads 'Occupy today: give education a future'.

Another protest march, with Somme Barracks in the background, this time in 1986 when the University's recurrent grant had been cut yet again.

in its attitude to the work of universities. The CVCP predicted that 'disaster' would result from the attempt to reduce the income of universities by twenty per cent in one decade, and its chairman, Maurice Shock, spoke of 'the lingering and painful terminal illness' caused by it.[99]

In Sheffield the immediate result of the green paper was an announcement in 1985 of a further round of job cuts through early retirement and voluntary redundancy – and threats of industrial action by campus unions.[100] The ADC decided not to try to restructure, on the grounds that 'the broad shape of the University', with its current range of disciplines, remained appropriate.[101] The outcome has been described as 'equal agony for all' – it caused unease, even among some of the staff charged with carrying it out, but was definitely favoured by the Vice-Chancellor, Geoffrey Sims. Those who wished to retire were allowed to do so, almost without exception, and remaining staff coped as best they could.

The results of the first RAE, announced in June 1986, declared that Sheffield had six outstanding research areas and another large group of subjects judged 'above average'. Despite this, the recurrent grant was cut again for 1986/87, leading the Director of Finance, Terry Thomas, to speak of 'the biggest crisis I have had to face here in more than 20 years'.[102] Even more jobs were withdrawn. The ADC, guided by the RAE and the preference of the UGC for 'selectivity', reversed its policy in 1987 and embarked on an unprecedented restructuring of the University.[103] Departments which had done well, like Architecture, both Control and Electronic Engineering, Education, and Psychology were given development funding, while some of the others were ordered to amalgamate with a cognate department. A few small honours schools closed. The effect on individual departments is described in subsequent sections. On the whole, the University succeeded in retaining its range of disciplines, but Ancient History and Classics were effectively lost. Ron Johnston was distressed to realise, when the ancient historians left, that the 'big family' could no longer work. There is no doubt that 'people left who maybe shouldn't have done' – 'it was a pretty tough time'.[104] Between 1985 and 1987 there were 131 premature retirements from academic posts and 174 among the non-academic staff.[105]

Terry Thomas, Director of Finance 1980–93.

John Nicholson, pro-vice-chancellor 1983–87, who undertook the task of conveying sometimes unwelcome news about early retirement schemes to members of staff.

A second government paper, *Higher Education: Meeting the Challenge*, came out in April 1987. It was enthusiastic about staff management methods like appraisal, encouraged links with industry and extinguished the last traces of grant-funding for universities. The UGC, which had been established in1919 as an independent body to fund and supervise universities, was abolished in April 1989 in favour of the UFC (Universities Funding Council). 'Contract' funding was established, determined by a 'guide price' against which institutions could bid for student places and, indeed, every other item of provision. In the UFC's first year of operation, 1989/90, universities were required to undertake another huge consultative and planning exercise, in the expectation that funding would be offered for several years. The results of the second RAE, announced in August 1989, judged Sheffield to have five top-rated departments, scoring 5, with another fourteen scoring 4.[106] The UFC's decision, after all this, to offer only a one-year funding horizon caused bitter disappointment.

Those in the 'hot seats' during this time of prolonged crisis deserve particular recognition. The eye of the storm was at Western Bank, where the Finance Department was led by Terry Thomas, the Registry by John Padley and the Academic Secretariat by Reg Goodchild. These administrators could call on fewer subordinates, due to the moratorium on replacement of staff. They were aided, however, by experienced lay officers like the Pro-Chancellors Christopher Barker and Bernard Cotton. The Treasurer, Jim Eardley, was able to give more time to the University after his retirement as the chairman of British Syphon Industries in 1983.[107]

They could also rely on the pro-vice-chancellors, whose role grew in importance as that of the deans declined. The twelve pro-vice-chancellors during the 1980s (see Appendix 1 for their names) were often given the most difficult jobs. For example, John Nicholson interviewed, and sympathetically counselled, many of the staff to

The new Medical School, with its motto ARS LONGA VITA BREVIS on a stone tablet transferred from the 1829 Medical School building. This became a popular spot for graduation photographs.

266

whom early retirement had been suggested, earning the enduring esteem and gratitude of Geoffrey Sims. Vic Barnett followed him in this role. Peter Banks, another pro-vice-chancellor, recalled that while some staff members were happy to accept a good pension, others were deeply disturbed by the suggestion that their job, and their contribution to the University, should be sacrificed on the altar of its insolvency.[108]

The interests of academic staff were represented by the AUT, led by Gwyn Rowley and Stuart Bennett, and by the NPSA. One member of NPSA, David Bland, became a pro-vice-chancellor and the non-professorial staff also had a number of representatives on Senate. Some of these served on ADC in the 1980s, including Bob Moore, Ian McLure, Len Hill and Julian Kinderlerer, who felt in retrospect that he did 'very little else' for six years.

The adaptations which the University made in the face of the eighties' onslaught were due, above all, to the members of the ADC. Geoffrey Sims paid particular tribute to Ron Johnston, who was chairman 'at the most difficult time'. The collegiality of the Sims regime, in willingly sharing power in this way, is striking: it ensured that academic considerations were at the heart of decision-making, no matter how painful the outcome.

THE FACULTIES 1970–90:
DEVELOPMENTS AND PERSONALITIES

THE FACULTY OF MEDICINE AND DENTISTRY
IN THE 1970s AND 1980s

Sir Charles Stuart-Harris, who had been Professor of Medicine for 26 years, retired from that post in 1972 although, as chairman of the medical sub-committee of the UGC and Regional Postgraduate Dean until 1977, he remained a significant figure. He had become 'a world authority on chest diseases', partly because Sheffield was such a 'bronchitis blackspot' before the Clean Air Acts.[109] The Department of Medicine continued its chronic lung disease research under his successor, John Richmond, who also introduced new work on liver disease and oncology.[110]

A second chair of medicine, named after Sir Arthur Hall and based at the Northern General Hospital, was established in 1972 and filled by Donald Munro. Munro's reputation lay in the functions and problems of the thyroid. He contributed much to the establishment of the Northern General as a second site for teaching and research. Both Nether Edge and the Northern General became teaching hospitals in 1969/70: the anticipated increase in student numbers necessitated extra beds in Sheffield, as well as nearby towns like Rotherham, Barnsley and even Hull and Grimsby, in order to maintain the small-group teaching which was a strength of the school.[111] This successful major expansion was promoted by Stuart-Harris and Robert Kilpatrick, his successor as Dean (1970–73), together with the new Administrative Dean, George Hudson, who had succeeded 'Ian' McCrie in 1968. Herbert Duthie, Professor of Surgery and Dean 1973–76, ensured that a second chair of surgery was established at the Northern General Hospital.[112]

The new dissecting room at Western Bank, opened in 1969.

The new medical school on Beech Hill Road opened in 1973. It contained lecture theatres and offices, as well as facilities for the departments of Pathology, Anaesthetics and Community Medicine. Intake rose to 132 in 1975 and 150 in 1977, making 1977–79 a difficult period when change was fast and staffing was under-resourced.[113] By 1979 both the Royal Hallamshire Hospital and a new Clinical Sciences Centre at the Northern General were in full operation.

The Royal Hallamshire Hospital itself opened at last in the 150th anniversary year of the medical school, 1978. Its planning and development had taken forty years; 'a monument to the procrastination of our times', as *North-Wing* put it.[114] What Stuart-Harris described as 'tragic' cuts to NHS funding (after government reorganisation in 1974) caused the delays of the final few years and, even when almost complete, threatened to prevent the opening.[115] The new building was a large tower block with eighteen floors. John Richmond was concerned that there would be fewer general medical beds, since both the Infirmary and the Royal Hospital had to close, but he rated the new academic facilities as 'second to none'.[116] In contrast to the NHS provision, these were funded generously by the UGC and provided offices and laboratories for staff who in some cases had previously had none at all. The new provision included a full-scale medical library, moved from Western Bank where it had not been easily accessible to clinicians. The standard of the facilities owed much to George Hudson, Bert Duthie and Bill Crane, the deans during the final years of preparation.

The Department of Community Medicine expanded its range to include general practice. Although this was the likely final destination of most of their students, training in general practice was widely neglected in medical schools, and Sheffield was among the first to organise clinical attachments in training practices.[117] In 1972, Eric Wilkes became the first Professor of General Practice and Community Care. Wilkes was a Baslow GP who had just founded St Luke's Hospice to care for the terminally ill, the first outside London.[118] He remained medical director there for fifteen years and combined this with his academic post and even, for a time, with some surgeries in Baslow. His students often went with him. An immensely compassionate, energetic and modest person, his thinking was often ahead of his time. He once said that squash courts were better for health than coronary care units, because regular exercise prevents heart disease.[119] He was also dedicated to fighting alcoholism. His plea for a chair in medical sociology was, he said, 'greeted by the medical faculty with a silence so deafening it lasted over twenty years'. Even the chair in general practice was threatened and when Wilkes retired in 1983 it went into abeyance. It was revived in 1987, by special recommendation of the ADC, for David Hannay, a Scottish GP.

The University's most famous pathologist Alan Usher moved from highly unsuitable premises in St John's Church basement (the 'crypt'?) in 1977. Usher had taught Forensic Pathology in this basement since 1961, and was also the Home Office pathologist for the whole of South Yorkshire and much of the East Midlands. In this capacity he worked closely with the local coroner, Herbert Pilling. Their relationship is indicated by the occasion in Court when Usher, who had forgotten his notes, called

Eric Wilkes, the founder of St Luke's Hospice, who was Professor of General Practice and Community Care 1972–83.

for a sheet of paper on which to jot down the essential points. After he had extensively consulted this sheet during a masterly submission, Pilling asked to look at it, only to find five words – 'God bless her Majesty's Coroner'.[120] Their partnership created the first purpose-built medico-legal centre in Britain, opened on Watery Street in 1977. 'Magnificently equipped', it had a mortuary and post-mortem suite specially designed by Usher and a sixty-seat lecture theatre which doubled as the coroner's court.[121] Alan Usher became the first Professor of Forensic Pathology soon after the opening, when a chair was created – one of a handful in the country.

A book could, and probably should, be written about Alan Usher's career, since there are so many stories.[122] He was a great wit and raconteur, a 'bonnie lad' from County Durham, fond of a pint or two with his staff and students, and dashingly dressed in a suit and bowler hat for every call-out. He performed over 27,000 autopsies and worked on some famous cases, like the Hillsborough football disaster, the Flixborough explosion, and the death of Helen Smith in Jeddah. One case, the Perera murder, involved the reconstruction of a body cut into more than a hundred pieces, hidden in many different locations.

Usher was aided by devoted technicians, especially David Jarvis, who worked in the department for 39 years. Jarvis reassembled skeletal remains, performed laboratory analyses and accompanied Usher on call-outs all over his 'patch', often at night, acting as photographer and driver as well as assistant.[123] Usher was also famed for his enthusiasm, if not prowess, at cricket. When captaining the University staff team, he would explain to the visiting side that the Sheffield fast bowler was so deadly that it was advisable always to have a forensic pathologist on hand. When he retired in 1990, it was said that in thirty years he had never made an enemy, only multitudes of friends.

Professor Ronald Illingworth retired in 1975 from the Department of Paediatrics which he had created and taken to a position of eminence. Six hundred research papers emanated from the department during his thirty years as professor. In addition to his own work on the normal child and that of Zachary and Lorber on spina bifida (discussed on pp. 221–2), there was the work of John Emery and his team into the causes of cot death. Emery was created Professor Associate in 1973 for his work since 1947 in the field of paediatric pathology.[124] He conducted many thousands of post-mortems on babies who had died unexpectedly and found a number of different causes, including unnoticed disease, genetic disorder and, in a few cases, neglect or smothering. He became embroiled in national controversy in 1982 for saying this, even though he linked such cases to maternal depression.[125] His concern was to understand the home circumstances in every case and to develop ways of preventing cot death. The research of his Sheffield team found that infants at increased risk of cot death could be identified at birth, and developed a scoring system which enabled health visitors to give extra support to their families. During this project, the incidence of cot death in Sheffield remained well below the national average.[126]

Emery worked with John Knowelden, who led a three-year study in the early 1980s into the causes of 988 infant deaths nationwide. His report, which received widespread publicity in 1985, stressed the importance of informed action on the part

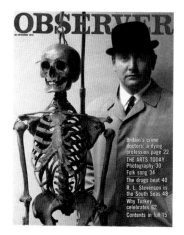

The 'man in the bowler hat', Alan Usher, Professor of Forensic Pathology 1978–90, and a lecturer since 1961. This photograph was taken for the cover story of The Observer Magazine, 28 October 1973.

John Emery, Consultant in Paediatric Pathology at the Children's Hospital 1947–80 and an Associate Professor, who pioneered research into cot death. An enthusiastic amateur artist, he was one of the founders of the University Fine Art Society.

Tony Barker (Medical Physics) and Ian Freeston (Electronic Engineering) demonstrating the Magstim equipment which they developed together. The project won the IEE Prize for Innovation in 1987.

Ian Cooke, Professor of Obstetrics and Gynaecology 1972–2001, with Dr Elizabeth Lenton and a patient at the Jessop Hospital for Women.

of parents and general practitioners.[127] The 'back to sleep' campaign, which was adopted internationally, undoubtedly saved many babies' lives. John Emery, who never really retired, was awarded the gold medal of the British Paediatric Society in 1987 and an honorary MD from Sheffield in 1999, the year before he died. At the same degree congregation, his granddaughter Lucy received her MB ChB.

The Department of Psychiatry lost its MRC unit, and thus many of its staff, in 1977, but its head, Alec Jenner, embarked on a new crusade to improve the lot of drug addicts in Sheffield. In 1984 he opened Storth Oaks, a large house in Ranmoor, as a 'zero tolerance' rehabilitation centre for young drug users. 'Our aim is to show these people they can live a life without drugs', he said.[128] He also promoted unconventional, 'democratic' approaches to psychiatry, and founded a new magazine, *Asylum*.

Medical Physics and Clinical Engineering became a full department in 1975, when Harold Miller retired and Martin Black succeeded him. Its central role in health care was marked by the allocation of 11,400 square feet of space in the new Hallamshire Hospital, together with the opening of units in Barnsley, Rotherham and Chesterfield. The department was one of the largest in the country, had many research teams and was constantly innovative. For example, collaboration with the surgeon Professor Ron Clark produced one of the first ultrasonic Doppler blood flow measurements. Sheffield became a world leader in the design and testing of prosthetic heart valves.[129] The Mechanical Engineering department collaborated in the design of a new kind of knee joint and Ian Freeston from Electronic Engineering worked with Anthony Barker to develop the 'Magstim', offering painless magnetic stimulation of the brain and nervous system.[130] These examples alone show the truth of the comment that medical advances in the last one hundred years have often 'been as a result of the enabling technologies of physics and engineering'.[131]

Ian Cooke arrived from Australia as Professor of Obstetrics and Gynaecology in 1972, in succession to Scott Russell.[132] His department was spread over two sites, at the Jessop and the Northern General hospitals, and challenged by heavy patient case-loads. He set about encouraging his colleagues to 'sub-specialise' in order to develop excellence in a particular area and produce high-quality research. His own interest was in reproductive medicine, where practitioners were beginning to unlock the causes of infertility and to provide effective treatment. The first Sheffield innovator was Douglas 'Tiger' Bevis, who began work on *in vitro* fertilisation in 1969.[133] Ian Cooke had considerable laboratory experience and had taken the chance to learn, from the inventor, a new microsurgical technique for unblocking fallopian tubes. His first researches were funded by private tubal surgery at the Beechwood Clinic, since the NHS refused to finance this work. He was finally able to secure the facilities to pursue his research in 1985, when he and Elizabeth Lenton were awarded half a million pounds from the Birthright Trust. A full-scale IVF treatment programme started, after the members of the new team trained themselves by investigating the impressive total of 200 patients in the first six weeks. The first Sheffield IVF babies were born in October 1986.

G. L. Roberts, who created the modern dental school and watched over it for 32 years, died suddenly in 1967. Paul Bramley proved a worthy successor. A UGC review in 1970 showed that the standards of the school were high, but that new departments and building extensions were needed if it was to expand beyond its forty-student intake.[134] In the unfavourable financial climate, significant expansion took almost twenty years: in 1988 a highly favourable UGC review (which recommended the closure of the dental schools in two other universities) approved an increase to fifty.[135] Plans which had been ready for years for a five-storey building, adjacent to the Charles Clifford Dental Hospital, were activated and it opened in 1991.

THE BIOLOGICAL SCIENCES

In the 1970s and 1980s, Botany was a highly successful research department, but struggled to attract undergraduates. The subject was unfashionable, but the degree in natural environmental science, run with Geography and Geology, proved successful. Arthur Willis succeeded Roy Clapham in 1969 and was a popular head of department for the next eighteen years. The department was home to a NERC unit in comparative plant ecology, sited in Sheffield because it is on an ecological boundary, as the northernmost limit of survival for Mediterranean plants and the southern limit for Arctic plants. By 1986, according to *The Guardian*, the staff of this Unit, led by Ian Rorison and later Phil Grime, had ensured that it had 'the most completely documented plant communities' in the world.[136] David Walker, a plant biochemist who became FRS in 1979, established a research unit to study photosynthesis, later known as the Robert Hill Institute. David Read conducted long-term research into the fungal infections of forest trees, was elected FRS in 1990 and later became Biological Secretary and Vice-President of the Royal Society. The research strength of the department ensured that Botany at Sheffield was one of only two departments in the country judged 'excellent' in the 1985 RAE.

Ecology became a major focus for the Department of Zoology when Peter Calow, a fresh-water ecologist, took over as head: Professors Chester Jones, Ebling and Ball all retired in the early 1980s. Ecology was a popular subject with students, particularly behavioural ecology, a field which expanded rapidly under the leadership of Tim Birkhead who acquired an international reputation for his work on birds and was elected FRS in 2004. His studies extended from magpies in the Rivelin Valley, to seabirds around the shores of Britain and in the Canadian Arctic.

Pauline Harrison was awarded a personal chair in biochemistry in 1978. At that time the only female professor in the University, her research was in the structures of protein, particularly ferritin. She and David Rice collaborated with colleagues in Chemistry and Information Studies to found a research group on protein engineering in 1985. Directed by Paul Engel, this became known as the Krebs Institute and thrives to this day.

The new subject of plant cell biotechnology took off like a rocket during the 1980s. It was pure research with huge commercial potential – the isolation of plant cells to grow artificially in 'bioreactors' as a basis for new drugs, food additives and other chemicals. Mike Fowler of Biochemistry attracted a large grant from the

Sir Paul Bramley, Professor of Dental Surgery 1969–88. Trained as both a dentist and a doctor, and a man of great energy, friendliness and modesty, his interests extended well beyond Sheffield. He advised on appointments to chairs all over the world and had close working relationships with dental schools in the Far East in particular. Knighted in 1984, he was Dean of the Dental faculty of the Royal College of Surgeons in 1980, President of the British Dental Association and a member of the Royal Commission on the National Health Service, 1976–9.

Professor Arthur Willis and his wife Dorothy carrying out their annual survey of the plants on a grass verge in Gloucestershire, a task which they began in 1957. The results form the world's longest-running data set for land vegetation by one person using the same methodology.

David Walker, Professor of Biology 1970–93 and Director of the Research Institute for Photosynthesis, conducting a study of the biochemistry of spinach leaves with a view to stepping up productivity and yield through improved photosynthesis.

Pauline Harrison joined the University as a demonstrator in 1954 and was awarded a personal chair in biochemistry in 1978. Tutored by the Nobel Prize-winning crystallographer Dorothy Hodgkin at Oxford, before moving to Sheffield she worked at King's College London on the structure of the protein collagen, which proved to be a triple helix. In an adjacent laboratory Rosalind Franklin was working on the double helix structure of DNA.

Wolfson Foundation in 1978 to establish a Unit of Plant Cell Biotechnology, which became the Wolfson Institute in 1981.

The government was enthusiastic about the possibilities of biotechnology; experts in this field were said to be 'the most highly sought after research scientists in the world'.[137] In the financial climate of the 1980s, every university tried to join the bandwagon, with its lure of lucrative industrial sponsorship. Plant Sciences Ltd (PSL) was formed to develop the commercial potential of this research in Sheffield – the University's first spin-out company. By 1992 commerce rather than the research councils was proving to be a more reliable source of income. The entire research team, including Fowler, moved out of the department and, indeed, the University when Phytera Inc, an American firm, acquired their technology. Phytera's British operation continued thereafter to be based in Sheffield.

Departments like Physiology and Zoology, which relied on animal research, had to endure a spate of anti-vivisection protests in the 1980s. This seems particularly ironic in view of the fact that David Smyth of Physiology promoted alternatives to animal experiments after he retired in 1973. He also became chairman of the Research Defence Society, which helped to draft a new law on the protection of laboratory animals. Animal Liberation groups began to target the Lodge Moor laboratories in 1980 and made several raids on the building. On the first occasion they took away some dogs, one of which was, quite wrongly, said by newspapers to be a stolen family pet.[138] The University was forced to defend itself against charges of cruelty and acquiring animals improperly. Some of the claims were repeated in a BBC2 programme in 1982 entitled *Rabbits don't cry*, upon which the University sued the BBC for defamation and won the case. Even though the perpetrators of the raids were imprisoned, security problems made the upkeep of isolated laboratories increasingly difficult. The Lodge Moor laboratories were closed and the land sold for housing.

Rod Quayle of Microbiology departed to become Vice-Chancellor of Bath University in 1983. Quayle, a former student of Krebs, was elected FRS for becoming 'the godfather of methylotrophy', the study of a novel form of bacteria.[139] There were two professors in this department by 1985, one of them another FRS, John Guest, who pioneered molecular-genetic studies leading to the cloning of genes which encode respiratory enzymes. Like Genetics, however, the Microbiology department was small.

The long-standing 'Balkanisation of Biology' into small departments (eight in Sheffield) was challenged in the 1970s and 1980s by economic reality and the academic desirability of closer integration. There was already an Integrated Biology first-year course and in 1970 an inter-departmental Committee for Biology was formed. In 1984 this became a more powerful Board of Biological Studies (later School of Biological Sciences) which was chaired by Len Hill.[140] Every department lost staff and at least one key professor in the 1980s, and some were not immediately replaced. The logic of further integration was too strong to resist. The Board of Biological Studies decided to pool scarce resources and formed, for example, the Electron Microscope Unit to manage microscopes which were originally owned mostly by Anatomy. Finally, in 1988, three new departments were created. Zoology

Mike Fowler, the founder of plant cell biotechnology in Sheffield. Here he explains the workings of the 100-litre air-lift reactor to the presenter of the BBC2 programme on biotechnology, Factories of Life, broadcast in August 1984.

and Botany agreed to come together to form a department of Animal and Plant Sciences under David Lewis and Genetics joined Biochemistry, Biotechnology and Microbiology to form Molecular Biology and Biotechnology.[141] Ernie Bailey of Biochemistry was the first head of the latter department which, like Animal and Plant Sciences, scored 4 in the 1989 RAE.

The third grouping, which united Anatomy and Cell Biology with Physiology, caused some bitterness.[142] Professor Tim Scratcherd fought fiercely for Physiology's independence and retired before the new department, Biomedical Science, was formed. Robert Barer had been succeeded as head of Anatomy in 1984 by Andrew Rogers, who continued the tradition of research in cell biology, especially image analysis, but lost several key staff in the 1980s. Rogers was the first head of Biomedical Science, but died in post in 1989 (within a month of Barer).[143] The physiologist Tony Angel took over as head of the department.

Having lost both staff and morale in the 1980s, Anatomy and Physiology scored poorly in the RAEs – a result which was disputed by the professors.[144] An additional problem was the low level of recruitment of anatomists, needed to maintain the level of research but also to teach dissection and gross anatomy to medical students. Anatomists in post were under great pressure, retired members of staff were called in to demonstrate, and the new Professor of Neuroscience, Carl Pearson, devoted himself to the anatomical teaching.

The 'pigs in space' episode caused national headlines and hilarity in 1987/88. The 'Institute of Space Biomedicine' was launched at the behest of Margaret Thatcher, who had signed a space co-operation agreement with the Russians, and it brought experts from several departments together to explore the effects of space travel on ordinary humans. Specially raised 'minipigs' were to be used in trial flights because of the pig's metabolic similarity to humans. The use of the 'minipigs', which were still large enough, according to Len Hill, to be 'capable of knocking over a fully-grown professor', was criticised by animal rights campaigners. The Institute survived only two years and, sadly, the pigs never did fly.

Boffins breed porkers to send into orbit to save our bacon

PIGS IN SPACE!

Douglas Northcott, Professor of Pure Mathematics 1952–82.

Geoffrey Sims created seven new posts, in biology and genomic medicine, shortly before he left in 1990. By then the biology departments were located in Western Bank, the Biology (now 'Alfred Denny') building and the Medical School, to which Pharmacology, Bacteriology and Pathology had moved. Apart from administrative offices, Western Bank was now entirely occupied by biology. This is a striking thought since, with the exception of Applied Science, this building once housed the whole University.

MATHEMATICS AND CHEMISTRY

The head of the Pure Mathematics department for almost thirty years was Douglas Northcott, the Professor from 1952 to 1982, elected FRS and remembered as 'the smartest mathematician we ever had'.[145] His colleagues recalled that a 'good morning' greeting might result in a few seconds delay while he considered whether this was true or not. He wrote seven textbooks on commutative algebra, a field in which the fruits of his research endured decades after his retirement, due to the concepts, theorems and theories in current use which bore his name.[146] Leon Mirsky, a Russian exiled from his parents as a child, was 'a great communicator' who managed to make his inaugural lecture, 'The Elements of Mathematics', enthralling both to his colleagues and friends.[147] He was awarded a rare personal chair in 1971 and continued to wear a gown to deliver lectures until his retirement in 1983 – one of the last members of staff to do so.

In 1980, the year that Deryck Allen, its founder, retired, the Department of Applied Mathematics spawned a separate Department of Computer Science. This was headed until 1986 by Julian Ullmann and then by Doug Lewin, who was just beginning to make an impact when he died in 1988. The fastest-growing subject in British universities thus had a difficult start in Sheffield.[148] Probability and Statistics, however, went from strength to strength, headed by Bob Loynes and Vic Barnett. In collaboration with the Polytechnic, the department set up a Centre for Statistical Education in 1984 and then, as its 'commercial arm', a Statistical Services Unit in 1986.[149] A good example of 'technology transfer', this unit provided a consultancy service to local industry, as well as to other departments.

Tony Miles won the World Junior Chess Championship in 1974 when he was a 19-year-old student of mathematics. He became the first ever British Grand Master in 1976 and was the first, and only, undergraduate to whom the University has awarded an honorary degree.

The research reputation of the Chemistry department remained high. It was enhanced when Peter Maitlis came in 1972 from McMaster University in Canada as Professor of Inorganic Chemistry. He was elected FRS in 1984 for his work on complexes of palladium, platinum, rhodium and iridium, and served as head of department 1973–76 and as a member of the ADC. Roy McWeeny, Neil Atherton and Eddie Haslam succeeded him in the role of head of department.[150] The eighties were, however, a troubled period, when David Ollis became an even more demanding colleague and Chemistry had to make painful sacrifices. The department had traditionally employed numerous secretaries and technicians to support its intensive research and teaching programme. This tradition was bound to come under scrutiny in an era of cuts. Academics and senior technical staff, led successively by Jack Davis and Derrick White, were forced to divert their energies into the battle to save resources, but many posts were lost.

When Ollis retired as Professor of Organic Chemistry in 1990, the department secured Charles Stirling FRS as his replacement. A distinguished senior organic chemist, he took a particular interest in the public appreciation of science, and in 1992 delivered the prestigious Royal Institution Christmas Lectures on 'Chemistry Through The Looking Glass'.

PHYSICS AND GEOLOGY

The high-energy physicists, especially Bill Galbraith and Fred Combley, divided their time between Sheffield and Geneva as the CERN accelerator developed, culminating in the first observation of new particles, called bosons, in 1989.[151] Space physics remained popular and astronomy became a combined honours degree subject in 1973. The lecturers 'really seemed to enjoy what they did and passed on the enthusiasm', recalled one student. David Hughes became known as the 'Halley expert' when the comet was visible from earth during 1985–86, and was part of the team which launched the 'Giotto' probe to investigate it.[152] Grenville Turner, another member of the Space Physics group, was elected FRS in 1980. He was particularly interested in investigating and dating moon rocks, using samples donated to him by NASA scientists.[153]

Left: *David Hughes, an expert on comets and asteroids, was a co-investigator on the European Space Agency's space probe Giotto, which encountered Halley's Comet in March 1986. An authority on the history of scientific instruments, Hughes also became well known for his 1979 book on the Star of Bethlehem.*

Below: *In February 1986 the Post Office issued a set of commemorative stamps designed by Ralph Steadman, to mark the passage of Halley's Comet. A special presentation pack, with text by David Hughes, accompanied the first day covers: this one shows the Giotto probe.*

Above: *Grenville Turner, who had worked at NASA , was one of the first British researchers to receive samples of moon rock after the original landing. The rock was the focus of great interest, not least from local schools; Turner is seen here with six-year-old John Burns during National Astronomy Week, April 1981.*

Right: *A sample showing various kinds of moon rock. The Sheffield team measured the age of lunar samples by assessing the argon content and made an important contribution to the establishment of a lunar chronology. The team was one of 200 research groups based in twenty countries looking at the characteristics of the moon.*

The links between Space Physics and Geology were thus very close. Physics and Geology were considered, together with Chemistry, in one of the funding groups for the ADC's sixth report in 1987 (ADC6). The research record of both departments had been assessed by the RAE as 'below average' and the ADC decided to limit their resources in order 'that the standing of Chemistry should be protected as far as possible'.[154] Physics had had no new lecturers for some time and, after ADC6, went from five professors to one, John Crangle, by 1988/89. 'That was our low time', he recalled, when they had to fight 'in order to survive'.[155]

Physics did survive; two new professors were appointed before Sims retired and it prospered in the 1990s. Geology struggled. ADC6 concluded that 'a viable presence in Physics' was essential and that therefore 'the bulk of the reduction must inescapably be borne by Geology'. The Geology department pointed out that it had valuable industrial sponsorship, for example for research in petrology and palynology, and that it was rated one of the top ten departments by industrial employers.

276

In its large teaching programme, it collaborated with several other departments and it had the second largest number of postgraduates in the faculty.[156] ADC6 nevertheless proposed to cut the size of the department by half, to eight, 'the threshold of viability'. Shortly afterwards, the UGC conducted a review of earth sciences prior to restructuring the whole sector. The UGC's report, published in 1988, recommended that a select group of six Geology departments should be built up with extra funding and, at the other extreme, that ten departments, including Sheffield, should close.[157] The recent decision to cut the size of the department undoubtedly influenced the UGC's verdict.

Two of the professors, Barry Dawson and Charles Curtis, together with several lecturers, moved to Manchester and Edinburgh, which did well in the review. Grenville Turner from Physics also left for a chair in Geology at Manchester. Those who were left felt, not surprisingly, that Sheffield had been asset-stripped and lamented the University's failure to fight for Geology. The single honours programme stopped in 1988 and the remaining staff, under Alan Spears, formed a Unit of Earth Sciences in 1990, together with a new Centre for Palynological Studies.

The interest of both staff and students in space physics and astronomy led to the construction of a new Observatory at Lodge Moor. It houses a 24-inch telescope built by the Astronomy department at the University of Edinburgh, which is on permanent loan to Sheffield.

THE APPLIED SCIENCES IN THE 1970s AND 1980s

The raising of overseas students' fees had an especially cruel effect on the applied science departments, which relied on them heavily and were also hit by a 'severe national shortage of applicants'.[158] Fortunately, postgraduate recruitment was healthy: the faculty liked to characterise the intake in 'waves'. For example, there was a 'Mexican wave' to train experts for its new steel industry.[159] Malaysian ceramics students were part of the first collaboration with the Perak campus, built on a former tin mining site. In Turkey, Sheffield's ceramics department had the reputation of being the 'best in Europe'.[160] A dispute between Turkish students erupted in 1977, when one of them rushed across Portobello Street brandishing a Beretta pistol and locked himself in the technicians' tearoom. He was disarmed by police and completed his studies in prison in the company of another Turk who had stabbed someone in the Students' Union.[161]

The Glass Technology department merged with Ceramics (including Refractories) and Polymers in 1974, a historic change which entailed the move of the Ceramics department to Elmfield – a long walk from St George's. Ronald Douglas was the first head of the consolidated department until his retirement in 1975. For most of the 1970s the Department of Metallurgy was run by two longstanding and dedicated professors. Bernard Argent came to Sheffield as an undergraduate in 1950 and was appointed a lecturer while still a postgraduate. Geoffrey Greenwood arrived even earlier, in 1947, and studied physics as an undergraduate before taking up metallurgical research. He left Sheffield to work in specialist laboratories, including Harwell, before returning to a chair in 1966. He was later elected FRS. Both he and Argent served the University centrally, Greenwood as a pro-vice-chancellor and Argent as a chairman of ADC.

Bernard Argent, left, and Geoffrey Greenwood, middle, both came to the University as undergraduates in the immediate post-war years (1948–50) and stayed for the rest of their careers. Both became professors in the Metallurgy (later Engineering Materials) department and acted as Dean. Argent was a chairman of ADC and Greenwood a pro-vice-chancellor. In 2004, both were still actively engaged in their department as Professors Emeritus.

Far right: Graeme Davies, Professor of Metallurgy 1978–86, was head of department, warden of Tapton Hall and leading light of the ADC in the 1980s.

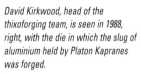

David Kirkwood, head of the thixoforging team, is seen in 1988, right, with the die in which the slug of aluminium held by Platon Kapranes was forged.

Graeme Davies was researching the steel industry from Cambridge until a chair in metallurgy at Sheffield was suggested, 'a much more logical place' and 'a good department [which] had strong links with industry'.[162] He arrived in 1978 and was elected to the ADC only a year later after Walter Bartley stopped him one day on the campus and said, 'We desperately need an engineer'. University administration proved to be his forté; he became chairman of the ADC in 1983 and left Sheffield in 1986 to become Vice-Chancellor of Liverpool. Later he chaired the UFC and HEFCE (the successors to the UGC) and then became, in impressive sequence, Vice-Chancellor of Glasgow and of London. David Kirkwood, a senior lecturer in metallurgy, inherited a seat in the House of Lords and served on the Select Committee on Science and Technology from 1987. His team invented thixoforming, a process for the precise and intricate shaping of steels and high performance alloys. Very valuable to industry, it was developed further in the 1990s by Helen Atkinson, by which time the department was recognised as a world leader in the technique.[163]

The University's Metals Advisory Centre (SUMAC), set up in 1980, was the result of a deluge of industrial requests for special equipment, expert advice and research facilities. In the first four years more than 300 companies used the service.[164] However, the decline in the British metal industries, combined with the general crisis in university funding, had an inevitable effect on metallurgy. The UGC reduced the number of materials undergraduates in 1987, with the result that three universities closed their departments. Even Sheffield, with the largest materials sector, experienced a sharp drop in student numbers.[165] In 1987 the University made the decision to merge the Materials faculty with Engineering.

As Geoffrey Sims recognised, Metallurgy was a 'magic' name in Sheffield and the degree of Bachelor of Metallurgy was a real loss.[166] However, the future for both Engineering and Materials lay in collaborative research in 'the high technology areas which lie at the interface between disciplines'.[167] Single disciplines were no longer viable and a separate Faculty of Materials no longer sustainable. The work of welding together the Materials school after 1987 was led by John Bailey, who had come to Sheffield in 1985 from a chair at the University of Surrey. He also ensured the success and expansion of polymer research.

278

Optical fibres were a focus of important collaborative research. Harold Rawson, who succeeded Ronald Douglas as Turner Professor of Glass Technology, demonstrated for the first time in Britain that silicate glasses could be made sufficiently free from impurities to be used for fibre-optic communications. The transmission of information via light pulsed through optical fibres is known as opto-electronics and the light-emitting crystals used are III–V semi-conductors, so named because they combine elements from the third and fifth elements of the Periodic Table. Sheffield became a world-class centre for research in semi-conductors, led by Peter Robson of the Department of Electronic and Electrical Engineering.[168]

The first widely-used semi-conductor was silicon, hence the achievements of Silicon Valley in enabling the swift transmission of huge quantities of digital information. Peter Robson was amongst the first in this country to demonstrate some of the unique electronic properties of the III–V semi-conductor gallium arsenide. A subsequent sabbatical at Stanford University in 1966–67 convinced him of the need to create dedicated III–V crystal growth facilities on his return to Sheffield. This was achieved in collaboration with Arnoldo Majerfeld and it led in 1978 to the creation of a National Centre for III–V Semi-conductors funded by the Science Research Council.[169] The Centre supplied a range of semi-conducting crystals and devices to the individual requirements of the academic research community.

The department of Ceramics, Glasses and Polymers carried out major work in fibre optics, sponsored by British Telecom. By 1990 more than 70 per cent of the UK telephone system used optical fibres and the department had developed even more efficient fibres for transmitting data across the Atlantic. The picture shows two types of fibre passing through the eye of a needle.

The Electronic & Electrical Engineering department, led for twenty years by Frank Benson, expanded greatly during the 1970s and 1980s and was rated 'outstanding' in the first RAE, as was the Department of Control Engineering under the continuing, astute, leadership of Harry Nicholson.[170]

The Mechanical Engineering department, under Ken Royle, had a heavy teaching load and research had taken rather a back seat. When Keith Miller arrived from Cambridge in 1977, he developed a new area of fracture research. Described by Geoffrey Sims as 'a man who made things happen', Miller was highly energetic, had contacts in all the right places and started an international journal. Miller secured funding from Rolls Royce and fourteen other firms to found the Institute of Fracture (later SIRIUS) in 1981. By 1985 it had installed the world's most advanced fracture test rig, and supported a wide range of research activity.

Peter Robson, Professor of Electronic & Electrical Engineering 1968–96, in the SERC-funded laboratory which he headed. Renowned for his work on semi-conductors, he was awarded the OBE in 1983 and elected FRS in 1987.

Keith Miller was also a highly enthusiastic mountaineer who, when asked why he forsook Cambridge for Sheffield, replied, 'There are no mountains in Cambridge'.[171] He was not the first academic to come to Sheffield because of the Peak District, but his achievements were on a scale undreamed of by most of his colleagues. He led several expeditions to Greenland and Iceland and then, in 1980, to the Karakoram in the Himalayas. On all of these, he recalled, 'I could honestly say that I was doing my research work', because he and his teams investigated the shape of glaciers and crevasses, avalanches, rockfalls and faults in the earth's crust. The Karakoram lies on a fault 600 miles long; earth tremors are a daily occurrence and the expedition carried sophisticated seismographic equipment to measure their impact. The venture attracted substantial funds from all the main research councils, since hardly any scientific data existed at that time. On the invitation of the Royal Geographical Society, Miller put together a 66-strong international team which

Keith Miller, Professor of Mechanical Engineering 1977–97 and outstanding mountaineer. On his return from the Karakoram in 1980 his stories so fascinated an audience at the City Hall that the lecture had to be repeated; he also produced a book, Continents in Collision. Miller claimed to be the only person to have been classified as both a Russian and a CIA spy. His many honours include Founders' Gold Medallist of the Royal Geographical Society and Fellow of the Russian Academy of Science.

The Buxton Experimental Station at Harpur Hill. These concrete bunkers were originally built to store munitions for the Ministry of Defence. Many experiments took place here, especially those involving rocketry and explosions.

included Ron Waters from Geography. He had to engage in high-level diplomacy, since the Karakoram is on the 'politically dynamite boundaries between Russia, Afghanistan, China, India and Pakistan'. The expedition was a great success, although overshadowed by the death of his best friend in a fall.

On his return, Miller became head of the Mechanical Engineering department and entirely restructured it: 'really pulled the department up by its boot-straps', said Philip Neal; 'a whirlwind', said Robert Boucher.[172] Miller took in the Theory of Materials department, which the ADC considered too small, and in 1988, by which time Robert Boucher was head of department, Chemical Engineering was also incorporated.[173] The enlarged department became Mechanical and Process Engineering, and research ratings improved in the 1989 RAE.

Jim Swithenbank (Chemical Engineering) became President of the Institute of Energy in 1986, three years after winning the Queen's Award for Export, which recognised his invention of an opto-electronic device for measuring the size and concentration of particles and spray droplets.[174] By now his research team had gained an international reputation for devising the basic integrated software package for computational fluid dynamics, arguably one of the most important innovations in modern engineering practice. The FLUENT code provided a quick and reliable method of modelling complicated industrial processes and revolutionised product design, operation and manufacture. Swithenbank also developed the technology for Sheffield's District Heating Network, which utilised the energy generated from municipal waste incineration to heat residential, commercial and public buildings in the city, including the two universities.

Much of the research in chemical engineering was conducted at the Buxton site, which contained laboratories and equipment for testing structures and devices under extreme conditions. This facility led to the award of numerous contracts from agencies like the power industry and the Ministry of Defence. Jim Swithenbank recalled that a visiting research fellow based at Buxton had formed the habit of keeping his propane gas cylinder warm by wrapping it in an electric blanket. This worked well until he went away for the weekend and forgot to switch it off. At 1.30 in the morning the cylinder burst and filled the bunker with a propane/air mixture nearly twice as powerful as TNT. There was an oil-fired stove at one end and the entire concrete roof slab, as Swithenbank later calculated, rose one hundred feet into the air, folded double and dropped down again. Unfortunately, the research fellow had left his car in the bunker for safe-keeping . . . The explosion was heard several miles away and was, the Buxton police assured him, bigger than anything experienced during the war.

The Department of Civil and Structural Engineering also used the Buxton laboratories, to monitor the behaviour of concrete and steel structures subjected to explosions, high velocity impact and fire using sophisticated equipment. The department was a leader in the use of microcomputers to analyse complex data, and for many years its staff were involved in writing software packages for the structural engineering industry. After the departures of two professors for private practice – Bill Eastwood in 1970 and Barry Rawlings in 1975, there was a difficult period in the

The Sir Henry Stephenson Building, funded by the Engineering and Technology Programme and opened in 1988. Designed by the Building Design Partnership in red brick with reconstituted stone dressings to reflect the original buildings in Mappin Street, it contains three lecture theatres, together with seminar rooms and laboratories.

1980s when the next head of department's behaviour towards both students and staff prompted an internal enquiry in 1986 and the threat of a boycott by overseas students in 1988.[175] There was no shortage of applicants for civil engineering at Sheffield from both home and abroad, however, – in 1986, for example, only two other universities admitted more British students onto their courses.[176]

In November 1985, a few months before the Technical School's centenary, Sheffield was among the top four universities to win Engineering and Technology Programme (ETP) awards. This was a feather in the cap of the Electrical and Control Engineering departments in particular. The programme was a UGC initiative to increase the number of graduates with high-level technological skills. Sixty extra students were admitted to a new degree in Information and Control Engineering in 1986, with five new lecturers appointed. The former Lucas company works, renamed the Portobello Centre, was extensively refurbished to provide additional laboratories and workshops for these two departments. In addition, new lecture theatres and more laboratories were planned in a new building on the adjacent Mappin Street car park. This was opened as the Sir Henry Stephenson building in 1988, with more than thirty members of the Stephenson family present.

In 1989, the UGC also decided to fund the long-awaited purpose-built Applied Science Library, an achievement of which Geoffrey Sims was justly proud. This was built on the site of the Caledonia Works next to the Stephenson building, a four-storey building with a Blackwell's Bookshop at ground level. The budget allowed for 'a relatively inexpensive shell with high-specification furniture, equipment and fittings'.[177] Peter Stubley, the first Librarian, emphasised the importance of the IT provision, to facilitate student-centred learning. A bank of open-access PCs and Macintosh computers on the first floor was seen as an 'interesting feature'. Eighteen workstations were considered sufficient when the Library opened in 1992, but it was designed for future flexibility, with trunking to allow data cabling for up to 100.

Right: *Looking down the staircase of the St George's Library to the main entrance from Mappin Street.*

Facing page, top: *The award-winning St George's Library for applied science, also designed by the Building Design Partnership. The Library reflected the importance of IT facilities in modern library design and facilitated student-centred learning. The concept was high-tech within an exterior that harmonised with its more traditional neighbours.*

Facing page, bottom left: *Glass panel incorporated in the library staircase, the design showing the stresses in a crane hook.*

Facing page, bottom right: *The stele, donated by the Fine Art Society, mixes symbols of engineering with those of Sheffield. Both pieces were designed and made by Sally Scott and David Peace, who studied architecture at the University and became one of Britain's foremost glass engravers.*

Another welcome development of the late eighties was the STEPS scheme, an access course which brought students without scientific qualifications into engineering. This doubled the normal intake of women and mature students into applied science. More female students had already been encouraged by the Women into Science and Engineering (WISE) initiative. In 1983 Heather Powell won the 'outstanding UK woman graduate in engineering' award.[178] The number of female undergraduates in Engineering rose from 13 in 1970 to 53 by 1979 and 125 by 1989.

St George's was at the centre of the University's attempts to capitalise on its research and thus increase its income from non-government sources. This was heavily promoted by both the government and the CVCP in the early 1980s. The University formed its own private marketing company, Unisheff Ventures Ltd, in 1984, and in the following year Bob Handscombe was appointed as director of the

283

University's Commercial and Industrial Development Bureau (CIDB), to develop industrial collaborations and license new products based on academic research. Regulations approved in 1986 gave academic researchers new incentives and greater scope for marketing the products of their research.[179] External consultancy was charged at commercial rates by 1988. A successful example of commercial enterprise in the 1980s was Biofouling and Corrosion Control Ltd, developed by CIDB and the departments of Zoology and Electronic Engineering to combat the build-up of marine life (such as barnacles) on ships, oil rigs and coastal power stations. The company became a major operating division in the Bates Corporation.

A novel feature was the creation of work space for private firms on university premises: the earliest was the 'Unit for Materials Processing' which opened in 1985 on Shepherd Street.[180] This also marked a new phase in relations with Sheffield Polytechnic, whose Pond Street campus had developed so rapidly in its first decade that, it was said, 'the concrete never sets'.[181] The expertise of the University and the Polytechnic was combined in a number of projects, including the National Transputer Centre, one of six in the country, which was established at the new Science Park in the city centre in 1988. Science Parks had been successful in the USA and spread through British university towns in the 1980s.[182] Entrepreneurial projects like the Transputer Centre, however, could sometimes promise more than they delivered. Sheffield, and the four other universities involved in developing transputers, found it difficult to compete with multinational firms which had a vested interest in resisting alternative forms of computing.[183]

The Engineering faculty entered the nineties in a more positive mood, encouraged by the potential of new developments, the 'record level' of admissions and the fact that it was one of the few parts of the University to have a recent new building.[184] The Korean steel firm POSCO decided to endow a Chair in Iron and Steel Technology for Mike Sellers in 1988. Traditional materials still had their place in this brave new world.

THE ARTS FACULTY IN THE 1970s AND 1980s

William Empson retired as Professor of English Literature in the summer of 1971. At his retirement party he commented to a colleague, 'I'm glad they feel it has worked out all right, because at the time I was considered a bold appointment'.[185] He maintained the tradition of the department to 'cover the field' of English literature in three years (something, he commented, that many other universities had given up). He left his successor a pair of dice, the 'sporting' method, which he believed students preferred, of deciding who should write the essay for the following week's discussion.[186]

Empson was one of the most remarkable personalities and intellects to grace the University. He was also one of the most eccentric, but that may be regarded as a *sine qua non*. A distinctive aspect of his career is that his finest poems were produced as a very young man, but he remained a stimulating critic and thinker to the end of his life. He was knighted (belatedly, one might think) in 1979 and died in 1984. Among the many obituaries, Richard Boston noted 'the quickness of his mind, the totally unconventional, original and provocative insight, and the wonderful wit'.[187] He recalled that, at one of his memorable poetry readings, Empson was using a copy of his *Collected Poems* which 'visibly bore the label of the London Library. I couldn't help feeling that it showed a certain style not to have a copy of your own book'.

Empson was succeeded by Brian Morris, whom a student remembered as 'one of the most articulate people I have ever known . . . His lectures were amazing . . . models of clarity and style of which any teacher of classical rhetoric would have been proud'.[188] Morris was a small man with a fondness for large dogs – the experience of driving behind his MG Midget with a Great Dane in the passenger seat was unforgettable.[189] Under his leadership (which lasted until 1980) the department responded to the high demand for places by doubling the number of staff. Even so, the student/staff ratio was the highest in the University. The department moved to the old Law faculty premises at the top of Shearwood Road and Morris promoted practical drama courses by developing a Theatre Workshop behind the Drama Studio. He also introduced the first Fellows in Creative Writing, Barry Hines and Angela Carter.

Sheffield was one of the few British universities to retain separate departments of English Language and Literature. The head of the 'other' English department was Norman Blake, an authority on the history of the English language with a particular reputation for his work on Chaucer, Caxton and the language of Shakespeare.[190] In addition, Blake served as both pro-vice-chancellor and public orator.

A new Prehistory & Archaeology department developed under Keith Branigan from 1977. Originally housed in the Arts Tower, Branigan made a successful bid for proper laboratory space, which became available when the Anatomy department relinquished 3 Clarkehouse Road. The new enterprise had some affinities with the old, with its 'defleshing unit' for animal bones and ten laboratories, as well as drawing and surveying offices.[191] The field-trips linger in the memory of students: 'Three weeks . . . in the Tuscan countryside digging out a medieval hilltop village was hard work but also thoroughly enjoyable, washed down with endless carafes of Chianti'. Branigan encouraged the development of new areas, like environmental and biological archaeology. He also positioned the department within both the Arts and Pure Science faculties, by adding a BSc in archaeological science and dual degrees with geography and earth science. The numbers of staff and postgraduate students grew quickly and the department's research earned it a place among the top seven British departments of Archaeology in the 1989 RAE. It was placed in the highest tier of Archaeology departments by the UFC in 1988/89 and awarded 'science-based status', with funding at the level of the physical sciences.[192]

Brian Morris, Professor of English Literature (1971–80) and later Lord Morris of Castle Morris, left Sheffield to become Principal of Lampeter College and Chairman of the Museums and Galleries Commission. He made regular appearances on Question Time and other BBC programmes, and his Collected Poems were published in the year of his death, 2001.

The Department of Music

Music moved to its first permanent home, appropriately renamed Hadow House, in 1971.[193] It proved to be ideal, even though it was a long, steep walk from the Arts Tower. The drawing room of the still-elegant Victorian house, the former Tapton Elms, became the library, and the dining room was used for lectures and occasional

Peter Hill, member of the Music department, Professor since 1994, and world-class concert pianist.

Above right: *The Lindsay String Quartet, teachers and performers in the Department of Music 1972–78. Despite moving their academic base to Manchester they continued to live in Sheffield and in 1984 founded the Chamber Music Festival, later called 'Music in the Round', based in the Crucible Studio. Particularly renowned for their interpretations of Haydn and Beethoven, they became internationally acclaimed as one of the greatest British string quartets. Each member received an honorary MMus in 1985 (pictured) and DMus in 2001.*

chamber concerts. Basil Deane, the new Professor, ensured that there were, at last, sufficient practice rooms. Deane was a 'wonderful person' in student memory and facilitated a happy rapport between students and staff. Annual summer music festivals, primarily organised by the students, began in 1974 and the Lindsay String Quartet took up residence in the department for six years from 1972. The Quartet was formed by fellow-students at the Royal Academy of Music, Peter Cropper, Ronald Birks, Roger Bigley and Bernard Gregor-Smith, and had already played together for five years at the University of Keele. In Sheffield they taught in the department and gave a series of recitals, especially acclaimed for their interpretations of Beethoven and Haydn and twentieth century composers like Bartok and Tippett. Although the Quartet moved to the University of Manchester in 1978, the players continued to live in Sheffield and to enrich the cultural life of the city.[194]

When Edward 'Teddy' Garden became head of department in 1975 there were still only four full-time lecturers, but the growing popularity of the BMus and new MMus degrees ensured rapid expansion.[195] David Cox, the department's principal composer, started an Electronic Music Studio and the University Orchestra and Chorus were conducted by members of staff. There were memorable performances of Verdi's *Requiem* and Beethoven's *Ninth Symphony* – 'a high point for all those involved'.[196] The new Firth Hall organ was installed under the direction of Teddy Garden, himself an organist. He was also an expert in Russian music and later supported the scholarly investigation of performance practice. Such research brought the department top ratings in the RAE by the early 1990s.

Peter Hill won countless awards for his piano recordings, especially of the complete music of Olivier Messiaen. He embraced all the challenges of this composer, including the marathon *Vingt regards sur l'Infant Jésus*, which lasted two and a quarter hours.[197] He has continued to be a leading recording artist in the piano music of a variety of composers. Colin Lawson gained an international repu-

tation as a scholar and player of the clarinet and its predecessor, the chalumeau. Roger Bullivant had joined the department in 1949 and was, a student remarked, 'a total inspiration' and a 'brilliant intellectual performing musician'. Both he and Alan Brown were scholars of the baroque period and expert players of the harpsichord and organ. Bullivant played at almost every degree congregation, and conducted the Sheffield Bach Society (founded by a previous Professor of Music, Stuart Deas) for forty years.[198]

Roger Bullivant was not only a long-serving member of the Music department but well-known across the campus for his work with the University Chorus and Orchestra, and his organ-playing at degree ceremonies. He was awarded the MBE in 1984.

Small Arts departments in the 1980s

The cutbacks in the eighties fell especially hard on small departments, of which there were many in the Arts faculty. Biblical Studies, for example, led by John Rogerson (who had succeeded James Atkinson in 1977), had seven lecturers in 1980 and was judged in the ADC1 report (1982) to be over-staffed because of its relatively small number of first year students.[199] None of the staff (who were all quite young) wished to retire and the department fought back with an enthusiastic recruitment campaign for overseas students to finance their perceived 'deficit'. The extra workload was immense and there was a time when a transfer to Manchester seemed possible, but the postgraduates came in increasing numbers and Biblical Studies ended this nightmare decade with a top grade of 5 in the 1989 RAE.

In addition to everything else, the staff made time to establish and develop their own publishing enterprise. Frustrated by the slow pace of the process in existing journals, they founded international journals for the study of the Old and New Testaments, and produced academic monographs in Biblical studies. The press was so successful that it became the leading publisher in the field. Its staff were among the first in the University to use word processing equipment, which included Greek and Hebrew typefaces. With forty new titles planned and a wider remit, the enterprise became Sheffield Academic Press in 1986.[200]

The struggle of Russian to survive was even more severe, as it was included on a list of fourteen departments of Russian which the UGC considered to be surplus to requirements in 1980.[201] Alan Waring, the head of department, fought back strongly, pointing out that Sheffield had little difficulty in filling 100 undergraduate places and taught eight East European and Balkan languages in addition to Russian, 'a linguistic group which covers one-sixth of the earth's surface'.[202] Geoffrey Sims, determined that Russian should survive, encouraged staff to stay and persuaded the UGC to change its decision in 1982.[203] It went on to become an extremely successful department. Sussex was the only other department reprieved. Like Biblical Studies, the department worked hard to justify its existence and succeeded admirably. There was a similar story with Spanish. Although eleven university departments of Spanish were recommended for closure by the UGC in 1986/87, Sheffield's department, under Tony Heathcote, not only survived but was commended for its 'above average' RAE result.[204]

Far from finding it impossible to justify its own existence, the Philosophy department remained, although it lost staff. Philosophy was a popular first year

From right to left, John Rogerson, David Clines and Philip Davies, three of the academics who decided to publish their own work, and became the founders of Sheffield Academic Press. They are seen here at the launch of the Press's landmark Hebrew Dictionary.

Peter Mayo, a lecturer in Russian and Slavonic Studies, won the national final of The Times Crossword Championship in 1993, having been a finalist on five previous occasions.

Eric Laughton, Professor of Latin 1952–1976 and a pro-vice-chancellor 1968–72. In addition to his knowledge of obscure and difficult Latin authors he also understood Japanese, after a stint as an Intelligence Officer during the war. He and his wife played violin in the University Orchestra and helped to bring the Lindsay String Quartet to the city.

subject and was regarded by the ADC as an essential part of an Arts faculty. Peter Nidditch, the head of department and an expert on John Locke, died in post in 1983. He was succeeded by John Skorupski and the department secured a major Leverhulme research grant in 1986/87. German, however, ordered to forfeit its single honours degree and three staff in the ADC6 report, lost its eminent professor, Hamish Ritchie, who felt obliged to accept the offer of a chair at Aberdeen University.[205] Italian, which had only two lecturers, was discontinued in 1981.

Classical Studies also proved to be unfortunate. The Firth chair of Latin was not filled after Eric Laughton retired in 1976. Laughton, who began his Sheffield career as an assistant lecturer in 1936, ran the department for 24 years.[206] He presided over the heyday of Latin, when there were plenty of students trained to 'A' Level standard in school. When this supply began to wane, he devised and taught a course for beginners, with the textbook *Latin for Latecomers*. He was an expert on the oratory of Cicero, and himself an eloquent Public Orator. His counterpart in the Greek department was Ron Crossland, who held the chair from 1958 to 1982, and ran a beginners' course in classical Greek as well as a dual degree with Biblical Studies.[207] Together with colleagues in Ancient History, they introduced a new degree in Classical Civilisation in 1975. Sheffield and Cardiff were the pioneers of this approach, since adopted elsewhere and popular with students.[208] After Crossland's retirement in 1982, the staff had been led to expect a new Professor of Classical Studies, but no appointment was made. Instead, a new department was created to unite Latin and Greek under a senior lecturer. Disillusioned about their prospects, the staff began to look elsewhere. Negotiations with other universities, especially Nottingham, led to the transfer of the lecturers during the years 1984–87: thus the study of a discipline which had been taught since Firth College days came to an end.

This was unfortunate enough in itself, but it also had destabilising consequences for linked departments like Ancient History & Classical Archaeology. This department was in good heart at the time, built up by its veteran head, Robert Hopper, who ran the department from 1947 to 1975, initially as a single-handed lecturer.[209] Hopper, notorious for his outspoken comments on Senate and Council, was widely respected for his research. His interest in ancient silver mining led him to collaborate with geologists and metallurgists. Derek Mosley, who succeeded Hopper to the chair of Ancient History & Classical Archaeology, assessed his department as 'one of the strongest teams in the provinces'.[210] The existing work in Classical Archaeology, together with the new developments in Prehistory & Archaeology under Keith Branigan, meant that the University had 'one of the largest concentrations of archaeologists in the country' in 1981.[211] However, the ADC6 report decided to reduce the number of Ancient History staff and merge them within a combined History department. The lecturers were, apparently, receiving approaches from other universities at the time and left Sheffield: within two years, none of the original staff remained.[212]

Ancient History was a loss to the History and Archaeology departments in particular. By the time ADC6 was published in 1987, however, it was very difficult

The official opening of the Department of Prehistory and Archaeology by Magnus Magnusson (second right). The new department's head, Keith Branigan, is to the right of him with, on the left, Kenneth Haley, the head of History, and Geoffrey Sims.

to maintain small, or even medium-sized, departments. The solution proposed by ADC6 was to preserve the broad spectrum within merged departments. In the case of Ancient History, this attempt was stifled at birth, due to the departure of the staff.

The Department of History

The Medieval and Modern History department was in a strong position in this period, having benefited from a succession of able professors since the sixties. These included Edward Miller (1965–71), a gregarious Cambridge medievalist, who was followed by David Luscombe in 1972. Luscombe was appointed at a young age to the Medieval History chair and retired in 2003, an impressive tenure of 31 years. His particular expertise was the writings of Peter Abelard, whose work he continued to edit and publish while serving the University as a pro-vice-chancellor and as Director of Humanities Research. Both David Luscombe and Kenneth Haley, the Professor of Modern History 1962–82, became Fellows of the British Academy. Haley wrote 'a sustained succession of books on seventeenth century English, Dutch and Anglo-Dutch history' as well as making 'shrewd and successful' departmental appointments.[213] The department moved in 1977 from the Arts Tower to Victorian houses on the Glossop Road / Clarkehouse Road junction, previously occupied by the Institute of Education.

On Haley's retirement he was succeeded in 1984 by Patrick Collinson, who had already been a professor in two other universities.[214] Collinson was a leading authority on the English Protestant Reformation and especially on the Puritans, about whom he wrote a doctoral thesis which was so enthusiastically long that London University imposed word limits thereafter. It subsequently became a somewhat shorter classic, *The Elizabethan Puritan Movement*. Collinson was appointed Regius Professor at Cambridge in 1988. The 'dissenting Victorianist'

David Luscombe, Professor of Medieval History 1972–2003, a pro-vice-chancellor 1990–94, and Director of Research for the Arts and Humanities 1996–2003.

The leaders of the Hartlib project: from right, Mark Greengrass and Patrick Collinson from History, Michael Hannon, the University Librarian, and Michael Leslie from English Literature. Bill Hitchens, Research Fellow to the project, is absent from this photo.

Clyde Binfield was head of department when the 'triple marriage' of the history departments took place in 1988.[215]

The third partner in this marriage (the second being the ancient historians) was the Department of Economic and Social History. When its founding head, Sidney Pollard, moved to Germany in 1980 that department was regarded as vulnerable by the ADC, despite the strong protests of students.[216] In the eighties it was run by Tony Sutcliffe and Colin Holmes, the former an expert on urban development and the latter on the immigrant experience in British society. By the time of ADC6, arguments that the department should stay with the Social Science faculty were discounted; History was in future to straddle two faculties. The new History department melded, despite difficulties, under Binfield's guidance.

The Hartlib Project

In 1987, 230 university research teams entered a competition for humanities research projects, funded by the British Academy and the Leverhulme Trust.[217] The 'Hartlib collection' proposal by Mark Greengrass and Patrick Collinson from the Department of History and Michael Leslie from English Literature, together with the Library, won one of only three grants of £150,000. Samuel Hartlib engaged in correspondence with many of the leading scholars and thinkers of the seventeenth century and amassed a huge collection of letters, pamphlets and other documents. This immensely valuable resource for seventeenth century scholars had been in the University's hands since 1933, when the collection was discovered in a London solicitor's office and given to Professor Turnbull of the Education department, who had already become an acknowledged expert on Hartlib.[218] The award funded a five-year project to make these papers available to scholars in a computerised form, with searching facilities. Key features of the project were its innovative use of computer technology and the interdisciplinary nature of the research, which the British Academy wanted to encourage. The Hartlib Project was ongoing, producing a set of definitive CD ROMs in 1996 and a second edition in 2002. Its success laid the foundations for other Humanities projects creating digital texts and employing new techniques: it has proved to be a genuine pioneer in this field.

THE SOCIAL SCIENCES IN THE 1970s AND 1980s

Although the sixties were a boom time for social sciences, the seventies were years of consolidation and the eighties ones of struggle. The overall numbers of social science students did not drop, except in 1983–85, but, as in the Arts faculty, some small departments teetered on the brink of closure. Others, like Psychology, strode forward almost regardless. Harry Kay left Sheffield in 1973, but the department he created continued to attract large numbers of applicants and to sustain its research under his successor, Kevin Connolly. The new building, which was opened in 1975, reflected Psychology's status and also managed to preserve the informal atmosphere of the old house. Christopher Spencer, a member of staff since 1968, suggested that

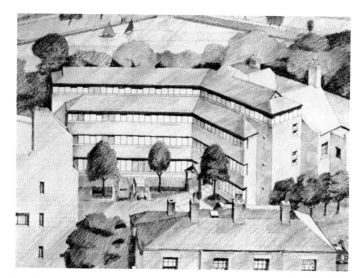

A preliminary sketch of he MRC/ESRC Social and Applied Psychology building, opened in 1988, which was the work of a team from the University's Architectural Consultancy, led by Kenneth Murta and David Bannister. Particular emphasis was laid on energy conservation, low external maintenance and long-term internal flexibility.

'the design incorporated good social and environmental psychology [with] no physical distance between staff and students and little social difference either'.[219] It was 'a very successful teaching, researching and living building'.

The work of the child psychologists received much press publicity, since they had a unique research tool, a nursery school on site which was 'a functioning nursery school and not a crèche for staff'.[220] It met both the city's criteria and the department's needs. Peter Smith conducted topical research in the early eighties on the impact of having a working mother.[221] His conclusions were that fewer than twenty per cent of his child subjects had difficulty accepting a familiar substitute carer.

The Social and Applied Psychology Unit, established in 1968, had by far the largest component of research workers – eleven in 1972, rising to 36 by 1992.[222]

The Nursery in the Psychology department.

Eric Sainsbury, above, and John Westergaard, below, the mainstays of the Department of Sociological Studies until the mid-1980s. Sainsbury began teaching social work at Sheffield in 1960 and first came to Yorkshire to work in the mines as a 'Bevin Boy'. He was the leader of a number of prestigious research projects and created client studies to focus on 'the people at the receiving end'. Westergaard, regarded as one of the most distinguished sociologists in Europe, was, in the words of a colleague, 'responsible for putting rigour into sociology'.

They were all employees of the MRC who, in addition to their world-class research, ran a MA in Occupational Psychology. Under Peter Warr, funds for a separate building were generated, which was opened on the Psychology site in 1988. The staff were known as 'the gnomes at the bottom of the garden' thereafter. Psychology retained its position at the top of the national tree, securing the highest RAE scores, together with Oxford, Cambridge and a small number of other universities, in 1986 and 1989.

Speech science teaching, with a four-year honours degree recognised by the College of Speech Therapists, began in 1977. Originally under the guidance of Colin Stork in the Linguistics department, it came to Psychology in 1988. One young lecturer, Philippa Cottam, co-authored the standard book on the value of 'conductive education' (pioneered by the Peto Institute in Hungary), but died tragically young in 1990.[223] Her name was commemorated in the Communication Centre opened on Claremont Crescent in 1992. Speech Science became an independent department at that time.

In the early 1970s Sociology was a relatively new discipline in most universities and received a bad press, partly because of Malcolm Bradbury's *The History Man* (1975), which caricatured the life and times of a sociology lecturer at a new university. The parties and leisurely life-style were not unknown in Sheffield, and Ankie Hoogveldt recalls that there was passionate commitment to ideological debate and a 'deeply engaged political bent' of about half the department, including herself, which 'saw politicising students as an entirely moral duty'.[224] All this changed in the 1980s, when theory collided with the pragmatic reality of cuts and demands for accountability.

A few departments of sociology, including Birmingham, closed at this time but most survived and Sheffield's department was, in any case, rather unusual in combining social administration and a post graduate social work degree with pure sociology. Under the leadership of Eric Sainsbury and John Westergaard, who replaced Keith Kelsall as Professor of Sociology in 1975, Sheffield's department survived, although not without trauma. Sainsbury and Westergaard formed a close working relationship and the department agreed to use social policy as a 'bridging interest' between theoretical sociology and social administration. Issues of social policy became a major theme in the undergraduate curriculum and the department's research became increasingly empirical. Alan Walker, among others, was appointed to strengthen this work and went on to become a national expert on ageing, poverty and community care. He was awarded a personal chair at the age of 36 in 1986.

When Westergaard took early retirement in 1986 his chair was not filled and the single honours degree in sociology fell into abeyance as student interest waned. Eric Sainsbury, who had directed social work education for 27 years, retired in 1987.[225] Alan Walker was the only professor left and kept the department going by focussing on social policy. After three years Lena Dominelli was appointed to Sainsbury's chair, and the swings of fortune revived interest in sociology among undergraduates in the 1990s, so that Westergaard's chair could be reinstated in 1995 for Richard Jenkins.

The Department of Politics evokes vivid student memories: Patrick Seyd, 'a favourite' with many, Anthony Arblaster 'sporting pink corduroy trousers', Andrew Gamble, 'head full of ideas, written some great books', and Howard Warrender 'highly eccentric' but 'brilliantly funny' in lectures. He appeared to live in the seventeenth-century world of the political philosopher Thomas Hobbes, on whom he was an international expert.[226] Several lecturers were lost in the early 1980s. When Warrender died in 1985, eight lecturers remained and there was a real chance that the department would have to merge with others.[227] What saved it was a 'buoyant student demand' and the support of Ron Johnston when he became chairman of the ADC.[228] Andrew Gamble was awarded a personal chair in 1986 and took over as head of department. Politics at Sheffield was to revive dramatically in the 1990s.

David McClean was Professor in the Law faculty from 1973 until his retirement in 2004. He served twice as Dean and as head of department and held the post of pro-vice-chancellor for five years during the 1990s. He was appointed Queen's Counsel honoris causa in 1995 and received his letters patent at a ceremony in the House of Lords. In 1992 he became a Chancellor of the Diocese of Sheffield.

LAW, ARCHITECTURE AND EDUCATION IN THE 1970s AND 1980s

Law was now a popular undergraduate subject and the faculty recruited large numbers of overseas students. David McClean humorously recalled that, in the 1980s, 'Hebrew was the second language of the department', since they 'scooped the undergraduate market in Israel' and had up to 150 students from there.[229] They even held degree ceremonies in Israel. When this supply began to dry up as Israel's own provision improved, Chinese students replaced them.

David McClean was, in his own description, a 'generalist' who published a great deal on the subject of international law, particularly air law, and contributed to many major textbooks. One of Roy Marshall's 1960s protégés, he was awarded a chair at 33 and served as Dean and head of department. He was also the leading Anglican layman for many years, as chairman of the House of Laity of the General Synod. In this role he steered the Synod through the legislation which permitted women's ordination in the Church of England. John Wood also arrived in the early 1960s, and became well-known nationally as a 'fixer' in industrial disputes.[230] He believed that arbitration was a far better solution than the courts and, as chairman of the Central Arbitration Committee, dealt with the 1978 Firemen's Strike and the Halewood dispute of 1983, when Ford sacked an employee for 'vandalism' of a bracket worth 83p. He also chaired the Police Arbitration Tribunal, the Mental Health Review Tribunal, and the Standing Committee on Pay Comparability – which led him to recommend pay rises for university clerical staff to the Conservative government in 1981. His work brought him much publicity, and a knighthood, but he preferred the anonymity of Saturday afternoons on the terraces supporting Huddersfield Town. Perhaps his favourite role was as chairman of the professional footballers' negotiating committee. It was widely believed among law students that a willingness to play for the faculty football team would get you straight into the BJur course.[231] He was an engaging teacher: one student recalled that he began a session on 'sexual offences' by saying, 'I assume you have already spent hours reading the chapters in the textbook on this topic and so instead we will talk a bit more about the Theft Act which we were studying last week'.

Professor Sir John Wood at the time of his retirement from Law in 1993.

John Wood and David McClean initiated the department's important work on criminology. McClean recalls their search for a lecturer to lead this new subject: 'We remembered a bright chap we had come across at these conferences in Cambridge. His name began with a 'B'. We looked down the list and there was a man called Bottomley so we asked him up to have lunch with us and have a chat. When he came in the room we both realised it wasn't him. We'd confused Bottomley with Bottoms'. Tony Bottoms was subsequently located and appointed and went on to create a master's degree and, with Norman Lewis, to pioneer the teaching of socio-legal studies.[232] In 1976 a Centre of Criminological Studies, only the third in a British university, was opened.[233]

By 1989, the faculty had seven professors, including the new chairs of Public International Law (John Merrills) and Commercial Law (John Birds), a post which was funded by the legal firm in which Chris Barker, the Chairman of Council, was a partner. The faculty lost eight members of staff during the eighties but, relatively speaking, survived with limited damage.

When John Needham retired as Professor of Architecture in 1972, the University made an unusual choice of replacement. George Grenfell-Baines was not an academic but the founder of a successful firm, the Building Design Partnership (BDP), which brought together architects, engineers, interior designers and other specialists to work in teams which were democratically organised.[234] Grenfell-Baines, who was knighted in 1978, was a great admirer of co-operation, workers' ownership and staff democracy; he agreed to become Professor only if a staff meeting ratified his appointment. Under his leadership the department changed direction, as 'teaching practices' in the city were set up (not least, a parallel BDP) and students received far more 'hands on experience' of real-life design and implementation. The approach was cemented by the appointment of David Gosling, an architect from the public sector, to a second chair in 1973.

Some staff and students regretted the reduction of theoretical education and artistic study, 'the aesthetic approach'.[235] The profession was changing, however, because of modern construction methods, computer-aided design, and the importance of costing, which brought quantity surveyors into the faculty for the first time. The success of the new approach was apparent in the number of prizes won – a world-wide contest to build an administrative centre in Barbados in 1978, for example, and a constant stream of student prizes, like the RIBA Silver Medal twice in the late 1980s.[236] Under Bryan Lawson, the department developed one of the most sophisticated and useful systems of computer-aided design, called Gable. It was marketed to other universities and architectural practices, forming another lucrative scheme of 'technology transfer'.[237]

Grenfell-Baines, who was already 64 when he came to Sheffield, continued teaching until 1980. His successor in the chair was Ken Murta. Despite the department's success, which included 'outstanding' in the 1986 RAE, lecturers were lost in the 1980s. Gosling commented, 'Our staff-student ratio has fallen, but I doubt if the students have noticed it because everyone works much harder than they used to'.[238] This was true of most departments. One of the casualties was Landscape

Architecture: Arnold Weddle resigned in 1982 and was not permanently replaced until 1990. Building Science lost John Page in 1984. 'Jimmy' James, however, was succeeded by Ian Masser in 1979. James, the founder of the Department of Town and Regional Planning, died in 1980, two days after receiving an honorary doctorate in Firth Hall.[239] As Geoffrey Sims recalled, the ceremony was arranged at short notice when James was known to be dying, and was 'the most touching moment' of his time as Vice-Chancellor.

The early 1970s were years of great trauma for teacher training. The government was keen to reduce student numbers because of the falling birth rate and the 1972 report of a committee chaired by Lord James of Rusholme recommended radical change. Small colleges with proud traditions were summarily closed and the work of those administered by the Sheffield Local Education Authority was taken over by the Polytechnic. The Institutes of Education disappeared. John Roach, the director of Sheffield's Institute, remembers that his meeting with Lord James was 'not a pleasant occasion, being conducted very much on the principle that we had been condemned before we ever arrived'.[240] Thus the University lost its connection with colleagues of education. The Area Training Organisations, which had linked colleges and universities, were abolished in 1976. The college-based BEd could no longer be run from the University and was phased out. However, the faculty launched a one-year full-time MEd for serving teachers which proved to be a great success, while recruitment to the postgraduate diploma was buoyant.

The Department and the Institute combined to form the Division of Education in 1971, with John Roach as the first head. Together with the Postgraduate School of Librarianship, they formed the new Faculty of Educational Studies, of which Harry Armytage was the founding dean. He retired in 1981. One PGCE student recalled that Armytage's office at the end of his career was 'stuffed with papers in

Above: Bryan Lawson, left, with an early example of his Gable software. Other computer-aided design systems existed but Gable had sophisticated software that was easy to operate and needed no specialised computer skills. Gable CAD Systems Ltd was established in 1984 to exploit its commercial potential.

Left: Design for a Performing Arts Centre in Barbados which won the 1983 RIBA Building Design Prize for students of architecture.

every cupboard and drawer'. His mind was as eclectic as ever and he tossed her a copy of his *Social History of Engineering* which had to be read from back to front because it had been translated into Japanese.

Research became an increasing concern and was rated 'above average' even in 1986. In view of future developments, it is worthy of note that tables published by David Jesson and John Gray in 1987 were the first to distinguish the performance of English Local Education Authorities by 'value-added' criteria.[241] Jesson and Gray collaborated in research with Jean Rudduck who was an invigorating leader, one of a number of colleagues who served as head of department after Armytage retired.

COMPUTING, INFORMATION STUDIES
AND THE LIBRARY

It was clear by 1970 that the University needed a dedicated service to supervise its new mainframe computer, the ICL1907, and the growing staff of operators and technicians.[242] Dermot McLain, an academic mathematician who was a Principal Scientific Officer at GCHQ, Cheltenham, was appointed as director of the new Computing Services. He served the University in this role for 25 years and proved a pragmatic guide through the years of breakthrough and byway which lay ahead. He invariably preferred systems which benefited a large number of users over ingenious ideas which could be of value only to a few specialist users.

By the mid-1970s the ICL1907 was the most heavily used machine of its kind in the country and a further mainframe, an ICL1906S, was lined up for the Service's new centre which opened on Leavygreave in 1976. The first small interactive computer, a Prime with 160MB of disc space, arrived later the same year. It could support a total of 32 'dumb' terminals (that is, lacking individual processing power). The old ICL1907 mainframe was decommissioned by 1979, liberating space in the Hicks building. The University continued, however, to find mainframes valuable: the 1906S lasted until 1986, by which time it was a museum piece, and it was replaced by an IBM 3083BX.

A digital communications network within the University was originally envisaged in 1976 by Julian Ullmann, the Professor of Computer Science, at a time when the first, very expensive microcomputers were starting to appear. A trial network for 96 machines in 1982 utilised both 'dumb' terminals and microcomputers; it was soon discovered that a single weakness, or a build-up of sub-critical faults, could cause these early networks to break down. It was at this stage, the mid-1980s, that the academic community nationally began to develop the potential of networks between universities through the Joint Academic Network (JANET).[243]

Office systems which had successfully relied on card indexes for decades were converted to computer during the 1970s and 1980s. Sheffield was the first university to adopt a computer-assisted admissions system in 1972; 'a matter of great prestige' to Alex Currie and appropriate in view of Sheffield's pioneering role in UCCA.[244] An Administrative Data Processing Unit was created in 1975/76; by then Sheffield was a latecomer to the computerisation of its student records.

The idea of 'word processing' was so new in 1980 that its advantages, in comparison with the typewriter, had to be carefully explained to staff in the *Newsletter*.[245] At that time a 'simple system' cost around £8,000. Two years later, however, the University took the plunge by installing 22 Compucorp word processors in various departments, seen as secretarial gadgets with which academics must not interfere. Staff training began and a sub-committee monitored the explosive development of ever more efficient, cheaper, machines. By 1985 the cost of an Amstrad, with printer, was £399 (plus VAT): cheap enough for academics to purchase their own.

The Postgraduate School of Librarianship, which changed its name to the Department of Information Studies in 1981, shortly before Wilf Saunders, its founder, retired, was the first in a British university to install an integrated office computing system for its secretarial and academic staff, in 1986. Tom Wilson, the new head of the department, realised the future potential of a critical mass of office PCs with modems, so that the benefits of electronic mail and file-sharing might be realised.[246] By 1988 Peter Mason of Computing Services had developed a university-wide email system, called 'Sheffield Post', for Prime Computers, who provided £114,000 worth of equipment in exchange for the marketing rights. 'Sheffield Post' enabled staff without expert computing knowledge to use email: it was replaced by the Pegasus mail system, developed at the University of Otago in New Zealand, as staff moved over to using IBM-compatible PCs.

Dermot McLain was founding director of the University's Computing Services, which moved into its own building in 1976. He presided over years in which the development of the service outstripped the most optimistic predictions: word processing and networks revolutionised the way the University worked.

'We have not only survived, we have thrived' was Tom Wilson's upbeat assessment of the fortunes of the Department of Information Studies in 1989.[247] Information technology, while not immune from the cuts, was of such potential to academia that its development was unstoppable. The research record of the department was among the best in the world and it successfully generated funds: the chemical information systems project under Michael Lynch and, later, Peter Willett, raised millions of pounds in industrial sponsorship and a company was formed to handle the resulting commercial rights.

In the Main Library, the IT revolution began with computerised library loans, announced in the *Gazette* in 1973, but taking many years to implement fully because of the need to fix a barcode label in every book. This project was initiated by Jim Tolson before he retired in 1974, and administered by Bill Hitchens. Computerised searches came next. Susan Frank recalled that when she arrived as a science librarian in 1974, the only electronic search engine was Medline, run on the computer at the British Library at Boston Spa, and delivered as a list of references several days later.[248] Other databases followed, mostly in science and technology, since these were funded by commerce. The librarians controlled all the searches, conducting interviews with staff and postgraduate students to determine their requirements. Electronic databases for personal use came later.

The existing libraries at Western Bank and St George's were supplemented in the late 1970s by the Hallamshire Hospital Library and the Crookesmoor Library. When graduates from these years were questioned about their favourite place to study, these new libraries were mentioned but, unexpectedly, the Main Library

John Padley, Registrar and Secretary
1982–98.

The Arts Tower on the move, from an
article written by John Padley for the
Newsletter, tellingly dated 1 April 1988.
Because the 'Ranmoor Rift' had been
discovered under the Arts Tower, the
building was to be moved to a safer
site. The relocation was scheduled for
a weekend, and was expected to be a
popular tourist attraction, boosting
catering income. The University's
television service had been granted
exclusive rights to film the move for
the world's TV networks.

stacks also proved popular. One said, 'I would spend hours buried deep beneath the library delving into journals and loving it all'. Another went to 'the dark dungeons' at exam time for a reason which lured many – the lack of distraction.

The Library was a rather easy victim in the eighties. There were cuts in both staffing and library budgets, despite the efforts of the University Librarian (first Colin Balmforth, then his successor Michael Hannon), the student 'work-ins' and the protests of staff. Linda Kirk of NPSA represented the interests of arts and social science staff on Senate. She recalls that 'it was hard to persuade people for whom the library was a sort of *extra* to the real work which they did [in laboratories or work-shops], so much so that we developed jargon phrases to defend ourselves, like "it is our laboratory"'.[249] The acquisition of funds for the new St George's Library was a major boost at the end of the 1980s, but also symptomatic of resources directed at technology rather than the humanities.

INNOVATIONS OF THE 1980s

Francis Orton, the Registrar and Secretary, was forced by ill health to retire early in 1982, and Dr John Padley was welcomed as his successor.[250] Padley was only 39 but a high flyer with considerable experience, most recently as Academic Secretary of the University of Liverpool. He described himself as a 'working-class lad' from a mining village in North Nottinghamshire, who was 'overjoyed' to be returning, as it were, to his roots in Sheffield.[251] Padley was dazzlingly innovative and energetic, someone who could quickly polish off routine work and be ready to entertain, and progress, new ideas. 'Dynamite', in one colleague's words. His *modus operandi* differed quite markedly from that of previous Registrars. Padley found the slow pace of university committees frustrating. He preferred rapid action. It was said that if you had a good idea in John Padley's office it would be implemented before you left. Inevitably, as Geoffrey Sims pointed out, some of these ideas were inspired and some not. But the sheer dynamism had many good results. Staff were galvanised into action and into believing that improvement was possible, at a time when spirits and optimism were low.

Padley expected, and received, particular support from the Estates department, under Brian Mayes, as he set about improving the public image of the University. Many buildings got a much-needed face-lift, including Firth Court (his new name for the Western Bank building), which under his care became more impressive and even luxurious (the pink décor and chaise-longue in the ladies' cloakroom are often mentioned). Landscaping received attention, several buildings were externally cleaned and the Hicks building was reclad. On these occasions Padley indefatigably sought out pockets of available money, actually persuading the UFC to pay for the Hicks work. He strongly believed in public relations and never missed an opportunity to present the University in its best light. He acted as the University spokesman to the press and responded to negative publicity with a plethora of positive news – commonplace today, but novel in the early 1980s.

The balance of power between management and academics shifted significantly at every university in the 1980s. The constant external pressure for speedy action and accountability inevitably undermined the culture of monthly committee meetings. Academic input to day-to-day decision making declined. Although the ADC's power was greater than ever, about half the other central committees ceased to exist. This change was endorsed by the Jarratt Report of 1985. Less than two years after he arrived, Padley proposed the University as one of six to take part in this government 'efficiency study'. It amounted to a management inspection lasting four months, during which Sir Alex Jarratt's team attended many committee meetings and looked at a mountain of documents. Jarratt's report made detailed proposals, as one would expect, but generally concluded that the University was well managed.[252] It recommended staff appraisal schemes for all universities and the development of performance indicators to measure the quality of departments. The report was resisted by the AUT, especially since it became part of the excuse for the next round of cuts in 1985/86.[253]

In December 1981, the *Sheffield Telegraph* announced that the University planned to spend £1.75 million on a 'dance hall'. At a time of funding crisis and threats to jobs, this seemed like a bad joke. A spokesman for the AUT criticised the plan and *The Star* talked about a 'danse macabre'.[254] The building was, in fact, the long-awaited extension to the Students' Union, to be built on the Clarkson Street car park. The UGC offered £1.5 million of the cost, and the University decided to provide the remaining £250,000, even at such a politically delicate time. It was never, of course, to be simply a dance hall, although that was its role on Saturday nights. The University's financial stake, however, gave John Padley the chance to change its use and to extend its benefits to the whole university community. The Union was persuaded to share the new hall with the University, in return for control of parts of University House. The 'Octagon Centre', so named after a competition, became a multi-purpose venue for exhibitions, conferences and concerts, quite as much as an exciting student facility. Opened in 1983, it proved to be a great success, not least for its potential to draw in the lucrative conference trade. *The Star* was forced to admit that 'it seems like a good investment'.[255]

Stephen Ware was appointed manager of the Octagon, and he and Padley worked hard to put Sheffield on the conference map. By 1985 *Conference Britain* described Sheffield as one of the 'top ten conference towns in the UK', surrounded by beautiful countryside and with the Octagon as a major venue.[256] The Social Democratic Party held a conference of 1,000 delegates at the Octagon in January 1988 and the University moved its degree congregations there from the City Hall in 1984, thus returning them to the heart of the central campus. Banqueting facilities for functions were introduced, following the construction of a bridge to link the Octagon with the kitchens of University House. The income was considerable – £420,000, for instance, in 1988.[257]

Catering all over the University was improved by Stephen Ware and the new catering manager, Stan Beresford, whom Ware described as 'very creative, capable, technically competent'.[258] They expanded the small Arts Tower café into The Plaza

Right: *The guitarist Segovia gave the inaugural recital in Convocation Hall, which was designed as a multi-purpose space for dances, concerts, degree examinations, art exhibitions and conferences. With the retractable seating in position, the hall holds 1,200.*

Below: *The Octagon Centre, opened in 1983, was built on the steeply sloping site of the former Graves mail order building. Designed by Gollins, Melvin and Ward, its facilities included Convocation Hall and the Union Council Chamber, together with bars and committee rooms.*

300

and in 1985 spent £120,000 on removing the 'cream gloss paint' from the Clerical and Technical Staff Club on Brook Hill and turning it into the Victorian-themed Club 197. Later they updated the St George's restaurant, closing the 'green hut', and turned the Upper Refectory in University House into Loxley Food Court. The SCR was refurbished and a Carvery established (later Abbeydale Restaurant). The aim was to provide quality catering and facilities in University House; the Union's catering was cheaper.

In 1981 the University acquired St George's Church, which had been closed for three years. Its potential as a library or chamber music concert hall was debated. Peter Cropper of the Lindsays promoted the latter idea, as the acoustic was perfect; George Grenfell-Baines drew up some plans.259 The idea was popular within the University, but the cost of the project could never be found. In 1991, Terry Thomas and John Padley drew up a proposal in collaboration with a local builder to convert the church into a lecture theatre, with the aisles and gallery utilised as student flats. The St George's Lecture Theatre, of which Padley was justifiably proud, opened in 1994

International links had always been important to the University, but they became crucial in the 1980s for financial reasons and to offset the negative effects of the rise in fees. Each *Annual Report* recorded liaison agreements with universities throughout every part of the world and an Overseas Liaison Office was launched in 1984. The prime aim was the recruitment of more overseas students. John Padley took the lead here; academic and administrative staff travelled abroad more than ever before, as ambassadors for Sheffield. By 1987/88 the proportion of international students was back to ten per cent, many of them postgraduate (see Appendix 4). A second aim of the overseas enterprise was the generation of funding through collaborative projects, research contracts and grants. The EEC proved to be a particularly fruitful source of grants and an EEC Office was established in 1985.

An early example of joint degrees with an overseas university – one of the first of its kind – was the Town Planning degree with Bangladesh developed by 'Jimmy' James and Alasdair Sutherland in the mid-1970s.260 The students spent their first year studying planning practice in Sheffield and then returned to Dhaka University for practical studies. The department opened a Centre for Development Studies in 1987. 'Jimmy' James and Geoffrey Sims were among the many academics who approached overseas projects as a contribution to the autonomous development of the countries concerned. Sims was devoted to the work of the Association of Commonwealth Universities and was awarded their Symons medal for services to commonwealth education in 1991. He made many visits to East and Central Africa, the Far East and Papua New Guinea, in addition to a heavy programme of committee work in London. Sims was also on the board of the European Rectors Conference for many years, as well as taking the chairmanship of the three main standing committees of the CVCP.

A veteran academic once commented that 'it has always been assumed in universities that competence in teaching is acquired naturally by an empirical process that relies more on mother wit and flair than on informed advice and counsel'.261 The

The fluctuation in overseas student numbers is indicated by this graph.

Full-time Overseas Students

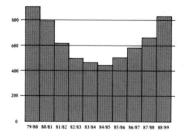

301

Jarratt Report preferred the latter approach, which had in fact been in place in Sheffield since the induction course for lecturers started in the 1960s. Jarratt recommended the extension of training to cover managers (including heads of departments) as well as lecturers. In 1985 the University appointed Pat Luker (later Partington) to the new post of training officer; among the early recruits to her courses was Bob Boucher, the future Vice-Chancellor.[262] Sheffield's management courses were offered to all the northern universities, so it was a natural progression for the National Staff Training Unit, funded by the CVCP, to be established in Sheffield in 1989. Pat Partington moved across to become its first leader.[263]

The Division of Continuing Education (previously the Department of Extramural Studies) developed strongly under Gordon Roderick (1975–83) and then Bill Hampton. The annual programme of 'Courses for the Public' offered hundreds of possibilities, in locations which ranged from South Yorkshire to Derbyshire, Nottinghamshire and Lincolnshire. Many of the tutors attracted loyal followings. To give one example, Mary Sharrock, the warden of Halifax Hall, taught Literature for over thirty years with 'a vitality and skill that generated student participation and creative activity in unparalleled quantity'.[264] The Division ran a part-time BEd for serving teachers in the seventies, and expanded its degree programme to include a MEd and the first part-time BA, in Social and Political Studies, in the eighties. By then, the increasing emphasis on vocational outcomes led the Division to set up the Centre for Continuing Vocational Education.

Mature students who aspired to the conventional degree programme but lacked 'A' Level qualifications were offered a part-time 'Mature Matriculation' (later 'Mature Access') programme, which began in 1977. Liz Hall, an early student who later became a university administrator, recalled that Gordon Roderick asked the first class how many thought they were middle class. When only two put up their hands, he was satisfied that the course was reaching its desired target group.[265] It continued to do so and also attracted significant numbers of students from ethnic minority groups, recent immigrants often among them.

STUDENT LIFE IN THE EIGHTIES

Sheffield hits the headlines

There was a fearful atmosphere in the autumn term of 1980, after a Leeds student, Jacqueline Hill, became the thirteenth victim of the Yorkshire Ripper. None of the attacks had taken place in Sheffield, but many women were afraid to go out and especially to walk through the red light district which at that time included Broomhall, across the road from the Union. One woman student recalled that 'it became quite a reflex for someone to walk a girl home' and that Eric, one of the 'fantastic' porters in the Union, often arranged an escort or lent taxi money to women going home alone after discos. Bill Hitchens organised similar assistance for the female library staff on evening duty. These precautions were prescient. On 2 January 1981, Peter Sutcliffe came to Sheffield, picked up a woman in Havelock Square and drove her to

Melbourne Avenue – both within a few minutes walk of the University.[266] There the false number plates on his car were spotted by two policemen, who arrested him and later discovered weapons he had concealed at the scene. Two days later Sutcliffe admitted that he was the Yorkshire Ripper. There is every reason to be grateful to the Sheffield police, who, as the trial judge commented, ensured the Ripper's capture through attention to 'humdrum, routine duty'.

This was not the only national event to have a deep effect on Sheffield. On 4 May 1982, HMS Sheffield was hit by an Exocet missile during the Falklands campaign. 'I will never forget the way that affected the student body', recalled David Bland.[267] The OTC contributed much equipment to the war, including a much-prized airportable Land Rover which never returned. Two years later, groups of South Yorkshire miners, their wives and supporters were on the streets and the campus collecting for their strike fund. There were violent clashes between busloads of police and the Miners' Union's 'flying pickets', and mass rallies of striking miners in Sheffield City Hall. On the 1984 'Spider Walk' one student reflected while 'trudging past Orgreave coking works in the dark and drizzle of the early hours' that a taxi driver had recently been killed there.

The worst event of all was the Hillsborough football stadium disaster on 15 April 1989, during the FA Cup semi-final between Liverpool and Nottingham Forest. The crush in the crowd at the Liverpool supporters' end caused the deaths of 96 people. Two of these were Sheffield students, Tracey Cox and Joe McCarthy, a Sorby JCR

Above and below: *Geoffrey Sims presenting a set of three cut-glass ship's decanters to Captain Tony Morton of HMS Sheffield in June 1988. Rosemary Gorton, Chairman of Stuart Crystal, is on the left. The decanters replaced similar pieces lost when the previous HMS Sheffield was sunk during the Falklands campaign in 1982.*

President, and another was a recent graduate, Richard Jones. Medical students (as well as staff) were among those who gave emergency help to victims and their relatives, and the Union raised £3,000 for the Disaster Appeal.[268]

Social life

'From Western Bank I could see green at almost every point of the compass.' 'Sheffield was the first (the only) city where complete strangers said hello to me on the day I visited.' 'I had a room at the top of Sorby Hall facing west, so that I could watch the sun set over the Peak District.' 'The cheap buses in David Blunkett's Socialist Republic of South Yorkshire' (for example '12p out to Fox House') and the ticket machines which took a rubbing of the coins, so that everyone had long tickets with 24 halfpennies stuck on their walls. These are some of the reasons why students chose to come to Sheffield and enjoyed their Sheffield life so much. Rag also prospered and, apart from a lull in mid-decade, raised impressive amounts of money for charity. In 1988, *Twikker* sold out so fast that appeals went out for people to return their copies so that they could be sold again.[269] It was more acceptable than the previous year's effort, which was condemned as 'racist and sexist' by Union officers in both the University and the Polytechnic.[270] This was, of course, a familiar pattern. Rag stunts were fewer and less daring. The zebra crossing on Chapel Walk in 1982 was not as impressive as its famous sixties' counterpart on the M1. Rag parades continued, but could be very disappointing; the *Sheffield Telegraph* reported 'stunningly forgettable' floats in 1981 and *The Star* advised 'sane, thinking people' to leave the city on Rag Day 1983.

The 'Fox and Duck' in Broomhill, bought by the Union in 1988.

The real success story of Rag by this time was Pyjama Jump. This pyjama party cum pub crawl began in 1965 in one of the city night-clubs and was almost compulsory ten years later. Every night club was booked and thousands of tickets sold: 3,000 in 1984, for example, and 6,000 in 1987. The memories are indelible and often shaming:

> 'I was arrested . . . and released from the police station at about 5 am to walk back to Earnshaw wearing only a nightie and a leather jacket !!!' (Male, 1977–80)

> 'I used to love the Pyjama Jump night, I loved dressing up in fish net stockings, a little pyjama top and not much else and getting very drunk, the later it got the more guys we kissed and we usually ended up at a club in town' (Female, 1981–85)

> 'Only time I got away with wearing suspenders in public' (Male, 1985–88)

> 'A couple were caught bonking on the pool table . . . It was in the 'Sun' and the 'Mirror' the next day . . . it gave the whole thing a frisson' (Male, 1983–6; this incident was in 1983.)

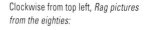

Clockwise from top left, *Rag pictures from the eighties:*

Bearded six-foot Rag Fairy (Robert Bloor).

Eye-catching Rag float passing the Town Hall.

Group of gnomes fishing in the Goodwin Fountain.

A printable scene from Pyjama Jump in the 1980s.

Apart from having a good time, the purpose of Rag was to raise money for local charities and organisations. In 1980 Rag donated a Spiderbus, named after the Rag symbol of a money spider, to Meynell Youth and Community Centre.

Darts *and* Arrows *won 'Best College Newspaper' and 'Best College Magazine' at* The Guardian/ NUS Student Media Awards *in 1983. The awards were accepted by Pat Mackl, left, editor of* Arrows, *and Mark Morreau, editor of* Darts.

'Seeing a fellow engineering student dressed up in a winceyette nightie was a sight never to be forgotten' (Female, 1985–88)

These memories can be summarised as 'too few clothes, too much alcohol'. But perhaps it is not too fanciful to see Pyjama Jump as 'Sheffield's Rio Carnival or New Orleans Mardi Gras' – a time to let all inhibitions go, just for one night.

Sheffield's clubs were now providing serious competition for the Union – many former students mention the 'brilliant' Limit Club ('so smoky and seedy') on West Street, the Leadmill and even the Polytechnic Union, which put on concerts to rival some of those at the University. Top acts now expected top facilities and in 1989 the Union voted in favour of having a professional entertainments manager, instead of the sabbatical Social Secretary – the end of an era.[271] The commercial operations of the Union were becoming increasingly slick and creative under its experienced managers John Windle and Paul Blomfield. Bar One was refurbished out of all recognition in 1985/86 and 'The Fox and Duck' in Broomhill was acquired the following year as a way of making extra money for the Union – bars and entertainments generated profits which could be ploughed back into student services, according to Blomfield. This income, however, was tempting to a cash-strapped University; a proposal in 1987 to impose a levy on Union profits was withdrawn after protests, but the issue returned in the 1990s.

The Union laid down a blueprint which other universities copied when it established a 'welfare rights and advice' service to deal with students' many queries. It was run by trained student volunteers during lunchtimes and offered personal advice as well as a wide range of leaflets. In 1985 a full-time worker was appointed to offer training and support to the volunteers and take over the more complex problems. The Union increased the number of permanent managers during this period, but the sabbatical officers were still in charge – an arrangement that worked because the managers were, as Mary Holding put it, 'on the same side as the students'.[272] The post of Women's Officer, which began in 1986 and was sabbatical from 1990, inaugurated a programme which included the Women's Health Handbook, the women's late-night minibus and self-defence classes.

306

Darts was again chosen as the best student newspaper by *The Guardian* in 1980, 1983 and 1986, and was runner-up in several other years. Esther Oxford won the 'Journalist of the Year' award in 1989 and again in 1991. *Darts* was a proving ground for careers in national journalism – 'a great confidence builder'. The launch pad of comic Eddie Izzard, a student of accounting and financial management 1980–81, was the Fringe Theatre Company (later the Alternative Productions Society), which he formed in 1981 to stage comic revues like 'Sherlock Holmes sings Country' and a five-person re-enactment of 'Ben Hur'.[273] 'Eddie Izzard was brilliant then and brilliant now. He stood out as someone of special talent', recalled a member of his audience.

Top: *Members of the Alternative Productions Society receiving the 'Students on Stage Award', jointly sponsored in 1983 by* Cosmopolitan *magazine and Lloyds Bank. Eddie Izzard is on the left. The judges were impressed by the group's 'eclectic and informal approach, and their prolific record in staging events, as well as their energy and imagination'.*

Below: *The chorus line from Eddie Izzard's production of* Cabaret *which played to sell-out audiences for eight nights at the Drama Studio in February 1983.*

Right: Frank Hayes, who graduated BSc in Applied Mathematics in 1969, achieved the rare feat of scoring a century on his England debut, in a match against the West Indies at the Oval in 1973.

Far right: Tim Robinson (BA Accounting and Financial Management, 1980) followed his University cricket career by becoming opening bat for both Nottinghamshire and England, and hit centuries against India, Pakistan and Australia during his 29-test career in the 1980s.

Below right: Members of the University Lacrosse team after a resounding victory in the Iroquois Cup Final in May 1982. In a good year for the University's teams, Men's Golf won the UAU Golf Championship for the first time and Ladies' Squash became UAU Champions.

Below: Sally Ann Hales ran the second fastest time ever by a woman marathon athlete in 1985, the same year that she gained her medical degree. In 2004 she was working as a pathologist – and still running.

Among student memories of this decade, the cuts featured surprisingly little. Enjoyment continued to be the theme – 'far and away the best three years of my life', for example. Allan Barnes, the Union President 1982/83, was deeply disappointed that only 1,000 people on the campus signed a well-advertised Union petition against the cuts, whereas 14,000 signatures were collected locally from the general public. He concluded that 'the social pressures on young people to gain a place at university, and then obtain a good degree in order to secure a job, were now so great that inward-looking and selfish attitudes were inevitable'.[274] This seems a more balanced assessment than 'creeping Conservatism', although this was the high water-mark of the Tories' national success, following the Falklands campaign. Three Conservatives were voted into sabbatical posts in 1983; the left-wing opposition was, apparently, disastrously split. The new Conservative Union President David Stubbs, however, disagreed with his party's higher education policy and

organised a march to London to protest against it.[275] The government had been threatening to introduce student loans instead of grants since 1979 and there was persistent campaigning by both the NUS and AUT against this threat to long-standing arrangements for student finance. No provision for inflation was made in the grant after 1986. In 1989, grants were frozen, supplementary loans were introduced and, to add insult to injury, student entitlement to housing benefit and income support was taken away. Financially, students would never have it so good again.

Retrospect

Geoffrey Sims retired as Vice-Chancellor in 1990, after over sixteen years in office. Looking back, he commented that 'no-one could have foreseen . . . how much national needs and attitudes would alter'.[276] The university world changed out of all recognition during his time in office. Quinquennial planning was replaced by contract funding, as the government scrutinised universities' internal affairs and became increasingly keen on external accountability and selectivity. UGC enquiries threatened the survival of certain departments and, in Sims's view, were 'unparalleled intrusions into our freedom to manage our own institutions'.[277]

Geoffrey Sims at the time of his retirement.

The RAE changed both research and teaching: 'Research output multiplies in the fields which are most measurable. The teaching of undergraduates slips still further down the list of priorities', wrote Andrew Gamble of Politics in *The Times*.[278] The results of the first RAE in 1986 were a disappointment to many, but Sheffield adjusted to the new game and received its reward in the second RAE of 1989. This was only possible, however, because of the inherent soundness of the system and because academics adapted, albeit sometimes reluctantly, to the new emphasis on short-term research objectives.[279]

As if staff cuts and research scrutiny were not enough, departments were also expected to generate money. In some cases, like the arts departments, this was extremely difficult and caused tension with senior management.[280] One successful venture was the Japan Business Services Unit which provided language courses and commercial information for British firms trading with Japan and Korea.[281] Degrees combining a language with Business Studies recruited well. Other faculties, of course, could offer research ripe for 'technology transfer' and staff worked hard to improve these prospects. In 1988 the University reported that its non-UGC income had increased by 66 per cent over the previous year.[282] Yet even this increase was below the income of universities which Sheffield regarded as its peers.[283]

Bids for research council funding assumed greater importance – and complexity. But the pressure meant that even enterprises with substantial research council income, like the Unit of Comparative Plant Ecology, were asked to consider the commercial potential of their work. The effect was to prioritise 'applied' over 'pure' research, and many argued that the pendulum had swung too far. Lord Dainton described the government's attitude as 'characteristic of the short-sighted accountant who wants quick returns to appear in this year's balance sheet and dislikes "patient" money for investment in the longer term future'.[284]

Three cartoons highlighting the grants situation. (Sources: Darts *and* South Yorkshire Student Handbook *1986/87*)

"This is your office, Mr. Baker — any little extras are usually provided by your mum and dad"

Many older members of staff, at all levels, were lost during this stressful time. Everyone remaining had to cope with vastly increased workloads. This experience was not, of course, in any way peculiar to Sheffield. Many other universities fared much worse. But the general depression of higher education had an effect on everyone and caused almost a crisis of conscience among staff about what they were doing. Although the University of Sheffield emerged strengthened in the 1990s, it is a source of regret that so much was lost which may never be regained – the interaction of staff and students at ratios which allowed strong personal relationships to develop, the respect of society for academic values and pure long-term research, the collegiality across departments which pressures of time and workload just swept away. 'A much more sociable way of living' disappeared, said one senior administrator.[285] Yet sociable living could make for more effective living.

Students responded by putting their heads down and working harder. Sims's period of office saw both the beginning and the end of serious student disruption. A 2003 postgraduate who conducted some interviews for this History could hardly believe that the Union had ever sanctioned an occupation of the Edgar Allen building. The student culture of the seventies could be described as adult freedom without adult responsibility, due to generous grants and the indulgence of administrators from a paternalistic generation. 'We older people paid too much attention to

them and that fuelled rather than quenched their conviction of the correctness of their views', concluded Lord Dainton.[286]

The student body was different in two other ways by 1990. Few limits had been placed on the number of postgraduates and so this group grew by twenty per cent in the 1970s and by a further 25 per cent in the 1980s – it was to expand much faster in the 1990s. The proportion of women undergraduates was higher, reaching forty per cent of the total by 1982 (see Appendix 4): numbers increased particularly in the pure sciences, social sciences and law. Among the staff, the number of women academics was only 8.4 per cent in 1985/86, with a small increase to eleven per cent by 1990/91. Promotion prospects continued to be much lower – only sixteen per cent of women academics had reached senior lecturer grade in 1982 and only one (Pauline Harrison) was a professor.[287] This was the common pattern; a study of five universities published in 1983 concluded that 'the inequality of women as university teachers in England in the post-Robbins era has not been markedly reduced'.[288] Even in 1990, a *Hansard* report described institutions of higher education as 'bastions of male power and privilege'.[289] By 1989/90 Sheffield had four female professors.

One academic who served on many committees during Sims's time, commented that, 'a university's principal function, like that of a Pope, is to survive.' What Sims did, ably supported by the pro-vice-chancellors, the lay officers and the chairmen of ADC, was to 'keep the ship afloat and that was a job he did very well'.[290] His 'liberal-minded collegial governance' was appreciated by many, who found him 'always approachable'.[291] However, by the end of the 1980s, the university world had become competitive and even ruthless. As late as 1987, Sims resisted the idea of deliberately buying in 'centres of excellence', arguing that 'our experience . . . shows that they tend to grow around able people, who can emerge in unexpected places'.[292] He believed that it was 'not gentlemanly' to poach staff to the detriment of another university.[293] This was the liberal approach, hallowed by tradition but now overtaken by events. Other universities were head-hunting the most able academics and even their research teams. Sheffield had to do the same. Focused management and tough decision-making were the way of the future.

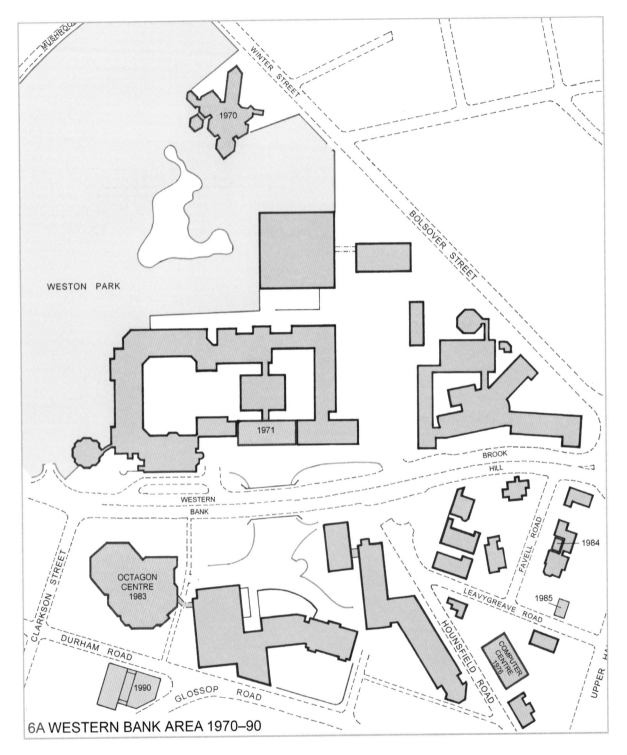

6A WESTERN BANK AREA 1970–90

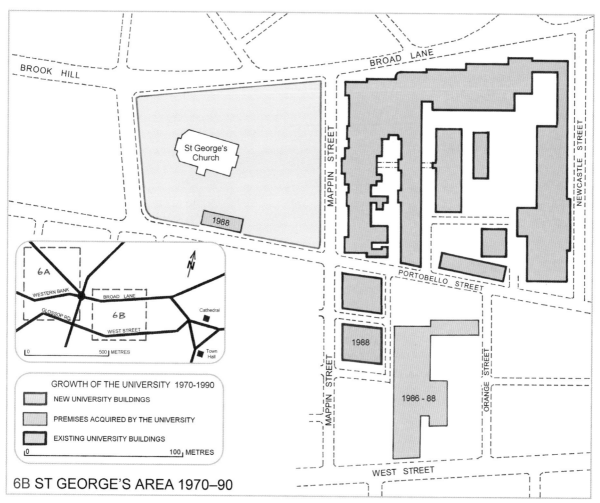

BROOK HILL

BROAD LANE

St George's
Church

1988

MAPPIN STREET

NEWCASTLE STREET

PORTOBELLO STREET

MAPPIN STREET

1988

ORANGE STREET

1986 - 88

WEST STREET

6A

WESTERN BANK

GLOSSOP RD.

BROAD LANE

6B

WEST STREET

Cathedral

Town
Hall

0   500 METRES

GROWTH OF THE UNIVERSITY 1970-1990

NEW UNIVERSITY BUILDINGS

PREMISES ACQUIRED BY THE UNIVERSITY

EXISTING UNIVERSITY BUILDINGS

0   100 METRES

6B ST GEORGE'S AREA 1970–90

7

Relentless Initiative: the Nineties

THE NEW VICE-CHANCELLOR

A WHIRLWIND BLEW THROUGH THE UNIVERSITY in January 1991, when Gareth Roberts took over as Vice-Chancellor. By his own description 'a bit of a control freak' and 'very competitive', he had an ambitious strategy for the University – to make it one of the country's leading 'research-led' institutions. Although other universities had approached him, he saw Sheffield as a 'sleeping giant' with 'huge potential'. In a local press interview conducted just before he arrived, he said, 'The University is beautifully balanced in . . . the spread of subject mix. It is situated in a lovely part of the world, but also it is a place with a social conscience . . . I'm a Welsh working-class lad and it appeals to me.'[1]

Professor Roberts was brought up in Penmaenmawr, the son of a quarryman. Ill for two years as a child, and small for his age, these experiences taught him to 'be sagacious and think strategically'.[2] He spoke Welsh at home, learned English at school and attended chapel every Sunday. He played football in the North Wales League and became a passionate, lifelong supporter of Tottenham Hotspur. Encouraged by 'excellent mathematics and physics masters', he read theoretical physics at the University of Wales, Bangor, obtained a first class honours degree and a PhD, and was appointed a lecturer there. A conversation with Charles Evans, the Principal of Bangor, gave him the ambition to become a vice-chancellor. Realising the need to expand his horizons, he moved to the laboratories of the Xerox Company in New York as a research physicist – an experience which, he recalled, 'was the making of me'. The atmosphere was 'daunting' and 'much more competitive'; he was expected to write a weekly research progress report.[3]

Facing page: Silk wall hanging, Academia, by Jacqueline Guille, 1993. The intertwined motifs reflect the work of the University's faculties.

He produced his best theoretical research papers there and was invited to move to the New University of Ulster as Senior Lecturer in Physics. In Northern Ireland he was promoted to professor, head of department and dean, but the 'Troubles' eventually caused Roberts to move, at the age of 36, to Durham as head of the Department of Applied Physics and Electronics. In 1985 he was appointed Professor of Engineering Science at Oxford, a post he combined with that of Director of Research at Thorn EMI. He was responsible for strategic planning in this large multinational firm.

Industrial research was a crucial aspect of Roberts's academic career. He returned to Xerox in New York during Ulster vacations, worked on semi-conductors and, while at Durham, pioneered an alternative to the silicon chip for ICI, ultra-thin molecular films for incorporation in electronic devices like transistors and infra-red detectors. He called this new field 'molecular electronics' and was elected FRS in 1984. He was invited to serve on the Prime Minister's Advisory Council on Science and Technology (ACOST), to which Mrs Thatcher was so committed that she chaired a meeting on the day that Britain embarked on the Falklands campaign.

Roberts became a member of both the UGC and its successor the UFC and was, by 1990, ideally placed to become the vice-chancellor of a university with a strong science and engineering base, like Sheffield. The Chancellor, Lord Dainton, took action, approaching him in Oxford and inviting him to Sheffield to meet the chairman of Council, Jim Eardley, lay officers and pro-vice-chancellors like Peter Banks who, in time-honoured fashion, drove him round the Peak District (in pouring rain). Roberts was impressed: 'I was well handled'.

Roberts was an extraordinarily hard worker, often starting work at 5.00 am and not finishing until late in the evening. In the months before he assumed office he made many visits, with introductory meetings in almost every department. Some staff have vivid memories of conversations with him by mobile phone as he commuted between Oxford and Sheffield. The result was that he 'hit the ground running' when he took over in January 1991, and change happened very quickly. Staff transfers within the central administration took place during his first month.[4] Roberts assumed control of the Strategic Planning Committee and announced that, in future, it would be the key executive committee with its own 'task forces'. Thus a committee which had met infrequently and made few decisions became all-powerful. The 'Monday morning meeting' (often stretching into the afternoon) was the crucial forum. Its membership was small and consisted of the Vice-Chancellor, the pro-vice-chancellors, the Registrar, the Deputy Secretary and the Director of Finance. With the addition of Pro-Chancellors and representatives of the ADC, this group became the Strategic Planning Committee. The power of the ADC itself was considerably reduced, and with it the tradition of allowing elected academics to run the University, which Geoffrey Sims had supported and fostered. Roberts also insisted that the chair of ADC could only be taken by a pro-vice-chancellor. The role of pro-vice-chancellor became a key appointment to which he gave a great deal of thought. Nominations were submitted by members of staff and considered by the Pro-Vice-Chancellorships' Committee, but the final decision

Gareth Roberts upon his appointment as Vice-Chancellor.

Gareth Roberts with his first team of pro-vice-chancellors, from the left, Professors Ron Clark, Peter Banks, Ron Johnston and David Luscombe. To the right is John Padley, the Registrar and Secretary.

was primarily that of the Vice-Chancellor. The contribution of the pro-vice-chancellors is discussed later in the chapter. Ron Johnston, pro-vice-chancellor and chairman of ADC at the height of its powers, moved on in 1992 to become Vice-Chancellor of Essex.

This change to a directorate suited Roberts's personality but was probably inevitable in the increasingly competitive university environment. His management style was combative and challenging, entrepreneurial and competitive. It was shaped by his industrial experience and came as a shock to the collegial instincts of many academics. Clyde Binfield recalled that he planned 'a nice lunch' when the new Vice-Chancellor proposed to visit the History department, to be attended by 'as many colleagues as possible in convivial circumstances'. Then he was told that Roberts preferred 'to meet me and my executive team. Well we had no such thing'. Roberts liked departments to have a management structure which mirrored his own central team.

The departments which had most cause to fear the new Vice-Chancellor's visitation were those with poor RAE scores or the perception of inadequate leadership and management. Peremptory action was taken in several cases: some heads of department took early retirement and new management was often imposed, after discussion in the Strategic Planning Committee. Roberts made his own selection of heads of department, who were not always professors, on the basis 'of their leadership qualities and national or international research reputation'. He was generous in availability to these heads, having an 'open door' policy for which many were grateful. Some, of course, were summoned. 'If I was happy with their planning there was a very light rein. If I was less happy there was more involvement'. This direct contact meant that the faculty deans lost some of their power during the nineties. Roberts perceived their role 'more as custodians of teaching quality than as budget-holders'. He introduced 'surgery' sessions which offered every member of staff direct access to the Vice-Chancellor; 'a superb corporate radar', in his view. His emphasis was on strategic planning by every sector of the University to maintain and enhance Sheffield's position in the 'super-league' of British universities.[5]

A tongue-in-cheek cartoon sent to Gareth Roberts, showing the Welsh dragon breathing fire on the ADC. Lest there should be any doubt about the identity of the dragon, it is wearing the scarf of Tottenham Hotspur, the football club supported by Roberts.

THE SURGE IN STUDENT NUMBERS 1991–95

In 1989 the government decided to fund an increase of at least ten per cent in higher education students by 1993. Every university wanted a share of this windfall. The ADC had a development plan ready and decided to bid to increase total numbers from 9,400 to 11,200 in the short term, and to 13,000 by the year 2000.[6] Undergraduate numbers increased by eight per cent from 1989/90 to 1990/91. For 1991/92 the UFC introduced a new system of funding, under which universities were required to bid against a 'guide price' for every course. Many vice-chancellors were apparently unprepared for this change and unwilling to go along with it, but Gareth Roberts had seen which way the wind was blowing and, while still in Oxford, directed a series of statistical projections aimed at securing the optimum balance of student numbers in different departments.[7] He was aided by Ron Johnston and a capable administrative team in a strategy which was so dazzlingly successful that all the other universities were out-manoeuvred.

The result was announced in February 1991, just after Roberts became vice-chancellor. The University of Sheffield was awarded both the highest increase in funding (19.6 per cent) and the highest increase in student numbers (14.7 per cent). *The Times* newspaper, in a feature on Sheffield, described it as 'a moment of triumph' after 'a number of years in which it had been known as a solid but unspectacular institution'.[8]

The extra funded student places went mostly to the social sciences, where the departments of Economics, Sociology and Geography had a 45 per cent increase and Politics and Law 23 per cent, and to the humanities, with average increases of 17 per cent, and as much as 31 per cent in Archaeology. The Biological Sciences had an increase of 12 per cent and Physical Sciences 17 per cent. During Roberts's first four years (up to 1994/95) the undergraduate population increased by 43 per cent. Not all of these increases resulted from the enhanced UFC funding. Some were 'fees only' students for whom the University received only a small fee contribution from their LEA. The reason for admitting them was tactical, since it was hoped that the UFC would fund them in subsequent years. Postgraduate numbers also took off, to the extent of a 72 per cent increase by 1995. There were 13,916 students by 1994/95 – more than the original goal for the year 2000. Sheffield's expansion during 1990–95 was 48 per cent. Other universities expanded to a similar extent: student numbers nationwide grew by fifty per cent during these years. This period has been dubbed the 'silent revolution', during which mass participation in higher education was quietly introduced.[9]

Resources did not, of course, keep pace. Many vice-chancellors, like Sir Michael Thompson of Birmingham, criticised 'expansion on the cheap'.[10] At Sheffield, the unit of funding per student went down by 28 per cent in the years 1990-96. This funding was still slightly above average for the university system as a whole; even Oxford and Cambridge were feeling the pinch.[11] University funding did not rise thereafter, and the period of expansion was abruptly curtailed in 1995. The government reversed its policy, capping student numbers and imposing financial penalties on universities which exceeded their allocation.

University staff were under tremendous pressure, especially during the early years of the student influx. Although extra academics were recruited, to the extent of 31 per cent by 1994/95, the student/staff ratio rose from 11.5 in 1990/91 to 14.0 five years later.[12] These averages conceal major variations between faculties. The highest ratios by 2000/01 were in Arts (17.7), Social Science (23.2) and Law (26.2). Seminar groups grew much larger and buildings were bursting at the seams. New lecture theatres seating several hundred were needed: Law, for example, had 400 students in some lectures. On the whole, departments which did not need to provide laboratory teaching shouldered the brunt of the increases, but Biology was an example of a scientific subject which coped with inflated numbers, initially without any additions to the staff. All first year lectures were duplicated and practical classes triplicated. Laboratories were in constant use and group projects replaced some individual final year submissions. A new, more flexible, degree was introduced which proved attractive to applicants.[13] The same story could be told of many other departments.

Inevitably, some students were disappointed. One mature student was quoted in *The Independent* as saying that 'you queue to see your lecturers, queue for the library . . . there are just too many people'.[14] The wonder must be, however, that the system managed to absorb so many extra students in such a short time. Staff and students adapted with remarkable resilience.

TEACHING QUALITY AND SEMESTERISATION

Assessment of teaching quality was one of the innovations of the nineties. It introduced a degree of external monitoring which previous generations of lecturers, accustomed to complete freedom at the lectern, would have regarded as unthinkable. The demands of the Quality Assurance Agency (QAA) were irksome: the paper chase was long and detailed, and inspections took several days. Roberts complained of methods which 'overwhelm the assessors with documentation and place virtually no emphasis on personal student experience'.[15] Ted Wragg of Exeter reported that his department had been audited ten times in one year by people wanting different sets of papers: 'proliferation becomes the enemy of quality because it sucks away so much time and effort'.[16]

The only plausible advantage was identification of, and reward for, good teaching. Sheffield was well-placed, having introduced training for lecturers in the 1960s and a staff development unit in 1985. These were augmented by a MEd course for lecturers in 1992 and the SOLAR resource centre in 1996.[17] Gareth Roberts believed that the extra funding awarded by the UFC in 1991 was largely due to Sheffield's strength as a teaching institution.[18]

Sheffield volunteered for the dubious honour of being among the first universities to have an Academic Audit, in June 1991. The University was praised for publishing its report, which suggested changes applicable to many universities, like

Bernard Kingston, Director of the Careers Advisory Service from 1975 to 1997, was responsible for the development of the service into a leader in its field. He also made a significant contribution to careers services at the national level.

the introduction of student feedback.[19] Concern about the teaching demands of 'mass higher education' were met by introducing training for both staff and students in the facilitation of independent study. A Flexible Learning Centre was established in 1992 to support the development of open learning and new technologies. One of the most successful of the new media proved to be 'networked learning', interactive course materials on an internet-delivery system called 'Web CT', which was beginning to have a real impact by 2000. Pilot disciplines included Chemistry, History, Biomedical Science and Medicine.

Independent learning was less controversial than 'enterprise' learning, which encouraged universities to improve the employability of their graduates by putting more emphasis on vocational outcomes. Bernard Kingston, the energetic head of Sheffield's careers service, set up the first university 'Personal Skills Unit' in 1988 and persuaded *The Times* to develop a comprehensive national league table for the career destinations of graduates.[20] Sheffield launched one of the first 'Enterprise in Higher Education' units, funded by the government to the tune of £1 million, in 1990.

A fundamental reshaping of the curriculum was gaining momentum at the same time, as the University considered whether to introduce modules of standard academic value.[21] At a time of concern about widening participation, the Board of Part-time and Access Studies chaired by Alan Walker, where the idea originated, hoped that modules would facilitate the introduction of part-time degrees. They would also give students the flexibility to choose courses from a wider range of departments and even from different universities. Modules were a popular idea with departments like the biologies, which had a wide range of interdisciplinary degrees more easily organised on a modular basis. They were unpopular with others, like Law, which had a fixed curriculum, because of the demands of external professional validation. The original scheme envisaged 'short, fat' modules extending over half a year and 'long, thin' ones lasting a full session.

Agreement in principle to introduce modules in every faculty except Medicine and Dentistry was reached in 1989, after 'a hell of a battle' in Senate.[22] To ensure academic progression, pre-requisites were to be attached to many modules. Honours degrees in named subjects would require study of specified modules. When Roberts arrived, he proposed the introduction of an academic year made up of two semesters, each of fifteen weeks duration. A working party chaired by Ron Johnston proposed that each module should be 'short, fat' and each semester consist of twelve weeks teaching, followed by three examination weeks. This was accepted by Senate in 1992.

Such a revolutionary change affected all the dates of time-honoured University operations. The consequent workload was enormous. Before the first 'modularised' year, 1994/95, academic staff devised a total of 1,493 modules, each containing a syllabus, bibliography, pre-requisites and, a new requirement, module 'outcomes'.[23] Administrative staff, with no additions to the workforce, wrote new regulations, co-ordinated the mountain of paperwork and organised the second examination session in January. Anonymity of examination candidates was introduced later, after a Students' Union campaign. The 'sixteen point scale' was devised to standardise a plethora of different marking schemes across the University.[24]

Most other universities implemented semesterisation at the same time. Only a few, like Oxford and Cambridge, held out against what Ron Johnston later described as a 'bandwagon'.[25] His experience in Sheffield led him to reject calls for a similar change in Essex when he moved there.

In 2002, during a review of the effects of modularisation, the majority of departments were keen to continue with it. However, some of the promised benefits had not been realised. Part-time degrees did not take off and, on the whole, students did not embrace the flexible possibilities, preferring to stay with traditional degree programmes. A reader in engineering said that his students found it almost impossible to choose modules outside the faculty because of timetable clashes – 'the opposite of what was promised'.[26] Departments with a high number of interdisciplinary degrees liked the system because it regulated student workload and made the degrees easier to organise. Unlike the sixteen point scale, which was abandoned in 2000/01, modules and semesters became part of the fabric of the University.

Incidentally, there is little evidence to suggest that modularisation, in itself, contributed to 'grade inflation'. The number of first class degrees jumped by an average of fifty per cent nationwide during the 1980s.[27] The percentage of first class degrees awarded by Sheffield remained stable at between eight and nine per cent from 1990 to 1995, and actually dropped below this in 1996–98. From 1999 the proportion of first and 2.1 degrees rose considerably. In 2003, 69.7 per cent of degrees awarded were first or 2.1; in 1989 it was 51.7 per cent.

Modularisation and Teaching Quality Assessments (TQA) led to an unprecedented focus on teaching methods and learning outcomes. This was happening nationwide, but Sheffield's teaching strength was affirmed when 29 disciplines received the rating of 'excellent', or equivalent, during the assessment period 1993–2001 (see Appendix 5). The promotions policy was revised, at Gareth Roberts's instigation, in order to acknowledge and reward staff who had proved to be particularly creative teachers.[28] He paid tribute to the 'brilliant' way in which his pro-vice-chancellor Phil Jones orchestrated the TQA visits.

'WIDENING PARTICIPATION' AND REGIONAL INITIATIVES

Sheffield has a proud record on student recruitment, which dates back to the creation of Student Reception in 1965 and the Schools Liaison Service, which began in the seventies and ran sixth form day and residential conferences. Both were 'something of a prototype' for other universities.[29] During the eighties, school visits were undertaken by schools liaison officers Malcolm McCormick, Stephen George and Allan Johnson. Stephen George recalls that they had access to Geoffrey Sims's official car, a blue Ford Granada, when he was not using it[30].

Gareth Roberts's contribution was the 'Early Outreach' scheme, a characteristically ambitious attempt to address the 'poverty of aspiration' of working-class pupils who never considered applying to university. This project was especially close to the Vice-Chancellor's heart and he visited schools in some of the most deprived parts of Sheffield and South Yorkshire in order to create direct links with the University. The programme was launched with the support of local head-teachers and the LEA and targeted fourteen-year-old pupils in selected schools. These pupils were invited to visit the University and offered an extra programme of study in school years 9, 10 and 11. The Students' Union recruited student mentors to work in their classrooms and act as 'positive role models'.[31] One head-teacher reported that his first group of pupils on the programme scored the best GCSE grades in the history of the school.[32] Over 1,000 pupils from 22 schools were involved annually in the three-year programme by 1994.

The aim of Early Outreach, explained Allan Johnson, who managed the programme, was to 'raise awareness' among pupils rather than recruit them specifically to Sheffield. It was 'very innovative' for that reason. It was not feasible to extend the full Early Outreach programme beyond 22 schools, but a far greater number made 'compact agreements' with the University. 'Compact liaison officers' were appointed from among the University's admissions tutors. They helped to identify pupils with academic ability whose circumstances might lead them to under-achieve in examinations. Experience showed that they performed very well upon entrance to the university environment. Hardly any other comparable university was investing so heavily in access schemes in the nineties, as a 1998 CVCP report, *From Elitism to Inclusion*, revealed. In 2003 the *Financial Times* concluded that Sheffield had outpaced every other university by starting its 'widening participation' schemes so early: 'building a socially inclusive university takes years of hard work'.[33]

ADMISSIONS TO THE UNIVERSITY OF SHEFFIELD FROM STATE SCHOOLS AND LOW-PARTICIPATION GROUPS
1998/99

Young entrants from state schools/ colleges		Young entrants from social classes IIIM, IV, V		Young entrants from low-participation neighbourhoods		Mature entrants with no previous HE experience and from low-participation neighbourhoods	
of all entrants	Benchmark (ie. target)	of all entrants	Benchmark	of all entrants	Benchmark	of all entrants	Benchmark
80%	74%	17%	18%	9%	9%	18%	15%

Source *THES* 3.12.99

Allan Johnson promotes the University of Sheffield to potential applicants.

The Medical School joined the Compact scheme in 1994 and found that students recruited in this way performed well.[34] In 1999, funding from HEFCE (the Higher Education Funding Council for England, which replaced the UFC) was secured to develop this scheme by offering twenty reserved places on the medical degree.

Roberts explained that the aim was to attract 'a previously untapped pool of potential doctors. They will provide the NHS with a clinical workforce that more accurately reflects the socio-economic basis of society'.[35]

Early Outreach pupils from Hinde House School, who re-enacted the 1905 opening ceremony on the University's ninetieth anniversary in July 1995, seen with Gareth Roberts in the Firth Court quadrangle.

A rather different access scheme involved the accreditation of further education college courses at degree level. The idea was pioneered by the University's 'Mundella Programme' in the eighties, but took firm and lasting shape in the 'Board of Collegiate Studies' from 1993.[36] It allowed students, who were often mature, to take home-based study to a high level. Not all the colleges were local to Sheffield: Wirral, Accrington and Peterborough were included, together with Thessaloniki in Greece. The facilities, staff and curriculum of each were carefully vetted by the University to ensure that the standards were comparable. Barnsley College had an especially large programme, with five validated degrees by 1995, including Creative Music Technology and Brass Band Studies, and a foundation year in Pure Science.[37] The graduation ceremonies were held at the University – a particularly special occasion because the new graduates had studied at a distance from the University, and often under challenging circumstances.

By far the most ambitious regional outreach scheme was Dearne Valley College. Dearne Valley was in the heart of the devastated South Yorkshire coalfields and the target of economic regeneration funds. In 1992 the University was invited by the Dearne Valley Partnership to establish a university college there.[38] Within nine months, however, it was clear that HEFCE would not fund the proposed student intake and plans for the higher education element of the college were drastically scaled down. The building which opened in 1996 had a higher education centre developed by the University, with a large IT suite, but the College was primarily devoted to further education. The most successful higher education programme has since proved to be Nursing Studies, which was based in Dearne Valley College until the University's Humphrey Davy House, with a library and IT centre, was built nearby in 1998.

Dearne Valley College, opened in 1996.

Roberts recognised the need for the University to become a central player in regional matters, at a time when 'significant structural changes' to the 'industrial and economic base' of Sheffield and South Yorkshire were being made.[39] He became a director of both the Sheffield Development Corporation and the

Gareth Roberts with Dr John Stoddart, Principal of Sheffield Hallam University.

Health Authority, and co-founded the City Liaison Group (later renamed 'Sheffield First') with Mike Bower, the leader of Sheffield City Council. These groups made many of the most crucial planning decisions about the future of Sheffield and its region.

The Vice-Chancellor was adept at promoting partnerships. The seedbed of many an important development was a dinner party at The Croft in Fulwood, previously the home of Pro-Chancellor Jim Eardley and selected by Roberts as the new vice-chancellor's residence. It had a large, secluded garden and a suite of reception rooms, ideal for entertainment. The visitors' books show the formidable range of guests who were regularly welcomed by Gareth Roberts and his wife Carolyn. Business was conducted up to the dessert course, and dinner was followed by a light-hearted quiz devised by the Vice-Chancellor to encourage his guests to mingle.

Relations with Sheffield Polytechnic (Sheffield Hallam University from 1992) were good, helped by the friendship between Gareth Roberts and John Stoddart, the Principal. Links with two other universities in the Yorkshire region, Leeds and York, were formalised in the 'White Rose' partnership, of which Roberts, the prime mover, was very proud. After the inaugural vice-chancellors' dinner at The Croft, rotating meetings were arranged and plans made to strengthen co-operation between the three institutions in teaching, research and regional activities. Joint bids for research funding were submitted, with the result that in 1999 the partnership was awarded £4.5 million from the University Challenge Fund and £2.9 million from the Science Enterprise Challenge. The Vice-Chancellor regarded White Rose as the model arrangement for collaboration between like-minded universities. He also became a member of the Board of the Yorkshire and Humber Regional Development Agency in 1998/99, a demanding commitment which continued until he left the University.

The Regional Office, opened in 1992 and directed by Marilyn Wedgwood, was designed to provide a central focus for the University's regional activities. One of its projects was the 'Materials Forum', led by Doug Liversidge, which supported research on industrial problems identified by a cluster of local companies.[40] Liversidge, who became Master Cutler in 1998, also formed 'Medilink', which brought small medical technology companies, the university and the hospitals together.[41] A new programme, given the name PLUS, linked local companies with students who could carry out specific project work as part of their degree course and for the benefit of work experience. Regional initiative was of such importance to Roberts that he included the development of regional projects within the criteria for academic promotion. The office he created was the first of its type in the country, in anticipating by several years the 'third leg' funding for regional projects which was introduced nationally in 2002.[42]

The World Student Games

Student sports champions from many nations came to Sheffield in July 1991 for the World Student Games. The event was conceived and run by the City Council, with

University involvement spearheaded by John Padley. It was an ambitious attempt to promote regeneration of the city through sport. Two swimming pools of international standard were built, together with an athletics stadium and an indoor arena on the site of obsolete steelworks in the Don Valley. Unfortunately, the cost of the Games, despite high hopes, was covered neither by sponsorship nor television rights, since the BBC and ITV chose not to show the Games at any length.[43] Rows about the cost to the local council taxpayer (eventually a £10 million deficit plus the annual interest on loans for buildings costing £140 million) formed a backdrop to the event and proved to be the main item of interest to the national press. Even the NUS was equivocal in its support.[44]

Sheffield's own Students' Union, however, was enthusiastic and its President, Dave McClements, was one of a group which travelled to Japan to collect the flame from the previous hosts. The Union ran the bar and entertainments in the Games village, including 'Sheffield's biggest party', attended by 5,000 competitors and volunteers, on the last night of the Games.[45] Many of these volunteers were students and members of staff, co-ordinated by Christine Sexton. The University hosted a range of events for the parallel Cultural Festival, which celebrated the diversity among the 101 countries which sent athletes to the Games. This Festival brought the spirit of the 'Friendly Games' to the heart of the City.

The University also had its own sporting star in Curtis Robb, a first-year medical student who won a silver medal in the 800 metres and went on to qualify for the final of the Olympic Games in Barcelona the following year. Hailed as the 'new hope' of British middle-distance running, he opted to concentrate on his studies, qualifying as a doctor in 1998.[46]

The Games gave Sheffield sports facilities which were second to none: Ponds Forge pool was described by the governing body of swimming as the best in the world.[47] Two years later, it became apparent that a British city might be selected as the host for the Commonwealth Games in 2002 and Sheffield decided, at very short notice, to enter the bidding against London and Manchester. The University's offer to take the leading role in the bid was crucial, since the City Council was reluctant to take another political battering when it was still paying the price for the World Student Games. A University team prepared the bid, which included use of the student halls as the athletes' village. Sheffield's proposals, based on the city's hard-won experience, were the 'most realistic' and estimated the cost at £38 million, mostly for operating expenses.[48] London and Manchester's estimated costs were far higher, since both needed to build facilities which Sheffield already had. Despite this huge advantage Sheffield's team, in Mike Bower's words, 'was shown the red card before we'd even set foot on the park'.[49] On the morning of the presentations, it was told that the bid would be disallowed unless the University signed an open-ended promise to underwrite the cost of the Games. Sheffield expected that the government would cover some of its costs, but since no promises had been made, it could not sign a 'blank cheque'.[50]

Members of the Sheffield team were aggrieved at the outcome. Mike Bower was openly suspicious that Manchester, which won the Games, had privately been

A performance of A Midsummer Night's Dream *at the Drama Studio by the Comedy Theatre Company of Bucharest, one of 23 events hosted by the University during the Cultural Festival.*

The World Student Games

Clockwise from above:

Postage stamp issued to mark the Games.

Using 10-ton overland vehicles, members of staff challenged a team from the Students' Union to a truck pull in February 1990 to raise money to help athletes from third world countries to participate in the Games.

Women's 3,000 metres final, won by Sonia O'Sullivan (in green and white) who went on to become one of the world's greatest female athletes.

Curtis Robb with his 800 metres silver medal.

Volleyball competition at Ponds Forge.

The Canadian team entering the Don Valley Stadium at the opening ceremony.

New synthetic turf pitches installed at the Bramley Fields in 1993/4, to be used mainly for hockey and six-a-side football. The University also made them available for community use, especially during vacations.

promised government aid.[51] Whether that was true or not, Manchester ultimately received over £200 million from the government and the National Lottery to stage the Commonwealth Games in 2002, after they were threatened with financial meltdown during the previous year.[52] Sheffield was not competing on a level playing field.

The University's own sporting facilities were improved during the nineties – an urgent project because of the influx of extra students. John Padley took forward a scheme which would have built new pitches on Oakes Park in Norton, and sold part of the original Warminster Road ground for housing. The proposal was turned down by the city planners in June 1992 because of the volume of protest from local residents.[53] More successful was the plan, announced in the same month, to build floodlit synthetic pitches on Bramley Fields.[54] These were opened in November 1993 with a men's hockey match between the University and Sheffield Hallam.

During 1992–96 the University made what should have been a successful attempt to take over the running of Weston Park.[55] Once regarded by local people as 'the showpiece of South Yorkshire', the park had been neglected for many years. The University simply wished to smarten it up; the park would have remained a community resource controlled by the City Council. However, the short-term lease offered by the Council, combined with the hostility of certain local residents, led to the breakdown of negotiations and the abandonment of the project. The park continued to be neglected, but in 2004 there were plans to improve it through an application to the Heritage Lottery Fund, following the restoration of the Mappin Art Gallery and Weston Park Museum.

OVERSEAS ENTERPRISE

Many universities sought imaginative ways to enhance the number of overseas students during the nineties. It was, indeed, a highly competitive market involving not only British, but also other European, Australian and American universities. The most valuable projects created a 'twinning' between a university and a particular college abroad, either to provide an access course or to teach part of the main degree course in the home college. In 1992 Sheffield established a successful partnership with Taylor's College in Kuala Lumpur, Malaysia, initially to provide law and management degrees, later expanded to include engineering.[56] Students studied in Kuala Lumpur for their first year and in Sheffield for their second and third years. In the mid-nineties, this arrangement provided 25 per cent of the University's overseas undergraduates. It thus formed the bedrock of overseas undergraduate recruitment.[57] For the students, studying abroad became a far less intimidating experience because they left Malaysia for Sheffield with a group of class-mates.[58] The students appreciated the expertise of the Sheffield staff, even if they found it 'a bit intimidating to be in a lecture with 200 other students'.[59] For their part, University staff could find themselves teaching classes in which a majority of the students came from overseas.

The success of the Taylor's College link established such a good profile for the University in Malaysia that Sheffield, despite competition from other universities, was invited in 1994 to enter a partnership to establish a medical school in the state of Perak.[60] According to Malaysian practice, a private firm, Suci Teguh Sdn Bhd consortium, was set up to build and run the Medical College. Both the University and the state government held shares in this company, and the University also stood to gain a percentage of student fees and a new building in Sheffield. The plan was that Sheffield would provide the initial, pre-clinical, training and students would return to the new medical school in Perak for their clinical experience. As its Health Minister explained, Malaysia preferred this part of the training to be based at home because students 'will be more familiar with treating diseases and ailments found in this part of the world.'[61] Graduates of this programme would receive a Sheffield medical degree, which was highly prized by the Malaysians as a passport to jobs worldwide. In these early stages the University had no reason to expect that this aspect of the proposal would prove to be a problem, and believed it had received assurances from the General Medical Council to this effect.[62] The chief concerns, with which the Medical faculty in particular had to grapple, were the cultural and ideological differences in healthcare between Britain and Malaysia, and the need to ensure that the facilities for clinical training were of a standard comparable to those in Sheffield. The medical school and biology departments in Sheffield also had to expand their provision to take an extra group of 100 students in the pre-clinical years.

The air miles accumulated over the next two years as Sheffield staff, both medical and administrative, made arrangements in Malaysia. Dinners and meetings

An artist's impression of the Asean Sheffield Medical College

Left: *An artist's impression of Perak Medical College, opened in 1999 next to Ipoh General Hospital, seen in the background.*

Above: *The atrium of Perak Medical College.*

were held and plans were drawn up for courses and for the College building, to be constructed next to Ipoh General Hospital and called the Asean-Sheffield Medical College. The first contract was signed on 31 October 1995 and the 'ground-breaking' ceremony on the site was performed by the Malaysian Prime Minister, himself a doctor, in July 1996. He was presented with a set of Sheffield-made surgical instruments by John Padley.[63] Nigel Bax from the Medical School was appointed as the first Dean and worked from the newly created South East Asia office in Kuala Lumpur, in order to supervise developments and recruit staff and students. Student interest was high and a preliminary cohort of thirty arrived in Sheffield in 1996, with 103 the following year. The pre-clinical building in Firth Court, named the Perak Laboratories, opened in 1997. Shortly afterwards, however, the first major crisis hit the project, when the Malaysian currency collapsed and the funding company withdrew from the project.

Months of uncertainty followed, with concern about the potential financial loss to the University and the fact that the first cohort of students was due to return to Ipoh in September 1998. It proved impossible to save the posts of the recently appointed professors of surgery and general practice in Ipoh. A rescue package was finally devised in 1999, by which the state government of Perak, which was strongly committed to the scheme, arranged to assume the debt and to finance and manage the College through a wholly state-owned enterprise.

The Ipoh building, just completed, was renamed the Perak Medical College. A franchise agreement, which gave the University responsibility for quality control but not for administration or the employment of staff, was signed in September 1999. The obstetrician Robert Fraser was seconded from Sheffield as Foundation Dean in December. He was joined by a rheumatologist, Michael Snaith, and the recently retired virology professor, Chris Potter. They worked with locally recruited colleagues to establish the clinical teaching. Within a few months, however, there was a second crisis, when in March 2000 the General Medical Council in Britain refused to ratify the Perak degree which, being franchised, they regarded as different from the original proposals.[64] It may be significant that the GMC was under fire at the time. Issues of quality control, revealed by the Bristol

The Chancellor Lord Dainton meets University of Sheffield graduates at a ceremony in Hong Kong.

heart scandal, were in the headlines.[65] No further salvage was possible and the project had to be unstitched. Students who had already enrolled were allowed to proceed with their Sheffield degrees, and the University of Malaya stepped in to offer its own medical degree at the College.

While all this was going on, several universities were negotiating with the Malaysian government to proceed to a further stage, in which they would run a franchised campus there. Monash University, Australia, won the first of these licences in 1998. For two years Gareth Roberts pursued the possibility of a Sheffield campus in Kulim, offering a range of courses, until the currency crisis of 1997–8. 'Sun sets on lucrative student market' was his inevitable conclusion.[66] This was the point at which the University turned back from increasingly risky enterprises, in which staff had to negotiate with private companies whose business practices could be very different from those of a publicly accountable British institution.

John Padley did a great deal to improve the recruitment of overseas students, by setting up marketing opportunities which enhanced the profile of the University in many countries. He also secured important research and consultancy links for the University, and was chairman of UNECIA, a consortium which sought overseas contracts on behalf of ten northern universities.[67] In 1998 he took early retirement, stating that, 'I've done sixteen years here and it's time for a younger person to have a go . . . UNECIA has become a big operation and I need to dedicate more time to it'.[68] He subsequently retired to Worcestershire.

Padley was behind the idea of holding degree ceremonies for university graduates in their home country. He was supported enthusiastically by the Chancellor, Lord Dainton, who enjoyed his visits and was an excellent ambassador for the University. 'These occasions were absolutely wonderful', Padley recalled, 'it was often the case that a student would be supported by the whole family in raising sufficient funds to send him or her abroad . . . giving students their degrees with all their families present was really heart-warming.'[69] Alumni who had never had the chance to be presented to the Chancellor at the time of their graduation, some as long ago as the 1950s, swelled the numbers.[70] The first were held in Tel Aviv, Singapore and Kuala Lumpur in 1992, with ceremonies to follow in Hong Kong and the West Indies. Some of these graduates had studied for Masters degrees by distance learning – an important growth area for the international market.

John Padley welcomes Junior Year Abroad students in the Department of Ceramics, Glasses & Polymers in 1987.

The 'Year Abroad' Programme, a Padley initiative of the 1980s, brought many students to Sheffield and had 22 partner universities in Australia, Canada and the USA by 2003. The corresponding ERASMUS exchange programme with other European universities involved most departments in the University and was the fifth largest in the country.[71] The Northern Consortium, linking twelve universities in the north of England, brought several hundred students to Sheffield from countries like Kenya, Jordan, Pakistan and China during the nineties and thereafter. The Consortium arranged a foundation year, either for an undergraduate or a masters' degree, in the home country. This was 'one of the success stories of the late eighties and nineties', according to Tim Crick, director of the International Office from 1998.[72] He stressed that the market for overseas students to come to Sheffield to

study was far larger than the market for franchised courses abroad. Sheffield's overseas student population increased exponentially and shows every sign of continuing to do so in the future.

Left: Students serve traditional Afro-Caribbean dishes at an International Food Evening in the Octagon Centre.

Right: Chung Man Cheung, a member of the Meet and Greet Scheme, welcomes overseas students arriving at Heathrow Airport at the start of the 1990/91 academic year.

International students in Sheffield

The number of overseas students registered on full-time courses at the University increased by 53 per cent between 1990 and 1995, and had reached 2,300 by 2002 (see Appendix 4). These students came from over 100 different countries, with Malaysians forming the largest single group. The number of postgraduate students was particularly high – 36 per cent of the total in 1993/94, for example.

Although most students arrived with adequate English, the need to develop their skills led the University to establish the English Language Teaching Centre, under Kevin Dunseath, in 1986. Other services were added; in particular Debora Green was appointed to Student Services in 1990 with the specific task of supporting overseas students. The Union had just decided to create the post of sabbatical International Student Secretary, only the third British Students' Union to do so. More and more societies for different nationalities emerged, about thirty by 2000. These groups were co-ordinated by the International Students' Committee, which organised events designed to 'celebrate the difference', like the International Food Evening, held in the Octagon from 1993 and attracting over 1,000 people: 'guests were able to sample traditional foods from all over the world – borekas from Turkey, mango ice-cream from Thailand, pakoras from the Indian sub-continent'.[73] The International Cultural Evening (first held as early as 1972) celebrated every kind of traditional music and dance. 'Globalspan', launched in 1993, organised trips to places of historic and cultural interest in Britain and Europe.

Debora Green established an orientation programme for newly-arrived freshers.[74] A student arriving from Uganda recalls, 'At Sheffield railway station I was received by members of the Meet and Greet. If there is anything of immediate relief to a new student in the UK, it is this!'[75] Others were met at Manchester Airport by students carrying a board saying 'Sheffield University'. One Chinese girl recalled that all the arrangements for her to reach her residence were made and

Careers Fair for graduates returning to Hong Kong, held in the Octagon Centre in April 1992. It was attended by 500 students from sixty British universities.

she was left 'with nothing to worry about'. This student, like the majority, arrived with no idea of what Sheffield would be like, beyond photographs in the prospectus or on the website, and with no friends in the vicinity. During the orientation week they met fellow-students, visited Chatsworth House, discovered bar quizzes and found their way around the city centre.

The *International Student* newsletter recorded early impressions.[76] A Chinese architecture student was surprised by Sheffield's buildings: 'I expected a modern metropolis full of skyscrapers and giant glass complexes, but the reality seems to be a rural place with rows of small houses not more than three storeys'. In Hong Kong, said another, 'buildings over 25–30 years are considered to be too old and are scheduled for demolition'. Some of the Chinese were surprised that the University campus was not fenced in, but was part of the city. The weather came in for predictable comment: 'as a foreign student, you have to face problems like home-sickness, a language barrier, culture shock and loneliness. You are thinking matters cannot get much worse, then it starts to rain!' 'I have learnt that spending fifty English pounds on a good jacket is worthwhile.' Reflections on the food, both quality and price, varied, but almost all mentioned the helpfulness and friendliness of local people, despite the occasional difficulty of understanding the accent.

There is little doubt that Sheffield has proved to be a worthy host of international students and at the forefront in developing services for them. The policy of 'internationalising' the Union was a great success, later recommended to other universities.[77] Among the University's other initiatives was the suggestion by Bernard Kingston of the Careers Advisory Service that it might prove economic for foreign employers to travel to Sheffield to do a 'milk round'. The first South East Asian Careers Fair was held in the Octagon Centre in 1991, and a Hong Kong Fair was added in 1992.

MANAGING THE UNIVERSITY IN THE NINETIES

The chairman of the CVCP and the Dearing Report

Gareth Roberts was a key player in the establishment of the Russell Group, formed at the time when the university community was extended dramatically, to include the polytechnics, in 1992. The need for a 'premier division' was seen as urgent by the vice-chancellors of leading universities and, according to Roberts's account, London, Oxford, Cambridge and Warwick universities were already meeting together.[78] He and Mike Carr, the Registrar of Liverpool University, organised meetings of the leaders of nine civic universities at the Hotel Russell in London in 1992. At the third meeting they decided to unite with the London, Oxford, Cambridge and Warwick group. The Russell Group, which by 2004 was nineteen-strong, still met at the hotel six times a year. It became 'the mouthpiece for the research-led, internationally-based British universities'.[79]

Gareth Roberts was elected chairman of the Committee of Vice-Chancellors and Principals (CVCP) in February 1995. This was a vote of collegial confidence in both his work in Sheffield and his contributions at national level, for example as

Director of the Higher Education Quality Council. Within months of taking the CVCP chair, he was plunged into conflict with the government over the twelve per cent cut in university income (plus at least thirty per cent in capital funding), announced in November 1995. This was on top of a freeze on expansion, enforced through fines for overshooting publicly funded places.[80] In an article in *The Independent*, Roberts wrote:

> Over the last few years universities have delivered what the Government asked for – a substantial move to a high-quality, mass higher education system. We have continued to provide a high-quality service with less and less money available for each student – down 28 per cent since 1989. However, we have now reached the limit for further 'efficiency gains'. The pressures on staff have been enormous, and with no reward.[81]

Graeme Davies, by now Vice-Chancellor of Glasgow, 'compared the universities to turtles being herded towards a cliff. Only when one of them fell over would the process be stopped'.[82] The CVCP, strongly steered by Roberts and the Russell Group vice-chancellors, decided to turn and fight. It threatened to impose top-up fees of £300 on students from September 1997 – a charge which the government opposed. Many vice-chancellors, like Roberts, saw the fee simply as a stop-gap pending the introduction of a proper loans system, linked to graduates' ability to pay. Within days, the government agreed to set up an enquiry under Lord Dearing into every aspect of higher education finance. Thus Roberts became known as 'the man behind the Dearing review'.[83]

The threat of the levy was withdrawn but the campaign against the cuts continued. A large rally was held at the University of Sheffield in April 1996, when national officials from all the campus trades unions joined the vice-chancellor on the platform.[84] Sheffield also played host to the vice-chancellors and principals at their annual meeting in September. Another round of voluntary redundancies and a recruitment freeze had to be introduced, at a time when lecturers' salaries were so deflated that 'a lecturer starts on £13,000 a year and can work up to the dizzy heights of around £35,000 as a senior professor of international repute'.[85]

Above: *Representatives of the campus unions brave the snow on 20 November 1996 on a national day of action to protest against the cuts. This photograph was published in the Yorkshire Post.*

Left: *Gareth Roberts, as Chairman of the CVCP, chairs a briefing meeting with national officials from all the campus unions including, on his left, David Triesman of the AUT and, on his right, Jim Murphy of the NUS during the 1996 national campaign against the cuts in higher education funding. A meeting in the Octagon Centre was attended by 1,000 staff and students from the two Sheffield universities.*

Large numbers of students from the two Sheffield universities, and local further education colleges, demonstrate in November 1997 against the imposition of tuition fees.

Right: Cartoon from Darts *showing the axe about to fall on the Department of Earth Sciences in November 1998. The department, originally Geology, was founded in 1913.*

The results of the 1996 RAE, announced in December, boosted the general level of morale at Sheffield and the University's allocation from HEFCE rose by 4.53 per cent, well above the national average, the following February. Roberts derided the overall level of higher education funding as 'grossly inadequate' but praised the decision to concentrate money 'where excellence is highest'.[86] His term as the chairman of CVCP concluded with the award of a knighthood in the Birthday Honours of June 1997 and with the publication of the Dearing Report the following month. The Report reproduced John Masefield's words during the installation of Sheffield's Chancellor Lord Harewood in 1946:

'There are few earthly things more splendid than a University . . .'[87]

It advocated lifting the 'cap' on entry to higher education, supported the widening participation strategy and recommended that tuition fees amounting to about 25 per cent of the average cost could be charged.[88] Roberts welcomed the report, pointing out that eight of Dearing's recommendations were identical to those advised by the CVCP.[89]

The Sheffield MP and graduate David Blunkett was now in pole position, as Secretary of State for Education and Employment in the newly elected Labour government. He welcomed the Report and, on 23 July 1997, announced the introduction of a means-tested annual tuition fee of £1,000. The arguments he adduced in his speech to the House of Commons became a familiar mantra: 'Students should share both the investment and the advantages gained from higher education. Rights and responsibilities should go hand in hand. The investment of the nation must be balanced by the commitment of the individual'.[90] Despite a fee exemption for students from poorer families, there was dismay among some MPs on the Labour benches, as well as among parents and students. Many argued that they were already

334

in debt, owing to the low level of the grant. Adam Matthews, Sheffield's Union President, said that he knew students who were holding down two or three jobs to make ends meet. He led a delegation which picketed the Labour party conference in October 1997, and a demonstration in Sheffield in November.[91] A 'Stop the Fees' protest prevented the Senate meeting in December, but was denounced by student leaders as 'counter-productive': its organisers, the Socialist Workers party, were fined by the Union.[92] Marches continued the following year, with a rent strike in Sheffield after the tuition fee was imposed for entrants in September 1998.[93]

UCAS applications nationally fell by 2.9 per cent in 1998 and 2.5 per cent in 1999. The drop in applications to Sheffield was somewhat greater – 3.4 per cent in 1998 and 5.0 per cent in 1999.[94] Recruitment of students from South East Asia was hit by the financial crisis there. More economies, including a second freeze on recruitment, had to be imposed in May 1998: *The Independent* reported that Sheffield was £5 million in debt due to funding the 1996 early retirement scheme.[95] This was, however, the only year of deficit during the 1990s. Industrial action by campus trades unions continued; threats to disrupt the admissions system were called off at the last moment in August 1999.[96]

The Pro-Vice-Chancellors

The Roberts management regime gave a particularly important role to the pro-vice-chancellors (see Appendix 1 for their names). They were the most powerful academics in the University and their role was pivotal, since they belonged to the key decision-making committees and headed some of the task forces which the Strategic Planning Committee had set up to deal with pressing issues. Each had a portfolio of responsibilities and chaired the appropriate committees, thus the pro-vice-chancellor for academic planning was chairman of ADC. On top of this, they remained members of their own departments with commitments to research. The term of office was normally four years, although it could be extended to five and early in the following decade there were two instances of six-year terms.[97]

The limited term and the continuing link to a department ensured, in the view of one pro-vice-chancellor, that the executive group was not isolated from the academics.[98] It retained the element of 'self-government' which had been such a prominent feature of the eighties – albeit by placing most of that responsibility on four pairs of shoulders. The load was heavy, but pro-vice-chancellors seem to have enjoyed their term of office.[99] More than one suggested that it had enabled him to have another type of career within the same institution. Tony Crook spoke of 'the best job in the world'. David McClean recalled the 'cracking team' of which he was a member, along with David Luscombe, Ron Clark and Bob Boucher. For his part, Luscombe spoke of a 'tremendous sense of camaraderie' and his sense that he was 'walking on clouds' with the whole of the university's administrative and committee structure to support him. Most of the pro-vice-chancellors had been professors for several years, had served on the ADC and other committees, and knew the University well.

From left to right: Stuart Johnson, Treasurer, Jim Eardley, Chairman of Council, and his successor, Peter Lee.

Particular demands were placed on the pro-vice-chancellors who served while Roberts was chairman of the CVCP, and he paid tribute to their 'professionalism and commitment'.[100] Roberts also used them as troubleshooters in certain departments – David Lewis, for example, was sent to the Department of Earth Sciences. The decision to close Earth Sciences was made after a review in 1998.[101] Roberts made it clear that research performance and the size of the department were the crucial factors. The department's staff moved to the departments of Animal and Plant Sciences, Geography and Civil Engineering. The closure was phased over three years, however, because of parental protest and the strong desire of the students to complete their degrees within the department. Ernie Bailey, a senior member of ADC, assisted in the management of these final years and later also helped to manage the Economics department.

The School of East Asian Studies had a strong business portfolio, with the Japan Business Services Unit run by Rosemary Yates, and the Asia Pacific Business Services, established in 1987. The success of Japanese Studies led to the creation of a programme in Korean Studies with a focus on the modern Korean language and study of the country from a social science perspective. This was introduced in 1980 and a separate Institute was formed in 1987.[102] The department needed some revitalisation in 1991, however, and Norman Blake, a former pro-vice-chancellor, became chairman, to be followed in 1993 by Ian Gow. A BA in Chinese Studies began in 1996 and an exchange programme with China started in the following year.[103] The number of staff increased significantly, and the department became one of the leading centres in its field under Tim Wright, the Professor of Chinese Studies and chairman from 2000.

The Lay Officers

The University continued to be fortunate in its lay officers. Jim Eardley, who retired in 1996 after almost twenty years of service, was, in Roberts's view, a 'superb' chairman of Council.[104] Stuart Johnson, the managing director of a company supplying equipment to the glass industry, was the University's Treasurer from 1987 to 1998, a longer period than that served by any of his predecessors, and at a time when research and fee income rose rapidly.[105] Peter Lee, who succeeded Eardley as Chairman of Council and was like him a former Master Cutler, had a long career as a managing director in the local steel and engineering industry. Such men brought their knowledge and daily experience of the commercial and industrial environment to their role as 'critical friends' of the University. Indeed, Peter Lee, who had been a member of Council since 1966, described the most important part of his new role as the maintenance of a continuing dialogue with the Vice-Chancellor and the Director of Finance.[106]

Lord Dainton, the University's Chancellor since 1978, died on 5 December 1997, ten days after the opening of the new British Library building at St Pancras, a project which he had steered for seven years through considerable controversy. He was the recipient of 26 honorary degrees from universities at home and abroad. At

Peter Lee formally installs the new Chancellor, Sir Peter Middleton, at a ceremony in Firth Hall on 9 October 1999.

Sheffield he presided over 187 degree ceremonies and awarded degrees to nearly 60,000 students.[107] He introduced the Chancellor's Medal to reward outstanding achievement within the University community and in 1993 he was delighted that the Chemistry building was named after him. His autobiography, *Doubts and Certainties*, in a draft form at his death, was edited within the University and published in 2001. His papers were donated to the University Library to form the wide-ranging Dainton Archive.

Dainton's successor as Chancellor was Sir Peter Middleton, a member of Council since 1991. Like Dainton, Middleton was brought up in Sheffield, but unlike him he also studied at its University, reading economics and living at home, which he

> found a distinct plus. Almost all my lectures were in the morning – amazingly convenient. I used to lunch with my friends in the Union, then down to town to the Reference Library in Surrey Street, then home, where I saw my *Sheffield* friends. It was one of the most enjoyable times in my life.[108]

David Fletcher, Registrar and Secretary from 1999.

After national service he had no 'real idea what to do', but joined the civil service and, in an apparently effortless ascent, eventually became Permanent Secretary to the Treasury. He thus worked closely with several Chancellors of the Exchequer. Like Lord Dainton, Middleton was appreciated by Mrs Thatcher, who found him 'fun', perhaps because he had the reputation of a 'man of action', bounding up three stairs at a time. In 1991 he left the Treasury, after almost thirty years, for Barclays Bank, where he became Chairman in 1999. Sir Peter was installed as Chancellor at a ceremony in Firth Hall in October 1999.

Changes to university governance and administration

Reg Goodchild was appointed to the new post of Deputy Secretary in 1993, a time of change among senior administrators when John O'Donovan became Academic Secretary and David Bearpark succeeded Terry Thomas as Director of Finance. Roy Eddy continued as Academic Registrar. They made the necessary, but demanding, adjustments to the 'Roberts revolution' in management.[109]

David Fletcher replaced John Padley as Registrar in January 1999. Like Peter Middleton, Fletcher was a Sheffield graduate, with both a BA and a PhD in History. After working as an administrator at Manchester University, he was Registrar of Loughborough University before returning to Sheffield. Fletcher spearheaded the significant changes to the governance of the University which were necessary following the Dearing Report.[110] Dearing proposed that universities should streamline the membership of their governing bodies and clarify their roles. A smaller Council was needed, exercising its functions in a more proactive way. After extensive consultation, a retirement age of seventy and a maximum period of office were introduced. This resulted in the departure of a number of faithful Council members in June 2000, for whom a special dinner was held in University House. Among them was Stephen de Bartolomé, who had served on Council since 1950 and

Stephen de Bartolomé, Treasurer 1965–71 and Pro-Chancellor 1971–80, an outstanding friend of the University. His grandfather Mariano Martin de Bartolomé was president of the Medical School in the late nineteenth century.

had been its chairman, as well as Pro-Chancellor and Treasurer. He had 'exceptional prowess as a public speaker' and 'a wit that was always amusing and never unkind'.[111] Bartolomé liked to recall that he had upset the University's bank manager by moving £300,000 to a deposit from a current account, where it had customarily been kept 'in case the University was caught short'.[112]

The Court was a large committee which normally met only once a year, but had, according to the Charter, the status of supreme governing body. Its members were asked to accept the termination of this role, a process which was 'like the House of Lords voting to abolish itself'.[113] The Court is now a consultative body, but retains the power to elect the Chancellor.

The academic governance of the University also came under Fletcher's scrutiny and a new structure was put in place. The main change was the abolition of the Graduate School in 2000. The Graduate School had been introduced in 1994 to promote the 'research led' strategy and was the product of considerable work by pro-vice-chancellors Bob Boucher and David Lewis.[114] It was seen as a means of attracting even more postgraduates, in competition with universities which already had such schools. However, a review concluded that the strength of the University's faculty system was such that an extra layer of bureaucracy was undesirable. Successful initiatives like the Research Training Programme continued. This review also endorsed the role of the Strategic Planning Committee and led to the incorporation of the Faculty of Educational Studies into the Faculty of Social Sciences.

The new Registrar restructured the administrative services into 'directorates' which could co-ordinate and focus the rather disparate working practices which had developed over the years. The most important directorates were Information Services, to cover Corporate Information and Computing Services (CiCS) and the Library, and the Facilities Management Directorate, for accommodation, catering, estates, safety, and sport. Each was required to develop a 'service level agreement', a method of quality assurance widely employed in the public sector. Service quality teams included representatives of the clients, who might be internal or external, in order to ensure that the service was working closely to their needs.[115]

ACADEMIC DEVELOPMENTS OF THE 1990s

THE INCORPORATION OF THE NURSING SCHOOL

Since the Medical School, Firth College and the Technical School came together in 1897 to form University College, every department and faculty has been home-grown. Nothing was acquired by merger until the Sheffield and North Trent College of Nursing and Midwifery joined the University almost 100 years later, in 1995.

The College had been formed in 1990 as the school of nursing for South Yorkshire and North Derbyshire. Based in Sheffield and run by the Regional Health Authority (RHA), it was charged with implementing a new nursing curriculum, for which accreditation was provided by Sheffield Hallam University. The College was only two years old when the Conservative government decided that nursing schools should be taken from the control of health authorities and relocated within higher education. This caused concern within the College, because nursing was not a graduate profession and at that time (1991/92) fewer than sixty per cent of the staff had degrees, let alone the higher degrees which could underpin the growth of a research ethos.[116] Both the nursing schools and the universities were thrown an enormous challenge when this policy was adopted by the Trent RHA in 1992.

At that point there was no working relationship between the College of Nursing and the University of Sheffield, apart from three masters' courses which were under collaborative development. Gareth Roberts was never slow to spot an opportunity, however. He and Frank Woods, the Dean of Medicine, organised an attractive bid. The College would become a School of Nursing and Midwifery within the Faculty of Medicine, with equal status to the two existing schools of medicine and dentistry. The University promised strong support to the staff in moving towards a 'research-led' ethos. This bid, which was in competition with one from Sheffield Hallam University, offered integration as 'part of the family', which the staff much preferred over being a tacked-on addition, a mere 'pimple on the body'.[117] Both David Jones, the Principal of the College, and the Trent RHA were enthusiastic and the bid was accepted in February 1993.

Plaster figurine of Florence Nightingale, who had family connections with Sheffield, which now stands in the entrance hall of the nursing school.

The task ahead was gigantic. The College had six departments, five teaching centres and almost 300 staff.[118] There were 2,400 full-time students, with a profile quite different from the rest of the University – more mature, locally-based, and admitted in two intakes each year. Although nursing degrees were developing quickly, the primary qualification was the three-year advanced diploma. Lecturers carried a heavy teaching load, with students on placement and in college throughout the year. The College also ran an impressive programme of post-registration courses, catering for another 700 students, many of them from overseas.

The leadership of Gareth Roberts, and the patient work of Bob Boucher and Reg Goodchild were critical between 1993 and 1995 in creating the structures of integration.[119] To take just one example, the staff had to be assimilated into academic-related salary scales and pension schemes. The difficulties of bringing the NHS pension and the Universities' superannuation schemes together almost derailed the entire project.[120] Accreditation of the College's courses required flexibility on both sides and considerable negotiation, as the University extended its embrace to the non-graduate diploma student, a species exiled since the 1960s.[121] These negotiations coincided, however, with government pressure for more 'non-traditional' access to universities and the proposed school 'ticked all the right boxes' on the equal opportunities agenda.[122] For their part, the Nursing staff prepared for the change by ensuring that, by 1995, over ninety per cent had first degrees and sixty per cent had achieved, or were pursuing, a higher degree.[123]

As luck would have it, a possible building for the new school was standing empty across the road from the main campus. The Winter Street hospital for infectious diseases had been built in 1881 and designed to isolate patients in four two-storey blocks, with flat roofs on which convalescents could take the air.[124] It became a dedi-

The former St George's Hospital on Winter Street, built in 1881, was converted by Race Cottam Associates as the School of Nursing and Midwifery. Named Bartolomé House to reflect that family's contribution to the development of the University, it was formally opened by Stephen de Bartolomé in July 1998.

cated tuberculosis hospital in 1912; treatment with tuberculin was tried out in Sheffield, and University staff conducted some of the research. The advent of antibiotics made such hospitals redundant, and Winter Street ended its days as the dilapidated St George's geriatric hospital, closing in 1990. After a major conversion project (funded by the Health Authority), it became the new home of the nursing school and was opened by Princess Anne in 1997.

New-build projects provided two further bases for the school. Samuel Fox House, on the Northern General Hospital site, was opened in 1997 and accommodated forty staff. Its Health Sciences Library on the ground floor was available to all medical personnel at the Northern General. Humphrey Davy House near Dearne Valley College, opened in 1998, was the base for training in mental health and learning disability nursing. In this redundant mining area, a number of ex-miners retrained as mental health nurses.

The formal integration of the nursing school with the University took place on 31 March 1995. David Jones became a professor and the Dean of the school. It was difficult to combine the heavy teaching load with time for research and the 1996 RAE came cruelly soon. Even so, Sheffield scored a 3, which was bettered only by Manchester, Surrey and King's College, London. Thereafter the number of research active staff quadrupled and staff with PhDs tripled.[125] The school's success in meeting the research challenge can be judged by the fact that it was one of four to score 5 in the 2001 RAE.

There were three fellows of the Royal College of Nursing (RCN) in the school by 2003. These were David Jones, Susan Read and Dame Betty Kershaw, who succeeded Jones on his retirement as Dean in 1998. At the time of her appointment Professor Kershaw was President of the RCN, and in previous posts had been a pioneer in the integration of nursing research into curriculum design. She was, and continued to be, an adviser on nursing education to governments worldwide.

David Jones and Betty Kershaw, the first two Deans of the School of Nursing and Midwifery.

Betty Kershaw argued that, while the school gained a great deal from the University, it made a major contribution in return.[126] The number of nurses who undertook research in other departments of the University rose substantially (from a total of two in 1993) and the school's diverse student intake included 'the global community of nurses', passing through the school on post-registration short courses and, increasingly, in touch through the medium of distance learning, which the school developed enthusiastically. Integrating the nursing school was a challenge which continued to tax the staff involved long after 1995. Looking to the future, however, as nursing gradually becomes a graduate profession and 'nurse-practitioners' become more common, the role of the school in the evolution of the Faculty of Medicine is likely to be significant.

THE REORGANISATION OF THE MEDICAL FACULTY

Frank Woods, Dean of the Faculty of Medicine 1988–98.

The advent of the RAE had a profound effect on British medical schools. On the whole, clinical subjects performed poorly (grades of 2 or 3) and so were singled out for criticism by the hierarchies of higher education. Yet medical academics, unlike their colleagues in other faculties, had a responsibility to spend part of every week, throughout the year, attending to the needs of patients. The Sheffield faculty had an extra problem, since it was contributing a higher proportion of staff time to the NHS than other universities; this reduced its capacity for research, as a report presented to the Strategic Planning Committee in 1991 showed.[127] Gareth Roberts conducted negotiations which eventually attended to this anomaly, reallocating staff time between the NHS and the University.

After the 1989 RAE, Frank Woods, the Dean of the Faculty of Medicine, began to promote a strategy to increase the numbers of research-active staff and provide an environment more conducive to successful research.[128] That became the driving force behind a decade of change. Its results were seen in a twenty-fold increase in research funding and a rise in research ratings from 4 in 1996 to 5 in 2001. Three important changes were made under Woods's strategy, which began under Sims and was strongly supported by Gareth Roberts and by senior professors like Ian Cooke, Gordon Duff and Graham Russell. First, the school secured higher levels of investment in laboratories and research facilities and keenly pursued lucrative grants. Secondly, Woods had noted that the medical schools which did best in the 1989 RAE had increased the volume of their research, by bringing in a much higher ratio of non-clinical, scientifically qualified, lecturers and professors. He set out to do the same in Sheffield. Some clinical staff were reassigned to the NHS rather than the University. Finally, it was argued that the existing departments were too small for the success of a 'research-led' strategy – some of the 'fiefdoms . . . like medieval Italian states' would have to go. The synergy released by bringing separate areas of expertise into closer conjunction would generate fresh ideas for research and new, fruitful staff teams.

This was an enormous agenda for the nineties, one which inevitably involved pain as well as gain for the faculty. The reorganisation was prolonged and difficult, as departmental structures were dismantled and new lines of management created.

341

Frank Moody, in gratitude for treatment and tests carried out at the Royal Hallamshire Hospital , donated £1 million in November 1990 to enable the foundation of a Department of Clinical Neurology. He is seen at the presentation of the cheque, with Frank Woods in the background.

Morale was badly affected in some cases. In 1989/90 there were twenty independent clinical departments within the fields of medicine and surgery, with another seventeen sub-departments. These were re-organised, at various times over the following ten years, into three divisions within the medical school: Clinical Sciences (South), Clinical Sciences (North) and Genomic Medicine.[129] The Dean of the school from 1999 was Tony Weetman, who in 1991 at the age of 37 was the youngest appointment yet to the Arthur Hall Chair of Medicine and highly respected for his research in endocrinology.[130]

The School of Health and Related Research (ScHARR)

This new school within the Faculty of Medicine was the result of the University's desire to increase its research output and the Trent Regional Health Authority's wish to invest in research. In 1992/93 the RHA invited bids for a Trent Institute of Health Service Research and decided that it should be run collaboratively by the three universities of Sheffield, Leicester and Nottingham.[131] The Health Authority's 'Operational Research Unit' was awarded to Sheffield, together with posts in health economics and nursing research.

The Trent Institute was only one part of a greater scheme, first proposed by Alan Walker, Professor of Social Policy, to create a centre which would link healthcare and the social sciences for research purposes.[132] As this centre evolved, it brought in staff from Psychiatry and the Medical Care Research Unit, under Jon Nicoll. Originally established in 1966, the Unit undertook commissions such as the national review of the 'NHS Direct' service.[133] A new Health Economics department was led by Ron Akehurst, who was also appointed director of the centre in 1994. It was based in a new building, Regent Court, on Leavygreave.

Two years later, the School of Health and Related Research, known as ScHARR, came into being when existing departments in the general area of primary and community care – Health Care for Elderly People, Public Health and General Practice – were added. These clinical departments, formerly in the medical school, had a different ethos, yet the focus of ScHARR was health services research and management, symbolised by the appointment of Brian Edwards, a regional director of the NHS, as Professor of Health Care Development and Dean of the school. Health Care for Elderly People did not remain in ScHARR for long. It had three professors, two of whom, Ian Philp and Anthony Warnes, were appointed at the same time because when faced with two good candidates, Gareth Roberts characteristically appointed both of them.[134]

Pam Enderby, the first female Dean of the Faculty of Medicine.

The clinical departments which remained in ScHARR, Public Health and General Practice, generated marked increases in research funding under their heads, Allan Hutchinson and Nigel Mathers. The staff of the Institute of General Practice & Primary Care, for example, grew to over 100 by 2000, among them David Hall, who was elected President of the Royal College of Paediatrics and knighted in 2003. He was the author of the influential Hall report on the development of children's community health services.

Thus by 1996 the Faculty of Medicine had a total of four schools: the medical school, the dental school, the nursing & midwifery school and ScHARR. There was also one separate department – Human Communication Sciences. Each school had a dean and there was an overall faculty dean, who could (unofficially) be given no other title than 'superdean'. In 2000 Pam Enderby achieved a double distinction: she became not only the first female dean of the Faculty of Medicine (and thus superdean), but also the first non-medically qualified dean. By this time the faculty comprised about one-third of the total size of the University. Pam Enderby stressed the variety of health professional training and research taking place within the University. Co-operation between professionals from different disciplines was the way of the future.

Nigel Bax with medical trainees.

Medical Education

By the end of the decade, the winds of change had blown through every aspect of the faculty's work except teaching. Only General Practice had 'radically restructured' its curriculum, introducing, for example, problem-based learning and the teaching of communication skills.[135] The rigorous division of the degree into preparatory and clinical phases had already been abandoned in a number of other universities in favour of greater clinical experience from the start. Sheffield began to make a similar change after the establishment of a Department of Medical Education in 1998, and the appointment of Tony Weetman as Dean the following year. Nigel Bax became Director of Teaching and won a National Teaching Fellowship award in 2003, the year in which the new MBChB curriculum was introduced.[136] A Clinical Skills Centre, providing training on 'virtual' patients, was set up at each of the two main hospitals and a three-week 'Intensive Clinical Experience' programme was introduced in 2001. The number of students grew during the nineties from an intake of 148 (not including students coming from Perak) to 223, with more increases planned after that.

Tony Weetman, Dean of the medical school, welcomes one of its oldest graduates, Dr Frank Ellis, on its 175th anniversary in 2003. Under Weetman's leadership the school introduced a new MBChB curriculum in that year and was developing plans to consolidate the school's laboratories on a single site by 2006.

Medical Research

It is impossible to do justice here to the abundance and range of Sheffield's medical research, but the growth of new centres of excellence should be noted. During the nineties, these included bone disease, genomic medicine, gall bladder disease, and tissue engineering, as well as a major expansion of cancer research.

Graham Russell, who joined the Department of Chemical Pathology in 1976, took over the headship the following year and renamed it Human Metabolism & Clinical Biochemistry. During his 25 years at Sheffield, the department became a centre of excellence in a wide range of diseases of the musculoskeletal system, including rheumatoid arthritis and osteoarthritis. Russell himself played a major role in the discovery and application of disphosphonate drugs, now widely used in the treatment of Paget's disease and osteoporosis. His hope that Sheffield would become 'one of the world's leading centres for bone research' was fulfilled in the

The Sheffield film star Sean Bean, second left, opens the Osteoporosis Centre at the Northern General, accompanied by Professor Richard Eastell, far left, Linda Edwards (Director of the Osteoporosis Society), and local artist Don Cameron who sculpted the bronze figures.

1990s; it was awarded collaborating status by the World Health Organisation and centres of expertise were established in three hospitals in Sheffield.[137]

One of these, at the Royal Hallamshire Hospital, was the result of a campaign by John Kanis to keep his Metabolic Bone Unit open when it was threatened with closure in 1989. He offered £12,000 of his own money and attracted strong public support.[138] At the Children's Hospital, Nick Bishop conducted research into childhood osteoporosis, while at the Northern General, Richard Eastell established the Academic Unit of Bone Metabolism and opened a dedicated Osteoporosis Centre in 1995. A pioneer in the use of biochemical markers to assess bone formation and bone resorption, he was described by an American colleague as 'a giant in this field and recognised as a world authority on all aspects of osteoporosis'.[139] In 1999 the University was placed fourth in a league table of the world's osteoporosis research centres, based on the number of citations in the scientific literature.[140]

Genomic (molecular) medicine developed into a research area of exceptional potential during the 1990s and Sheffield was a leader in the field, with the appointment in 1990 of Gordon Duff, the country's first Professor of Molecular Medicine, and the award of a second chair to Ian Peake.[141] These chairs were named after the faculty's illustrious former professors, Edward Mellanby and Howard Florey. Genomic research sought to describe and understand disease at the molecular level, in order to develop new diagnostic techniques and therapies. The idea that normal genetic variations in the population might affect susceptibility to disease, and its severity, was generally resisted by medical science before the 1990s. Taking advantage of the large populations served by the Sheffield hospitals, the new department pioneered a series of studies that brought together clinicians, molecular geneticists, molecular biologists and statistical geneticists in the same research teams.

The research contributed to the growing consensus that common illnesses, such as heart disease, arthritis, diabetes and asthma, were 'multifactorial' in nature and had a significant genetic component. The Sheffield department also established a new concept – that the genetic programme controlling inflammatory response plays a previously unsuspected role in many common diseases, for example coronary artery disease.

Genomic Medicine was the largest of the three divisions in the medical school by 2003, with about 450 staff and full-time research students. It pursued a policy of

Left: Gordon Duff, Professor of Molecular Medicine, in his laboratory.

Right: Graham Russell, Professor of Human Metabolism 1977–2000.

recruiting 'top international talent', a good example being Steven Dower, a 'major British scientist' who had worked at the National Institute of Health and in industry in the USA before coming to Sheffield in 1995.[142] Chris Cannings, on the other hand, was recruited from the University's own department of Probability and Statistics, where he was already a leading figure, in order to strengthen the crucial mathematical base of the research. The Division of Genomic Medicine formed productive research links with international institutes, as well as with the Molecular Biology and Biotechnology, Biomedical Science and Chemistry departments within the University. High levels of funding were attracted from the Wellcome Trust and from pharmaceutical giants like Glaxo.

The opera singer José Carreras, who had himself suffered from leukaemia, talks to Malcolm Goyns at the opening of the Institute for Cancer Studies.

Gordon Duff and Graham Russell were the 'movers and shakers in the medical school' during the 1990s, according to an experienced observer, Ian Cooke. Russell, however, left Sheffield in 2000 for the University of Oxford. Duff's role was even more central thereafter, and he also became chairman of the national committee on the safety of medicines and the national standards board, regulating vaccines.

The Department of Oncology & Pathology was located within the Division of Genomic Medicine in order to foster a genetic approach to its research. As Barry Hancock, the first Professor of Clinical Oncology, put it, 'If we can identify what makes cancer cells different at a molecular level, we will be able to make them the target'.[143] The faculty had excellent relations with Yorkshire Cancer Research which gave an initial £1 million, and later £4.5 million, for the Institute of Cancer Studies, opened by José Carreras in 1993.[144] A Cancer Research Centre followed in 1999, the director of which was Robert Coleman, an expert in cancer-induced bone disease and the development of drugs to treat breast and ovarian cancer. John Lilleyman, Professor of Paediatric Haematology, conducted seminal research on childhood leukaemia for twenty years at the Children's Hospital, which became a national centre for the treatment of this disease. Lilleyman became President of the Royal College of Pathologists in 1999, after he had left Sheffield. He was followed in that position by James Underwood, Professor of Pathology and a member of the University since 1969.[145] This seems particularly appropriate in view of the fact that a group of Sheffield pathologists, including C.G. Paine, had been instrumental in shaping the formation of the College in the 1950s.[146]

Alan Johnson, the Professor of Surgery, developed a leading centre for research into, and treatment of, gall bladder disease. Johnson, who came to Sheffield in 1979, immediately won over his new colleagues by converting his large office in the Royal Hallamshire Hospital into a clinical research unit. On the national stage, he served as chairman of the government's Standing Medical Advisory Committee, describing its philosophy as 'taking the ideals of the National Health Service and soaking them in reality'.[147] He also played a significant role in the field of medical ethics, chairing the Senate of Surgeons' committee that produced definitive legal and ethical guidelines for practising surgeons. He became President of the Association of Surgeons in 1993.

The engineering of tissues and materials to improve the quality of patient care became a major field of research by the late 1990s. The Centre for Biomaterials and

Tissue Engineering was formed, within which cell biologists, clinicians, computer specialists, engineers and chemists collaborated in the development of novel replacement tissues for use in clinical situations. Sheila MacNeil from the medical school and Robert Short of Engineering Materials developed a revolutionary 'biological bandage' for treating patients suffering from severe burns and persistent wounds. Novel high-strength bioceramic materials were designed for both dental and bone repair work, while the computational biology group, led by Rod Smallwood (Computer Science), carried out sophisticated modelling of heart valves and epithelial tissues in a way that accurately reflected the behaviour of living tissue.

The Dental School [148]

The Dental School's score of 3 in the 1996 RAE was an improvement on the 2 awarded four years earlier, but still short of the 5 rating that Gareth Roberts considered appropriate for Sheffield. Alan Brook was recruited from the London Hospital Medical College to address the matter and he concentrated the school's research into three multidisciplinary areas. The oral neurosciences portfolio was built round the expertise of Peter Robinson, an international authority on the treatment of facial pain and nerve injuries, who succeeded Sir Paul Bramley as Professor of Dental Surgery in 1988. The other research clusters were concerned with the genetic and environmental factors involved in tooth development, and the repair of damaged bone and cartilage using new biomaterials and the latest tissue engineering techniques. At the same time, some non-clinical research scientists were appointed to work alongside dental clinicians.

The research strategy was handsomely rewarded in the 2001 RAE, when Sheffield received a 5 rating, a score bettered by only two other institutions. The Dental School also gained a national reputation for its training programmes aimed

Below: Colin Smith CBE, Professor of Oral Pathology 1973–2003.

Right: The new Dental School building, designed by the James Totty Partnership and opened in April 1992. Four of the school's five departments, which had until then been in nearby houses, were brought under one roof.

at the entire primary care dental team – dentists, hygienists, nurses, practice managers and receptionists. A national centre for research into oral health, sponsored by Boots, was established at the school. By 2004 the number of full-time academic staff had risen to 37, a fifty per cent increase over the 1991 figure. Alan Brook was Dean of Dental Studies for three years before his appointment in 2003 as Dean of the Faculty of Medicine, the first representative of the Dental School ever to hold this senior post.

Colin Smith, who retired in 2003, was head of the Department of Oral Pathology for thirty years and helped establish the discipline worldwide, particularly through his work with the World Health Organisation. He served as Dean of Dental Studies for a total of eighteen years. His most visible legacy is the magnificent five-storey Dental School building which was opened in 1991. He also helped establish courses in dental hygiene and dental therapy. During his time in office, the undergraduate curriculum was extensively revised and extended from four to five years; undergraduate student numbers were increased by fifty per cent (to 278); and the score of 23 out of 24 was achieved in the QAA assessment of 2000, his final year as Dean.

THE 'RESEARCH-LED UNIVERSITY' [149]

One of Gareth Roberts's most prized visual aids was a matrix which showed Sheffield in the 'top right hand corner', as the university with the highest combined achievement in teaching and research after the 1996 RAE. Seven departments (all three Biologies, both Automatic Control and Electrical Engineering, Politics and Russian) achieved the top score (5* and 24) in both the 2001 RAE and their QAA teaching quality assessments. These results were the ideal demonstration of his strategic commitment to the 'research-led university', strong in both teaching and research.

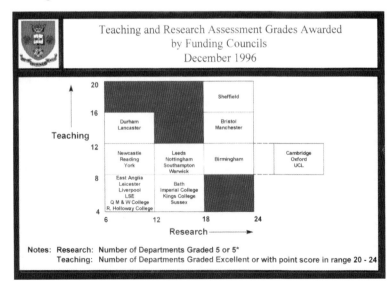

An example of Gareth Roberts's favourite visual aid – a chart showing Sheffield in the top right-hand corner.

High RAE scores were pursued relentlessly. Seven departments achieved 5 (then the top score) in 1992, five gained 5* in 1996, and nine in 2001. Sheffield's total of departments scoring 5 or 5* was eighteen in the 1996 RAE and 35 in 2001 – a considerable achievement. Research income doubled between 1990 and 2000.

One of Roberts's key contributions to the 'research-led' strategy was the recruitment of 'star' academics to many departments and research teams. The Vice-Chancellor chaired every professorial appointment committee, a considerable task by the 1990s, and was prepared to negotiate special deals to secure particular members of staff.[150] He was particularly proud of his willingness to promote young talent. His behaviour has been likened to 'a football manager, buying in high profile strikers'.[151] This was the brave new competitive world of British universities. In the run-up to the 1996 RAE whole research teams, not just individual professors, were being sought by many universities. 'Active poaching' was taking place, with generous expenses and 'non-teaching packages' on offer in order for the 'stars' to concentrate on their research.[152]

Roberts's policy was a mixture of injecting new blood and giving overdue promotion to established staff who had weathered the storms of the eighties. In several cases the new policy turned the fortunes of a department around. In addition, teaching and laboratory space was reconfigured as part of the drive to provide appropriate research facilities.

Roberts was prepared to reorganise an entire faculty in the pursuit of high RAE scores, as Medicine discovered. The following account will look at the effect of the 'research-led' strategy on the rest of the University, concentrating on those departments and teams which did particularly well during the nineties. It is impossible to acknowledge adequately all the successful research of these years, or to feature every department that maintained a high standard. The focus will be on the research which was nationally, and internationally, acknowledged as among the leaders in its field. Departments which improved dramatically during the nineties are also noted. For reference, Sheffield's RAE results for 1992, 1996 and 2001 in every subject area are reproduced as Appendix 5.

David Howe at the wheel of a Formula 3000 racing car, which his research group aimed to convert into an electric vehicle with a powerful electric motor inside the hub of each wheel. This was one of the projects of the Electrical Machines and Drives Group during the 1990s.

Research in the Faculty of Engineering

The Department of Electronic and Electrical Engineering was one of the top three in the world outside the USA, according to the Institute for Science Information.[153] Its semi-conductor research, in particular, was 'cutting edge' and secured substantial grants totalling at least £6.4 million during the nineties.[154] There were facilities for sophisticated growth of microelectronic devices and ultra-high resolution microscopy. Colin Whitehouse and Tony Cullis, who was elected FRS in 2004, led this field. Whitehouse also acted as pro-vice-chancellor for research from 1999 to 2003. Their colleague David Howe led a team which developed electrical machine and controlled drive systems that were of considerable interest to the aerospace, automotive and maritime industries.

In the Department of Automatic Control and Systems Engineering, which co-operated with many departments, including medicine, Derek Linkens developed techniques enabling anaesthetists to measure the extent of a patient's consciousness. These have been tested and implemented in Sheffield hospitals. Peter Fleming secured long-term funding from Rolls-Royce in 1994 to develop its next generation of engine control and monitoring systems. The success of this first 'University Technology Centre' (UTC) led Rolls-Royce to establish two more in 1998. One of these, for materials damping technology, was led by Geoff Tomlinson of Mechanical Engineering and went on to produce novel materials for suppressing vibration in gas turbine engines. A fourth UTC was established in 2003, giving Sheffield a total matched only by Cambridge.

The Civil and Structural Engineering department was revitalised under David Lerner, who joined the University in 1998. Research activities were concentrated into the areas of water engineering, groundwater pollution and structural engineering. The Centre for Cement and Concrete, brought to the University by Peter Waldron, who also became a pro-vice-chancellor, developed into the largest academic unit of its kind in Britain. The department was ranked second in the country by 2004 for its undergraduate teaching.[155]

The School of Materials was amalgamated within the refurbished Hadfield Building, after the difficult decision to move Ceramics, Glasses and Polymers from Elmfield in 1992. The faculty was painfully aware of the historic significance of leaving W. E. S. Turner's purpose-built creation on Northumberland Road, but the need to merge the accommodation of the school was urgent. The Elmfield-based staff came to regard the move as a success, and the Turner Museum of Glass was skilfully rehoused in a large common room, which became the heart of the building.[156] The school was renamed the Department of Engineering Materials. Its important role within the faculty was demonstrated in 1996, when Mike Sellars secured funding for the launch of IMPETTUS, 'a huge research centre', bridging three departments.[157] John Beynon of Mechanical Engineering moved department to take over the POSCO chair and the directorship of IMPETTUS when Sellars retired in 2001. These interdepartmental links led to the introduction of a popular MEng course in Aeronautical Engineering and laid the foundations for the Advanced Manufacturing Research Centre with Boeing, established in 2001. Gareth Roberts believed that Sheffield had 'arguably the best collection of materials

The Turner Museum of Glass in its new setting in the Hadfield Building, where the collection was made accessible to all in a multi-purpose coffee bar, meetings space and common room. The collection's significance was acknowledged in 1995 when it received full registration from the Museums and Galleries Commission.

research centres in the country' by 2004, not only in the Faculty of Engineering but also in Medicine, through Medical Physics and the work of Alan Brook in the dental school, and in the Pure Science faculty where Molecular Electronics under Richard Jones (Physics) formed part of the Molecular Materials centre, set up in 1993 with Chemistry and Engineering Materials.

Research in the Faculty of Pure Science

Physics, Roberts's own subject, had suffered the loss of most of the department's professors by the late 1980s. Gillian Gehring, a specialist in solid state physics, had been recruited as the second professor in 1989. She came from an Oxford laboratory where, unusually, almost one-third of the staff were women, and when appointed was only the second female professor of physics in the United Kingdom.[158] Fred Combley, a popular head of department, was promoted to a personal chair in 1991. He had worked in the department since 1963, specialising in high energy and particle physics, and was described by a colleague as an 'ideal academic'.[159] Maurice Skolnick was recruited from a government research laboratory to a chair in experimental condensed matter the following year. He collaborated, in what Roberts dubbed the 'Holy Trinity', with Colin Whitehouse and Tony Cullis on semiconductor research.[160] Neil Spooner was recruited to work on dark matter, once described as 'hunting for a galactic needle in a haystack'. Spooner, who by 1999 was regarded as the leading national expert, secured £3.2 million to build a laboratory deep underground in mines near Whitby.

Chemistry, a large and independent department, took longer to respond to Roberts's initiatives. Physical Chemistry was boosted in the second half of the decade by the recruitment of Tony Ledwith and Tony Ryan. They enhanced the links with engineering and physics and both acted as head of department. Ryan had a particular interest in polymer science and worked closely with colleagues in

Chemistry graduate Helen Sharman (BSc 1984) was selected to become the first Briton to go into space. She trained in Moscow for an eight-day flight in 1991 in a Soyuz spacecraft. On her return, she promoted science education, and worked closely with the University's Schools Liaison Service. In 1992 she opened the refurbished Automatic Control building, named after Amy Johnson, another female air pioneer and Sheffield graduate.

Left: Richard Roberts, joint Nobel Prize winner for Medicine/Physiology in 1993, in the laboratory in the Department of Chemistry where he undertook postgraduate research. He graduated BSc in 1965 and PhD in 1968 before moving to the United States, where he discovered the split gene arrangement within DNA. He became the fourth Nobel laureate associated with the University.

Right: Sir Harry Kroto who, like Richard Roberts, graduated with a PhD from the Chemistry department (1964), gained the Nobel Prize for Chemistry in 1996 for the discovery, with two others, of 'fullerenes', a new form of carbon. On receipt of his prize he publicly complained about the paucity of funding for scientific research in the UK, adding that his latest funding bid had just been turned down by the Engineering and Physical Science Research Council.

several departments, including Physics and Engineering Materials, to establish a centre of research and training in this field. With the aid of HEFCE, the entire team of polymer scientists at Lancaster University moved to Sheffield. The Polymer Centre was launched in 2001 and by 2004 it drew on the skills of 41 academic staff, together with over a hundred research staff and students, in seven University departments.[161]

Pure Mathematics increased its RAE score from 3 in 1992 and 1996, to 5 in 2001 under the leadership of John Greenlees. Several mathematicians applied their expertise to multidisciplinary areas, including Chris Cannings in Genomic Medicine and Shaun Quegan in the Centre for Earth Observation Science. The Computer Science department was re-energised after Yorick Wilks was appointed as its head in 1993. The RAE score improved steadily thereafter.

The Information Studies department gained the top score in all four of the RAEs 1989–2001. It is the only Sheffield department to have achieved this standard, and one of only 51 nationwide.[162] 'The department is one of the leading ones in the world. I am quite certain we are competitive with the USA', said Peter Willett, the head of Information Studies.[163] Willett's own work, started with Mike Lynch, on the use of computers to discover new pharmaceuticals, created a centre of excellence and attracted generous funding from top drug companies. Bob Usherwood had an outstanding reputation in the world of library management and became President of the Library Association. In 1994, Information Studies became one of the first British departments to put its course prospectus on the World Wide Web.[164] Its MA in Librarianship continued to be 'the best in Europe', while the Masters degrees in Information Systems and Information Management were especially attractive to 'high quality' overseas students.[165]

Noel Sharkey of the Department of Computer Science, an expert in artificial intelligence and robotics. He became a media star as an on-screen consultant to the television programmes Robot Wars and TechnoGames. Sharkey credited Robot Wars with attracting many more young people, especially girls, into engineering courses.

Biological sciences [166]

All three biology departments moved from a score of 4 in the 1996 RAE to 5* by 2001 and, in addition, achieved the top grade in their teaching quality assessments. This placed Sheffield in fourth place nationally on *The Times* league table in 2002 and 2003.[167] There was considerable investment in both staff and buildings during those years, but the foundations of success had already been laid by Ernie Bailey, David Lewis, Peter Banks and Len Hill. The Krebs Institute for Biomolecular Research, led by David Rice, was distinguished for its work on protein structure. The Institute had the reputation among postgraduates of being the best in the country for its combination of skills and technical equipment.[168] Reproductive biology was developed by Harry Moore, an innovative joint chair appointment with the Faculty of Medicine in 1992.[169] In Biomedical Science Peter Andrews, a cell biologist, was recruited in 1992 to the Arthur Jackson chair and began work on embryonic stem cells with Moore, a controversial area with great potential for medicine.[170] Another new field was developmental genetics, introduced to Sheffield by Philip Ingham and his research team in 1996. Ingham's work gave insight into the cell biology of embryonic development in humans. Alan North, who also brought a

A pre-clinical medicine tutorial in a study bay in the Perak Laboratories, which were opened by the First Minister of Malaysia in 1997.

Dr Riadh Dinha and his family with Terry Croft from the Department of Animal and Plant Sciences. Dr Dinha gained his PhD at Sheffield, but he and his family were refugees from Iraq stranded in a camp in Turkey when Croft recognised them on a television news programme in 1991. Croft began negotiations with a number of authorities which secured the family's return to Sheffield, and was awarded the Chancellor's Medal.

large team to Sheffield, founded the Institute of Molecular Physiology in 1998, which became central to research on membrane proteins.

In 1999, the molecular life sciences research was awarded a significant share (£23.6 million) from the government's Joint Infrastructure Fund (JIF), introduced in 1998 to promote high quality scientific research in universities. This, together with other grants, was predominantly used to refurbish biology research laboratories in Firth Court, with £5 million set aside for a new building on the 'fourth side of the quad'.[171] The biology departments also benefited from the Perak Laboratories for pre-clinical medical students, which opened in 1997 behind the Alfred Denny building.

JIF funding provided new 'environmental growth rooms' under Tower Court and refurbished laboratories for environmental biology and behavioural ecology. The effect of climate change on plant growth had, for many years, been studied at both the Robert Hill Institute and, until its demise in 1999, in the NERC Unit of Comparative Plant Ecology led by Philip Grime. Arctic and Physiological Ecology were new areas, introduced after the recruitment of Terry Callaghan and Malcolm Press from Manchester, together with John Lee, regarded by his colleagues as 'one of the leading environmental biologists in the country'.[172] Terry Burke, an expert in DNA fingerprinting, was recruited from Leicester to expand behavioural ecology.

Research in Social Sciences and Education

Politics was 'contracting' so fast during the eighties that amalgamation with a cognate department was seriously considered.[173] Those academics who remained, headed by Andrew Gamble, were, however, determined and enthusiastic. In the first month of the Roberts regime, January 1991, they seized the opportunity to offer a chair to David Marquand, a former Labour MP who had joined the breakaway Social Democratic Party.[174] He was the author of major works of political analysis and a biography of the Labour Prime Minister Ramsay MacDonald. Marquand set up the 'Political Economy Research Centre' and recruited high-profile advisers like

Ralf Dahrendorf and Shirley Williams.[175] In 1994 another chair was created for Paul Whiteley from the USA, who was already collaborating with Patrick Seyd on a major study of the membership of British political parties. They surveyed 8,000 Labour party members in 1990 (with a follow-up in 1999) and went on to analyse the Conservative party and the Liberal Democrats.[176] Their research concluded that the Conservative party was 'dying', since almost all its members were over sixty.[177] The Politics department had six professors by 2000 and was regarded as one of the best departments in the country.

Psychology continued to be a success story: it achieved 5 or 5* in all four RAEs. Peter Smith became a 'leading authority' on bullying and attracted much press attention and funding from the Department of Education.[178] Rod Nicholson's research on dyslexia also proved outstanding, together with John Frisby's work on human vision.[179] The MRC Social & Applied Psychology Unit reached the end of its funding in 1996, but the staff attracted alternative support from a range of bodies and it was reconstituted as the Institute of Work Psychology, led by Toby Wall.[180] The Faculty of Educational Studies consistently scored 5A in the 1990s, despite the departure of Jean Rudduck and John Gray in 1993. Jerry Wellington, a member of staff since 1979, received major grants for his research into science and technology education, and on the interface between education and employment. Peter Hannon was known for his work on early literacy development and family learning. A satisfying feature was that this strong research across a broad spectrum of educational subjects was matched by a placing among the top three British departments for its postgraduate training course.

Research in the Faculty of Arts

In 1992, the Russian department had no professors.[181] Within two years it had three, after Bob Russell was promoted to the chair of Russian, David Shepherd was recruited from Manchester University and Bill Leatherbarrow was awarded a personal chair. Shepherd established the Bakhtin Centre to explore the intellectual context of this Russian theorist and philosopher; a wide range of publications, in print and electronic forms, followed.[182] Czech and Polish became named degree subjects and the department's disciplinary range expanded to include the Russian visual arts. Its RAE scores rose to 5 in 1996 and 5* in 2001. By then it was regarded as the best Russian department in the country, with 'clear blue water' separating it from its closest competitors.

Bob Pullin of the Department of Education was responsible for Britain's largest programme of teacher training for Russian specialists. He was awarded the Pushkin Medal for services to Russian teaching in 1991.[183]

Ian Kershaw succeeded Patrick Collinson as Professor of Modern History in 1989. Kershaw had already written extensively on the Third Reich before coming to Sheffield, but his massive two-volume biography of Hitler was produced entirely at Sheffield and, apart from one year of study leave, while also head of the History department.[184] It ran to 2,000 pages and was published simultaneously in six

Sir Ian Kershaw, author of the acclaimed biography of Hitler and many other works, in his office in the Department of History.

A tutorial for the MA in Creative Writing for Film and Television, which was established in 1999/2000. Tutors included well-known writers such as Jack Rosenthal, shown here, a Sheffield graduate and former holder of the University's Maisie Glass Associate Professorship in Theatre.

languages. The German version of the biography was promoted and read as enthusiastically as the English original. The international lecture tours, television appearances, and newspaper interviews which followed the publication of each volume raised the profile of the University and its History department, which received increasing numbers of applications. Ian Kershaw was knighted 'for services to history' in 2002; a notable double since his wife Dame Betty Kershaw had been honoured for services to nursing before her arrival in Sheffield. The department attracted increasingly impressive levels of funding from the Arts and Humanities Research Board (AHRB), and Richard Carwardine won the Lincoln American History Prize for his biography of Abraham Lincoln. Carwardine was Dean of the Arts faculty 1999–2001 and received the prize shortly after his recruitment to Oxford as Rhodes Professor of American History.

The French department was transformed by the demands of RAE assessment, according to David Williams, a professor since 1976.[185] It became 'research driven' and increased its score from 3 in 1992 to 5 by 2001. Williams, an expert on Voltaire, served as Dean of the Arts Faculty 1992–95 and was later succeeded in this role by his colleague David Walker, an expert on André Gide who discovered and edited some 900 of his lost letters. The Department of Hispanic Studies also dramatically improved its RAE score during the 1990s. Nicholas Round, the Hughes Professor of Hispanic Studies 1994–2003, stands out for his contributions at international level to Hispanic research. Previously a professor in Glasgow for 22 years, in Sheffield he focussed on the realist novelist Pérez Galdós and directed a project to complete English translations of his work. Round's *Who's Who* entry endearingly lists his honorary life membership of the Belfast Students' Union as his only club – the university in which he began his career.

The RAE scores for English rose from 3 in 1992 to 5 by 2001. Sally Shuttleworth, a specialist in nineteenth-century literature and culture with an interest in Victorian science, was appointed to the chair of English Literature in 1994. She subsequently became head of department and encouraged interdisciplinary research, as did David Burnley, Professor of English Language 1993–2001. His enthusiasm for computer

Left: *Keith Branigan, Professor of Archaeology from 1977, sorts early Bronze Age pottery in the Stratigraphic Museum, Knossos, Crete.*

Right: *The dendrochronology laboratory in Archaeology, where the ring patterns of ancient timbers can be matched against known recorded patterns to facilitate accurate dating. The laboratory is a nationally recognised centre of excellence employed, for example, to date timbers damaged in the 1992 Windsor Castle fire and to help to date the 'Sea Henge' discovered in North Norfolk.*

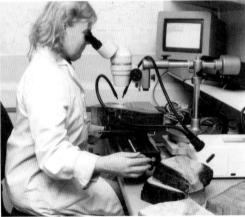

technology led him to produce *The Sheffield Chaucer Textbase*, a collection of machine-readable Middle English texts.[186] Both Shuttleworth and Burnley contributed to the Faculty by acting as Dean and their departments were closely involved, with others, in the development of the Humanities Research Institute, described on pp. 359–60. Dominic Shellard, who became head of the School of English in 2004, had produced acclaimed works on theatre censorship and on the theatre critics Harold Hobson and Kenneth Tynan. His research interests centred on British theatre since the war, and he had been awarded a research grant from the AHRB to develop the British Library Theatre Archives.

There were never more than eight members of staff of the Philosophy department in the 1970s and 1980s: by 2004 this figure had risen to eighteen, including five professors, and the department had become one of the top half dozen in the country, based on its RAE results in 1996 and 2001, and its maximum score for teaching quality. The architects of this success were David Bell, an analytic philosopher, and Peter Carruthers, who had a special interest in the philosophy of psychology. Supported by the Hang Seng Bank of Hong Kong, Carruthers set up the Hang Seng Centre for Cognitive Studies in 1992, to promote interdisciplinary research in this field. The department subsequently received a substantial grant from the AHRB for an international project on innateness and the structure of the mind, which embraced over seventy academics in Europe and America.

Archaeology was regarded as one of the best three departments in the country in the first half of the decade (the other two were Oxford and Cambridge). Its expertise in applying biological research techniques to archaeology (bioarchaeology) was a prime reason for this. For example, the methods of plant ecology were applied to the study of early farming methods in a number of countries.[187] The many departmental projects of great interest and significance included the 'outstanding excavation' of John Collis, the leading expert on the European Iron Age.[188] Robin Dennell directed excavations of Stone Age sites in Pakistan, where the tools proved to be the oldest found outside Africa. Both he and Collis acted as head of department during the 1990s, together with Keith Branigan, Archaeology's founder and senior mentor. His research in the Outer Hebrides of Scotland was the largest project of its kind ever undertaken.

By 1993 the department had eighty postgraduates and urgently needed a new home, which was provided at Northgate House and West Court on West Street.[189] Postgraduate numbers increased even further after it opened in 1995, making it the largest such department in the country. The specialist laboratories included the principal British centre for tree ring studies (dendrochronology), funded by English Heritage, and the headquarters of ARCUS, the department's consultancy service undertaking excavations for clients, who include private developers and public institutions.

The Biblical Studies department continued its strong research tradition: David Clines secured grants amounting to £1.2 million for an eighteen-year project to produce a definitive *Dictionary of Classical Hebrew* in eight volumes.[190] Cheryl Exum, who was appointed to a chair in 1993, represented an important new field, feminist Biblical criticism.

Law, Geography and Architecture

The University pioneered a specialist field when it created the Sheffield Institute for Biotechnological Law and Ethics (SIBLE) in 1995. This was the work of Derek Beyleveld, a professor in the Law faculty, and Julian Kinderlerer from the Molecular Biology and Biotechnology department, who introduced a popular MA course.[191] Kinderlerer worked closely with both Conservative and Labour Environment ministers as a government adviser on genetic manipulation. He became an international expert on biotechnological law and was seconded to the United Nations in the late 1990s. At that time he moved to the Law faculty, where the award of a personal chair completed a remarkable metamorphosis.

Law maintained its standing as one of the most popular subjects for undergraduate study, and the faculty continued to make weighty contributions to research. In addition to the professors mentioned in Chapter 6, Roger Brownsword was the author of many books and articles on contract law and was also interested in the law in relation to human genetics. Paul Wiles, Professor of Criminology, maintained the strong tradition established by Tony Bottoms, and went on to become the Chief Scientist at the Home Office. Bottoms returned to the faculty from Cambridge in 2003. Joanna Shapland, also a criminologist, founded the Institute for the Study of the Legal Profession; her work included a pioneering study on training for the Bar.

Ron Johnston left Sheffield in 1992 after eighteen years in the Geography Department but his field, electoral and political geography, continued to thrive under colleagues like Charles Pattie. The Sheffield Centre for International Drylands Research, set up by David Thomas in 1994, provided a focal point for international collaboration on the susceptibility of drylands, which occupy two-fifths of the earth's land surface, to become deserts. Louise Heathwaite's work on the impact of agriculture on surface water quality attracted large grants from research councils, government departments, water utilities and the Environment Agency. By 2004 the department had twelve professors, one of whom, Paul White, became a pro-vice-chancellor, the latest in a long line of geographers to hold this senior position.

Ian Masser, who took over from Jimmy James in 1979, was an influential figure in the Department of Town and Regional Planning for almost twenty years. An international authority on the development of geographic information systems as an aid to the planning process, he was instrumental in setting up the Sheffield Centre for Geographic Information and Spatial Analysis with colleagues in Geography. Tony Crook, a member of staff from 1968 and an expert in the field of housing policy, guided the fortunes of the department in the second half of the nineties, helping it to secure excellent scores in both the research and teaching quality assessments. He recalled that he told his colleagues, 'Anything less than the best was unacceptable'.[192]

Anne Beer, a specialist in urban environmental planning who joined the department in 1974, was appointed to the chair of Landscape in 1990 and acted as its head for eleven years.[193] She was succeeded in 1995 by Carys Swanwick, who, like her predecessor, had considerable professional experience in private practice before joining the University. She played a major role in guiding the Countryside Commission's approach to landscape assessment, which was thereafter applied throughout Britain and, indeed, abroad.[194] The department grew substantially: by 2004 it had over 200 students and twelve academic staff, including four professors, double the number at the beginning of the nineties. It remained the only independent landscape school in the country. The department's expertise was applied to many community projects over the years: it prepared the successful lottery bid for the refurbishment of Sheffield Botanical Gardens in 1996–97, provided the chair of the partnership group which oversaw the restoration, and offered technical advice.

There were two schools of thought about the architects who daily and nightly beavered away at the top of the Arts Tower. To Bryan Lawson, who was head of department from 1991 to 1999, 'we are like a beacon shining out over the city'.[195] In the popular mind, they were marooned at the summit of one of their own creations. Computer-aided design, as pioneered by Lawson, continued to flourish and was applied to the prediction of environmental conditions.[196] The school linked with Civil and Structural Engineering to form the Sheffield Academy of Steel Construction. A professorial team, Jeremy Till and Sarah Wigglesworth, partners in a forward-thinking London practice, were recruited in 1999. There was much press interest in their 'straw house' project and in Till's unorthodox choice of another tower, the Park Hill flats, as his Sheffield home. He became head of department, describing Sheffield as 'one of the three top schools in the country' – a judgement which was endorsed by a poll of 100 top practitioners in 2004.[197]

Research funding and new collaborations

Gareth Roberts was strongly committed to interdisciplinary research: he 'believed passionately that seminal developments occurred at the interface between subjects'.[198] This reflected his experience in the field of molecular electronics. He persuaded the Senate and senior colleagues to top-slice a significant part of the University's research income and devote it to an internal competition to start new research centres and institutes – a project which was in his view extremely successful.

The need to attract research funding was a constant feature of academic life and the source of much uncertainty. No grant was a foregone conclusion, as Harry Kroto pointed out when he won his Nobel Prize.[199] Competition between research teams, often at international level, was intense and much work could go into a bid which was ultimately unsuccessful. Research Councils and European funding streams began to place far greater emphasis on the assembly of multidisciplinary teams, hence the creation of centres to combine the expertise of several departments. Sheffield's examples include the Centre for Molecular Materials, the Polymer Centre and the Centre for Chemical Biology.

The largest and most ambitious research teams became multi-faceted, increasingly spanning a number of universities, involving relevant external organisations, and drawing on several income streams. An example was the research on ageing carried out by Alan Walker of Sociological Studies. His pan-European research on the sociological effects of an ageing population was funded by the European Commission, the Economic and Social Science Research Council, and the Department of Education and Science. The ESRC 'Growing Older' programme, for example, commissioned 24 research projects from experts in 26 different higher education establishments and seven specialist centres.[200]

The University's research on ageing was later co-ordinated by the Sheffield Institute for Studies on Ageing, which, in addition to Alan Walker, included Ian Philp, Tony Warnes, Richard Eastell and Sheila Payne from the medical school, Mike Nolan from the nursing school, and Pam Enderby of ScHARR. In 2002 the Institute won a Queen's Anniversary Prize for Higher and Further Education, for its work on improving the quality of life of older people. The University also won this influential biennial prize in 2000 for its work in the field of pollution control and sustainable development. The successful entry included Jim Swithenbank's Waste Incineration Centre, David Lerner's Groundwater Protection and Restoration Group and ECUS (Environmental Consultancy Unit University of Sheffield) led by Chris Routh.

University consortia added new dimensions to research. The White Rose Group, already mentioned, created research studentships; the World Universities Network (WUN) built on this success.[201] WUN was formed, under the chairmanship of Gareth Roberts, when the 'White Rose' universities, Leeds, Sheffield and York, together with Southampton and, later, Manchester and Bristol, went international by establishing links with leading American state universities in 1999. Exchange programmes in research training were arranged, as well as a number of jointly-developed masters' programmes. Following two visits to China, Roberts's friendship with the Presidents of Nanjing and Zhejiang Universities led them to join the network in 2002, a collaboration with untold future potential.

The Library and the Humanities Research Institute

Computing continued to transform the Library: the computerised catalogue was converted to the 'Star' system in 1996.[202] 'Star' was immediately accessible via the University's internal network and, shortly afterwards, over the internet. Staff and students no longer had to visit the Library to search the catalogue, and the accessibility of 'Star' to all internet users put Sheffield in the forefront of library development. This initiative was due to the enthusiasm of Michael Hannon, the University Librarian, and Martin Lewis, his deputy. Journal access was transformed by the availability of BIDS, in 1990, and other search engines, the first being Medline. Hannon and Lewis were early enthusiasts of electronic journals, the articles of which could be accessed directly from the internet. This facility offset some of the problems of the high inflation in journal subscriptions and subsequent purchasing reductions. Such economies were essential when the 'student surge' was putting heavy pressure on library funding. The Library was only able to cope with this through electronic resources and computing. Listed as 40th in the country for library spending per student in 1996 and 47th in 1999, the University took positive steps to reinvest in library purchasing over the following years.[203] Conventional loans continued to grow, but by 2001, the number of electronic uses of the Library exceeded the number of books borrowed – an information revolution.

The Library's Special Collections, one of Michael Hannon's priorities, acquired the literary papers of Richard Hoggart, the Cornish poet Peter Redgrove and the playwright Jack Rosenthal. The papers of Sir Hans Krebs were received in 1984, the first of a number of collections from contemporary scientists. The Music Library of the conductor Sir Thomas Beecham, purchased in 1997, was a major resource for music research containing autographed pieces presented to him by their composers and his own annotated scores.[204] Premises for the National Fairground Archive were opened in 1994, the creation of Vanessa Toulmin, a postgraduate in the Centre for English Cultural Tradition and Language. Describing herself as 'the most over-qualified candyfloss spinner in the country', she grew up on her grandparents' fairground in Morecambe and, having made the transition into higher education, was determined to preserve the history of her community, especially the personal narratives. 'You can preserve a fairground ride but you can't pickle a showman. The way of life, the tales and the memories can't be recaptured once they're gone'.[205] The collection has continued to grow, funded by numerous external grants, including a Heritage Lottery Fund award to digitise some 50,000 photos. Many families have donated their entire collections of memorabilia and there is a complete run of *The World's Fair* newspaper.

The Hartlib Papers project (p. 290) established a new approach to textual analysis and preservation, using the resources of IT. The Humanities Research Institute

Eric Clarke, Professor of Music, centre, with the University Librarian Michael Hannon, right, and Tom McCanna, the Music Librarian, at work on the Sir Thomas Beecham Music Library. Acquired in 1997, the collection includes 3,000 musical scores, many of them personally annotated in blue pencil by the conductor.

Sir Thomas Beecham.

(HRI) was formed in 1991 to develop further interdisciplinary projects; a partnership between the Library and humanities departments which was promoted by the first chairman, David Luscombe. He described the Librarian, Michael Hannon, as 'the perfect bridge-builder between the Library and the arts research constituency'.[206] The transcription of the 25,000 pages of the Hartlib collection was completed in 1995 and made available on CD-ROM. The computerisation of Chaucer's *Canterbury Tales*, under the direction of Norman Blake and David Burnley, began.[207] Gareth Roberts took a personal interest in the project and in his Dainton lecture used an analogy with pure science to explain it: a 'family tree' of eighty manuscript versions of the original text existed and 'the subtle textual differences are, for literary scholars, what mitochondrial DNA is for evolutionary biologists'. Mathematical analysis would be used to identify the different strains in the various versions of the text.[208] In 1998/99, David Loades and Mark Greengrass received one of the first grants of the Arts and Humanities Research Board (AHRB) for a definitive electronic version of the sixteenth-century history of the persecution of English Protestant martyrs known as *Foxe's Book of Martyrs*.

These were annotated transcriptions to the highest standards of scholarship and with corresponding research value. Sheffield has been at the forefront of these developments and received its first Queen's Anniversary prize, in 1998, for the work of the HRI. David Luscombe was also appointed Director of Research for the Arts and Humanities, 1996–2003. The HRI increased the opportunities for humanities research and created interdisciplinary links which were unprecedented and of considerable significance for the future.

The Times Higher Education Supplement enjoyed revealing 'leaked' letters detailing Sheffield's 'freemason pact' in 1999.[209] The freemasons had offered access to their archive, a treasure trove of under-researched material going back 330 years, and few strings were attached. This was the attraction to supporters like Philip Davies and David Luscombe, who pointed out that research into British freemasonry had been badly neglected. This was a unique opportunity to develop scholarly research. The University established the Centre for Research into Freemasonry,

One example from the tens of thousands of photographs on fairground life held in the National Fairground Archive: the Nottingham Goose Fair in the early twentieth century.

Geoffrey Chaucer's medieval poem *The Canterbury Tales was transcribed in many different versions; this is a page from a facsimile produced in 1911. A collaborative research project between the universities of Sheffield and Oxford, based in the Humanities Research Institute, began in 1994/95. The aim was to transfer all the versions to computer to allow comparisons to be made, and to determine the best approach towards producing a modern edition of the poem.*

with freedom to appoint the staff and control the research output. Andrew Prescott, a curator at the British Library, became the first professor in 2000, based in the HRI but closely linked to the History department.

Computing and corporate information

Computer networking came of age in the 1990s, as the technology advanced and the number of PCs increased.[210] The first significant purchase of PCs for student use was made at the start of the decade, with 250 machines placed in open-access 'clusters'. (Some of these were not replaced until 1999, by which time they were, in technological terms, antique). Staff use of microcomputers and networks grew so fast and so enthusiastically that seventy per cent of the Academic Computing Services' effort was devoted to their support. The University's last traditional mainframe computer, an IBM 3083, was decommissioned in 1993, by which time most users had transferred to newer and far more powerful microcomputers. By 2004 Sun Microsystems provided virtually all the University's large-scale computing power, for the Library, the central administration, the network servers and even the latest 'mainframe', which survived as a 'number cruncher' deemed essential to support certain areas of research. Its power was equivalent to that of at least eighty processors working in unison.

Email access from PCs was introduced as a managed service in 1991/92, simplified from the start by the use of software which made addresses logical and memorable. Email quickly became the communication mode of choice within the University. In comparison to the telephone, the time-delayed response and facility to compose phraseology, which could then be copied, saved and forwarded, were of matchless advantage to an articulate and highly literate staff group. The telephone system itself was renewed in 1995/96, with the introduction of voicemail and other services. The deregulation of telecommunications made it possible for the University to install its own ducts, cables and optic fibres for both data and voice transmission, even as far as the halls of residence: previously, it would have had to commission British Telecom to do the work, at far greater cost.

The telephone system was under the control of the Estates department until this time, but the convergence of data and voice networks brought this to an end. Estates reluctantly passed it over to Corporate Information and Computing Services (CiCS), which was set up in 1996. Directed by Christine Sexton, with Chris Cartledge as her deputy, CiCS subsumed and co-ordinated the academic and administrative functions of the previous Computing Services.[211]

An early task of CiCS was to oversee the implementation of systems created under the Management and Administrative Computing (MAC) Initiative, which had been in development at national level since 1988. This collaborative project aimed at no less than the computerisation and integration of every university's administrative procedures; inevitably, there were many delays and cost overruns. Jokes about 'Big Macs' of dubious quality were frequent.[212] Sheffield implemented its new staff and student record systems for the first time in 1996. There were serious problems of data transfer, to the extent that it might have been quicker and easier to print out all the existing student records and key them afresh into the new system. Data quality improved once departments were allowed to maintain and amend student records directly, with the benefit of their local knowledge. The MAC Initiative eventually delivered on its promise to generate accessible, definitive data sets – and there was no going back.

The new department of Journalism

Journalism is a popular subject with students, but is taught by surprisingly few of the Russell Group universities.[213] Indeed, ten years after its foundation Sheffield's department was the only one to run a single Honours BA combining press and broadcast journalism. This degree was an accredited training programme for journalists; the department also offered a range of postgraduate degrees. Seven of the lecturers were professional journalists with backgrounds in newspapers, magazines, radio, television and web-site journalism.

The department was set up in 1994 as a result of the efforts and enthusiasm of Maurice Roche from Sociological Studies, the Registrar John Padley, and Neil Sellars of the Mundella Programme, which accredited Sheffield College's course in Journalism. There were over 1,000 applications for the first intake of about seventy students. Donald Trelford, editor of *The Observer* 1975–1993, was an ideal choice as the first professor, because of his high profile and his affection for Sheffield, where he had worked as a novice journalist on the *Sheffield Telegraph* and later developed a passion for snooker in the hothouse of the Crucible.[214] Barrie Gunter, head of research at the Independent Television Commission, took a second chair. Some of the lecturers were practising journalists, like Bob Bennett from the *Sheffield Telegraph* and Jonathan Foster from *The Independent*, while others had an academic background, like Bob Franklin, a political scientist.

This mixture took some years to gel but then succeeded surprisingly well, and the research ethos of the university encouraged a number of projects, like an early survey of violence on TV by Jackie Harrison and Barry Gunter. Later the 'METER' project, to detect the reuse of text in journalism, and 'Cub Reporter', to provide swift background information for journalists covering breaking news stories, were well funded by the Engineering and Physical Sciences Research Council. Both were joint projects with the Computer Science department.

The department was based in Minalloy House on Regent Street, which contained a student newsroom with an editing suite and a broadcast studio. Student demand continued to be buoyant and the intake increased over the years. Donald

Donald Trelford, former editor of The Observer *and the founding head of the Department of Journalism, with a group of students.*

Trelford left in 2000 and was replaced by Peter Cole, who had been the Deputy Editor of *The Guardian*.

Changes to Adult Continuing Education

The Division of Adult Continuing Education reached a 'high peak of achievement' by the early nineties under Bill Hampton and his successor Geoffrey Mitchell.[215] There were 13,000 enrolments annually to the 'Courses for the Public' programme, and the Division diversified its output, which doubled in size between 1989 and 1994. This was achieved despite the closure of the Miners' Day Release Programme, caused by the break-up of the industry. A new and larger building was acquired in 1991, with a 'shop front' on West Street. Gareth Roberts endorsed the idea of a 'network for education in the community', when Robert Cameron took over as head of department in 1994.[216]

The Division was in crisis shortly afterwards, however, because of a change to its funding. HEFCE, previously supportive of the entire teaching programme, had decided to limit its funding to courses carrying accreditation.[217] The Division responded by developing a number of part-time degrees and 'university certificates' in, for example, the humanities, local history and archaeology, French and Hispanic studies, natural history and women's studies. There were also taught Masters degrees in Historical Archaeology, Local History, and Literature & Cultural Tradition (a joint venture with John Widdowson at the Centre for English Cultural Tradition and Language). The majority of the 'Courses for the Public', however,

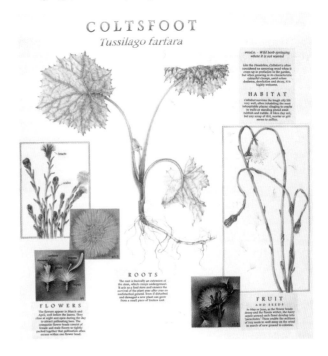

A course in botanical illustration run by Valerie Oxley of the Division of Adult Continuing Education was a resounding success. Students of the course won medals at the Royal Horticultural Society and were invited to mount an exhibition at the Natural History Museum in London. This illustration shows work by Amanda Willoughby, a member of the group.

Ken Hawley, pictured here with Joan Unwin, research associate, made a lifelong collection of Sheffield tools and cutlery, together with catalogues, photos, films and memorabilia which record the processes of a historic industry. The Hawley Collection, which is unique and of immense educational and research value, was housed by the University in a specially converted building in 1996.

were taken for pleasure rather than credit. Many of the students needed no extra qualifications and enjoyed the stimulating discussions and friendly atmosphere of the classes. Funding these courses was a 'real challenge' after 1994 and by the late 1990s could often only be achieved by offering them as part of a degree or certificate programme.[218]

These challenging adjustments were made while the demands of the RAE intensified. Because the Division was multidisciplinary, research fields varied widely: an issue which affected RAE returns and created a problem for adult education departments nationwide. At Sheffield, research into aspects of adult education was encouraged and a number of taught Masters degrees in education were developed. The innovative research in other fields continued, for example in local history and archaeology, led by David Crossley and David Hey, who supervised 12 PhDs during the nineties. The Hawley tool collection, a resource of unique value for research in the history of local industry, was housed in its own research centre at Portobello in 1996.[219]

The department was in deficit by 1997 and the University responded by setting up a task force which recommended a complete restructuring. As finally implemented in 1999/2000, the Division's postgraduate programme was redistributed to Education and other departments, to form a critical mass for RAE purposes. The remainder formed the Institute for Lifelong Learning with a part-time degree and certificate programme. Several of the professors took advantage of early retirement schemes and there were none left by 1999.

This sad story might have been worse; several university adult education departments closed at this time. Sue Webb, the new Director, stressed the positive adjustments to change which took place and the 'second chance' possibilities still available. By 2004 the Institute was financially viable and its courses had been 'mainstreamed' – included in the University's undergraduate programme. The recruitment of mature students to the University generally was encouraged and some departments, for example, Archaeology and Sociological Studies, prided themselves on attracting a large proportion. The glory days of traditional adult education at the University of Sheffield, however, have now passed.

Women at the top of the University

The 'glass ceiling' had hardly been penetrated in Sheffield, even by the mid-1990s. A particularly low point was a university league table showing that Sheffield had six female professors in 1994/95, 2.9 per cent of the total, compared with an average of 5.9 per cent for the other English civics.[220] Criticism of universities as 'bastions of male power and prestige' continued, especially at a time when the proportion of female to male students was approaching one to one.[221] Sheffield's six (full) professors in 1994/95 were spread across the University – Gillian Gehring in Pure Science, Cheryl Exum and Sally Shuttleworth in the Arts faculty, Joanna Shapland in Law, Anne Beer in Architecture and Lena Dominelli in Social Sciences. Numbers urgently needed to increase and Rosie Valerio, the newly appointed Director of Human Resources, played an important role by pursuing an equal opportunities strategy.[222] More women became members of the Academic Promotions Committee, for example. Valerio herself was one of a new generation of women directors of administrative departments who were appointed by John Padley – there were six by 1997.

Women's promotion prospects improved slowly, but steadily. One of the problems was that very few women applied for the top jobs.[223] However, six more female professors were appointed by 1996, including three to the faculty of medicine. Angela Seddon attained a senior position in the Engineering faculty, as director of the Centre for Glass Research. A major breakthrough came in Gareth Roberts's final year, 1999/2000, with ten female promotions to chairs, bringing the total to ten per cent of the non-clinical academic staff.[224] Roberts also appointed the first female Pro-Chancellor, Kathryn Riddle, in 1999, and encouraged Pam Enderby to apply for the role of Dean of the Faculty of Medicine. Enderby, a speech therapist by profession, has a place in the history of equal opportunities as the creator of a precedent equal pay case. While working in Bristol in 1986, she began a claim against the Department of Health, arguing that speech therapists were comparatively underpaid because the profession was predominantly female. Her main motivation was 'to keep people in this valuable job'. A succession of legal hearings followed before the claim was finally declared just in 1997; back pay for speech therapists totalling at least £30 million was awarded.[225]

Promotion for women lower down the pay scale also increased significantly from 1999 onwards. Appointments to readerships quadrupled in that year and the number of promotions to senior lecture rose from three in 1994 to eleven in 1999.[226] This was partly due to new policies which ensured, for example, that research time lost during maternity leave was taken into account in assessing a lecturer's overall output. It was also due to greater transparency in reporting trends and success rates, thus ensuring that the successful progression of academic women became a focus.

Kathryn Riddle, the University's first female Pro-Chancellor, had been a Law lecturer and had degrees from the University in both Economics and Law. She made many other contributions to the life of the city, including chair of the Health Authority, High Sheriff of South Yorkshire and Deputy Lieutenant.

THE NINETIES STUDENTS [227]

Student services

The Union urgently needed to expand its provision, following the intense growth in student numbers during the first half of the nineties. Adjustments to accommodate the influx of overseas students and the growing number of mature students, especially those in the new School of Nursing, were needed. It succeeded in impressive style and maintained its reputation for caring student services. The Union transformed its peer-group 'rights and advice service' into a professional Student Advice Centre with five full-time staff, including specialists in housing, finance and international issues. Advisers represented students at Discipline and Student Progress hearings and at Social Security tribunals. Mary Holding of the University's Student Services section rented space in the Union for a 'one stop shop', the Student Services Information Desk, in 1997. It could answer 97 per cent of enquiries and referred the remaining few.

The counselling service was needed more than ever in an era of rising staff/student ratios, in the opinion of its director Colin Lago. A degree profile with numerous options could mean that students were 'tearing around between different locations without a reference group'.[228] Lago developed a particular expertise in the culture shock experienced by overseas students and published a staff training manual on the subject.[229] Funding for student services from the University was tight; Gareth Roberts tended to favour charging students for some services, like health and sport. When this was tried in the case of the Student Health Service, however, in the form of an extra fee, it proved to be unworkable. James Burton, the long-serving director of Student Health, was relieved that it retained its original form.[230] During the decade, University subventions to the Union were reduced, with the result that it had to rely on its commercial performance to maintain services. This was, however, impressive: for several years turnover was the highest of any Students' Union in the country. Indeed, Sheffield's Union was seen as a beacon by many others, 'the best of its kind' for, among others, its entertainments, high-quality facilities, and strong welfare support in areas such as student advice, the nursery and the programme for international students.[231]

Dr James Burton, head of the University Health Service from 1988 to 1998. This photograph was taken in 1997, when he was admitted to the Fellowship of the Royal College of Physicians of London – a rare honour for a general practitioner.

Student finances

During the nineties, most of the financial cushions on which students had previously relied were taken away. The right to unemployment benefit during the vacations was withdrawn in 1990 and the grant was frozen, so that its value steadily fell. The Union estimated that eighty per cent of students had personal debts by 1992, and there was far worse to come, with the complete cessation of the grant and the introduction of tuition fees in 1998.[232] Part-time jobs during term-time became essential for many; they were one of the features which made the nineties different

The deteriorating financial outlook for students inevitably led again to campus protest – this is a grants demonstration on 8 December 1993.

Students' Union concert in the Octagon Centre.

from any previous decade. Our survey of Sheffield graduates found very few examples of term-time employment before 1990. The Careers Advisory Service, together with the Union, set up the 'Tempus' agency for part-time jobs, which signed up 200 students in its first month, October 1994.[233] One student interviewed by *The Star* said that he had a grant of £1,500 and a £1,000 student loan, but needed to work three nights a week in a pub to supplement this. Another said he was 'wary of loans' due to the unemployment rate.[234] The finances of postgraduate students were often even more precarious, and many did not expect to find jobs easily: a survey of Sheffield science research students by *The Times Higher Education Supplement* in 1994 showed that half of them planned to leave the country, on completion of their degrees, to look for work.[235]

Students in other parts of the country were even worse-off; a national survey in 1996 concluded that Sheffield offered the lowest cost of living for students.[236] Some problems were solved by the improving employment situation after 1997. It is undeniable, however, that students became dependent on debt. A national survey by *The Times* in 1998 concluded that the average debt of a Sheffield graduate was £3,040.[237] This survey was conducted just before the introduction of tuition fees; in 2004, student debt was much higher.

Building for changing needs

Under the inspired leadership of John Windle and Paul Blomfield, supported by an efficient management team and a host of well-organised sabbatical officers, the Union was strikingly successful not only in its consistent level of service but also in its ability to adapt quickly to the needs and desires of new students. Blomfield noted two major changes during the nineties. The first was the tendency for students to regard the Union as a service provider and themselves more as consumers and less as members of a self-governing organisation. This was reflected in the reducing participation in general meetings by the late nineties. The sheer number of students on campus made such meetings impractical anyway. They were discontinued, and referenda took their place. The second change was external competition from national pub chains, which opened outlets like 'The Cavendish' on West Street aimed specifically at the student market.[238] On a national level this, combined with the urban 'club scene', took business from students' unions.

Sheffield held its own with a succession of new ideas based on careful market research. In the early 1990s the club night of choice at the Union was 'Mrs Thatcher's Big Night Out', followed by 'Pop Tarts', which sold out every week.[239] 'El Tel's Midweek Fixture' was 'the UK's biggest student sports night' by 1997/98. In 2003 there were six different club nights every week, including a gay and lesbian night which began in 1990 (called 'Liberation' and later 'Climax'). Concerts continued to be popular; the 'supergroup' INXS chose Sheffield for its only campus performance on a national tour in 1993. In 2000 the Union won the *Club Mirror* award for entertainment venue of the year – not just among student venues but among the entire leisure industry.

The Union remodelled:

From the top left: *The first step in the remodelling of the Union building was the demolition in 1994 of the walkway across which generations of students had entered the Union.*

The curving north façade of the extension facing the Concourse, opened in 1996 and designed by Mott Architecture. The upper floor includes a gallery sponsored by Convocation.

The glass wall of the atrium at the point where it adjoins the original Graves building.

The Auditorium, a 400-seat lecture theatre and cinema.

The WorkSpace surrounding the atrium, formed by roofing over the space between the old and new buildings.

The glass-fronted lift tower and remodelled main entrance to University House, completed in 1993.

John Windle and Paul Blomfield, managers of the Students' Union since the mid-1970s.

The facilities of the Union grew ever smarter and more extensive. The old Graves restaurant closed in 1991 and was turned into offices and meeting rooms. 'The Park', with a sophisticated bar, café and dance floor, opened in 1991. Three years later the interior of University House was remodelled and extended in order to create an impressive new entrance with space for a shop, banks and travel agency, as well as a central situation for the box office and advice centre. The bridge leading to the Union was demolished and the lower refectory roofed over and made into 'The Foundry', a night club venue. During the second phase of this major refurbishment, an extra floor was added to the link building and a glass atrium created in front of it. The old Graves cinema (originally Graves Hall) reached the end of its days, but was splendidly replaced by the Auditorium with 400 raked seats.[240] The cinema became the 'Interval Café Bar', catering particularly for the needs of postgraduates and mature students. Committee facilities were provided in the open-plan 'WorkSpace' and there were new lounges and even a gallery, sponsored by Convocation, overlooking the concourse. The completion of this £4 million conversion was celebrated with a 'lift-off party' in October 1996, exactly sixty years after the original Graves building opened. It is still quite recognisable, from the outside at least.

The increasing number of international students, with their 'national societies', compensated for a decrease in committee activity by other students. A strategic review of student demand in 1999/2000 revealed a desire for the provision of casual activities requiring less commitment. This led to schemes like the 'Give it a Go' recreational activities, which were 'extraordinarily successful'.[241] Some traditional committee activities continued to inspire effort. The Newspaper Committee rebranded *Darts* as *The Steel Press* in November 1997 – thus *Darts* came to the end of its life after fifty years. *The Steel Press* won the 'Student Newspaper of the Year' award in 2000.[242] Success in the Student Journalist of the Year competition continued – Rachel Newsome won in 1994, Guy Adams in 2000 and Alice Tarleton in 2001 and 2002.

Rachel Newsome, centre right, winner of The Guardian 'Student Journalist of the Year' award in 1994.

The LGB society for lesbians, gays and bisexuals was established as an official Union committee in 1991. Sheffield was the first Union to be declared 'gay friendly', with a 'safe room' and a gay awareness week.[243] One memorable demonstration was held outside the Octagon after Ann Widdecombe, at that time the Conservative 'Minister for Sheffield', made a speech which was seen as anti-gay. Missiles were thrown, and Gareth Roberts was confined in the depths of the Octagon with Ann Widdecombe for two hours until it was safe to leave the building.[244]

In the 1993 Union elections, six of the seven sabbatical posts were taken by women, a result attributed by the outgoing President to the success of a drive 'to involve more students and end the influence of political factions'.[245] The success of women's representation was such that in 1998 the Union held a referendum to decide whether the post of Women's Secretary was still needed. The proposal to abolish it was resoundingly defeated.[246] An extra sabbatical post of 'Education and Representation Secretary' was created in 1998/99, in acknowledgement of the Union's

Left: *The University's Culinary Competition Team competing for one of many awards it has won – the Gold Medal and Challenge Trophy at the 1998 British Universities Chefs' Challenge. Left to right: Debbie Gooder, Tracey Carr, Kerry Crocker, David McKown.*

Right: *Another prize for Residential, Catering and Conference Services – the National Training Award in December 1996. Left to right: David McKown, Stan Beresford (who was also voted Catering Manager of the Year), Pat McGrath and Stephen Ware (Conference Manager).*

important campaigning role. For example, anonymous marking of examinations became universal in the 1990s after a student campaign. The three-week vacation originally allowed at Christmas under the new semester system was extended to four after student protests that they had no time to take holiday jobs and revise for semester one examinations.[247]

The end of traditional Rag

Most of the traditions associated with Rag, which was started by ex-service students in 1919, ended by 1996/97. The main reason was, ironically, the incredible success of Pyjama Jump. In 1990 the *Sheffield Telegraph* declared it to be possibly the largest ticket-only annual event in the world.[248] It was certainly 'the world's biggest open-air underwear party' and attendance was still rising, with Sheffield acting as a beacon for young people from all over the country. The disruption to normal life became more apparent each year, as local newspapers printed photos of the litter left after all-night queuing for tickets and stories of drunken behaviour on the routes of the pub crawl. Forged tickets led to a serious crush outside Roxy's night club in 1992. Security grew tighter and patrols of minibuses, with first-aiders on board, were organised by the Union to respond to the cases of drunken collapse and imminent hypothermia. Cleaning squads followed the revellers. A Channel 4 film about the Jump was made in 1995 and numbers reached at least 20,000 in the following year. 'It's absolutely brilliant – the one night in the year when anything goes', said one student.[249]

The last year of Pyjama Jump was 1996. The police's concern had become stronger by the year: parts of the city had to be closed off and the supertram service stopped for safety reasons. 'It became too dangerous for the participants', said Paul Blomfield, and its character had changed because it began to attract large numbers of people from all over the country who had no interest in the student charity aspect.[250] Adam Matthews was the unfortunate President who had to announce that the Jump 'has grown and grown to the point where it can no longer be controlled or altered. Cancelling is the only answer'.[251] The Rag Committee made several unsuccessful attempts to arrange an alternative, and there were even 'single issue' campaigners for the return of Pyjama Jump at the sabbatical elections of 1999, but

A new Sheffield Student Charities Fund gradually took over from Rag; a bungee jump for charity was held in May 1993.

Left: *The Comic Relief fashion show in the Octagon Centre, 1997.*

Right: *The 24-hour musical* Bugsy Malone, *1998.*

they were heavily defeated.[252] Nightclub owners who tried to revive the Jump were stopped by the Union, which held the trademark on the name.

The Rag parade lasted one further year. It had been overshadowed by Pyjama Jump since the early eighties and some of the parades were of an embarrassingly low standard. Attempts were made to improve them in the nineties, but times had changed. Paul Blomfield, who has watched the Union develop since 1978, suggested that 'there was a very distinctive Rag culture which just petered out', particularly after the age of majority was lowered to 18 (in 1969); gradually the 'Rag culture of pranks and being a bit naughty' began to seem immature. The Rag Committee tried to keep the parade going 'beyond its sell-by date' and the last one, in 1997, was 'a shadow of its former self'.[253] Of the traditional Rag activities, only Spider Walk continued.

A new Student Charities Fund was launched in 1992/93. A fashion show for Comic Relief in 1997 produced the highest contribution from outside London.[254] The Octagon was packed in March 1998 for a performance of the musical *Bugsy Malone*, produced and rehearsed by over 200 volunteers during the previous 24 hours. 'The atmosphere was incredible' and the event raised about £3,000.[255] The 'End of Year Carnival' in 1998 realised more than £10,000 for the Children's Hospital and in 2004 a sponsored hitchhike to Budapest raised a similar amount for rural development in Ethiopia. Even so, the great fundraising totals of Rag may never be regained, and the traditions associated with it are dead and buried. In 2002, *The Steel Press* commented that 'most people have never heard of Rag Week because it was discarded before they arrived at university'.[256]

Student accommodation and the community

The University built hardly any student accommodation during the cash-strapped 1980s, but the 'student bulge' of the early 1990s called for instant remedy. Even the small increase of 1988/89 left students homeless at the start of term and the proposed solution, raising the proportion of first years in hall from 70 to 85 per cent, was overturned after protests that this would damage the atmosphere in the

The 'student surge' of the early 1990s caused a temporary accommodation crisis. Some students were even housed in Nether Edge Hospital for a short time.

halls.[257] The short-term expedient of converting surplus university houses into flats solved this crisis and plans were drawn up for new flat complexes. Some of these were in the grounds of existing halls, like the attractively designed Endcliffe Vale Flats next to Sorby, opened in 1992. Stephenson Hall acquired three new blocks in 1990 and both Halifax and Tapton were extended in 1995/96. Crescent Flats, built at 16 Endcliffe Crescent, and Carrysbrook Court on Westbourne Road housed 224 students between them. Most of these developments had a dual purpose, with en-suite bedrooms designed for conference letting during vacations. This was very important to the conference manager, Stephen Ware. Earnshaw Hall acquired a large meetings room and a further conference room was opened in 1992, named after its long-serving warden Tony Heathcote, the Professor of Hispanic Studies.

These developments aroused new protests from local residents, spearheaded by BANG (Broomhill Action Neighbourhood Group), but gaining support from the residents of other suburbs with large student populations. They claimed that there was 'a growing colonisation of some parts of the city by students' leading to 'the destruction of communities by the sheer weight of transient residents'.[258] There were plenty of residents who disagreed, and wrote to the newspapers to support the students; the Union pointed out that many lived in Sheffield throughout the year and supported suburban food and entertainment outlets which benefited the whole community.[259] The 'swamping' argument was powerful, however, since it fuelled not only objections to planning applications (the extension to Tapton, for example, had to be scaled down twice), but also to the purchase of houses for student occupation and even the conversion of unused buildings. The University was not allowed to develop the old Co-operative store on Crookes Road, for example, because of the number of students already in Crookes.[260]

Whatever the effect of the protests, the number of new students forced the University to look further afield. Urban regeneration was on the agenda and groups like Sheffield First were attracting inward investment. The University decided to develop sites close to the city centre. The first residential complex, Mappin Court on Mappin Street, which opened in 1991, was followed in 1993 by the much larger

Left: *Crescent Flats on Endcliffe Crescent, which were designed by David Bannister of the University's Architectural Consultancy Service, housed 128 students and were opened in 1992.*

Right: *Endcliffe Vale Flats, opened in 1992, had places for 126 students. The development, by HLM Architects, won the 1993 RIBA White Rose Award for design excellence.*

The Unitarian church on Crookesmoor Road became 'a desirable residence' for 59 students in 1991. Some of the stained glass and architectural features were retained, as a feature of the building.

Top left: *St George's Church, seen here from Mappin Street, had been the University Church but closed as a place of worship in 1978. It was acquired by the University and in 1994 an imaginative conversion by the architects Peter Wright and Martyn Phelps of Buxton created self-catering en-suite accommodation in the north and south aisles.*

Top right: *Inside the new west entrance, showing some of the memorial tablets retained by the architects and a stained glass back-lit panel by Wendy Taylor representing the eight faculties of the University.*

Bottom: *The nave, converted into a 380-seat lecture theatre.*

Broad Lane Court, on a University car park close to the Engineering buildings. This provided for 228 students in 37 flats. The following year, distinctive flats were created as part of the St George's Church conversion. As with Crookesmoor House, many original features were retained. The flats were placed in the old gallery and aisles, since the central nave became a lecture theatre.

This building programme enabled the University to maintain its policy of providing a guaranteed place to first-year students in either flats or halls.[261] Some halls took excessive numbers of first-years: Sorby, in particular, usually had a proportion of around 85 per cent , far higher than the 75 per cent generally thought to be the desirable maximum.[262] For other students, the housing service kept a register of some 3,500 beds in privately-owned and regularly-inspected houses and flats. Co-operation with Sheffield Hallam helped to maintain standards. Sheffield topped a national league table for good relations between students and the local community in 1999.[263] Initiatives in community liaison, like the 24-hour campus control telephone lines, must have helped.

One unresolved, indeed growing, problem was parking. The University admitted in 1993 that it only had spaces in its own car parks for around a quarter of those issued with permits.[264] Those who parked on local streets were competing not only with residents but with visitors to the hospitals and to Sheffield Hallam's Collegiate Crescent site. Staff living less than two miles from the University were not issued with parking permits from 1993 onwards, but there was hesitation about actively pushing staff towards using public transport.[265] The possibility of getting the bus, however, was supplemented in 1995 by the chance of boarding the smooth and spacious supertram at its university stop. Unfortunately, the route which would have been of greatest value to the university/hospital community – towards Broomhill and the western suburbs – was exactly where it failed to go. A 'park and ride' scheme from a University car park in Endcliffe Crescent was provided for staff travelling from these areas. Staff parking was restricted further in 1997 when a new permit scheme was introduced which required staff to pay a charge for the first time.[266] Combined with yellow lines and meters around the University, however, one of the effects was to create informal park and ride (or walk) arrangements in all the streets of adjacent neighbourhoods. This issue was ongoing.

THE NEW ESTATE AT PORTOBELLO

One of Geoffrey Sims's greatest regrets was the restriction on the development of the University estate during his time as vice-chancellor. Government cuts were the main reason, but the University was also refused permission to borrow money on the security of its existing building stock. As he recalled, this rule was changed as he left office.[267] Plans existed when he retired for at least one development on the 'Portobello strip'.[268] Gareth Roberts injected new enterprise, recognising that University property might attract a high commercial rent which would offset some of the building costs. Money also followed the extra student places and the RAE successes. The result was that buildings which had been eagerly anticipated for years at last materialised. David Luscombe, who was the pro-vice-chancellor responsible for physical planning in the early 1990s, was delighted to see 'the University sprouting and growing on a scale far greater than most other institutions'.[269] The first new building was Regent Court on a large site on Regent Street, designed with a central quadrangle and with the intention of using half the 80,000 square feet of offices for high-technology departments and letting the other half to outside companies. In the event, the University's needs became so pressing that the building was almost entirely used as a home for ScHARR and the departments of Computer Science and Information Studies. They have benefited from the fact that the building was finished to a superior standard because of its commercial potential.

There was space on the site for another building; hence the Management School, designed to complement the other buildings in the area, including the Sir Frederick Mappin building across the road. The Management School was opened in 1993 and moved the departments of Economics, Business Studies and Accounting away from the lawyers at Crookesmoor to the other end of the campus. They were joined in adjacent buildings by Adult Continuing Education and, on West Street, by Archaeology. The Hadfield Building for Engineering Materials was refurbished and the Hicks Building for Mathematics and Physics reclad.

The University published its 'Central Campus Masterplan' in 1995, placing the heart of the development plan at Portobello.[270] Much had already been achieved and one further building, the Innovation Centre was completed in 1998. This was entirely funded by British Steel in a successful example of 'technology transfer', encouraging private industry to fund 'incubator' buildings in which small firms could grow and benefit from the expertise on the campus.[271]

The Masterplan also proposed the new and refurbished Biology laboratories (see p.352), for which JIF money was in place before Roberts left office – an achievement of which he was particularly proud because of the University's success in a highly competitive bidding process. As head of the HEFCE Research Committee, he helped to draw up a new, later permanent, scheme called the Science Research Infrastructure Fund (SRIF) which was less competitive than JIF. Sheffield's first

The supertram at the new University stop, opened in February 1995. The Vice-Chancellor and the Student President, Dominic Carr, formally opened the university section by riding on an inaugural tram.

Below top: Part of the Portobello strip in 1990, prior to re-development, seen from the top of the Jessop Hospital. This area became the site of Regent Court and the Management School. The Sir Henry Stephenson Building can be seen in the middle distance: to its left is the Caledonia Works, the future site of the Applied Science Library.

Bottom: The model for the Regent Court building, designed by HLM Architects, which opened in September 1992.

The Management School from Mappin Street, designed by HLM Architects and opened in 1993. Regent Court can be seen to the rear. For both projects, building materials were chosen to harmonise with the nearby St George's Engineering buildings.

allocations from SRIF were announced at the time of his departure from the University and guaranteed capital funding to support the future of biology and chemistry. The building programme by 2001 totalled £160 million.

When all the buildings mentioned in this chapter are taken into account, it is clear that the 'Roberts estate' is considerable. Moreover, the centre of gravity of the campus had shifted significantly towards St George's. Many of Roberts's aims, for example, to introduce private finance to the estate, were achieved and the University was on course to continue these developments in the following decade.

Retrospect

Gareth Roberts left the University in December 2000, on his appointment as President of the Science Council and President of Wolfson College, Oxford. One newspaper described this as 'one of the best post-VC jobs in the business', offering the opportunity to 'enhance his reputation as the networker supreme, continuing to advise the government on science, biotechnology, university funding and researchers' careers'.[272] At an emotional farewell reception, he expressed his profound regret at leaving Sheffield.[273] He departed in full expectation of 'an excellent set of results' in the 2001 RAE. The results did, indeed, endorse his strategy for research development: 35 of the University's 48 units of assessment scored 5 or 5*, a result bettered by only five universities. 81 per cent of the academic staff were based in these top-rated departments and 27 subjects had improved their rating since 1996.[274] This was a formidable baseline for the 'research-led university' of the 21st century. Another statistic in which Roberts took much pride was the 82 per cent entry from state schools in 2000, with eighteen per cent from lower social classes. This was better, he said, than Manchester, Leeds or Nottingham.[275]

The University changed profoundly during Roberts's ten years in office. This was not only due to his energy and vision, but to the external forces driving the transformation of every British university. In his reflective Dainton lecture of 1998,

Tapestry showing Stanage Edge in the Peak District, commissioned from Sue Lawty in 1995 and hung in the refurbished Mappin Hall.

376

he remarked that 'the system has been almost entirely reinvented and transformed from a colonial antique to a modern mass-education system'. Autonomy no longer existed, since the funding councils retained 'punitive powers to discipline any institution that attempts to ignore pre-determined constraints'. This control was described as 'almost Napoleonic' by another commentator.[276] Its effect on academic staff may be summed up in the words of Peter Banks, a pro-vice-chancellor: 'research is now better funded, possibly more dynamic but more precarious. More students are taught at much greater staff/student ratios. There are real gains but very real losses'. Of the latter, the loss of a sense of collegiality across the university world was, he suggested, the most profound.[277]

Competition between universities was enforced and inescapable in the nineties. Almost every aspect of higher education was expressed in numbers on a league table which compared the performance of each institution. Many academics found this disturbing and an affront to traditional values. But there is no doubt that it also inspired enterprise and drove high levels of achievement in certain areas. It also brought universities together in a different way, through partnerships designed to maximise creative and financial potential, like the World Universities Network (WUN). Gareth Roberts was one of the leaders of this development, which he believed would be the hallmark of higher education in the 21st century.

Roberts espoused strategic planning, relentless initiative and hierarchical management. He was an entrepreneur who seized every opportunity and created many more. Not all of his ideas came to healthy fruition and some have withered since he left. Staff energy was sometimes diverted to little effect. Yet there is no doubt that by the time Roberts left the University was immeasurably stronger. It survived and flourished in a decade which saw the swiftest increase in student numbers in the University's history – a 75 per cent rise from 9,406 to 16,481. Few members of staff relished the challenges posed by government policy, but Sheffield under Roberts proved not only equal to them, but capable of using them to the University's own advantage.

Left: Mappin Hall restored to its former glory after many years as the Applied Science Library; part of a programme of improvements and modernization in the Mappin Building.

Right: The very first Applied Science Library was restored as the John Carr Library in 1995. This room was used by the city's Munitions Committee during the First World War; King George V attended one of their meetings here during his visit to the University in 1915.

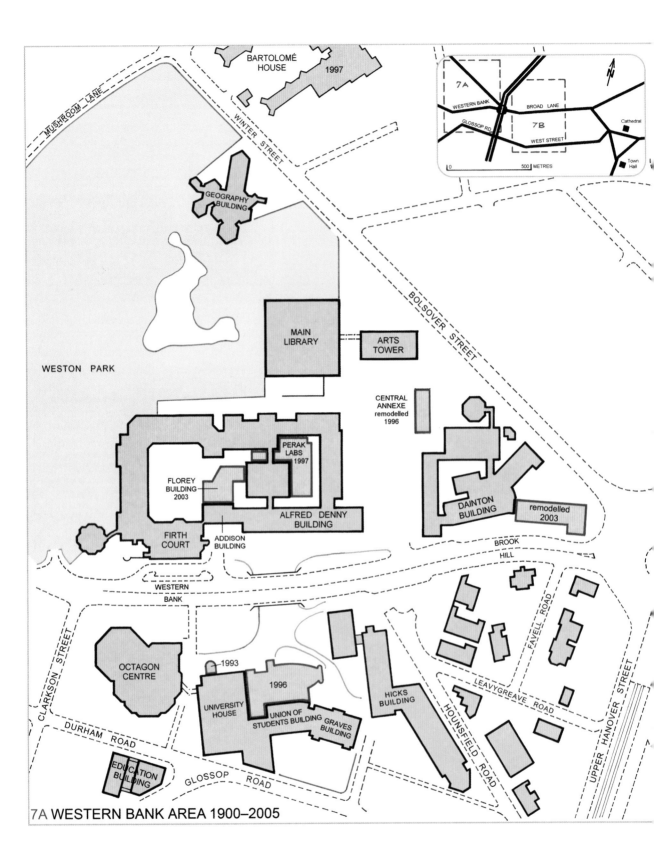

BARTOLOMÉ HOUSE 1997

MUSHROOM LANE

WINTER STREET

GEOGRAPHY BUILDING

WESTON PARK

MAIN LIBRARY

ARTS TOWER

BOLSOVER STREET

CENTRAL ANNEXE remodelled 1996

PERAK LABS 1997

FLOREY BUILDING 2003

DAINTON BUILDING

remodelled 2003

ALFRED DENNY BUILDING

FIRTH COURT

ADDISON BUILDING

BROOK HILL

WESTERN BANK

FAVELL ROAD

CLARKSON STREET

OCTAGON CENTRE

1993

1996

LEAVYGREAVE ROAD

UPPER HANOVER STREET

UNIVERSITY HOUSE

UNION OF STUDENTS BUILDING

GRAVES BUILDING

HICKS BUILDING

HOUNSFIELD ROAD

DURHAM ROAD

EDUCATION BUILDING

GLOSSOP ROAD

7A WESTERN BANK AREA 1900–2005

7A WESTERN BANK

BROAD LANE

GLOSSOP RD

7B

WEST STREET

Cathedral

Town Hall

0   500 METRES

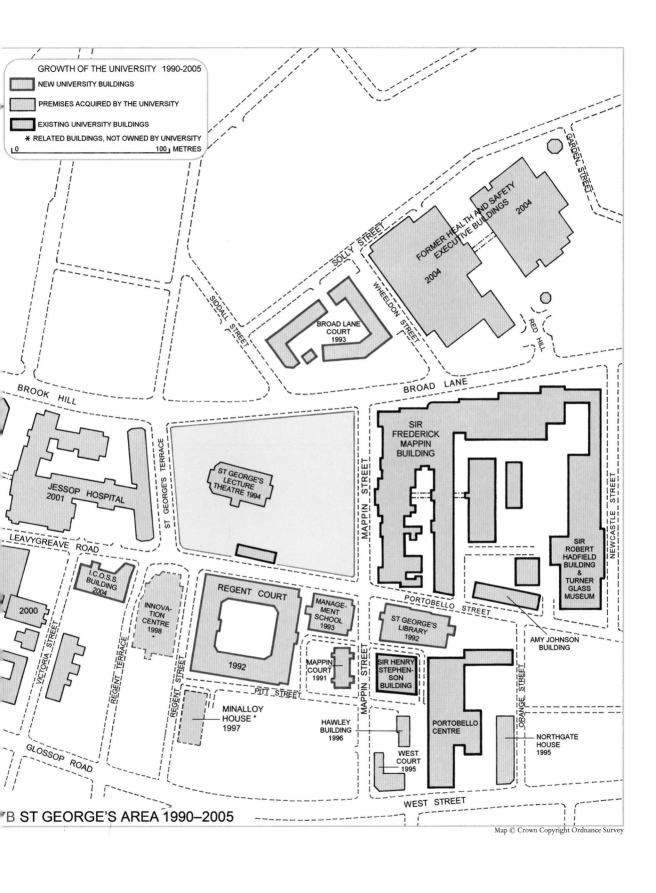

GROWTH OF THE UNIVERSITY 1990-2005

NEW UNIVERSITY BUILDINGS

PREMISES ACQUIRED BY THE UNIVERSITY

EXISTING UNIVERSITY BUILDINGS

✳ RELATED BUILDINGS, NOT OWNED BY UNIVERSITY

0   100 METRES

GARDEN STREET

SOLLY STREET

FORMER HEALTH AND SAFETY EXECUTIVE BUILDINGS

2004

2004

WHEELDON STREET

SIDDALL STREET

RED HILL

BROAD LANE COURT 1993

BROAD LANE

BROOK HILL

JESSOP HOSPITAL 2001

ST GEORGE'S TERRACE

ST GEORGE'S LECTURE THEATRE 1994

SIR FREDERICK MAPPIN BUILDING

MAPPIN STREET

NEWCASTLE STREET

LEAVYGREAVE ROAD

I.C.O.S.S. BUILDING 2004

INNOVA-TION CENTRE 1998 ✳

REGENT COURT

MANAGE-MENT SCHOOL 1993

PORTOBELLO STREET

SIR ROBERT HADFIELD BUILDING & TURNER GLASS MUSEUM

2000

VICTORIA STREET

REGENT TERRACE

1992

ST GEORGE'S LIBRARY 1992

AMY JOHNSON BUILDING

REGENT STREET

MAPPIN COURT 1991

SIR HENRY STEPHEN-SON BUILDING

ORANGE STREET

PITT STREET

MINALLOY HOUSE ✳ 1997

HAWLEY BUILDING 1996

PORTOBELLO CENTRE

NORTHGATE HOUSE 1995

GLOSSOP ROAD

WEST COURT 1995

WEST STREET

B ST GEORGE'S AREA 1990–2005

Map © Crown Copyright Ordnance Survey

Postscript

Into the Twenty-first Century: 2001–05

By David Fletcher, Registrar and Secretary

THE CHARACTER OF THIS FINAL CHAPTER is inevitably different from all the others since it deals with events in progress and a future in the making. An objective view must be left to a later history. However, this Centenary History would be incomplete without an account of current developments and concerns within the University, and of the hopes and plans for its next century.

Government policy in the 1980s and 1990s suggested a lack of confidence in the university system, which was clearly unjustified when one considers the dramatic increase in student numbers, and the evidence from research assessment and teaching quality review that standards were steadily improving. Year after year universities were faced with funding reductions described as 'efficiency gains' which in fact had the result of severely under-funding both the teaching and research infrastructure. In the late 1990s the attitude of government changed. There was a recognition that this policy could not continue if the country wished to maintain institutions that bore comparison with the best in the world. The Labour government's 2003 White Paper stated that there was a funding gap, paid tribute to the quality and success of the university system, and accepted that significant funding was required to maintain international competitiveness and quality. The White Paper also emphasised the importance of greater social inclusion, to be achieved through widening participation. Controversially, it proposed the charging of higher tuition fees to be recovered through a graduate contribution. The legislation to implement this policy, supported by all the Russell Group universities, was

Facing page: Rerum Cognoscere Causas *by Brendan Neiland RA, 2002, a painting which takes the façade of the Main Library as its theme and the University motto as its title.*

381

Robert Boucher, Vice-Chancellor of the University of Sheffield from January 2001.

adopted by Parliament after extensive debate in 2004. Fees of up to £3,000 per annum could be charged from September 2006.

The White Paper also supported the allocation of research funding in a more concentrated way and stressed the importance of activities which reached out to business and the community. As a research-intensive university with an excellent record in widening participation Sheffield was well positioned to take advantage of this agenda.

In its new Vice-Chancellor, Sheffield had a man who understood its traditions and had already made significant contributions to its development, as a pro-vice-chancellor and chairman of ADC in the early 1990s. Robert Boucher, who took over in January 2001, was in many ways the people's choice – well-known to colleagues, including the previous Vice-Chancellor, and a member of the Mechanical Engineering department from 1970 to 1995.

Boucher's early academic training was unusual, since he was advised to study for a PhD ('the foundation of my career') at Nottingham after he shone as one of the top students in the country on the Higher National Diploma course run at that time by the Council of Engineering Institutions.[1] He wrote his first paper immediately afterwards, based on his final year project. Awarded a postdoctoral fellowship at Queen's University, Belfast, he became a lecturer there in 1968. He and his wife, Rosemary, built their own house in Northern Ireland, but the increasingly troubled political situation, and the fact that this University offered specialist facilities for his research, caused them to move to Sheffield in 1970. His research was in the area of fluidics, the control and measurement of liquids and gases without the use of moving mechanical parts. Boucher was promoted to a personal chair in 1985 and succeeded Keith Miller as head of department in 1987. He enjoyed academic administration; his first experience of this as an admissions tutor was, he recalled, 'very satisfying'. As head he 'enjoyed enabling people to do well for themselves and for the department'. It achieved the grade of 5, then the maximum, in the RAE of 1992 and 'excellent' in the TQA.

By this time Boucher was a pro-vice-chancellor, having become involved in university committees in the early 1980s as a representative of NPSA (Non-Professorial Staff Association). He chaired the Technical Staff Sub-Committee, moved on to the ADC, and became a member of the powerful Planning Committee under Ron Johnston in the difficult years of the later 1980s. As a pro-vice-chancellor (1992–5), he undertook the academic development portfolio, including the chairmanship of ADC, and established a Teaching Quality Framework as the foundation for the new assessments – one which served the University well. In 1994 he was invited to apply for the post of Principal and Vice-Chancellor of UMIST (University of Manchester Institute of Science and Technology). His experience at Sheffield made him an ideal candidate, particularly as UMIST needed to develop its biological and environmental sciences. At the time of his appointment, Boucher was chairman of the Graduate School and a pro-vice-chancellor with responsibility for the University's research development.

Boucher enjoyed his time in Manchester, but commuted from Sheffield because of the lack of a Principal's residence: thus he and his wife never really left Sheffield.

Left: *Bob Boucher, centre, with his senior management team in 2001: from the left, David Bearpark, Director of Finance; pro-vice-chancellors Geoff Tomlinson, Colin Whitehouse, Phil Jones and Tony Crook; and the Registrar and Secretary, David Fletcher.*

Boucher was the ideal choice to succeed Gareth Roberts. 'Sheffield is in the blood', he said on his appointment, 'I genuinely think this is a very bright period in the development of the University and the city'.[2]

Bob Boucher's style of management chimed with the maturity of the University after an era of unprecedented growth. The ADC took a stronger role in decision-making and, particularly, resource allocation to departments. Boucher was committed to the devolution of power, and to the provision of training to enable academic staff to take on greater managerial responsibility. The ultimate goal within departments was devolved budgeting. Many strongly supported this aim; as Andrew Gamble, Professor of Politics and a former pro-vice-chancellor, put it: 'What really makes a department work is the involvement of all its members in governing it and that is enormously helped by having control of finances'.[3]

The recruitment of women to senior posts continued in the Boucher era; by 2003/04 eighteen per cent of professors were women. Women's success in gaining promotion was closely monitored at every stage, and the results were openly reported, in order to encourage further progress.

In 2001, Sheffield was named as 'University of the Year' by *The Sunday Times*, in recognition of its 'outstanding' performance over the previous twelve months. The award was based on

> a range of qualities: chiefly teaching; the overall academic health and robustness of the institution; the student experience; and the university's role on regional, national and world stages. In all these areas, Sheffield does exceptionally well.[4]

It noted that the most recent TQA scores of 'excellent' were all in arts or social sciences: 'a strong showing for an institution best known for science and engineering. While these subjects remain jewels in Sheffield's crown, the latest assessments provide compelling evidence of all-round academic excellence.' The number of top ratings by the QAA (26) was 'a record few institutions can approach', especially since another eight subjects missed the top grade by a single

Professor Tony Ryan of the Chemistry department making his entrance for one of his 2002 Royal Institution Christmas Lectures, entitled 'Smart Stuff' (a photograph taken from the video recording). Another Sheffield chemist, Professor Charles Stirling, gave the Christmas Lectures in 1992.

Professor Freddie Hamdy of the Academic Unit of Urology, the director of a comprehensive Department of Health study of prostate cancer which will survey 230,000 men over a period of five years.

Professor Neil Spooner of the Department of Physics at the opening of the laboratory in Boulby Mine designed to facilitate his research into dark matter. The facilities are sited one kilometre below ground level to avoid interference from cosmic rays and other external forces. Spooner is seen (left) in discussion with Lord Sainsbury, Minister for Science, and the Vice-Chancellor.

point. The drop-out rate was 'one of the lowest in Britain', indicative of a high level of student satisfaction.

This successful year was crowned in December by the publication of the results of the 2001 Research Assessment Exercise. No fewer than 35 (73 per cent) of the University's 48 units of assessment were ranked in the top two grades of 5 and 5*.[5] Sheffield achieved sixth place in the number of these ratings which it achieved – a strong endorsement of the 'research-led' policy pursued since 1991 and a firm basis for further development. Research funding followed RAE success. In 2000/01 the value of new research awards secured by staff had reached an impressive £100 million, an increase of 61 per cent on the previous year's figures. After the 2001 RAE results were announced, HEFCE increased its research allocation to Sheffield by another thirteen per cent (equivalent to an extra £3.5 million). 'This has indeed been an *annus mirabilis*', said Boucher in his address to staff in June 2002.[6] In the next two years, over 200 new academic posts were advertised, proof of the University's determination to invest for the future and, in particular, for the RAE due in 2008.

Among the notable research awards of the years 2001–04 were £13 million from the Department of Health, the largest grant the University had obtained to date, to co-ordinate a nationwide clinical trial on the diagnosis and treatment of prostate cancer. Sheffield also received £1.15 million, the highest in the country, from the AHRB (Arts and Humanities Research Board).

The White Rose alliance of the universities of Sheffield, Leeds and York continued to flourish, with particular success in technology transfer, science enterprise and the development of high speed computer grid technologies, and raising funds to support the spinning-out of companies from University research. By 2003 the Worldwide Universities Network, of which Sheffield had been a founder member, had expanded to include six British, five American and two Chinese universities. These were all universities of high international standing, collaborating across a range of research areas. Sheffield was the lead partner in Stem Cell Biology and Advanced Materials & Nanotechnology.

The 'long-standing expertise' of the University in metals and cutting technology brought a giant aerospace and communications company to the city.[7] Boeing wished to develop new processes for the manufacture and structural analysis of titanium, with the aim of developing lighter, stronger materials which would improve the efficiency of its aircraft. After twelve months of negotiation in 2000/01, Boeing agreed to become a major partner in an Aerospace Manufacturing Research Centre based in Sheffield. The University's new Vice-Chancellor was able to announce the plans during his first months in office: 'This illustrates how a leading university such as Sheffield can act as a magnet for regional development'.[8] The new centre was jointly sponsored by Yorkshire Forward, the regional development agency, which provided a former mining industry site near the Sheffield Parkway. The Centre became a vital component in Yorkshire Forward's plans for an Advanced Manufacturing Park there. The aim was to create a major metals and engineering cluster which would attract high technology companies and provide a significant number of jobs.

The University continued to play a key role in the economic regeneration of the city and its sub-region. Sheffield had been an innovator in this field, but government policy increasingly emphasised the importance of so-called 'third stream' activities, alongside research, and learning and teaching. The result was that the University's links with the city of Sheffield became better and closer than they had been for many years. The University was an important member of the Sheffield First partnership, the local organisation of civic and business leaders which acted as a catalyst for the regeneration of the city, aided by its designation as an Objective One area, which made it eligible for special financial support from the EU. The University saw no difficulty in 'thinking locally while acting globally' – in being a major international institution of higher education which at the same time played a crucial role in the economic renaissance of the city and the sub-region.

Channel 4's Time Team *records excavations at several sites in Sheffield supervised by ARCUS (Archaeological Research and Consultancy at the University of Sheffield). The resulting programme, entitled* Steel City: a Time Team Special, *was broadcast in March 2004 and attracted an audience of 2.7 million viewers.*

The University's technology transfer and spin-out activities were relaunched under the name of Sheffield University Enterprises Ltd (SUEL) in 1998.[9] SUEL aimed to commercialise University research projects in order to enhance the University's reputation and create a culture of enterprise. A number of facilities existed to support this, including the University Challenge Fund, which from 1998 made a total of £9million available to the White Rose universities to establish the Technology Seedcorn Fund. Later, a partnership with the University, the city and Sheffield Hallam University known as Knowledge Starts secured a budget of almost £6 million, half of which came from the European Commission. By 2003, the support of the University and the availability of both sources of funding had assisted SUEL to establish some forty spin-out companies, and had brought several to the point where significant funding for a second stage of development had been secured. For example, Celltran Ltd successfully launched its first product, MySkin,

The Queen and the Duke of Edinburgh presenting the Queen's Anniversary Prize Gold Medal and Scroll to the Vice-Chancellor and Professor Alan Walker in recognition of the University's contribution to the study of ageing and to improving the quality of life of older people.

Keith Ridgeway, Professor of Design and Manufacturing Engineering, left, and Adrian Allen of Technicut Ltd, the driving forces behind the establishment of the Aerospace Manufacturing Research Centre in partnership with Boeing in 2001.

A cover from the new alumni magazine, Your University, launched in 2003.

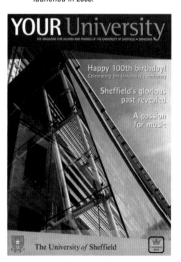

a 'biological bandage' developed by the Centre for Biomaterials and Tissue Engineering. It used the patient's own skin cells, cultivated on a specially-synthesised polymer layer, to improve the healing of burns and other chronic wounds.[10] The Polymer Centre, launched in 2001, involved staff from seven departments by 2004, and created a range of 'demonstrator projects' to show the commercial potential of its products and processes.[11] Its first spin-out company was Farapack Polymers Ltd.

The most ambitious enterprise of all, Biofusion plc, was established in 2002 to exploit the commercial potential of the University's intellectual property in medical life sciences. The company signed a ten-year exclusive agreement to provide investment capital and management support to existing and future spin-out companies. The University had an initial 70 per cent shareholding, later reduced to 49.59 per cent. In 2005, Biofusion was listed on the Alternative Investment Market. Sheffield is believed to be the first university in the world to approach spin-out commercialisation in this manner. Biofusion raised £8.2 million on 2 February 2005, giving the company a valuation of £28.2 million: proof of the enormous potential of this model for the commercialisation of university-based research.

The White Rose Centre for Enterprise co-ordinated plans to develop the enterprise skills of creativity and commercial thinking in both undergraduate and postgraduate students, especially in science and engineering departments, by introducing a range of course modules. One example was 'Physics in an Enterprise Culture' to 'provide students with an insight into the chain of events occurring between project conception and product launch'.[12] A second-year student of this course, during a summer vacation placement, devised a software suite for a Silicon Valley company which saved $40,000 compared with the commercial alternative.

The University established a Development office in 2002, to work in partnership with the Alumni Relations office. Its aim was to develop the University's wide circle of contacts, as well as to raise funds. The renewed focus on alumni emphasised their role not only as potential donors but also as friends of, and ambassadors for, the University. As part of this task there was an extensive and successful drive to update the mailing list: within twelve months reliable contact had been made with some 20,000 alumni.

Students in the new century

In 2003 HEFCE awarded the University an additional 866 student places to be introduced in phases over the following three years. This represented more than fourteen per cent of the total national allocation and provided £3.9 million of additional funding. The numbers related to areas of growth and demand, mostly in the arts, law and social sciences, and new academic staff were appointed. The number of overseas students continued to rise – 2,495 were registered on full-time degree courses in 2001/02, 2,657 in 2002/03 and 2,859 in 2003/04.

The proportion of entrants from state schools had risen to 84 per cent by 2002/03, the highest in the Russell Group.[13] Eighteen per cent came from social classes III, IV and V in 2003/04 and ten per cent from low participation neigh-

Above: *Students welcome visitors to the University on one of its Open Days.*

Above left: *The 'Coffee Revolution' café in the Students' Union.*

bourhoods. These were the fruits of the widening participation schemes of the 1990s, which continued to be developed and extended. New educational activities encouraged pupils and their parents to consider the idea of higher education, and they were given tours of the campus, since 'some of the families have never set foot in a university before'.[14] The Compact Scheme, which had started in 1994 with sixteen schools, expanded to include 85 schools and colleges in the region by 2003. The aim was to identify young people with academic potential whose circumstances or experiences had caused them to under-achieve at school. Such pupils were 'flagged up': brought to the special attention of admissions tutors, although they were not identifiable to other students. Liaison officers were there to offer discreet support, if they needed it, after they entered the University.

The tradition of student protest goes on: *left,* The Steel Press, *Sheffield students responding to the NUS call for a day of action in March 2001 to draw attention to the issue of fees and financial hardship; right, a 24-hour occupation of the Sir Henry Stephenson Building on November 2002 to protest against the threatened Iraq War.*

Examples of the work of student volunteers: (Left) *Members of the Malaysian Society encourage children with special educational needs at Mossbrook School, Rotherham, to make cards and sample traditional Malaysian foods.* (Right) *This group renovated a children's playground, one of many projects completed in a 'Just Do It' weekend. (Photos from The Steel Press).*

Architecture students created this daffodil on the Arts Tower during March 2004 to draw attention to the Marie Curie Cancer Campaign. They used 500 square metres of paper, which was donated by the local firm A. Pinder Ltd.

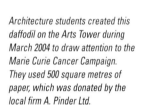

The widening participation strategy sought to extend the intake into degree courses which led to professional careers. The Sheffield medical school became the pioneer of a new approach, after it was allocated twenty additional places as the result of a successful bid to HEFCE in 1999. These places were to be taken by people from backgrounds currently under-represented in the medical profession. The Outreach and Access to Medicine Scheme (SOAMS) was launched in 2001 with the aim of recruiting 100 Year 9 students annually to follow a five-year programme of awareness, mentoring and support which would lead the most able students to gain entry to the medical degree. In 2003 the first twenty reserved places were awarded –the result of a 'fast-track' programme for Year 12 pupils which began in 2001.

Such programmes were crucial when the government had announced its commitment to extend entry to higher education to fifty per cent of school-leavers. The University also took steps to address the financial hurdles for such students. In 2000 a bursary scheme entitled 'Enough to Learn On' was introduced, providing scholarships of £2,000 per year for young people from lower socio-economic backgrounds.

The nature of the campus – integral to the city and with an easy-going and informal style – has always been an important factor in attracting students to Sheffield, and in the low drop-out rate. The Students' Union continued to be professionally run and very popular: it was rated the best in the country in the 2001 *Virgin Alternative Guide to British Universities*. The Union had also been picked as the 'entertainments venue of the year' by *Club Mirror* in 2000 because of its 'excellence in the club sector' – a notable achievement since *Club Mirror* surveyed the entire entertainments industry.[15] In market research conducted by the Union at this time, 87 per cent of students described the Union as 'excellent' or 'good'. In 2002 a new subvention agreement was reached with the University, which stabilised the

Union's finances for the next three years. The Union became owners of the 'Coffee Revolution' franchise in 2002 and ran these classy coffee shops on the campus and on Ecclesall Road.

Sheffield students of the new century took to volunteering in a big way. The Sheffield Volunteering scheme, which was introduced in 2002 and supported by the Higher Education Active Community Fund, recruited students to help a wide range of local charities and organisations. The befriending scheme, for example, matched an 8–11 year old child in need of extra support with a student volunteer who organised regular meetings or outings over a defined period of a few months. The strong emphasis on targets suited many students: 'I wanted to do something where I would notice a difference straight away. Volunteering for the impatient – excellent!'[16] The experience was also valued as a training-ground in vocational and leadership skills. By May 2003 almost 1,000 students had shown an interest in this kind of voluntary work – five per cent of the student population. The role of tutor in a primary school, supporting the teacher during the literacy and numeracy hours, was especially popular, and greatly appreciated by the recipients. The volunteers 'exceeded expectations' and were 'a credit to the University', commented one teacher.

The 'Give it a Go' scheme, offering students the chance to 'pick and mix' a range of leisure and sports activities, continued to be popular. The sports facilities at Goodwin were improved at a cost of £6 million during 2001/02. The new 'S10 Health' provision had 150 exercise stations, together with an aerobics studio and indoor climbing arena. Additional synthetic pitches were provided, and the gymnasia were refurbished. 'USport' was created to run the facilities and to take over the responsibility for sports clubs, after the University and the Union agreed to have a single body in charge of sporting provision. 'USport' facilities were made available to the public as well as students, who, for the first time, had to pay a membership fee. Even so, take-up was extremely high – there were, for example, at least 4,000 student members of the fitness suite in 2004/05.

May 2002 saw an attempt to revive Rag Week and the tradition of streakers on the Paternoster.

The fitness suite at S10 Health, part of the new USport facilities.

The Sunday Times designated the University's sports facilities as 5* – one of the reasons that it became 'University of the Year' in 2001 . The excellent provision for sport within the city generally was augmented in 2003, when Sheffield finally opened its regional 'English Institute of Sport' (EIS) in the Don Valley.[17] In addition to an indoor athletics arena and sports halls, it housed the national netball centre, a regional judo facility and a large table tennis centre.

The Estate

A major building programme began in Firth Court in Bob Boucher's first year of office. In 2003, after almost a century, the fourth side of the quadrangle was completed with a new building for Biomedical Science, named after Sir Howard Florey, the Nobel Prize-winner who had been Sheffield's Professor of Pathology in the 1930s. This building was funded by the JIF (Joint Infrastructure Fund) competition, which secured capital funding amounting to £36.4 million in 1999 to improve the scientific infrastructure. A further £56.4 million from two rounds of applications to the Science Research Investment Fund was announced during 2001/02. This funded a two-year programme (2002–4) of refurbishment of the biology accommodation in Firth Court, which was now extended to areas used by Finance and Human Resources. After the staff of these departments moved to other premises, the biology departments were left as the sole occupiers of Firth Court, with the exception of ceremonial rooms like Firth Hall and the offices of the Vice-Chancellor and Registrar in the Edgar Allen building.

Biology also benefited from the installation of controlled environment facilities beneath the Arts Tower concourse. The 32 underground chambers were capable of simulating all the major ecosystems of the world and had a carbon dioxide injection facility to allow experiments on the likely impact of 'global warming', an important research theme for the Department of Animal and Plant Sciences. The East Wing of the Dainton building, opened in 1960, was stripped to its basic structure and rebuilt in dramatic style to improve the research and teaching facilities of the Chemistry department.

The Medical School was also refurbished, with funding of over £10 million from the Wellcome Trust, to form a medical sciences institute, particularly for the Division of Genomic Medicine. By 2002/03, this division had raised the highest level of research income in the University, over eleven per cent of the total.[18] Basic laboratory sciences were to be transferred from the Northern General Hospital to the Royal Hallamshire Hospital in order to concentrate this research on one site.

In the Portobello area, the Social Sciences Informatics Collaboratory on Victoria Street opened in 2004 to support multidisciplinary research particularly in healthcare and socio-economic planning. At the same time a new University Health Centre at the corner of Gell Street and Glossop Road succeeded the original building in Claremont Place.

From the late 1990s, the University had been keen to dispose of some of its increasingly ageing stock of residential accommodation, both in houses and halls, and thus

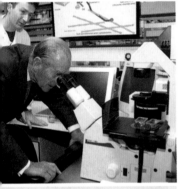

Below, top: *The Duke of Edinburgh at the opening of the Howard Florey building in October 2004.*

Bottom: *The Howard Florey Building for Biomedical Science in Firth Court, designed by the Bond Bryan partnership.*

Left, from top to bottom: *The original East Wing of Chemistry, remodelled by CPMG Ltd. The top two floors of the building house research facilities, including the Centre for Chemical Biology devoted to investigating the functional properties of biological systems at the molecular level.*

The Health and Safety Executive buildings on Broad Lane, conveniently situated across the road from the Engineering buildings, and acquired by the University for use as the new North Campus for scientific research and development.

The new University Health Service building, designed by CPMG Ltd, opened in time for the academic year 2004/05. The Claremont Place building, in use since 1977, had long proved inadequate. Under the directorship of Dr Melvyn Osborne, and with the support of the new Vice-Chancellor, the Service acquired the accommodation and facilities it needed to meet the requirements of a much-expanded student population.

Below: *The Informatics Collaboratory for the Social Sciences (ICOSS), designed by CPMG Ltd, nearing completion in October 2004. The main areas of initial activity in this building are urban and regional planning, environmental criminology, and public health. The research has an interdisciplinary focus, and features large data sets and state-of-the-art information and communication technologies.*

The Jessop Hospital site, purchased in 2001 after the new Jessop Wing was opened at the Royal Hallamshire Hospital. The original 1878 Jessop building, Grade II listed, will be retained for academic use; further development is planned for the rest of the site.

One hundred years after the Western Bank foundation stone was laid, workmen accidentally broke through a 'time capsule' left there in 1903. The contents included a print of the architect's design, a copy of the ground plan, and a list of all those invited to the stone-laying ceremony.

to release funds to invest in academic development. A 'Public Private Partnership' was sought as a means of managing the residences, providing new accommodation, and transferring the demand risk to the private partner. After several years of work, an agreement acceptable to the University could not be reached and this project was abandoned. Council decided to retain and redevelop the Endcliffe site and to dispose of some peripheral sites and street properties, in favour of new student accommodation in the city centre. The street properties were to be sold with covenants to ensure that the properties returned to private family ownership, a response to previous criticism by neighbourhood groups that students were 'swamping' Broomhill and Crookes.[19] Meanwhile, an ambitious plan was developed to update the accommodation at Endcliffe and Ranmoor by creating a 'student village' with a central social building. Some halls would be demolished in order to create new residences with modern en-suite bedrooms, and greater provision of flats. The number of students accommodated on these sites would rise from 3,500 to about 5,000, but existing green spaces like 'The Paddock' would be retained. As the University approached its Centenary, these plans were presented for public consultation. They represented the University's most ambitious attempt to rethink its residential strategy. At the start of its second century, student residences would be updated, some unpopular buildings would be demolished, and the balance of student and family accommodation in neighbourhoods like Broomhill and Endcliffe would be improved.

Plans for a Learning Resources Centre (LRC) on Upper Hanover Street were agreed in 2002. This was the flagship project of the Learning and Teaching Strategy, with the aim of facilitating student-centred learning. The LRC would provide the most modern electronic resources in a prominent building next to the Brook Hill roundabout. The Library and CiCS (Corporate Information and Computing Services) designed the interior resources, to include multiple copies of course textbooks and a range of electronic facilities. Unfortunately significant reductions in the teaching grant which affected all Russell Group universities meant that the original scheme could not be built. The University agreed a revised investment for learning and teaching, which was still some £16 million. The modified plans for the building were approved by the City Council in the summer of 2004, and the opening of the Learning Resources Centre is scheduled for 2006.

Two developments of the greatest strategic significance for the future planning of the estate occurred in the years 2001–4. The first was the acquisition in 2001 of the Jessop Hospital site from the Sheffield Teaching Hospitals Trust. This large site is of immense importance, since it lies between the two parts of the campus and provides an invaluable future academic land bank for the University. The University has thus been given the chance to complete the 'Portobello link' between its two sites – the dream of every Vice-Chancellor. The second development was the acquisition of the Health and Safety Executive site and buildings on Broad Lane. The existing modern building will be named the Kroto Research Institute and Centre for Nanoscience and Technology; and the site can accommodate a multidisciplinary engineering research centre as well as 'incubator' space to foster the development of new companies. SRIF funding of £10 million has already been awarded for these developments. A 'bio-incubator' is to open in 2005 as one of the first new buildings on the Jessop site. In 2003 the University completed a Development Framework to assist its planning and the development of the estate over the next ten to twenty years.

Our University, by Joe Scarborough, commissioned to celebrate the Centenary, represents a kaleidoscopic view of the University and the activities of its staff and students over its first 100 years.

The Future

As it reaches its centenary the standing and strength of the University has never been greater. For example, in 2004 it was listed as seventh in the United Kingdom in a league table produced by Shanghai Jiao Tong University which rated universities worldwide by the standard of education, quality of the faculty, research output and size of the institution.[20] This recognition would have delighted Sir Charles Eliot, Sheffield's orientalist Vice-Chancellor (1905–12). Such achievement at the highest levels was undreamt of for many years, and is a tribute to the members of staff who maintained and improved the University of Sheffield during the first century of its development.

The challenge in 2005 is to build on this position of strength, particularly in the areas of research excellence, which now encompass every faculty. The current opportunity to develop the estate is the best that the University has had for several generations. Postgraduates will become an even more important sector of growth within Russell Group universities. Higher undergraduate fees, to be introduced in September 2006, promise additional income and investment in the learning and teaching environment, but challenge the universities to maintain the diversity of the student population. Sheffield has, however, shown itself to be sensitive to this issue over many years and is well prepared. Visionary leadership, sound strategic direction and academic excellence remain the keys to continued future success.

Arthur Chapman concluded his Jubilee history of the University with the following words:

> So the University approached its fiftieth birthday, after a career marked by many vicissitudes and some perils. It had grown greatly in numbers; the range of its activities far exceeded the dreams of its founders; from a local college it had become a national institution, and not a few of its members had known the good fortune of which the ancient poet sang,
>
> *Felix qui potuit rerum cognoscere causas*[21]
>
> (Virgil *Georgics* ii.490)

In its first century the University of Sheffield has developed into an institution renowned internationally for the excellence of its research, and for learning and teaching enhanced by a research-informed environment. It has become one of the finest universities in the country. And yet it has remained true to the aspirations of its founders; it is a University for the people and for its city. It can look forward to its second century and to the achievement of even greater things with confidence.

Sic itur ad astra[22]

(Virgil *Aeneid* IX.641)

Sources and Acknowledgments

Steel City Scholars is based almost entirely on sources collected or generated by the University of Sheffield. The University Archive includes copies of its major publications, especially the *Annual Report* and the annually produced *Calendar* in complete runs going back to Firth College days. The minutes of the main University committees are preserved in bound volumes and there are many collections of correspondence and other records. Although faithfully preserved by generations of university administrators, these records were scattered in several locations around the campus when the Centenary History project started and only those held in the Main Library were listed. Matthew Zawadzki was appointed to the new post of Records Manager in 2002 and has been engaged since then in locating and listing Archive materials and in uniting them in a single repository in the Main Library.

The University has an impressive collection of newspaper cuttings in a full run dating back to its foundation. These helped to provide the essential external perspective. Sheffield's local newspapers gave the viewpoint of the city and its more vocal inhabitants on the activities of the University. The University of Sheffield hit the national headlines on a number of occasions (*The News of the World* only once) and the advent of serious higher educational journalism, represented by *Times Higher Education Supplement* and the Education sections of *The Guardian* and *The Independent*, provided invaluable material for the later chapters of this History.

The Students' Union published its own newspaper, beginning with a handwritten gem entitled *IT* and progressing to *Darts*, which regularly won the *Guardian* award for student newspapers and lasted for fifty years. It was recently replaced by *Steel City Press*. The first University publication for staff was *The University of Sheffield Gazette* (1948–80), which contained articles, often several pages long, about the work of departments, together with retirement and obituary notices. The *Newsletter* was introduced in 1970 and evolved into a newspaper format – snappy articles, generously illustrated, with publication at shorter intervals. This was edited for much of its existence by Roger Allum, the University's long-serving Director of Public Relations. In 2003, *Overview* and *E-view*, a web publication, took its place.

The tone of the University's publications changed markedly around 1980, when public relations became an important consideration. Before that, the details of failures and disappointments were recorded along with the successes and the *Annual Reports* could be unnecessarily modest about genuine achievement. Thereafter the reverse is the case and it can be difficult for the historian to separate the truly significant advance from the multitude of initiatives which promised much but proved transitory. Sheffield was simply following a national trend, of course; universities were in competition with each other and every publication had to present a positive image.

We thought it essential to supplement the material within the University's collections with the direct personal reminiscences of students and staff. In the case of students, a Convocation appeal for written contributions was spearheaded by David Bradshaw, who was delighted to receive a warm response, particularly from students who were then of retirement age. These letters, some very expansive, are preserved as the Convocation Centenary History Archive. In order to extend the number of responses from post-1960 graduates, an email questionnaire was sent to all those for whom the Alumni Office had an email address. The database had recently been updated and we were gratified to receive almost 1,000 replies. Inevitably, only a small amount of this material could be quoted but the size of the collection means that the stories chosen are always representative of many more. They are cited anonymously as 'Alumni Questionnaire' in the notes. We thank all the graduates who responded to our requests for help.

The staff interview project got off to a flying start when the retired Registrar and Secretary Francis Orton presented us with a collection of cassettes. These were interviews he had conducted in the early 1980s with leading members of the University during the previous three decades, including the former Vice-Chancellor Jack Whittaker who died two years after the interview. The Centenary History would be poorer without his memories of the Jubilee and the many candid comments made during these conversations with Orton. Other interviews were conducted by members of the Editorial Board; the choice of subjects was designed to encompass the breadth of the University and the experience of its most senior members of staff. These are an important source for the last three chapters of the History and are not specifically referenced except where the context demands it. It is our intention to place all this material in the University archives in due course. We are most grateful to all those who agreed to be interviewed.

Francis Orton interviews

Arthur Connell, Alex Currie, Robert Hopper, Billy Ibberson, Roy Johnson, Harry Kay, Eric Laughton, Peter Linacre, Frank Pierce, Arthur Quarrell, Jim Tolson, Roderick Urquhart, Jack Whittaker, Gerard Young.

Centenary History interviews

Neil Atherton, Eric Bagnall, Chris Barker, Stephen de Bartolomé, Stuart Bennett, Frank Benson, Clyde Binfield, Martin Black, Norman Blake, David Bland, Paul Blomfield, Robert Boucher, Keith Branigan, Kate Carr, Ian Cooke, Tony Crook, Alex Currie, Gordon Daniels, Graeme Davies,

Alec Daykin, Eileen Denman, Frank Ellis, David Fletcher, Heather Foster, Dorothy Freeman, Andrew Gamble, Reg Goodchild, Eddie Haslam, John Hawthorne, Mary Holding, Ron Johnston, Ian Kershaw, Julian Kinderlerer, Bernard Kingston, Linda Kirk, Colin Lago, Peter Lee, David Luscombe, Nigel Mathers, David McClean, Ian McLure, Peter Middleton, Keith Miller, Roy Millington, Lucy Mitchell, John Nicholson, Francis Orton, John Padley, Helen Pollard, Gareth Roberts, Alan Roper, Christine Sexton, Patrick Seyd, Geoffrey Sims, Geoff Tattersall, George Tolley, Stephen Ware, John Widdowson, David Williams, Arthur Willis, John Wood, Frank Woods, Diana and Gerard Young.

We sought to supplement the interviews with a general appeal for the written reminiscences of members of staff, both current and retired. We thank all those who troubled to respond: many of these reminiscences are specifically cited in the Notes under the heading 'Staff Centenary History Archive'. Discussions were held with selected groups of staff, in particular retired administrators, departments in the Engineering faculty, the School of Nursing & Midwifery, and the departments of Physics and Mathematics.

Roger Harper prepared an outline history of the University's buildings which was used as the basis for the account of its architectural history. Len Hill's history of the biology departments was used in the same way, and both acted as consultants throughout the project. Bernard Argent, Robert Edyvean, Geoffrey Greenwood and Adrian Taylor gave particular help with the history of applied science. Harold Swan's knowledge of the history of the early Medical School is unrivalled and he gave copious and invaluable advice. George Hudson provided information on the later history of the medical faculty, and David Jones and Betty Kershaw advised on the School of Nursing & Midwifery. Gareth Roberts provided information for chapter 7 and gave his opinion on the selection of featured research; Geoffrey Sims commented on chapter 6 and Bob Boucher on the Postscript. In addition to the Editorial Board, those who read chapter drafts included Paul Blomfield, who advised on the history of the Students' Union, and Reg Goodchild. Many members of staff, both current and retired, answered queries and checked drafts of particular sections: their contributions are specifically acknowledged in the Notes. To all those who provided information for *Steel City Scholars* we are most grateful. None of them is, of course, responsible for the final interpretation.

Lawrence Aspden was a helpful guide in the early stages of finding material in the Special Collections and Archives of the Main Library. Roger Allum and Ann James of the Public Relations office located many items of information among their own collection of records. Librarians at the Local Studies Collection of the Sheffield Central Library, and at the Sheffield Newspapers Library, provided extra material, including some photographs. GMW Architects (formerly Gollins, Melvin and Ward) made their archives available to us.

Charlotte Brownhill compiled the original database of student and staff statistics used for Appendix 4. An enthusiastic group of postgraduates, Marco Ajovalasit, Joe

Langley, Sebastian Sethe, Alan Smalley and Raymond Yeap, conducted several interviews and supplemented our material on the history of the Students' Union. Interviews were transcribed by Pam Broadhead, Ellie Button, Pat Holland, Jeanette Newcombe, Shirley Rhodes, Margaret Rose and Jane Zambouras. Pam Broadhead also gave secretarial help to the author.

As the author, I would like to give my personal thanks to Ian Kershaw, who encouraged me to undertake the project, and to my History colleagues, who have been consistently interested in my progress. My family and friends have been unfailingly supportive. David Tomkins provided the perspective of an external reader and both my husband Nigel Mathers and my father Keith Robinson read drafts of every chapter.

This History would not have been possible without the help of a dedicated team, the Editorial Board, which collectively represented well over two hundred years of experience of the life and work of the University of Sheffield. All facts have been checked, all statements scrutinised and all opinions debated. In the final analysis, however, it is not the University nor the Editorial Board but the author who must take responsibility for the selection of material and for the opinions expressed in this Centenary History.

Helen Mathers

PICTURE CREDITS

The great majority of the illustrations in this book are drawn from the University's own collections, including those in the Union of Students. The Editorial Board is most grateful to all who have helped to locate items and to make them available.

In addition, sincere thanks are due to the following organisations and individuals who have supplied materials or given permission for images to be reproduced:

Clyde Binfield; Bridgeman Art Library; Michael Cable; Chris Dowd; Guardian Newspapers Ltd (proprietors of *The Observer*); Anne Murdoch; Douglas Northcott; John Robson; Royal College of Art; Sheffield Galleries and Museums Trust; Sheffield Teaching Hospitals NHS Trust; Sheffield Libraries, Archives and Information Services (Local Studies Library); Sheffield Newspapers Ltd; Trustees of the Firth Almshouses, Sheffield; David Welsh; *Yorkshire Post*.

British stamps are reproduced by kind permission of Royal Mail Group plc.

Maps are based upon Ordnance Survey mapping with permission of the Ordnance Survey on behalf of the Controller of Her Majesty's Stationery Office, © Crown Copyright reserved ED100018617.

Every effort has been made to trace copyright holders; any omissions notified to the publisher will be corrected as opportunity offers.

ABBREVIATIONS USED IN NOTES AND BIBLIOGRAPHY

AR	*University of Sheffield Annual Report*
Gazette	*University of Sheffield Gazette*
NL	*University of Sheffield Newsletter*
USL	*University of Sheffield Library*
US	*University of Sheffield administrative archive*

Collections within the University Archive

US/CHA	*Chapman collection*
CHI	*Centenary History Interview*
FOI	*Francis Orton Interview*
Biog. Coll.	*Staff Obituary and Biography Collection*
CCHA	*Convocation Centenary History Archive*
AQ	*Alumni questionnaire*
SCHA	*Staff Centenary History Archive (written submissions)*
USUS	*University of Sheffield Union of Students*

Local Newspapers

SI	*Sheffield Independent*
S Tel	*Sheffield Telegraph (daily morning paper until 8. 2. 86; reissued as a weekly from 6. 10. 89)*

Star	*The Star* (daily evening paper)
YP	*Yorkshire Post*

National Newspapers

THES	*Times Higher Education Supplement*
Indep	*The Independent*
Guardian	*The Guardian*
Times	*The Times*

Others

FRS Biog Mem	*Biographical Memoirs of Fellows of the Royal Society.*
DNB	*Dictionary of National Biography**
BMJ	*British Medical Journal*
UP	*University Press*
AP	*Academic Press*
Pam.	*pamphlet*
T/S	*typescript*

*note: The new Oxford Dictionary of National Biography (ODNB) was published too late for inclusion in these Notes.

Notes

CHAPTER 1

1. Quoted by Sheldon Rothblatt, *Tradition and change in English liberal education*, London 1976, p.186.
2. One of the traditional milestones of civic progress is the building of a town hall commensurate with its size and wealth. Sheffield's was opened in 1897, far later than these other cities.
3. See Gordon W. Roderick and Michael Stephens, *Education and Industry in the nineteenth century*, London and New York 1978.
4. Rothblatt, *Tradition and change*, pp.164–5.
5. Michael Sanderson, *The universities in the nineteenth century*, London and Boston 1975, p.79.
6. Bristol gained its royal charter in 1909, Nottingham in 1948 and Newcastle in 1963.
7. Michael Sanderson is unusual among historians in not recognising this. See *The universities in the nineteenth century*, p.10 and *The Universities and British Industry 1850–1970*, London 1972, p.104.
8. Sir Isambard Owen of Bristol, quoted in Sanderson, *Universities and British industry*, p.82.
9. Sanderson, *Universities and British industry*, p.104; See also P. H. J. H. Gosden & A. J. Taylor, *Studies in the history of a university 1874–1974*, Leeds 1975, pp.11–12.
10. W. H. G. Armytage, *Civic Universities, Aspects of a British tradition*, London 1955, p.256.
11. Quoted by Thomas Kelly, *A History of Adult Education in Great Britain*, Liverpool 1970, p.227.
12. Sarah Barnes, 'Crossing the invisible line: establishing co-education at the University of Manchester and Northwestern University', *History of Education* Vol 23, No 1, 1994, pp.39–48.
13. See Carol Dyhouse, *No distinction of sex? Women in British universities 1870–1939*, London 1995, pp.33–5.
14. Helen Mathers, 'Scientific women in a co-educational university. Sheffield 1879–1939' to be published in *History of Education*.
15. Julie Gibert, 'Women students and student life at England's civic universities before the First World War', *History of Education* Vol 23, No 4, 1994, p.406.
16. J. Yates, *Thoughts on the advancement of academical education in England*,

quoted by Sanderson, *The universities in the nineteenth century*, p.57.

17. Hugh Kearney, *Scholars and gentlemen: universities and society in pre-industrial Britain 1500–1700*, London 1970, p.180.

18. Sanderson, *The universities in the nineteenth century*, p.208.

19. Kearney, *Scholars and gentlemen*, pp.179–80.

20. Sanderson, *The universities in the nineteenth century*, p.7.

21. The phrase is that of Moore, first Professor of Biochemistry at Liverpool University, quoted by Roderick and Stephens, *Education and Industry*, p.102.

22. Quoted Sanderson, *The universities in the nineteenth century*, p.115.

23. Sanderson, *The universities in the nineteenth century*, p.19.

24. From George Gissing, *Born in exile*, London 1892, 1894 edn, p.11. Quoted Sanderson, *ibid*, p.160.

25. Figures from the 1871 census cited by Dennis Smith, *Conflict and compromise: class formation in English society 1830–1914*, London 1982, tables 10,12,13, pp.65–72. 'Persons of independent means' are included in the middle-class total.

26. David Hey, *A history of Sheffield*, Lancaster 1998, pp.177–184.

27. A. K. Osborne (ed), *An encyclopaedia of the iron and steel industry*, London 1956, 2nd edn 1967, pp.159–60.

28. This was the first Ranmoor House. See chapter 4, p.141.

29. A. W. Chapman, *The story of a modern university: a history of the University of Sheffield*, Oxford 1955, p.14. The Extension movement is described by Kelly, History of adult education, pp.218–240.

30. Miss Shrewsbury and Miss Keeling are named in an article in *Floreamus* Vol 1 (1897–1901), p.113. This was only the second year of Extension activities in the north of England, see N. A. Jepson, *The beginnings of English university adult education – policy and problems*, London 1973, p.41.

31. Quoted by Kelly, *History of adult education*, p.227.

32. Statistics from Chapman, p.17.

33. Kelly, *History of adult education*, pp.220, 225, 232. Moulton later wrote a book about the University Extension movement.

34. *SI* 1 May 1877. This comment confirms that it was mostly middle-class people who attended at this stage – a common experience of the Extension movement, see Jepson, *The beginnings*, pp.105–6.

35. Quoted Chapman, p.22. He includes the full text of this crucial Executive Committee memorandum.

36. Prince Leopold's address to the opening ceremony; *SI* 21 October 1879.

37. See Chapman's comments, p.23.

38. See speech at opening ceremony, quoted by Chapman, p.24.

39. W. M. Hicks, 'October 1879 and after', *Arrows* Vol 1, No 3, Dec 1929; Chapman, pp.26–7.

40. See Kelly, *History of adult education*, p.224.

41. *SI* 21 Oct 1879.

42. Sanderson, *The universities and British industry*, p.119.

43. This episode is described by W. M. Hicks, 'October 1879 and after'.

44. These were transcribed in some detail in a biography written by his wife, Katharine Viriamu Jones, *The life of John Viriamu Jones*, London 1915, pp.50–85. Subsequent quotations in this paragraph are taken from pp.64, 61, 72, 69. Jones was named after the missionary martyr, John Williams – 'Viriamu' was the closest that his south seas converts could come to pronouncing 'Williams', *ibid*, p.12.

45. Quoted *ibid*, p.71. Other quotations in this paragraph are taken from p.73.

46. *Ibid*, p.60.

47. Comment by A. E. Barnes in letter to A. W. Chapman, 16.4.55, US/CHA/13/4. For Hicks, see Royal Society obituary by S. R. Milner, Hicks MSS, US. *Arrows* 18, Dec 1934, pp.10–11.

48. Firth College, AR 1888, quoted by Milner, *ibid*.

49. See correspondence between A. W. Chapman and Morris W. Travers, US/CHA/13/4. Travers wrote a biography of Ramsay: *A life of Sir William Ramsay*, London 1956.

50. 'Do you remember: the memoirs of Albert Ernest Dunstan', T/S, US/CHA/1/1.

51. *IT* Vol II, Spasm 5, October 1895.

52. 'Do you remember: the memoirs of Albert Ernest Dunstan', T/S, US/CHA/1/1.

53. *S Tel* 26.6.22.

54. A. E. Barnes, letter to Chapman.

55. See T/S notes by Chapman, US/CHA/13/2(iv).

56. This paragraph has been compiled from US/CHA/8/10 (job applications) and Firth College, *Prospectus*, 1886–7; 1887–8; 1888–9; 1889–90; 1890–91. A further interesting aspect was that the chair of Classics was vacant when this post was advertised and was offered to W. C. F. Anderson shortly afterwards.

57. Chapman, p.82. For Moore Smith, see obituary by J. Dover Wilson, *Proceedings of the British Academy* 30(1944), pp.361–377 and by C. J. Sisson and G. R. Potter, *Biog Coll*.

58. Dover Wilson, *ibid*, p.12. Even Chapman says that he was 'ill at ease' with women students, p.82.

59. *Floreamus* Vol XI, June 1924, p.249.

60. E. D. Mackerness, *Somewhere further north: a history of music in Sheffield*, Sheffield 1974, pp.86–121; H. Coward obituary *S Tel* 12.6.44.

61. For this paragraph, see H. Dent, *The training of teachers in England and Wales 1800–1975*, London 1977 p.33; Roy Millington, *A history of the City of Sheffield Training College*, Sheffield 1955, pp.13–18.

62. 'Memoir of Mrs Lysbeth Dawson

Henry 1856–1946', T/S, *Biog Coll*. With thanks to her grand-daughter Anne Murdoch for supplying this. See also Millington, *City of Sheffield Training College*, p.18.

63. Report quoted by Chapman, p.84.

64. See comments by A. E. Barnes in letter to Chapman, 16.4.55, US/CHA/13/4.

65. Letter from Ernest Cotton to Chapman, 15. 5. 55, US/CHA/13/4.

66. See Chapman, pp.87–8 for Stephenson's letter, which in one business-like paragraph surmounted not only the decision to build but also the methods of funding.

67. See Chapman, p.39.

68. See *History of the University of Sheffield to the time of its coming-of-age, 31 May 1926*, pamphlet (USL) pp.3–4.

69. CH Firth later became Regius Professor of Modern History at Oxford University, D. N. B. 1931–40 pp.272–275.

70. Jones, *John Viriamu Jones*, p.64.

71. J. H. Stainton, *The Making of Sheffield 1865–1914*, Sheffield 1924, pp.345–6; W. Odom, Hallamshire Worthies, Sheffield 1926, pp.91–2.

72. See, for example, *History of the University of Sheffield to the time of its coming-of-age*, p.4.

73. *Ibid*, pp.4–5.

74. John Roach, 'The Company and the community. Charity, education and technology' in *Mesters to masters: a history of the Company of Cutlers in Hallamshire*, eds. Clyde Binfield and David Hey, Oxford 1997, p.248. Roach stresses that the Company had very little money at this time.

75. *S Tel*, 2.2.1886.

76. *S Tel*, 2.2.1886

77. Chapman believed these grants secured the future of the school – see letter to Morris Travers, 26.1.54, US/CHA/13/4.

78. For example, Stuart Uttley, a 'Lib-Lab' file cutter, who was also on the Technical Committee of the School.

79. Chapman, pp.42, 72.

80. J. O. Arnold, Royal Society obituary, *Biog Coll*.

81. J. H. Andrew, Memorandum, US/CHA/2/14.

82. J. H. Andrew, Memorandum. Information given to Chapman by W. E. Harris, US/CHA/1/2.

83. W. G. Fearnsides, Memorandum, 1944, US/CHA/2/4.

84. Chapman, pp.20–21; 225, Sorby MSS (US) and *Biog Coll*.

85. Obituary of W. R. Ripper by F. C. Turner, *Sheffield University Magazine*, Vol 1. No 1, Dec 1937.

86. *Ibid*

87. Extract from Technical School Prospectus 1896–7, quoted by Chapman, p.79; J. H. Andrew, Memorandum.

88. The main sources for this section are Harold T. Swan, 'Sheffield Medical School: origins and influences', *Journal of Medical Biography*, 1994, 2: 22–32 [Swan]; Porter, *The medical school in Sheffield 1828–1928*, Sheffield 1928 [Porter]; Arthur J. Hall, Notes on the *Sheffield School of Medicine*, T/S, 1944 (USL) [Hall]; Chapman, pp.103–132. I am grateful to Harold Swan for further information and advice.

89. For early nineteenth century medical education, see E. M. Brockbank, *The foundation of provincial medical education*, Manchester 1936, which is mostly about Manchester; *The history of the Birmingham Medical School*, Birmingham 1925 and Charles Newman, *The evolution of medical education in the nineteenth century*, Oxford, 1957.

90. Swan, p.24.

91. *History of the Birmingham Medical School*, p.4.

92. *Sheffield Iris* 19 Feb 1828.

93. *Sheffield Iris* 27 Jan 1835 and 3 Feb 1835 (letter from Samuel Roberts). The premises were described as a 'museum' but Swan believes this to be incorrect.

94. The lecturers 1844–97 are listed in

Chapman, App.C, pp.474–478. For Bartolomé, see S. Snell, *Sheffield General Infirmary*, pp.71–76. *Biog Coll*; Hall, pp.47–8.

95. Sanderson, *The universities in the nineteenth century*, p.81.

96. Porter, pp.98–99.

97. The story of the curriculum is complex and too detailed to tell here. See Newman, *The evolution of medical education*, pp.207–224.

98. See Council's report to the lecturers quoted in Porter, pp.37–8.

99. Hall, p.8. Subsequent quotations taken from pp9, 18, 21, 27–8.

100. Newman, *The evolution of medical education*, pp.41–7. Swan points out that Newman's research is based on London and that the Edinburgh School appears to have been more salubrious.

101. See Chapman, pp.90–1 and the next section of this chapter.

102. *S Tel*, 23.10.1886.

103. A. E. Barnes, *Medical student days*, T/S, US/CHA/2/7; Chapman, p.124. Barnes's story was confirmed by Arthur Hall.

104. For Arthur Hall, see also *Gazette* 10, Feb 1951, pp.2–4 and Hall MSS, (USL).

105. A. E. Barnes, *Medical student days*, p.18.

106. *SI* 22.6.1893.

107. *SI* 6.2.1897.

108. *IT*, reproduced in Chapman, p.101

109. For Stephenson, see Chapman, pp.19–20; *Floreamus*, No. 10, Dec 1900.

110. Chapman, p.132.

111. It is extensively analysed by Chapman, pp.133–48 and App.A.

112. The report was eventually sent by the Vice-Chancellor, after a second request, on 4 November.

113. See Chapman, App.A. The report is included together with the College's detailed comments. These comments were never sent, or made public in this form.

114. Chapman, App.A, p.449. See also A. N. Shimmin, *The University of*

Leeds: the first half-century, Cambridge 1954. Shimmin quotes the opinion of the Bryce Commission, 1894/5, that the Yorkshire College could not claim, outside its Medical School, to be doing much work of university standard, pp.19–20.

115. Chapman, p.449.
116. See Chapman, pp.176–8; Sanderson, *The universities in the nineteenth century*, pp.217–8. Armytage emphasises the example set by Birmingham on becoming an independent university in 1900, *Civic universities*, p.245.
117. Quoted by Chapman, p.177.
118. *SDT* 10.6.1898.
119. Hicks, 'October 1879 and after'.
120. References and quotes in this paragraph taken by Chapman from *IT*, 1897–99. See US/CHA/2/25.
121. *Floreamus* No. 13, Dec 1901, pp.20–21.
122. MS sent to A. W. Chapman, 8.11.51, US/CHA/13/2(iv).
123. In a sample year, 1901–2, there were eight in a total membership of thirty which also included nine lawyers, three doctors and six members of academic staff. University College, Sheffield, *Calendar*, 1901–2; *White's Directory of Sheffield*, 1902.
124. Chapman, p.153. For parallel developments in other colleges, see Sanderson, *The universities and British industry*, pp.208–9.
125. AT Baker, *Biog Coll*.
126. See Chapman, pp.154–6.
127. The following account is based on Roy Millington, *A History of the City of Sheffield Training College*, Sheffield 1955, pp.18–28.
128. See Chapman, p.162. The exact nature of the lack of provision is not clear from the surviving records, as quoted in Millington, *History of the City of Sheffield Training College*, p.19.
129. Morris W. Travers, letter to Irvine Masson 11.10.49, US/CHA/13/4.
130. W. P. Wynne, speech at dinner to honour his 21 years as Professor of Chemistry, 12 Sept 1925, US/CHA/2/3.
131. A. S. Barnes, *Medical student days*.
132. University College, Sheffield, *AR 1904/5*,
133. 20.12.00. US/CHA/5/2.

CHAPTER 2

1. For a valuable account of these years, see Sanderson, *The universities in the nineteenth century*, pp.207–14.
2. Eric Ives, Diane Drummond and Leonard Schwarz, *The first civic university*. Birmingham 1880–1980, Birmingham 2000, p.117.
3. Elizabeth J. Morse, 'The English civic universities and the myth of decline', *History of Universities* Vol XI, 1992, 177–204, pp.182–3.
4. Quoted by H. C. Dent, *The Universities in Transition*, London 1961, p.61.
5. W. Ripper to James Mair, 27.3.19, US/CHA/1/19.
6. Ives, Drummond and Schwarz, *The first civic university*, p.117.
7. Report of the University Colleges Committee, 1907, quoted by Dent, *Universities in transition*, pp.63–4.
8. Ives, Drummond and Schwarz, *The first civic university*, pp.111–27.
9. See Shimmin, *The University of Leeds. The first half-century*, p.49.
10. 1897 was the first occasion that the Council expressed interest in buying property 'near Weston Park'. See Chapman, p.170.
11. The Council was advised that the Wesley College building could not be converted for less than £8,000 and would even then not be satisfactory. Soon afterwards it became King Edward VII Grammar School for Boys.
12. Minutes of the New Building Committee, 1 April 1903, University College, Sheffield, *Sundry Committees Minute Book*, 1891–1905.
13. Letter from Ensor Drury, 16.1.02, quoted Chapman, p.179.
14. Meeting of the College Court on 18th May 1903, reported in *1903 A University for Sheffield*, Sheffield 1903, p.16. In March 1903 the College prepared a statement to prove, statistically, 'the practical equality of the two Colleges at Leeds and Sheffield in relation to their fitness for University powers'. USL/CHA/1/5(i).
15. *1903 A University for Sheffield*, p.11. Further quotations in this paragraph are taken from pp.10 & 13 and *Floreamus*, Vol II, p.166.
16. Drafts of the petition sent to the King in 1903 are preserved in USL/CHA/1/5(i).
17. Mappin to Hall, 31.3.03, USL/CHA/1/5(i)
18. *Floreamus*, Vol II, Dec 1904, pp.300–04.
19. 3 Mar 1904, USL/CHA/1/5(ii). Sheffield's petition against the proposal to create the 'Victoria University of Yorkshire' in Leeds went to the House of Lords, as subsequent correspondence shows.
20. Drafts of the Charter are preserved in USL/CHA/1/5(i). A first version provides that 'women shall be eligible for any office in the University and . . . all degrees and courses of study in the University shall be open to women'. Another Ordinance stated that 'no religious test shall be imposed upon any person . . . and that no theological teaching shall be given by or under the authority of the University'. This last *proviso* was omitted from the final version.
21. *Floreamus*, Vol II, pp.374–5. There is a full account in *SDT* 3.6.05 & 5.6.05.
22. See ref. 1, Chapman, p.196 and the programme, 'Visit of His Majesty King Edward VII and Her Majesty Queen Alexandra to open the new building, July 12 1905' (USL).
23. See *Floreamus* Vol V June 1912,

p.239, for an assessment of his time in Sheffield. The Senate passed a resolution supporting Eliot's appointment but deploring the omission of the academic staff. This was rectified for all subsequent vice-chancellor appointments, see Chapman, pp.194–5.

24. *SDT* 30.6.05. *The Telegraph*, a Conservative newspaper, took Lansdowne's side in this dispute, calling Eliot an 'erring subordinate' with 'extraordinary pretensions'.

25. 'Coming of Age celebrations 1926, Conferment of Honorary degrees 1st July 1926' Programme, US/CHA/7/9.

26. Comparable figures: 1913/4, Sheffield – £17,226; Leeds – £16,022; 1921/2, Sheffield – £39,691; Leeds – £28,766. Taken from *UGC Statistics* quoted by Steve Sturdy [see note 66], pp.53–4.

27. Chapman, p.206. Wynne is referring to the Old Testament story of Jacob who served seven years to marry Rachel (Genesis ch. 29)

28. Minutes of Senate, 18 Mar. & 5 May 1908, Vol II.

29. The university ordinances were changed to allow 'substantive' doctorates, see Minutes of Senate, Vol II, 2 & 6 June 1908.

30. Chapman, p.209.

31. *SI* 10.2.06. See also *Floreamus* Vol III, March 1906, pp.56–9.

32. *SDT* 10. 2.06

33. W. E. S. Turner, 'The early years of the University Chemistry department', T/S, US/CHA/2/3.

34. Thomas Kelly, *For advancement of learning: the University of Liverpool 1881–1981*, Liverpool 1981, p.169.

35. Dyhouse, *No distinction of sex?*, p.24

36. See W. P. W[ynne], 'The playing fields at Norton', *Floreamus* Vol IV, March 1910, pp.49–53.

37. *SDT* 17.10.10.

38. *The Blade* No. 1, April 1905. (USL)

39. W. P. Wynne, Speech made at dinner to honour 21 years as professor of chemistry, 1925, T/S,

US/CHA/8/15; W. E. S. Turner, 'The early years of the University Chemistry department'; Emily Turner MSS, USL; A. W. Chapman, Obituary of Wynne, *Biog Coll*. Quotations in this paragraph are taken from Chapman's Obituary.

40. W. E. S. Turner, *ibid*.

41. This was C. R. Young, see W. E. S. Turner, *ibid*.

42. Obituary of Emily Turner by A. W. Chapman, *Biog Coll*.

43. Letter from Emily Turner, 13.7.50, Emily Turner MSS.

44. Turner, 'The early years of the University Chemistry department'.

45. I am grateful to Gary McCulloch for showing me a proof copy of his article on Green in *ODNB*.

46. Article by J. A. Green, *Floreamus*, Vol III, June 1906, pp.68–70.

47. See chapter 1, Dent, *The training of teachers*, p.61.

48. In a letter to Albert Hobson (University Treasurer) on 18 May 1906, Eliot stated that it 'cannot be businesslike' to adopt a policy which resulted in the loss of these grants. Quoted Chapman, p.215.

49. C. Eliot and J. A. Green, 'Report on the relations of the Training College to the University of Sheffield', May 1906, T/S, US/CHA/2/17.

50. The scheme made the Principal of the Training College a member of the Arts faculty and Senate. During this period, the College took the title 'University of Sheffield Teachers' College'. See Roy Millington, *A history of the City of Sheffield Training College*, pp.34–5 and Dent, *The training of teachers*, p.61.

51. Quoted by Chapman, p.215.

52. See A. B. Robertson, *A Century of change: the study of education in the University of Manchester*, n. d. 1990, chapter 1.

53. R. Mather, 'Early days at St George's Square', *Journal of Sheffield University Metallurgical Society*, Vol 1 1962, p.30.

54. *Sunday Chronicle*, 8.3.08.

55. See reports on the mining department, 1909 and 1918–19, US/CHA/2/12(i) and Professor's memo, quoted in Chapman, p.247.

56. Obituary of Armstrong, *Floreamus*, Vol X, Dec 1921, pp.112–4. For new building, see letter from D. Hay to Gibbons, Feb 1924, US/CHA/2/12(i).

57. E. J. Thackeray, 'Some personal reminiscences of the Department of Metallurgy of the University of Sheffield', T/S, US/CHA/2/14.

58. See Michael Sanderson, *The universities and British industry*, pp.88–89. Letters from Arnold declining to publish in *Times and Nature* can be found in his correspondence files (USL), Feb 4 & 6, 1909.

59. Arnold to Hughes, Feb 11 1909, Arnold correspondence.

60. See Arnold to Hatfield, Mar 3 1909 and to Hughes, the solicitor for Sheffield Steel Manufacturers Ltd, Mar 8 1909, Arnold correspondence.

61. Arnold to Hughes, Feb 11 1909, Arnold correspondence.

62. Sanderson, *The universities and British industry*, pp.102–3.

63. Arnold made his case in letters to W. E. Clegg, the chairman of the Applied Science Committee, pointing out that although the department's degrees were 'unique' they were presented by Ripper, as head of the faculty, August 30 1916, US/CHA/1/2(ii).

64. Chapman talks about 'a period of quiet development', p.228, but it will become clear that this is an under-estimation of what was going on.

65. Porter, *Appendix*, p.95. [The appendix, which deals with 1905–28, was actually written by Arthur Hall, after Porter's death.]

66. Steve Sturdy, 'The political economy of scientific medicine: science, education and the transformation of medical practice in Sheffield, 1890–1922', *Medical History* 36 (2), April 1992, 125–59, p.136. This

article is a major source for this section [hereafter Sturdy].

67. Hall, *Appendix to Porter*, p.96.
68. The tradition of appointing the Medical Officer of Health as a lecturer in public health continued until 1946, when the city established its own laboratories. See Sturdy, pp.131–2.
69. See copy of memorandum by P. E. Barber, US/CHA/2/7(ii); Sturdy, p.142.
70. Sturdy, pp.133–4.
71. Sturdy, pp.134,138. In the 1920s Hall and Barnes advised the local health authority over an outbreak of enchephalitis; Hall's extensive research made him an 'authority of international standing' on the disease, *ibid*, pp.138–9.
72. Even so, Sheffield was the last of the civic universities to have a full-time physiology lecturer; Leeds had one in 1884. See Stella V. F. Butler, 'Centers and Peripheries: The development of British Physiology 1870–1914', *Journal of the History of Biology*, Vol 21, No. 3, 1988, 473–500, p.478.
73. Sturdy, pp.141–2.
74. Hall, p.66.
75. Hall, p.74.
76. See Sturdy, p.140. The grant for clinical teaching was awarded in February 1911 after interminable correspondence with the hospitals, preserved in US/CHA/2/7(i).
77. Minutes of the Faculty of Medicine, 6 June 1905.
78. Catriona Blake, *The charge of the parasols. Women's entry to the medical profession*, London 1990, is a history of this campaign.
79. Minutes of the Faculty of Medicine, 6 June 1905, 12 Oct 1907.
80. Lydia Henry MSS, 110/12, USL.
81. Florence Millard's career is described by Alice Robson in T/S, *Biog Coll*; Lydia Henry's career is described by Eileen Crofton, *The Women of Royaumont. A Scottish Women's Hospital on the Western Front, East*

Linton 1997. I am grateful to Eileen Crofton, Anne Murdoch, Lawrence Aspden and Harold Swan for help with this section. Lydia Henry was the first female medical graduate at Sheffield, with Florence Millard behind her, alphabetically, in the queue for degrees in 1916.
82. Obituary, *North-Wing*, Spring 1948, pp.4–7.
83. Norah Naish, 'Dr Lucy', T/S, USL. I am grateful to Catherine Spencer for information and for donating this family memoir to the Library. See also 'Dr Lucy and Daddy Naish', chapter 2 of Gayle Greene, *The woman who knew too much*, Ann Arbor, Michigan 1999.
84. Fred Davies in *SDT* 12.12.06. The 'Lib-Lab' Councillors Holmshaw and Wardley also objected, see *SDT* 10.11.06.
85. Chapman, p.212.
86. Letter from Flockton and Gibbs, Minutes of Library Committee, 23 Jan 1906. The final capacity of the library is discussed in chapter 3.
87. US/CHA/1/17. Chapman is being kind when he suggests that Loveday had 'relevant experience' of book management, p.213.
88. Loveday ended his varied career as Vice-Chancellor of Bristol.
89. University College London had the first degree in English Law, see W. L. Twining, 'Laws' in F. M. L. Thompson, *The University of London and the world of learning 1836–1986*, London 1990, p.95.
90. Quoted by Chapman, p.221.
91. Details in this paragraph derived from correspondence in US/CHA/2/11. See also Chapman, pp.221–3.
92. Munby and Sparkes to Gibbons, 18 July 1913, US/CHA/2/11.
93. The Department of Biology was divided into Zoology and Botany in the same year.
94. See Chapman, p.224.
95. See Visitors' Report, 1911, US/CHA/2/16.

96. For the development of social sciences, see Reba N. Soffer, *Ethics and Society in England. The revolution in the social sciences 1870–1914*, California 1978, pp.1–11.
97. Peter Warr, *Psychology in Sheffield: The early years*, Sheffield 2001, pp.3–8.
98. For Marshall, see Soffer, *Ethics and Society in England*, pp.58–88.
99. Eliot to George Franklin, 14 Sept 1909, US/REG/2/2, pp.829–30.
100. These books are in USL. David Bland recalls that Knoop 'wept piteously' at his retirement party, CHI.
101. Quoted in Chapman, p.227.
102. Hicks to Higgins (President of the Royal Society), 18 Oct 1904. Quotation supplied by Robert Edyvean. I am grateful to him for making his unpublished paper on Sorby's contribution to the University available to me. See also N. Higham, *A very scientific gentleman: the major achievements of Henry Clifton Sorby*, Oxford 1963.
103. Chapman, p.228.
104. Information from Robert Edyvean, the Fellow appointed in 1984. There has been one subsequent Fellow, P. G. Higgs, 1992–1995.
105. Letter to Sadler of Leeds University, quoted by Chapman p.255, during his analysis of these returns. See also 'Twenty-five years', *Arrows*, Vol 1, No 5, June 1930, p.226.
106. As before, the main opposition was from Labour members of the Council.
107. Chapman to G. T. Clapton, 13 Mar 1953, US/CHA/13/4. See also Chapman, pp.355–6.
108. Chapman p.233 and statistics retained in US/CHA/2/18.
109. For the history of the WEA, see Kelly, *A history of adult education*, pp.248–58; J. F. C. Harrison, *Learning and living 1790–1960: a study in the history of the English adult education movement*, London 1961, pp.261–75.

110. See Joseph I. Roper, *The challenge of adult education. The record of a partnership 1910–1960 between the University of Sheffield and the Workers' Educational Association*, Sheffield 1993, pp.7–12. Ezra Fisher, 'The university and the workers', *Sheffield University Magazine* Vol II, No. 1, June 1939, pp.18–23. The WEA's first lecture courses at the University were in 1907 – see *Floreamus* Vol III, March 1907, p.141.

111. Arnold Freeman, see Roper, *The challenge of adult education*, p.15.

112. Obituary, *Arrows*, Vol 1 No 8, July 1931, p.386. Eliot published 15 papers during his time at the University, according to the annual reports.

113. H. A. L. Fisher, *An Unfinished Autobiography*, Oxford 1940, reprinted 1941, p.87. One of the 'unfinished' sections is an account of his time in Sheffield!

114. Chapman, p.260.

115. *SI* 29.6.14.

116. *SDT* 25 & 27.7.14. The correspondents refer to the most splendid country houses within a thirty-minute drive of the university.

117. Fisher, hand-written letter to Treasurer, 26 Oct [1913], US/CHA/6/1; Gibbons, notes to Treasurer. 16 Aug 1913, quoted Chapman p.237.

118. *SDT* 8.2.13. The 'Lloyd George' coffin has been added from a very similar description in *SI* 8.2.13.

119. *SDT* 2.7.17.

120. Kelly, *For Advancement of Learning*, p.136. Sheffield statistics derived from Chapman, Fig 2, p.7.

121. See article by Douglas Laurie, reprinted in Sanderson, *The universities in the nineteenth century*, pp.226–8.

122. Preface to American edition of *British Universities and the War: a record and its meaning*, London 1917, p.xii. The quotations from Dale and Green are on pp.20–1 & 27. Stuart Wallace, *War and the image of Germany: British academics 1914–1918*, Edinburgh 1988, is a study of the response to the war in British universities.

123. See Roderick and Stephens, *Education and Industry*, p.107, 109. The criticism has been made by many commentators on British higher education, one of the first being Charles Grant Robertson, *The British Universities*, London 1930, p.51.

124. In an address delivered to the Sheffield Society of Engineers and Metallurgists in 1907 he said 'War can only be waged successfully if those who are responsible for its conduct are possessed of methods which nothing but the closest study and the most anxious devotion to principle can give.'

125. Sanderson, *The universities and British industry*, p.215.

126. Sanderson, *ibid*, p.240.

127. Taken from *History of the university to the time of its coming- of-age May 31 1926*. The un-named author was W. Ripper. Further war statistics compiled by Len Hill from University records.

128. *SI* 6.8.15.

129. One of these women, Violet Dimbleby, stayed in the University until 1956. *Gazette* 26 (June 1956) pp.4–6.

130. *History of the university to the time of its coming-of-age*, p.21.

131. The Council believed that Sheffield University was the only one to have made its resources available 'for the public welfare' in this way. Minutes, 29 Nov 1915, Vol VI.

132. Arnold to Board of Education, 15 May 1916, US/CHA. 2/14.

133. *History of the university to the time of its coming-of-age*, p.17. Ripper's pride in the faculty's war-work is evident from the fact that his pamphlet is disproportionately concerned with the war; it occupies more than one-third of the whole.

134. *Ibid*, p.18.

135. *Arrows* 18, Dec 1934, p.11.

136. Fisher describes this episode in detail, *An unfinished autobiography*, pp.90–92.

137. Fisher asked for his job to be kept open but resigned in January 1917, presumably because he had been adopted as Member of Parliament for the Hallam division. (See Minutes of Council, 11 Dec 1916 & 22 Jan 1917, Vol VII). However, in March 1917, A. J. Hobson, the Pro-Chancellor, said at the Council meeting which adopted Ripper that he still hoped Fisher would return. Ripper concurred and was not relieved of his role until 1919. (Report of Council meeting, *SDT*, 6.3.17.)

138. *Floreamus* Vol XI, Dec 1923, p.149. Ripper was certainly easier to work with than Arnold, whose fiery temperament has already been noted.

139. Fisher to Hichens, 22 Feb 1916, US/CHA/2/1.

140. Freund to Gibbons, 12 Dec 1916, US/REG/1/27, Vol 34, p.33. See also G. Newton, *German studies at the University of Sheffield: a historical perspective 1880–1980*, Sheffield 1988, pp.55–69.

141. *Floreamus* Vol X, Dec 1921, pp117–8; Jonas obituary, *SDT*, 23.8.21; Newton, *German studies*, pp.91–2; N. D. Ballin, *For King and Kaiser: the Life of Sir Joseph Jonas Lord Mayor of Sheffield*, pamphlet 1998 [Sheffield Central Library]. I am grateful to Gerald Newton for advice on Jonas.

142. See article by T. M. Sparks, *SDT*, 8.7.20.

143. W. E. S. Turner, *Report on the Glass industry*, submitted to the Scientific Advisory Committee, May 1915, T/S, US/CHA/2/15.

144. R. W. Douglas, Obituary of Turner, *Gazette* 44 (Oct 1964), pp.117–9.

145. In 1937 he explained that 'having pleaded so strongly for the new department he was unable to resist the argument that the least he could do was undertake its organisation',

R. W. Douglas, 'The first W. E. S. Turner memorial lecture', p.6, Nov 1966, T/S US/CHA/2/15(ii). This lecture summarises Turner's most important research projects.

146. Turner, article in *Journal of the Society of Glass Technology*, 1937, quoted by Chapman, p.269.

147. Professor M. W. Travers, who had worked in Sheffield, wrote to Chapman, 23 Jan 1954, to say, 'I regard [Turner's] work for glass as one of the most remarkable academic efforts within my experience'. (US/CHA/13/4).

148. See Turner's report on this project, October 1920, US/CHA/2/15.

CHAPTER 3

1. Quoted by Shimmin, *The University of Leeds. The first half-century*, p.37

2. A. H. Halsey, *The decline of donnish dominion: the British academic professions in the 20th century*, Oxford 1992, p.43.

3. For technology students in the period, see Sanderson, *Universities and British industry*, p.263.

4. Dyhouse, *No distinction of sex?*, p.18.

5. Cited Armytage, *Civic universities*, p.275.

6. Robertson, *The British universities*, p.59.

7. Brian Simon, *A student's view of the universities*, London 1943, p.68.

8. Armytage, *Civic universities*, pp.275–6.

9. The full history of the PhD is told by Renate Simpson, *How the PhD came to Britain. A century of struggle for postgraduate education*, Guildford, 1983.

10. Armytage, *Civic universities*, p.251.

11. The history of the CVCP is described by H. Hetherington, *The British University System 1914–54*, Aberdeen 1954.

12. For the History of the UGC, see Christine Helen Shinn, *Paying the Piper: the development of the University Grants Committee 1919–1946*, London & Philadelphia 1986.

13. Hetherington, *The British University System*, p.6. Hetherington was vice-chancellor of Liverpool, and later Glasgow.

14. Robertson, *The British Universities*, p.53. Robertson was vice-chancellor of Birmingham, 1919–38.

15. Harold Perkin, *Key Profession. The History of the Association of University Teachers*, London 1969. For Sheffield, see pp.42–44.

16. Research by Len Hill. See also *THES* 15. 2.80.

17. M. Rendel, 'How many women academics 1912–76?' in Rosemary Deem (ed.), *Schooling for Women's work*, London 1980, Tables 11.2 & 11.4.

18. Carol Dyhouse, *No distinction of sex?*, p.240.

19. Minutes of Discipline Committee, February 1919, quoted by Chapman, p.299; Jennifer R. Simmons, *So deft a builder: an account of the life and work of Sir Henry Hadow*, University of Sheffield PhD thesis, 1978, pp.228–9.

20. Hadow to Miss Dickinson, 19 June 1922, US/CHA/2/25.

21. Chapman, p.298.

22. Chapman, p.299.

23. Donald Bailey, Sheffield B Eng 1923, Hon D Eng 1947. See *Biog. Coll.*

24. *Arrows*, Vol 1 No 6, Dec 1930; Chapman, p.303.

25. Armstrong College was part of the federal University of Durham until 1963.

26. Hadow to Hatfield, 21 Oct 1919, US/CHA/2/14.

27. See Hadow letter to Sir William McCormick of the UGC, 29 Sept 1925, quoted in Chapman, p.346.

28. Letter to his sister, 13 Nov 1926, quoted in Simmons, *So deft a builder*, p.231.

29. Sharp to Gibbons, 19 Jan 1925, US/CHA/1/2. This particular dispute was over the payment of superannuation costs, which Sharp accused Gibbons of 'burying' in his estimated costs. H. K. Stephenson supported Gibbons's actions, see letter to Gibbons, 7 Apr 1925, US/CHA/1/2.

30. Report of consultations between Sheffield University and representatives of the Education Committee, May 1927, US/CHA/1/2.

31. Chapman, p.348.

32. Chapman, p.349.

33. Hadow, Memorandum to the University, 8 April 1927, US/CHA/1/2.

34. *SDT* 23.6.27.

35. Desch to Gibbons, 23.6.27, US/CHA/1/2.

36. Sharp to Sir William Clegg, 12.3.28, 26.3.28, 16.3.28; Hadow to Clegg, 3.4.28, Sharp to Clegg, 16.4.28, US/CHA/9/2.

37. Hadow to Pickard-Cambridge, 30 July 1930, quoted Chapman, pp.348–9.

38. Jennifer Simmons, *So deft a builder*, p.229.

39. Amy's letters to her lover, Hans Arregger, are preserved in Hull Central Library. Quotations are taken from 18 Oct 1922 & 3 Dec 1922. The latest biography is Midge Gillies, *Amy Johnson*, London 2003. I am grateful to the author for information about these letters.

40. See letters to Gibbons from Allison and other members of SRC, 1925, US/CHA/2/25. These requests continued until the Graves Union building was opened in 1935.

41. SRC minutes 6 Oct1916, 14 Nov 1916, 18 May 1917, copied in US/CHA/12/2. The officers of the SRC demanded to interview the Registrar about their 'unjust and extraordinary treatment'.

42. *AR 1919/20*. The students were enthusiastic about the 'War Memorial' see *Floreamus*, Vol IX, Dec 1919, p.169. The Council included it in their general appeal of 1920, see Minutes, 7 Feb 1920, Vol

IX.

43. Minutes of Council, 12 Jul 1921, Vol X.

44. *Floreamus* Vol X, Dec 1921, p.149.

45. *Floreamus* Vol X, Dec 1920, pp.43–4.

46. *Floreamus* Vol X, Dec 1920, p.30.

47. *Floreamus* Vol X, March 1922, pp.182–4.

48. Douglas Haigh, CCHA.

49. See *AR 1925/26*, p.7.

50. The site was actually in the front gardens of four houses which the university had purchased. The houses were later used by departments in the Arts faculty, see Chapman, p.336.

51. See report of the Gymnasium Committee, quoted by Chapman, p.336.

52. Aldous Huxley, *Point Counter Point*, London 1941.

53. E. A. Ovens, 'The University Careers Service 1928–1978', T/S, USL.

54. Hadow to Gibbons, 12 Sept 1919, US/CHA/6/2.

55. Jennifer Simmons, *So deft a builder*, p.230.

56. Kay Rogers, CCHA. Kay and Margaret lived at the Hall in the early 1930s, just before this regime changed.

57. *SI* 3.12.24.

58. Hadow to Mrs Stephenson, Chairman of the Women's Halls Committee, 21 June 1926, US/CHA/8/1.

59. AR 1924, quoted Chapman, p.330.

60. This correspondence, Sept–Oct 1919, is in US/CHA/6/2.

61. 5 July 1930, US/CHA/7/9.

62. *Times Educational Supplement* 23.12.59.

63. Noted by an anonymous contemporary who commented on Chapman's draft section on Pickard-Cambridge, see US/CHA/12/2. Also Chapman, pp.351–2.

64. Quoted Chapman, pp.372–3.

65. Chapman, p.371.

66. Chapman's view, p.375. He implies that corridors were more noisy.

67. *Oakholme* (The Magazine of Crewe Hall), No. 3, 1937. See also A. W. Chapman, 'Crewe Hall', *Sheffield University Magazine*, Vol 1 No 1, Dec 1937, pp.41–3.

68. Pickard-Cambridge to Archbishop of Canterbury (who opened the Hall), 13 Nov 1936, and to the Marquess of Crewe, 6 Feb 1937, US/VC/1/32.

69. See Chapman, p.369–70. The Halls report to Council for 1932–3 said the decline was due to 'decrease in the number of students recognised by the Board of Education', US/CHA/6/1.

70. Oakholme became part of Crewe Hall, while Tapton Cliffe was eventually sold. The name 'University Hall for Women' was later changed to 'Halifax Hall'.

71. Kay Rogers, CCHA.

72. Vera Haigh (née Rose), CCHA.

73. *Ibid.*

74. There were 41 residents (the lowest point) in 1936–7, 46 in 1937–8, 56 in 1938–9 and then 79 resident women, 1939–40; notes by Chapman, US/CHA/12/2 and *AR 1939/40*.

75. *Arrows*, No 12, Dec 1932, p.17.

76. Donald Tomlin, CCHA.

77. Margaret Tomlin (neé Bond), CCHA.

78. This episode is analysed by Carol Dyhouse, *No distinction of sex?*, p.75.

79. Francis Knight, CCHA.

80. Margaret Robinson, neé Wolstenholme, CCHA. Two other accounts in the CCHA confirm this story.

81. *Arrows* No 12, Dec 1932, p.18. Dyson was the main porter 1905–32.

82. *AR 1932/33*, p.5.

83. 'Memorandum with regard to the Library', Minutes of the Library Committee, January 1944, SUA 9/1/1. Some material in this paragraph is taken from earlier minutes of the committee, especially when the information in the Memo is contradicted by earlier evidence.

84. Minutes of the Library Committee, 5

June 1929, 28 Oct 1929. See also Chapman, p.319.

85. Minutes of the Library Committee, 27 Jan 1936.

86. Minutes of the Library Committee, 17 Oct 1933, 31 Oct 1933, 10 May 1934.

87. Hadow to Mawer of Liverpool University, 12 Sept 1922, US/CHA/2/2. The text of this letter, omitting Boult's name, is transcribed in Chapman, p.317.

88. Hadow to Sharp, 31 March 1920, reprinted in Chapman, p.316. The previous lecturer in music, Henry Coward, had just resigned.

89. Hadow to Sturt (solicitor), 6 May 1927, US/CHA/2/2. For the offer to Vaughan Williams, see *Annual Report of the Senate*, 1926/27.

90. Quoted by Jennifer Simmons, *So deft a builder*, p.234. Rossiter Hoyle was a past Master Cutler.

91. *Calendar*, 1927.

92. See report of RIBA Visiting Board, 26.1.34, US/CHA/2/16.

93. Alec Daykin, CCHA.

94. Black spent most of his professorial career at Aberdeen University (1930–53); he was an expert on Elizabeth I.

95. Francis Knight, CCHA.

96. Donald Tomlin, CCHA.

97. There are many letters from Pickard-Cambridge to Turnbull on selection issues in US/CHA/2/17.

98. Chapman, 'The early days of the Chemistry department' part 2, 1. 2.

99. Obituary of Milner by J. R. Clarke, *Biog Coll*.

100. Connell was Professor 1919–30. 2. Clarke bequeathed his skull to the University for medical research and it was put on display in the medical school in 1983. *S Tel* 4.6.83.

101. D. Tomlin, CCHA.

102. I am grateful to Nick Bingham and John Pym for information on Daniell; see also Obituary, *Journal of the London Mathematical Society*, Vol 22 (1947), pp.75–81.

103. I am grateful to Milton Wainwright

and Harold Swan for advice on this section.

104. There is a detailed account of this relationship in Sturdy, pp.144–46.

105. A full account of the negotiations is given by Sturdy, pp.148–50.

106. Hadow to Johnson, 12 Jan 1921, US/VC/1/8.

107. Obituary by A. E. Barnes, *Sheffield University Gazette*, Feb 1955, pp.6–7.

108. May Mellanby, Honorary degree oration, 1 July 1933, US/CHA/7/9; Obituary, *Times*, 9.3.78.

109. H. Swan, 'Medicine in Sheffield', p.1046.

110. Hall, *The Sheffield School of Medicine*, pp.73–74.

111. *My Medical School*, ed D. Abse, London 1978, p.19. Lord Platt became Professor of Medicine at Manchester and President of the Royal College of Physicians.

112. Frank Ellis, CCHA. Frank Ellis, who was brought up in Upperthorpe and later Ranmoor by parents who were chapel caretakers, was 96 when he wrote these memories in 2001.

113. Story told by Lord Platt, *My Medical School*, p.17.

114. Invitations and programmes are preserved in US/CHA/2/7.

115. Letter to Hall from MRC (signature indecipherable), 5 July 1933, US/CHA/8/21.

116. Hall's achievements are summarised by G. A. Clark in an addendum to Hall's *The Sheffield School of Medicine*, pp.82–87.

117. T. E. Gumpert, *Recollected in Tranquillity: Reminiscences of a Sheffield Physician*, 1978 (USL).

118. Hall, p.76.

119. R. G. Macfarlane, *Howard Florey: the making of a great scientist*, Oxford 1979, has a chapter on his time in Sheffield, pp.205–225. See also Macfarlane's article on Florey in DNB 1961–70, pp.370–374. Trevor I. Williams, *Howard Florey: Penicillin and after*, Oxford 1984, focuses on Florey's later career.

120. See Macfarlane, *Howard Florey*,

pp.236–7. Florey was sorry to leave Sheffield; his resignation letter to Pickard-Cambridge spoke of 'my great regret at leaving a University where I have been so happy'. 1 Feb 1935, US/CHA/8/23.

121. The story of the development of penicillin is too complex to describe here; see Harold Swan, *Medicine in Sheffield*, pp.1046–48; M. Wainwright, *Miracle cure: the story of penicillin and the golden age of antibiotics*, Oxford 1990.

122. See M. Wainwright and H. T. Swan, 'C. G. Paine and the earliest surviving record of penicillin therapy', *Medical History* 30 (1986), pp.42–56. Milton Wainwright, a Sheffield University lecturer in microbiology, established the significance of Paine's work while doing historical research in the 1980s. Paine received an honorary degree from the University in 1987, at the age of 82.

123. *S Tel* 19.5.67; *Gazette* 47, Nov 1967, pp.143–4.

124. His work on lyosozyme was 'constantly frustrated by the lack of adequate biochemical collaboration' in Sheffield, *DNB* 1961–70, p.371.

125. Hans Krebs, *Reminiscences and reflections*, Oxford 1981, p.95.

126. The annual applications for the Rockefeller grant, 1935–46, are preserved in US/CHA/2/10. Krebs gave all his papers to the University Library (MS 116).

127. Krebs, *Reminiscences and reflections*, pp.97–8, 105–118; M. Wainwright, 'William Arthur Johnson – a postgraduate's contribution to the Krebs cycle', *TIBS* 18, Feb 1993, pp.61–2.

128. There was a course in pharmacy in the University College which later lapsed.

129. Wynne to Hadow, 9 Aug 1928. Memo by Wynne, and summary of meeting, T/S, US/CHA/2/6.

130. *AR 1920/21*, p.31. In 1933 external examiners reported that knowledge

of dental anatomy and physiology among the students was 'poor'. Minutes of the Faculty of Medicine, 6 Oct 1933, Vol V.

131. Minutes of Council, 8 Feb 1935, Vol XIX.

132. See Chapman, pp.367–8 for further biographical details about Clifford.

133. *Sheffield University Magazine*, Vol 1, No 1, Dec 1937 pp.25–31; *Gazette* 3, Nov 1948, pp.6–7; John Roach, 'The Company and the community', pp.271–5. According to Jim McQuaid, a historian of the TTS, they started to decline in the 1960s and ceased to exist around 1985.

134. Correspondence 1919–20, eg Arnold to Gibbons, 18 July 1920, US/CHA/2/14.

135. See correspondence preserved in Desch papers, USL, CHD 14/SHE/2.

136. W. Ibberson, FOI.

137. J. W. Jenkin, 'Fifty years in Metallurgy', *The Metallurgist and Materials Technologist*, Nov 1973, p.580.

138. *Gazette* 33, Dec 1958, p.19.

139. Desch Papers, CHD 15/10.

140. Address by Sir R. A. Hadfield, 2 July 1926, pamphlet, US/CHA/1/2.

141. J. H. Andrew, Report to Vice-Chancellor, 8 Mar 1932, US/CHA/2/14.

142. E. J. Thackeray, 'Some personal reminiscences'.

143. Report by J. H. Andrew to Council, 8 Mar 1940, Minutes Vol XXIV.

144. G. N. Critchley, *A Short History of Fuel Technology at the University of Sheffield*, T/S, p.111, MS 104 (USL).

145. June Rose, *Marie Stopes and the sexual revolution*, London 1992, pp.93, 99–100. I am grateful to Peter Foster for extra information.

146. Correspondence in US/CHA/9/3.

147. W. G. Fearnsides, 'Memorandum on the department of geology', Nov 1944, US/CHA/2/4.

148. Douglas Haigh, CCHA.

149. *Centenary of the Sheffield Technical School: an illustrated account*, p.25

(comment by Keith Miller).

150. Pickard-Cambridge to Swift, 19 Oct 1936, US/VC/1/32; Minutes of Applied Science Committee, 18 May 1931, Vol IV; Minutes of Senate 24 Nov 1931, Vol XXI.

151. Memories of Eric Tomlin, who worked there, CCHA.

152. Minutes of Council, 12 Feb 1943, Vol XXV.

153. Stanley Ellam, CCHA.

154. Minutes of Applied Science Committee, 23 May 1938, Vol VII.

155. Minutes of Senate, 4 Feb 1938, Vol XXVIII.

156. Annual Dinner of Old Students Association, 1931, US/CHA/8/15.

157. Minutes of Senate, 1 June 1928, Vol XVIII.

158. Quoted Chapman, p.376.

159. *SI* 10.2.34.

160. Stanley Thomas, CCHA.

161. See Brian Simon, 'The student movement in England and Wales during the 1930's', *History of Education* 16 (3), 189–203.

162. Tomlin, CCHA; *Arrows* Summer 1939, pp.8–9.

163. *Arrows* Vol 1, No. 2, June 1929, p.77.

164. See letters from Pickard-Cambridge to Feasey 17 Feb 1936, Smart 17 Jan 1936, Robertson, nd 1936, US/VC/1/31.

165. SDI 12.5.36. See also *Arrows* Dec 1936, p.7.

166. Dr Peter Gifford, 'Forty years of Student Health', *Gazette* 57, Dec 1977, pp.42–47.

167. These were completed by 1938. Chapman, pp.378–9. The ground by that stage extended to 38 acres with three football and two rugby pitches, hockey pitches, tennis courts, a netball pitch and a running track.

168. The next Vice-Chancellor, Masson, thought the Crewe site would privilege its residents at the expense of the other students. Unfortunately, no alternative site could be found and UGC funding was lost. See Masson correspondence Dec 1938–June 1939, US/VC/1/34.

169. Ives, Drummond and Schwarz, *The first civic university*, pp.193–5.

170. Sarah V. Barnes, 'England's civic universities and the triumph of the Oxbridge ideal', *History of Education Quarterly* Vol 36, no 3 (Autumn 1996), pp.271–305.

171. Elizabeth J. Morse, 'English civic universities and the myth of decline', p.196.

172. Eric Bagnall, CHI. Bagnall joined Gibbons's department in 1930.

173. Tom Smart, Student President 1935–6, CCHA.

CHAPTER 4

1. Comment by the Professor of Latin, Eric Laughton, *Gazette* 54, Nov 1974, p.8. See also Masson Obituary in *University of Durham Gazette*, 1962, News cuttings Vol 13, p.2,346.

2. Gerard Young, FOI. Young had also married into the Stephenson clan and so had family connections with the previous generation of Pro-Chancellors.

3. *S Tel* 13 & 17.11.42. Masson pleaded 'war exigencies' but this Committee was considered to be too important for that to be an excuse.

4. C. R. Tottle, *Now and Then*, 6, 1991, p.37.

5. See comments by Mavis Hitchcock, J. R. Carr, CCHA.

6. Derek Mosley, SCHA.

7. *North-Wing*, Summer 1939, p.11.

8. The OTC was known as the 'Senior Training Corps' until 1948. There was also an air squadron commanded by Kenneth Mellanby.

9. Report by Major Orme to University Council, Feb 12 1943, Minutes Vol XXV, pp.224–9.

10. *S Tel* 5.7.43.

11. Committee appointed by the Senate to report to the Ministry of Labour on students reserved from military service, Sundry Committees Minutes, Vol VII, meetings 1942–4.

12. *North-Wing*, Winter 1940, p.10.

13. *Arrows* 42, Dec 1942, p.9. 'Stygian' was presumably intended.

14. Geoffrey Ardron, 'A very personal recollection – Sheffield University sixty years ago', *Convocation News*, Spring 1999.

15. C R Tottle, *Now and Then* 6, 1991, p.36.

16. The university was criticised for this by a student who had witnessed the London blitz. *Arrows* 37, Mar 1941.

17. Robert Brian, CCHA. Another student, Hazel Dewhurst, recalls taking an examination in Firth Hall that day, even though 'the dust of many years had been shaken down from the roof'.

18. This story is told by both Alec Barron, CCHA, and Eileen Denman, CHI. In 1991, the pedal powered air filter was discovered rusting in the basement, *Star* 14.9.91.

19. Alec Barron, CCHA.

20. Margaret Rogers, née Cooper, CCHA.

21. *Arrows* 35, June 1940. (Also next quote)

22. Chapman, pp.393–4.

23. Chapman, p.431.

24. Geoffrey Ardron, 'A very personal recollection'. Clyde Binfield provided the explanation of this stunt.

25. *S Tel* 3 Nov 1941.

26. *Arrows* 44, Dec 1943, p.6. A newsletter called 'Union Weekly News' was published 1936–7 and resumed early in the war. *Arrows* mentions a fortnightly news-sheet in 1939 and 1940.

27. *Arrows* Dec 1939.

28. Minutes of University Council, Vol XXV, 12 March, 12 May, 11 June 1943; *North-Wing* Summer 1943.

29. Minutes of Finance and General Purposes Committee, Oct 12 1942, Council Minutes, Vol XXV, p.141.

30. Margaret Queening, CCHA.

31. Masson, *FRS Biog Mem*, Vol 9, 205–221, p.211; Brynmor Jones, *University of Sheffield. Record of War work 1939–45*, pamphlet 1946, p.8.

32. Willie Sucksmith, *FRS Biog Mem*, Vol 28, esp. pp.577–8; Obituary, *Times*, 6.10.81.

33. These and other aspects of the University's war work are described in Jones, *Record of war work*.

34. Margaret Rogers, (née Cooper), CCHA.

35. Minutes of University Council, Vol XXV, 13 Nov 1942, 11 June 1943.

36. Jones, *Record of war work*, pp.16–17.

37. Both Krebs and Mellanby wrote accounts of this research; see Kenneth Mellanby, *Human Guinea Pigs*, 1st edition London 1945, 2nd edition 1973; Krebs, *Reminiscences*, pp.119–123.

38. Krebs, *Reminiscences*, p.119.

39. Wilfred Harrison, CCHA. Another C. O., Hedley Drabble, contributed memories to CCHA.

40. Margaret Queening (née Bradshaw), CCHA.

41. Mellanby, *Human guinea pigs*, pp.70–1; see also *S Tel* 20.9.41.

42. Krebs, *Reminiscences*, p.119

43. Eric Bagnall, Honorary degree oration, *Gazette* 52, Nov 1972, pp.29–30; also E. Bagnall, CHI.

44. A.W. Chapman, Obituary of Harold Rayfield, who worked for Gibbons, *Gazette* 48, Nov 1968, pp.83–4.

45. Gibbons to Andrew, 14 Feb 1935, US/CHA/2/14.

46. Bycroft gives Gibbons the credit for this day to day work, but the Vice-Chancellor said that Bycroft 'handled practically all the business'; 'Appreciation', *Gazette* 14, July 1952, p.4.

47. Obituary of Gibbons by J. Bycroft, *Gazette* 13, Mar 1952, pp.2–3.

48. 'Appreciation', *op cit*, p.5.

49. Margaret Bennett (née Cooper) SCHA.

50. *Arrows* 47, June 1945, pp.7,13.

51. W. R. Maddocks, 'The ex-serviceman at the university', *Gazette* 1, Feb 1948.

52. David Payne, CCHA.

53. In comparison to the 1939 cohort, there were four times as many students coming from homes more than thirty miles distant in 1948.

54. A. Feltzer, 'Re-awakening', *Arrows* 50, Dec 1946, pp.32–35. See also *Arrows* 47, June 1945, p.27.

55. M. Woodruffe, 'A study in adaptation', *North-Wing*, Winter 1947, pp.9–16.

56. Masson's address to the University Court, *AR 1945/46*, pp.6–9.

57. Chapman, p.407. 'General post' is the moment in the game 'Stations' when every player changes trains.

58. The figure of 54% is taken from Masson's address to the University Court, *AR 1946/47*, pp.5–8. He gave Sheffield's increase as 120%, but our figures, taken from the *Annual Reports*, suggest 105%.

59. For the history of Ranmoor College, see W. H. G. Armytage, 'Ranmoor College', *Gazette*, March 1952, pp.4–5.

60. Douglas Rimmer, CCHA.

61. Sheila Gladwell (née Banks) CCHA.

62. Article on Miss Ball's retirement by W. H. G. Armytage, *Gazette* 49, Nov 1969, pp.54–5. For previous student complaints, see *Darts*, 1.11.46.

63. E. T. M. Ball, 'Looking back on lodgings', *Hallmark* 3, Summer 1964, pp.26–7.

64. J. F. Watkinson, CCHA.

65. *The Gargoyle*, (Ranmoor House Magazine) Summer 1997.

66. Geoff Moll, CCHA.

67. John Lello, Alec Barron, CCHA.

68. John Lello, Alec Barron, CCHA.

69. Douglas Rimmer, CCHA.

70. *Star* 24.10.49.

71. J. F. Watkinson, CCHA.

72. *S Tel* 4.11.46.

73. Jean Brittan, née Beeley, CCHA.

74. 'Record of meetings of Developments, Sites and Buildings Committee', 19 Feb 1951,T/S, US/CHA/5/7.

75. University's response to UGC, drafted by Masson, April 1944, quoted by Chapman, p.401.

76. Minutes of Council, 12 June 1946, Vol XXVII.

77. *S Tel* 20.1.47.

78. 'Report by J. S. Beaumont on scheme of extensions, 1946', T/S, SUA 5/1/84.

79. *Star*, 10.3.48.

80. *Yorkshire Post* 26.6.46.

81. Reprinted as the frontispiece to Chapman's history. The speech was given without notes and so fast that reporters could catch only snatches, according to *S Tel* 20.4.49.

82. *S Tel* 3.7. 48. Halifax was a prominent Anglo-Catholic.

83. Masson's address to University Court, reprinted in *AR 1948/49*, pp.5–10.

84. There was fear that it would become a 'technical school', *Arrows* 50, Dec 1946, p.5.

85. Minutes of the Committee on Social Studies, 25 Oct 1945, Sundry Committees Vol VII.

86. Eric Sainsbury, 'Social Work education and training in Sheffield'. T/S, USL.

87. Quoted by Peter Warr, *Psychology in Sheffield: the early years*, Sheffield 2001, pp.13–14.

88. G. R. Potter, untitled T/S dated Feb 1980, SCHA.

89. One example of this is the letter he wrote to F. F Bruce in 1948 enquiring about textual details of a copy of the Septuagint which he had bought. See David Bradshaw, CCHA.

90. Frederick Bruce, obituary, *Guardian*, Sept 21.10.90.

91. F. F. Bruce, *In retrospect: remembrance of things past*, London 1980, p.142.

92. Alec Daykin, SCHA.

93. Ralph Carr, CCHA.

94. D. Rimmer, *Gazette* 58, Dec 1978, p.61.

95. John Salt, CCHA.

96. Ian Kershaw, obituary of William Carr, *Indep* 24.6.91.

97. Comment by David Williams, a successor as Professor of French; *Gazette* 45, Nov 1965, pp.121–22.

98. *Rutland*, Aug/Oct 2003. Lawton was still alive at the age of 104 in 2004.

99. Francis Berry, 'William Empson' in Roma Gill (ed.), *William Empson, the man and his work*, London and Boston, 1974, pp.208–212, p.210.

100. Jerome Hanratty, Alec Barron, CCHA; *S Tel* 30.6.65. Berry wrote thirteen volumes of poetry and two of criticism. Francis Berry, *Collected Poems*, Bristol, Redcliffe, 1994.

101. For Empson's poetry, see John Haffenden's introduction to *William Empson: the Complete Poems*, Penguin 2000, pp.xi–lxv. A chronology of his life appears on pp.lxx–lxxv. The notes, pp.139–405, give fascinating insights into Empson's personality and quote from his letters, eg p.399 on his politics. Haffenden, a Sheffield Professor, plans to publish a full-length biography of Empson. See also Roma Gill (ed.), *William Empson: the man and his work*. Other information has been taken from *Yorkshire Post*, 21.2.53, Neil Roberts, SCHA; Greene, *The woman who knew too much*, pp.103–10.

102. Haffenden, *ibid*, pp.xxi–ii. These are the facts although precisely what happened 'has become the stuff of legend, with as many versions as there were gossips to embroider them'.

103. Marian Smith, AQ.

104. D. L. Linton, Obituary, *Gazette* 51, Nov 1971, pp.80–81.

105. This is the judgement of D. L. Linton, *Gazette* 48, Nov 1968, p.68.

106. *Gazette* 7, Feb 1950, p.8.

107. Malcolm Lewis, CCHA.

108. The first was Aileen Guilding, see chapter 5. Garnett was short-listed for the chair of Geography as early as 1945; see Minutes of appointment committee, 29 May 1945, Sundry Committees Vol VII.

109. Geoffrey Ardron, 'A very personal recollection'.

110. *S Tel* 2.2.54, 16.2.54. Also *Gazette* 19, March 1954, pp.4–5.

111. R. D. Haworth, *FRS Biog Mem*, Vol 37, esp. pp.267–269.

112. For Porter, see Obituary, *Times* 2.9.2002; *Indep* 4.9.2002, *New York Times* 4.9.2002.

113. *Gazette* 1, Feb 1948, p.5.

114. *Ibid*

115. *S Tel* 30.4.49.

116. *Gazette* 27, Dec 1956 , pp.31–2; *Gazette* 31, Mar 1958, p.26.

117. 'Pegasus', *Gazette* 33, Dec 1958, p.8. See also pp.21–2.

118. 'Statistics as a university discipline', *Gazette* 28, Mar 1957, pp.18–20. This article claims that statistics was placed from the start in both the faculties of pure science and medicine, but the Calendars do not confirm this.

119. Chapman, p.427.

120. For details, see Chapman, pp.423–4. The report was published as *Report of the Inter-departmental Committee on Medical Schools*, HMSO, 1944.

121. The other two candidates were the future Sir George Pickering and Lord Platt. For Stuart-Harris, see Frank Woods, 'Address given to the service of thanksgiving for the life of Prof Sir Charles Stuart-Harris', 4 Mar 1996 (*Biog Coll*). Two obituaries repeat many of the points made in this address: *Daily Telegraph*, 15.3.96, *Times* 20.3.96.

122. R. M. Urquhart, FOI.

123. R. Illingworth obituary, *Indep* 9.6.90; *NL* Vol 14, 3.8.90.

124. *Star* 11.2.59.

125. R. M. Urquhart, FOI. For Russell, see Mathers and McIntosh, *Born in Sheffield: a history of the women's health services 1864–2000*, Barnsley 2000, pp.138–9; C. Scott Russell, *The World of a Gynaecologist*, Edinburgh 1968.

126. *Gazette* 12, Nov 1951, pp.5–6.

127. David Smyth, *FRS Biog Mem*, Vol 27, 525–553, p.532.

128. Research by Len Hill.

129. In the care of David Rice, who kindly brought them to the attention of the author. Quotations are taken from the first volume, 1947–58.

130. Krebs, *Reminiscences*, pp.132–3.

131. *Ibid*, p.135.

132. Reg Hems, the co-author of many of his papers, worked with him for over forty years.

133. Krebs, *Reminiscences*, pp.180–1.

134. Hans Kornberg, CCHA.

135. *Star* 10.12.47.

136. 'The Sheffield Dental School', *The Dental Practitioner*, Vol IV, No 5, pp.152–6.

137. Chapman gives a detailed account of the schemes, pp.412–5.

138. N. R. Tempest, 'The Institute of Education', *Gazette* 14, July 1952, pp.6–7.

139. *Gazette* 37, July 1960, pp.8–9.

140. *S Tel* 12.8.45.

141. The Regional Committee to organise adult education in the forces during the war, which was chaired by the Vice-Chancellor; its report is transcribed in Chapman, pp.506–17.

142. Maurice Bruce, *The University of Sheffield Department of Extramural Studies, 1947–68: a personal survey*, pamphlet, USL.

143. Geoffrey Mitchell, *Responsible body; the story of fifty years of adult education in the University of Sheffield 1947–97*, pamphlet 2000, p.18.

144. *AR 1947/48*, p.13.

145. Comment by Robert Hopper, FOI. Hopper liked Bruce and thought that he deserved more support from the university.

146. The WEA slowly declined after the war, see Joe Roper, *The challenge of adult education: the record of a partnership 1910–1960 between the University of Sheffield and the Workers Educational Association*, pamphlet 1993, pp.56–7.

147. This account is taken from Mitchell, *Responsible Body*, pp.21–7.

148. Quoted by Mitchell, *Responsible Body*, p.26.

149. 'Too long' is a quote from Chapman, p.420.

150. See Brian Hanson, 'The post-war development of further and higher

education', in C. Binfield et al (ed), *History of the City of Sheffield, Vol II*, pp.337–41; *S Tel* 20.6.53.

151. '1879. A Centenary lecture by Professor W. H. G. Armytage', T/S, p.12, SCHA.
152. Stephen F. Cotgrove, *Technical education and social change*, London 1958, pp.143–4.
153. Arthur Quarrell, FOI.
154. A. W. Chapman, 'The University' in D. L. Linton (ed), *Sheffield and its region: a scientific and historical survey*, Sheffield 1956, p.211.
155. I am grateful to Philip Neal for this information.
156. I am grateful to Adrian Taylor for information on Tuplin.
157. *YP* 22 & 28.4.55, *Star* 27.4.55, among others.
158. *Centenary of the Sheffield Technical School*, pamphlet 1986, p.25.
159. *Gazette*, May 1959, pp.1, 4. Peter Robson, a subsequent professor, has paid tribute to the foundation laid by Cullen.
160. John Gamlin, Harold Priest, Russell Brown, CCHA.
161. *S Tel* 28.6.50; Russell Brown, CCHA.
162. *S Tel* 8.6.59.
163. W. G. Fearnsides, 'Memorandum on the Department of Geology', Nov 1944, US/CHA/2/4.
164. Norman Butcher, CCHA.
165. The donation was made anonymously but recorded in Minutes of Council, 11 May 1944, Vol XXVI.
166. Alan Dunkley, CCHA.
167. Margaret Butcher (née Nutter), CCHA.
168. 'The Expedition to Kilimanjaro', *Gazette* 18, Nov 1953, pp2–3; 'Return to Kilimanjaro', *Gazette* 30, Nov 1957, pp.2–14; C. Downie and P. Wilkinson, *The Geology of Kilimanjaro*, Dept of Geology 1972. The late Peter Wilkinson kindly supplied extra information.
169. W. E. Lee, 'Refractories Education in the UK', T/S, USL.

170. Elizabeth J. Morse, 'English civic universities', pp.6–7; Thomas Kelly, *For advancement of learning*, p.292.
171. 'Bruce Truscot' (E. A. Peers), *Red Brick University*, Faber and Faber, London, 1943; Elizabeth J. Morse, 'English civic universities', p.198.
172. Manchester, for instance, completed Chemistry laboratories, arts and library extensions and the huge Dover Street building for Education, Economics, Music and Law.
173. J. B. Headridge, SCHA.
174. The idea for the *Gazette* came from W. 'Billy' Ibberson, a former student and lay member of Council.
175. Bernard Argent, SCHA.
176. J. M. Whittaker, FOI. Unless otherwise noted, subsequent Whittaker quotes are taken from this interview.
177. Testimony of both Gerard Young and J. M. Whittaker, FOI.
178. W. Ibberson, FOI.
179. See notes on Empson's 'The Birth of Steel' by Haffenden, *William Empson: the complete poems*, pp.403–5. The full text of the masque is printed on pp.104–110 and was first published in *Gazette* Jubilee Number, 21, Nov 1954, pp.5–7.
180. Quoted in Haffenden notes, *ibid*, p.405.
181. Peter Linacre, FOI; Eric Bagnall, CHI.
182. W. Ibberson, FOI.
183. Chapman's album of reviews is preserved in the University archives.
184. *Gazette* 21, Nov 1954, pp.8–10. This review, unusually, was published several months before the book appeared.
185. In 1914, the Building Committee hoped to obtain the Old Great Dam, but failed.
186. Whittaker, Address to Court, 9 Dec 1955, US/CHA/7/16.
187. Masson, Address to Court, 14 Dec 1951, bound with *AR 1950/51*.
188. Edward Bramley, Address to Court, 14 Dec 1951, *ibid*.
189. As in the case of the Edgar Allen

library, the university gave some of its land in exchange, so that the overall size of the Park was unaffected.
190. *S Tel* 19.9.53.
191. *S Tel* 10.4.56.
192. See Gerard Young, 'Architectural Competition', *Gazette* 16, Feb 1953, pp.6–7; Gerard Young, FOI.
193. J. Bycroft, 'The Master Plan', *Gazette* 19, Mar 1954, p.2.
194. Quoted by Bycroft, *ibid*, p.3.
195. *S Tel* 28.11.53.
196. *The Builder*, 15.1.54, p.85.
197. *Gazette* 19, March 1954, p.2.
198. H. R. Johnson, 'The Western Bank buildings. The evolution of the development plan', *Gazette* 36, Feb 1960, p.13–19. This article describes the changes to the Plan.
199. 'Memorandum on the future development of the Medical School'. 17 June 1955, Minutes of Standing Committee of Faculty of Medicine 1948–60, pp.195–212.
200. Prof G. W. Pickering of Oxford, *S Tel* 30.11.56.
201. *S Tel* 16.12.58.
202. Gerard Young, FOI.
203. *S Tel* 7.2.59.
204. 'Memorandum with regard to the Library', Minutes of the Library Committee, Jan 1944. Although unsigned, this was clearly written by Peyton.
205. 'Proposed new Library; the case for urgent action', Minutes of the Library Committee, 22 Feb 1944.
206. The original plans are described by Stanley Peyton, 'The University Library. Past, present and future', *Arrows* 55, June 1949, pp.39–40.
207. Comment by Roger Harper.
208. *Gazette* 25, March 1956, p.4.
209. *Guard* 12 May 1959.
210. J. M. Whittaker, FOI.
211. *Star* 12.5.59.
212. *Guard* 13.5.59.
213. Bill Hitchens, SCHA.
214. J. Whittaker, FOI.
215. Alf Walker, CCHA.
216. Angela Dixon, CCHA.

217. Brian Lothian, CCHA.
218. Alf Walker, CCHA.
219. *S Tel* 4.1.58.

CHAPTER 5

Unless separately referenced, all student memories cited in this chapter are taken from the questionnaire sent to alumni (AQ). The views of Jack Whittaker, Roderick Urquhart, Roy Johnson, Arthur Connell and Gerard Young, which are extensively cited, are taken from their interviews with Francis Orton (FOI).

1. Paul Sharp, 'Central and Local Government' in Richard Aldrich (ed), *A century of education*, London 2002, p.102. The provisions of the Butler Act are described on pp.102–105. Butler mentioned Fisher and Hadow in his inaugural address as Chancellor, *Gazette* 37, July 1960, p.18.
2. Whittaker (FOI) states that a Yorkshireman, Sir John Cockcroft, was seriously considered for the post and Butler refers to the Yorkshire roots of his predecessor in his inaugural Chancellor's address, *Gazette* 37, July 1960, p.17.
3. Francis Orton during his interview with Whittaker.
4. Gerard Young, speech at installation of Butler, *Star* 4.5.60.
5. These were East Anglia, Essex, Kent, Lancaster, Stirling, Sussex, Warwick, and York.
6. Roy Lowe, 'Higher Education' in Aldrich (ed), *A century of education*, p.83.
7. B. Simon, *Education and the social order 1940–1990*, London 1991, pp.258–9.
8. *AR 1963/64*, p.1. The target of 4,600 set in 1957 had previously been increased by small amounts, including 100 extra places in Medicine.
9. See Harold Silver, *Higher education and opinion making in twentieth century England*, pp.187–196. Anthony Crosland, its progenitor, later regretted the policy.

10. *AR 1966/67*, p.17.
11. Dainton comments on this in *Doubts and certainties: a personal memoir of the 20th century*, Sheffield 2001, p.256. See also Sanderson, *The universities and British industry*, pp.379–80.
12. Urquhart, for example, mentions this criticism made by some in the University, one he did not share, FOI.
13. *AR 1969/70*, p.1.
14. By 1970 staff numbers had also risen by 87%, according to AR statistics, 1960–70.
15. A. H. Halsey and M. Trow, *The British academics*, London 1971, p.158.
16. H. R. Johnson, 'The Western Bank buildings. The evolution of the development plan', *Gazette* 36, Feb 1960, pp.13–19.
17. *Star* 19.4.61.
18. *YP* 12.10.62. *Gazette* 42, 1963, pp.5–10 gives a full description of the accommodation.
19. According to *The Observer* 8.5.66.
20. AQ.
21. John Jackson, AQ.
22. J. Whittaker, FOI.
23. R. Urquhart, FOI.
24. A. W. Chapman, 'Tribute to the late Sir Stuart Goodwin', *Gazette* 49, Nov 1969, pp.10–11. See also obituaries in *Times* 9.6.69, *S Tel* 7.6.69.
25. Cofield is the most likely source of the information, suggested by both Connell and Urquhart.
26. *S Tel* 21.10.60.
27. Roderick Urquhart, FOI.
28. Roy Johnson, FOI.
29. Whittaker discusses these plans, FOI. See his comments on wedge-shaped rooms in *S Tel* 24.6.61.
30. Description in *Guardian*, 30.10.64.
31. Robert Hopper, FOI.
32. *Star* 7.1.60.
33. *Financial Times* 23.6.66.
34. Robert Hopper, FOI.
35. Peter Linacre, FOI.
36. Frank Pierce, FOI.
37. *S Tel* 24.6.66.

38. *Gazette* 46, Nov 1966, p.34.
39. *YP* 2.9.61.
40. *Gazette* 48, Nov 1968, p.28. The Vice-Chancellor in this case was Hugh Robson.
41. Bill Hitchens, SCHA.
42. *S Tel*, *YP*, 4 March 1961. The 'ostrich egg' was coined by W. Mainland, quoted in an unidentified news cutting, Vol 13, p.2395, June 1964.
43. See *Gazette* 39, June 1961, pp.16–17.
44. See *Star* 7.9.62.
45. *S Tel* 15.1.63.
46. Roderick Urquhart, FOI.
47. Comments by David Burley, lecturer, SCHA. Urquhart described it as an 'eyesore', as did Eric Laughton, 'The University of Sheffield. Some reminiscences of the period 1955–1970', T/S, USL.
48. W. Mainland, as ref 42.
49. Gerard Young, FOI. He pointed out that a wing planned for the west side of Stephenson Hall was never built.
50. Urquhart found that this happened in Southampton when he moved there in 1966.
51. The University had already acquired Endcliffe Grange and bought Endcliffe Vale House in 1957/58. The plan was made available to the Centenary History project by Alec Daykin.
52. Gerard Young, FOI.
53. Accounts of the protest are given by Young, Urquhart and Johnson in their interviews.
54. See Urquhart's comments to *Star* 15.9.60 and Gerard Young, FOI.
55. Arthur Connell, FOI.
56. *S Tel* 27.3.63.
57. *AR 1964/65*, p.17.
58. *S Tel* 19.8.65.
59. The Deputy Warden, who was a Catholic, strongly disagreed, AQ.
60. The Clean Air Act of 1956 gave manufacturers and householders seven years to install smoke-free equipment.
61. First referred to in *AR 1963/4*, p.3. See also Jack Whittaker, FOI.

62. *Gazette* 45, Nov 1965, p.73.
63. *S Tel* 7.11.61. The previous age limit was 25.
64. *AR 1968/69*, p.19. By 1963/64 third-year students aged under 21 could live in a flat approved by the Lodgings officer and in 1966/67 this was extended to second years.
65. P. H. Mann and G. Mills, 'Living and Learning at Redbrick. A sample survey at Sheffield University', *Universities Quarterly*, Vol 16, 1961–2, pp.19–35.
66. *Gazette* 47, Nov 1967, pp.100–101. Confusingly, this Headquarters is called Tapton Hall.
67. *Gazette* 47, Nov 1967, p.102.
68. The decision was made by the Committee on Student Accommodation, 1968/9. See also *AR 1968/69* p.18.
69. AQ.
70. Tribute by Brynmor Jones, *Gazette* 43, March 1964, p.52. Jones suggests that Chapman was unfortunate not to get a chair in Chemistry, but does not include the claim made by the *Star* 28 March 1963 that he invented a chemical device for Miles Phillips at the Jessop Hospital, which indicated when sterilisation of medical instruments was complete. Also *Star* 26.9.63
71. Mentioned by the Public Orator, Eric Laughton, *Gazette* 44, Oct 1964, p.19.
72. CVCP, Third Report of an Ad Hoc Committee on procedure for Admission of Students, App.B, pp.17–40, London 1961. Chapman's copy of the three reports is held in the University Archives.
73. CVCP, Second Report, 1960, p.2.
74. Alex Currie, 'Peter Linacre; a personal note', obituary, 28 Jan 2002, T/S, *Biog. Coll.*
75. Lucy Mitchell, a member of staff in the Pure Science faculty office at this time, CHI.
76. *S Tel* 26.9.63.
77. V. H. H. Green, *The Universities*, p.165.

78. This account is derived from Francis Orton's interviews with several of the 'young Turks', especially Frank Pierce.
79. Harry Kay, FOI. This account is based on this interview and that with Frank Pierce.
80. The members included Frank Pierce (Spanish), Harry Armytage (Education), Robert Hopper (Ancient History), Harry Kay (Psychology), John Page (Building Science), Sidney Elsden (Microbiology), Ron Mason and George Porter (Chemistry) and Robert Kilpatrick (Pharmacology).
81. Eric Laughton, FOI.
82. B. W. Clapp, *The University of Exeter: a History*, Exeter 1982, p.175.
83. This paragraph is based on memos and minutes of the Academic Development Committee, 3 Nov 1964 and 12 Jan 1965.
84. *Gazette* 50, 1970 p.34.
85. Until 1965/66, all students took four subjects, to include Economics, in the first year. (*Gazette* 36, Feb 1960, p.10).
86. AQ.
87. Jack Gilbert, Obituary by George Clayton, *Indep* 6.3.2000.
88. Sidney Pollard, Obituary by Colin Holmes, *Indep* 10.12.98. The following account is based on this obituary.
89. Recollection of Helen Pollard, CHI. The department at this time is described by Pollard in *Gazette* 45, Nov 1965, pp.43–48.
90. Bernard Crick, *In defence of Politics*, London, 1st edition 1962. Four editions had been published by 1992.
91. Bernard Crick, *Now and Then* 7, 1992, pp.30–31.
92. Bernard Crick tells this story himself, *ibid*. David Blunkett adds some details in *On a clear day*, revised edition London 2002, p.99.
93. Patrick Seyd, CHI.
94. AQ.
95. David Blunkett describes his time at the University in *On a clear day*,

pp.96–102; 113–121.
96. *Star* 13.1.45. The story was also covered by national papers, including the *Daily Mirror*.
97. Richard Jenkins, *The department of Sociological Studies, University of Sheffield: an outline history*, T/S, USL; Keith Kelsall obituary, *Indep* 9.5.96.
98. Quoted in Jenkins, *ibid*.
99. *Guardian* 17.4.64. The project is mentioned by Keith Kelsall in an article in *Gazette* 39, June 1961, pp.7–9.
100. I am grateful to Martin Howe for help with this section.
101. *S Tel* 14.6.63; see also M. Howe, 'Department of Business Studies', *Gazette* 45, 1965, pp.48–55. Gerard Young was keen on Business Studies and believed 'we were ahead' of Manchester.
102. The following account is based on obituaries of George Clayton by David Chappell and Kevin Dowd, *Indep* 11.5.2002; Jonathan Foster in *Times*, 20.5.2002.
103. Chappell and Dowd, *ibid*.
104. Obituary of Denis Browne by CA Whittington-Smith, *Gazette* 45, Nov 1965, pp.119–20.
105. Account of Sir Roy Marshall's career taken from *Who's Who 2001*, *Gazette* 52, Nov 1972, pp.28–29. See also *S Tel* 18.10.68.
106. O. R. Marshall, 'Preface' to *The Jubilee Lectures. The Faculty of Law, University of Sheffield*, London 1960, p.xiv.
107. Roy Marshall, 'The department of Law', *Gazette* 34, May 1959, p.12.
108. *S Tel* 7.4.69.
109. David McClean, CHI.
110. *Gazette* 34, May 1959, p.13
111. Bramley died a year later. Obituary, *Star* 18.12.68.
112. Aileen Guilding, *The Fourth Gospel and Jewish Worship*, 1960. F. F. Bruce describes Guilding in *In retrospect*, p.142.
113. Account of James Atkinson taken from *Gazette* 59, 1978/9, pp.25–6.

See also Anthony C. Thistleton, 'James Atkinson: Theologian, Professor and Churchman' in WP Stephens (ed), *The Bible, The Reformation and the Church. Essays in honour of James Atkinson*, Sheffield 1995, pp.11–35. Atkinson wrote six books on Luther, including *The great light: Luther and Reformation*, London 1968; *Martin Luther and the birth of Protestantism*, revised edition London 1982.

114. Thiselton, 'James Atkinson', p.13.

115. Frank Pierce, obituary by Geoffrey Ribbans, *BHS*, LXXVII (2000), pp.239–241. See also obituary by George Clayton, *Indep* 27.7.99.

116. G. Ribbans, *ibid*.

117. F. W. Pierce, 'The Department of Spanish', *Gazette* 42, May 1963, pp.24–27; Ribbans, *ibid*.

118. Obituary by DEL, *NL* Vol 12, 25.5.88.

119. *AR 1969/70*, p.6.

120. Quotation from Gordon Daniels, CHI. The following account is based on this interview and further information from Daniels, one of the first three members of the department. Charles Fisher wrote a book about his Japanese experiences, including his imprisonment: *Three times a guest: recollections of Japan and the Japanese, 1942–1969*, London 1979. See also obituary of Fisher, *Times* 11.1.82.

121. J. M. Whittaker, FOI. See also *Gazette* 42, May 1963, p.36.

122. Quoted by Eric Laughton (Professor of Latin), FOI. Harry Kay speaks of the 'diehards' on the faculty in his interview.

123. English Language had a professor and three lecturers; Greek and Latin had two professors and a lecturing staff of seven between them in 1969.

124. Harry Kay, FOI.

125. Alec Daykin, who was the architect to the expeditions, SCHA.

126. *Who's Who* 2001.

127. John Widdowson, 'The Sheffield Survey of Language and Folklore', *Gazette* 49, Nov 1969, pp.41–2. This paragraph is based on this article, plus John Widdowson, CHI.

128. AQ.

129. Alec Daykin, CHI.

130. Information from Ian Ward.

131. The following account of James's career is taken from *AR 1966/67*, p.7; *Gazette* 58, 1978, pp.42–3; J. R. James, Honorary degree oration, *Gazette* 60, 1979/80 pp.16–17; Obituary, *Gazette* 60, 1979/80, pp.41–2; Tony Crook, CHI.

132. *Gazette* 52, 1972, pp.10–13.

133. Arnold Weddle, obituary by Anne Beer, *Landscape design*, Sept 1997, pp.10–12.

134. See *Hallmark* 4, autumn 1964, p.27; *Star* 7.1.60: 'It is proposed to create new departments of Russian, Italian and fine arts when the Arts Tower opens'.

135. *A celebration of the life and work of Professor Harry Armytage, a commemorative record*, 1998, USL, p.14. This contains appreciations from colleagues and family. The following account is taken from this booklet and from honorary degree orations at Sheffield, 1991, and Hull, 1980.

136. Story told by Geoff Stephenson. The incident took place at Henry Fanshawe School, Dronfield.

137. Gary McCulloch in *A celebration of . . . Armytage*, p.18. John Roach mentions the taste for the 'recondite' on p.11. See also Gary McCulloch's entry on Armytage in the *ODNB*.

138. John Roach in *A celebration of . . . Armytage*, p.12.

139. Obituaries of Boris Ford in *Times* 21.5.98; *Daily Telegraph* 25.5.98, *Guardian* 22.5.98. John Roach's books include *Social reform in England 1780–1880*, London 1978; *A history of secondary education in England 1800–1870*, London 1986; *Secondary education in England 1870–1902: public activity and private enterprise*, London 1991.

140. John Roach gives an account of this period in his unpublished autobiography, kindly shown to the author.

141. Maurice Bruce, *1947–1968: a personal survey*, p.1.

142. See *Gazette* 48, Nov 1968, pp.13–15.

143. Peter Warr, *Psychology in Sheffield: The early years*, p.87. See also *Gazette* 40, March 1962, pp41–3; *Gazette* 47, 1967, pp.65–67.

144. *S Tel* 20.11.65. The first full-scale course in teaching and lecturing methods took place in 1971, held over two days (*Gazette* 51, 1971, pp.11–12). The attendance was 145 (37% from medicine).

145. *Gazette* 49, 1969, pp.11–12.

146. Quoted by Peter Warr, *Psychology in Sheffield*, p.41. (Later quote, p.38).

147. Comments by Chris Spencer, SCHA. Peter Warr has written a history of the Unit, *Work, Well-being and effectiveness: A history of the MRC/ESRC Social and Applied Psychology Unit, Sheffield* 1999.

148. This account of the school is taken from W. L. Saunders, 'The University of Sheffield Department of Information Studies, 1964–89', *Journal of Information Science* 15 (1989), pp.193–202. See also *Gazette* 44, October 1964, pp.65–7; *Gazette* 47, Nov 1967, pp.69–72. Jim Tolson discusses the foundation of the School in FOI.

149. A course was held describing the potential for library use of computers, attended by representatives of 26 university libraries in 1966, *S Tel* 3.7.66. See also *S Tel* 10.5.65.

150. David Henry Smyth, *FRS Biog Mem*, Vol 27, pp.544–5.

151. T. S. Stevens, 'Professor R. D. Haworth', *Gazette* 43, March 1964, pp.55–6.

152. *Star* 23.3.65. See also *Guardian* 24.3.65; *S Tel* 24.3.65.

153. In 1959, the Lectures were given by a former student, Thomas Allibone (BSc 1924, PhD 1926) who was 'one of the world's leading authorities on

the use of electrical and atomic power' (*Star* 12.7. 1969). Gareth Roberts, future Sheffield vice-chancellor, gave the lectures in 1988.

154. Minutes of Senate, 10 July 1963. See also P. A. H. Wyatt, 'A. S. C. Lawrence', *Gazette* 47, Nov 1967, pp.122–3; T. S. Stevens, *FRS Biog Mem*, Vol 49, 2003, pp.523–35.

155. Administrators' seminar.

156. This account is the consensus of opinion from both inside and outside the department.

157. See William David Ollis, *FRS Biog Mem*, Vol 47, pp.397–413. Quotations in this paragraph are taken from pp.387 and 400.

158. Richard Roberts, CCHA.

159. See his article in *Gazette* 47, Nov 1967, p.21.

160. This account is based on obituaries of Tom Kaiser in *Times*, 17.7.98; *Guardian*, 5. 8.98, *Indep* 13.8.98 and *MIST Newsletter*, No 9, July 1998 (www.nerc-bas.ac.uk).

161. *Gazette* 31, Mar 1958, pp.1–6; 26. A building opened there in 1962 – see photo in *Gazette* 44, Oct 1964, p.38.

162. *Star* 15.8.62, *S Tel* 7.6.63, 29.8.63, 26.3.65, *Star* 17.1.66.

163. G. E. Bacon, Honorary degree oration, 22 July 1998.

164. Bill Galbraith, unpublished autobiography, kindly shown to the author.

165. J. M. Gani, Honorary degree oration, 15 July 1989. Gani reviews the history of the department in *Gazette* 47, Nov 1967, pp.58–61.

166. C. Heyde, 'A conversation with Joe Gani', *Statisical Science*, 1995, Vol 10, No 2, pp.214–230. The following account is based primarily on this paper. See also J. Gani, 'Adventures in Applied Probability', *Journal of Applied Probability* Special Volume 25A (1988) pp.13–15.

167. Heyde, *Ibid*, p.221.

168. Heyde, *Ibid*, p.220.

169. Roger Webb, 'Be a man, Mrs. Fisher', unpublished autobiography kindly shown to the author.

170. In 1965, of 13 academic staff, eight were comparative endocrinologists and two others had an endocrine aspect to their work. Four research staff helped with the work. A Unit for Endocrine Chemistry was established in the department under Dr J. K. Norymberski in 1968.

171. Comment by Len Hill, who was a Zoology student from 1957 and thereafter postgraduate and lecturer until 2000.

172. *North-Wing*, Vol 30, no 2, Summer 1966, p.9.

173. Information from Michael Williams, a member of the department 1963–1996. A degree in anatomy had existed since 1935, but there had been no graduates.

174. Quotes from letters collected by Michael Williams and his own contribution in SCHA.

175. Roger Webb is one of several staff to describe David and Gilbert.

176. *Gazette* 47, Nov 1967, pp.119–121.

177. Alan Roper, CHI. The following account is based on this interview.

178. *Star* 20.4.64.

179. Five Biochemistry academics left to take up posts in North American universities, 1961–64.

180. Obituaries: *Times*, 2.9.94; *Indep* 30.8.94.

181. An extension to the design to cover the intake of 120 students was approved in 1964, *AR 1963/64*, p.2, *1965/66*, p.4.

182. Taken from AQ.

183. Obituary, *North-Wing* Vol 33, no 2, spring 1970.

184. Stengel was an honorary professor from 1956. The following account, with quotations, is taken from *Gazette* 47, Nov 1967 pp.123–5; 51, Nov 1971, pp.21–2; *S Tel* 1.9.67 and Obituary, *Times* 9.6.73.

185. Christopher Knapper, CCHA.

186. Information from Alan Roper, CHI.

187. The Unit's research is described in *Gazette* 48, Nov 1968, pp.49–51; *Gazette* 49, Nov 1969, pp.13–14.

188. For example, Dorothy Rowe, *The experience of depression*, Chichester 1978; *Depression: the way out of your prison*; London 1983; *Beyond fear*, London 1987.

189. The chair was originally entitled 'Social and Industrial Medicine'. From 1949, under William Hobson and John Pemberton, the department developed a special interest in the healthcare of the elderly, but both left in 1958. John Knowelden obituaries: *Times*, 21.8.97; *Indep* 15.9.97.

190. John Emery's research is discussed in chapter 6.

191. This centre was part of the Department of Paediatrics. A sub-department of Paediatric Surgery, under Robert Zachary, was established in 1968/69. See *Gazette* 48 Nov 1968, pp.17–19.

192. This account is largely based on John Emery's obituaries for John Lorber, *Times* 2.8.96 and Robert Zachary, *Indep* 18.3.99.

193. John Lorber obituary, *ibid*.

194. Harold Miller, *A brief history of Medical Physics in Sheffield, 1914–1982*, T/S, 1982, USL. The following account is based on this history.

195. Frank Ellis was interviewed, at the age of 96, during this project. The Radium Centre was later renamed the Centre for Radiotherapy.

196. Miller, *ibid*, p.8.

197. Miller, *ibid*, p.19.

198. *Gazette* 42 1963, p.30.

199. Mathers and McIntosh, *Born in Sheffield*, p.133.

200. Harold Miller, Obituary by Donald Munro, T/S, *Biog Coll*.

201. See Thring's comments to *S Tel* 16.5.55 and interviews with Gerard Young and Roy Johnson.

202. *S Tel* 3.11.61. Further articles on this robot appeared in *The Observer* 13.1.63 and *Star* 26.2.63. In the latter he admitted that it would take several hundred thousand pounds to develop, but believed it would be very worthwhile.

203. Peter Linacre, FOI. Others present have corroborated this story.
204. Jim Swithenbank, Materials History seminar.
205. *S Tel* 1.4.66.
206. *S Tel* 10.11.66.
207. The following account is taken from staff memories collected by Peter James in an obituary of Ronald Douglas, 2000 (*Biog Coll*), and from the Materials history seminar.
208. Michael Cable, SCHA.
209. American universities were the first to make this change, see *AR 1963/64*, p.6.
210. Materials History seminar.
211. Descriptions by John Hawthorne.
212. Alex King, *MRS Bulletin*, July 1999, p.80.
213. *Gazette* 43, March 1964, pp.15–16.
214. Reported to Engineering History seminar.
215. *Gazette* 43, Mar 1964, p.9.
216. *Gazette* 41, Oct 1962, p.20.
217. Gerard Young, FOI.
218. Stuart Bennett (a founding member of staff), CHI.
219. *Gazette* 46, Nov 1966, p.43.
220. Comment by Adrian Taylor.
221. Engineering history seminar.
222. Gerard Young, CHI.
223. Jack Whittaker, FOI.
224. *S Tel* 17.10.64.
225. *Gazette* 54, Nov 1974, p.6. This account is also based on the memories of Frank Pierce, Gerard Young and Harry Kay, who were members of the Committee.
226. *Gazette* 54, Nov 1974, p.5.
227. Alice Robson, FOI. See also Alice Robson, *My Life with Hugh Robson*, Edinburgh 1988.
228. Two versions of this story are recounted in memoirs of Robson: Magnus Magnusson's tribute, Jan 1978 and obituary, *Year Book RSE*, 1979, p.60. Both in *Biog. Coll.*
229. Arthur Connell, FOI.
230. Quote from Harry Kay, FOI.
231. Alex Currie, 'Peter Linacre; a personal note', *Biog. Coll.*
232. Alex Currie, FOI.

233. Harold Perkin, *Key Profession*, p.223. See also Robson's comments about 'an unaccustomed degree' of national planning in *AR 1967/68*, pp.1–2.
234. See, for example, *AR 1966/67*, p.1 and *1967/68*, p.2. The UGC's operations were externally audited by the Comptroller and Auditor General from 1967, leading to a huge increase in paperwork to justify requests for funds.
235. Alice Robson, *My Life with Hugh Robson*, p.45.
236. *Gazette* 47, Nov 1967, p.5.
237. *AR 1967/68*, p.25.
238. R. Dahrendorff, *LSE, A History of the London School of Economics and Political Science*, pp.460–463.
239. For the following, see *S Tel* 26.4.69, 30.4.69; *YP* 29.4.69, 1.5.69.
240. Kelly, *For advancement of learning*, pp.323–4. The vice-chancellor of Liverpool resigned at this time (Dec 1968) over the issue of government policy towards the universities.
241. Colin Crouch notes sit-ins at twelve British universities in 1968/69: *The Student Revolt*, London 1970, pp.97–127. This includes every English civic university except Liverpool, which had an occupation of the Senate House in 1970, and Sheffield, whose first occupation was in 1974.
242. *S Tel* 12.7.65.
243. Eric Laughton, *Gazette* 54, Nov 1974, p.11.
244. Alex Currie, FOI.
245. See *AR 1969/70*, pp.9–10. Initially, students were allowed to speak and ask questions but not to vote.
246. The origins of NPSA are obscure; it is mentioned in *Gazette* 23, June 1955, p.6 but probably goes back to the 1930s.
247. *Gazette* 49, Nov 1969, p.3.
248. Two films from this era, 'Freshmen's Week' and 'The Redbrick University' are held in the Archive.
249. One of the perpetrators contributed to AQ. His next Rag stunt was more

sober: 'a team of six of us hit a croquet ball with regulation mallets through the night from Birmingham Town Hall to Sheffield Town Hall'.
250. Very few answered positively when asked in the AQ about exposure to drugs.
251. *Darts* 9.11.67.
252. For comments on the sculptures, see *Star* 25. 2.64 and Bill Hitchens, SCHA.
253. The following account is based on the regular reports carried by the *Gazette* between March 1964 and Dec 1971. See also *Star* 3.2.64, *YP* 25.6.66; *S Tel* 27.5.67; *Star* 1.11.67.
254. Bill Galbraith gives an account of his role in his T/S autobiography, lent to the author.
255. Gerard Young, FOI.
256. The following is derived from *S Tel* 12.3.66, *Star* 16.6.66, 22.6.66.
257. Roy Johnson, FOI. Young and Urquhart, in their interviews, independently agreed that the idea was entirely Johnson's.
258. Gerard Young, FOI.
259. *S Tel* 5.3.73.
260. *Gazette* 50, Nov 1970, p.11. This article describes the design in detail.
261. Harry Kay, FOI.

CHAPTER 6

1. Gareth Roberts, Vice-Chancellor 1991–2000, also chaired the CVCP.
2. That he saw this as a crucial part of his task is confirmed by Alice Robson in *My Life with Hugh Robson*, p.49.
3. *My life with Hugh Robson*, p.56.
4. Recalled by Alex Currie, FOI & CHI.
5. Sanderson, *The Universities and British Industry*, p.381.
6. *S Tel* 3.3.70. Robson described the expression of some students in the audience as 'mindless hatred': Alice Robson, *My Life with Hugh Robson*, p.50.
7. Alex Currie, FOI & CHI.

8. *Star* 20.7.70. See also *YP* 5 & 6.3.70, *Star* 5.3.70.
9. Anthony Arblaster, SCHA. See also Brian Pullan with Michele Abendstern, *A History of the University of Manchester 1951–73*, Manchester 2000, pp.211–16, and *Guardian* 19.10.70.
10. In his book *Academic Freedom*, pp.143–4, he describes how he and three colleagues sent a circular letter to staff during the postal workers' strike of 1971 asking for contributions to their hardship fund. The response was 'meagre' and included criticism of the 'political' content of the letter. They were shocked by the apparent conservatism they perceived among Sheffield staff at the time.
11. Letter about incidents in Birmingham, *Times* 20.10.70. Renfrew stood as a Conservative candidate, see *S Tel* 29.2.72.
12. *S Tel* 5 & 6.11.71, *YP* 6.11.71, *THES* 8.6.73 (letter from Arblaster).
13. Alice Robson, *My Life with Hugh Robson*, p.54; Robson's comment to *Star* 18.4.74.
14. *S Tel* 5.11.71, *YP* 6.11.71.
15. *Gazette* 50, Nov 1970, p.14.
16. Alice Garnett obituary, *NL* Vol 13, No 12, 3.5.89.
17. Alec Daykin, CHI. See also *Gazette* 50, Nov 1970, pp.12–13
18. Quote from Tony Heathcote, SCHA. I am grateful to Mrs Winifred Whitehead for memories of the Staff Dramatic Society.
19. 'The University of Sheffield. Long-term development', report, July 1966.
20. Alex Currie (interviews) used the term 'wider' particularly about the Crookesmoor plans. He remembers Harry Kay saying to him that 'this would be a university to be proud of'.
21. The initial idea for the 'strip' existed in Whittaker's day and he was a great enthusiast for it, *Gazette* 44, Oct 1964, pp.4–8.

22. Arup's scale model is reproduced in *Gazette* 51, Nov 1971, p.10. See also pp.9–11.
23. *AR 1972/73*, pp.6–7.
24. See, for example, 'University expansion in Sheffield: a critical examination of the development proposals', prepared by Crookesmoor Mooroaks Association and Broomhill Action and Neighbourhood Group, T/S, Oct 1975.
25. Alex Currie, FOI & CHI.
26. *S Tel* 30.9.74.
27. *S Tel* 30.9.74.
28. This was estimated at £20–25 million in 1975, *THES* 1 Aug 1975.
29. *S Tel* 3.8.79.
30. See Roy Lowe, 'Higher education', p.85.
31. *AR 1973/74*, p.7.
32. *THES* 20.9.74.
33. Mentioned by Magnus Magnusson, Rector of the University of Edinburgh, in his 'Thanksgiving and Memorial Address for Professor Sir Hugh Robson', 21 Jan 1978, *Biog. Coll.*
34. Magnus Magnusson, *ibid*. The many obituaries include one by Alex Currie, *Gazette* 58, Dec 1978, pp.78–80.
35. Geoffrey Sims, CHI.
36. Comment by David Bland, the NPSA representative on the panel, CHI.
37. *S Tel* 22.2.74.
38. See, for example, *AR 1974/75*, p.3.
39. Comment by Bill Hampton.
40. *AR 1977/78*, section 2.
41. Fred Dainton, *Doubts and certainties*, Sheffield 2001, p.311.
42. *AR 1973/74*, p.8.
43. *Gazette* 60, 1979/80, p.21.
44. *Gazette* 53, Nov 1973, pp.94–6.
45. *AR 1974/75*, pp.27–33.
46. The rate had remained stable, though discriminatory, since 1967. See *AR 1976/77* for a full account of the crisis, pp.3–5.
47. *S Tel* 1.11.75. See also *Star* and *S Tel*, 20. 11.75, 3.12.75, 4.12.75.

48. *S Tel* 23.11.76. It was covered daily in the local press from 23.2.77 to 3.3.77.
49. *S Tel* 11.10.76 describes Hamilton. His predecessor, Andy Tucker wrote a similarly uncompromising report to the Court, *AR 1975/76*, pp.31–39, which was heavily criticised by some of its members, see *S Tel* 17.12.76.
50. This was even true of left-wing members like Pauline Harrison and Julian Kinderlerer, who wrote to *S Tel* 9.3.77.
51. I am grateful to Hamish Ritchie for this information and his account of the occupation.
52. Speech to the Court, reported in *S Tel* 17.12.76.
53. Sims's speech to the Court reported in *S Tel* 23.12.77; letter to *Times*, 18.11.77. For Currie's views, see *Star* 16.3.77.
54. Quotes in this paragraph taken from Alex Currie, FOI & CHI.
55. *The Observer* 19.8.79.
56. The story was reported without this detail in *S Tel* 10.11.79.
57. *AR 1980/81*, p.19.
58. This story was reported in many newspapers, including *S Tel* 5.5.78; *Sunday Times, Daily Mail, YP*, 7.5.78; *THES* 19.5.78 & 28.7.78, *Star* 30.5.78, 8.6.78, 21.7.78, *THES* 28.7.78. I am grateful to Hamish Ritchie for his comments on this section.
59. Hamish Ritchie, SCHA.
60. Dorothy Freeman, CHI. I am grateful for her comments on this section.
61. *Star* 6.10.71.
62. *AR 1974/75*, pp.28–9; *S Tel* 26.2.75; Alex Currie, FOI & CHI.
63. *Star* 2.7.73. David Blunkett was one of a number of Councillors who opposed the Riverdale development.
64. *S Tel* 6.3.74. Bill Michie and George Wilson (Council leader) spoke out against house conversions. *S Tel* 6.3.74, 4.6.75.
65. Squatting took place in a number of properties during the 1970s, often

encouraged by the Union. The first squat was probably 18 Endcliffe Crescent in autumn 1971.

66. *Gazette* 60, 1979/80, p.9.

67. W. R. Maddocks, *Gazette* 53, Nov 1973, p.25.

68. For the flats rule, see minutes of the Student Accommodation Committee, 16.12.75.

69. *Star* 23.7.73.

70. It was discovered after the meeting that some votes against had not been declared. R. A. Nind to S. M. de Bartolomé, 18 Dec 1979, US.

71. *AR 1975/76*, p.33.

72. *Gazette* 58, Dec 1978, p.74. See also AR 1982/83, p.29.

73. This account is based on Paul Blomfield, CHI.

74. Mary Sharrock, SCHA.

75. For details, see *Gazette* 57, Dec 1977, p.58, *AR 1977/78*, section 9.

76. AQ. See also *Star* 3 & 4.3.80, *S Tel* 5.3.80, 17.5.80. The campaign resumed a year later, see *Star* 16.3.81, *S Tel* 17.3.81, *THES* 1.5.81.

77. Paul Blomfield, CHI.

78. Dainton, *Doubts and certainties*, pp.11–14. This autobiography is the main source for the following account.

79. Dainton, letter to A. Heathcote, 25 July 1984, passed to the author by the recipient.

80. Stephen de Bartolomé, CHI.

81. *NL*, Vol 4, no 4, Jan 1980, gives details of the UGC letter and the University's response.

82. See *NL*, Vol 2, no 8, *Financial Times* 11.5.81. Target admissions for higher education were revised downwards in 1977, with the new policy being justified in the 1978 report, 'Higher Education into the Nineties'. See R. Aldrich (ed), *A century of education*, pp.85–6.

83. *NL*, Vol 5, no 6, March 1981 and Vol 5, no 7, April 1981.

84. Administrators' History seminars.

85. Figures taken from *Times* 3.7.81. The results were reported in very different ways in the press at the

time. *S Tel* said Sheffield's cut was 11 per cent.

86. *S Tel* 4.7.81.

87. *Gazette* 58, Dec 1978, p.6. See also *Financial Times*, 4.7.81

88. *THES* 9.7.82.

89. *NL*, No 6, no 15, 5 July 1982.

90. Report of the Premature Retirements Committee, Minutes of Council, July 1987

91. These reports were all made to Senate and may be found in the Senate Minutes as follows: ADC1, 12 May 1982, Vol CIII, pp.905–936; ADC2, 16 June 1982, Vol CIV, pp.29–38; ADC3, 11 May 1983, Vol CIV, pp.1005–1026; ADC4, 23 May 1984, Vol CVI, pp.189–226; ADC 5, 11 Dec 1985 (omitted from Senate Minutes but to be found in the Minutes of the Council, Vol LXXV, pp.405–509); ADC6, 4 Mar 1987, Vol CVIX, p.462 (App.B, separately numbered.)

92. ADC2.

93. *S Tel* 13.5.82.

94. *S Tel* 6.2.82, 11.2.82, 18.2.82, 24.2.82. See also his account of the protests in *AR 1981/82*, p.29.

95. *Darts* 8.3.84.

96. *S Tel* 9.3.84, 23.5.84.

97. *THES* 6.4.84.

98. *AR 1984/85*, p.2, 32–4.

99. Quoted *NL* Vol 10, No 8, 12.2.86 and *AR 1984/85*, p.32.

100. *NL* Vol 9, No 16, 2.8.85; *S Tel*, 13.8.85, 16.8.85, *THES* 28.6.85.

101. ADC5, see also *AR 1985/86*, p.3.

102. *YP* 20.6.86.

103. ADC6; *NL* Vol 10, No 14, 11.6.86.

104. Ron Johnston, CHI; John Nicholson and Graeme Davies made similar comments in their interviews.

105. Report of the Premature Retirements Committee, Minutes of Council July 1987

106. *THES* 1.9.89, *NL* Vol 14, No 1, 6.10.89.

107. *Star* 8.9.81; *S Tel* 15.3.83.

108. Peter Banks, SCHA.

109. *S Tel* 1.1.70.

110. John Richmond, Hon degree oration

22 July 1994. See also John Richmond, *Life's Jigsaw: a medical man finds the pieces*, Durham 2001.

111. G. Hudson, *North-Wing*, Vol 43, No 2, May 1978. I am grateful to Professor Hudson for his written account of the school at this time.

112. Herbert Livingston Duthie was Professor of Surgery, 1964–79. He became Provost of the Welsh National School of Medicine in 1979 and was knighted in 1987.

113. M. Hardman, 'Student Increases', *North-Wing*, Vol 42 no 1, May 1977.

114. *North-Wing* Vol 40 no 1, Oct 1975.

115. See articles by Charles Stuart-Harris and John Richmond, *North-Wing* Vol 43 No 2, May 1978, on which the following account is based.

116. *North-Wing* Vol 40 no 1, Oct 1975, Vol 43, No 2, May 1978.

117. Article by John Knowelden, *Gazette* 51, Nov 1971, pp.27–9.

118. Interviews with Eric Wilkes, kindly made available by the Hospice History Project at the University of Sheffield. These form the main source for this section.

119. *S Tel* 2.5.78.

120. Alan Usher, Honorary degree oration, 16 July 1992.

121. *S Tel* 18.5.77; *Gazette* 57, Dec 1977, pp.40–42.

122. The sources for this account are Usher's honorary degree oration; Obituaries in *Times* 17.8.98, *Indep* 20.8.98, *Guardian* 21.8.98, *Daily Telegraph* 24.8.98.

123. See interview with David Jarvis and honorary degree oration, 23 July 2003.

124. Information on John Emery taken from articles in *Times* 2.5.2000, *Gazette* 60, 1979/80 pp.26–7; Obituaries in *Indep* 13.5.2000; *Times* 2.5.2000; *Guardian* 15.5.2000; *Daily Telegraph* 2.5.2000; and by Robert G. Carpenter and James Underwood, *Biog. Coll.*

125. *Star* 1.11.82 and other newspapers at the time.

126. *NL* Vol 9, No 8, 13.2.85.

127. *AR 1984/85*, p.22; *Times* 21.1.85, *Daily Mail* 22.1.85 and many other papers at this time.
128. *Star* 10.11.83; *Guardian* 20.6.87.
129. Sheffield was the first official government centre for the testing of heart valves, *Star* 29.7.86
130. *S Tel* 19.5.77, *Star* 7.11.85 , *AR 1986/87*, p.16. The 'Magstim' won the Institute of Electrical Engineers Prize for Innovation.
131. Brian Brown, *Now and Then*, 10, 1995.
132. This account is based in interviews with Ian Cooke conducted for both this project and the 'Born in Sheffield' project. See Helen Mathers and Tania McIntosh, *Born in Sheffield*, pp.154–157.
133. His final achievements are still open to speculation. See *ibid*, pp.156–7.
134. UGC Dental Sub-Committee visitation, 26 Feb 1970, US/CHA/2/8.
135. *AR 1988/89*; *NL* Vol 13, no 8, 15.2.89.
136. *Guardian* 24.10.86.
137. *Sunday Times* 12.4.81, *Financial Times* 4.5.83. The government's enthusiasm followed the Spinks Report of 1980. Birmingham, UCL and UMIST were awarded £10,000 each and Sheffield was among a group of five universities invited to bid for up to £50,000 each.
138. *S Tel* 20.10.80, for example.
139. J. R. Quayle, Honorary degree oration, 11 Dec 1992. The quotation is from *The Biochemistry of Methylotrophs*, by C. A. Anthony.
140. It was later renamed the School of Biological Sciences.
141. In practice, geneticists were shortly appointed to the other two departments as well.
142. This strong word is justified by comments made by both Barer, before his death, and Michael Williams, a member of the department.
143. Their obituaries appeared in the same edition of the *NL*, Vol 14, no 1,

6.10.89. See also obituaries of Barer in *Daily Telegraph* 19.7.89 and *Indep* 10.7.89; obituaries of Rogers in *Indep* 15.8.89 and *Times* 5.8.89.
144. Rogers and Scratcherd, *THES* 7.11.86.
145. Mathematics history seminar.
146. I am grateful to Rodney Sharpe for this information.
147. Leon Mirsky obituary, *Linear Algebra and its applications*, 61: 1–10 (1984), pp.1–10; *Bulletin of the London Mathematical Society*, 18 (1986), 195–206.
148. *University Statistics 1988–9*, cited by *NL* Vol 14, no 7, 22.2.90
149. *AR 1983/84*, p.25; *NL* Vol 10, no 2, 23.10.85; Vol 14, no 3, 15.11.89.
150. I am grateful to Ian McLure, Neil Atherton and Eddie Haslam for information on this period.
151. *NL* Vol 14, no 6, 1.2.90.
152. *NL* Vol 10 no 8 12.2.86.
153. See *Star* 26.3.80, 6.4.87 and *Gazette* 50, Nov 1970, p.38.
154. ADC6 (1987), Funding Group P.
155. Physics history seminar.
156. Charles Curtis, Report to Pure Science Faculty Board Meeting, 1 Feb 1987. This is one of a number of items supplied by Alan Spears, including a written recollection used for the following account. See also D. A. Carswell, letter to *THES* 18.3.88, quoting survey in *THES* 9.5.86.
157. *Indep* 8.3.88, *THES* 11.3.88.
158. Quote from *AR 1974/75* referring to Materials recruitment.
159. Materials history seminar.
160. AQ.
161. *S Tel*, YP, *Daily Telegraph* 8.3.77; *Star* 7.3.77; information from G. Sims.
162. Graeme Davies, CHI. Other quotes are taken from this interview.
163. *AR 1987/88* p.33, *1995/96*, p.28. *NL* Vol 12, No 8, 10 Feb 1988, p.1.
164. B. B. Argent, 'One hundred years of the Department of Metallurgy in Sheffield', pp.24–5.
165. See graphs in Argent, *ibid*, p.22.

166. Geoffrey Sims, CHI.
167. *Centenary of the Sheffield Technical School*, p.30, *NL* Vol 8, No 11, 1.5.84, p.3.
168. I am grateful to Peter Robson for help with this section.
169. Majerfeld joined the department as a lecturer in 1972 and left for a chair at the University of Colorado in 1978. He was replaced by Peter Houston.
170. Its activities ranges from coal-cutting machinery to biological systems.
171. Keith Miller, CHI. The following account is based in this interview, plus *S Tel* 31.3.80.
172. Engineering history seminar: Robert Boucher, CHI.
173. This department was causing concern in the 1980s, see *THES* 23.1.81, 8.5.81.
174. I am grateful to Jim Swithenbank for help with this section.
175. *Star* 12.5.88.
176. ADC Report to Senate, March 1988.
177. Peter Stubley and Nick Cole, *The Architects' Journal*, 21.7.93; *Now and Then* 7, 1992, pp.42–3. Other quotes are taken from the first article.
178. *Star* 11.6.83.
179. *AR 1985/86*, p.7. See also *NL* Vol 13, No 2, 19.10.88, p.3.
180. *NL* Vol 10, No 1, 9.10.85; *AR 1985/86* pp.7–8, *S Tel* 26.9.85.
181. John Salt, 'The Polytechnic at Sheffield 1969–92', in Binfield et al (ed), *The History of the City of Sheffield*, Vol 2, p.342.
182. There were 27 in existence before Sheffield's, *Financial Times*, 9.12.86.
183. *Guardian* 13.4.89. *Star* 7.3.88 has a good description of the potential of transputers.
184. *NL* Vol 11, no 2, 22.10.86.
185. Speech by Empson, *Gazette* 54, Nov 1974, p.30.
186. Speech by Brian Morris, *Gazette* 54, Nov 1974, p.23. One version of the story is that the dice were loaded.
187. *Guardian* 16.4.84
188. Andrew Braybrook. 'Halcyon days at Sheffield University (1970–1974)', CCHA. This account is also based

on the honorary degree oration for Brian Morris (Lord Morris of Castle Morris), 26 July 1991; *Gazette* 53, Nov 1973, pp.49–53.

189. Comment by John Hawthorne.

190. See Geoffrey Lester, 'Norman Blake and his work' in G. Lester (ed.), *Chaucer in Perspective: Middle English essays in honour of Norman Blake*, Sheffield 1999, pp.13–25.

191. 'Department of Prehistory and Archaeology. Opening Ceremony', Tuesday 3 April 1979, pamphlet, USL.

192. *AR 1988/89*, p.5. The department was placed jointly in the Arts and Pure Science faculties from 1986.

193. See Judith Brown's history of this house (T/S, USL) which was used as Stephenson Hall, c1920–45. It had a brief life as a women's hall before being taken over as the OTC headquarters for fifteen years prior to the Music department's incumbency. See also Basil Deane's article in *Gazette* 50, Nov 1970, pp.47–9.

194. Information on the Lindsay String Quartet from *Gazette* 52, Nov 1972, pp.13–14, 58, Dec 1978, p.9, *S Tel* 13.2.80, *Star* 29. 5.85 (when Roger Bigley left, replaced by Robin Ireland), Honorary degree oration for all four 'Lindsays', 20 July 2001.

195. Taken from Edward Garden's written account of his years in the department, 1975–1993.

196. Alan Brown, SCHA.

197. *S Tel* 25.1.91. See also *NL* Vol 10, 30.4.86.

198. Roger Bullivant was appointed MBE for his work with the society in 1984 and awarded a Sheffield honorary degree in 1999.

199. John Rogerson, 'The Storm before the Calm? The department of Biblical Studies in the 1980s', T/S, USL.

200. *NL* Vol 11 no 4, 19.11.86. Sheffield Academic Press was taken over by Continuum in 2002.

201. *S Tel* 18.1.80; *Daily Telegraph*

19.1.80. *Times* listed 18 departments, 20.6.80.

202. *S Tel* 6.2.80.

203. Information from Bill Leatherbarrow, Bob Russell and John Nicholson.

204. *AR 1986/87*.

205. Hamish Ritchie, SCHA. He called 1987 the 'annus terribilis'. A new professor, N. M. McGowan, was appointed in 1989.

206. The following account is taken from *Gazette* 56, Dec 1976, pp.32–3 and obituaries in *NL* Vol 13, no 11, 15.10.88; *Indep* 13.9.88 and *Daily Telegraph* 9.9.88.

207. *Gazette* 52, Nov 1972, pp.60–62.

208. Information in this and the subsequent paragraph supplied by Derek Mosley.

209. Obituary of Robert Hopper by D. J. Mosley, *Biog. Coll.* ; also *Times* 13.7.82.

210. Derek Mosley, SCHA. This view is confirmed by David Luscombe.

211. *AR 1980/81*, p.18.

212. Three went to Nottingham, one to Oxford, one to the USA; Mosley himself went to Warwick.

213. K. H. D. Haley obituaries, *Times* 21.7.97; *Indep* 11.8.97.

214. This account is taken from a profile of Collinson in *The Historian* Summer 1988; honorary degree oration, 21 July 1995, and comments from colleagues.

215. These are Clyde Binfield's phrases. The following account is based in part on his CHI.

216. See, for example, Union President's report in *AR 1981/82*, p.29.

217. This account is drawn from *THES* 2.10.87, *Star* 30. 8.87, 9.10.87, *NL* Vol 12, no 2, 21.10.87.

218. Turnbull published *Samuel Hartlib: a sketch of his life and his relations to J. A. Comenius*, London and Oxford, 1920 and later wrote *Dury, Hartlib and Comenius*, London and Liverpool, 1947. For the story of Turnbull and the Hartlib collection, see *Gazette* 2, May 1948, p.4; 20, June

1954, p.5; 40, May 1962, pp.59–60.

219. Chris Spencer, SCHA.

220. Comment by Kevin Connolly.

221. See, for example, *YP* 19.1.83, *Star* 15.1.86

222. Details contained in Peter Warr's history of the Unit, *Work, Well-being and effectiveness*.

223. *S Tel* 21.11.84, *NL* Vol 14, no 11, 30.4.90; 'Department of Human Communication Sciences', T/S history supplied by department.

224. Ankie Hoogvelt, comments quoted in 'The department of Sociological Studies, University of Sheffield: an outline history', T/S, USL. This history is the source of subsequent comments, along with John Westergaard's written contribution (SCHA).

225. An interview with Eric Sainsbury on his retirement was published in *Community Care* 13 August 1987. He has written his own account, 'Social Work Education and Training in Sheffield 1949–85', T/S, USL.

226. These comments are all taken from the AQ.

227. This was the conclusion of ADC5 (1985)

228. Anthony Arblaster, SCHA, and Patrick Seyd, CHI.

229. David McClean, CHI.

230. The following account is taken from interviews with colleagues, article in *Times* 14.10.80 and honorary degree oration, 22 July 1995. See also *Star* 18.8.78, 6.9.80, *THES* 9.1.81, *Financial Times* 12.4.83 (and others), Education 7.3.86.

231. AQ.

232. A. K. Bottomley later became Professor of Criminology at the University of Hull.

233. *Gazette* 56, Dec 1976, pp.5, 10–12, 38–9. See also *Gazette* 60, 1979/80, pp.46–47.

234. The following account is based on obituaries of Grenfell-Baines in *Indep* 19. 5.2003, *Daily Telegraph* 3.6.2003, *Times* 14.5. 2003 and *Building Design* 16.5.2003. None of

these were written by Sheffield colleagues and the obituary by Ken Murta, T/S *Biog. Coll.* is useful here and corrects some misapprehensions about Grenfell-Baines's politics. Ken Murta's article on the subsequent direction of the department, 'Sheffield Studies', *RIBA Journal* Feb 1986, pp.41–3, and his clarifying comments have also been very helpful.

235. Alec Daykin, CHI.
236. *Star* 18.8.78, *NL* Vol 13, no 9, 1.3.89.
237. *NL* Vol 9, no 3, 7.11.84.
238. *Architects Journal* 11.6.86.
239. *Gazette* 60, 1979/80, pp.16–17, obituary pp.41–2.
240. The following account is based on information supplied by John Roach.
241. *NL* Vol 11, no 8, 11.2.87. They related to 'O' Level achievement. Newspaper accounts persisted in describing the former as 'Dr Lesson', eg *Times* 19.11.92.
242. This section is based on research by John Hawthorne.
243. 'A brief history of JANET', which started in 1984, may be found on the Superjanet website.
244. Currie's assessment in a paper to Policy Committee, 17 June 1972.
245. *NL* Vol 4, no 9, June 1980.
246. *NL* Vol 11, no 5, 22.12.86; *THES* 25.10.85. See also article by Chris Brown of Computing Services, *Unix Systems* Nov 1985. Wilson pointed out that Europe and the USA were ahead of Britain in this area.
247. Quoted in W. L. Saunders, 'The University of Sheffield Department of Information Studies, 1964–89', T/S, USL. This history is the source for the following paragraph.
248. Susan Frank, SCHA.
249. Linda Kirk, CHI.
250. *S Tel* 22.4.82. The following account is based on comments made by colleagues, including Roger Allum, John Hawthorne, Ian McLure, Bill Galbraith and Ron Johnston.
251. John Padley, CHI. This is the source for subsequent comments attributed

to Dr Padley.
252. See *NL Supplement* 1.5.85; CVCP, Report on the University of Sheffield, Vol 1: General Study, Vol 11: Purchasing Study, 1985.
253. See comments by Jarratt in *THES* 2.5.86, also letter from G. Rowley and S. Bennett in *NL* Vol 9, no 13, 29.5.85.
254. *S Tel* 2.12.81, *Star* 2.12.81.
255. *Star* 4.10.83.
256. *Conference Britain* May 1985.
257. *Now and Then* 4, 1988.
258. Stephen Ware, CHI. This is the source for information in this paragraph.
259. *YP* 23.4.86, *Star* 17.10.88.
260. *Gazette* 57, Dec 1977, pp.37–8.
261. Michael Argyles, *South Kensington to Robbins: an account of English technical and scientific education since 1851*, London 1964, p.79.
262. Bob Boucher made complimentary remarks about the course, CHI.
263. See interviews with Pat Partington published in *THES* 16.12.88, 19.3.93; *Daily Telegraph* 19.10.89.
264. Geoffrey Mitchell, *Responsible Body*, pp.73–4.
265. Liz Hall, SCHA.
266. Details taken from the Yorkshire Ripper official website.
267. David Bland, CHI.
268. Sheffield University Students' Union, *AR 1988/89*, p.8.
269. *Star* 20.10.88, 31.10.88.
270. *Star* 7.10.87, 9.10.87, 22.10.87. A UGM supported it, however, see *Star* 17.10.87.
271. Sheffield University Students Union, *AR 1986/87*, 1989/90.
272. Mary Holding, CHI.
273. *NL* Vol 8, no 9, 6.3.84.
274. *AR 1982/83*, pp.28–9.
275. *Darts* 23.2.84.
276. *Quality of Sheffield* Jan/Feb 1985.
277. Geoffrey Sims, CHI.
278. *Times* 17.7.85.
279. I am grateful to Reg Goodchild for these comments.
280. This was the work of a Committee of Council, implementing ADC6.

Clyde Binfield describes his experience, CHI.
281. *S Tel*, 17.7.85, *NL* Vol 10, no 10, 12.3.86.
282. *AR 1987/88*.
283. *AR 1988/89*.
284. *THES* 6.1.87.
285. Administrators' seminar.
286. Dainton, *Doubts and certainties*, p.213.
287. *S Tel* 8.12.82.
288. R. Szreter, 'Opportunities for women as university teachers since the Robbins report of 1963', *Studies in Higher Education* Vol 8, No 2, 1983 pp.139–150.
289. Quoted by Halsey, *Decline of donnish dominion*, p.222.
290. Ian McLure, CHI.
291. Comments by John Westergaard, Clyde Binfield and David McClean.
292. *AR 1986/87*, p.2.
293. Geoffrey Sims, CHI.

CHAPTER 7

1. *S Tel* 28.12.90.
2. The views of Gareth Roberts cited in this chapter are based, unless otherwise stated, on Centenary History interviews and further information supplied to the project. I am grateful to Sir Gareth for his considerable help with this chapter.
3. Vice-Chancellor's Address to Court, 11 Dec 1991.
4. *NL* Vol 15, 20.2.91.
5. Annual Address to Staff, *NL* Vol 16, no 9, 18.3.92.
6. Unless otherwise referenced, statistics quoted in this section have been compiled by Len Hill from University records.
7. Reg Goodchild, CHI.
8. *Times* 4.3.91. See also *Guardian* 27.2.91, *THES* 1.3.91, *S Tel* 1.3.91.
9. Gareth Roberts, *AR 1995/96*, p.3, also p.4.
10. *THES* 28.2.92, *Times* 2.3.92.
11. See table in *THES* 13.1.95. Sheffield is fifth above average. A

league table published in *THES* 27.5.94 gives staff/student ratios of 12 for Sheffield and Oxford, and 11 for Cambridge.

12. Research by Len Hill estimates the change to student-staff ratios over forty years as: 1960/61: 8.7; 1970/71: 9.1; 1980/81: 9.5 1990/91: 11.5; *1995/96*: 14; 2000/01: 13.6 2002/03: 14.9.

13. Len Hill, SCHA.

14. *Indep* 5.1.95.

15. *AR 1992/93*, p.2. See also *THES* 5.2.93.

16. *THES* 28.1.2000.

17. *AR 1991/92*, p.8, *NL* Vol 21, 27.10.96.

18. Vice-Chancellor's Address to Court, 11 Dec 1991.

19. TES 15.11.91.

20. Bernard Kingston, CHI. He collaborated with John O'Leary, The Times Education Editor and a former Union President. Sheffield's destination statistics go back to 1963, see E. A. Ovens, 'The University Careers Service 1928–78', T/S, USL.

21. I am grateful to Alan Walker and Len Hill for help with this section.

22. A member of staff who supported the change.

23. *AR 1993/94*, p.8, 1991/92, p.5.

24. The Sixteen point scale: 1–3 = fail; 4 = pass; 5–7 = class 3; 8–10 = class 2.2; 11–13 = class 2.1; 14–16 = class 1.

25. Ron Johnston, CHI.

26. Peter Foster, SCHA.

27. *Times* 28.6.93. This paragraph is also based on research by Len Hill.

28. Information from Gareth Roberts. He stressed that they should also have 'some involvement in research'.

29. Mary Sharrock, 'Receiving Students', *THES* 10.2.78.

30. Stephen George, SCHA. I am also grateful to Allan Johnson for help with this section.

31. *NL* Vol 16, No 8, 26.2.92. See also *Star* 7.2.92, 6.4.92, 21.9.93; *Wakefield Express* 16.4.93; *AR 1991/92*, p.14.

32. *Guardian* 8.9.98.

33. *Financial Times* 3.5.2003.

34. Carole Angel and Allan Johnson, 'Broadening access to undergraduate medical education', *British Medical Journal*, Vol 321, 4.11.2000, pp.1136–8.

35. Press Release, 11.3.99.

36. Information on Collegiate Studies supplied by Tom Rhodes and Anthea Stephenson. The Mundella Programme was named after the Sheffield Liberal MP, A. J. Mundella, who supported Firth College in its earliest days.

37. *AR 1995/96*, p.13.

38. The Partnership linked Doncaster, Rotherham and the Dearne. For the College plans, see *NL* Vol 16, 1.7.92, Vol 17 1.4.93 ; *AR 1991/92*, pp.3 & 15; *S Tel* 19.6.92, 15.1.93; *YP* and *Guardian* 19. 6.92; *Star* 18.3.93 12.4.95, *South Yorkshire Times* 17.5.96.

39. *S Tel* 31.1.92.

40. *NL* Vol 20, 1.4.96, Department of Engineering Materials, *Research in Progress 2002*, p.21.

41. *Star* 9.9.98, *YP* 18.7.96, *Daily Telegraph* 10.5.99.

42. The office was disbanded in 1999 when Marilyn Wedgwood left for Manchester University. Its functions were incorporated, as the Regional Advisory Board, within the University's Committee structure.

43. There are many accounts of the troubled build-up to the Games, see for example *S Tel* 12.7.91.

44. *Star* 16.4.91, *S Tel* 26.7.91.

45. USUS, *Annual Report 1990/91*, p1.

46. *Indep* 9.7.92, *Observer* 9.4.95. He took time out of his career in 1999 to train for the World Championships, but had to abandon this and the Olympics because of recurrent injury. *Independent on Sunday* 4.7.99, *Daily Post* 7.9.2000.

47. *S Tel* 26.7.91.

48. Gareth Roberts, Memo to University staff, 8.2.94; *NL* Vol 18, 12.1.94.

49. *S Tel* 9.2.94. Mike Bower was the

leader of the City Council at this time.

50. *S Tel* 4.2.94. The team had been attempting to negotiate on this point for some time.

51. *YP* 4.2.94.

52. *Daily Telegraph* 22.6.2001; *Indep* 3.7.2001, *Manchester Evening News* 24.7.2003.

53. See, among others, *S Tel* 12.1.90, 26.1.90, 26.10.90, 13.9.91, 20.9.91, 7.2.92, 5.6.92.

54. *S Tel* 19.6.92, 10.7.92. A plan for two sports halls on Northumberland Road, announced at the same time, was later abandoned.

55. This account taken from *S Tel* 31.7.92, 27.8.93, 16.6.95, 2.8.96; *Star* 14.7.95, 16.8.95.

56. The Engineering courses were originally run by a consortium of five universities. Minutes of the Strategic Planning Committee, 23.9.96.

57. Reg Goodchild, CHI.

58. Kevin Kam, 'It was a rainy day', *So what's it really like? International Students' own views of Sheffield life*, (Student Services dept) edition 1, pp.7–8.

59. 'Taylor's College at the University of Sheffield', pamphlet, 1999, p.7.

60. This account is based on CHIs with Gareth Roberts, John Padley, Reg Goodchild, Frank Woods, Robert Fraser, Nigel Mathers, Campbell Murdoch, Abu Bakar (CEO Perak College); Minutes of Strategic Planning Committee, 9.5.94, 6.6.94, 15.5.95, 10.2.97, 14.4.97, 6.2.98, 5.3.98, 5.5.98, 12.5.98, 8.6.98, 6.7.98, 21.9.98, 26.10.98, 23.11.98, 22.2.99, 26.4.99, 28.6.99, 27.9.99, 27.3.2000; *BMJ* 21.11.98; *THES* 6.11.98.

61. *The Star* [Malaysian newspaper] 23.11.97.

62. Evidence of Reg Goodchild and Robert Fraser.

63. *Star* 5.7.96, *AR 1995/96*, p.18.

64. Comment by Robert Fraser, who attended the meeting with the GMC.

65. Three doctors at the Bristol Royal

Infirmary were found guilty in June 1998 of serious professional misconduct by the General Medical Council, since they failed to stop performing heart operations despite evidence that the death rate was much higher than the national average.

66. The title of the vice-chancellor's presentation to Council on 18.5.98. Minutes of Strategic Planning Committee, 12.5.98; for Kulim also 19.2.96, 10.6.96, 16.2.98, 5.3.98, 9.3.98, 5.5.98, 8.6.98.

67. *UNECIA in Action 1992–3*, *UNECIA* (nd), *UNECIA and the Environment* (nd), *Yorkshire Business* June 1997; *Star* 1.2.90, 7.2.96, 11.12.96, 31.10.97, *Financial Times* 5.12.97.

68. *S Tel* 1.5.98.

69. John Padley, CHI.

70. *AR 1992/93*, p.17.

71. Information from Tim Crick.

72. Information from Tim Crick.

73. University of Sheffield, *International Student*, Feb 1994, p.6.

74. It became a model for other universities, since Debora Green performed the national training for UKCOSA, the UK Council of Overseas Student Affairs.

75. *International Student*, Feb 1996, p.6. Other quotations in this paragraph taken from *So what's it really like?* edition 1, pp.2; 12–13, 7–8.

76. Quotations in this paragraph taken from *International Student*, March 2001, pp.6 & 7; *So what's it really like?* edition 1, p.6.

77. Jo Holliday, *International Student* Adviser, wrote the pamphlet 'Internationalising Student Unions', which is distributed by UCOSA.

78. Gareth Roberts, CHI; see *Times* 4.11.91 for comments by the editor of the *THES* on the inevitability of a 'premier league'.

79. Gareth Roberts, CHI.

80. *Indep* 3.3.95, *Guardian* 25.1.96. The cut was over two years, 1996–98.

81. *Indep* 31.1.96. For this story, see also *Times*, *Indep* 30.1.96, *Times* 31.1.96,

Financial Times 3.2.96, *Star* 21.2.96.

82. *Guardian* 5.3.96.

83. *THES* 18.7.97, 30.11.2001.

84. *AR 1995/96* p.4, *S Tel* 19.4.96.

85. Julian Kinderlerer, quoted in *S Tel* 19.4.96.

86. *Indep* 28.2.97.

87. See p.146 for Masefield's speech; *AR 1996/97* p.4.

88. The National Committee of Enquiry in Higher Education (The Dearing Report), 1997, Recommendations 1, 2 & 79.

89. *Guardian* 29.7.97.

90. *Hansard* 23.7.97.

91. *Star* 11.7.97, 1.10.97, 3.11.97.

92. *Steel Press* 15.12.97.

93. *Star* 27.8.98. There was also a non-payment campaign at several universities, including Oxford.

94. *Indep* 19.3.98, *Times* 12.5.98, *Star* 20.2.99.

95. *Indep* 28.5.98, *NL* Vol 22, 5.6.98.

96. *S Tel* 13.8.99, 20.8.99.

97. Phil Jones and Tony Crook.

98. Andrew Gamble, CHI.

99. Interviews have been conducted with a number of pro-vice-chancellors, including Tony Crook, David McClean, David Luscombe and Andrew Gamble, from which the quotations in this paragraph are taken.

100. *AR 1994/95*, p.3.

101. The Earth Sciences Unit became a department in 1992. For its closure see *S Tel* 20.11.98, 4.12.98, *Star* 28.11.98, *THES* 4.12.98, 18.12.98 (letter from Roberts), *NL* Vol 23, 13.4.99. I am also grateful for information from Ernie Bailey.

102. James Grayson, 'Korean Studies at the University of Sheffield', *The Korean Foundation Newsletter*, March 2002.

103. I am grateful to postgraduate student Raymond Yeap for information on Chinese Studies.

104. Gareth Roberts, CHI.

105. Stuart Johnson, Honorary degree oration, 21.7.2000.

106. Peter Lee, CHI.

107. Lord Dainton obituary, *AR 1997/98*, p.3. Obituaries appeared in all the national newspapers on 8.12.97.

108. Peter Middleton, CHI. See also *Star* 25.1.83, *Indep* 21.3.90.

109. Reg Goodchild, CHI.

110. David Fletcher, CHI; see also *AR 1999/2000*, pp.14–15.

111. Obituary, *NL* Oct 2001.

112. *NL* Vol 25, 27.10. 2000.

113. David Fletcher, CHI.

114. *AR 1993/94*, p.21; Bob Boucher, CHI.

115. David Fletcher, CHI, *AR 1999/2000*, p.16.

116. Information from David Jones, the Principal of the College. I am grateful to him for help with this section, including a written account and discussion of the school's history hosted by Betty Kershaw, 10.11.2003. See also *NL* Vol 17, no7, 24.2.93, Vol 19, no 10, 28.4.95.

117. Betty Kershaw's inimitable comment, 10.11.2003.

118. These are the figures at the time of integration in 1995, see *NL* Vol 19, no 10, 28.4.95.

119. Comment by David Jones

120. Reg Goodchild, CHI.

121. The Certificate in Social Studies was abandoned in 1962 and a short-lived diploma in the Institute of Education was the only subsequent initiative.

122. Comments by David Jones and Betty Kershaw.

123. Figures supplied by David Jones.

124. *The History of our Hospitals (III)* [Sheffield Central Library] pp.9–11. See also *NL* Vol 22, 28.11.97.

125. Gordon Grant, *International Nursing and Midwifery Link-Up 22*, 2002, p.3.

126. Comment during the discussion of the school's history.

127. Gareth Roberts and Frank Woods, CHIs; Minutes of Strategic Planning Committee, 13.5.91, App.F.

128. This account is based on Frank Woods, CHI. He produced a 'blueprint for change' in 1989. Quotes attributed to Woods in this section are taken from his interview.

Ian Cooke's CHI has also been helpful.

129. There was an interim stage of seven divisions in 1997, which are listed in *AR1997/98*, p.29.

130. *NL* Vol 15, 13.3.91. Minutes of the Strategic Planning Committee, 7.12.92, 19.4.93, 7.6.93, 6.12.93, 17.1.94 (Appendix C).

131. Defined as 'research into the costs and effectiveness of health care interventions', *ibid* 17.1.94 (App.C).

132. I am grateful to Alan Walker for help with this section.

133. *NL* Vol 16, 4.9.91, Vol 20, 31.5.96; *British Medical Journal*, Vol 321, 15.7.2000, pp.150–153; *Indep* 21.3.2000, *Pulse* 11.3.2000 and many others.

134. Gareth Roberts, CHI, see also *AR 1993/94*, p.13. These chairs were funded by the Marjorie Coote Trust.

135. David Hannay, *North-Wing*, Spring 1990, pp.19–21.

136. For this section, see *AR 1998/99*, p.10; 2001/02, p.9; 2002/03, p.11.

137. *Star* 21.3.90, 9.5.90, 16.11.90.

138. *YP* 1.3.90, 27.6.90, *S Tel* 27.6.97. For Kanis's campaign, see also *NL* Vol 14, 15. 3.90.

139. B. L. Briggs, Distinguished Investigator, Mayo Clinic, Rochester, USA, in correspondence submitted as part of the University's bid for a Queen's Anniversary Prize, March 2002.

140. Table compiled by the Institute for Scientific Information, on behalf of Osteoporosis International. (Queen's Anniversary Prize bid)

141. Letter from Gordon Duff, *British Journal of Hospital Medicine*, Feb 1991. I am grateful to Gordon Duff for help with this section.

142. Quotations from Gordon Duff.

143. *Star* 11.5.93.

144. *AR 1987/88*, p.10; *NL* Vol 18, 12.1.94.

145. John Lilleyman, Honorary degree oration 23.7.2003; James Underwood, SCHA.

146. W. D. Foster, *Pathology as a profession in Great Britain and the early history of the Royal College of Pathologists*, n.d., pp.67–68. With thanks to James Underwood for supplying this reference.

147. A. G. Johnson, Honorary Degree oration, 15.1.2004.

148. I am grateful to Alan Brook for help with this section.

149. I am grateful to Gareth Roberts for specific help with this section, especially in the selection of research featured.

150. Gareth Roberts, CHI.

151. Gareth Roberts, Honorary Degree Oration, 25.7.2002.

152. *Times* 15.5.96.

153. *Star* 25.3.92. The others were Southampton and Tokyo. See also *THES* 18.5.2000.

154. *THES* 18.5.2000. *AR 1993/94*, p.20, 1998/99, p.8.

155. *EducationGuardian.co.uk*, University Guide 2004.

156. Materials staff Centenary History seminar; Michael Cable, SCHA.

157. Materials staff Centenary History seminar; AR 1996/7, p.18, Department of Engineering Materials, *Research in Progress 2002*, p.20.

158. *New Scientist* 14.4.90.

159. Obituary by John Williams, *NL* Vol 25, 5.6.2001.

160. *Star* 23.10.97; Physics Centenary History seminar, *AR 1999/2000*, p.9.

161. *NL* Vol 25, 3.8.2001; *Overview*, issue 3, Feb 2004.

162. Research by Mark Sanderson. Fifteen of these departments were at Cambridge, seven at Oxford and six at University College, London.

163. Peter Willett, CHI. He was head of department 1997–8 and from 2002.

164. *Guardian* 7.7.94. Bradford University claimed to have been the first to use the Web for this purpose, in 1992.

165. Peter Willett, CHI.

166. I am grateful to Len Hill and Ernie Bailey for help with this section.

167. *Times Good University Guide*, 2002 & 2003.

168. Comment made by postgraduate to author, 1.11.2001.

169. Ian Cooke, CHI. Moore hit the headlines when he was said to be working on a contraceptive pill for squirrels, see *Guardian* 19.10.94, *Daily Mail* 20.10.94, *S Tel* 15.5.98, *Sunday Telegraph* 13.6.99.

170. *Daily Telegraph* 16.8.2000; *Overview*, issue 2, Dec 2003.

171. The additional grants for refurbishment of Firth Court were from the Wolfson Foundation and the Royal Society. JIF funding also established a centre for Chemical Biology and supported Neil Spooner's work on 'dark matter' (Physics).

172. Ernie Bailey, CHI.

173. This account is based on Pat Seyd and Andrew Gamble, CHIs.

174. *S Tel* 18.1.91, *Star* 25.1.91, *NL* Vol 15, 23.1.91. Also *THES* 6.12.91.

175. *NL* Vol 18, 2.2.94.

176. *Tribune* 12.1.90, *Guardian* 2.10.90, *Glasgow Herald* 11.5.92, *Independent on Sunday* 26.6.94, *Guardian* (and others) 20.9.99, *Times* 30.5.2000. Also *NL* Vol 15, 23.1.91, Vol 19, 28.10.94.

177. Paul Whiteley, Patrick Seyd and Jeremy Richardson, *True blues: the politics of Conservative Party membership*, Oxford 1994.

178. *AR 1993/94* p.22; *Daily Telegraph* and *Times* 24.7.90, TES 31.8.90, *S Tel* 5.4.91.

179. *AR 1992/93*, p.23; *Indep* 24.9.99.

180. Peter *Warr, Work, well-being and effectiveness*, pp.21–22.

181. I am grateful to David Shepherd and Bob Russell for help with this paragraph. Quotations come from them.

182. *AR 1996/97*, p.28.

183. *NL* Vol 16, 26.2.92.

184. Ian Kershaw, CHI. The Hitler biography was published by Penguin as *Hubris* (1998) and *Nemesis* (2000), with simultaneous publication in German, French, Spanish, Dutch and Italian.

185. David Williams, CHI.
186. Obituary, *NL* Vol 26, Oct 2001.
187. *NL* Vol 21, 10.1.97.
188. Archaeology department website, 2003/04.
189. Dept of Archaeology and Prehistory, 'The opening of Northgate House and West Court, Jan 29 1996', pamphlet.
190. *AR 1999/2000*, p.7; information from David Clines. The project spanned 1988–2006.
191. Julian Kinderlerer, CHI; *NL* Vol 19, 9.6.95, Vol 23, 26.3.99 and David McClean, CHI.
192. Tony Crook, CHI.
193. 'Architecture' was dropped from the title of the department in 1993, reflecting a broadening of the profession to embrace planning, design and management – all of which it taught.
194. All the others are small parts of larger schools or faculties.
195. *Star* 1.12.92.
196. *NL* Vol 21, 21.2.97.
197. *The Architects' Journal*, 25.3.2004, listed Sheffield as third choice of university architecture departments in a poll of 100 top practitioners.
198. Gareth Roberts, comment to the author.
199. *Indep* 10.10.96; see photo and caption.
200. *AR 1999/2000*, p.7; *Indep* 24.4.97, *Star* 1.6.99, *THES* 19.11.99.
201. Account based on Gareth Roberts, CHI; *AR 2001/02*, p.16.
202. I am grateful to Michael Hannon and Martin Lewis for help with this section.
203. *THES* 17.5.96, 23.4.99.
204. *Times, Daily Telegraph, Star, YP, THES*, 29.8.97.
205. *S Tel* 1.8.97. See also *Star* 11.8.97, *YP* 21.11.94, *NL* Vol 19, 9.12.94.
206. David Luscombe, CHI.
207. *AR 1994/95*, pp.17–18.
208. Gareth Roberts, Dainton lecture, 29.9.98. This lecture draws on a paper published by Blake and his colleagues in *Nature*.
209. *THES* 25.6.99, 2.7.99.
210. I am grateful to John Hawthorne for further research on this section.
211. *NL* Vol 20, 26.1.96.
212. 'Big Macs' are burgers produced by the fast food chain McDonalds.
213. I would like to thank Jonathan Foster and Bob Bennett for help with this section; see also *NL* Vol 13, 15.3.89, Vol 19, 7.10.94, *AR 1993/94*, p.12.
214. *Now and Then*, 7, 1992, pp.32–33.
215. Geoffrey Mitchell, *Responsible Body*, p.123. See also chapter 3. I am grateful to Sue Webb and David Hey for help with this section.
216. Minutes of the Strategic Planning Committee, 14.3.94, App.G.
217. This was first proposed in a 1984 UGC Report on Continuing Education. See John McIllroy and Bruce Spencer, *University Adult Education in Crisis*, Leeds 1988, pp.65–72.
218. Geoffrey Mitchell, *Responsible Body*, p.114. Sue Webb points out that Sheffield was better prepared for these changes than many other universities.
219. *AR 1995/96*, p.14.
220. *THES* 26.7.96. This table does not count Associate Professors.
221. Hansard Society report quoted by Helena Kennedy, *THES* 3.11.95.
222. I am grateful to Rosie Valerio for help with this section.
223. John Behagg quoted in *Star* 16.5.98, responding to a league table in *THES* 15.5.98 which continued to show Sheffield lagging behind.
224. University of Sheffield, *Annual Staffing Report 1999/2000*.
225. *Star, Indep, Daily Telegraph, Guardian* 4.4.97 & 8.5.2000, *BMJ* 12.4.97.
226. University of Sheffield, *Annual Staffing Report 1994/95; 1999/2000*.
227. This account draws on the *Annual Reports* of the Union of Students, 1990–2001 and interviews with Paul Blomfield, Heather Foster and Mary Holding. I am grateful to David Bradshaw for further research on
Student Services.
228. Colin Lago, CHI.
229. Colin Lago and Alison Barty, *Working with Overseas Students: A Staff Development and Training Manual*, edition 2, London, UKCOSA, 2003.
230. Evidence from James Burton, director of Student Health, and David Luscombe.
231. See quotes from national newspapers etc inside the cover of USUS, *Annual Report 1999; Guardian* Higher 10.3.98.
232. Letter to *Star* 1.2.92.
233. *Independent on Sunday* 6.11.94, *Star* 30.11.94.
234. *Star* 28.1.94.
235. *THES* 22.7.94.
236. *Star* 28.9.96. A *Guardian* survey, 19.8.99, showed that only St Andrews was cheaper for a university room.
237. *Times* 19.3.98.
238. This opened in 1997, part of the Bass Taverns national drive to create alternatives to the Students' Unions, *S Tel* 14.3.97.
239. *AR 1992/93*, p.28, *1995/6*, p.34, *1996/7*, p.32.
240. This later became the venue for meetings of the Senate – an example of the mountain coming to Mahomet.
241. Paul Blomfield, CHI.
242. *Darts* was also runner-up for best newspaper in 1994.
243. Information from Matt Watson; USUS, *Annual Report 1990/91*, p.11. The LGB Society was first established in 1973.
244. Gareth Roberts, CHI.
245. *YP* 24.2.92.
246. USUS, *Annual Report 1998*, p.11.
247. *Darts* 14.12.95; *NL*, Vol 20, 5.1.96.
248. For this section, see *S Tel* 2.11.90, 13.11.92, 12.11.93, 3.11.95, 10.11.95, *Star* 15.11.94, 13.11.95, 25.11.96, 26.11.96, 25.2.97, 3. 10.97.
249. *Star* 26.11.96.
250. Paul Blomfield, CHI.
251. *Guardian* 10.10.97. Matthews was,

however, upbeat enough to pronounce 1996/97 'one of the Union's most exciting years', USUS, *Annual Report 1997*, p.1.

252. *Star* 18.2.99, 24.2.99, 1.3.99, 11.3.99.
253. Paul Blomfield, CHI, Adam Matthews quoted in *S Tel* 27.2.98.
254. *S Tel* 20.2.98.
255. *NL* Vol 22, 1.4.98, *S Tel* 13.3.98.
256. *Steel Press* 15.5.2002.
257. USUS, *Annual Report 1989/90*, p.7; *Star* 4.10.88, 1.3.90, 21.9.90.
258. *S Tel* 23.9.94.
259. *S Tel* 1.11.96; a reply to a letter in *S Tel* 18.10.96. The vicar of St Mark's, Broomhill, wrote to distance himself from accusations of 'swamping', *S Tel* 30.9.94.
260. *Star* 11.6.98, *S Tel* 12.6.98.
261. Information for this paragraph supplied by David Bradshaw.
262. At the same time, student aspirations were increasing, as an annual survey of student satisfaction with services, introduced in 1993, showed. There was, for example, demand for *en suite* facilities, which were hard to meet in the short term. *En suite* 'pods' were fitted in some bedrooms but plumbing problems often proved insuperable.
263. *YP* 30.11.99.
264. *NL* Vol 17, 19.5.93.
265. *NL* Vol 17, 19.5.93.
266. *S Tel* 25.4.97, *Star* 27.6.97. The

charge was linked to income. There had previously been limited use of charging in specific, reserved places.
267. Geoffrey Sims, CHI.
268. *NL* Vol 14, 1.2.90. This was 'St George's village', an early version of Regent Court.
269. David Luscombe, CHI.
270. *NL* Vol 19, 9.6.95.
271. *NL* Vol 22, 26.6.98, *S Tel* 15.11.96, *Business North* Jun/July 1998.
272. *Guardian* 30.5.2000.
273. *NL* Vol 25, 22.12.2000.
274. *AR 2001/02*, p.6.
275. Gareth Roberts, CHI.
276. Michael Shattock, *The creation of the British university system*, Oxford 1996, p.24.
277. Peter Banks, SCHA.

POSTSCRIPT

1. This paragraph is based on Bob Boucher's Centenary History Interview, with further comments, and the profile by Roger Allum produced for the Special Meeting of Court, 18 July 2000.
2. *The Sunday Times University Guide*, 16.9.2001.
3. Andrew Gamble, CHI.
    4. *The Sunday Times University Guide*, 16.9.2001.
5. These results have already been

described in chapter 7 and are summarised in App.5.
6. *Newsletter*, Vol 26, August 2002.
7. Press releases 31.1.2001, 23.3.2001, 12.10.2001, 7.11.2001, 18.6.2003; *Newsletter* Vol 25, 16.3.2001; Vol 26, Feb 2002; AR 2000/01, p.20.
8. Press release 31.1.2001.
9. SUEL was the successor to Unisheff Ventures, set up in 1984 and described in chapter 6, pp.282–3.
10. See chapter 7, p.346.
11. *Overview* No 3, Feb 2004, p.3.
12. *AR 2001/02*, p.12.
13. Figures supplied by Student Recruitment and Admissions Office. They exclude students from EU countries.
14. *Financial Times* 3.5.2003
15. Allan Johnson, quoted in *ibid*.
16. Information from Paul Blomfield.
17. Sheffield Volunteering, *AR 2002/03*. See also *AR 2003/04* for comments in this section.
18. www.archive.sportengland.org, *S Tel* 5.12.03.
19. Information from Gordon Duff.
20. *S Tel* 9.7.2004; 10.9.04.
21. *Independent on Sunday* 29.8.2004; University of Sheffield website.
22. Chapman, p.446. The University's motto may be translated as 'Happy is the person who understands the reasons for things'.
23. 'Thus we travel to the stars'.

Select Bibliography of Secondary Sources

This Bibliography is limited to works cited in the notes. Full length biographies are included, but not biographical articles.

Works about Sheffield University (available in USL)

Argent, B. B., 'One hundred years of the Department of Metallurgy in Sheffield', T/S 1984.

Boylan, Maureen & Riley, Gillian, *The University of Sheffield: an illustrated history*, pam. 1981.

Boylan, Maureen, *The University of Sheffield: a pictorial history*, pam 1985.

Bruce, Maurice, *The University of Sheffield Department of Extramural Studies 1947–68: a personal survey*, pam. 1968.

Chapman, A. W., *The story of a modern university: a history of the University of Sheffield*, Oxford UP, 1955.

Chapman, A. W., *The early days of the Chemistry department*, pam. 1959/60.

Critchley, G. N., *A Short History of Fuel Technology at the University of Sheffield*, pam. 1980.

Edyvean, R. G. J. (ed), *Centenary of the Sheffield Technical School: an illustrated account*, pam. 1986.

Gifford, Peter, 'Forty years of Student Health', *Gazette* 57, Dec 1977, pp.42–4.

Hall, Arthur J., *Notes on the Sheffield School of Medicine*, pam. 1944.

Hill, Len, 'A history of Biology in Sheffield 1828–2000', T/S.

Hoath, David (ed), *75 years of Law at Sheffield, 1909–1984*, pam. 1984.

[Jenkins, Richard], 'The department of Sociological Studies, University of Sheffield: an outline history', T/S.

Jones, Brynmor, *University of Sheffield: record of War work 1939–45*, pam. 1946.

Mann, P. H. and Mills, G, 'Living and learning at Redbrick: a sample survey at Sheffield University', *Universities Quarterly*, Vol 16, 1961–2, 19–35.

Marshall, O. R. (ed), *The Jubilee Lectures: the Faculty of Law, University of Sheffield*, Stevens & Sons, London 1960.

Mathers, Helen, 'Scientific women in a co-educational university: Sheffield 1879–1939', to be published in *History of Education*.

Miller, Harold, *A brief history of Medical Physics in Sheffield, 1914–1982*, pam. 1982.

Mitchell, Geoffrey, *Responsible body: the story of fifty years of adult education in the University of Sheffield 1947–97*, pam. 2000.

Newton, Gerald, *German studies at the University of Sheffield: a historical perspective 1880–1980*, pam. 1988.

Ovens, E. A., *The University Careers Service 1928–1978*, T/S 1978.

Porter, W. S., *The medical school in Sheffield 1828–1928*, Northend, Sheffield, 1928.

Ripper W., *History of the university to the time of its coming-of-age, May 31 1926*, pam. 1926.

Roach, John, 'The University of Sheffield', in C. Binfield et al (ed), *The History of the City of Sheffield 1843–1993*, Vol 2, Society, Sheffield AP, 1993, 347–63.

Rogerson, John, 'The Storm before the Calm? The Department of Biblical Studies in the 1980s', T/S.

Roper, Joseph I., *The challenge of adult education. The record of a partnership 1910–1960 between the University of Sheffield and the Workers' Educational Association*, pam. 1993.

Sainsbury, Eric, 'Social Work education and training in Sheffield 1949–85', T/S.

Saunders, W. L., 'The University of Sheffield Department of Information Studies, 1964–89', *Journal of Information Science* 15 (1989), 193–202.

Swan, Harold T., 'Sheffield Medical School: origins

and influences', *Journal of Medical Biography*, Vol 2, 1994, 22–32.

Warr, Peter, *Work, well-being and effectiveness: a history of the MRC/ESRC Social and Applied Psychology Unit*, Sheffield AP, 1999.

Warr, Peter, *Psychology in Sheffield: the early years*, Sheffield AP, 2001.

General and Biographical Works

Abse, D., (ed), *My medical school*, Robson, London 1978.

Aldrich, Richard, (ed), *A century of education*, Routledge Falmer, London 2002.

Arblaster, Anthony, *Academic freedom*, Penguin 1974.

Argyles, Michael, *South Kensington to Robbins: an account of English technical and scientific education since 1851*, Longmans, London 1964.

Armytage, W. H. G., *Civic universities: aspects of a British tradition*, Benn, London 1955.

Barnes, Sarah, 'Crossing the invisible line: establishing co-education at the University of Manchester and Northwestern University', *History of Education* Vol 23, no 1, 1994, 35–58.

Barnes, Sarah V., 'England's civic universities and the triumph of the Oxbridge ideal', *History of Education Quarterly* Vol 36, no 3, 1996, 271–305.

Binfield, C., Martin, D. et al (ed), *The history of the City of Sheffield 1843–1993*, Vols 1–3, Sheffield AP, 1993.

Blunkett, David, *On a clear day*, Michael O'Mara Books, revised edition London 2002.

Bruce, F. F., *In retrospect: remembrance of things past*, Pickering & Inglis, London 1980.

Cotgrove, Stephen F., *Technical education and social change*, Allen & Unwin, London 1958.

Crouch, Colin, *The Student Revolt*, Bodley Head, London 1970.

Dahrendorf, Ralf, *LSE: a history of the London School of Economics and Political Science 1895–1995*, Oxford UP, 1995.

Dainton, Fred, *Doubts and Certainties. A Personal Memoir of the 20th Century*, Sheffield AP, 2001.

Dent, H. C., *The universities in transition*, Cohen & West, London 1961.

Dent, H. C., *The training of teachers in England and Wales 1800–1975*, Hodder & Stoughton, London 1977.

Dyhouse, Carol, *No distinction of sex? Women in British universities 1870–1939*, UCL Press, London 1995.

Fisher, H. A. L., *An unfinished autobiography*, Oxford UP, 1940.

Gibert, Julie, 'Women students and student life at England's civic universities before the First World War', *History of Education* Vol 23, No 4, 1994, 405–422.

Gill, Roma, (ed.) *William Empson: the man and his work*, Routledge & Kegan Paul, London 1974.

Gillies, Midge, *Amy Johnson*, Weidenfeld & Nicolson, London 2003.

Gosden, P. H. J. H. & Taylor, A. J., *Studies in the history of a university 1874–1974*, Arnold, Leeds 1975.

Greene, Gayle, *The woman who knew too much*, Ann Arbor, Michigan UP, 1999.

Gumpert, T. E., *Recollected in tranquillity: reminiscences of a Sheffield physician*, pam. 1978.

Haffenden, John, (ed.), *William Empson: the complete poems*, Penguin 2000.

Halsey, A. H. and Trow, M., *The British academics*, Faber, London 1971.

Halsey, A. H., *The decline of donnish dominion: the British academic professions in the 20th century*, Clarendon Press, Oxford 1992.

Harrison, J. F. C., *Learning and living 1790–1960: a study in the history of the English adult education movement*, Routledge & Kegan Paul, London 1961.

Hetherington, H., *The British university system 1914–54*, Oliver & Boyd for University of Aberdeen [1954].

Hey, David, *A history of Sheffield*, Carnegie Publications, Lancaster 1998.

Higham, N., *A very scientific gentleman: the major achievements of Henry Clifton Sorby*, Pergamon Macmillan, Oxford 1963.

Ives, Eric, Drummond, Diane and Schwarz, Leonard, *The first civic university: Birmingham 1880–1980*, Birmingham UP, 2000.

Jepson, N. A., *The beginnings of English university adult education – policy and problems*, Joseph, London 1973.

Kearney, Hugh, *Scholars and gentlemen: universities and society in pre-industrial Britain 1500–1700*, Faber, London 1970.

Kelly, Thomas, *A history of adult education in Great Britain*, Liverpool UP, 1970.

Kelly, Thomas, *For advancement of learning: the University of Liverpool 1881–1981*, Liverpool UP, 1981.

Krebs, Hans, *Reminiscences and reflections*, Clarendon Press, Oxford 1981.

Lester, Geoffrey (ed.), *Chaucer in Perspective: Middle English essays in honour of Norman Blake*, Sheffield AP, 1999.

Linton, D. L., (ed), *Sheffield and its region: a scientific and historical survey*, Local Executive Committee for the British Association, Sheffield 1956.

Macfarlane, R. G., *Howard Florey: the making of a great scientist*, Oxford UP, 1979.

Mackerness, E. D., *Somewhere further north: a history of music in Sheffield*, Northend, Sheffield 1974.

Mathers, Helen and McIntosh, Tania, *Born in Sheffield: a history of the women's health services 1864–2000*, Wharncliffe Books, Barnsley 2000.

McIlroy, John and Spencer, Bruce, *University adult education in crisis*, University of Leeds, 1988.

Mellanby, Kenneth, *Human guinea pigs*, 1st edition Gollancz, London 1945, 2nd edition 1973.

Millington, Roy, *A history of the City of Sheffield Training College*, City of Sheffield Training College, 1955.

Morse, Elizabeth J., 'The English civic universities and the myth of decline', *History of Universities* Vol XI, 1992, 177–204.

Newman, Charles, *The evolution of medical education in the nineteenth century*, Oxford UP, 1957.

Perkin, Harold, *Key profession: the history of the Association of University teachers*, Routledge & Kegan Paul, London 1969.

Pullan, Brian with Abendstern, Michele, *A history of the University of Manchester 1951–73*, Manchester UP, 2000.

Rendel, M. 'How many women academics 1912–76?' in Rosemary Deem (ed.), *Schooling for women's work*, Routledge & Kegan Paul, London 1980, 142–161.

Roach, John, 'The Company and the community: charity, education and technology 1914–1994' in Clyde Binfield and David Hey (ed), *Mesters to masters: a history of the Company of Cutlers in Hallamshire*, Oxford UP, 1997, 259–283.

Robertson, A. B., *A century of change: the study of education in the University of Manchester*, University of Manchester 1990.

Robertson, Charles Grant, *The British universities*, Methuen, London 1930, revised edition 1944.

Robson, Alice, *My life with Hugh Robson*, Edinburgh UP, 1988.

Roderick, Gordon W. and Stephens, Michael, *Education and industry in the nineteenth century*, Longman, London and New York 1978.

Rose, June, *Marie Stopes and the sexual revolution*, Faber, London 1992.

Rothblatt, Sheldon, *Tradition and change in English liberal education*, Faber, London 1976.

Sanderson, Michael, *The universities and British industry 1850–1970*, Routledge & Kegan Paul, London 1972.

Sanderson, Michael, *The universities in the nineteenth century*, Routledge & Kegan Paul, London and Boston 1975.

Shattock, Michael, *The creation of a university system*, Blackwell, Oxford 1996.

Shimmin, A. N., *The University of Leeds: the first half-century*, Cambridge UP, 1954.

Shinn, Christine Helen, *Paying the piper: the development of the University Grants Committee 1919–1946*, Falmer, London & Philadelphia 1986.

Simmons, Jennifer R., *So deft a builder: an account of the life and work of Sir Henry Hadow*, University of Sheffield PhD thesis, 1978.

Simon, Brian, *A student's view of the universities*, Longman, London 1943. Simon, Brian, 'The student movement in England and Wales during the 1930's', *History of Education* 16 (3), 1987, 189–203.

Simon, Brian, *Education and the social order 1940–90*, Lawrence and Wishart, London 1991.

Simpson, Renate, *How the PhD came to Britain. A century of struggle for postgraduate education*, Society for Research into Higher Education, Guildford 1983.

Smith, Dennis, *Conflict and compromise: class formation in English society 1830–1914*, Routledge & Kegan Paul, London 1982.

Soffer, Reba N., *Ethics and society in England: the revolution in the social sciences 1870–1914*, Berkeley, California UP, 1978.

Stephens. W. P., (ed), *The Bible, the Reformation and the Church: essays in honour of James Atkinson*, Sheffield AP, 1994.

Sturdy, Steve, 'The political economy of scientific medicine: science, education and the transformation of medical practice in Sheffield, 1890–1922', *Medical History* 36 (2), April 1992, 125–59.

Thompson, F. M. L., (ed), *The University of London and the world of learning 1836–1986*, Hambledon, London 1990.

Truscot, Bruce, (E. A. Peers), *Red Brick University*, Faber, London 1943.

Turnbull, G. H., *Hartlib, Dury and Comenius: gleanings from Hartlib's papers*, Hodder & Stoughton, London 1947.

Turnbull, G. H., *Samuel Hartlib: a sketch of his life and his relations to J. A. Comenius*, Oxford UP, 1920.

Viriamu Jones, Katherine, *The life of John Viriamu Jones*, Smith Elder, London 1915.

Wainwright, M. and Swan, H. T., 'C. G. Paine and the earliest surviving record of penicillin therapy', *Medical History* 30 (1986), 42–56.

Wainwright, M., *Miracle cure: the story of penicillin and the golden age of antibiotics*, Blackwell, Oxford 1990.

Wallace, Stuart, *War and the image of Germany: British academics 1914–1918*, Donald, Edinburgh 1988.

APPENDIX 1

The Governance of the University

Under the original Charter and Statutes of the University of Sheffield, the principal governing bodies were the Court, the Council and the Senate. The officers of the University were the Chancellor, Pro-Chancellors and Treasurer – all lay positions – together with the Vice-Chancellor and Registrar. The bodies authorised to govern the University in 1905 continued to do so thereafter, but the statutes were amended at various times. The most significant changes, described below, were approved by the Privy Council and adopted on 1 August 2000. The Court's powers became advisory and the membership of Council was reduced to its original total.

The Court, with a membership of several hundred, was the supreme governing body until 2000. Ex officio members, life members and representatives of other universities and of a wide variety of local and regional bodies met once a year to receive the *Annual Report* and *Statement of Accounts*. The Court was responsible for electing the Chancellor, Pro-Chancellors, Vice-Chancellor, Treasurer and Auditors, and nominated members of the Council. In 1905 the majority of places on Council were in the gift of the Court, but this proportion was gradually reduced.

In 2000 the Court became a consultative body and lost the power to make ordinances and to appoint Pro-Chancellors, the Vice-Chancellor, Treasurer and Auditors. These powers were transferred to Council. The Court continues to meet once a year and retains the right to elect the Chancellor.

The Council is the executive body of the University: it manages the revenue, property and general business and is responsible for staff appointments. The chairman is a Pro-Chancellor; the majority of members are ex officio or lay officers, and the academic community is represented by the faculty deans and by elected members of Senate. After student representation on Council was implemented in 1972, the proportions of Council membership became: lay and ex officio members 57 per cent, staff 37 per cent and students 6 per cent. In 1905 there were 37 members of Council but gradual additions had taken the total to 69 by the 1990s. In 2000 the number of Council members was reduced to 35; the proportion of representation from lay and ex officio members, and the staff and student body, remains the same.

The Senate is the supreme body of academic governance. It is chaired by the Vice-Chancellor and includes the heads of all academic departments, and representatives of the non-professorial staff. Its most significant sub-committee is the Academic Development Committee (ADC), formed in 1964. The Vice-Chancellor is a member ex officio but not the chairman, who is elected by ADC. From the late 1980s onwards the chairman has always been a pro-vice-chancellor.

Convocation was created, by the Charter and Statutes of the University, as an advisory body through which graduates could play a part in the counsels of the University. It has the right to elect representatives to Court and Council.

The Officers of the University

The Chancellor, Pro-Chancellors and Treasurer are lay officers, independent of the University, who offer their services as governors. The Vice-Chancellor is the leading academic and administrative officer, while the Registrar and Secretary oversees the day-to-day administration and is Secretary to Court, Council and Senate. Since 1946, pro-vice-chancellors have been appointed from among the academic staff to act as deputies to the Vice-Chancellor for a minimum period of three years. The officers include the current Dean of each faculty; the names of former Deans, too extensive to be included below, are listed in the University *Calendar*.

THE OFFICERS OF THE UNIVERSITY OF SHEFFIELD 1905–2005

Chancellors

1905–17	His Grace the 15th Duke of Norfolk	1959–77	Rt. Hon. Richard A. Butler, Baron Butler of Saffron Walden
1917–44	Most Hon. The Marquess of Crewe	1978–97	Rt. Hon. The Lord Dainton of Hallam Moors
1944–47	Rt. Hon. The Earl of Harewood	1999–	Sir Peter Middleton
1947–59	Rt. Hon. The Earl of Halifax		

Pro-Chancellors

1905–10	Sir Frederick T. Mappin	1965–72	Arthur H. Connell
1905–16	Sir George Franklin	1972–79	Howard P. Forder
1910–47	Sir Henry K. Stephenson	1971–80	Stephen M. de Bartolomé
1916–23	Sir Albert J. Hobson	1980–82	Denis B. Harrison
1923–32	Sir William E. Clegg	1979–87	Christopher S. Barker
1932–34	Walter Newton Drew	1982–87	Bernard E. Cotton
1934–37	James H. Doncaster	1987–97	James E. Eardley
1937–46	Sir Samuel Osborn	1987–	Peter W. Lee
1946–51	Edward Bramley	1997–98	Peter E. Middleton
1947–56	Sir H. Francis B. Stephenson	1997–00	Raymond A. Douglas
1956–65	William H. Olivier	1997–	Peter W. Lee
1951–67	Gerard F. Young	1999–	Kathryn E. Riddle
1967–71	Sir Charles Sykes	2001–	G. H. Neville Peel

Treasurers

1905–10	Sir Henry K. Stephenson	1937–41	Joseph Ward	1965–71	Stephen M. de Bartolomé

1905–10 Sir Henry K. Stephenson
1910–16 Sir Albert J. Hobson
1916–17 Herbert Hughes
1917–26 Douglas Vickers
1926–32 Walter Newton Drew
1932–34 James H. Doncaster
1934–37 Sir Samuel Osborn

1937–41 Joseph Ward
1941–46 Edward Bramley
1946–47 Sir H. Francis B. Stephenson
1947–51 Gerard F. Young
1951–56 William H. Olivier
1956–65 Arthur H. Connell

1965–71 Stephen M. de Bartolomé
1971–79 Christopher S. Barker
1979–87 James E. Eardley
1987–99 H. Stuart Johnson
1999–02 Sir Hugh R. Sykes
2002– A. M. C. (Kim) Staniforth

Vice-Chancellors

1905 William M. Hicks
1905–12 Sir Charles N. E. Eliot
1913–17 Rt Hon. Herbert A. L. Fisher
1917–19 William Ripper
1919–30 Sir W. Henry Hadow

1930–38 Sir Arthur W. Pickard-Cambridge
1938–52 Sir J. Irvine O. Masson
1952–65 John M. Whittaker
1966–74 Sir Hugh N. Robson
1974–90 Prof. Geoffrey D. Sims

1991–00 Prof. Sir Gareth G. Roberts
2001– Prof. Robert F. Boucher

Pro-Vice-Chancellors

1946–50 Prof. Leonard E. S. Eastham
1950–54 Prof. Denis Browne
1954–58 Prof. A. Roy Clapham
1958–62 Prof. Arthur G. Quarrell
1961–64 Prof. Harold W. Lawton
1962–66 Prof. David H. Smyth
1964–68 Prof. W. Harry G. Armytage
1966–70 Prof. Deryck N. de G. Allen
1967–71 Prof. Harry Kay
1968–72 Prof. Eric Laughton
1970–74 Prof. John R. James
1971–75 Prof. J. Alan Roper
1972–76 Prof. Frank A. Benson

1974–78 Prof. Ronald S. Waters
1975–79 Prof. James M. Ritchie
1976–80 Prof. Walter Bartley
1978–82 Prof. George Clayton
1979–83 Prof. Geoffrey W. Greenwood
1980–84 Prof. Stanley Gregory
1982–86 Prof. William Galbraith
1983–87 Prof. R. John Nicholson
1984–88 David E. Bland
1986–89 Prof. Victor Barnett
1986–90 Prof. Norman F. Blake
1987–91 Prof. Peter Banks
1989–92 Prof. Ronald J. Johnston
1988–93 Prof. Ronald G. Clark
1990–94 Prof. David E. Luscombe

1992–95 Prof. Robert F. Boucher
1991–96 Prof. J. David McClean
1994–98 Prof. Andrew M. Gamble
1995–99 Prof. Ian T. M. Gow
1995–99 Prof. David H. Lewis
1996–00 Prof. Peter Waldron
1998–04 Prof. Philip A. Jones
1999–03 Prof. Colin Whitehouse
1999–05 Prof. Anthony D. H. Crook
2000– Prof. Geoffrey R. Tomlinson
2003– Prof. Peter J. Fleming
2004– Prof. Paul E. White

Registrars/Registrars and Secretaries

1987–02 Ensor Drury
1902–44 William M. Gibbons
1944–63 Arthur W. Chapman

1963–65 George Clark
1965–78 Alexander M. Currie
1978–82 Francis J. Orton

1982–98 John S. Padley
1999– David E. Fletcher

Bursars/Directors of Finance

1944–52 John Bycroft
1952–66 Roderick M. Urquhart
1966–72 Eric Walker

1972–80 John H. Barker
1980–93 Terence A. Thomas
1993–03 David R. Bearpark

2003–04 Euan T. McGregor

Union of Students Presidents: 1906–2005

1906/07	Frank G. Belton, Richard Mather	1938/39	Howard Robinson	1972/73	Roland Hayes
1907/08	Douglas Green	1939/40	William A. Armstrong	1973/74	John O'Leary
1908/09	Cyril J. Peddle	1940/41	Kamel M. Hanna	1974/75	Patrick Hughes
1909/10	Edward M. Holmes	1941/42	Thomas E. Cleghorn	1975/76	Andrew R. S. Tucker
1910/11	Lionel E. Sutcliffe	1942/43	Denis C. Burnham	1976/77	Robert J. H. Hamilton
1911/12	Cecil H. Wilson	1943/44	John D. Glendenning	1977/78	Andrew Palazzo
1912/13	Claude O. Hudson	1944/45	Eric W. Bradford	1978/79	Linda G. Miller
1913/14	Claude O. Hudson	1945/46	William R. Souster	1979/80	Stephen Grabiner
1914/15	Ralph B. Gibson	1946/47	Alan G. Bradford	1980/81	Lynne Bowles
1915/16	Margaret M. Surtees *	1947/48	P. Owen, Owen McGirr	1981/82	K. K. Tan
1916/17	Frances E. Hawkins *	1948/49	B. Hart, Douglas H. S. Robson*	1982/83	Allan D. Barnes
1917/18	John V. Mainprize, William P. Hildred	1949/50	Eric N. Walker	1983/84	David T. Stubbs
1918/19	James H. Marsden	1950/51	Richard M. Burton	1984/85	Aleks A. Szczerbiak
1919/20	Gordon A. Milne, Alexander J. Jack	1951/52	Harold Clark	1985/86	Caroline Stockdale
1920/21	William R. Chapman	1952/53	John F. Watkinson	1986/87	Birgit I. Pierce
1921/22	Kenneth C. Bruce	1953/54	Michael Walker	1987/88	Jon A. Colman *
1922/23	Olive D. D. Dickinson	1954/55	Alan Walker	1988/89	Tom D. Goodhill *
1923/24	Hyman Stone	1955/56	Alan G. Cox	1989/90	Helen E. Pitts *
1924/25	Douglas Chandler	1956/57	Ramnath Swamy	1990/91	David A. McClements
1925/26	Ernest W. J. Nicholson	1957/58	Peter Rogers	1991/92	Jon Gerard Baker
1926/27	P. A. R. Senior	1958/59	William Moore	1992/93	Philippa A. M. Dodd
1927/28	Geoffrey M. Willis	1959/60	Michael R. Ashburner	1993/94	Mark Fletcher
1928/29	F. S. Clark	1960/61	Keith R. McNeil	1994/95	Dominic Carr
1929/30	Muriel Musgrove *	1961/62	David M. Heap	1995/96	Claire L. Geener
1930/31	Eric J. Widdowson	1962/63	Baden S. Prince	1996/97	Sophie Ansell
1931/32	Roland E. Richardson	1963/64	John H. Wilson	1997/98	Adam Matthews
1932/33	John H. Hazeldene	1964/65	Eoin S. Hodgson	1998/99	Rachel Garnham
1933/34	Frederick L. Ralphs	1965/66	Viv Astling	1999/00	Hayley Rose
1934/35	Arthur W. Cutts	1966/67	William J. Griffiths	2000/01	Andrzej Nowakowski
1935/36	Thomas B. Smart	1967/68	Jon G. Bush	2001/02	Robert Forbes
1936/37	Ali A. Yousef, Robert R. S. Ward	1968/69	Julian B. Allitt	2002/03	Katie Buckle
1937/38	Philip H. Moneypenny	1969/70	Helen H. Davidson	2003/04	Daniel S. Mitchell
		1970/71	David J. Serjeant	2004/05	Jamie Bristow
		1971/72	Abdul S. Gani		

* General Secretary

Academic Distinction

Readers are referred to the University *Calendar*, published annually, which lists deans and professors, with their dates of office, for the whole of the University's history.

Academic honours are noted in the text of *Steel City Scholars*; in particular, election to a Fellowship of the Royal Society (FRS) has been acknowledged in every case. Non-scientific disciplines award a variety of distinctions, for example Fellowship of the British Academy (FBA) and the Vautron Laud prize in Geography. Recipients of these have also been noted. During the preparation of this History, however, it was hard to avoid the conclusion that, while some disciplines justly honour their most distinguished practitioners, others do not. Even-handedness has been the watchword as far as possible.

Nobel Prize-winners associated with the University

Howard Florey
Pathology 1932–35
Nobel Prize for Medicine/Physiology, 1945

Hans Krebs
Pharmacology 1935–38; Biochemistry 1938–54
Nobel Prize for Medicine/Physiology, 1953

George Porter
Chemistry 1955–66
Nobel Prize for Chemistry, 1967

Richard Roberts
Chemistry BSc 1965; PhD 1968
Nobel Prize for Medicine/Physiology, 1993

Harry Kroto
Chemistry Bsc 1961; PhD 1964
Nobel Prize for Chemistry, 1996

University Statistics

Compiled by Charlotte Brownhill and Len Hill

Student Numbers in University College, Sheffield and the University of Sheffield 1898–2003.

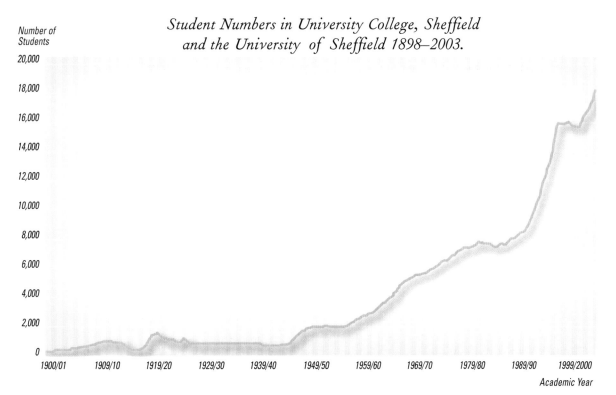

This table shows the total numbers of day students. Until 1914 less than half of these students were full-time. By 1924 80 per cent were full-time; by 1930 this had risen to 90 per cent, and after 1945 all the students represented by these statistics were full-time. The table does not include evening students.

Source: *All statistics are derived from the relevant University* Annual Report *or* Calendar.

Number of
Students

Full-time Undergraduate Degree and Diploma Students, 1905–2003

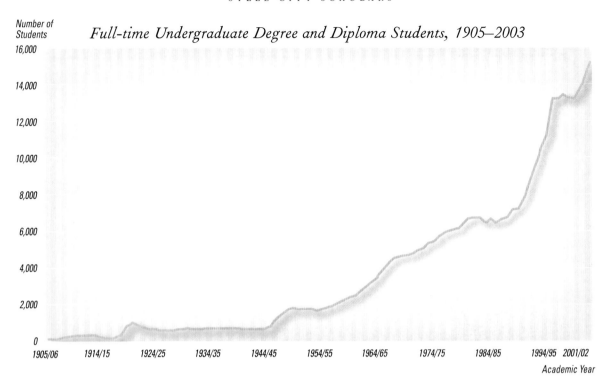

Academic Year

Number of
Students

Postgraduate Students, 1905–2003

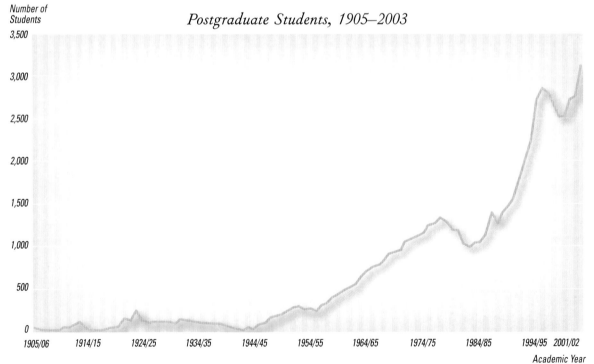

Academic Year

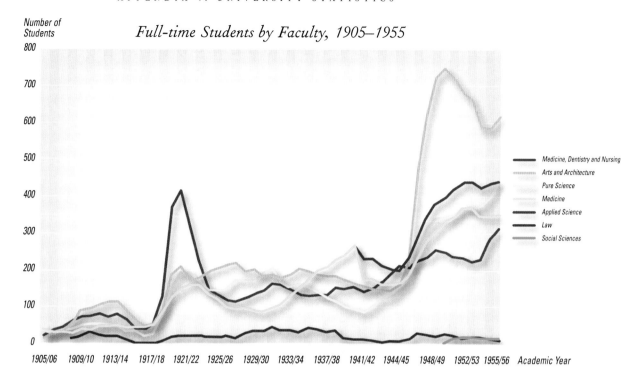

Number of Students

Full-time Students by Faculty, 1905–1955

Legend:
- Medicine, Dentistry and Nursing
- Arts and Architecture
- Pure Science
- Medicine
- Applied Science
- Law
- Social Sciences

Academic Year

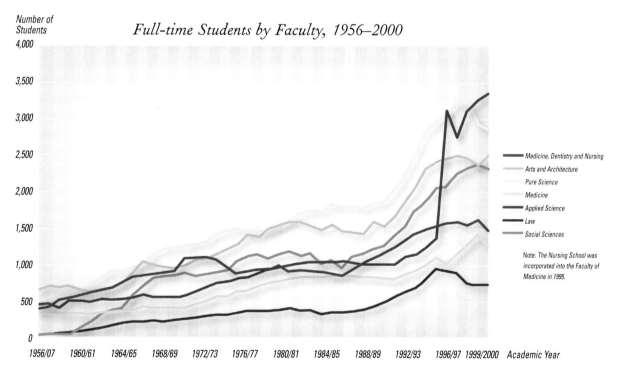

Number of Students

Full-time Students by Faculty, 1956–2000

Legend:
- Medicine, Dentistry and Nursing
- Arts and Architecture
- Pure Science
- Medicine
- Applied Science
- Law
- Social Sciences

Note: The Nursing School was incorporated into the Faculty of Medicine in 1995.

Academic Year

439

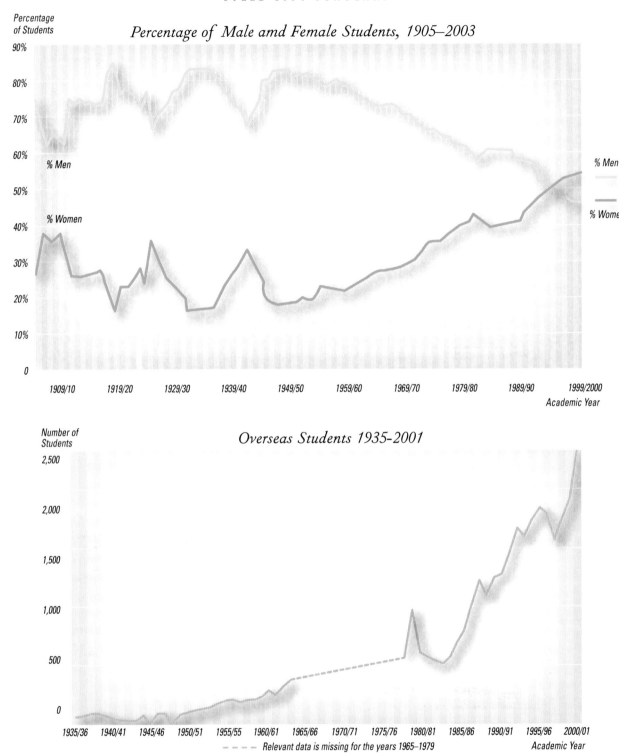

Percentage of Male amd Female Students, 1905–2003

Overseas Students 1935-2001

Relevant data is missing for the years 1965–1979

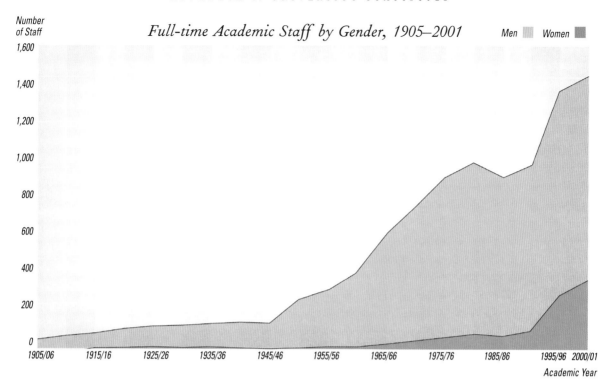

Full-time Academic Staff by Gender, 1905–2001

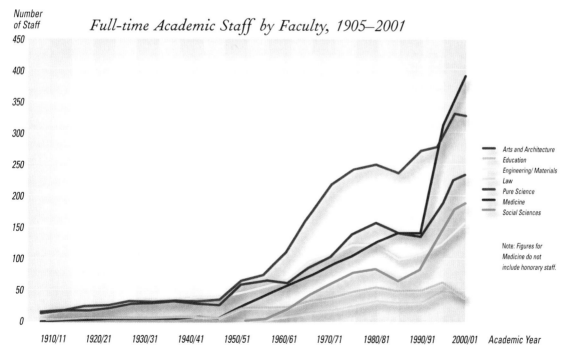

Full-time Academic Staff by Faculty, 1905–2001

441

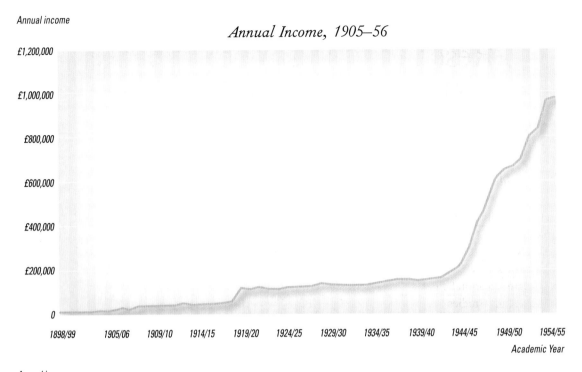

Annual income

Annual Income, 1905–56

£1,200,000

£1,000,000

£800,000

£600,000

£400,000

£200,000

0

1898/99   1905/06   1909/10   1914/15   1919/20   1924/25   1929/30   1934/35   1939/40   1944/45   1949/50   1954/55

Academic Year

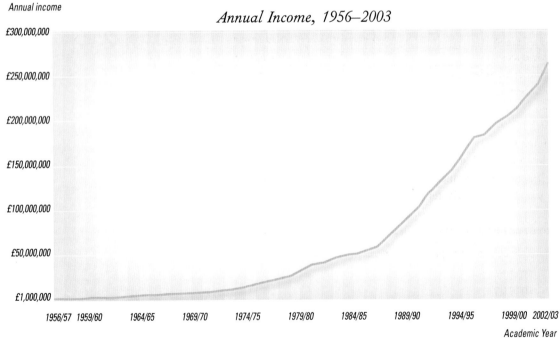

Annual income

Annual Income, 1956–2003

£300,000,000

£250,000,000

£200,000,000

£150,000,000

£100,000,000

£50,000,000

£1,000,000

1956/57 1959/60   1964/65   1969/70   1974/75   1979/80   1984/85   1989/90   1994/95   1999/00 2002/03

Academic Year

APPENDIX 5

Research Assessment Exercise (RAE) results, 1992–2001

Department/Unit of Assessment	Rating 1992	1996	2001
School of Health & Related Research			
	–	2C	4B
Hospital-based Clinical Subjects	2A	4C	5C
Dentistry	2B	3aC	5C
Biomedical Science	2A	(4A)	5*C
Nursing & Midwifery	–	3bA	5D
Human Communication Sciences	1A	3aB	4B
Psychotherapeutic Studies	–	(2C)	3aC
Psychology	5A	5A	5A
Animal & Plant Sciences	(4A)	(4A)	5*A
Molecular Biology & Biotechnology	(4A)	(4A)	5*B
Chemistry	4A	4A	5B
Physics & Astronomy	3A	4B	5B
Medical Physics	(3A)	(2C)	5A
Earth Sciences	3A	3bA	3aD
Environmental Sciences	(4A)	(4A)	4B
Pure Mathematics	3B	3aC	5B
Applied Mathematics	4A	4B	4B
Statistics	4B	4B	5C
Computer Science	3B	4B	5B
Chemical Engineering	(5A)	(5A)	4B
Civil & Structural Engineering	4B	4A	5B
Automatic Control & Systems Engineering			
	(4A)	5A	5*B
Electronic & Electrical Engineering	(4A)	5*A	5*B

Department/Unit of Assessment	Rating 1992	1996	2001
Mechanical Engineering	5A	5A	5A
Engineering Materials	4B	5*A	5*A
Architecture/Landscape	4B	5A	5B
Town & Regional Planning	5A	5B	5A
Geography	4A	5A	5A
Law	4A	5B	5C
Economics	(3A)	(4B)	3aB
Politics	4A	5A	5*A
Sociological Studies	4B	4B	5B
Management	3A	4B	4B
East Asian Studies	2A	3aB	4D
English	3A	4B	5B
French	3A	4A	5B
German	3A	4B	4A
Russian	4A	5A	5*A
Hispanic Studies	3B	4A	5A
Archaeology & Prehistory	5A	5*A	5A
History	4A	5A	5B
Information Studies	5A	5*A	5*A
Philosophy	4A	5A	5A
Biblical Studies	5A	5*A	5A
Journalism	–	–	4C
Music	4C	5A	5B
Education	5A	5A	5A
Leisure Management	–	3aB	4A

Ratings in brackets were part of larger submissions in 1992 and 1996.

A = 95–100
B = 80–94.9
C = 60–79.9
D = 40–59.9   A, B, C, D denote the percentage of academic staff whose research output was assessed.

Teaching Quality Assessment

1993–1995

Subjects	Result	
	Excellent	Satisfactory
Architecture	●	
Business and Management		●*
Chemistry		●*
Computer Science		●
English Literature	●	
Environmental Studies		●*
Geography	●	
Geology		●*
History	●	
Initial Teacher Training	●#	
Law	●	
Mechanical Engineering	●	
Music	●	
Social Policy	●	
Social Work	●	
Sociology	●**	

* These subjects did not receive an assessment visit.

** Graded 'Excellent' by HEFCE after self-assessment and a previous visit to examine Social Policy

\# An HMI assessment of this course was converted into an 'Excellent' by HEFCE in 1994

Numerical scoring was introduced in 1995; whereupon scores of 22–24 were deemed to be equivalent to 'excellent'. External grading was replaced by internal audit in 2001.

1995–2001

Subjects	Result
Animal & Plant Sciences	24
Archaeology	22
Biblical Studies	24
Biomedical Science	24
Chemical & Process Engineering	21
Civil & Structural Engineering	21
Dentistry	23
East Asian Studies	22
Economics	21
Education	24
Electronic & Electrical Engineering and Automatic Control & Systems Engineering	24
Engineering Materials	22
English Language & Linguistics	22
French	21
Germanic Studies	20
Hispanic Studies	21
Information Studies	22
Mathematics and Statistics	21
Medicine	19
Molecular Biology & Biotechnology	24
Nursing & Midwifery	21
Other Subjects Allied to Medicine	21
Pharmacology	21
Philosophy	24
Physics & Astronomy and Medical Physics	22
Politics	24
Psychology	22
Russian & Slavonic Studies	24
Town & Regional Planning and Landscape	23

Establishment of Departments

Compiled by Len Hill

Where subjects were taught by one or more full-time members of staff in Firth College, the Technical School, or the University College, this has been taken as the date of establishment of a department, although this terminology was not used until the founding of the University in 1905. Otherwise the date of the establishment of a department is taken as the session in which it was first included in the University Calendar. Where a subject was taught before the establishment of a department this is indicated.

ACCOUNTANCY & FINANCIAL ADMINISTRATION
Department of Accountancy & Financial Administration established in 1948. Included in the Division of Economic Studies in 1970 and the Management School in 1986.

ADULT CONTINUING EDUCATION
Department of Extramural Studies established in 1947. Renamed Division of Adult Continuing Education in 1977 and Institute for Lifelong Learning in 2001.

ANATOMY
Taught in the Medical School from 1829. Department of Anatomy established in 1897. Renamed Department of Human Biology & Anatomy in 1962 and Anatomy & Cell Biology in 1982. Merged with Department of Physiology to form Department of Biomedical Science in 1988.

ANIMAL & PLANT SCIENCES
Department of Animal & Plant Sciences established in 1988 by the merger of the Departments of Botany and Zoology.

APPLIED MECHANICS
Postgraduate Department of Applied Mechanics established in 1951 and closed in 1968.

ARCHAEOLOGY
Taught in the Department of Ancient History until 1977.

Department of Prehistory & Archaeology established in 1977. Renamed Department of Archaeology & Prehistory in 1984 and Department of Archaeology in 2003.

ARCHITECTURE
Department of Architecture established in the Faculty of Applied Science in 1908. Transferred to the Faculty of Arts in 1911.

BIBLICAL STUDIES
Department of Biblical History & Literature established in 1947. Renamed Department of Biblical Studies in 1968.

BIOCHEMISTRY
Department of Biochemistry established in 1938. Merged with the Departments of Genetics and Microbiology and the Wolfson Institute of Biotechnology to form the Department of Molecular Biology & Biotechnology in 1988.

BIOLOGY
Department of Biology established in 1884. Divided into separate Departments of Botany and Zoology in 1908.

BIOMEDICAL SCIENCE
Department of Biomedical Science established in 1988 by the merger of the Departments of Anatomy & Cell Biology and Physiology.

BIOTECHNOLOGY
Wolfson Institute of Biotechnology established in 1978 as part of the Department of Biochemistry. Given departmental status in 1981. Merged with the Departments of Biochemistry, Genetics and Microbiology to form the Department of Molecular Biology & Biotechnology in 1988.

BOTANY
Department of Botany established in 1908. Merged with the Department of Zoology to form the Department of Animal & Plant Sciences in 1988.

BUILDING SCIENCE
Department of Building Science established in 1965. Incorporated into the Department of Architecture in 1989.

BUSINESS STUDIES
Department of Business Studies established in 1962. Included in the Division of Economic Studies in 1970 and the Management School in 1986.

CERAMICS
Originated as Department of Refractories Technology in 1956. Renamed Department of Ceramics with Refractories Technology in 1964 and Department of Ceramics in 1971. Merged with the Department of Glass Technology to form Department of Ceramics, Glasses & Polymers in 1974. Incorporated into the School of Materials in 1987 which was renamed Department of Engineering Materials in 1992.

CHEMISTRY
Department of Chemistry established in 1879.

CHEMICAL ENGINEERING
Department of Fuel Technology & Chemical Engineering established in 1955 and merged with Mechanical Engineering in 1988. Department of Chemical & Process Engineering re-established in 1996.

CIVIL ENGINEERING
Taught from 1892. Department of Civil Engineering established in 1917. Renamed Department of Civil &

Structural Engineering in 1965.

CLASSICS
Department of Classics established in 1880. Divided into separate Departments of Greek and Latin in 1909. Departments of Greek and Latin replaced with Department of Classical Studies in 1983, which closed in 1987.

COMPUTER SCIENCE
Department of Computer Science established in 1980.

CONTROL ENGINEERING
Department of Control Engineering established in 1968. Renamed Department of Automatic Control & Systems Engineering in 1991.

DENTAL SCHOOL
Dental School established in 1898. First full-time Chair of Dental Surgery established in 1935.

EAST ASIAN STUDIES
School of East Asian Studies established in 1990.

ECONOMICS
Department of Economics & Philosophy established in 1897. Divided into separate Departments of Economics and Philosophy in 1910.

EDUCATION
Taught from 1891. Department of Education established in 1906. Institute of Education established in 1948. Department of Education and Institute of Education merged to form a Division of Education in 1971.

ELECTRICAL ENGINEERING
Taught from 1889. Department of Electrical Engineering established in 1917. Renamed Department of Electronic & Electrical Engineering 1964.

ENGINEERING
Department of Engineering established in 1884. Divided into separate Departments of Mechanical, Electrical and Civil Engineering in 1917.

ENGINEERING MATERIALS
School of Materials renamed the Department of Engineering Materials in 1992.

ENGLISH
Department of English & History established in 1882. Department divided into separate Departments of English Language & Literature and Ancient & Modern History in 1896. Department of English Language & Literature divided into separate Departments of English Language and Literature in 1926. Department of English Language renamed Department of English Language & Linguistics in 1988.

FRENCH
Taught from 1880. Department of French established in 1901.

FUEL TECHNOLOGY
Department of Fuel Technology established in 1920. Renamed Department of Fuel Technology & Chemical Engineering in 1955.

GENETICS
Department of Genetics established in 1954. Merged with the Departments of Biochemistry and Microbiology and the Wolfson Institute of Biotechnology to form the Department of Molecular Biology & Biotechnology in 1988.

GEOGRAPHY
Department of Geography established in 1908.

GEOLOGY
Department of Geology established in 1913. Incorporated into the Department of Animal & Plant Sciences as the Earth Sciences Unit in 1990. Re-established as Department of Earth Sciences in 1992. Incorporated into the Department of Geography in 2001.

GERMAN
Taught since 1880. Department of German established in 1901. Renamed Department of Germanic Studies in 1966.

GLASS TECHNOLOGY
Department of Glass Technology established in 1915. Merged with the Department of Ceramics to form Department of Ceramics, Glasses & Polymers 1974.

GREEK
Department of Greek established in 1909 and incorporated into the Department of Classical Studies in 1983.

HISTORY
Taught from 1880. Department of History & English established in 1882. Department divided into separate Departments of Ancient & Modern History and English Language & Literature in 1896. Department of Ancient & Modern History divided into separate Departments of Ancient History and Modern History in 1920. Department of Modern History renamed Department of Medieval & Modern History in 1959. Department of Economic & Social History established in 1963. Department of Ancient History renamed Department of Ancient History & Classical Archaeology in 1976. Departments of Medieval & Modern History, Ancient History & Classical Archaeology, and Economic & Social History merged to form Department of History in 1988.

HUMAN COMMUNICATION SCIENCES
Department of Linguistics established in 1976. Renamed Department of Linguistics & Speech Science in 1986. Linguistics incorporated into the Department of English Language in 1988 and Speech Science formed a Speech Science Unit in the Department of Psychology in 1988. Department of Speech Science established in 1995. Renamed Department of Human Communication Sciences in 1996.

INFORMATION STUDIES
Established as the Postgraduate School of Librarianship & Information Science in 1963. Department of Information Studies established in 1981.

JAPANESE
Centre for Japanese Studies established in 1963. Incorporated into the School of East Asian Studies in 1990.

JOURNALISM
Department of Journalism Studies established in 1994.

LANDSCAPE ARCHITECTURE
Department of Landscape Architecture established in 1967. Renamed Department of Landscape in 1993.

LATIN
Department of Latin established in 1909 and incorporated into the Department of Classical Studies in 1983.

LAW
Taught from 1899. Department of Law established in 1906.

MANAGEMENT
School of Management & Economic Studies established in 1986 including Accountancy & Financial Administration, Business Studies and Economics. Economics later established as a separate department.

MATERIALS
School of Materials established in 1987 by the merger of the Departments of Metallurgy and Ceramics, Glasses & Polymers. Renamed Department of Engineering Materials 1992. Department of the Theory of Materials established in 1966 and closed in 1983.

MATHEMATICS
Department of Mathematics & Physics established in 1879. Department divided into separate Departments of Mathematics and Physics in 1892. Department of Mathematics divided into separate Departments of Applied Mathematics, Pure Mathematics and Statistics in 1955. Department of Statistics renamed Department of Probability & Statistics in 1965. Department of Applied Mathematics renamed Department of Applied Mathematics & Computing Science in 1967 and then divided into separate Departments of Applied & Computational Mathematics and Computer Science in 1980.

MECHANICAL ENGINEERING
Taught from 1884. Department of Mechanical Engineering established in 1917.

MEDICAL SCHOOL
Medical School established in 1828. Dates of establishment of full-time clinical Chairs: Pathology 1906; Pharmacology 1920; Bacteriology 1932; Medicine 1946; Child Health 1946; Community Medicine 1949; Obstetrics & Gynaecology 1950; Surgery 1954; Psychiatry 1959; Anaesthetics 1970; General Practice 1972; Chemical Pathology 1974; Medical Physics 1975.

METALLURGY
Department of Metallurgy established in 1884. Incorporated into the School of Materials in 1987.

MICROBIOLOGY
Department of Microbiology established in 1952. Merged with the Departments of Biochemistry, Genetics and the Wolfson Institute of Biotechnology to form the Department of Molecular Biology & Biotechnology in 1988.

MINING ENGINEERING
Taught from 1883. Department of Mining Engineering established in 1892 and closed in 1965. Postgraduate School of Mining established in 1952 and closed in 1968.

MOLECULAR BIOLOGY & BIOTECHNOLOGY
Department of Molecular Biology & Biotechnology established in 1988 by the merger of the Departments of Biochemistry, Genetics, Microbiology and the Wolfson Institute of Biotechnology.

MUSIC
Taught from 1880. Department of Music established in 1928.

NURSING & MIDWIFERY SCHOOL
The School of Nursing & Midwifery joined the University in 1995.

PHILOSOPHY
Department of Philosophy & Economics established in 1897. Department divided into separate Departments of Philosophy and Economics in 1910.

PHYSICS
Department of Mathematics & Physics established in 1879. Department divided into separate Departments of Physics and Mathematics in 1892. Department of Physics renamed Department of Physics & Astronomy in 1998.

PHYSIOLOGY
Taught in Medical School from 1829. Department of Physiology established in 1898. Merged with Department of Anatomy & Cell Biology to form Department of Biomedical Science in 1988.

POLITICS
Political Theory & Institutions established in the Department of Economics in 1959. Established as a separate department in 1965. Renamed Department of Politics in 1987.

PSYCHOLOGY
Taught from 1948. Department of Psychology established in 1960.

REFRACTORIES TECHNOLOGY
Department of Refractories Technology established in 1956. Renamed Department of Ceramics with Refractories Technology in 1964 and Department of Ceramics in 1971.

RUSSIAN
Department of Russian established in 1917 and closed in 1943. Department of Russian & Slavonic Studies established in 1966.

SCHOOL OF HEALTH & RELATED RESEARCH
School of Health & Related Research established in 1996.

SOCIOLOGICAL STUDIES
School of Social Studies established in 1949. Renamed Department of Sociological Studies in 1959.

SPANISH
Department of Spanish established in 1918. Renamed Department of Hispanic Studies in 1966.

TOWN & REGIONAL PLANNING
Department of Town & Regional Planning established in 1965.

ZOOLOGY
Department of Zoology established in 1908. Merged with Department of Botany to form Department of Animal & Plant Sciences in 1988.

ESTABLISHMENT OF FACULTIES

ARTS, PURE SCIENCE, MEDICINE AND APPLIED SCIENCE in 1905

LAW in 1908

APPLIED SCIENCE divided into the FACULTIES OF ENGINEERING AND METALLURGY in 1917

ECONOMICS & SOCIAL STUDIES in 1959

ARCHITECTURAL STUDIES in 1965

ECONOMICS & SOCIAL STUDIES renamed the FACULTY OF SOCIAL SCIENCES in 1967

METALLURGY renamed the FACULTY OF MATERIALS TECHNOLOGY in 1969

EDUCATIONAL STUDIES in 1972

MATERIALS TECHNOLOGY renamed the FACULTY OF MATERIALS in 1973

MATERIALS incorporated into the FACULTY OF ENGINEERING in 1987

EDUCATIONAL STUDIES incorporated into the FACULTY OF SOCIAL SCIENCES in 1999

Index

Compiled by Penny Draper

Page numbers in **bold** indicate a main reference for that entry in the text. Page numbers of illustrations are shown in *italics*.
Current departmental titles are used wherever possible; see Appendix 6 for the history of departments.